ARMING AMERICA
THROUGH THE CENTURIES

ARMING AMERICA THROUGH THE CENTURIES

War, Business, and Building a National Security State

Benjamin Franklin Cooling

Legacies of War
G. Kurt Piehler, Series Editor

The University of Tennessee Press / Knoxville

The Legacies of War series presents a variety of works—from scholarly monographs to memoirs—that examine the impact of war on society, both in the United States and globally. The wide scope of the series might include war's effects on civilian populations, its lingering consequences for veterans, and the role of individual nations and the international community in confronting genocide and other injustices born of war.

Copyright © 2022 by The University of Tennessee Press / Knoxville.
All Rights Reserved. Manufactured in the United States of America.
First Edition.

Library of Congress Cataloging-in-Publication Data

Names: Cooling, Benjamin Franklin, III, 1938- author.

Title: Arming America through the centuries : war, business, and building a national security state / Benjamin Franklin Cooling, Legacies of War, G. Kurt Piehler, series editor.

Description: First edition. | Knoxville : The University of Tennessee Press, [2022] | Series: Legacies of war | Includes bibliographical references and index. | Summary: "This book examines the roots of the military industrial complex (MIC) in the eighteenth and nineteenth centuries, the MIC's full flowering in the wake of the Cold War, and how America's current MIC evolved after the events of 9/11 and throughout the War on Terror. Benjamin Frankin Cooling argues that the MIC has transformed into a problematic demand for absolute security that is neither practicable nor financially sound. While emphasizing many aspects of Eisenhower's broad conception of the MIC, and Eisenhower's own warning at the close of World War II, Cooling's synthesis provides historical perspectives on American industry as a matter of national security, the rise of outsourcing practices, and the changing nature of modern warfare"—Provided by publisher.

Identifiers: LCCN 2021055864 (print) | LCCN 2021055865 (ebook) | ISBN 9781621905868 (hardcover) | ISBN 9781621905875 (pdf)

Subjects: LCSH: Military industrial complex—United States—History. | Weapons industry—United States—History. | Defense industries—United States—History. | Eisenhower, Dwight D. (Dwight David), 1890–1969—Oratory. | Rhetoric—Political aspects—United States—History.

Classification: LCC HC110.D4 C594 2022 (print) | LCC HC110.D4 (ebook) | DDC 338.4/735500973—dc23/eng/20220127

LC record available at https://lccn.loc.gov/2021055864
LC ebook record available at https://lccn.loc.gov/2021055865

To the memory of mentors
at the University of Pennsylvania
Roy Franklin Nichols,
Thomas C. Cochran,
and Richard Shryock

at Rutgers University
Richard P. McCormick,
Sidney Ratner,
and Peter Charanis

Contents

Foreword	ix
G. Kurt Piehler	
Preface	xi
Chapter 1. Colonial Security Shaped by War and Trade, to 1783	1
Chapter 2. Manifest Destiny, Industrial Revolution, Public Enterprise, 1783–1860	19
Chapter 3. Resourcing the Civil War and Arming the People, 1860–1865	53
Chapter 4. Continental Defense, Imperial Pretensions, and Formation of the MIC, 1865–1917	89
Chapter 5. Arsenal of Democracy in Two World Wars, 1917–1945	127
Chapter 6. The Cold War MIC and Eisenhower's Warning, 1945–1990	177
Chapter 7. Cold War Legacy and the Grave New World, 1991–2001	237
Chapter 8. National Security since 2001	275
Postscript. The National Security State for Posterity	317
Notes	339
Selected Bibliography	431
Index	459

Foreword

American attitudes toward war remain complex and contradictory. Although Americans have not viewed themselves as a militarized people, they have fought a major war every generation since the founding of the republic. For much of its history, the United States has relied on volunteers to fill the ranks of the armed forces but has also turned to conscription during the Civil War, the world wars, and the early Cold War. Until the 1940s, the United States upon entering a conflict dramatically increased the production of war materials and with the arrival of peace demobilized. At the end of the Civil War the American navy possessed one of the largest and technologically sophisticated fleets in the world only to see Congress allow it to quickly dissipate. World War II and the Cold War that followed changed everything and led to unprecedented spending on defense. Even with the collapse of the Berlin Wall in 1989 and the Soviet Union in 1991, the much heralded peace dividend proved elusive and spending on defense escalated to unprecedented heights after the terror attacks of September 11, 2001.

Shedding new light on the topic is Benjamin Franklin Cooling who has written an audacious and daring book. In this wide-ranging study, Cooling examines how the United States procured arms and war material from the Revolutionary War through the administration of Donald Trump. Covering this broad span highlights both continuity and change over time. As Cooling recounts, the trend by defense contractors to spread out manufacturing work to different political constituencies is nothing new. Indeed this pattern emerged during the Revolutionary War when the Continental Congress had ships for the new navy built in both northern and southern shipyards.

Moving to the twentieth century, Cooling sees that in response to the threat posed by the Axis and later Soviet Union the United States underwent a pivotal transition of America from a democratic Athens to a militarized Sparta. Until the 1940s the United States relied on the industrial sector to supplement the production of army arsenals and navy yards to supply the war materiel necessary for a major conflict. Once peace arrived industry converted to needs of civilians. But after 1945, companies started specializing in serving the needs of the Defense Department, and over time the number of major defense contractors shrank. As Cooling observes, the warnings of President Dwight D. Eisenhower regarding the military-industrial complex have largely fallen on deaf ears. Despite the vast sums spent on weapons, it has evoked little outcry or genuine efforts at retrenchment or reform.

These massive sums deserve the attention not only of scholars but the broader public. As the industrial base of the United States has shrunk since the 1960s under the growing weight of globalization, the Pentagon and Congressional allies through defense contracting allocate a significant portion of spending in this sector. The United States no longer builds commercial merchant vessels, but as Cooling points out, the shipbuilders that have survived live off the largesse of naval contracts. By the early 2000s, American defense spending exceeded those of Russia and China as well as our major Allies combined. Despite these trends, Cooling makes the case the sheer acquisition of weapons has not engendered a great sense of national security among the public. There is in Cooling's estimation a heavy price to the republic of the United State emerging as an armed Sparta in terms of democratic values and devotion of inordinate number of resources to weapons.

G. Kurt Piehler
Florida State University

Preface

Was the United States destined to be America's Sparta rather than America's Athens? Was the one word—"security" what did it? Was it by conscious or unconscious action? Peace historian Charles Debenedettii offered sage observations before his death in 1987. While "explosive weapons" had become a dominant feature of American life during the twentieth century, he advanced, "the American people have long led industrialized nations in the possession and use of arms." He cited that by 1980, an estimated 140 million rifles, shotguns and handguns circulated in a population of 223 million people. At the other end of the explosive spectrum stood a nuclear stockpile of an estimated 24,000 weapons while Americans trafficked in almost $20 billion worth of arms at home and abroad. "The dollar value of the country's total investment in weaponry is incalculable," he contended. Examining why American historians and their textbooks were so loathe to examine the issue, he wondered "why Americans have attached such importance to the production, acquisition and use of armaments." He found problems abroad, revolutionary changes in technology, reflections of different social pathologies and matters of tradition among the reasons. Yet, for Debenedettii, among others, guns and bombs were more than just material objects. They were cultural objects, "subjective attitudes felt . . . deep within the larger culture." He used the word "armamentism" as the label.[1]

Debenedetti's views surely warrant further reflection in the twenty-first century. True, the textbook coverage might differ but perhaps the themes would not. Broad themes like expansion, industrialization, triumphalism, exceptionalism continue to resonate as fertile ground for explaining the American Sparta. Economic, political, social-cultural security (reality) and geography mix with idealistic rhetoric. Interests overshadow values. Possibly the industrial revolution even more than the atomic age might guide our understanding. Yet, protean signs were always there. Finance historian Robert Hormats asserts that America was "a country born of war and debt." It remains so today. Yet, it has always been shaped also by war and trade. Conflict and economics merge when providing the sinews of defense, an inherently state function. The state mobilizes resources. It provides structural and legal authority, raises revenues and sets the need, goal and strategy simply for its survival. Yet, it must tap (extract) societal and natural *elements* of power for conversion to *instruments* of power. That is where both public and private sectors come together to provide goods and services (resourcing) in a contract between the government and the people. Americans long ago discovered that security is a costly business.[2]

Political economist Ethan B. Kapstein contends that the cost of war can disrupt "national strategy no less than enemy forces." Popular constraints upon state power attach to excessive taxation, unmonitored abuse of power and the moral and political imperatives of war-making (even preparations for such) were traditionally ingrained in the American ethos. They seem less so today. Historian of government contracting James F. Nagle points to recurring themes, like tempestuous public-private relations over cost and profit, government-contractor sourcing and ethics as well as competition, accountability and processing as running through the story of American defense enterprise. So too do fear of standing armies, strong central government and "the man on horseback" (generals exercising Cromwellian authoritarianism). Or, at least they used to be of concern. Now, an Age of Fear has reinforced a Gun Culture, police state surveillance and even diminution of democratic institutions and human worth as a march toward artificial intelligence gains blind acceptance more indicative of George Orwell's "1984" than Locke and eternal verities advanced as underpinnings of free men by the Founding Fathers. The fact that a militarized, hegemonic America rests largely upon an entrepreneurial defense industrial base, large standing military force, laughingly obscene national security (much less defense) budget, and obsequious government worthy of a late Roman senate raises hardly a whimper among a bread and circus populace. It wasn't always that way, of course.[3]

This leads to a second major theme, intricately bound to the first. In the beginning was the Word. In this case, the word is an acronym—"MIC." "God" was the saintly military hero of World War II victory and later president, Dwight D. Eisenhower. He coined the term for a potentially sinister "military-industrial complex" in his 1961 farewell address. For political reasons, he avoided including Congress for an explicit political dimension. He did add a "scientific-technological elite" to the warning without changing the lettering of the mix. Possibly he could have underscored a "G" for government (agencies/bureaucracies with their own vested interests) or even economic (E) to include Wall Street financiers. Thus, the influence of a "MIC" thenceforth attached to a Cold War and unceasing global interventionism. Still, historian Robert F. Smith dates its seed corn to American "manufacturing independence" of the Revolution. It certainly began no later than the industrial age, overseas expansion of the turn of the twentieth century and participation in two world wars. It sweeps effortlessly into the future with endless conflict plus a self-serving national security state. Together they permit a late American empire to prosper not in spite of but because of this full-flowering phenomenon. Whether or not America has lost some moral compass is another story. Of course, there always has been a symbiotic relationship between public and private sectors providing sinews of common defense and war. Yet, it is the size and influence raised in Eisenhower's remarks that transfix our curiosity. Witness scholar Paul A. Koistinen's five detailed volumes and the bibliography of the present volume to illustrate why MIPC and America's security state excite further scrutiny.[4]

On May 10, 2013, sometime Pentagon official and president/CEO of the influential Washington think-tank Center for Strategic and Internal Studies, John Hamre, penned "An Honest Look at the 'Military-Industrial' Complex." Despite the obligatory paean to Ike, Hamre discounted the enduring myth "that the defense industry is an ominous, all-powerful puppeteer, manipulating the actions of politicians, political appointees, generals and admirals." "The truth is," he proclaimed, "it is the weak partner to the Defense Department." Departing the government arsenal system that had served the republic since its founding, Hamre espoused, harnessing "the energy and creative power of the profit motive to national security" by commercially produced aviation had introduced "a qualitative military edge" and indispensable partnership that won the Cold War. Now, the country threatened to seriously damage the private partner with long range consequences. Here then lay the MIC apologist view. It hinted at vested interest and unswerving acceptance of existence, not Eisenhower's plea to manage and control. Various reasons accounted for the problem in Hamre's view.[5]

First, claimed Hamre, "the defense industry is not sitting at the table when hard budget choices are made in the Pentagon." Sitting there were acquisition officials charged with end strength and force structure. Hovering over all "is the specter of Congress," insistent that no base or installation could be cut. Present too are the demands of combat units so that "among these powerful forces, the defense industry is a feeble voice." Second, Hamre railed against "an accretion of laws, regulations, reporting requirements and mandated procedures," choking the system, most government employees lacking experience in the private sector "so they don't understand what it takes to run business," and worse still, public policy ethics" that are being forced on the defense industry," sending a signal to talented businessmen—"stay away from government contracting." Third, Hamre told his think-tank family, a budget stalemate was crippling the economic future and "damaging an essential component of our national security in the process." Nine years later, this refrain still echoes in a Washington, fiscally challenged, ideologically divided and periodically shut down by politics, power grabs and issues broadly touching national security as *the* health of the nation. Hamre's concerns were real inside MIPC's inner circle. Yet, Eisenhower's original concern about MIC itself has faded from John Q. Public's awareness.

The "military-industrial complex" is the simple manifestation of arms and the State. Its pervasive strength, not necessarily dependent upon size, is part of historical lore. This book traces the evolution of America's military-industrial-business experience as the basis for what I suggest is an American Sparta. The insidious and ubiquitous presence of a vast spectrum and hierarchy of arms and services, public and private enterprise, mindsets and perceived goblins has integrated the nation's evolution. If the United States was itself a "Great Experiment" it was also a "Great Endeavor," inextricably glued together by demands of vast political, economic and cultural implications assuredly implicit in how the Founding Fathers' Constitution has evolved and been interpreted ever since. Therefore, the book examines the relationship of the public-private *provider* base over the course of American history. The story is not necessarily sinister but is fraught with implications and ramifications for power and mischief. In a sense that is what Eisenhower warned about. However, it can only be understood today when set against the context from President George Washington's own farewell enjoinder to the People and modern mores and needs of that People. It should remain the People's call. But, asking why the People have bought into the scheme that can be said to have profited mainly Elites remains unanswered.

Scholars from various disciplines have continued to broaden or deepen the epistemology although perhaps with less passion than shown in historian Keith L. Nelson's survey of "the 'Welfare State': History of a Concept." Critics lurk in the shadows; proponents like Hamre and others more openly on Capitol Hill, the Pentagon, Washington think-tanks and even the intelligentsia. As a result, while successive generations occasionally continue chants against war profiteering, merchants of death and militarization or demonstrate about far distant imperialist pretensions or rally herd-like to patriotism when tribe and homeland seem threatened, such expression reflects little more than proud tradition. Lost in translation is the futility of Ike's angst. For Americans, in particular, the revealing journey from Founding Generation to today evaporates in a tempestuous dystopia of globalization versus nationalist/populist pushback, non-state sponsored terrorist disruption paralleling a rejoined government-trumpeted great power competition and renaissance of eternal struggle between autocracy versus democratic liberalism. We have met "the MIPC," its off-shoot the "defense industrial base" and now, the "national security state." Pogo-like—it is us! Can we do anything about it?[6]

American business historians Keith Bryant and Henry Dethloff advance that for over three centuries, "the business of America has been business" (echoing President Calvin Coolidge's famous adage), but the characteristics of the society, the economy, and the culture have been in a constant state of change." Today, the business of America is largely about security, if not the common defense. Imbedded are other key themes, themes as prosaically traditional as the fate of the administrative state, the human inequality or have/have-not paradigm of large corporate power versus small business and common folk and mischief-making of plutocracy in the name of "patriotism and profit." Scholar Koistinen (who did the most comprehensive study of the political economy of American warfare) posits three major stages over the course of American history attaching to three familiar and pivotal wars—the Revolution, the Civil War and the twentieth-century wars. He conveniently labeled the stages as preindustrial, transitional, and industrial. Of course, a post-industrial appellation will obtain the further we move into the twenty-first century. Whether or not "transformational," "modificational" or "hybridal" will win out remains unresolved as long as industrial age legacy systems integrate with post-industrial informational cybernetics. Thus, technological now overtakes economic, political and military in Koistinen's quad. At the moment, the epoch moves into a new aspect of an Age of Fear still dominated by terror yet complicated by a return to Great Power competition/confrontation in addition to migrations, climate change, economic inequity and pandemics.[7]

Befitting a work of history, I advance the following scheme for the present book:

A Six Epoch Story

Tradition During Transition—from Colonies to Nation, Pre-1860
A Brave New World of Revolution and Emerging States
Government, Arsenals, Yards and a Cottage Armaments Industry
A People Numerous and Armed

Industrial Revolution and National Unification, 1860 to 1915
Wartime Military-Industrial-Commercial Complexes
Navalism, Imperialism, Industrialism and Advanced Technology
Arms Partnerships for the State

Total War/Mobilization of State, Government, Private Sector, 1916–1945
- Industrialized War and Managerial Capitalism in Public-Private Partnering
- Warfare/Corporate State, Merchants of Death/Arsenal of Democracy
- Sanctuary for Production

Cold War/Hot War and Warfare State, 1946–1990
- Nuclear Armageddon—the Ultimate Weapon
- Permanent State of Common Defense—the Military-Industrial Complex
- Hot Base/Cold Base/Warm Base—Rheostat Mobilization and Supplicant State

Millennial Transition and Uncertainty, 1991–2001
- Peace Dividend Transformation—"Last Suppers" and Supplicant Providers
- Revolutions in Military Affairs, Business Affairs
- Globalization, Destabilization and MIC's Survival

Back to the Future—9/11 and the Age of Fear and Upheaval from 2001
- Changing Threats, Benevolent Interventionism, Endless Instability
- Innovative Technology versus Legacy Production and Services
- Launching Backward to Make America Great Again as the Modern Sparta

Separate chapters will examine this schema. The end state today seems to be the business of security is now a core value and a vital national interest of an American Sparta. A living, breathing military-industrial-political complex is its driving force. Perhaps, it always has been that way.

The author would like to acknowledge the invaluable assistance, hard work, and patience of the University of Tennessee Press family associated with this work, including Scot Danforth (Director), Thomas Wells (Acquisitions Editor), Jonathan Boggs (Editorial Assistant), Patricia Ford (Copyeditor), and Holly Day (Indexer).

Chapter 1

COLONIAL SECURITY SHAPED BY WAR AND TRADE, TO 1783

Perhaps it started with Captain John Smith, a hired gun to train seventeenth-century Virginia colonists in self-protection. Captain Myles Standish filled a similar role for the Plymouth, Massachusetts experience. They brought their own weapons with them. Here began a "service sector" dimension of American defense followed by other facets of statist versus anti-statist attitudes, power of the purse, self-sufficiency (autarky) versus collaborative dependency, civilian control of the military and strategic unity in the country's formative years. We can also discover emergence of a gun culture and seeds of a prototypical "iron triangle of executive, legislative and private resource provider base from the era of the Founding Fathers. Eventually, we encounter public accountability, cost, efficiency and effectiveness in "a people numerous and armed." Pro and con security leaders and theorists are there also. Most of all, strategic geographical isolation vied with globalized mercantile system to set strategic parameters for safety and survival. Hundreds of years later we still ask, was the future United States of America destined to be an American Sparta rather than an American Athens?

The answer should bedevil us even in the twenty-first century. The answer lies certainly not before the Industrial Revolution or even perhaps the Atomic Age, yet protean signs were there. Finance historian Robert Hormats asserts that America was "a county born of war and debt." It should then be no surprise that today, America remains a country of war and debt. Even so, it has always been shaped by war and trade. Chalk it up to American security fears. Conflict and economics go hand-in-hand in resourcing a nation's security, a state function under the guise of mobilizing resources for war and peace. The state provides the structural and legal authority that sets the needs, goals and strategy. It then raises revenue to pay for execution, which in its most basic form is simply *survival*. It draws upon societal and natural elements of power to muster the instruments of power. Public and private sectors provide goods and services by contract between government and the people. The American state continues in debt because of the "sinews of war." Security is an expensive enterprise.[1]

Political economist Ethan B. Kapstein contended in 1992, the cost of war could disrupt "national strategy no less than enemy forces." The strength of governments in relation to their societies and relative popularity of causes, as well as conditions of its natural resource base, dictates the process. Popular constraints upon the state's power regarding excessive taxation, debt instruments employed by banking and credit markets, and moral and political imperatives of war-making must be considered. While the nature of the threat forever changes, the defense resource-base for securing ways and means adjusts even as the ends of policy change. The quandary—should strategy dictate resourcing or vice versa remains the determinant.[2]

An expert on the history of government contracting, James F. Nagle suggests recurring themes attend the three centuries since European-American governance was established on our shores, including tempestuous public-private relations over cost and profit, and government-contractor sourcing, ethics, competition, and contracting processes. Yet, other themes also exist including fear of standing military and strong central government. Emergence of a people numerous and armed, rising from the idea of an organized common militia, has paralleled aversion to government extraction, whether by taxation or conscription, regulation or surveillance. These are issues of statism versus anti-statism, along with self-sufficiency versus collaborative dependency (coalitions, alliances and partnerships). Humble beginnings "for the common defense" can be traced from America's germinal period, carefully crafted by centuries of civilian control of the military and strategic unity *for national security*.[3]

THE NEW WORLD AND IMPERIAL ECHOES

America was born and bred of empire, somebody else's empire. The Americas (for there were several) emerged from a transformative period in world history. This period can be characterized as globalization through contact with other cultures and peoples, commerce and colonization. It was mainly European expansion that also brushed with China and Islam, buttressed by trade and conquest. Proselytization of Christian faith, facilitated by maritime and military technological revolutions, aided and abetted a brave new world. The search for land and riches benefiting a home country characterized "mercantilism" and fueled an unrelenting projection of European civilization through force more than persuasion. Colonies were spokes, and mother country was the hub. Over several centuries, "the movement to settle America" occurred in a "world of mixed and conflicting tendencies," notes historian Richard D. Brown.[4]

Commercial expansion, readiness for high-risk investment, and power-based competition coupled with colonization, provided a grand strategy. Public and private investment and protection came within the purview of relations between Crown and subject. Subsumed within friction between rulers in the Old World and colonists in the New, emerged irrepressible questions. Who was to protect whom and whose investments, and at what price to each party? Who provided the "sinews of war" and what responsibilities fell to home governments via contractual dependence or self-sufficient autarky? The wealth of empire had to be tapped for God, Sovereign and State from subjects, whether at home or abroad. But, were colonials to expect a free ride or incur certain obligations? Geographical distance between crown and colony resulting in a consequent communication time-lag, and no "rationality of a modern bureaucratic system" to establish regularity, precision and punctuality, shaped defense of the realm. A certain sour note emerged from public-private enterprise known as "colonial expeditions" during various imperial campaigns of the British, French, Spanish and Native Americans. Weaponry and uniformed regular regiments marched, following logistics mainly contracted with colonists and indigenous peoples that were not always to everyone's satisfaction. The theme that colonial field operations conveyed cost, inefficiency and ill-effectiveness also took root.[5]

Historian John Shy once suggested 90,000 pounds sterling in provisioning and 94,000 pounds sterling in monetary beneficence flowed to American colonial economies between 1768 and 1774. This, set against British expenditures in North America that reached a million pounds per year, plus reimbursing the colonies nearly one-half the 3 million pounds spent on the French and Indian War alone. Afterward, the home government left 20,000 firearms and 200,000 pounds of powder, expecting colonial authorities to pay the expense of self-defense from that point on. Global Great Power conflicts moved elsewhere after the Seven Years War. Strictly orchestrated land fights as well as great sea battles between monarchial fleets remained the staple of the time, with irregular ancillary actions against merchant vessels by pirates, corsairs and freebooters. Special private contractors engaged in home-government bidding melded the New World contexts of irregular fighting between indigenous natives, settlers and crown militia. "The gun-carrying sailing ship remained the military-technological system of the modern era" and a European monopoly, claims technology historian Barton

Hacker. Colonials shifted from providing auxiliary help to Crown regulars to become first-defenders against both Crown tyranny and terrorism from the original inhabitants of the New World.[6]

Historians through the years have been skeptical of colonial military prowess. Nagle claims the French and Indian War "gave the colonies experience in fighting a war, including experience in supplying troops." It should have been "a training ground for the contracting and mobilization to come," but it was not. Naval historian James Bradford sees solid foundations "on which to build two of three necessary political-military institutions: experience with colonial governments, and with intercolonial congresses for sporadic cooperation. Yet, any colonial naval antecedents were largely chimerical. Lack of truly unified effort required to win wars especially stood out, but proved the greatest fault. Somehow forgotten is the fact that the colonial experience did introduce the climate of fear—fear of foreign and domestic threats (French, Spanish, native Americans, slaves, Crown power), mischief, and cost of standing militaries, as well as a strong and expensive but perhaps oppressive central government—in short, the theme of "anti-statism."[7]

The 1763 Treaty of Paris concluded the Seven Years War of Great Britain and Prussia against France and Austria, but shifted tectonic plates in North America. A vast British Empire now stretched from Labrador and Hudson Bay to Florida, and inland to the mountainous Appalachians. According to English historian Edmond Wright, these scattered and diverse bits of empire "casually and haphazardly acquired, were not parts of a system." The Board of Trade and Plantations lightly directed it and laws were evaded as much as honored. London, Bristol, Liverpool and Glasgow linked with Boston, New York, Philadelphia, and smaller American seaports, spawning an entrepreneurial merchant elite independent in mind and wealth but inextricably linked as part of mercantilism. Strategic priorities repositioned British resources to Canada, Appalachia, the West Indies, and even India. The home government posted nine under-strength battalions on a great arc, from Halifax in Canada to Pensacola on the Gulf of Mexico, for North American security. Postings were mostly detachments of the Sixtieth Royal American Regiment, to guard against French resurgence. Their purpose and cost to the colonial elite suddenly yielded unrest and rebellion.[8]

TECHNOLOGY TRANSFER VIA TOOLS OF WAR

Over the years, European colonists brought with them crafts and knowledge useful to security. Some historians see resultant "preindustrial craft traditions" and innovation underscoring this transplantation. Yet, they cite slow pace of technological change in weaponry, and Hacker particularly asserts that scientific and engineering technology in the art of fortification proved less transferable. This might seem unsupportable from remnant relics of Louisbourg, Ticonderoga and archeological digs elsewhere. Nonetheless, the uncontested superiority of European ships and guns provided foundational elements for conquest of the Americas while all nations standardized their cannon and adopted systems of artillery in the period 1689—1783. From matchlocks to flintlocks and iron to bronze cannon tubes, the mother country provided tools of war. Brightly-colored uniforms soon yielded to duller garb for colonial warfare, while Native American tomahawks and frontier Pennsylvania long rifles joined the tools of war. American oak trees remained indispensable to a wood-starved Royal Navy. A colonial shipbuilding industry could turn out small naval as well as commercial vessels.[9]

Charles Winthrop Sawyer contended in his 1919 study of firearms in America that "Colonists in America were the greatest weapon-using people of that epoch in the world." Everywhere, the gun was "more abundant than the tool." They were mainstay providers of food, protection of the homestead against aboriginal owners of the occupied land, as well as helping the mother country win possession of territory and resources. So, conditions were ripe for developing a gun culture. While the provider base for heavy ordnance and official martial arms stayed with home governments, émigré settlers eventually changed the provider paradigm through emergence of a home-grown metals industry. Historian of colonial metals James A. Mulholland discerned copper and iron as indispensable strategic materials in the convergence of an "American" political, economic, business and military experience. Long before the industrial revolution metals for tools, iron-bladed plows, wheelbands for mills and transport, conveyance hardware, something so commonplace as horseshoes, and chains and anchors of sailing ships, spawned objects critical to enterprise. No wonder historian Robert F. Smith stresses the application for potential military use.[10]

Tools and humanity, ideas and techniques, together crossed the Atlantic in "a feat of monumental importance in world history." Yet, under mercantilism, advances in colonial trades were tightly controlled so as to protect homeland enterprise. The Iron Act of 1750 severally stunted development of the North American iron industry. Independence of economic, political or cultural identity never entered mercantilist thought. Even so, "Enlightenment" military institutions themselves "underwent a sea change in passage to America," claim Hacker and Ian C. Hope. Highly-stylized "cabinet" warfare designed for *la grande guerre* of the continent competed with "a looser, more independent style" of *la petit guerre* combat in America. Bloody disasters like General Edward Braddock's defeat in western Pennsylvania underscored a sense of need for resourcefulness and individualism. Each colony bore responsibility for the costs of its militia under the principle of the assize of arms requiring weaponry and ammunition for the common defense. The 1689 English Bill of Rights granted the right of ordinary Englishmen to possess weapons and their American offspring also embraced this principle. Those able to purchase arms were to do so; those who could not looked to provincial governments to supply them. Hence the American tradition of possessing arms from offshore procurement and domestic provisioning, via mobilizable citizen-manpower service.[11]

Colonies were not intended to be self-sufficient, although Smith, in fact, supplements firearms historian M. L. Brown's computation of nearly 100 "British-American iron furnaces and forges" in the colonies before the Revolution, with latent capacity for domestic conversion to military purposes. Subsistence supplies like naval stores, wagons, conveyances, textiles, and leather goods, even human resources augmentation, could be locally provided in the colonies. Rudimentary support facilities succoring Crown military and naval forces, dual-use shipyards at ports like Philadelphia, New York and elsewhere, and niche-application scientific or engineering skills, enabled American subjects to begin their own technological base. Notably lacking was a centralized agency or system for cohesive wartime coordination. Smith questions "domestic availability of weapons, the productive design to make weapons, or the trade connections to import well-made weapons." Yet, he suggests the more fundamental problem may not have been technological at all, but rather the invertebrate condition of North American administration for mobilizing the implements of modern warfare, and employing them efficiently and effectively. Colonial military operations uncovered that notable deficiency.[12]

Moreover, the resourcing dilemma, unanswerable then or now, suggests the eternal issue of "how much is enough." Royal arsenals and armories tightly guarded the technologies of arms production. They had spawned an arms industry, whether Britain's London and Birmingham manufactories (with subcontractors as far afield as Scotland), or St. Eienne, Mauberge and Charleville in France. Home governments protected such a strategic asset so that from 1689 to 1763, suggests Sawyer, England alone "produced, used, and exported to America an enormous number of muskets of various sizes and shapes, and a large number of fowling pieces and pistols." There, they could be serviced by a cottage industry of emigrant gunsmiths who, according to arms expert Arcadi Gluckman, "repaired and made rifles and muskets, and made their parts in small quantities."[13]

When technology historians Alan Marcus and Howard Segal refer to colonial emergence of "large scale enterprise," they cite ironmaking and shipbuilding. These two key sectors, which later undergird a national military-industrial complex of the machine age, even in the colonial period pointed the way to a protean industrial base for American defense. These sectors coalesced with other factors when, as E. Wayne Carp sees it, British ministries "began to rationalize imperial administration" through taxation to pay for colonial defense by enforcing neglected trade regulations plus adding new ones. In 1774 the final blow of Coercive Acts—the Boston Port Act, Administration of Justice Act, Massachusetts Government Act and the Quebec Act—shifted the era from colonial dependency to rebellion and independence. Mobilization held the key.[14]

Perhaps the most fascinating part of the story lies with the seaboard ports which hosted industries most closely tied to mercantile trade and empire. It may have been inevitable that the technologies and manufacturing techniques of commercial shipbuilding tied into wartime necessity. Despite such religious aversion to conflict in a pacifist Quaker area like Pennsylvania, vested-interest colonial merchants, tradesmen, and shipbuilders resorted to survival-need defense against roving pirates, and Spanish and French privateers, when home-provided fleets failed them. Civic-minded politicians like Benjamin Franklin teamed with shipping entrepreneurs John Wharton, James Penrose, and Wharton's cousin, ship constructor Joshua Humphrey, "to complete the family linkage to an American naval establishment," claims historian Jeffrey Dorwart. Simplifying this phase of the enterprise, suffice to say, a naval/maritime shore establishment for acquisition and logistics emerged, based on the early Philadelphia waterfront of Southwark and Kensington where modest manifestations of a local Defence Committee authorized warships for a Pennsylvania navy (row galleys at first and later more advanced platforms), thus forming a growing provider-base for cannon and ammunition that supplied orders even from outside this particular colony. Need and profit, attitude and "patriotism" gelled, together with facilities, as a security establishment by the eve of revolt.[15]

Revolution to War, Government to Enterprise Institutions may have been more important than military technology at this point. English law and institutions had migrated to colonies, spanning Georgia to Massachusetts. Variations naturally existed and localism stood paramount, yet provincial assemblies, royal governors, and courts had become governmental mainstays until London's tyranny and oppression prompted a new American scheme for security and stability. That came with the protests, organizing of rebellion against the Crown, and a revolution in 1776 with subsequent confederation for independence. Philadelphia became the governing/strategizing centerpiece with the survival purposes of organizing and sustaining military force, and searching for partners and allies from abroad (mostly for arms and money), acutely aware that the loose arrangement of former colonies (now termed states) and a deliberative coordinating body (Continental Congress) faced major impediments attempting to mobilize and manage a war effort. Talk of unification had been voiced for decades by colonial leaders like Benjamin Franklin. The 1754 meeting at Albany, New York only proved again that disparate colonies had difficulty coming together even when confronting external threat. Now another armed conflict tested resolve and enterprise and Anglo-American aversion to standing armies. [16]

Still, if an American populace remained enigmatic in commitment, the Congress, its committees, and a Board of War working through a Commissary General of Military Stores (CGMS), tried to resource strategy and develop a "managed production system." The CGMS's "department" oversaw public production arsenals with government managers, and skilled and unskilled craftsmen at prototype Government Owned/Government Operated (GOGO) facilities in Philadelphia, Springfield, Massachusetts, and Carlisle, Pennsylvania. CGMS also coordinated quality standards at such facilities and provided material support through cash, resources and transportation to private contractors as part of a developing wartime military-industrial complex. Such a system joined the military during the conflict as more than mere trappings of sovereignty: it sufficed for mobilization.[17]

Army historians would later declare, "The primary commodity of any military mobilization is manpower." State militias sprang to the colors, seamstresses in towns made flag bunting (plus bandages, uniforms, and other civilian-convertible items) while iron furnace owners at Principio and Catoctin in Maryland, or Hopewell and Cornwall in Pennsylvania, showed how public purse and private America put shoulders to a new common weal. Whether in state governments or Continental Congress, the central issue quickly became finances. Taxation without representation under the empire gave way to anti-statist antipathy to any authoritarian hand of central governance, with money-raising a crucial rub even amid necessity of supporting a war for freedom. Certainly, the revolutionary elite—northern merchant and southern planter—understood the stakes of power. A people in revolt came face to face with the political necessity of organizing a military and an economy for war against a superior enemy overrunning the land. American revolutionaries learned on-the-job how to fund and resource from hand to mouth as part of self-governance. Their earlier experience with local colonial home rule vying with rule from home by King and Parliament conveyed to the new Continental Congress that rights and responsibilities formed part of the struggle over wartime common defense. The elite colonial governing class, as well as tradesmen, farmers, and small artisans, sought to balance individual self-interest and the welfare of larger society When individual colony-states failed to provide for America's common defense then Philadelphia had to step in with an invertebrate method for linking means to the ends (independence) through loans, liens, requests, cajolery, and economic diplomacy for underwriting the endeavor.[18]

In a way, the Founding Father dubbed "The First American," typified the ersatz revolution and war. Benjamin Franklin of Philadelphia—that classic combination of businessman, scientist, politician, and much else—was drawn into the intricacies of common defense against French, Indian, and even political discord within his province of Pennsylvania. He had experienced firsthand from the building of colonial forts the disunity of providers, from fellow provincials and the governors of Maryland and Virginia to Braddock's imperial campaign. It was only through personal contacts and emptying of his own purse that he effected resourcing under the anticipated partnering expected by His Majesty's government. Franklin and some other colonial figures like Thomas Hutchinson of Massachusetts had already faced the dilemma. Writing to London friend and fellow scientific dabbler Peter Collinson in May of 1754, Franklin pronounced: "Britain and her Colonies should be considered as one Whole and not as different States with separate interests." Only with unity of purpose could evolve unity of effort and defined organization, plans, procedures and proper staffing. After signing the Declaration of Independence, Franklin went off to find resources in Europe. He left others to secure unity at home. Still espousing American "first principles" of preparedness and reliance on citizen arms, Franklin theoretically reflected Britain's own 1757 Militia Act reform that stipulated all males of a certain age group had an obligation to state service.[19]

To later Americans, the major fault of the revolutionary generation was failure to build a truly cohesive effort necessary for winning wars and ensuring security. Yet, why fault the Founding Fathers when their phobia included fears of central government, standing armies and tyranny of what later would be styled "the administrative state." Moreover, profits could be made from war by the elite. A subsequent philosophy of business pacifism—that war hurts economic activity and prosperity—hardly moved beyond the common man's realization of a "rich man's war and poor man's fight." Accountability and misuse of excess profits traced directly to the business of defense and security in this period. Vested interests draped the costs of protest, rebellion and war in public virtue, and hid material gain. The chance, even probability, of malfeasance together with virtue coursed through hearts and minds. Bowing to reality, the Continental Congress jettisoned its earlier economic sanctions against trade with Mother England and opened global commerce with all parts of the Empire in April 1776. Logistics historian James A. Huston called this "the real declaration of independence" which, as it turned out, became absolutely crucial to building an enterprise.[20]

Merely proclaiming independence and styling some new entity a "United States of America" was not enough. Wresting an identity from Great Britain's restrictive "Mercantile Theory of Colonial regulation" still demanded proof of sovereignty. Full implementation of what today we label DIME—diplomatic, informational, military and economic power—required credibility of government. If central government was to shape attitudes and institutions to larger purpose, it required legitimacy, stature, and communicative power beyond the capabilities of the era. Whether judged by any previously estimated "1/3–1/3–1/3" equation (patriot, loyalist and uncommitted) or subsequent "1/5, 1/5, and 3/5" assessment, in the words of historian Michael Zuckerman, "we're no longer talking about a revolution that was the glorious emanation of the spirit of the people." Today's view that "about 20 percent who stole the country for their interests, ideology, politics–and who used force to bring the other 80 percent around" complicates analysis, as to how a Continental Congress and its fielded military acting under rudimentary Articles of Confederation might "secure the fruits of liberty."[21]

Identity had to be forged by force of arms on the battlefield, through sustainability, and frankly, in the self-interest of others. Taxation remained idiomatic anathema to authors of those Articles. Monetary analysts advance that congressional leaders at the time assumed the war would be financed by other means like foreign and domestic loans (hence the mission of Franklin and others), impressment of necessary matériel, and paper money–"lots and lots of paper money." Millions of this fiat money only resulted in non-acceptance by public and private users of such "currency finance." Large-scale indebtedness ($27 million from French, Spanish and Dutch lenders) plus services-in-kind (land, sea, and material), and extracting from a populace reluctant to sell matériel to the army, produced promises of ultimate payment which kept men in the ranks plus manning forges and tool benches, to accomplish eventual victory. Foreign governments sought advantage, discomforting Great Britain for their own gain not American rights.But it was messy.[22]

Procurement of manpower, matériel and financing ironically, proved troublesome to both Philadelphia and London. Generations of patriotic Americans have airbrushed heroic if questionable battlefield performance, much less procurement practices carrying whiffs of fraud, waste and abuse. General George Washington and his generals had to combat not only British regulars and hired mercenaries, but also their own politicians and tradesmen. The British watched the Americans broker rebellion and independence into resource multipliers via French, Dutch and even Spanish alliances, while King George III secured Hessian grenadiers. Yet, in the end, America's first war turned on tapping a domestic resourcing system, however shaky its financial underpinning. The Continental Congress and the various colony-states muddled through, setting precedents with policies and procedures, recruiting manpower, setting up production facilities for direct manufacture of munitions, and contracting for goods and services but almost always in competition with one another. Meanwhile, British generals and home government bungled actual conduct of the war.[23]

American revolutionaries produced their own share of misunderstood lessons. Battlefield captures scarcely augmented domestic procurement or foreign acquisition. Hauling captured artillery from Fort Ticonderoga to the siege of Boston made for good legend, but prolonged conflict required a more systematic and sustained resourcing effort. Congress worked to manage the war but, says Huston, "it hardly was to be expected that the colonies would at once grant to a congress, even of their own representatives, powers for regulating a common defense which they were determined to deny to Parliament even at the expense of war." Thus, could be found fourteen logistical systems—one each for the colonies plus the Continental Congress—attempting to mount a war effort. Resorting to an approach of both a "command" as well as a "market economy" eventually resulted, when rebellion turned into prolonged conflict and internationalization threatened an expiration date unsatisfactory to both sides in this cousin's war.[24]

FURNACE, FORGE, AND ENTERPRISE

Of two Continental Congresses, the first "was not a planning agency; it was a grievance forum," while the second "simultaneously began planning and legislating but [was] hobbled all the time by its inability to execute *forcibly*," explained Army mobilization historians Marvin A. Kriedberg and Merton G. Henry in 1955. Lacking power to tax or conscript significantly handicapped central direction. Under then-current philosophy, policy, and laws, the militia-draw from states would provide necessary units to a central army. At that time, as combat attrition supplanted protest and rebellion, the nearly decentralized system of state and national agency competition for resources produced conditions of trial and error. Other approaches were tried, including a requisition system whereby each state would furnish supplies in-kind on a fixed quota. It failed. So too did the civilian-contractor system that operated at the whim and prerogative (and honesty) of individuals not directly under army control. Finally, a system under unified, coordinated control and supervision emerged late in the war; this is what Smith, Carp and others have explored. [25]

Their scholarship discloses a natal military-industrial complex. Stretching from Congress in Philadelphia through a board of war, to a department of Commissary General of Military Stores under unsung but indispensable bureaucrats Colonel Benjamin Flower and Samuel Hodgdon who supervised arsenal facilities in Philadelphia and Carlisle, Pennsylvania, Springfield in Massachusetts, Albany in New York, and after 1781 in Virginia. Similar commissaries with superintendents of arms and ordnance also existed in Philadelphia, Carlisle, Springfield, and Boston. Notable generals Benjamin Lincoln and Henry Knox also populate a shifting framework of arsenals, armories, and private parties contracted for logistical enterprise. It was a "start-up" way of war.[26]

Meanwhile, a controversial portrait emerges of businessmen drawn into government service, who saw little difference in mingling public and private interests. Senior officials understandably sought merchants as deputies for various positions and places; as historian E. James Ferguson suggests, businessmen were the only individuals "who knew how to get things done" in an era prior to business professionalization. They possessed connections and expertise to deal with details of a supply chain operation, since as merchants they already engaged in such transactions. Public acceptance sans any developed codes of conduct for government-business officials also seemed apparent. However, Smith's detailed account of the small maze of both government and contracted gunsmiths, blacksmiths, ironmongers, and other artisanal craftsmen entering into the Revolutionary enterprise, found no culpable fraud, waste or abuse at the next level.[27]

Resourcing the Revolution and the War for Independence requires understanding public-private partnering in both the domestic and international context. They involved continental and state agents, private sector providers as well as globalized arms and manpower suppliers accessed via a network of friends and contacts ("elites" as Paul Koistinen styled them). Military operations interrupted supply chains and forced innovative solutions to some extent Re-outfitting a French fleet at Boston in August 1778 disrupted the Continental army's supply system in New England. But, evaporation of soldier exemptions for critical skills affecting ironmongers' cannon production that same year in Pennsylvania also affected resourcing. These occurred off stage from Congress and its business practices involving nepotism, limited authority, mingling of public and private ventures, funds and relationships that added questions to methods for winning independence.

Demand from Congress and colony-states for gunpowder, lead, small arms, artillery, clothing and equipment, forage, and food preeminently taxed domestic availability. Production, stockpiling and distribution among competing jurisdictions tested supply and demand with diverse practices such as contracts and impressment. County committees assisted state committees of safety in acquisition of military supplies and raising of troops. Virginia was especially active at that level, with the manufacture of hemp for clothing and rope even styled "a war-inspired industry." Firearms like muskets and pistols termed "Committee of Safety" and "Continental" weapons, for instance, reflected states' augmentation to a variety of European arms put in the hands of the insurrection. Lack of standardization plagued patriotic domestic arms makers as did procurement of materials, skilled labor, and uncertain money supply. It provided quite a learning experience although a partial list of musket makers supporting province/state committees from 1775 to 1777 counted 116 names. At the close of the Revolution the army of the fledgling United States held a heterogeneous collection of firearms including British Queen Anne (Brown Bess), French royal armory from Charleville, Mauberge and St. Etienne, as well as those makes from Committee of Safety and state armory. Over 100,000 French arms were procured at about $5.00 per musket. American-produced arms cost $12.30 per weapon. Importing firearms, "largely purchased by money borrowed in France," totaled $7,000,000.[28]

Resourcing war also extended beyond procurement of weaponry. Scarcity of some commodities like salt, indispensable in meat preservation and cheaply provided from Europe and the Caribbean before the war, led to rationing in Virginia. Gunpowder suffered in quality and cost from French competition, as well as inadequate domestic production facilities. "Lack of circulating hard cash and high prices hurt Pennsylvania's efforts to encourage both saltpeter and gunpowder production," observed David L. Salay in 1975. Such was the scarcity of lead that Daniel Roberdeau, a sometimes-wealthy Philadelphia merchant, delegate to the Continental Congress, and Pennsylvania brigadier, personally led a small expedition to the Juniata Valley in the central part of the state, to finance and direct construction of one of the earliest leadworks in both the state and new nation. Then suddenly, as was the case with saltpeter and gunpowder, the 1778 French treaty of alliance rendered it unnecessary to support and defend a frontier leadworks enterprise. Roberdeau's scheme collapsed.[29]

THE ONSET OF HEAVY WEAPONS ENTERPRISE

The Revolution surfaced two weapons requirements for America's defense and security. One, they would require industrial skills and infrastructure as well as raw materials and process. Second, they would be set apart from normal procurement due to size and technological sophistication as well as production capacities. The two types were artillery and warships. Both weapons systems drew upon foreign imports as well as domestic production. At the outbreak of the war, American artillery was an accumulation of diverse sorts of guns, mortars, and howitzers in thirteen different calibers. Until importation sources from Europe could be reopened, underdeveloped colonial casting industries assumed the burden of cannon fabrication. By contrast, colonial maritime industries were better able to convert merchant shipbuilding to naval use, fabricating distinctly American-made frigate-class warships.[30]

True, domestically made American cannon might not surpass European counterparts, but they could and did supplement what artillery eventually made the trans-Atlantic crossing. As early as the winter of 1776, a Congressional committee explored artillery requirements, production capabilities, and procurement opportunities that led to domestic fabrication of 250 twelve-pounders, 60 nine-pounders and 62 four-pounders within a year. Foundries were already casting both bronze and iron guns by 1775, and additional facilities sprang up at Reading and Warwick in Pennsylvania, Bridgewater in Massachusetts, Westham in Virginia, Salisbury in Connecticut, and the Hope Foundry in Rhode Island, for instance Labor shortages and necessary proximity to iron sources, such as Salisbury in the Connecticut region, affected production. Still, proprietors like Charles and Joseph Hoff, managers of the Hibernia furnace near Morristown, New Jersey, could be seen as prime contractors of heavy ordnance for the Continental Army.[31]

Yet, above all, independence demanded a navy. By December 13 of 1775, the Continental Congress had decided to build an American fleet. There were to be thirteen frigates, five of which would mount 32 guns, five with 28 guns, and three with 24. These were commerce raiders, preying on enemy trade yet capable of engaging enemy warships This legislation introduced a pattern of economic patronage to maritime communities with obvious patriotic overtones. Possible construction locales divided the shipyards among New Hampshire (one), Massachusetts (two), Rhode Island (two), Connecticut (one), New York (two), Pennsylvania (four) and Maryland (one). Estimated cost reached well over a half-million dollars apiece. All the materials to outfit them for sea, excluding canvas and gun powder, could be procured in America—a sort of predecessor to "buy American" in later years. A powerful body of representatives from each of the thirteen states (not just the construction states), known as the Marine Committee, took charge of building and fitting out these vessels. Special agents were selected to superintend the construction, usually determined by local advice, influence, and local residents.[32]

The story of construction established a pattern. The New Hampshire 32-gun frigate *Raleigh* was built at Portsmouth under direction of John Langdon, a former Naval Committee member and now Continental Agent. He and three master-builders completed the frigate within sixty days of raising there. Massachusetts frigates *Hancock* (32 guns) and *Boston* (24 guns) were constructed at Salisbury and Newburyport under an agent's direction. Rhode Island frigates *Warren* (32 guns) and *Providence* (24 guns) were built at Providence under superintendence of twelve prominent citizens of the city appointed by Stephen Hopkins, the Rhode Island member of the Marine Committee. Controversy over cost erupted when some of the local committee employed workmen and stock of privateers on their outfitting, and eventually relinquished authority over the Rhode Island vessels to Hopkins.[33]

Chatham on the Connecticut River was the site for Connecticut's frigate, *Trumbull* (28 guns) while two other vessels underwent construction in 1777: 28-gun *Bourbon*, also at Chatham, and *Confederacy* (36 guns) on the Thames River between Norwich and New London. Each was constructed by a superintendent, responsible to Governor Jonathan Trumbull and the Connecticut Council of Safety. Two commissioners at Poughkeepsie in New York had charge of that state's work on *Montgomery* (28 guns) and *Congress* (24 guns). The Marine Committee kept direction of the Pennsylvania frigates in its own hands. Philadelphia was the site for building *Randolph* (32 guns), *Washington* (32 guns), *Effingham* (28 guns), and *Delaware* (24 guns). The frigate *Virginia* (28 guns) was built at Baltimore, assisted by the local Committee of Observation. Omission of maritime Virginia and the south, perhaps due to their own initial opposition to thirteen frigates as "a Yankee scheme designed to fatten northern purses," was obviated by congressional resolves of November 29, 1776 which designated Gosport, near the mouth of Chesapeake Bay in Virginia, a shipyard site for constructing two frigates. In charge were two commissioners and a master-builder, with the state's member on the Marine Committee, Richard Henry Lee, handling contract arrangements. The Marine Committee also constructed and purchased other vessels, for a fledgling navy of twenty-seven vessels by 1776, including John Paul Jones's famous *Ranger*. However, three years later it had shrunk by over half, and to three warships in total by 1781, with *Bourbon* and *America*, a magnificent 74-gun ship of the line, still on the stocks under construction.

No wonder the preeminent naval historian Oscar Paullin once opined, "with its pygmy fleet the Maine Committee was able to inflict but little injury upon the British navy," an armada of 468 vessels, many of them powerful frigates and ships of the line, by war's end. Apparently only the *Randolph*, from the Wharton and Humphreys shipyard in Philadelphia, out of thirteen American frigates laid down under the Naval Act of December 1775, actually saw combat. No less ignominiously, all the ships were sold off at the end of the war; from the sale of the last, *Alliance*, until establishment of a new navy under the Constitution, "it was left to the stars and stripes floating from American merchantmen to familiarize foreign ports and seas with the symbol of the new nation." The United States might be a maritime nation, but it was born of land war.[34]

DEMOBILIZATION AND PROTO-INDUSTRIAL REVOLUTION

The new United States knew no more about how to "demobilize", than it had to "mobilize" in the first place. Demobilization after the Revolution would produce another of two hallowed American traditions, along with basic unpreparedness for war. However dangerous a post-independence world was, still dominated by major powers like Great Britain, France and Spain—all retaining colonial footprints in the New World and threatening the very existence of the nascent republic—America's citizen-soldiers returned to their plows, equipment went to rust or rot in storage bins, and infrastructure became moribund. A postwar slump hit hard in places like Philadelphia's maritime industries. True of the war itself, who could contradict logistical historian Huston's later conclusion that "the American effort, with all its shortcomings and times of crisis, ultimately was successful." French aid had been indispensable, but "all the French aid could not have brought about American independence." Perhaps republican ideology had not exclusively won the Revolution either, but Robert F. Smith's studies advance a real contribution of matériel by a home-grown defense-industrial base (DIB). Possibly some false sense of self-sufficiency, virtue and "a people numerous and armed" emerged from the experience. Naval historian William Fowler decided that constructing those thirteen frigates was no easy task. "They were the biggest and most expensive vessels ever laid down on this side of the Atlantic," he observes. "Millions of dollars [were] spent–some of it wisely, some of it foolishly," but "it was our first grand experience with defense contracting and then, as now, politics was always a consideration."[35]

Nobody could be quite sure how to handle demobilization in the practical sense of sending soldiers home, auditing outstanding contracts, paying off accounts, disposing of war surplus, or storing matériel at places like

Springfield, West Point and Philadelphia- as well as maintaining some form of standing force for common defense. An attitude of who was going to fight us, plus pecuniary necessity, defrayed serious question by the Confederation Congress on the nature of governance and paying lip service to independence. Only much later could mobilization historians Kreidberg and Henry visualize lessons like "inescapable value of centralized, coordinated control and supervision of the war effort," or the need for control of a national economy and public opinion, clearly foretold by events of that fiery trial. A nation which could produce only few surpluses for war must have some other assured source of war material, said the pair. In contrast, the "militia style" myth of a minuteman, like Cincinnatus springing from his plow in time of danger, went forward with a symbolic Yankee Doodle experience. Everyone might agree that mobilization accomplished during a war without adequate prior planning, "is wasteful, clumsy, inefficient, and potentially dangerous." But, in 1783, Americans wanted to forget war.[36]

* * *

Was it worth it? Certainly not for the "twenty-percenters" (loyalists), and a fair number of "sixty-percenters" (non-aligned). The revolutionary experience costs are largely unknown, aside from a war debt of perhaps $27 million and worthless paper money. Upwards of supposedly 25,000 American lives were lost in military service (during imprisonment, mostly from disease and starvation), with possibly another such number disabled or otherwise lost to productive activity. Direct costs in pay and equipment drained $37 to $40 million from national coffers and $114 million from states. Dislocation from a prewar economy as part of the British imperial system was palpable. How to break back into globalized trade but now as outsiders provided a challenge. War debt presented another one. Also, hostile European powers and aborigines still occupied portions of the new frontier beyond the Appalachian horizon. How to protect an infant republic against those predators?[37]

While it remains "difficult to determine if government operations were effective in meeting the needs of the Continental Army," traditional interpretation by E. Wayne Carp suggests that they did not. Still, Robert J. Smith contends the department of Commissary General of Military Stores "provided the most significant impact" by equipping the army with the weapons "it needed to fight and win the War for Independence." Moreover, the effort acquainted American manufacturers and craftsmen "to large-scale production" through innovative ideas, workspace organization, and labor methods. Smith stands by "the successful introduction of the Industrial Revolution to America" through the Revolution's "revelation" that large-scale manufacturing and industrial organizations could be productive in the domestic economy." To him, the enterprise "influenced the role of the federal government in guiding national manufacturing," and encouraged producers to "push the boundaries of manufacturing innovation and develop more effective large-scale operations." Moreover, Brown lists some 500 domestic "patriot arms makers" contributing to the manufacture of firearms or related war matériel for the American cause. Fellow historian Larrie Ferreiro, however, insists that it was French and Spanish intervention with volunteers, money and arms, especially the latter, that tipped the scales. Overall, "over 90 percent of the arms" and $30 billion equivalent in direct financial aid kept "the sinews of war from unraveling." Such lessons in overseas dependency would factor prominently in the psyche of the young new nation.[38]

The marginally successful combat soldier but discerning logistician and postwar Secretary of War, Benjamin Lincoln, told Congress in 1783 that war was not the moment to establish manufactures "which are . . . perfected by time and long experience, and "not [to be] deferred until the necessities of such a situation declare its propriety." He went on to say: "Manufactures should be erected under the immediate inspection of the public–and such bounties be given as would be sufficient inducement for individuals to attempt their establishment and perfection." Here was a prescription for survival in a dangerous world, a useful lesson from his generation's experience. As Carp perceptively suggests, the conflict changed attitudes toward two institutions that many Americans had heretofore deplored: professional armies and a strong central government. Joyce Malcom isn't as sure when it came to either or both. Just how such perceptions carried forward remained to be seen now that America was on its own.[39]

Chapter 2

MANIFEST DESTINY, INDUSTRIAL REVOLUTION, PUBLIC ENTERPRISE, 1783-1860

Americans may have awakened afraid, the day after the Treaty of Paris was signed. True, the war for independence was over. They were free from British rule. A vast future beckoned. But Congressional ratification of the peace treaty would take months, and few citizens of the new republic really understood the implications of their success. The new nation would lack British protection. Trade within constraints of the mercantilist world would continue as Great Britain prescribed new navigation act restrictions. Legal provisions regarding property restoration, debt repayment and slave removal in the new nation would be soon disregarded by individual states, with the power of central government so weak. Boundary details of the treaty did not match geographic reality in North America. Any safety value for land-hungry, restless Americans still confronted roadblocks to the west. War debt and economic uncertainty loomed, as Americans now bore responsibility for their own survival. Most of all, American leaders sought a national identity.[1]

DETERMINING A PEACE ESTABLISHMENT

Survival and self-determination, together with the war debt, confronted leaders with what should be "the common defense?" How would it be paid for? How could the contemporary plight of European nations–the rise of the so-called "fiscal-military state" for war—be avoided in North America? The new nation rested on faith, hope and charity for the most part. Perceived "isolation" from world affairs, deficient means of defense, and a government too weak to implement responsibility for its citizenry symbolized the Confederation period. Yet, foundational cornerstones for a later United States had been laid. Present at its creation were confidence and messianic intent, appetite for territorial expansion, anti-statism, and disputed definitions of public/private enterprise. Would agrarian reality or commercial potential portend America's future? How was "power" to be defined, shared and protected via government in this new and perilous journey? Moreover, just who would want to fight us anyway?[2]

The answer lay with ill-wishers of various stripes: the British, French, and Spanish, and the original Native American tribes. The machinations among their agents to contain American expansion often involved a flourishing arms trade. Even domestic threats such as city mobs and plantation slaves posed potential dangers. Or, as Secretary of War James McHenry more simply told President John Adams in April 1797, the object of national defense should be "the protection of our commerce, the securing our cities from requisitional invasions, and the Southern part of the U.S. from domestic insurrections." Representatives in Congress advanced that "an energetic national militia is to be regarded as the *capital security* of a free Republic." Americans stood opposed to a costly, intimidating standing army benefitting elite-class interests, at the expense of common liberty. Fearful of some militaristic Cromwellian reincarnation, "militia theory" would undergird American military policy for decades, yielding rheostatic mobilization and demobilization of citizens and matériel in time of specific need. Overlaid with principles of liberty, justice and pursuit of happiness, helped by geographical isolation that rendered costly defense expenditures moot, the theory fit early grand strategy.[3]

The newly independent United States had to grapple with identity. It would pass through a period of gestation with periodic conflict, but in time, also by national development—compliments of an industrial revolution. The transition would alter how the State converted elements of power. Matters of cost and influence, and concern over potential misuse of public money shaped the thinking of the Revolutionary Generation. The names Washington and Henry Knox, Alexander Hamilton, Thomas Jefferson, James Madison, Benjamin Stoddert, John Marshall, and a host of lesser mortals, populated the years to the end of a second war with Great Britain. Then a new leadership team appeared, with names like James Monroe, Andrew Jackson, John C. Calhoun, Daniel Webster, Jefferson Davis and James Dobbins, who found national security to be of absorbing interest. "Manifest destiny," continental expansion and free trade, as strategic talismans, would be joined with defending America's interests of urban and rural investment enterprise, for elites and commoners alike. Slave labor as a troublesome underpinning for much of American capitalism, defined a struggling divisive nation into the mid-nineteenth century. Draped across the nation-building effort was the quest for a monolithic soul. But, at this point "these united states" dripped from American tongues still in the plural sense, not singular. Historians speak of "an empire of wealth" creating an American economic identity, with a limited, wise and beneficent government holding some sort of key. Immediately following revolution and independence, demise posed the real threat.[4]

Meanwhile, the Confederation Congress voted on June 2, 1784 to limit the standing army at eighty men and a small number of officers. They would be stationed at Fort Pitt (Pittsburgh) and West Point to safeguard military stores, principally gunpowder, along with a leftover surplus of firearms and equipment of domestic or foreign manufacture. This cache could be stored until needed again. A small complex of arsenals and armories eventually dispersed military storage to places like New London in Connecticut, Campbell County in Virginia, Philadelphia and Carlisle in Pennsylvania, West Point in New York, and Springfield in Massachusetts. Knowledge of logistics was kept alive by dedicated government bureaucrats like Samuel Hodgdon and Henry Knox, both veterans from wartime agencies such as the Department of Commissary General of Military Stores (DCGMS), and the army artillery establishment. Hodgdon managed to keep his agency afloat by selling off surplus while Knox badgered the legislators for a modernized, more structured arrangement. Forward depot facilities like Fort Pitt lamely resourced frontier protection. The Springfield arsenal gained notoriety in Daniel Shay's 1786–87 rebellion through linking that episode with a perceived need for stronger centralized government. This national facility continued to operate at reduced levels until its formal establishment by act of Congress in 1794, producing the first official American martial arm, a model 1792 musket based on its French Charleville counterpart.[5]

If no significant technological development in American firearms evolution surfaced in the Confederation period, as firearms expert M. L. Brown sees it, the thrall of the Founding Generation for British and French models of public manufactory tantalized officials like Ambassador to France Thomas Jefferson. Mainly because of standardization and parts-interchangeability concepts of Paris musket-maker Honore' Blanc, French influence would continue for decades, further helped by Napoleonic battlefield success, as much as any residual gratitude for the Marquis de Lafayette and his countrymen's role in helping win American independence. At the time, with freedom achieved, and the near-coup of Washington's officer-corps-inspired conspiracy at Newburgh, New York quashed, military stores were safely tucked away, contracts terminated and, in disdain of possible expensive military costs, with avoiding heavy taxation uppermost in mind, even the remaining ships of a wartime ersatz navy were sold off and foreign policy issues delegated to diplomats. To one historian, the United States was predominantly a maritime entity, "albeit a nearly defenseless one."[6]

The new nation's power truly lay with merchant fleets and foreign trade growth. Imposition of British postwar trade restrictions "sent shock waves throughout the American economy," much more than destabilized land frontiers. To legendary naval historian Charles Oscar Paullin, "it was left to the stars and stripes floating from American merchantmen to familiarize foreign ports and seas with the symbol of the new nation." Still, twentieth-century army mobilization historians claim that "all of the difficulties of manpower procurement, supply, transportation, and communications" encountered by the army along the western frontier for decades to come were already present in these early years. Following precedents, low-bid government contract agents handled supply and transport for clothing and feeding the meager frontier garrisons. War surplus sufficed, since no provision was made for a force large enough to deal adequately with a frontier problem, further exacerbated by a land ordinance of 1785 and the Northwest Ordinance of 1787, both of which opened the floodgates of potential conflict between white man's expansionism and Native American rights and way of life. The Confederation government proved inept at addressing basic military, commercial and financial needs of the young Republic.[7]

SECURITY BLUEPRINTS

The United States clearly needed a security blueprint at this point. To start with, aside from Benjamin Lincoln and Henry Knox, America's *pater familias* George Washington seemed the most logical advisor to the Confederation Congress on military matters. On May 2, 1783, he submitted "Sentiments on a Peace Establishment" to a congressional committee charged with envisioning "the defense of the Empire: involving the immediate safety and future tranquility of this extensive Continent." He spoke of "empire." And, military historian Dave R. Palmer later suggested Washington's thoughts provided the seed corn of vision and strategy, supporting "strong and broadly based military organization." The general particularly enunciated three distinct goals: defending the new nation's territory and citizenry, protecting commerce and trade, and promoting the opening of western lands for settlement. Sufficiently powerful deterrence would keep all foes at bay. Washington then optimistically rested his case on four pillars of a "strategic concept for the defense of the continent." To Palmer, they included, "forces in being for immediate reaction, others having an efficient mobilization capability, a system permitting rapid movement to threatened areas, and a sustaining base." The general drew upon classical Greece and Rome "in their most virtuous and Patriotic ages" and superimposed Anglo-American recognition that militia, not standing armies, were synonymous with liberty and prosperity. Washington also advocated a national military school to perpetuate appreciation of science, while reducing from five to three grand Arsenals as advocated by the secretary of war at the time.[8]

Hardly a scientist of Benjamin Franklin's stature, yet deferring to those who were, Washington touched chords resplendent with scientific and engineering overtones. "That some kinds of Military Manufactories and Elaboratories [sic] may and ought to be established, will not admit a doubt; but how far we are able at this time to go into great and expensive Arrangements and whether the greater part of the Military Apparatus and Stores which will be wanted can be imported or Manufactured, in the cheapest and best manner," was the question. His opinion held "that if we should not be able to go largely into the business at present, we should nevertheless have a reference to such establishments hereafter." Interim work could be carried on "wherever our principal Arsenals may be fixed, as will not only be sufficient to repair and keep in good order the Arms, Artillery, Stores &c of the Post, but shall also extend to Founderies [sic] and some other essential matters." Thus the "Father of His Country" gave sentiments "without reserve" that they might prove useful "in forming an Establishment which will maintain the lasting Peace, Happiness and Independence of the United States." Two centuries later, historian Palmer thought that Washington's "prescription for preparedness" would prove "every bit as valid in 1883 or 1983." Opposition would be too.[9]

Unready to embrace the need, Congress rejected Washington's proposals. Yet, international uncertainty, government insolvency, and frontier instability eventually drove a strategy meeting, in Philadelphia in 1787, "to form a more perfect union". What emerged was *The Constitution of the United States*, a national security document, or as distinguished analyst Walter Millis once observed, "a military, no less than a political charter for the infant republic." It could be cited as the first national security strategy with "First Principles," "military clauses" grappling with thorny issues of standing military versus militia, financing and strong central government. Article I grants authority over purse and sword to Congress. Article II accords commander-in-chief, treaty and appointment provisions to the presidency. Article III inserts the Judiciary with regard to treason. The Second, Third and Fifth Amendments chime in as afterthoughts or conscience-tweaks of the signers concerning well-regulated militia, the eternally contentious issue of the people's right to bear arms, the quartering of troops, and military exemptions to capital crimes. Only Article IV of the Constitution arguably provides "The Basic Law" regarding national security, where Section 4 ensures: "The United States shall guarantee to every state in this Union a republican form of government, and shall protect each of them against invasion; and on application of the legislature, or of the executive (when the legislature cannot be convened), against domestic violence." We could ask why this Article is not the first in the sacred text? Nonetheless, the Constitution provides a fundamental blueprint for America's modern security state.[10]

The Constitutional Convention resulted from unmet needs. The Confederation government at least had set up a contract-managed national postal system ensuring national security communication. By 1791, ten amendments had been added as a Bill of Rights, most if not all of which spoke to security. Other tinkering continued when the critical issue of centrism versus diffusion plagued the first presidential administration. Embryonic political factions, later called parties, emerged. Embracing "the militia tradition" as a baseline for volunteerism and still fearing what revolutionary pamphleteer Thomas Paine might term a monarchic "war system," Congress produced the Militia Act of 1792 (Paine would soon react to upheaval in France with his pivotal *Rights of Man*, and at one point, advocate general disarmament). A national government could call forth the states' militia "to execute the laws of the Union, suppress insurrections and repel invasions," another semi-success for the centrists. Would that be enough? To Millis it was unrealistic, "attempting to create a great army, which should arm itself with the muskets and rifle equipment carefully prescribed," but which he suggests, "in fact produced only a paper system that was never of much military value." In the 1790s, this prescription was about rationally resourcing men and matériel between the states and the populace.[11]

The nation-building continued, notwithstanding anti-federalist politicians working hard to counterbalance centralization of power. By mid-decade they succeeded in limiting construction for only a small, independent federal navy and relegated responsibility for coastal defense to the states. The national government would build and garrison inland frontier forts. Federalists got their arsenal/armory arrangement, a corps of artillerists and engineers to assist in maritime defense, and eventually a military school for science and technology at West Point. In the eyes of one visiting French engineer the coastal forts, proved to be "either good for nothing or at least defective." They were good money "said to be thrown away." Persistent unrest on the frontier, domestic unhappiness like the Whiskey Rebellion in Massachusetts and Watauga disillusionment in western North Carolina, quasi-war troubles with the French or irritating tweaks by Great Britain, ruffled progress in domestic development. Yet, more blueprints appeared, such as Alexander Hamilton's "Report on Manufactures", sent to Congress on December 5, 1791.[12]

Historian Edward Meade Earle once contended Hamilton was "an economic nationalist," promoting manufacturing to make "the United States independent of foreign nations for military and other essential supplies.

Best known for his financial and fiscal acumen, Hamilton envisioned that solvency could be a "national blessing" or "powerful cement to our Union." A single national currency. federal financing of a massive system of internal improvements, and a strong professional military including, encouragement of government munitions-making, could support commercial and industrial liberty, and above all promote national unity thereby contributing to political and economic power of the nation. In all cases, Hamilton's focus was strategic, with national defense pervading his advocacy. Numbered among his themes were autarky, annual purchase of military weaponry, government encouragement of a weapons industry, and protective tariffs leading to a truly diversified economy that included agriculture, manufacturing, and commerce. But, as a maritime nation, a national navy would be the great resource integrator. Dependent upon the sum of its parts for power, Hamilton saw Southern supply of wood for construction, as well as naval stores of tar, pitch and turpentine, melding with Middle-States iron ore, and Northeastern supply of seamen. To him, "the necessity of naval protection to external or maritime commerce does not require a particular elucidation, no more than the conduciveness of that species of commerce to the prosperity of a navy."[13]

Congress was unready for Hamiltonian progressivism, just yet. His program, if not his ideas, proved premature for moneyed interests continuing to embrace merchant capitalism. Earle places Hamilton squarely between Scottish economist Adam Smith with his 1776 anti-mercantilist ideas in *Wealth of Nations*, and the later German-émigré intellectual Frederick List, who preached autarky and protectionism during the blossoming of the industrial revolution. Self-sufficiency made sense in the 1790s, a decade fraught with a revolutionary Europe and fractious American unification wobbling under its first trammels of presidential succession. Once more, Washington rose to the occasion with final ruminations. His much-cited *Farewell Address* of September 1796 provided yet another blueprint for American state development. Florid in style, his words hung out new and essential pillars of public felicity and liberty: National Unity, Political Moderation, Fiscal Discipline, Virtue and Religion, Education, and Foreign Policy. In the last, however, he contravened the very tenet that had underscored independence—alliance with foreign powers who might help with resources necessary for effective security and defense. His view brimmed with self-sufficiency and self-determination.[14]

Washington was all in favor of coalitions as temporary collaborations "for extraordinary emergencies" but hardly capable of permanent entanglements. A centrist/nationalist, presiding over launching the unification movement for national development, with Hamilton drafting the message anyway, who would have expected anything less than a paean to self-sufficiency and self-determination? So was born that hoary American espousal of disengagement if not outright isolationism, by keeping to "harmony, liberal intercourse with all Nations," and freedom of impartial trade. Perhaps Washington's annual message to Congress at the end of the year held greater importance for later development of a military-industrial complex and national security state. Here, he elaborated upon what public service had actually taught him. "Indispensable" naval protection, encouragement of manufactures, agriculture, and stimulation of education seemed inseparable from "individual or National Welfare." A national university and military academy for "the education of our Youth in the science of Government" were most pressing as "future guards of the liberties of the Country." [15]

Thus, Washington preached self-reliance. He saw congressional encouragement of manufacturing aligned with the trend we have come to understand as "industrialization." As a country squire he may have been less cognizant of the phenomenon than compatriot Hamilton, although more so than their agrarian contemporary Thomas Jefferson. Not that Washington advocated "manufactures on public account." But, he posited, where conditions left "little hope that certain branches of Manufacture will, for a great length of time obtain; when these are of a nature essential to the furnishing and equipping of the public force in time of War, are not establishments for procuring them on public account, *to the extent of the ordinary demand for the public service*, recommended by strong considerations of National policy, as an exception to the general rule." Should the country remain dependent on precarious foreign supply, liable to interruption? "If the necessary Articles should, in this mode cost more in time of peace," would not the resulting security and independence "form an ample compensation?" Government-owned and operated establishments "commensurate only with the calls of the public service in time of peace, will, in time of War, easily be extended in proportion to the exigencies of the Government," and "could even be made to yield a surplus for the supply of our Citizens at large; so as to mitigate the privations from the interruption of their trade." However, Washington concluded, such facilities must not endanger private industry.[16]

Interestingly enough, the final "blueprint" of this formative period came in 1798, from secretary of the fledgling Navy department Benjamin Stoddert. He proposed a major and continuing program, or as Millis styled it, "a powerful instrument of protective sea power." As major war with France threatened, Stoddert claimed twelve ships of seventy-four guns, as many frigates, and twenty or thirty smaller vessels, would ensure respect from the Maritime

Nations, protection of coastline, security from invasion, and safety of important commerce. Whether to buy them or build them was the question of the day; the first one was most expeditious, the second "will be the most honorable and most advantageous," in Stoddert's view. Purchase from a foreign nation would not net the best quality and "the sum given for them will not be kept at home, and distributed amongst our own Citizens; but will operate against us like an unfavourable balance of trade." He calculated the annual expenditure of this new navy at $5.5 million, double that at present. The attraction came from domestic procurement including hemp, possibly copper, to the iron for cannon. Here was Hamilton's "infant industry" argument or the later "American System" notion that blended economics seamlessly with the national security. What Stoddert, like other nationalists, saw was an America blessed with boundless resources and geographical advantage, the "means of annoying the Trade of the Maritime powers" but requiring "force sufficient to insure our future peace with the Nations of Europe." He spoke to a battle fleet that could protect American commerce, guard against invasion, and make powerful nations "desire our friendship and the most unprincipled respect for our neutrality." He stressed that a navy would be for defense and "not for Conquest."[17]

NECESSITY FOR A DEFENSE INDUSTRIAL BASE

Congress did little with any of these blueprints for the moment. Ironically, the first United States census in 1790 might almost have provided another blueprint. Population hovered at 4 million souls but the national debt was about $54.1 billion. Of federal expenditures at $4.27 million, some $2.35 million went to reducing that debt. Interestingly, Federal government expenditures teetered around $1.3 million of which the Department of War demanded $633,000, and an additional $176,000 to veterans. However, federal expenditures teetered under $10 million of which the Department of War commanded about half during the decade of the 1790s. Meanwhile, President Washington had signed into law the tariff of 1789, setting precedent for funding government and national security by yielding revenue without unduly restricting trade. The infant United States stumbled through insults from European powers, Algerine corsairs, and Native Americans.[18]

Alarmed by punitive disasters on western frontiers, Congress contracted with seven Pennsylvania gunsmiths to supply unembellished American long rifles for a new battalion. It was, notes firearms historian M. L. Brown, "perhaps appropriate that the first firearms made under United States contract" added public-private partnership to the seedling domestic defense provider base of government manufacture. Six of the seven contractors had supported the patriot cause during the Revolution. Furthermore, contracting out such munitions production (eventually including French émigré powder maker Eleuthere Irene du Pont in Delaware plus Connecticut River valley gun producers Simeon North and Eli Whitney), together with government armories at Springfield and Harpers Ferry, Virginia, offered what Brown suggests as "a climate ripe for the propagation and exploitation of practically unlimited techonomic development in the struggling United States."[19]

Meanwhile, the tariff of 1789 set precedent for funding government and especially national security by "yielding revenue without unduly restricting trade." It worked well until 1815, providing roughly 90 percent of total revenue although the Federalists resorted to a direct property tax in 1798 to boost a naval buildup. Although the early days of a political party system promised a stormy future, the president finally started a navy with four 44-gun and two 36-gun frigates, constructed for about $6.9 million by Henry Knox's War Department. Heated arguments attended House floor debate when one Virginia representative spoke of "certainty and enormity" of expensive fleet procurement. It would be "a complete dereliction of the policy of discharging the principle of the public debt," he raged. History afforded no instance of a nation "which continued to increase their navy and decreased their debt at the same time." Naval competition between European powers had only "produced oppression to their subjects and ruin to themselves." A South Carolina colleague countered that he saw no reason why the country with increasing population, much individual wealth, and considerable resources in building its own navy, "should involve us in an insupportable expense." This argument would be heard in the future.[20]

Meanwhile, responsibility for negotiating contracts, and ordering and assembling construction materials for building the warships passed from Knox to Secretary of the Treasury Hamilton, who in turn assigned it to revenue commissioner Tench Coxe. Knox consulted with renowned Philadelphia shipbuilders, eventually engaging Joshua Humphreys and John Hackett of Salisbury, Massachusetts to draw up plans for the warships. Humphreys's designs won out even though based on French plans for a heavier 74-gun craft. The live oak and red cedar hull materials would come from Georgia and Carolina coasts but the woodcutters and carpenters went south from Connecticut, Rhode Island and Massachusetts, under supervisors, to do the work. A Boston company would supply sailcloth. Maryland and Rhode Island furnaces would forge the cannon while cannon balls would come from two New Jersey providers. Home industries were to be patronized although hull-sheathing copper, bolts, nails, bunting and iron kitchens, even cloth flags, had to come from abroad. Six naval captains were appointed to superintend each ship's construction. President Washington himself chose to spread construction to six port cities (the "44s" at Boston, New York, Philadelphia and Norfolk and the "36s" at Portsmouth and Baltimore). The administration decided to build the ships through leasing or purchasing shipyards, not by contract with private builders.[21]

Thus began the United States government's first experience with constructing major weapons platforms in dispersed, politically sensitive locations, and by contracting with a variety of suppliers while also incurring production issues, time delays and cost overruns. From the start, material procurement difficulties arose. Climate in the southeastern states affecting timber-cutting schedules, and transport to construction sites, political haggling over whether or not to continue with the work at all when peace with Algiers returned in 1796, predictable criticism from private competitors concerning Humphreys, and unscrupulous practices. All contributed to the saga. In the end, the government decided to concentrate on just three of the vessels—frigates *Constitution* at Boston, *United States* at Philadelphia, and *Constellation* at Baltimore. Subsequent French intransigence and an outbreak of yellow fever the next year disrupted work. Ordnance and equipment delays produced further delays into 1797, and individual preferences of ship commanders regarding a particular ship also interfered. By 1798, Congressional investigations disclosed a rocky learning experience. Final costs for completing the three frigates plus the others left unfinished, totaled $1,114,179.94.[22]

Explanations attributed the causes for such overruns to building in different locations, design changes, unexpected procurement costs, price increases of labor and matériel, losses incurred in matériel transport, and launching mishaps. Most of all, Knox told the House of Representatives, there had been the lack of what would later be called a national stockpile: "magazines of timber, materials or system" to facilitate "the building and equipping of heavy ships of war." Ultimately, Knox blamed excess profit and exploitation, for "when everything is thus to be suddenly procured, will there not be found, in every community, too many persons ready to profit by the occasion?" Who could reliably estimate "with precision, what an article will finally cost, or say, with certainty, when a work can be finished?" From conception to launch the three frigates intended in 1794 still cost $804,762; $115,874 more than was planned for all six ships. The estimated cost overrun was in excess of $450,000. The young nation did gain experience, reputation and patriotic pride when those ships were judged "the best of their class which influenced later naval design." Moreover, with pressure from experts like Humphreys,

Philadelphia would become the place for a government navy yard, ninety miles up the Delaware River from blue Atlantic waters. Politicians, entrepreneurs and sailors had discovered lucrative business in defense.[23]

To Benjamin Stoddert, whose "reasoning is . . . still a landmark in the development of American military thinking" and ranked with Washington's in the same period, "the good policy of paying the difference to our own Citizens, to render ourselves independent of Foreign Countries, for articles essential to our defense cannot for a moment be doubted." While big 74-gun warships might be purchased abroad (no such behemoth had yet been constructed in America), Stoddert saw merit in home production. He urged purchase of a couple of Georgia's sea-islands for securing live oak to supplement yellow pine and white oak from the Chesapeake region; also, to build a reserve stockpile for the future and establish dockyard repair facilities "convenient to the sea but not readily accessible by the enemy." The cost of all this—$5,383,540 annually—would be nearly $3,000,000 more than was currently expended on the navy. Nevertheless, claimed Stoddert, a fast-growing young nation would doubtless be capable of bearing "any expense necessary for their present safety and future tranquility."[24]

Stoddert's dream was not for a navy to subdue pirates but to confront the world. His push for a domestic industry base reflected timeless aims of emerging nations. His goal to spread construction largesse "more equally amongst the states" was very Hamiltonian. His subtle chide that "it may be in the public interest that the Congress . . . should rely a little more on Executive discretion, than may hereafter be necessary" suggested a "whole-of-government" unified approach. Indeed, it would be Josiah Parker, chairman of the House Committee on Naval Affairs, coupled with a federalist Congress, that overall helped set some of Stoddert's construction in motion. Temporarily hawkish in mood, legislators may have been willing to expend upwards of fifty percent of budget on national defense. At any rate, iron ore extractors of the Keeptryst and Salisbury mines or Cecil, Hanover, Schuylkill, Eagle, Hope and Foxall furnaces to make naval cannon, and portside shipbuilders (not counting the equippers and their wares), together formed a naval acquisition base. Fleet strength in the early nineteenth century could point to an increase from twenty-four to thirty-five ships, as well as fifteen revenue-cutters and galleys mounting 1,044 guns and manned by over 7,600 officers and seamen.[25]

Stoddert's search for self-sufficiency and efficiency also bore fruit with establishment of government navy yards at Gosport (now Norfolk) in Virginia, Portsmouth in New Hampshire, Philadelphia in Pennsylvania, Brooklyn in New York and at Charlestown, a Boston, Massachusetts suburb. He bought the two Georgia Sea Islands for timber reserves, and expanded the policy of commissioning navy agents in major maritime cities to include less important ports up and down the Atlantic coast. Subsidies went to Samuel Lyman of Springfield, Massachusetts for canvas manufacture, to Boston's Paul Revere for copper (plus $10,000 to secure a mill for dry-rolled sheathing), and hemp growers along river valleys ranging from the James, Potomac and Susquehanna in the east, to the Ohio and Mississippi in the emerging west. Additionally, augmenting the government's own shipbuilding response to French provocations, merchant interests allied with maritime entrepreneurs in several cities raised money and contracted for warship construction. Whether this enterprise arose out of necessity driven by weak national protection or mutual self-interest, the story is a fascinating one. Economist Larry J. Sechrest tweaks the question of whether government has to provide a public good directly or that it might come, as in this case, from private subscription.[26]

Notwithstanding source, cost, and performance of this add-on to national defense, Sechrest shows, "a number of self-interested citizens undertook to provide nine additional, privately funded frigates and sloops-of war" that not only were "outstanding examples of naval architecture" but "served with distinction." Moreover, Congress also authorized the traditional form of legal piracy by issuing 365 letters of marque and reprisal, enabling merchants to revive the potentially lucrative privateering business of the Revolutionary period. Before it ended, the Federalist splurge on defense saw Congressional appropriation of $1,000,000 for six 74-gun ships-of-the-line and six additional sloops-of-war. One of its last naval acts, passed March 3, 1801, appropriated a half-million dollars to continue construction of six 74-gun ships, and complete navy yards, docks, wharves, and Marine barracks at shore-establishment infrastructure. Philadelphia vested interests, like Joshua Humphreys as surrogate for an official naval constructor, lobbied hard for an official navy yard in his neighborhood (if not on his own and neighbor-specific waterfront land) while several other government and private special-interest persona chose an alternate place for a new navy yard in the recently-transformed swamplands along the eastern branch of the Potomac River at the new capital. Of great interest, this naval armament program also demanded heavy ordnance contracting for numerous cannon. Time was precious—a sea-change impended as newly elected Jeffersonian opponents of the burgeoning navy returned a large part of unspent Treasury appropriation as they re-focused policy.[27]

Such developing internal political battles between federalists and anti-federalists translated to political factionism for a peculiar American approach to a fiscal-military state. Size and power of central government remained in flux. Naval build-up cost money and the abiding issues of how much is enough and how to pay was reflected even then in philosophies and models of security. Unpopular federalist taxes spawned discontent. Excise taxes on whiskey and other items, a property "war–tax" on homes, land, and slaves to offset the Quasi War with France , and a federal bankruptcy law to protect merchants, all symbolized the strengthening of national government, the policy abhorred most by anti-federalist Republicans. About the only interest President Thomas Jefferson seemingly showed in national security lay with developing the new, emblematic national capital named after George Washington, coincidentally included a local naval-marine base of barracks, dry dock and navy yard. Two years into Jefferson's term all but thirteen frigates had been sold off, work on dry docks and harbor fortifications halted, the navy downsized and the number of agents reduced. Naval expenditures slumped to their lowest point in five years, at less than a third of those when the Federalists left office.[28]

Jeffersonian defense posture would rest upon more economical, shallow-draft gunboats for harbor protection, with neutrality as a grand strategy. Forty gunboats could be built at the cost of one frigate, small-government advocates decided. They could be constructed at more remote places, like Havre de Grace in Maryland at the head of Chesapeake Bay, or inland at Middletown on the Connecticut River, thus spawning political and local industrial enterprise. Of some 257 such craft estimated to protect harbors, coasts and commerce, 176 stimulated the maritime industry by $1,584,000. When the War of 1812 erupted, supposedly 165 warships comprised active and reserve fleets, eventually supplemented by a class of vessel termed "the barge." Naval historian Charles Paullin found it "the irony of fate that a President devoted to peace and to retrenchment in naval expenditures should have had to conduct one naval war [Tripoli] and to face the probability that others might break out at any time [with Spain or Great Britain]" by resorting to this "largest naval increase that "at the same time the most useless." The "actual protection that [the gunboats] they afforded was small." To Paullin and others, this pecuniary approach "was a blunder and a misdirection of the national resources." Not necessarily so if a diversified, more economical defense industrial base was intended. Great Britain would test the hypothesis.[29]

A BRITISH WAKEUP CALL

Wars produce strange bedfellows. A second war with Great Britain could not have come at a worse time. Pieces of a defense industrial base derived from public-private partnership were congealing, but slowly. The highly successful, lucrative gunpowder mills of (E.I. Du Pont de Nemours and Company) in Delaware achieved sole source status with the War Department in 1805. The company would supply virtually all the required powder in the subsequent contest with England. Yet, as long as peace reigned, the young Navy department showered favor on the emerging local Washington navy yard, just as Capitol Hill contentedly targeted the facility and nearby Marine barracks for perceived fraud and mismanagement. Unprepared "in every essential means, instrument and material of naval warfare," all navy yards except Washington were in a state of neglect and decay.[30]

Parsimony and political wrangling took their toll. Emergency appropriations for arms and ammunition, repair timber, repairs and equipment for frigates *Chesapeake, Constellation* and *Adams*, plus $1,000,000 for fortifying the coastline, seemed too little too late. A tradition of unpreparedness and niggardly financial support had entered the nation's psyche. Of seventeen warships in the navy's inventory, perhaps only twelve could put to sea. The others needed extensive repair. Possibly 500 shipboard guns could be brought to bear on the British foe, whose North American squadron alone counted a ship-of-the-line and five frigates. The Speaker of the House of Representatives facetiously suggested lending the American navy to any other power then engaged with the mutual enemy. Once hostilities began, however, the floodgates typically opened as authorization of naval construction poured forth millions of dollars for four ships-of-the-line, six frigates, and twenty-eight 10-gun vessels. The result that actually fought the British was a mottled, mostly federalist period navy. Yet, fed by Du Pont gunpowder, its guns (and those of the army) managed to counteract the veteran British.[31]

Hasty mobilization and throwing money at the problem began another American pattern: war finance had again proved that peacetime provided inadequate preparation. Jeffersonian austerity, the war's unpopularity, and absence of any balanced tax system all hindered success. Historian Donald Hickey correctly discerned that the war hawks "appeared to support the conflict more with their heads than their hearts and more with their hearts than their purses." There were additional resourcing limitations as well. The militia system proved remarkably inept. Geographic sanctuary collapsed, along with only marginal coastal defenses, a raider navy was swept from the seas despite noteworthy tactical success, and yet another abortive attempt to capture Canada only reinforced the sense of national identity north of the border. Strategically, the war was a disaster as when the Chesapeake region proved no challenge for a joint army-navy British foray that ravaged southern Maryland, burnt Washington's government buildings, and helped hapless defenders themselves destroy the local arsenal and navy yard. American smuggling, trade with the enemy, privateering, ransoming, and profiteering all emerged. Financial historians claim the fiscal history of the war "was not an abject failure," since Congress did enact a wide range of wartime internal taxes (mostly repealed after the conflict), and such revenues which "paid for more than 40 percent of the war's total cost," outstripped tariff duties before peace returned. Taxing-power "so earnestly sought" by the federalists, and so "unwillingly employed" by Jeffersonian republicans, proved adequate to finance war. When peace returned, the federal government reverted to financing security from tariffs.[32]

Nonetheless, naval-shore infrastructure and contracting procedures had weathered government inconsistencies over two decades, and established a baseline for the war's resourcing efforts. Supporting those efforts were six navy yards, and various naval stations for ship repair and servicing, storing naval supplies, and recruiting manpower. Wartime operations spread out resourcing efforts, while expansion of public-private partnerships for production could be seen in Paullin's anecdotal remark that "from 1798 to 1816 when many naval vessels were built by contract, it is said that Baltimore constructed more ships for the navy than any other city in the Union." The navy expanded first-line combatants from eighteen to seventy-five armed vessels (sporting 10 to 74 guns) in addition to the gunboats and barges. Still, three 74-gun and three 44-gun ships authorized by the act of January 2, 1813, lay only partially completed and some sixty "largely insignificant craft" plied the Great Lakes.[33]

A case could be advanced that British destruction at the nation's capital was more injury than insult to the young nation. Wrecking the Capitol and Executive Mansion, the Washington Navy Yard, the army's arsenal and the navy's capital ship, the 74-gun *Columbia*, was a distinct blow to the nation's defense resourcing capacity if not ego. A thunderstorm spared the cannon-making Foxall Foundry in Georgetown—it too was a legitimate military target if several miles from the epicenter of destruction. The catastrophe was coupled with new navy secretary William Jones, "whose meddling with the plans for the ships constructed in 1813–1815 certainly delayed their completion, if it did not harm their sailing qualities." The ships in question, the first two 74s, *Independence* and *Washington*, were "notably unsuccessful" in some judgements. And, Jones was equally inept when it came to the Jeffersonian gunboats, ordering all boats east of Boston to be laid up at Portsmouth, thus leaving the east coast devoid of protection.[34]

On the other hand, fighting at sea handicapped replacement capacity in wartime. Losses of frigates *President, Chesapeake, Essex,* and *Adams,* as well as another half-dozen sloops and brigs, allows maritime historian Linda

Maloney to speculate that those were offset by addition of fourteen vessels constructed or captured. These included three ships-of-the-line, three frigates and eight sloops, thus aggregating a seagoing force nearly double what was available at the war's onset. Maloney suggests that the wartime building program for sea and lake operations "had enlisted a new group of constructors" like Adam and Noah Brown, Henry Eckford, and William Doughty, who in the postwar era would continue the American tradition "of building the finest ships afloat." The period additionally stimulated authorization, funding, and construction of America's capital ships, 74-gun "line-of-battle" ships of Stoddert's sea-going navy. Yet, policy not capacity would govern future peacetime direction. To be sure, with major departmental reorganization in 1815, a new Board of Navy Commissioners focusing on resourcing and working closely with the secretary) and a Congress chastened by its close escape from the British - no "postwar decimation of the service" came, as had occurred after the Revolution.[35]

The army, meanwhile, also had suffered compounding perils of unpreparedness, army and War Department pattern-setting, internal disarray for mobilization and surge, and a supply and service contracting system that failed to placate field generals. A virulent, antiwar sentiment in certain northern locations had imperiled prosecution of the conflict and made it easier for British forces to obtain food and forage than even for American counterparts. In typical wartime profiteering, colorful manipulative characters abounded, like David Parish, a German-born land developer of St. Lawrence and Jefferson counties on the Canadian border in New York, who attempted but failed to exploit iron deposits for making cannon balls. Although the militia system generally proved deficient, unexpected benefits came from having a parallel system for manpower extraction. The governor of Tennessee flatly proclaimed that in issuing privately made firearms "it was desired to avoid smoothbore muskets as much as possible" since "they may be good enough for Regular Soldiers but not the Citizen Volunteers of Tennessee." Army Commissary-General of Purchases Callender Irvine established a clothing factory at Philadelphia that employed 3,000–4,000 workers, turning out 2,000–3,000 uniforms per week for the Frankfort Arsenal. Transportation and distribution to front-line units also relied on private providers, although accountability still seemed weak. Nonetheless, the arsenal system adequately supplied small arms during the war and seemed "the only bright spot in the procurement picture." The return of peace would cause re-evaluation and reassessment. For instance, the Watervliet Arsenal on the west bank of the Hudson River north of Albany, New York (created on July 14, 1813 to support the war), was re-designated in 1817 and became the oldest continuously active arsenal in country. Similarly, The Watertown Arsenal, established in 1816 on the north shore of the Charles River at Boston, Massachusetts, replaced a similar facility at nearby Charlestown.[36]

Army mobilization historians later determined the War of 1812 forecast that "procurement for the armed forces in war must be based on sound assessment of the nation's economic and industrial capacity and must include some arbitrary allocation of resources to ensure a flow of supplies to sustain the war effort." This was entirely premature for a government still in an artisan-based, pre-industrial age. Where critical shortages existed in national resources, they declared then "some assured means of supply must be secured whether it be by stockpiling or other means." Washington, Hamilton and Stoddert could have agreed, addressing fiscal-military power of the central state.[37]

ISOLATED SECURITY, NATION-BUILDING, AND INDUSTRIALIZATION

What came next has been termed "The Era of Good Feeling" in international affairs, an untrammeled continental expansion labeled "Manifest Destiny", and the domestic rise of popular democracy, courtesy of President Andrew Jackson. Historian Brian Balogh speaks of the mystery of national authority out-of-sight while Max Edling points to a Hercules in the cradle. Old World Powers largely left the United States on its own to develop strength, identity and self-sufficiency. Its security rested on geography, an expanding sail-and-wood (and eventually steam) navy, a second system of stronger coastal masonry fortifications, and a small, expeditionary frontier army wresting land from the environment and its hostile inhabitants. The militia system would continue to deter any domestic insurrection from servile Blacks and urban working whites, against enterprise owners. Profits from the War of 1812 moved merchant capitalists into manufacturing as a source for wealth-accrual, in much the same manner as southern slaveholders and yeomanry looked to cropland. Changes after 1815 in social and political structure, and attitudes about tariffs, taxes and business, pointed toward a protectionist policy for national development. Jackson could tell his fellow countrymen upon leaving office, "You have no longer any cause to fear danger from abroad," as "your strength and power are well known throughout the civilized world."[38]

To historians Keith Bryant and Henry Dethloff, a new relationship between business and manufacturing and rising interdependence between manufacturing (particularly in textiles) and agriculture (cotton and wool producers) would take hold in this period. Southern cotton would become the key strategic resource. Lowell, Massachusetts and Manchester, England, symbolizing how cotton became King, paralleled in development with transport, machinery, and resulting sociological divides. Hamiltonian promise of the 1790s made sense to a breed of "New Americans." Creation of industry-based "know-how," general expertise, and a domestic technology seemed indispensable for converting elemental fruits of the land, hard-working labor and "Yankee Ingenuity", into instruments of national power. That process, achieved by mill, machine and human inventiveness, translated to an "American System" of uniformity with standardized interchangeable parts throughout industrialization. Perhaps DuPont gunpowder truly undergirded new national expansion and enterprise. With the huckstering flare of Americans' unquenchable faith in themselves, and innovation combined, the period between the War of 1812 and the Civil War was exciting and promising.[39]

This was the age of Henry Clay of Kentucky, Daniel Webster from Massachusetts, and John C. Calhoun in South Carolina, wedding their parochial political bases with national bombast and strategic aspirations. Calhoun warned about resurgence of Anglo-American conflict, and spoke feelingly in 1816 of the requirements of suffrage and universal military service as prerequisites for America's continued fulfillment of responsibilities and mission. Later, Jefferson Davis (Mississippi) and James Dobbins (North Carolina) added their nationalist weight as elected and appointed government officials seeking a stronger army and navy to protect special interests, namely cotton and slavery. Calhoun and Webster linked national security with development of internal improvements, notably canals and roads, fostering domestic cotton and woolen manufacture. Calhoun earlier had pushed for coastal fortifications (especially at the mouths of the Chesapeake Bay and Mississippi River) "by means other than the navy." A year later, new president James Monroe (Virginia) took up the cause for strong navy and coastal fortifications. Yet, his military policy, seen in his inaugural address, represented "a long line of Presidential statements, announcing generalized military policy to which the nation paid little or no attention," according to Walter Millis. Three years later when Congress demanded reduction of the standing army, Calhoun, by now Monroe's Secretary of War, detailed how such an austere force in peacetime might be readily expanded in time of crisis. Calhoun's "expansible army" blueprint codified as gospel well into the twentieth century.[40]

Built upon earlier Whig traditions, Calhoun's words from the 1820s still spoke to concepts like mobilizable reserves, adequate training for those reserves, and mobilization planning. They seemed a viable counterbalance to peacetime reduction of a standing military, based on ideological as well as fiscal grounds. Calhoun's tenure reflected continuing upgrades of resource institutions—arsenals, armories, navy yards and public-private partnership in acquisition and logistics—and costly engineering projects for forts up and down the coasts, which gave the army a share of strategic mission beyond expeditionary warfare. The period begat another American characteristic: phlegmatic peacetime interest in military matters. In a spate of reports after the War of 1812, accompanied by statements from war and navy secretaries laid out detailed, necessary plans for martial embrace of the attack and defense of the frontier, finding sites for naval depots, and protecting, "by the general system of defence [sic], the general system of internal navigation." One particular report supported by Calhoun's enjoinders conveyed the next set of blueprints, beyond those unveiled before.[41]

A three-member board, led by Brigadier General Simon Bernard (Napoleon's late chief engineer), plus navy Captain J. D. Elliott and army engineer Joseph G. Totten (whose name has been mostly attached to that body), projected strategic vision for a system of fortifications as part of a broader defense strategy. Their work, suggests Ian Hope, "anchored a comprehensive defense policy and set the course of military planning and preparations until disrupted by war in 1861." Their very words regarding "a defensive system for the frontiers" suggested an understanding of the problem. Its "bases," they observed, were first a navy, fortifications second, "interior communication by land and water" the third, and fourth a regular army and well-organized militia. "These means must all be combined, so as to form a complete system," they advanced. The navy was the first-line of defense, its protection looming large in actually locating positioning three levels of coastal harbor forts. The projected expense for maritime frontier fortification totaled $17.8 million, requiring a permanent peacetime garrison of 4,700 men and about 38,000 in wartime. According to the board, Congress should dedicate "considerable legislation and a sizeable portion of the monies appropriated for military matters" to implementing this strategy of fortified frontiers. Here was a jobs program worthy of later national government endeavors and another army engineer thought yearly average costs of $894,318 would consume over $41 million over time. Moreover, a March 1836 naval board wanted a large fleet of sail-powered warships, augmented by steam-powered craft, assigned for coastal work.[42]

The efforts of men like Calhoun and policy boards spoke to large and expensive projects—enterprise comes to mind—in support of the greatest endeavor of that time, nation-building. The army and navy searched for missions supporting a grand or national security strategy for that endeavor. Here could be found the ligaments for a complex of people and jobs, resources and matériel, business and government. If the navy's focus was more at sea, the army's investigations fit nicely into the idea of homeland defense combined with frontier bases to launch manifest destiny. Both army rationales were visible in Bernard board comments vis-a-vis internal improvements, serving as integrative vertebrae for the young nation. Like the twentieth century system of interstate highways, Bernard board recommendations suggested a similar military priority that also had commercial utility. National armories, arsenals and navy yards, plus private suppliers, would join with army engineers actively helping survey canals and railroads and keeping inland waterways clear for navigation in the interest of national security.[43]

By mid-century, forces of industrialization, nationalism and liberalism defined a United States just as they had Europe after 1815. Two, perhaps even three distinct geographic, socio-demographic, and political-economic sections determined America, standing in stark contrast to unifying national institutions. Army and Navy, including their educational institutions at West Point and Annapolis, together with canals, waterways, railroads, and proto-national roadways, all functioned as government-private enterprise for moving commerce and people. But labor, capital, and the industrial revolution were, if anything, dis-unifying. Rise of the particularly divisive issue of slavery even more greatly destabilized the Union. New territory acquired by war from Mexico added to what one historian has called "this vast southern empire", vying with new American territories in California and Oregon on "the Pacific slope." Here was a new wrinkle for national security, with forts and naval presence soon placing the flag over pine and palm. A seemingly integrative narrative of cotton/textiles from field to mill and beyond went inexplicably lacking. A later American leviathan would rest on technology, mechanization, innovation, and uniformity as well as democratization, but not just yet.[44]

MILITARY TECHNOLOGY AND AMERICAN INNOVATION

Artillery buffs tell us that, after the War of 1812 "artillery in the United States felt the impact of the Industrial Revolution." New fabrication methods employing power-drive machinery, improvements in methods of construction, scientific advances deriving better understanding of "pressures, ballistics, metallurgy, strain and stress," produced cannon-making innovations not always fully understood by contemporaries. The durability of iron supplanted brass and bronze for cannon (for the navy from the start, the army's motley array of foreign makes left over from the Revolution only slowly reflected such modernization). "The industrial revolution" which began in eighteenth-century Great Britain had impacted American shores by the 1830s. The advent of steam propulsion, mechanized production, uniformity via standardization, as well as speeding up processes between idea and product, together connoted drastic, unrelenting change. New England's fast-moving rivers in particular were well-suited textile manufacturing sites for southern cotton. Certain waterways like the Connecticut River Valley, for example, also spawned a burgeoning, private small-arms industry, with the town of Springfield, Massachusetts as the center of government production. Harpers Ferry at the confluence of Potomac and Shenandoah rivers in Virginia became the government's second site for musket and then rifle production. With industrialization also applied to arms making, firearms industry developments were transferable to new commercial industry through a so-called American System of Manufacturing.[45]

Interchangeability, machined-tool production, and precision measurement, "three of the salient features of modern American industry," declares Felicia Johnson Deyrup, "were well established in arms plants when much of this country's production was still on the handicraft level, or only slightly above it." Yet, other technology historians like Donald Hoke emphatically insist there was no technology transfer of any such "armory process" to private-sector clock and tool making. Nonetheless, from roughly 1815 to 1861, both the national government through its national armories and arsenals coupled with its private contracting system, produced the underpinnings of preparedness for the herculean tasks of later nineteenth-century endeavor. Inventors, entrepreneurs, national politicians, and uniformed scientist-engineers would create an expansive commercial-industrial base for domestic and later overseas ventures. Technology held a key, whether for convergence of munitions, transportation, mechanics, and management, or for cranking out goods like firearms, clocks, agricultural implements, sewing machines, padlocks, bicycles, typewriters and so forth—even improved Du Pont "soda" blasting powder. This story, much like maritime-naval complex development, centered on key locales, agenda-prone individuals, and special interests at all levels. War Department infrastructure was critical, as was public and private capital, with politics forever part of the process.[46]

Historians have long viewed the United States Military Academy at West Point as a major player. Ian C. Hope sees the academy as the essential dispenser of "military science," while Clive Bush contends establishment of this national institution in 1802 as "a basis for the encroaching power of the state and the military machine." It was "a supra-personal icon of a nation," based on "nationalistic principles of boundary, with the magical texts of physical science as its bible." Through engineering, its core, "the great principles it embodied of uniformity, security, predictability and progress" were discernable in the types and manufacture of war machines. He concludes these principles were "among the most important of the 'mechanical arts'" during the nation's formative years. . Bush advances that by 1860 American production of armaments would be on a scale unsurpassed by previous European levels, deriving from the American System of Manufacturing concepts of uniform production, interchangeability of parts, division of labor, and mass production. Some historians note the French-influenced transfers of a national military-scientific academy, patterns and techniques of small arms, and even a style of warfare, however, a distinctly American public-private partnership lay at its core.[47]

Perhaps a trend started when the Department of War by necessity tried to fulfill the mandates of providing small arms to both national army and militia. The Springfield Arsenal faithfully provided a uniquely American version of the famous French "Charleville" musket while the new Harpers Ferry counterpart embarked on rifled firearms. Manufacture slowly increased (a total of over 471,000 muskets were made at Springfield from 1795 to 1844, and 332,171 various arms models at Harpers Ferry between 1801 and 1842), although laborious manual filing and other artisan tooling still attended production. The pressure from strained Franco-American relations resulted in congressional appropriation of $800,000 on July 5, 1798 for 30,000 stands of domestic-made arms to augment government production. Following procurement experiences of the Revolution, this enterprise variant on government-owned/government-operated (GOGO) firearm provision would become standard American practice, with arsenal patterns supplied to private contractors in company-owned/company-operated (COCO) facilities. Some twenty-seven contractors responded, helping create an expandable industrial defense base, and the same procedure was followed for pistols. Famous among contractors would be the establishments of Eli Whitney for muskets and Simeon North for pistols. Separate Pennsylvania and Virginia state contracts (sixteen apiece) used the 1795 American musket pattern. But, results proved mixed for delivery and quality.

Still, this contract approach continued under an April 23, 1808 appropriation of $2,000,000 in twenty-five contracts let for 85,200 muskets with patterns supplied from Harpers Ferry. Some twenty-one to twenty-two contractors thus joined the War Department family of arms-suppliers for muskets and pistols, Springfield and Harpers Ferry provided arms-patterns (blueprints) plus a set of gauges for parts aimed at a uniformity system leading to efficiency and effectiveness in greater production capability. If the long road to standardization and interchangeability of locks, plates, furniture, and screws for musket and pistol models proved uneven and uncertain, arms authority Colonel Arcadi Gluckman felt this was the first time "in which a contractor agreed to a stipulation to produce an arm uniform and interchangeable." It "marked a revolutionary change in the manufacture of firearms" despite the interchangeability principle having somewhat "limited application" at this time.[48]

The contrast in development of Springfield and Harpers Ferry together with the private producers in the Connecticut Valley has been termed by one author as "the Silicon Valley of its day". Such likeness indicated the role played by cultural, demographic, institutional, even personal, relationships in evolution of a defense industrial base before the Civil War. Absolved from heavy industrial work like cannon making, the two government facilities illustrated acceptance of new technology, ever-present pressures for change (in firearm model style and types), cost-consciousness (budgetary and departmental oversight), and even in management (preferred superintendence by a military officer versus civilian). Washington interfered with site management early and Congress loomed in the wings as ultimate overseer. Government enterprise by the mid-1820s also included a GOGO complex of arsenals, predominantly for repair, at Augusta, Maine; Vergennes, Vermont; Watertown, Massachusetts; Watervliet, Rome and New York City in New York; Frankford (Philadelphia) and Pittsburgh, Pennsylvania; Baltimore, Maryland; Washington, D.C.; Fortress Monroe (Hampton) and Richmond, Virginia; Augusta, Georgia; Mount Vernon, Alabama; Baton Rouge, Louisiana; St. Louis, Missouri and Detroit, Michigan. The changing role of work at such facilities could be seen when Frankford transitioned from inspection, storage, repair and distribution of small arms purchased under contract, to a post-Mexican War role as the army's principal center for small-arms ammunition development, testing, and manufacture. Between all these public facilities, a considerable work force produced or repaired large quantities of small arms, swords and bayonets- a major contribution to national defense. They contributed to technological convergence with the machine tool industry, suggests technology historian Merritt Roe Smith, citing Ames Manufacturing Company of Chicopee and American Machine Works of Springfield, Massachusetts, Robbins and Lawrence of Windsor, Vermont, Brown and Sharp of Providence, Rhode Island, and Pratt and Whitney of Hartford, Connecticut.[49]

George Washington's hidden hand in selecting the second armory at Harpers Ferry as both competitor and collaborator in determining cost, efficiency and effectiveness, led to desultory searches for other armory sites (including Mount Dearborn, South Carolina as well as locations closer to the ever-receding western frontier). Also, the development of skilled labor from both public and private arms enterprises, transitioning into other areas of manufacturing in peace but still a mobilizable resource in war, further clarify the story. The path led beyond the entrepreneur Whitney, to North, to John H. Hall, Marine T. Wickham, Asa Waters, and on to the most famous, even revolutionary, inventor-manufacturer Samuel Colt, significant for his groundbreaking revolving firearms. North assumed production of Hall carbines when the inventor's employer, Harpers Ferry arsenal, could not meet the army's substantial orders. Standing with these names were lesser-known soldier-industrialists, armory and arsenal superintendents James Bomford, Roswell Lee and James Stubblefield.

Disposal of obsolete stock from American armories and arsenals through sales to Latin American clients for their own revolutionary wars set another pattern. Foreign sales opened new market outlets along with technologically advancing a prototypical American defense industrial base. The unquenchable westward expansion drew upon St. Louis gunmaker H. E. Dimick for his famous plains rifles, while Springfield armory's model 1842 musket represented the first-fruits of the armory uniformity system and also first to incorporate a new percussion cap firing mechanism. French captain Claude-Etienne Minie's conical shaped bullet became practical thanks to Harpers Ferry assistant master armorer James Henry Burton. Henry Maynard invented a different capping method and the notion of a rifled musket; both appeared with the government's model 1855 long arm. Breech-loading experimentation moved beyond Hall's design to that of his protégé Christian Sharp's model 1859 carbine.[50]

Contract-supplied munitions had its problems. Given to non-delivery and frequent delays such as those experienced with Eli Whitney, orders for heavier ordnance, dependent upon private makers under government contracts, often went only partially fulfilled or delivered marginal products. Samuel Hughes of the Cecil Furnace in Maryland, like Whitney, simply could not deliver 24-pounder cannon for fortifications, as well as the first frigates. Hope Furnace in Rhode Island filled the gap. Joseph McClung's Pittsburgh, Pennsylvania Foundry (later named Fort Pitt Foundry) ostensibly produced cast-iron cannon for Captain Oliver Hazard Perry's Lake Erie squadron in 1813. Also serving the army's defense industry base were the Phoenix Iron Works at Phoenixville, Pennsylvania, John Clarke's Bellona Foundry on the James River upstream from Richmond, Virginia, which was close to Joseph Reid Anderson's Tredegar Iron Works, Cyrus Alger's South Boston Iron Company Foundry, Nathan Peabody Ames works near Springfield in western Massachusetts, and Gouverneur Kemble's West Point Foundry at Cold

Spring, New York across the Hudson from the military academy. Perhaps, Henry Foxall's Columbia Foundry works at the edge of Georgetown, D.C., offered the best prospective provider before the War of 1812, but he bridled when the government asked him to construct a heavier ordnance foundry claiming (in a refrain that would echo down through subsequent years in the nation's history) cessation of government orders would be disastrous to keeping the foundry operating. He urged the government to build its own facilities to serve as a yardstick to determine cost and facilitate artillery standardization. Foxall's idea had to await ordnance needs later in the century.[51]

Technically, this was an era of ordnance experimentation with variants of iron, fabrication processes, design, and educational trial and error. Heavy manufacture of coastal guns and naval ordnance new contributors like Swedish-American naval officer/inventor John Dahlgren. Technically, dearth of copper for bronze guns kept American cannon to more durable iron fabrication in various forms. The Ordnance Department, which later became several separate Ordnance Boards, under Colonel Decius Wadsworth sought to standardize artillery types for land use but the period from the 1830s through the 1850s was one of deliberation and experimentation, with smoothbore as well as rifled gun tubes before the advent of the gun that excited American artillerists, the 12-pounder field gun of 1857, dubbed the "Napoleon" after Louis Napoleon who became Emperor Napoleon III of France. Naval ordnance also teetered on the brink of standardization, as Swedish-American John Dahlgren, inventor and naval officer at the Washington Navy Yard, experimented with a variety of ordnance, from boat howitzers to 8-to-11-inch shell guns. West Point graduates Joseph R. Anderson, Thomas J. Rodman and Robert P. Parrott became involved in cannon production by introducing new techniques and styles of rifled cannon in the field, at the Fort Pitt and West Point foundries respectively, thus continuing the government's policy of contracting for heavy ordnance production.[52]

Market fluctuation often kept the firearms business more experimental than productive. Simeon North, Nathan Starr, Remington, Robbins, Kendall and Lawrence, Tryon, and even Eli Whitney's firm, all managed to provide a superb Model 1841 contract rifle for Mexican War service. Supplanting Whitney's fame, earned more for masterly promotion than meeting delivery dates and interchangeable parts, was Samuel Colt who patented his revolving six-cylinder pistol on the uniformity system, secured Mexican War contracts, and vaulted onto the world stage at London's Great Crystal Palace Exhibition in 1851, as the epitome of Yankee ingenuity, mechanized production and assembly-line methods. While pistol work continued at the two government arsenals, by the 1840s contractor names like H. Aston, I. N. Johnson, Nathaniel Ames and Henry Deringer, even William Glaze's Palmetto Armory of Columbia, South Carolina, would supply handguns and pistol-carbines for army needs. With introduction of the pin-fire cartridge in 1847, flintlock conversions to percussion in 1848, 1850 introduction of the so-called "Minie" conical bullet and invention of the first practical metallic cartridge, 1856 advent of the breech-loading percussion carbine with breech-sealing cartridge, and the Deringer pocket pistol in 1857, inventions of the first effective and widely used repeating rifle, and the center-fire cartridge in 1860, the stage was set for carrying invention, testing, and constant tinkering with military firearms, to some larger arena.[53]

Of greatest uncertainty, perhaps, was the question of whether or not government facilities would continue as trailblazers for innovation or lag behind the private arms industry. Were they to be merely munitions laboratories or model establishments of quantity production and simplicity? Historians Donald Hoke and Robert A. Howard agree "that attainment of interchangeability was a function of the precision in the mechanism being produced and the market's desire for this feature." Clockmaking's relatively low level of precision hence interchangeability, was readily attained and eventually also with muskets. Not so with pistols and more sophisticated, technically advanced breech-loading carbines. Cost and market determined the latter; the government's desire for interchangeability and willingness to pay for it determined the former. Supply to mobilizable militia and volunteers depended upon volume and simplicity plus operational efficiency and effectiveness, not high precision. Even the private arms industry looked to a different market.

Howard suggests that interrelationships in the private arms making trade relied on work experience and cross-pollination of technique through family connections. But relatively few were innovators. Reasonably uniform manufacturing concepts arising through long-established tradition, as with small assemblers, or from consanguinity of the larger makers, marked the private sector. Roberts concludes that, based upon the overall record of antebellum arms production, "the use of machine tools was of paramount importance, but the interchangeable part was not achieved to any great measure" by private arms makers. He comments that even a century-and-a-half later not much had changed! Only the great American mobilization for a people's war in 1861 would test resourcing capabilities of public and private production. Demand for large numbers of weapons would test private sector abilities to provide quantities of firearms quickly and effectively, if not necessarily efficiently.[54]

INDUSTRIALIZATION AND NAVAL AFFAIRS

For reasons including ever-increasing foreign trade, Southern expansionist interests in the Caribbean, or coastline protection, the navy undertook what Walter Millis termed a "naval revival" before the Civil War. Here too, technological advance and industrial dynamics rose to the occasion. Steam propulsion and screw-propellers slowly intruded on wooden sailing ships and paddle-wheel locomotion. Shipboard ordnance transitioned through disasters, tests, redesign and new approaches to metallurgy. Steam engines relying on anthracite coal dictated new shore facilities for that fuel at the Philadelphia navy yard. Much of the ordnance and metallurgy experimentation took place at Washington's restored navy yard. Elsewhere, the Delaware River valley thrived on maritime activity, upon private entrepreneurial constructors, the naval shore establishment, and an array of Mid-Atlantic subcontractors feeding in from Maryland to New York. That nexus would gain national renown for ships ranging from domestic commercial craft to the 120-gun ship-of-the-line USS *Pennsylvania*. Of course, the region was also blessed by nearby gunpowder producer DuPont, as well as the coal fields of northeastern Pennsylvania.[55]

A small Navy department in Washington presided over the revival from its two-story brick building, scarcely two hundred yards west of the rebuilt White House. Thirty individuals, including Cabinet Secretary, the naval commissioner, administrators, clerks, and couriers hustled about, as major reform efforts restructured the department to better reflect naval modernization. Five independent bureaus, encompassing navy yards and docks, construction, equipment and repairs, provisions and clothing, ordnance and hydrography, and medicine and surgery, reported directly to the Secretary. Naval historian Kurt Hackemer feels naval bureaucracy in this era provided a footprint for contract education that heralded a "naval-military complex." Frank M. Bennett earlier had observed that it constituted "the end of the experimental period and beginning of the creationary period" of a steam navy.[56]

Indeed, the phrase "steam navy" best clarifies this point in the development of the modern fleet. The steam navy of the 1850s, ironclad navy of the 1860s and subsequent steel navy of the late-nineteenth century all demanded different design, fabrication and maintenance, than ships of oak. Earlier experimental design combining side-wheel and steam propulsion enabled naval constructors to move forward, but Swedish inventor John Ericsson's improved system of screw-propellers which replaced vulnerable side-wheels made this advance practical. Navy Secretary James C. Dobbin truly captured the spirit of the time. In his 1853 annual report, he advocated "at least six first-class steam-frigate propellers," also asserting that "Steam is unquestionably the great agent to be used on the ocean, as well for purposes of war as of commerce." Then, Dobbin almost undid his own words by suggesting steam be used as only auxiliary instead of primary power, due to cost of operation, a theme that hovered for generations as naval peacetime dogma. Policy implications of coaling stations and considerations of the coal industry as strategic resourcing aside, many worked synchronously to advance technical modernization: engineers like John Lenthal and B. F. Isherwood, ordnance wizards such as Lieutenant John Dahlgren at the Washington Navy Yard and Robert Parrott at the private West Point Foundry, also naval Lieutenant Mathew Fontaine, an expansionist publicist, scientist, and worthy predecessor to Captain Alfred Thayer Mahan, along with zealous naval officials including Dobbins, army-ordnance professional Colonel Decius Wadsworth, and arsenal superintendents Roswell Lee (Springfield) and James Stubblefield (Harpers Ferry).[57]

Public-private naval partnering moved ahead in this period continued much as it had for decades, via contracting. Construction of frigates *Merrimac, Wabash, Minnesota, Roanoke, Colorado, Niagara* as well as sloops *Pensacola, Lancaster, Hartford, Richmond, Brooklyn* went to government yards using prefab materials originally intended for other ships, to expedite completion, and were spread across key installations, as much for political purposes, as for technical proficiency. But now the navy realized it could not handle a building program completely in-house. Government had to look beyond its own technical capabilities for steam machinery, and in the case of the *Brooklyn*, officials in Washington opted for private bidding "in order to incite a healthful rivalry between the naval constructors and civilian ship builders." Jacob Westevelt of New York City won the prized contract, with machinery sublet to Fulton Iron Works. When the naval service determined in 1857 that the *Richmond* class sloops were too large for coastal duties both at home and in Chinese waters, seven screw-sloops and a shallow-draft side-wheeler, *Saginaw*, were added to the program with the side-wheel constructed on the Pacific coast. Mare Island Navy Yard and the Union Iron Works of San Francisco joined naval-industrial facilities in the San Francisco region.[58]

Bennett's 1896 account of the steam navy was first to pull aside the curtain on the naval-business matrix of mid-nineteenth century America. Bennett meticulously listed fifty vessels constructed or purchased for a new steam navy, beginning with the experimental *Fulton I* or *Demologos* in 1814. At an approximate total cost of almost $18 million, involving ship construction, steam-machinery fabrication at eight government yards and twenty-eight private manufactories, plus the myriad suppliers of other nautical matériel, joined by the army's government armories and arsenals, and a stable of private providers for food, clothing and transport, here was a formidable procurement complex, unsung in its time. Hackemer's paean to a naval-industrial complex and Thomas Heinrich's dissection of the Delaware Valley maritime-naval "complex" in the late period of wooden shipbuilding, still witnessed design and construction controversies accompanying introduction of new technology to the sea service. Ericsson's screw propulsion with two vibrating, lever engines, built by Philadelphia-based Merrick and Towne for the Philadelphia Navy Yard-constructed, ill-fated sloop *Princeton* with her large substandard wrought-iron cannon "Peacemaker" specially forged by Hogg and DeLamater of New York City. Explosion of that cannon (killing a party of viewing cabinet officials on the Potomac), produced a firestorm of accusations of culpability between designers and Ericsson and supposedly "delayed for years the development of screw propulsion." Nevertheless, no one should overlook influential private shipbuilders like Charles Cramp at Philadelphia, Harlan and Hollingsworth at nearby Wilmington, Delaware, together with major marine-engine builders like Merrick & Sons, I. P. Morris, and Reaney, Neafie & Levy, as "proprietary entrepreneurs," performing design, management and supervisory functions.

As Heinrich shows, proximity to one another on the Delaware waterfront ensured cross-fertilization of ideas, labor, and a production capability of infinite naval value in time of war. In truth, navy yards up and down the Atlantic, Gulf and California coasts relied on local subcontractors who supplied boilers, engines, and other marine stores, thus establishing a vital network of public-private enterprise. The Philadelphia Navy Yard, especially, "became the laboratory of the American steam navy during the 1840s." The Washington Navy Yard served in a similar capacity for ordnance. The *Princeton* disaster opened new vistas for ordnance testing, enabling inventor Dahlgren to make his distinctive bottle-shaped gun tube. Curiously, the earlier Six Frigate naval program suggested other themes of military procurement for decades to follow. I.W. Toll and defense analyst Mark Cancian claimed in 2006 that "all the pathologies of today's weapon systems acquisition were evident" at that time. They included: criticism of "innovative but unconventional" and "extravagant" designs, multi-mission requirement (great-power naval as well as irregular pirate threat), introducing conflicting design demands, use of exotic construction materials that raised costs and delayed completion, a divided political establishment, contracts spread across northeastern maritime states "to ensure political support," cost growth caused by schedule slippage and programmatic instability, congressional intervention, and search for fraud, waste and abuse. Cancian declares that these early sail frigates still "proved world class in operation."[59]

NOT TO NEGLECT THE SERVICE SECTOR

Army logistics historian James A Huston dubbing this period as "thirty-five years of trial and error" obscures what government contracting historian James F. Nagle portrays as a security service community, which included freight companies and overland mail service, supplying western expansion. Government subsidies for road, canal and rail, even regulatory oversight for steam propulsion, also flowed from the national security enterprise of the day. So, too, did clusters of supporting merchants and shopkeepers, provisioning and outfitting food and wares for warships around the navy yards. Nagle suggests that over time military contracting became more structured thanks to management practices of Congress and the departments of War and Navy, to ensure accountability, economy and efficiency. Except in specified circumstances, detailed records were kept of competition and advertisement for bidding on contracts and multiple copies of paperwork made. Meanwhile, "a reciprocal relationship developed between the regulations of the executive branch and the statutes enacted by Congress." Not merely what the army and navy procured but how they did so, came to be reflected in regulations. Such approaches spread to all government offices by 1842 as did contract-advertising requirements soon after, thus tightening centralized oversight and control. Expending public monies for national security became a pacesetter for controlling fraud, waste, and abuse.[60]

Economic historian Stuart Brandes nonetheless criticizes the Mexican War (another conflict unpopular in some sections of the country), for poor management of logistical needs, fiscal houses of Cochran and Riggs in Washington and E. B. Cox in Philadelphia for bond-purchase profit, as well as general conduct of "America's first foreign campaign." He discovers a surprisingly modernist refrain from the time by Transcendentalist reformer Theodore Parker: "War, wasting a nation's wealth, depresses the great mass of the people," but "serves to elevate a few to opulence and power." Parker called out the pecuniary advantage for army contractors, "when they chanced to be the favourites [sic] of the party in power." To Brandes, the war was conducted somewhat blatantly on behalf of a southern slave oligarchy and at a distance, which only induced great supply difficulties, cost, and opportunity for private contractual corruption. Still, military-spending graphs continued to show traditional peaks and valleys of war expenditure and peacetime austerity typically associated with an American way of security. Army and navy budgets combined shot to over $300 million during the War of 1812, rose up to $1.1 billion in 1847, then receded below $350 million by mid-century.⁶¹

Studies of the army's influence on the western frontier suggest a service sector paralleling the navy's maritime-industrial contribution. Texas was largely built upon army money and activity. As one army quartermaster put it, "the sword plants the banner and a city is built around it." Quite typical of military spreading civilization since ancient times, this latest American version has been labeled "a military-commercial cooperative" with Texas businessmen and agriculturists." Texas was the army's "largest theater of war," observes Timothy T. Smith, furthering goods and services exchange, economic development with political-economic pressures, and spawning urban settlement. The Army dollar pervaded everything, he says. Set beside Raymond and Mary Lund Settle's exciting account of the Russell, Major and Waddell freighting firm's virtual monopoly of army expeditionary experience, and overland civilian logistics link with California further north, one has a prelude to Brown and Root, even Halliburton, enterprise of the post-industrial age.⁶²

* * *

On June 18, 1860, Congressman John McRae from Mississippi's Fifth District, reported to the House Committee on Military affairs about national cannon foundries. He suggested how "the attention of Congress has been called to this subject at almost every session since the adoption of the federal Constitution." As early as May 4, 1798, he pointed out how an act was passed authorizing the president "to establish a foundry to cast the cannon required by the government." But, "owing to the want of means at the disposal of the government," nothing could be done. Over the years, the subject continued to attract attention from Congress, the Executive branch, and many of the state legislatures. Now, with 6,500 cannon needed for coastal fortifications (4,200 present) and 2,300 more for the navy (2,600 on-hand), "the present seems to be an auspicious time to inaugurate a new system." Arguing that all the European governments were "devoting much attention to the improvement of their means of offence and defence" and that America's national armories were turning out small arms unsurpassed elsewhere in the world, McRae worried that this nation should be the only great nation without its own establishment for the manufacture of cannon. "With a government foundry, under the direction of government officers," he argued, there would be no doubt "that our cannon would soon attain the same superiority that now exists with regard to our small arms." Eastern Pennsylvania's Lehigh County and Shelby County in, Alabama provided candidates for such a government venture, estimated to cost $300,000. Timing was everything. After the *Princeton* disaster would have been a more propitious time for getting this measure passed.[63]

The early national period produced a philosophy of self-sufficiency, together with a basic resourcing mobilization base for national security. "Buy American" became firmly entrenched. Despite parsimony, a stable of government arsenals, armories, and private firearms makers as well as navy and private shipyards could supply the adolescent nation's needs. That navy formed a first line of defense and protection for expanding foreign commerce, even power projection, abroad. As Secretary Dobbins dramatically proclaimed, this navy was indispensable to "the maintenance of our proper and elevated rank among the great powers of the world." For most Americans, however, the specifics of military and naval agendas barely touched their lives. Notions of nationhood floated more upon Yankee Doodle jingoism. The post office, customs service and Pony Express themselves were national security assets! Only a chosen few were defense contractors.[64]

The nation rushed unwittingly toward a modern, industrialized, "people's war," mostly with a spirit of Young America, a country of inveterate tinkerers, wannabe inventors, and aspiring entrepreneurs. Edward D. Tippett, a Washington, D.C., War of 1812 veteran and inventor of a balloon, repeatedly plied the government for subsidy of his brainchild, but to no avail. Undaunted, he came to the attention of a new president, Abraham Lincoln, who dubbed him "Tippett Crazy-man." Whatever he was, Tippett prophetically told an unnamed official in May 1861, "this is the age of wonders and great battles are before us." Indeed, within weeks, the greatest wonder would be Americans killing fellow Americans. Two rival governments would undertake that killing by mobilizing a resourcing base of material, functions and procedures, organizations and institutions. Star-struck individuals like Tippett, would be few and far between.[65]

Chapter 3

RESOURCING THE CIVIL WAR AND ARMING THE PEOPLE, 1860-1865

Was America ready for what has been styled "a people's war?" It actually began in 1859 as an insurrection at a government facility—the Harpers Ferry arsenal. The war started two years later at one of the government's prized coastal forts in Charleston Harbor, South Carolina. From the start, the Civil War embraced strategic resourcing. In retrospect, however, killing nearly a million fellow Americans might be the most significant thing about this conflict. To do so fundamentally changed the nation, its people, leaders, institutions and processes. Two Americas temporarily became security states. Even gathering people and resources proved remarkable.

A war of survival, it was the ultimate security test for a nation-state, the catalyst for modernizing the country. Later it came to reflect a unique "American *Way* of War," a war of annihilation but also of humanitarian intervention. The United States federal government officially labeled it a rebellion. Southern rebels thought it was a war for their independence. Not an emancipation war at first, it became so about the second or third year mainly because of resourcing demands. Along the way, a bitter fight unfolded over political abstractions, constitutional interpretation, and economic control. Mostly, it was about "the people", who had just grown tired of one another. The nation's first large-scale, modern industrial war, it involved a continent and spawned two wartime defense-industrial bases, North and South.

ABOUT PERCEPTIONS

The Civil War was sectional, regional, and local, yet national at the same time. What was supposed to be a short war became a protracted conflict, and has come to be seen since, as the tale of two nations, two governments, and two resourcing bases, mobilized for conflict. Though there were parallels between the warring sides and unforeseen directions for which neither had prepared, in itself, that was typically American. In part, technology lay behind such new directions. It was about cotton, iron and carnage. It was about administration and innovation. Circumstances forced organizational and managerial adjustments. To scholar Walter Millis, the war produced few generals, "who seemed to grasp the implications of the new and dreadful lineaments of war, as they were now appearing out of the womb of the industrial revolution."[1]

The significance of two events commands our attention. After initial stalemate produced inconclusive results, President Abraham Lincoln's calls for 75,000 volunteers in the summer and another 500,000 in the fall of 1861 required unprecedented public response. Such numbers needed arms, equipment, clothing, food, shelter, and transport. As logistics historian James A. Huston once observed, "there was no such thing as systematic war planning" or even much logistical preparation. In 1861 the regular standing army numbered about 16,000, and the navy forty-two vessels with 555 guns. A dozen years had passed since major expeditionary warfare against Mexico, and half that since suppression of the Mormons in Utah. Political compromise had previously averted the Union's breakup. Who knew that secession would produce a war, or that the war might achieve the intensity that it did? Huston thought that industrial mobilization was "the result of economic pressures," coming with recovery from four years of depression and the new demands for wartime military supplies. The generation which brought on the conflict could not have anticipated a resulting million under arms, well over 700,000 deaths (at latest count) in a population approaching 32 million, or "human capital" loss of $1.8 million plus direct government expenditures of some $3.3 billion for war. Still, it embraced Great Enterprise.

GREAT ENTERPRISE AND THE STAKES OF POWER

Enterprise stood at the heart of America's soul. So did competition for Power. Manipulating the former begat the latter. In 1861, the south wanted self-determination; the north wanted a re-structuring of the Union. True, this "was the first full-scale war shaped in major ways by the tools and weapons of the Industrial Revolution," observe technology historians Barton Hacker and Margaret Vining. They point to telegraph and railroad as increasing the pace of events, new weapons multiplying ranges "at which death could be dealt," thus extending "the scope and deadliness" of the battlefield "while at the same time reducing its decisiveness." They suggest agricultural mechanization permitted large armies to be fed and industrial growth supplied steam-powered transport to deploy and sustain the military, as well as making the tools of war. The sewing machine promised mass production of clothing and shoes. Innovation followed a traditional path. Vast as the accumulation of technical knowledge seemed by this point, it emerged from experience of craftsmen and tinkerers, "laboriously augmented over many years, unevenly developed, and slow to spread." Such antebellum advances as had begun modernizing America—common-school reform, science education, mechanics' institutes, agricultural fairs, building railroads, running steamship lines, even supervising plantations—the war expanded, for endeavors of a different sort.[2]

Whether it was technology, organization or management that won the Civil War, manufacturing loomed large, and sanctuary of production proved pivotal. Harnessing process and output ultimately laid out victory or defeat. Hacker and Vining conclude that the flowering of the uniformity system in rifle development, now applied in war by both sides through public-private production systems, "incorporated something more novel, a kind of systematic empiricism that began from the eighteenth century onward to accelerate the pace of change." Fellow technology historians Alan Marcus and Howard Segal advance that the most significant effect of the Civil War was actually the commonality it reinforced: "the archetypical mass experience in an era distinguished by attempts to provide common experience" through technology. The stakes of power were simply too high to do otherwise. Enter Brian Balogh's "government out of sight" into a more intrusive, visible central-state authority, and Max Edling's Hercules leaving the cradle to become Richard Bensel's Yankee leviathan through rebellion, war and reconstitution. Perhaps the Confederacy provided a junior partner.[3]

The redoubtable Columbia professor Allan Nevins once pictured antebellum America as "the gangling, adolescent" state, "a sprawling" nation where industrialization was "by far the most powerful force making for a greater degree of organization." He saw the Civil War as galvanizing "national character," concluding that this conflagration "measurably transformed an inchoate nation, individualistic [in] temper and wedded to improvisation" into "a shaped and disciplined nation, increasingly aware of the importance of plan and control." To Nevins' generation, organization was the key to the enterprise. He tallied all the forces of disorganization at play–farmers, labor, and professional groups. Aside from churches, business alone developed "organization on a general scale and of a powerful type." How, he wondered, "could a truly national utilization of the country's resources be achieved?" His contemporary, Pulitzer Prize recipient historian Roy Franklin Nichols answered the question as acquisition of power, when he pictured the United States as a failed state.[4]

Grasping those stakes of power involved both sides transforming elements of power into instruments of power. Large-scale albeit imperfect mobilization provided method. Northern and Southern resource-bases performed sufficiently well enough to send thousands to the killing fields more or less adequately equipped and supplied. Initially, both sides relied upon state regimes for their muster. Then, exigencies moved focus to national management. Twentieth century army historians decided that "it was a curious anomaly that centralized control over mobilization processes was asserted first by the Confederacy whose existence was predicated on state sovereignty rather than by the North which was fighting to maintain the Federal Union." They felt the South had within its borders "practically all of the materials necessary for waging war." The problem, they maintained "was to transform those materials into munitions and supplies for the army." The problem also was one of time to do so.[5]

Nation-building involves statistics. Generations of polemicists have cited 1860 census data as indicators of disparity between North and South hence impediments to national unity. Yet, U.S. census superintendent Joseph Kennedy at the time used the statistics to sound a note of optimism about national progress, despite "that unhappy state of affairs which has interposed to impede the ordinary course of events." If by the date of actual census publication in 1862 "the insurrection has tended to depress commerce, to paralyze many branches of industry," while plunging the nation into debt of unsurpassed magnitude with accompanying suspension of internal trade, Kennedy still found abundant indicators "that the mass of our population has thus far experienced but gently, the suffering and desolation usually attendant upon a revolution of so widespread and serious as nature as this has proved." The masses "feel some of the calamitous effects of the insurrection less" and "are prospering in every branch of industry" largely beyond "the direct influence of the rebellion." War always seems to favor some people.[6]

Kennedy's words championed power, mustered for a vast future. His confidence radiated themes of national government, based on northern manufactures and the agriculture of the vast west "progressing with a vigor altogether beyond expectation." Stoked by the influx of gold, exemplary exports of breadstuffs and, above all "the demand for army supplies, in provisions, forage, horses and various fabrics of our own production," these results "have protected the North and West from financial convulsions and pecuniary suffering" since the Panic of 1857. Even "the spirit of self-dependence, which the comparatively helpless condition of many of the Southern States, cut off from foreign supplies, has compelled them to encourage in the promotion of manufactures, will doubtless exercise a wholesome effect upon their future prosperity," Kennedy glowed. The "immense and unexampled exportations of grain and provisions," notwithstanding loss of labor to the military, yielded "an immense surplus of provisions," as "the strongest proofs of the energies of our people and the inexhaustible nature of the resources of the land." Future American omnipotence stood ready to spring forth.

Kennedy hoped his census "will teach us the importance of union and harmony, and stimulate a proper pride in the country and people as one and indivisible." A people "who have in twenty-five years doubled their numbers and much more than quadrupled their wealth need not apprehend with misgiving any inability to pay all the national debt which has been incurred" in fighting the war. Wartime mental and material suffering, and loss of national dignity were all transitory, "resulting in accelerated prosperity by the sweeping off of the feebler elements and bringing new energies and resources into action." This was Kennedy's version of "creative destruction" for an America that might hope a few years "will obliterate most of the painful reminiscences resulting from our present unhappy condition." Before the next census, Kennedy prophesied, the United States would be "restored to harmony, and profiting by the past, realize the importance of peace and the blessings of prosperity, with a good assurance of the long continuance of both."

Kennedy's account, as interpreted by modern Civil War historians like James McPherson, reinforces Nevins' perception of inchoate. McPherson points to a rump Union enjoying an 88-to-12 percent superiority in industrial capacity over its insurgent fraction. He cites the Union producing "eleven times as many ships and boats" and "fifteen times as much iron, seventeen times as many textile goods, twenty-four times as many locomotives, and thirty-two times as many firearms," not to mention in-excess of "twice the density of railroad mileage per square mile and several times the amount of rolling stock" of railway vehicles. He, like others, suggests a population disparity of twenty-two million northerners to about thirteen million white and chattel-slave southerners. But, while white southerners would never arm those slaves to fight, they could and did utilize them for logistics chores and production tasks. So did white northerners under the guise of liberated "contraband of war" or captured enemy property. Confederate president-elect Jefferson Davis assured fellow Mississippians, as he left home to take office, that should the North try to coerce the new Confederacy back into the Union, it would meet "Southern powder and feel Southern steel." Army historians Kreidberg and Henry found southern industrial expansion "remarkable considering its lack of manufacturing at the beginning of the war." It was "the first attempted economic mobilization of a nation for war." Today, we are less sure since the South ultimately lost.[7]

Kennedy's census suggested odds were stacked against the South in 1860, yet what about skill-sets? It was not numbers themselves but how the protagonists converted them to a Great Endeavor. People of color, whether free, slave or emancipated, come into perspective. The number of immigrants provide another data point. Their country of origin paled in comparison to who they were in person: a wide spectrum of merchant and manufacturers, mariners, farmers and miners, artisans in all aspects of textiles, clothing, and skilled trades, educators, those in professional and cultural arts, as well as common laborers and servants. Vital to a developing civilian economy, they were indispensable in wartime. Again, enter perception. Kennedy's census clerks saw immigrants as statistics. Some southerners saw immigrants like slaves as threats to heritage and control. The Union counted them as force multipliers. War's necessity involved them all.[8]

Man, machine and war clearly fused, for instance, when the 1860 census confirmed "that all the gunmakers in the county, private and public produced fifty thousand firearms, the highest level yet attained in the United States." Some 239 private firms made firearms, though more for specific customers than general sale. Entrepreneurial inventors like Samuel Colt had freed American gun manufacture from dependence on English locks, and achieved production levels equal to anything in Great Britain. Robbins and Lawrence were renowned for firearms and tools, even contributing to sewing machine technology before closing in the mid-1850s. As technology historian Merritt Roe Smith has suggested, Springfield Armory's "dissemination of the new technology to the larger American manufacturing economy" became important. Equally so, the experimental work of arsenal technicians took relatively simple, mass-producible long arms and married them with French captain Claude Minie's invention, the conical, rifled bullet. Government-owned and operated factories (GOCOs) set the direction, thanks to revived state militia needs. Then, in 1861 the massive people's war overwhelmed the system.[9]

The advent of steam power attached even greater potential for building and exerting power in peace and war. Progress accompanied steam locomotion by rail and boat, carrying strategic implications for time and distance travel, hence economic implications for profit and loss. Though horse and mule-drawn transport still had to fill the final gap to customer, steam transport spawned organization and management opportunity, particularly when associated with a new communication device called the telegraph. Indeed, its introduction enabled railroads to properly function, with consequences at strategic, operational and logistical levels. Yet another breakthrough paralleled the telegraph when coal offered a more efficient fuel than wood for generating steam power. The maritime and naval sector especially adopted conversion but abundance of wood on land stalled railroad embrace. It would be a question of coal-yard versus wood-pile in strategic planning for logisticians. How well either side used such tools at their disposal would be a tipping factor toward winning or losing the struggle.[10]

So, imbalance existed between north and south. The north counted 31,000 miles of railroad track compared to the south's 8,000. Long-distance hauling, indispensable to any war effort, was more concept than reality. Locomotive capabilities varied, with stronger engines in the north. Double-tracking versus single-tracking favored the north. A major drawback lay with railroad interconnectivity. Faster and cheaper, railroads had begun to supplant canals for freight transport from the Midwest to Atlantic port cities, still, steamboats on western rivers remained the preferred means for moving goods and people locally, and to the great port of New Orleans. All modes of transport held promise as well as risk. Beside mechanical risk also lay government seizure, and physical destruction by friend or foe in wartime. In truth, while government contracts might prove attractive, private ownership potentially could thwart the state's use of a resource, for political reasons. Nevertheless, Kennedy's statistics suggest an economic and political confluence critical to modern security, discernable explicitly through war. What they could not suggest, barring extrapolation and analysis, was the human factor: capital, labor, organization and management. Weighing statistics too heavily can be deceptive.[11]

A WAR OF SPACE, TIME AND RESOURCES

Davis and Lincoln, congressional delegations, and southern extremists bluffed their way into war. None of them truly appreciated geography or the vastness of distances for their peculiar endeavors. It was only when the hoary myth of a short war proved elusive that both sides tested process and adapted to necessity. Grand exposure to securitization took deeper root, stemming from the American tradition of improvised war. Two nations, now invertebrate, with limited notions of government, inflamed public will, and outdated militia rolls proffered incomplete, even inaccurate, guidelines. The American martial spirit that rested on English scholar Marcus Cunliffe's model of Quaker merchant, Yankee Doodle farmer, Southern cavalier, and non-participatory pacifist yielded amateur enthusiasm and quick-profit anticipation to demands of "a continent-wide theater of operations," in army logistics historian Charles R. Shrader's words. The eleven seceding states alone encompassed 750,000 square miles that had to be subdued. It took staggering amounts of men and matériel to do so, over distances in which the opposing armies operated and had to be supported. This required expansion of military administration—departments, divisions, and districts overseeing and administering an infrastructure benefitting forces in the field. Naval expansion likewise spawned more structure. If the Union and Confederacy added little to government bureaucracy and more to process, they nonetheless mobilized an "administrative state."[12]

For both sides, assembling and readying troops and supplies rested upon federal and state statutory agencies of the departments of War, Navy and Treasury, Congress and the presidency, as well as local government. A wartime generation would have to learn about shared responsibility and experience, as they went along. Land operations stretched from Pennsylvania to Arizona and from Ohio to the Gulf of Mexico. Naval operations in protecting commerce and hunting corsair predators proved global, while army-navy cooperation was needed for blockading and interception duties along southern coastlines and inland waterways. Such unprecedented demands dictated logistics as much as "the intricacies of national policy, industrial and agricultural procurement and distribution, and the detailed mobilization activities of the opposing governments." Underappreciated were the contributions of customs, revenue and tax officials, and provost and volunteer social-welfare administrators aiding the displaced dependents of those who went off to fight for Cause. When strategically prescient general-in-chief Winfield Scott at first gave Lincoln policy options for conquering the rebellion, such as conciliation, acquiescence to separation, or merely importation-duty collection at retained ports, he offered only conventional wisdom short of conflict. An alternative soon became imperative: invasion and conquest, stabilization and occupation. Jefferson Davis, on the other hand, vowed to defend "the whole of the territory of the Confederate States as the best hope politically, economically and patriotically for securing the blessings of independence." In his inaugural address a year later, formally as president, he confessed that "events have demonstrated that the government had attempted more than it had power to successfully achieve." His further exhortations for mustering the human spirit failed to redeem lost territory and resources; those drove the wartime experience.[13]

Union military operations into Confederate territory added unanticipated consequences. "As the Union armies advanced down the Mississippi valley" where the "lines of communications became longer," noted army historian John Beeler in 1954, conquered populations were bitterly hostile, despite pockets of unionism across the South. As such, "it became necessary to garrison or constantly patrol every mile of railroads and navigable stream to prevent, or at least control, acts of sabotage on the part of the Confederate sympathizers." He might have added the requirements of also protecting unionists and liberated slaves in Tennessee, Kentucky, north Alabama and

Appalachia, while exterminating partisans and guerrillas that infested the region. Beeler felt this tied up increasing numbers of troops in what were essentially occupation duties, and expedient measures to meet this situation were "almost always unsatisfactory and short-term, both in conception and effect." Combat casualties, disease, and occupation duties only necessitated more manpower calls, with age and race regulations eliminated over time. No less than fifteen Union calls for more manpower and perhaps half that for the Confederacy attempted to resupply the ranks. Aside from able fighting men or stevedores, even as Confederates tapped slaves to dig trenches or work in factories and fields, neither convalescents nor prisoners of war escaped exempt from labor dragnets.[14]

Then too, America's Civil War assumed distinctly international resourcing overtones from the beginning. Procuring tools of war and labor quickly turned on how the European factories, markets, governments, and people might be exploited. For various strategic and economic reasons, British and French governing classes favored the Confederacy. A rising, unified powerful United States always posed danger to their interests. Economics and geopolitics mixed, over King Cotton! In time, emancipation supplanted King Cotton as the equalizer, although foreign recognition and overt intervention remained distinct possibilities. Meanwhile, Europe supplied arms and equipment, immigrants, and plenty of diplomatic minuets to avert confrontation in America, as its own backyard simmered with the rise of upstart Prussia and threat of domestic proletariat unrest. Cotton and slavery may have been swing factors in Westminster and British mill towns, but the arms trade and the rise of technologically challenging American naval power cast a shadow for British and French naval ministries. In the end, simple soldier affinity for superior Enfield shoulder arms as well as continental immigrant recruits for Yankee ranks may have counterbalanced diplomatic subtleties of support and recognition of the Southern Confederacy.[15]

CENTRALIZED STATE BUILDING AND WAR ECONOMIES

Prolonged hostilities forced governmental centralization on both sides. Historians might argue whether to term it state socialism, expedient corporatism, command economy or modernization, or some combined variant. Traditionalists retreat to the standard competing paradigms of nationalism versus localism, and revolution versus counter-revolution. A famous quip from British Chancellor of the Exchequer and later Prime Minister William Gladstone, about the Confederacy creating armies and navies, and more than either making a nation, rings true. He could have been talking about the Union as well, except that Davis and his administration truly seemed to approach the concept of a modern, centralized state. Desperate times demanded desperate measures for the disintegrating Confederacy. Lincoln's Union seemed more respectful of state prerogative, adjusting its internal war management, and performing what historian Paul A. C. Koistinen terms "artificial dominance" from Washington. Traditional views that Lincoln's command conduct more amenably led to victory, while the meddlesome autocratic leadership of Davis spelled defeat, seem irrefutable.[16]

Interpretation notwithstanding, keeping with a prewar doctrine of state-by-state reporting of militia and inventoried matériel sufficed at first. Then, war managers on both sides had to discover a new resourcing paradigm. There was little time to incorporate evolving technologies into the questions of "how much is enough", or quantity versus quality. By 1862, for the north at least, economic recovery seemed to assure the modern litany that only war spending lifts a country out of financial distress. Business failures and unemployment declined, fiscal policy expanded money supply, and wartime inflation eased debtor woes. Business confidence returned as industry and commerce shifted to a market demand made by war. The Confederacy teetered on in the meantime, resting its faith on cotton by stockpiling and embargoing that commodity from trade. Oversupply abroad plus Union naval blockade thwarted this Confederate strategic design. The wartime cotton exploitation story retains its own opaque reaction to laws of supply and demand.[17]

Southern historian E. Merton Coulter thought decades ago that the South's antebellum economy, largely built on systems of barter and hard cash, was doomed when confronted by a protracted, large-scale, industrializing war. Still, the keys to surmounting such weaknesses in wartime depended upon time (duration), sanctuary (space), and leadership (guidance). If the integrity of Confederate territory could be preserved, if Confederate government could feed its military but also ensure adequate provender got to its civilian workforce then a viable nation forged in war by cooperative political action might lead to a prosperous new nation If not, this experiment in rebellion would fail and the Union would be restored. How the Union and Confederacy managed to balance antebellum laisse-faire tradition and emergent centralized administrative direction defined the fulcrum. The Union effected a mingling of approach or "a mixed system of supply that combined federal production and supervision with private enterprise," says Matthew Gellman. Koistinen employs his concept of political system, institutions and economic-elite execution to advance a prototype paradigm of civilian-military and public-private hybridization. Michael Bonner terms the Confederate counterpart "expedient corporatism." Paul D. Escott sees "military necessity" driving everything.[18]

When logistics historian Charles Shrader observed that Civil War armies had "to create or expand logistical infrastructure and to develop new procedures as well as the trained personnel needed to support widespread military operations of tremendous scale," he could have included navies as well. Superimposed on extant systems, the military encroachment by logistical expansion, organization and coordinative management into the civilian sector are hallmarks of the experience. Antebellum tradition and form had stabilized inside small government, but hardly survived the adjustments dictated by prolonged war. Preliminary mobilization via customary state and local efforts, private institutions and elites proved incapable of winning decisive victory and ending the conflict. Extended war came to demand "greater governmental intrusions as the price for achieving widely agreed-upon national goals," suggest historians Jerry Gallagher and Joan Waugh. In part, this led to violation of civil liberties, imposition of personal taxation, and intrusion into private lives through conscription, confiscation as well as destruction of property including slavery. Was this what it took to bend citizenry to the common weal?[19]

Maybe it did, as Koistinen thought so, observing that a generation of postwar entrepreneurs "gained invaluable training during the war in the techniques of large-scale manufacturing, transportation, distribution, and finance." Others, like Allan Nevins, Jeffrey Wert and Mark R. Wilson would have agreed. Yet, centralized direction from Washington or Richmond accompanied by dispersed execution in war zones depended upon persuading hearts and minds in democratic wars. Lincoln's grand vision was one of promise; for Davis it was duty. Lincoln employed this theme in the dedicatory Gettysburg address and conciliatory second inaugural message, while Union grand design, pointing long-term, came from congressional legislation through the Homestead, Pacific Railroad, Morrill Land-Grant and National Bank acts that opened the continent, agriculture, education and financing to a restless, forward-looking populace. A stolidly legalistic Emancipation Proclamation offered an evolving, if controversial, program for ending slavery and enhancing human dignity. By contrast, the Confederacy promised preservation of an idyllic status-quo, caste and class perpetuation, as well as defense of the homeland, wrapped in the garb of independence as a counter-thrust to perceived northern oppression. That southern self-determination for an equally bright future as seen by leaders like Davis came to rest on a war requiring systemization, centralization and industrialization directly contradicted the state-rights theory underpinning of the

Confederacy. Meanwhile, Yankee invasion and destruction incentivized defense of hearth and home as enterprise.[20]

Exigencies in a survival war that stemmed from squandered military opportunities and lost resources (human, material and geographic), caused a broadening of securitization. While accommodation of approach varied, the desire to maintain military control (subsistence, ordnance, and quartermaster) channelized acquisition of goods and services including wartime use of rail and telegraph by introducing them into existing military organizational structure. Addition of a signal corps and U.S. Colored Troops units within the Union's operational army ranked as possibly revolutionary, along with adding Bureaus of Refugees, Freedmen and Abandoned Lands to War Department administrative structure in early 1865. Frankly, the experiences of U.S. Military Railroads, U.S. Military Telegraph government organizations, as well as private social welfare commissions U.S. Sanitary and U.S. Christian, may have contributed equally to shaping an American identity. The Confederacy bumbled through establishment of a Railroad Bureau separate from the Quartermaster department, then back again thanks to congressional interference and meddling by Davis and others. Its greatest weaknesses—infighting, personal rivalries, and "fatal hesitation" at strong management application—may have obscured similar tendencies in their opponents, always present in any national mobilization.[21]

At the same time, both national governments may have seemed generally capricious toward their citizenry. Union attempts at censorship and prosecution for sedition, and Confederate taxes-in-kind with impressment of private goods, livestock and enslaved labor belied smooth accomplishment of war goals from obedience to war stocks. Government contracting historian James F. Nagle thinks that a prewar contracting process which "had been carefully structured to ensure accountability and competition," recoiled when a war "overloaded the purchasing infrastructure," and "haste battled accountability." The advent of citizen armies lacking experienced procurement officials to oversee the system, yielded "a large influx of strangers, numerous venal types [who] snuck in and found willing co-conspirators in a horde of equally venal contractors." Officials wanted results not delays; suppliers wanted assurance of fair prices and fair returns on those prices. Predictably, vendors looked to quick profit regardless of allegiance. Military needs requirements guaranteed a proliferation of state and national government agents, independent profiteers, manufacturers and merchants untrained for war. The experience suggested uncontrolled profiteering and scandal, thus prompting yet another wartime development—congressional investigatory committees.[22]

Emerging from decades of investigation and analysis of the Civil War experience come some simple truths. Reams of paper have touted why the North won or the South lost. A fair spread enumerates leadership, politics, economy, social cohesion, and military performance, with passions aroused over issues of slavery, emancipation, free labor, and immigration (and the list goes on) somehow related to resourcing two great endeavors. The simple fact rested on one word–*Sanctuary*–which fate decreed that the Union would enjoy; the Confederacy denied. Both sides employed similar procedures to secure munitions, equipment and supplies. Neither side hurt for firearms. As early as February 20, 1861, eleven days after assuming the presidency, Jefferson Davis signed an "Act to Provide Munitions of War and for Other Purposes." Both sides built upon caches in old national and state facilities. Both rushed to foreign purchase. Southern warriors brought flintlocks and hunting rifles from hearth and home to the fight. Union and Confederacy tapped production at government facilities (arsenals, depots and navy yards) and ensured new construction. Beyond recovery from captures and battlefield destruction, they contracted with private manufacturers for government-patterned arms or mixed in unique designs of private origin. In exchange, they resorted to contracts, hard cash, promissory notes and seizure of unfilled orders. Weaponry "varied from merely serviceable to useless." Short war offered certain lessons; protracted struggle taught public-private partnering was a necessity.[23]

By 1865, fourteen or fifteen Union calls or proclamations for volunteers had secured 2,666,999 of the 2,759,049 requested number of white males through recruitment or conscription, plus 186,017 African-American comrades. Five similar actions on the part of the Confederacy (with all manner of inducements, commutations and offsets), netted approximately 1,000,000 bodies. While the 1860 census had presumed a manpower pool of 4,559,872 northern to 1,064,193 southern men, manpower extraction via state mobilization was phlegmatic and even national conscription proved difficult. State orientation remained at the core of national effort. Only an invalid Corps and the United States Colored Troops joined with U.S. regulars; the Confederacy organized a small regular contingent but never meaningfully tapped its large African-American pool for military service.

Never has there been an accurate total of how many men, women, and children, regardless of race, experienced the war through fighting or on logistical and production fronts. The U.S. Sanitary Commission commendably attempted to compute ages of U.S. Volunteer soldiery toward war's end; other tallies at various levels also tried to sum up the human dimensions of this endeavor from a mountain of reports and official record. Overall, governors and elites stayed at the core of the extractive effort for manpower, supplies and equipment, superimposed on a civilian economy under national auspices. Organization became as important as function. Marginal degrees of bureaucratization and reorganization resulted but did not explode at Union and Confederate national levels. So-called "Treasury girls" recruited for Washington jobs, and war clerks kept pen and paper busy in Richmond and other locations. An unsung, hidden corps of female, black, and "walking wounded" helped with hospital work, munitions production and other rear-area work. Expanding departmental and district facilities from Baltimore to Louisville, Nashville, Memphis, and elsewhere in warzones replicated localized expansion of projects, labor and facilities. So too, at navy yards and stations. The pace was hectic, typically underscored by confusion and inefficiency in this Endeavor, as were later efforts of a more mature America.[24]

FINANCING WARTIME LEVIATHANS

The Civil War spawned two Leviathans, variously defined as "something large or formidable," or "a totalitarian state having a vast bureaucracy." Either way, how does one finance the voracious appetites of leviathans at war? As political economist Ethan B. Kapstein comments, national security has always been a costly undertaking and severely tests rulers and governments. Financed primarily by taxation and borrowing, successful states have been those that generally "were able to sustain the heavy financial burdens of war." According to a 2010 Congressional Research Service study, the Union reputedly funded twenty percent of its war expenditure through taxes; the Confederacy, just four percent. Mobilization and attrition of resources ballooned the financial burden for both sides. U.S. spending shot up from less than two percent of gross national product just before the war to twenty-five percent at war's end. The antebellum mindset rested on a philosophy of minimal to no national debt, financing chiefly from tariffs. Resorting to property tax had been so unpopular in the War of 1812 that Americans were "almost pathologically resistant to any other form of taxation" other than tariffs, claims historian Robert Hormats. Inflation had accompanied the Revolution and War of 1812. Increases in trade, with attendant tariff reductions, had enabled Washington to avoid raising taxes for the Mexican War. Following deficits from the 1857 market crash, loss of foreign investment, and territorial shrinkage from secession, the maw of Mars now demanded alternatives. Both Union and Confederacy employed their Treasury departments as mobilization agencies.[25]

Financing the Union's restoration war required a cooperative effort by Capitol Hill politicians and Executive Branch officials, to sell a combination of patriotic fervor and practical financial tools. Unsung heroes, from Senate Finance Committee chairman William Fessenden, Secretary of the Treasury Samuel P. Chase, to Philadelphia banker Jay Cooke, personified a crisis-response effort for alternative funding. Protective tariffs and internal development legislation could not underwrite war expenses in full. The war spawned income and excise levies, the creation of a Bureau of Internal Revenue to collect them, a national banking system, and nationalization of an identifiable, legal-tender paper currency called "greenbacks", in addition to borrowing through nationally issued bonds, backed by promise of postwar redemption. Concern for backup gold and silver receded in 1864 with Nevada's elevation to the Union as a state that October. As economist Sarah E. Kreps terms it, "war-related institutional developments" created an "internal revenue system for collection of direct taxes."[26]

The National Banking Act of 1863 made the national currency redeemable for all public and private debts, except interest on government bonds and customs duties, an obvious inspirational enjoinder to loyalism. The plethora of currency, from "several thousands of kinds and denominations of state banknotes, not counting counterfeit bills, then in general circulation," and general lack of a decisive tax program at the beginning of the struggle, observes James Huston, meant "the dearth of financial resources threatened the procurement effort." While inflation failed to spiral completely out of control, and "the nation's financial structure did not collapse," the 1863 act plus companion legislation the next year helped nationalize the Union. By imposing a ten percent tax on state bank notes to drive them out of existence, a subtlety only implemented almost at war's end, northerners were weaned away from state currencies, in favor of the national system. Unappreciated in nationalizing security, perhaps we could substitute the name "Civil" war with the title "War for National Unification."[27]

Make no mistake, northerners were not amenable to idealisms of shared sacrifice via higher taxation. When James McPherson somewhat facetiously suggests that the Internal Revenue Act of 1862 taxed "almost everything but the air northerners breathed," he was not far off the mark. Yankee initiative withheld taxes from salaries of government employees and from corporate dividends. Frankly, the financial credibility of the federal government depended on Union victory. According to a clause in the Fourteenth Amendment reaffirming article 6 of the Constitution, war debt would be repaid if the Union won! This promise, ultimately achieved through military means, enabled Washington to meet wartime expenditures totaling $3.34 billion and an unprecedented national debt of $2.75 billion, soaring to this from an 1861 projected prewar budget baseline of $74 million, and debt of maybe $1 million. What Hormats styles "a tax to save the Union" must be placed in context with 1864 military and political victories that finally underscored the full faith and credit of the national government. McPherson concludes "the relationship of the American taxpayer to the government was never again the same."[28]

It was a different matter for the Confederacy. In retrospect, the new nation committed mistakes from the beginning. It tried to practice short war. It attempted to barter its chief resource, cotton, by warehousing coupled with market denial. It failed to establish full trust and faith in its currency. It had to inspire patriotism without asking for too great a fiscal sacrifice. Maybe it could have better played its cotton card. Confederate Secretary of the Treasury Christopher G. Memminger assumed his duties by floating government loans, immediately creating a national debt. Treasury notes, a national paper currency, would pay bills, yet were not backed with gold or silver but warehoused cotton. They would not be held as legal tender. Printing money and issuing paper bonds along with state currency "produced hyperinflation unseen since the Revolutionary War." A Confederate paper dollar eventually stood at just five cents in gold value. The south's weak tax base, the same aversion to taxes and debt as northerners, plus the inability to raise sufficient capital from foreign investors stunted Richmond's war economy.[29]

A small tariff, while philosophically agreeable, proved totally inadequate for war funding. The Confederacy enacted a War Tax in August 1861, of one-half percent on real and personal property, but expected the states to collect the levy, a move that failed miserably, lasting but two years and netting only $20 million in revenue—when and if passed along by the states. Impressment of goods and conscription of manpower, as well as forcing or hiring out servile labor were other devices used for the war effort. Runaway inflation threatened by 1863. The government imposed a graduated income tax, and a ten percent tax in-kind on agricultural products. The French financial firm of Emile Erlanger marketed $15 million in bonds backed by cotton but while receiving good profits , only about $6 million accrued to the Confederate treasury Moreover, the 1864 Compulsory Funding Measure, which devalued Treasury notes that had not been exchanged for noncirculating government bonds, failed to stem inflation, Since the Confederacy's national debt exceeded $700 million and overall inflation was nearly 6,000 percent, government-issued paper provided only a marginal medium of exchange for goods and services. By 1864, taxation provided almost eleven percent of the

Confederacy's total revenues; by comparison, the Union raised 15 percent of its revenues from taxes.

Financing the purely military dimensions of its war economy was only one of many problems for the Davis government. The economic effects of military spending impacted locally and regionally. How to have kept home front and fighting front clothed, fed and functioning, when simultaneously invaded, raided and besieged, would have defied even the best statesmen of the time. Here was possibly the insurmountable obstacle of modern war, impossible to address much less resolve by money flow alone or any resort to passing patriotism. Confederate Treasury department collection of produce from Tax in Kind laws was inefficient. Even an assessment base fluctuated, due to premature army consumption in production areas, and the loss of such areas to early enemy occupation or destruction. Also, problems in transporting to distribution points, as well as permission for a taxable populace to pay those levies in inflated state currency, caused "blueback" national currency to feed inflation and create an inverse tax on Confederate citizenry. Home-front allegiance eventually buckled, "nationalism" never really gelled, and the Confederate constitution's preamble promises could not be fulfilled. The new nation had no time to effectively achieve a satisfactory, accepted financial and governmental system, nor consolidate an integrated agricultural-commercial empire. America's cotton mania survived the war, while slave labor and the southern social caste system did not. Destruction and revolution ended some institutions of the Old South, but prevented viable replacements.[30]

To historian McPherson, under pressures of blockade, invasion, and a flood of paper money, the South's agrarian economy "simply could not produce guns and butter without shortages and inflation." At times the moral imperative of Cause for both sides simply fell prey to self-interest. Historian Maury Klein's description of Union "boys who stayed behind" to partake of opportunity offered by family firms and paid-for military substitutes, may have enjoyed few southern counterparts. Nonetheless, the Confederacy offered loopholes and evasion. Philip Leigh's provocative examination of wartime cotton trading lends credence to late-war profit motive and capital, whether official or unofficial, legally and illegally draining the societal well of what was, by then, a Confederate illusion. The winter of 1864–1865 may have been as crucial as 1860–61 for innovative interpretation of capitalist enterprise on both sides. With Lincoln's reelection secured, Union military success assured by wider raids throughout Dixie, and capture of remaining southern ports, the subsequent disintegration of antebellum society and infrastructure rapidly pulled back the curtain on potential for a corrupt new postwar world.

Cotton remained at the center of capitalism south of the Potomac and Ohio rivers. Jeff Davis's model of strong central power stuttered off to await a distant resurrection.[31]

In many stretches of the south, a black-market economy simply defied codification. This shadowy "underground" activity was deemed "covert" even for cross-boundary trading. Indeed, it defined the war in certain areas, since resumption of cotton trading became the abject desire for belligerents both north and south, as well as foreign nations. Leigh exposes the lucrative exchange of cotton for weapons, among other commodities, through the lines especially in the Mississippi valley. This was no mere soldierly trading for coffee and tobacco. This was an openly flaunted trade, lying beyond the reach of Confederate-state prohibition that some northern contemporaries saw as prolonging the war, but others viewed as entrepreneurial opportunism. Here were antebellum realities carried over into wartime. While the southern Confederacy "depended primarily on cash crops such as cotton and tobacco," it relied on the states northwest of the Ohio River for provender, much of its manufactured goods from those in the Northeast. Conversely, says Leigh, the northern economy depended on southern cotton, since "that supported important Northern commercial sectors like shipping, finance, insurance, warehousing, and other services connected with cotton finance and maritime trade." He cites Stanley Lebergott's conclusion that the amount of cotton exported to Europe throughout the blockade "was only about half as much as what was traded through enemy lines to the Northern states," or nearly a million bales. Confederate government denial policy, and enemy, even friendly, destruction also spawned this wartime expediency.[32]

The cotton trade remains an under-stated link for reunification if not reconciliation or, put another way, a tool of national economic power that may have eluded meaningful utility by administrative state officials of the time. Innovative as well as disciplined, organized even draconian use of a financial siege to bankrupt the enemy had to await the Roosevelt administration's manipulation of Japanese assets and economy just before World War II. Neither side in the Civil War had the governmental apparatus nor sophisticated understanding of economics to do so. One might revisit weaponization of money and cotton economy by Washington and Richmond for bringing their opponent to the peace table in the 1860s. Certainly, the Confederate government tried to use that commodity to lure foreign recognition and aid if not northern business acquiescence. By comparison, the Federal government tried a combination of confiscation and Treasury department—issued permits for cotton trading. Corruption resulted although deeper study may now suggest a more positive result for conveying ersatz military-business exploitation into Reconstruction. Cotton mostly contributed to the wartime destabilization and disruption of a prewar norm.[33]

Here, on combat's edge, a mix of normality, instability and uncertainty thanks to invasion and occupation, guerrilla activity and downright brigandage and even loyalism defined adaptation to demands of modern war's centralized mobilization. At the heart of commerce in this eerie world of survival lay a barter trade beyond cotton—mostly illicit—for food, shelter, clothing with salt and sugar, medicine as well as weapons, equipment, and especially horses. Suggesting trading improvisation at this very basic level was farmer John D. Hart on Younger's Creek in Hardin County, Kentucky. In an unstable, lawless area, Hart's wallet counted paper currency from the United States, the Confederacy, the Michigan bank of Allegan, and Merchants Planters bank in Georgia, to pay his bills. Did such variety reflect Walt Whitman's "real Civil War?"[34]

BUILDING TWO DEFENSE INDUSTRY BASES

John Steele Gordon contends that, thanks to the war, "the industrialization of the American economy, already well under way, expanded exponentially." Resourcing what became the largest army in the world, and a navy second only to Great Britain's, drove productivity. Federal government expenditures exploded from $172,000 a day across departments in April 1861, to $1 million per day three months later at the time of First Bull Run, to $1.5 million *per diem* by Appomattox. New York City's Wall Street financial district, distant from daily battlefield scenes but happy to exploit their existence, consolidated in 1863 as the New York Stock Exchange, profiting immensely as securities trading increased. The adage "rich man's war, poor man's fight" became attached to the carnage, with public funds underwriting northern iron mills, gun foundries, railroads, telegraph companies, as well as textile and shoe factories, suggests Gordon. He also hails the growth of a southern war industry, "but from a much smaller base and with far greater constraints." Dislocation of cotton markets, destruction of the prewar Union's merchant marine to Confederate sea predators, and liberation of the south's slave labor force, garner attention. However, claims Gordon, it was the overall "Armageddon of the Civil War" that produced a dynamism "that could inspirit the next generation of both sides."[35]

Twentieth-century American wars have yielded prodigious statistical indicators. So did the Civil War. The Union army's expansion caused the Springfield armory to fabricate over 800,000 rifled muskets, with at least thirty private firms producing additional hundreds of thousands. Many were made according to government-templated specifications, others of innovative pattern. Barton Hacker thus concludes the war was "not just an industry-based conflict," it also "marked the advent of mass production." James Nagle further suggests "the uniformity system pioneered in the arsenals worked fantastically." Once a War Department commission sorted out the turmoil of early mobilization, preferred manufacturers like Colt, Remington, Sharpe, Ames, Jenks, and Spencer, along with lesser-known vendors like Lamson, Goodnow, and Yale of Windsor in Vermont, joined foreign producers to supply something like 1.2 million muskets and rifles, over 400,000 carbines and 372,800 revolvers. Colt's Patent Fire Arms Company received 267 contracts worth $4,687,031 million; J. T. Ames, Herman Boker, Alfred Jenks and Son, E. Remington and Sons, Sharpe, Starr, and Spencer makers cleared over $1 million each. Even the older Eli Whitney firm garnered $353,647 in contracts. At least fifty firms rushed to fulfill contracts and provide what turned out to be largely ornamental cavalry and artillery swords. Every northern state numbered arms makers, contends Merritt Roe Smith, with New England and mid-Atlantic states topping the list. Here was the mixed-economy resourcing base of Mark Wilson's "unacknowledged militarization of America." But this was wartime anyway.[36]

Of course, cannon demanded heavier industrial production facilities. Five prewar U.S. cannon foundries went to thirteen, producing 3,687 field and 2,172 heavy guns (5,859 total) during the war. With only two prewar facilities, southern makers nearly equaled the Union's wartime total, as twelve of them turned out 2,331 and 732 heavy cannon (2,063 total). Some estimates run as high as fifty-eight separate private and government facilities used by the Confederate government for cannon fabrication with perhaps 2,529 additional rebel ordnance coming from captures, prewar militia, military academies' stocks, and foreign acquisition. Of twelve major domestic facilities, however, Georgia's Central Ordnance Laboratory of Macon, Alabama's Naval Ordnance Works and National Foundry in Selma, the Powder Works in Augusta, Georgia, and Richmond's Tredegar Iron Works in Virginia all escaped Yankee capture and destruction, almost to the end of the war. This munition base even produced torpedoes or mines. True, the Confederacy lost one-quarter of its supplier base in the first year of the war thanks to Union invasion of Kentucky and Middle Tennessee, and inept Confederate response. But, as Union forces advanced, authorities transferred armaments manufacturing to less threatened regions. This move, like later World War II Soviet war-industry transfer east of the Ural Mountains, spared a Ruhr-like Confederate munitions strip in the deeper south until almost war's end. Production sagged more from lack of raw materials, tools and machinery, and skilled workers, either nonexistent or conscripted into the army; even slave labor was in short supply.[37]

Localized threats complicated production efforts by Confederate Niter and Mining Bureau officials. Niter, lead, iron, sulfur, and copper extraction suffered from Yankee raiders and irregulars. A combination of Confederate conscripts, bands of deserters, draft-dodgers, bushwhackers, and just plain outlaws supplemented the more formal destruction by Union forces, set against a backdrop of already-virulent anti-Confederate, even pro-Union sentiment, in some locales. Affected areas included southwestern Virginia, eastern Tennessee, northern Alabama, northwestern Georgia, northwestern Arkansas and southwestern Missouri. Certainly, no such fate befell the northern counterpart although one could argue that Confederate general Jubal Early's "hard war" actions that destroyed Pennsylvania congressman Thaddeus Stevens's ironworks during the Gettysburg campaign showed some appreciation for economic warfare. But, Early's initiative, whether self-directed or soldierly hooliganism, could have been more personally directed at the abolitionist congressman himself. Early's laying tribute at Gettysburg and York in route to the 1863 battle was more sinister and reactive to what Federals did to civilian property in Virginia.

Elsewhere, geography or distance shielded northern mines, furnaces and foundries in western and northeastern Pennsylvania, although Confederate intent to stir labor unrest and industrial action in the anthracite coal fields figured in Lee's campaign plan. Certainly foundries like Cyrus Alger's South Boston company (Boston), Ames (Chicopee-Springfield), Henry N. Hooper (Boston), Hinkley, Williams (Boston), Revere Copper (Boston) all in Massachusetts; Builders (Providence, Rhode Island); Marshall (St. Louis, Missouri); Greenwood (Cincinnati, Ohio), Fort Pitt and Singer, Nimick (both Pittsburgh) and Phoenix Iron (Phoenixville), Seyfort, McManus (Reading) all in Pennsylvania, Portland (Portland, Maine) and Robert P. Parrott's West Point Foundry, (Cold Spring N.Y.) escaped Confederate reprisal. Random raids against Union logistical facilities in Tennessee and Mississippi by Confederate raiders like John Hunt Morgan, Joseph Wheeler, Nathan Bedford Forrest, and lesser knowns, such as Hylan B. Lyon in Kentucky, even Morgan's famous 1863 foray north of the Ohio River, even raids as far north as St. Albans, Vermont, often held more psychological intent. Early on, Union mounted raiders, and later William T. Sherman, consciously aimed at more strident targeting of economic destruction and strategic resourcing.

Indeed, defeated Confederate general Robert E. Lee's post-Appomattox contention, which became postwar southern dogma, that he and his countrymen had been beaten not by their northern enemies, but merely overwhelmed by Yankee resources, holds some truth. Manifesting that conclusion, Union ordnance bureau chief A.B. Dyer in October 1865 reported impressive statistics, most of which had been acquired in wartime: 3,325 field, siege and seacoast guns and mortars on-hand, 571,690,504 projectiles for the same, 1,589 carriages and 464 mortar beds for the same, 948 caissons, 221 forges, and battery wagons for artillery. For hand-held weaponry, 1,195,572 rifles and muskets, 65,768 carbines, and 68,062 pistols were inventoried. Infantry accouterments numbered 419,639; cavalry accouterments 102,997. Horse equipment of 74,425, artillery harness for two horses numbered 5,843 and 120,277 saddle blankets added to Dyer's statistics. Ammunition seemed staggering: 1,263,844 artillery rounds, 282,167,898 for small arms. Indispensable percussion caps to fire the small arms stood at 91,078,071, artillery friction primers at 1,911,102, and 1,561,1883 artillery fuses. 3,366,825 pounds of gunpowder, (3.5 and 4.0 million pounds by supplier Dupont's own computation to army and navy), 8,098,986 pounds of niter, 408,932 pounds of sulphur, 39,661,103 pounds of lead and 5,517,991 pounds of lead balls attested to a national stockpile by war's end. The gunpowder maker Du Pont added measurably to family fortunes thanks to chemist scion Lamont's application of larger grained "Mammoth Gunpowder" to Captain Thomas Rodman's newer cannon thus enabling ever-larger calibers of both seacoast and naval ordnance for the war. [38]

Dyer would leave analysis of these details to future historians. Union industry overcame delays through tooling up factories, sharing technical ideas and expertise industry-wide, and building links if not actual partnership between public and private enterprise. Nonetheless, Confederate fighting men never lacked for weaponry. Illustrating the point was Chief of Ordnance Josiah Gorgas's report for the year ending September 30, 1864 that recounted how the Confederacy had imported 30,000 small arms, manufactured 20,000 and captured 45,000. He admitted the soldiers had lost 30,000 "leaving a gain of 15,000", or more than enough to arm a full corps. Many captured weapons went to the Confederate States armory at Richmond where master armorer Solomon Adams told his superiors, "I suppose there are in the north not less than thirty-eight armories, all on a large scale," capable of turning out 5,000 arms per day, including breech-loading types. By comparison, the embattled south created no fewer than fifty-five major ordnance arsenals, depots and stations from Virginia to Texas, and offshore in Bermuda and the Bahamas. Mary A. DeCredico's phrase "patriotism for profit" accounted for national and state contracts across the land.[39]

The Confederacy created its own set of statistics from entrepreneurs like Samuel Griswold of Georgia and Edward S. Spiller, David Burr and James H.

Burton of Virginia, to the redoubtable French émigré in New Orleans, Jean Francois Alexander LeMat. The south also had its equals to Samuel Colt and Nathaniel Ames although mostly in model copying. Better known to today's weapons collectors, famous makes flowed from arsenals, armories, naval works, foundries and ironworks, even pre-war plow works, located in Virginia, North Carolina, Georgia, Alabama and Tennessee. Names rolled from southern tongues like the Atlanta Arsenal, Atlanta Naval Works August Arsenal, Augusta Foundry and Machine Works, Columbus Arsenal, Augusta Foundry and Machine Works, Macon Armory, Macon Foundry and Machine Works, Columbus Arsenal, Columbus Naval Iron Works, Etowah Works and Noble Brothers and Company all in Georgia. Alabama added Brierfield Arsenal and Selma Works, North Carolina contributed Fayetteville Armory and Salisbury Arsenal and T. M. Bannon, Nashville Plow Works Whitfield, Bradley and Company as well as Quinby and Robinson from Tennessee before Union conquest and occupation. Virginia was also present with Bellona Arsenal, Bellona Foundry, Richmond Arsenal, Richmond Armory and Tredegar Foundry for the public-private endeavor. Outlying production and ordnance storage facilities ranged from Texas, Louisiana, Arkansas and South Carolina to places in Alabama such as the Arsenal, and Naval Ordnance Works, in Selma, and Petersburg Iron Works in Virginia.

Thus, Gorgas presided over a small empire of facilities that one tabulator of Confederate cannon manufacturers lists as sixty-five public and private manufacturers. Like the Union model, Gorgas's enterprise replicated the familiar GOGO, GOCO and COCO formulas. No less than thirteen British firms likewise made cannon to be shipped through the Union naval blockade. As Larry J. Daniel and Riley W. Gunter suggest, even domestic infrastructure comprised established foundries, improvised foundries and government foundries. Confederates like George W. Rains (Augusta Powder Works), Catesby ap Roger Jones, (at the Selma ordnance works), and John W. Mallet (Macon's research and development guru) merited Maurice Melton's point that "all over the Confederacy could be found good men trying to accomplish [such contribution] while meeting with moderate or no success." Eventually Gorgas's empire crumbled, thanks to Confederate material scarcities and Union military destruction.[40]

TWO PROTO-NAVAL/INDUSTRIAL COMPLEXES

The wedding of technology, industry and government could be seen best in naval historian Dana M. Wegner's suggestion that, "the monitor-type warship, though of limited value [in the Civil War], introduced the [United

States] navy to a new dependence upon private industry," just as "the use of mines and torpedo boats forecast [naval] combat of the future." At an earlier point, historian Oscar Paullin noted that "the rusty machinery" of the Union's Navy department "had to be repaired, lubricated, and enlarged" before forging "the thunderbolts of war", with officers, sailors and ships supplied in great numbers, just like the army. Both interpreters point to statistics of achievement: the number of ships increased from 90 to 671, officers from 1,300 to 6,700, seamen from 7,500 to 51,500, and annual expenditures exploded from $12 million to $123 million, peaking in 1863 at $144,000,000, and reaching $314,000,000 in sum for the war. Union Secretary of the Navy Gideon Welles modernized his department in 1862 but always retained his prerogative on final shipbuilding programs, operation plans, and general lines of policy. "He was held responsible for the blunders and failures of the Department and the navy," declared Paullin. So, too, was Confederate counterpart Stephen E. Mallory.[41]

Both administrators faced problems of improvised mobilization. For that reason, on February 15, 1862, Welles asked congress for $250,000 to enable the department at once "to commence the casting of the heaviest ordnance at the Washington Navy Yard" because of the "extraordinary demands for heavy ordnance" and "the fact that private establishments cannot produce near the quantity required." Ironically, both secretaries sequentially faced major resource losses early in the war, first from Confederate capture of United States property that included ordnance and stores at navy yards and coastal forts, then later changing back to Union hands at Forts Henry and Donelson, Columbus bluffs and Island Number 10, New Orleans, Vicksburg, and Port Hudson. Perhaps because the Confederacy needed every human and matériel resource for its survival the Richmond government blinked at culpable commanders like Tennessee politician-turned-general Gideon Pillow who, helped sacrifice numbers of heavy cannon and indispensable stores, plus a 12,000–15,000 corps-size army, while deserting his Fort Donelson post. Confederate special orders of August 22, 1862, declared "it is impossible to acquit" him "of grave errors of judgement," but since "there being no reason to question his courage and loyalty," his suspension was removed and he returned to the army on recruiting and training duty, trying to muster malingering human resources with his oratory. The Confederacy could ill afford losses on the scale of Forts Henry and Donelson, Island Number 10, other Mississippi River posts like Vicksburg and Port Hudson as well as eventually indispensable coastal forts guarding Mobile Savannah and Wilmington ports.[42]

In contrast to army mobilization primarily through state channels, both

Union and Confederate navies tried centralize mobilization through bureau and shore-establishment systems although southern states with water boundaries supplemented the national program. In truth, each antagonist developed two operational fleets, one comprising traditional "blue water" focus on command of the water well as commercial raiding (Confederate). The other a Union "brown-water" river flotilla working joint operations with land armies faced a Confederate embrace of harbor and river defense mostly by land forts and converted civilian craft mounting scarce guns. Both parties had their Marine corps. The two navies recruited human resources heavily from army volunteers as well as recruiting-rendezvous locations on their respective seaboards and waterways while also then setting up naval construction, repair and supply stations accordingly. Obviously, the Union navy enjoyed an edge—it had an established infrastructure in being. Fewer prewar naval officers than their army counterparts left for the Confederacy. The Union navy appointed volunteer junior officers largely from the merchant service and conducted "no experimenting corresponding to that of the War Department" with its general officers. Most naval "experimentation" for both sides went toward warship procurement, secured through conversion of civilian craft and new construction. At various points, the Union War Department went into business building a river gunboat squadron (eventually taken over by the navy), and the Quartermaster Department leased its own vast fleet of transport and supply vessels supporting army operations while the U.S. navy provided for its own fleet logistical support. The Confederacy managed only a pale simile.

Five U.S. navy yards—of which Pensacola and Norfolk, lost early to the insurgents, were subsequently recovered—formed the nucleus of depots, manufactories and repair facilities. Two floating drydocks, and naval station depots at wide-ranging locations such as Cairo and Mound City in Illinois, Memphis, New Orleans, Ship Island, Key West, Port Royal, Beaufort and Baltimore, were all temporary wartime additions serving river squadrons and blockades. Soon, a forward-thinking Welles sought a new navy yard, adaptable to the iron fleets. It would contain foundries, steam machinery with repair shops, as well as facilities for constructing metal ships and shafting. Competition between New London in Connecticut and Philadelphia hit shoals when Congress failed to secure Philadelphia's League Island where the Schuylkill and Delaware rivers joined, despite the willingness of city fathers to simply give the land to the navy. Wartime shipbuilding increases pitted the expanding Southwark city neighborhood against limited navy yard space, for building steam and iron monitors with a wartime labor force swelling to 2,000.[43]

Most statistics suggest Union naval expansion followed the army pattern of unplanned approach to mobilization, but tapped a flourishing private East Coast maritime support sector. The new Confederacy enjoyed no such luxury although enlisting watercraft within its jurisdiction even capturing and reusing those of the north. Oceangoing merchant ships, ferry boats, and steamboats used for blockade and riverine duties served the immediate problem of increasing Union numbers. The navy department purchased every available merchant steamer in the Northern ports which could be advantageously converted into a naval vessel and used on the blockade, states Paullin, in addition to many other watercraft unfit for such duty. New York was the best market, and Secretary Welles drew heat using his wife's brother-in-law, influential businessman George D. Morgan, as a purchasing agent. A team in Boston included the navy yard commandant and two businessmen who drew no charges for their services. Western river gunboats ranged from contracted Ohio River steamboats for both transports and converted gunboats, as well as new, special-combat designs from St. Louis civil engineer James B. Eads, facilitated by army Quartermaster General Montgomery C. Meigs. Public and private boat yards provided the base for a squadron that achieved the first river war success.

Like the War Department, the Union navy also suffered its share of alleged abuses and questionable practices. After all, if good money could be made supplying pork to the army at Louisville, then also purveying substitutes for sperm oil as well as purloined copper, pitch, rosin and other naval stores, plus selling copper bathtubs, brass filings and other government items to a local junk dealer, provided a lucrative black market in ports like Philadelphia. Even the low-bidding requirement hardly prevented fraud, waste and abuse. Cost overruns might be expected from constructing and completing 179 U.S. navy ships from 1861 to 1866, all steam vessels, with fifty-five built at northern navy yards and 124 constructed under contract. Prices for the newly constructed warships ranged from $75,000 to $650,000 apiece; *Madawaska*, the highest-priced, cost $1,673,000, while purchased vessels ranged from $10,000 to $60,000. Captured from the Confederates, the prize-ship *Tennessee* commanded $595,000. A stone fleet of seventy-eight vessels acquired for navigation obstruction and purchase of 313 transport craft for $18 million, further reflected wartime costs. Ship inventory-lists even enumerated 112 old sailing vessels.[44]

Transitions in heavy naval ordnance accompanied the revolution wrought by iron ships. The prewar 2,966 heavy guns and howitzers came chiefly in 8-inch, 10-inch and 32-pounders for a wooden fleet. The iron navy's 4,333 new guns manufactured using the Dahlgren, Fox or Parrott models demanded 9-inch, 11-inch, 15-inch, even 20-inches in size. Many were rifled and made by seven or eight private foundries at locations in Boston, South Boston, Providence, Cold Spring, Reading and Pittsburgh. Navy yards mainly provided the gun carriages, with the Washington yard employing 600 men fabricating boat guns, fuses, primers, percussion caps and ammunition, while conducting experiments, and providing specifications to other public and private facilities as well. During the first half of the war alone, nearly 7 million pounds of shrapnel, grape and canister were cast at that yard, and 2.6 million more were purchased. Huge ammunition magazines for the powder were situated near northern navy yards as well as at Baltimore and Fortress Monroe. Dependence on foreign niter from India was supplanted by the New Haven Chemical Works, and a depot established at Malden, Massachusetts in 1864.

Other ordnance depots could be found at New York and Boston, other northern yards at Fortress Monroe, Baltimore and Mound City, with store ships stationed at Port Royal, Key West, Pensacola, and New Orleans, in more direct support of naval coastal and river operations. Mare Island outside San Francisco serviced the Pacific squadron and intimated global reach for the future. Colliers supplied various blockading squadrons, and sixteen coaling depots located principally in Caribbean waters but also abroad at Lisbon, Honolulu, Rio de Janeiro, Halifax, and St. John, which were intended for foreign squadrons chasing Confederate raiders. Much of the coal was eastern Pennsylvania anthracite purchased by Philadelphia special agent Commodore H. A. Adams, Sr. and shipped via the Pennsylvania and Reading railroad to Philadelphia coal yards. Thus, war stoked yet another northern industrial sector, as the amount of fuel consumed reached about 500,000 tons in 1864. No naval vessels lacked fuel, according to historian Paullin.[45]

Introduction of these "mastless war vessels," Paullin's term for ironclads, spawned the defense industrial base necessary for resourcing those weapons systems. HMS *Warrior* in Great Britain and the French *La Glorie* and especially Confederate ironclad *Virginia/Merrimac* forced the American navy to embrace the new naval weapons platforms, complementing the army's coastal and harbor shore defenses. A customary naval board determined three different ironclad designs leading to contracts with Bushnell and Company of New Haven, Merrick and Sons of Philadelphia, and John Ericsson of New York. The *Galena* failed due to defective d armor, *New Ironsides* seemed the most successful, while the third was Ericsson's *Monitor*. The *Monitor* versus *Virginia/Merrimac* encounter in March 1862 settled the matter. *Monitor*-mania swept the north and navy department leaders. Twenty craft of that design underwent construction in 1863 with contracts geographically allocated, a la the old frigate idea, among a dozen cities from Portland, Maine to St. Louis, Missouri. Paullin thought this program was "of unsavory memory, for their construction was the principal blunder of the Navy department in the Civil War." Yet, Confederate naval secretary Stephen Mallory determined that "not only economy, but naval success, dictates the wisdom and expediency of fighting with iron against wood, without regard to first cost." Hampton Roads dictated expediency until deliberation could better wed platform with mission. Only wartime permitted such innovative adjustment.[46]

The war at-first stressed both army and navy prewar procurement apparatus. Experience with private contracting for steam power plants, when extended to entire warships like ironclads, ran into the need for production speed, not guaranteed product performance. Such demands led the navy to preprinted contract forms for constructing entire classes of ships or number of similar power plants, claims naval historian Kurt Hackemer, though not always with desired result or smooth government-private partnering. Yet, he suggests the process gave both government and private producer "a comfortable relationship" for the future. A result that began with frigate construction in the 1850s combined with monitor procurement in the 1860s via the process of acquiring steam power plants that then expanded to whole vessel procurement, government and contractors developed a method that Hackemer views as preparation for the expansion of a "new navy" of steam and steel 1880s and 1890s.[47]

However, grafting the new technology of using iron onto an inadequate manufacturing infrastructure, both private and public, still wedded to wood, by implementing the contracting experience of the 1850s, proved challenging. It could not be smoothly or swiftly done. Thomas R. Heinrich's examination of shipbuilding on the Delaware River, particularly at Philadelphia, affirms that conclusion. Wartime transition from wood to iron could be seen both in navy facilities and company yards such as Charles Cramp (Philadelphia), Raney & Archbold (Chester), Wilcox & Whitney (Camden) or Harlan & Hollinsworth (Wilmington) for ships or working with Merrick & Sons (Philadelphia) for engines and boilers was as much instructive as it was productive. Cramp's superb *New Ironsides* was more than offset by a disastrous "light-draft monitor scandal" of twenty vessels for inland waterway service that, by summer 1864 cost $500,000 apiece to produce, and were "entirely useless," in Heinrich's words. The disaster involved more than Cramp's company, and corrective measures by the public-private partners naturally took place. Nonetheless, it remained to be seen if any new way of business would join any new way of war emerging from the Civil War. As Heinrich implies, the future for any naval-private partnering after Appomattox lay with mothballing on "Monitor Row" not far from *New Ironsides* herself at the Philadelphia Navy Yard! Whether comparable Confederate naval experience had anything to teach posterity, evaporated in triumphant Union victory.[48]

Structurally and institutionally ill-prepared for modern industrialized war, the Confederacy actually had better opportunity than the Union for experiment and innovation. Thoroughly examined by various scholars like Raimondi Luraghi, William N. Still and Thomas H. Wells, the rebel naval program also naturally reflected conventional American strategy of harbor-defense and seacoast fortification supplemented by high-seas raiding of enemy commerce. Southern strategy also embraced contracted blockade running craft to exit tradable commodity cotton to Europe in return for war-sustaining goods That strategy in Confederate hands also led to an innovative use of technology for armored warships, a submarine, submersible mines and rifled heavy ordnance. Perhaps development of sleek and swift blockade runners in British yards as well as the famous Laird rams should be studied more closely for an underdog's resort to various technologies snuffed out in their cradle by superior enemy application of resources. Union and Confederate navies both hovered on the cusp of developing the requisite military-industrial complex as a natural reflex of waging major war. The Confederacy, however, facing competition for its meager resources, resorted to wedding steam and iron afloat, via the *Virginia (Merrimac)* and similar casemate types. The Union embraced both casemate and turreted models thus representing a transitional state in American naval architecture and warfare.[49]

Battleships and cruiser-raiders best reflected Confederate plans for a 150-ship fleet, maybe a third of which never slipped down launching ramps. But, twenty-one ironclads would have more than offset U.S. Navy superiority both in numbers and quality. The question was more one of securing adequate pig-iron in Alabama, the main source, and transporting it over rickety railroads to places like Richmond's Tredegar works or other fabrication points for making armor plate, then getting that to naval assembly yards. Officials like Mallory and Gorgas, ordnance genius John M. Brooke, and European agent James Bulloch cobbled together a domestic naval fabrication patchwork while tapping British yards for purchasing a fleet. If the famous Laird ram scheme from Scottish yards never came to fruition, the raiders *Alabama, Shenandoah, Sumter*, and others reduced the proud American merchant fleet by almost one-half.[50]

Italian scholar of Confederate naval development, Raimondo Luraghi seemed astonished when he chronicled the brief but remarkable resourcing effort. He recounted production of 150 warships while acknowledging fully half were never completed or made operational, also failing to recognize the proto-submarine experience of the CSS *Hunley* that would lead to further revolutions in future naval warfare. But, he did cite the "still more astounding" industrial success of setting up twenty shipyards (at least four for naval purposes), a rolling mill producing armor plate, two engine and boiler plants (of which the one at Columbus, Georgia became the most important in the South), a foundry for heavy and extra-heavy ordnance, a powder works, three artillery plants, a laboratory for caps, primers and torpedoes, a rope walk, plus food-producing and packing facilities, two clothing and shoe factories, a medical and sanitary laboratory, several hospitals, and warehouses for naval supplies and barrack equipment. Luraghi also added several partner enterprises "controlled by naval authorities even though still under private ownership. He discerned three Confederate patterns: direct institution of new government naval shipyards, control of private shipyards via agents, "either lawfully or not," with direct management, and contracts with private shipyards to which the navy supplied specific ship plans and closely controlled their work. Not unlike its Union counterpart, here was the military-industrial complex of the future—GOGO (government owned, government operated), GOCO (government owned, company operated) and even COCO (company owned, company operated)—a system that would surface by the 1880s.[51]

A PORTENT FOR THE FUTURE?

The Civil War was mainly one of size if not necessarily complexity. Yet, such size conveyed its own complexity. The Civil War enterprise dwarfed previous conflicts, with millions under arms, millions more supporting them in factory and field, seriousness of goals, and tenacity of purpose. Resourcing the endeavor encompassed new approaches, driven not only by these phenomena but above all by the geography of distance, time, technology of iron and steam, new types of munitions and a military-industrial base displaying public/private partnerships. Necessity begat technology-sharing between government armories and private contractors. Rival ordnance chiefs Ripley and Gorgas understood the difficulties of introducing new technology (breech-loading firearms) onto stabilized, logistically dependent military systems (armies) in the heat of war. Both sides drew upon technically skilled artisans and an organized, basic labor force. The stakes of power—survival of the state—dictated that devices which could be mobilized would be put into play, perhaps mainly as wartime anomalies. Nevertheless, a model was established, to be retrieved later as the need arose.

On the large front of human experience, University of Washington business professor Joseph W. McGuire advances that northern businessmen "adjusted to the new conditions of war and as in all wars, eventually began to prosper under the stimulus of increased government expenditures." The south, by contrast, took an inherently "maladjusted industrial structure" and unsuccessfully rushed to "build the enterprises essential to the waging of war." A bit simplistically, McGuire's wisdom nonetheless generalizes that, despite the Confederacy's "brilliant generals and heroic troops," the important thing was "the war ended with the star of business burning more brightly than ever in the North, pointing the way to a shining and profitable future." By contrast, the South's "economy stood in ruin, industries destroyed and fortunes shattered." Yet, both sides had experienced the venality of "patriotism for profit" and fears of corruption.[52]

Railroads provided living proof. Wartime conversion of even modest facilities for building locomotives and maintaining rolling stock such as lubricating car wheels to producing war matériel doomed Confederate rails while northern lines prospered. Neither Union nor Confederate governments took over railroads completely, yet both centralized their oversight. In the end, Keith Bryant and Henry Dethloff suggest war consumed the South's railway system due as much to military actions as resourcing deficiencies. Its northern counterpart prospered thanks to the flush of business, with possibly only the Baltimore and Ohio suffering recurring enemy damage. A rehabilitation program, stimulated in some degree to surplus U.S. Military Railroad rolling stock and Union generals like William T. Sherman needing wartime reconstruction for supply, enabled postwar southerners to view railroad expansion as promising for a New South. War's "creative destruction" stripped away impediments and generated opportunities of its own.[53]

Historians for decades have argued over the pros and cons of the Civil War's impact on industrialization and economic growth. The issue speaks directly to "national security." Following the lead of business historian Thomas C. Cochran, some decided that the direct economic impact of the war "must be considered limited" with the exception of effects on income, but "certainly no grand shifts or transformations in economic activity can be delineated." Earlier, however, Charles Beard and Louis M. Hacker had seen it differently, Hacker in particular, as a revolution with "its striking achievement" being the triumph of industrial capitalism. He advanced that industrial capitalists through their political voices, the Republican Party and Lincoln administration, "had succeeded in capturing the state and using it as an instrument to strengthen their economic position." In his view, it was no accident that while the war was "waged on the field and through Negro emancipation," Congress made victory more secure with the longer-term economic implications of legislating tariffs, central banking, public lands, railroads, and contract labor. The epic forged not only a more perfect Union but also a Leviathan for the future. It revised the political system by removing enormous obstacles to industrialization like southern slaveholding agrarians controlling affairs in Washington[54]

Fellow-scholar Walter Licht would contend that changes such as the first federal income tax law, establishment of the National Academy of Sciences to boost technological knowledge and development, creation of a Department of Agriculture to sponsor agrarian improvements, a Bureau of Printing and Engraving, an Office of the Comptroller of the Currency, and the Office of Immigration were "all new federal bureaucracies aimed at greater central-government leadership in economic affairs." Licht concludes that, the war put in place "a new political economic order long championed by those who sought to build the United States into a powerful nation-state through government promotion of growth and large-scale enterprise." Yet, Richard D. Brown adds that "no great bureaucracy was permanently established, nor was national centralization achieved," despite the war being "highly influential in the economy." The war spurred no permanent peacetime defense-industrial base or national security state. Separate ingredients were there: in the North, a concentration of capital in key modern industries, as well as an increase of labor-saving technological advances. None of this obviates Cochran's conclusion that war diverted rather than spurred production in such sectors as cotton-textile production and steel rails. The war period, to Cochran, was not a time of booming production like in future wars. Economist Robert Heilbroner posited that like all wars, this one merely created pent-up demand in normal civilian sectors, delaying the trend toward industrialism already in motion. He and Cochran saw no longer-term impact for economic security writ large but rather merely some war-dictated common defense of the moment. Surely, however, national security was effected merely by a war of reunification or resolution of national unification in the first place.[55]

At a more strictly military level, Army logistics historian James Huston felt that the procurement program during the war "was enough in itself to put the United States into the rank of first-class powers." Inefficiency of competitive purchasing, faulty early-war contract supervision and swarms of profiteers peddling faulty merchandise at high prices, along with general imperfections of bureaucratic processes notwithstanding, he determined that "the final achievement compares favorably with the best efforts of the major military powers of the world at that time." In Huston's view, the north's attempt to tap domestic production more than foreign sourcing may have temporarily given the Confederacy an upper hand, exploited by Confederate agents like C.R. McRae or James D. Bullock. A "New Plan" featuring far more centralization and rigid governmental control of purchasing agents abroad came too late to offset Union crescendo of wartime autarky. Nonetheless, Union and Confederate soldiers themselves preferred British Enfield rifles as their weapon of choice. Still, Huston clung to his position that domestic production "inspired confidence that, with the country's potential to meet any conceivable future wartime demands, it would not find itself at a serious disadvantage relative to any possible enemy."[56]

In the end, skepticism of Cochran's generation for war's economic and business effect presaged today's post-revisionist school of Civil War historians viewing the epoch more as a calculus of violence. Wrapped in social-cultural causes and effects of a turbulent early twenty-first reawakening of racial prejudice, they test the story in terms of executive power expansion, limits of sovereignty in property confiscation, loyalty oaths, trampling of accompanying of civil liberties, suspension of habeas corpus and rampant incarceration for treason, changes in law and society—yet without apparent connection between either Lincoln's or Davis's constitutions or government abuse of much of anything but necessary and temporary wartime limitations. Of course, construction of a slave republic rested on coercion and oppression (but, apparently only for a minority). The Free Republic rested on something else that would require plebiscitary codification after the war in national and state constitutions. The question of the Civil War and Reconstruction as "stage setter" for a later "American Sparta" remains lost in aversion to thinking about today's security state.[57]

Even Licht asks, was not the emplacement or triumph of a new, political and economic order brought about by the Civil War "more episodic than structural?" Was there any fundamental shift in the way the country was ordered or, given the "shift toward a market and industrial society in the particular mid-nineteenth century American context," was any "capture of government by manufacturing interests and the writing of a particular legislative agenda" required at this point? "Quantum and permanent leap in the presence of the central state in the lives of the American people and the building of a definitively new state corporate capitalist order," would take another generation, and would result from great developments and crises of the postwar period, suggesting "the rise of the corporation, pitched conflict between capital, boom and bust cycles of the economy, and upheavals caused by urbanization and massive immigration." These developments "reshaped the nation, not the Civil War."[58]

It would seem Civil War and Reconstruction together with, a Robber-Baron driven Gilded Age thereafter, linked as deterministic milestones for America's entrepreneurial, enterprise development. These periods realigned the business community through destabilization and creative destruction in route to great change. The war's fiery trial enabled new attitudes. Secretary of the Treasury Samuel P. Chase sensed it early on in 1863 when he penned how the country had begun the war without capital, and if the greater part of that, which was being accumulated to prosecute that war, was lost before the struggle ended, then enterprise would bring it back again "and with a power hitherto unfelt among us." A new swagger, and a national confidence would attend postwar America, "today the most powerful nation on the face of the globe." Congressman Goodlove S. Orth informed a Lafayette, Indiana audience: "This war has been the means of developing resources and capabilities such as you never before dreamed that you possessed." Hubris joined the "City on the Hill," exceptionalism and manifest destiny, as America's creed through military action.[59]

* * *

At some point during the war an unknown Union statistician estimated current war expenses at $3. 2 billion. He then added "bounties other than Federal" at $2.9 million; "estimated private contribution" ($50 million); "Loan of Soldier Productive Labor" (slightly over $1 billion); 'various war claims at $140 million; pensions on account of Civil War ($2.4 billion) and Interest on War Debt at $2.36 billion for a total of $8,425,185,017. He scoffed that according to the 1860, the value of all property in the Southern states (excluding slave states Delaware, Maryland, Kentucky and Missouri "was only $5,202,000,000. He figured then that "the cost of the war was almost double the present aggregate of deposits in all the national, State and private banks, savings banks and trust companies in the United States." Indeed, years later, after two world wars, army mobilization historians decided, "there was no precedent for a war of the magnitude of the American Civil War." Past mistakes were repeated; advance planning might have avoided waste and inefficiency. Centralized, coordinated, supervisory control of the war effort, a command economy of an administrative state, suggested alternatives. But these were hindsight observations underscoring a traditional benchmark of fighting war until the Atomic Age. Today, we might even make a case that next to development of the Union's ironclad fleet as a strategic deterrent against Great Britain, the most significant technological achievement of the war was "the advent of mass production, notably at the Springfield Armory," and that technology, logistics, and mobilization heralded the new industrial age of war.[60]

The Civil War harnessed latent to tangible power. Jeffrey D. Wert's "Civil War Barons–those tycoons, Entrepreneurs, Inventors, and Visionaries"— plus common labor, [Black and White] may have "truly forged victory and Shaped a New Nation." Yet, so did Ian C. Hope's legion of West Point graduates who expanded their knowledge and appreciation of a new military science at higher levels of experience in the war. Some officials concluded that procurement had to be based on sound assessment of a nation's economic and industrial capacity. Few besides Jefferson Davis thought necessary controls over a nation's economic life had to replace the traditional American free market. Allocation of manpower and resources to resolve wartime supply and demand certainly took more than cadre organization, rudimentary planning and unsophisticated process. Critical shortages in national resources warranted careful stockpiling. Promising research agencies, like the Smithsonian Institution or Confederate John Mallet's Central Ordnance Laboratory, were best left to peacetime development. Expediency demanded convention not revolution, and effectiveness more than efficiency. Paul A. C. Koistinen concluded that, all things considered, the Union, if not the Confederacy, did fairly well with war mobilization. Then, Americans turned to a hopeful peace in 1865, not a security state. They had had enough of death and carnage in war.[61]

Chapter 4

CONTINENTAL DEFENSE, IMPERIAL PRETENSIONS, AND FORMATION OF THE MIC, 1865-1917

War strains a nation's industrial and agricultural capacity, demanding resource redistribution, but can "encourage improved production techniques." Historian Richard Bensel concluded that while Civil War mobilization diverted resources from westward expansion, "the northern economy grew, "and unlike the South, "emerged almost unscathed." Technology historians Alan Marcus and Howard Segal claim "America's civil war was striking in how little permanent change it made in northern industry and agriculture." They saw greater similarities in northern and southern economic experiences than most historians. Colleague Barton Hacker agreed, contending that, however short-lived, an almost superhuman effort by the South more "nearly approximated the North's than it had for several decades." Marcus and Segal see the war's major impact as "a homogenizing experience," which reinforced "the most significant technological effect"—commonality. It was "the archetypical mass experience in an era distinguished by attempts to provide common experience." Peter Stearns thinks that "the second stage of U.S. industrialization took off with the expansion of war industries during the Civil War." Perhaps this singular event provided unparalleled opportunity to "systematizing America," a process of ordering, categorizing and standardizing elements of people, places and things, pointing toward operating at optimal efficiency. The armaments sector in particular evolved with Stearns asserting that American manufacturers even extended their reach, "beginning a tradition of arms sales abroad when the domestic market shrank after 1865."[1]

POSTWAR LETHARGY

Where better to pinpoint production success than the Civil War? Resulting from improvisation and the government's public-private enterprise system, prodigious statistics attended Brigadier General A.B. Dyer's ordnance stockpile and the navy's recitation of military-industrial potential. For instance, by the end of 1864 the fleet comprised nearly 700 warships and 5,000 guns, up from forty-two vessels and 555 guns at the beginning of the war. Navalists at the time could contend the American fleet "possessed armored ships and guns superior to anything afloat," citing 71 ironclads (the so-called monitor type) in commission, the largest mounting the "celebrated fifteen and twenty-inch smoothbore naval guns of the Dahlgren type." Absent enemy threat, maintaining such monuments to heavy industry cost money and they were soon "mothballed."[2]

Arguably, when the Civil War ended, the most powerful military in the world simply evaporated. Regular army numbers stabilized at about 54,000 but by 1877 at the end of formal southern Reconstruction, customary pecuniary dictated half that. The national government faced rebellion of a more muted stripe in an un-repentant south as it shied away from responsibilities toward freed people. There was a Reconstruction army occupying and keeping order in some states readmitted to the Union. Demobilization took sway, volunteers went home, the navy docked its vessels, army ordnance stacked cannon balls, and procurement officials cancelled all unfilled war contracts. Public agencies disposed of surplus stores at public auction for absurdly low prices. Du Pont, for instance, complaining about lost peacetime revenue (sunk profits from southern sales) and already criticized for war profiteering, reluctantly bought back much of its own war-supplied gunpowder at public auctions. He offered to be a sole-source option to a disinterested government and the auctions continued for six years. A heavily indebted ($30 million) army quartermaster department liquidated half its indebtedness by selling excess horses, mules, and oxen. The ordnance department also auctioned off "war surplus," spawned a private-arms trade in time for the Franco-Prussian war, until a State Department embargo put an end to that activity for fear of alienating an emergent Germany. Military railroads reverted to private owners as did a captured Confederate iron-rolling mill in Chattanooga, which the Union had used to support Sherman's operations but was no longer of military value at war's end.[3]

The American war model now embraced size through prompt mobilization, annihilative victory, and smooth return to peace. Army occupation duty in the conquered South, irregular war there as on the western frontier, plus a momentary flutter about French intrusion in Mexico and Fenian troubles on the Canadian border, hardly stirred a ripple. More serious were domestic disturbances between labor and capital by the 1870s which required military intervention on behalf of owners against strikers. Meanwhile, as the navy resumed patrolling the high seas, guarding commerce and showing the flag, it economized by using economical sail rather than coal-fired steam power. Few senior military officials, other than veterans like John Gibbon or Emory Upton, worried about mobilization issues *per se*, and few citizens cared that technologically advancing weapons might require more time and skill to produce. Except for occasional catastrophes like Custer's 1876 "massacre," Americans focused on making money, shedding wartime taxes, and embracing the "rise of consumerism."[4]

Of course, some sectors suffered. Revenues dropped eighty-seven percent for private arms makers in the two years after Appomattox. Cutbacks trimmed the overcapacity of what contracting historian James Nagle terms "the semiofficial arsenal system that had developed after 1808, died in the 1850s, and reappeared during the Civil War." Government facilities experimented with converting muzzle-loader production to breech-loaders while a few private firms developed advanced shoulder arms, but "could hardly sustain an industry that had been tooled to produce hundreds of thousands of weapons" during wartime. Government bureaucrats rebutted protests to Congress from companies like Remington, Winchester, Ames and Colt, that they were more innovative and efficient than government shops. The Spencer repeating Rifle Company of Boston disappeared in 1869, when acquired by Remington. A postwar pattern surfaced but without government intervention. Tycoons, entrepreneurs, inventors and visionaries who helped forge victory (according to author Jeffrey Wert), moved to parlay their wartime experiences into new great endeavors.[5]

AMERICA'S EVOLVING PARADIGM

Historians traditionally have differentiated Reconstruction, Gilded Age, Populist and Progressive eras of post-Civil War America. Some like Heather Richardson now view nineteenth-century attempts to balance freedom, taxation, and government power as the "central story." Industry supplanted agriculture in post-Civil War America, and what emerged defined "a desirable American citizen and an ideal American state." Richardson sees issues forming in this period like size and role of government whether benign or activist, individualism versus corporatism, and political influence from special interests corrupting process and institutions. All signaled a new country. The rugged individualist marched west with the receding frontier, personified by that anachronistic legend, the cowboy, improbable icon of equal opportunity superimposed on repressed social inequalities of race, gender and economics. All parties spoke to this "American rebirth," with "progress" preoccupying rejuvenated businessmen and public alike after the Civil War. The quest for profit characterized Mark Twain's quaint "Gilded Age," and Andrew

Carnegie's "Gospel of Wealth." America's passage to the twentieth century displayed an amalgam of religious conviction, strategic stridence, and messianic promise. American values and vision eventually transferred outward to reform the world. The old "manifest destiny" directive hardly missed a beat vaulting the Pacific and Caribbean moats, as Rudyard Kipling's "White Man's Burden" whetted American appetites. Whether trade followed flag or vice versa, late-century economic transformation translated, at some point, to America needing a modern military.[6]

America's security apparatus atrophied at the very moment the nation moved forward. Content with its success from the Civil War, the Gilded Age army and navy produced few strategic sages. Congressional pecuniary especially meant that "after 1867, the gap between the idea of naval greatness and actual American naval strength widened relentlessly," claims naval historian Lance C. Buhl. "Command of the sea" doctrine had not yet caught on, nor had Karl von Clausewitz's axioms about war as extension of politics. The navy still meant control of coastlines, harbors, and protected sea lanes of commerce. It had sufficient resources for that task and the spirit of Civil War admirals Farragut and Porter would suffice as leadership models. Land warfare took its lead from application of decisive force in the manner of Grant, Sherman and Sheridan. Nobody thought about overseas contingencies, for there were to be none. Development of a postwar professional trade education system would eventually point to some higher military art and science, but most senior and middle professionals seemed unfazed by innovation and reform. Ordnance and ship improvement through testing and experimentation only dimly registered as long as money for maintenance was in short supply and threats were opaque.[7]

The antebellum model of a military connection to machine industries, steam propulsion, and their application in nation-building had blossomed with the war. This particular public/private partnering assumed a different shape after the war. America's railroads, temporarily harnessed to public use via contract, morphed into nurturing post-bellum army mobility in the west and rehabilitating southern lines as part of recovery, reconstruction and reunification. The story of strategic networking for the common defense seemed evident from the 1862 "Act to Aid in the Construction of Railroad and Telegraph Line from the Missouri River to the Pacific Ocean and to Secure to the Government the Use of the Same for Postal, Military, and Other Purposes." As historian Robert Angevine notes, "the government provided the land, the army provided the protection, and private business built and operated the railroads," in other words a definition of postwar security. Yet, organizationally and even doctrinally, the Gilded Age army was unable or unwilling to resume constructing "a vast rail network" for strategic-defense purposes, leaving railways "dependent on private business to manage and operate." True, railroad expansion increasingly demanded a domestic iron and steel industry that could be linked to defense in time of need. It was centralized state planning and action that remained absent from the American ethos. Railroad lessons from Austro-Prussian and Franco-Prussian wars in rapid mobilization and logistics were not lost on the U.S. army. Public-private partnering for sealing connections between military and business in peacetime remained elusive.[8]

Ironically, impetus for a "Buy American" autarkic policy of establishing and sustaining a self-sufficient and independent national economy was supported in Washington at this time. The naval appropriation acts of 1865 and 1866, as well as that of the army in 1876, required a preference for domestic products, labor, and fabrication materials in public-improvement contracts. The fortification appropriation act of 1888 specified that all guns and materials "shall be of American production and furnished by citizens of the United States," a principle ultimately passed on to building a new navy. Such developments were designed to stimulate domestic production, though it may be argued whether or not such provisions slowed or even stifled quality procurement via the international market. Other formalized acquisition procedures and standardization, first applied in the War Department and subsequently transferred government-wide, suggest a transformational experience. If railroads may have appeared more strategic, the military's institutional rigidity remained more traditional with veteran military "tycoons" like generals Grant, Sherman, Sheridan and Schofield. The staff-and-line priesthood "reverted to prewar levels and tasks," or in Barton Hacker's words, in "a kind of enforced isolation" from American society. Much vaunted movement toward military professionalization in the period was not at the top level of war preparation.[9]

More fascinating was America's transformation itself, now about men, machines, money-making and power. The destiny of a reunified nation lay with an age of businessman and consumer, the technology of industrialization via machinery, and accumulation of private capital through manipulation, risk-taking and inadequate state controls. Development of an industrial heartland stretching from New England to Pennsylvania and westward across the base of the Great Lakes past Chicago, symbolized the new geography of an awakened giant. Steel, steam, and coal provided Vulcan with an immigrant workforce, a burgeoning agricultural sector providing food to feed it, and consumerism at home and abroad ravenous for finished products, from wool and cotton to iron and steel. Mass production and a transportation revolution expanded distribution, now freed from obstructionist antebellum issues that had paralyzed Washington politics. New Capital ruled the land.[10]

No doubt, post-Civil War America was greedy, restless and ambitious. Government regulation was weak or even absent in this period of wealth accrual. As historian Walter McDougall observes, manufacturers made the U.S. economy the largest in the world, financiers and railroad promoters often seemed voracious "wolves in sheep's clothing" while politicians "achieved little besides making immigrants docile, blacks invisible and democracy a bad joke." Robber barons, railroads and banks trampled farmers, small-businessmen, and an emerging middle-class. Wealth inequality, the "haves-and-have-nots," caste and class stratification so familiar to twenty-first century rhetoric, fueled late-nineteenth century domestic dissatisfaction. Railroad and steel strikes, Populist unrest, and Progressive reform attended debate in the 1880s and 1890s over the tariff versus income tax. Lost in the kerfuffle was the fact that the state now had at hand the ingredients for guiding a rapidly forming corporate America. Yet, merchandise giants Macy's, Sears Roebuck, Montgomery Ward, S. Kresge (later K-Mart) and Marshall Fields (now Marshall's), centralizing transportation empires from Union Pacific and Pennsylvania to New York Central as well as daunting Big Business entities like Standard Oil, U.S. Steel, Armour, General Electric, Westinghouse and American Tobacco eventually could be harnessed to serve the national weal in time of need. Kingpins of capital such as John D. Rockefeller, Andrew Carnegie, Jay Gould, the Du Ponts and J. P. Morgan might be enlisted to join government-private partner efforts. Yet, absent tangible reason, Great Enterprise remained beyond government marshalling men and organizations for their inventiveness, enterprise, and entrepreneurship. Nothing beyond the Civil War experience offered a guide.[11]

Military logistics historian James A. Huston felt "the surge toward military modernization stimulated by [the Civil War] once again declined to a slough of indifference, disturbed only now and then by the demands of Indian warfare and by a few imaginative officers seeking steady improvement, until a new national emergency should once more call forth the waves of progress." Army mobilization historians Marvin Kreidberg and Merton Henry added that the most important events of the period for the service, at least, were reorganization of the War Department and developments in professional military education. Professionalism and modernization set in motion with staff and war colleges, and the army's mobilization disaster in the Spanish-American War, were way stations until some new opportunity knocked. The 1890s sounded the trumpet when the Census Bureau declared an end to the free-land frontier in 1890. That same year, an obscure navy captain published his famous sea-power treatise while his equally unknown patron, an expansionist-imperialist secretary of the navy, connected with trade hungry Republican politicians in Congress to appropriate money for a battle fleet. New forces carried America outward-bound in an "idyllic crusade for national coherence and homogeneity." Fertile ground now existed for changing direction. Special providence if not hegemony beckoned for the future.[12]

MURMURS OF NEW DIRECTIONS

The late nineteenth to early twentieth century period was a transition that witnessed decline and then revival for the navy, and decline and reforms for the army. The army's ordnance chief touted in January 1872 that, from July 1865 to July 1871, over $11.5 million-worth of excess (many obsolescent and obsolescing) firearms and ordnance stores had been sold off with proceeds going to the U.S. Treasury. Markets removed major arms companies through closure and consolidation, with survivors often converting to other ventures requiring similar machinery and manufacturing processes, thus pioneering the machine-tool industry. This swords-to-plowshares approach led to inventing or perfecting sewing machines, typewriters, bicycles, high-speed printing presses, portable steam-engines, and mechanized agricultural machinery. Foreign sales offered another avenue for simply dumping obsolete products abroad. And, the United States "relinquished leadership in weapons production to Great Britain and Germany, where American designers of machine guns and armor plate were forced to seek business," comments Stuart Brandes, student of war profiteering. Along the way, powder maker Du Pont experienced anti-war criticism for Civil War profit-making and shifted to civilian sporting markets although occasional army-navy importunities to search European experience for new forms of propellants like smokeless powder beckoned. Dynamite replaced black powder as a more useful civilian product and Du Pont shifted accordingly. Indeed, munitions research and testing marked the period. Eventually, the navy and Du Pont teamed to make guncotton and smokeless gunpowder for military purposes. The company (that modernized out of family partnership into corporate status in the new century) became sole-source provider.[13]

Even as capitalists grabbed headlines and their places in history books, selective arms makers eventually joined them. Late-century wars (Russo-Turkish, Franco-Prussian, and in Venezuela and Columbia), and defense modernization involving Egypt, Spain, Brazil, Canada, Denmark, and Sweden opened convenient markets for company magnates Providence Tool,

Colt, Remington, and Whitney that had done so well in the Civil War. Small family firms joined familiar Colt, and Smith and Wesson revolver-makers revived their factories through conversion to a brass, center-fire, rimless cartridge. In fact, technical conversion and experimentation joined foreign sales, in stimulating the lagging American arms business. Russia's Tula and Izhevsk armories employed the American System of Manufacturing while tapping technology advice from Colt and Hiram Berdan.[14]

If the U.S. army spent thirty years searching for a repeating rifle to replace obsolete "trap-door," single-shot, black-powder fired breechloaders (mostly converted from Civil War musket production), dynamic new firearms appeared from the private sector in the United States as well as Europe. Old standbys like the Sharps Rifle Manufacturing Company of Hartford, Connecticut downsized, reorganized and moved to Bridgeport, making Sharps-Bouchard military rifles and sport rifles until 1881. Firms like Winchester as well as Hotchkiss and Chaffee-Reese entered the government's ordnance competition until finally, in the mid-1890s, a persnickety U.S. Army caught up the American decision-making process with newer technologies, embracing the Danish bolt-action Krag-Jorgensen rifle. Something of a resuscitated firearms renaissance emerged anyway as firms used Samuel Colt-style promotion of guns for private use, worries of race war in the south, images of a violent "Wild" west, cheapness of production, identification with "manly" security and the image of the government as guardian of the nation's freedom and safety of the family all contributed to the unquestioned presence of guns in American life. This gun culture re-energized America by the time of the nation's centennial.[15]

A National Rifle Association came into being in 1871, stoked by the changes in society and arms technology. Like the large pool of surviving Union veterans, here was a special interest group with political and security implications. The next year, seven of the largest gunpowder manufacturers formed a Gunpowder Trade Association and immediately set a price for their product. Systematic underselling forced independents "to the wall" while others fell into line from pressures of a "united front." As firearms expert Colonel Arcadi Gluckman once explained, the end of the Civil War marked new and innovative firearm technology "the end of the percussion period and the introduction of the cartridge era." Operating firearms became simpler and more mechanistic. Eventually, special ordnance boards were organized, bids advertised and various entrepreneurs as well as charlatans submitted proposals. Prototypes were tested, evaluated and judgment pronounced. Field testing by the troops reinforced conservative ordnance chief Stephen Vincent Benet's conviction that the times were unready for change.

Still, technological development like smokeless powder, quick-firing artillery and metallurgical advances engaged the attention of ordnance soldier and sailor/scientist types alike. The army, at least, turned its heavier ordnance production to rifled steel cannon made at Watervliet arsenal, while the navy already used a production plant at the Washington navy yard.[16]

As simple an item as a propellant for metal-jacketed bullets confounded American munitions makers for much of the era. The secret of smokeless powder, the 1884 invention of Frenchman Paul Marie Eugene Vielle, eluded American ordnance for another decade. The natural symbiotic bond between science and the military that increased professionalization through interaction of both, remained stunted by budgets and parochial government armaments establishments. The fact is, much of the period instead saw independent invention, whether from electricity/communication or transport mechanization/motorization with great potential for military purposes. Discovery, experiment, and testing provided a natural progression, whether in private or public shops and workrooms. However, institutional conservatism, evolution of inherently core-military technology, congressional parsimony and public apathy stood in the way, absent major conflict providing necessity. Such would only come with the twentieth century.[17]

If military and naval bureaucrats generally worked their separate spheres in isolation, they occasionally collaborated via some advisory, inter-service war, or strategy boards in what today would be styled "jointness." The sea service always took the lead for what torpedo historian Elizabeth Epstein colorfully cites as "convenient signposts on the Navy's whiggish march to administrative centralization." Reconstruction and Gilded Age legislators remained preoccupied with politics that tangentially involved the common defense, usually pet projects like patronage, graft and corruption in home district navy yards or land installations, leaving the American military generally to rot and rust on its own because nobody wanted to spend money. That, at least, has been the conventional wisdom. Scandals elsewhere in the American government fascinated reformers and journalists, for example leading to Civil Service reform in 1883, while the private sector provided frequent glimmers of rampant corporate and business jungle ethics, and scientific testing and experimentation remained disorganized and lacking modern, systematic research and development. Eventually a spectrum of the latest design and technology in small arms, field guns, heavy coastal and ship pieces, even self-propelled torpedoes, would emerge from the invention and testing churn. Foreign and domestic knowledge would be tapped since, as naval historian Charles Paullin thought, it was "doubtless inevitable, for a revolution, or several revolutions, were going on in naval science". That said, in his view, wood, and iron, versus steel and sheath-armor in ship design and construction, steam versus wind as motive power, even the rifled ordnance versus torpedoes were "all still undecided in the period 1869–1881." That was about to change.[18]

MIC'S CONGRESSIONAL BLUEPRINT

In the end, one congressional group prepared the way for a modern military-industrial-political complex (MIPC). The desultory naval renaissance had only just begun by the time Senator Joseph R. Hawley's Select Committee on Ordnance and War Ships weighed in with a pivotal 1886 report. Yet modern accounts slide past the significance of this particular document. Industrialized defense and war required synchronized partnering of industry and business with government. That was the direction of Hawley's blueprint. Previous army and navy ordnance boards, as well as uniformed and civilian navy officials under presidents James A. Garfield and Chester Allen Arthur, had begun studying and lobbying for new guns and projectiles, even a government gun foundry. But these were internal service affairs, even if tangential groundwork for a modern MIPC. The five-member Hawley group provided a more comprehensive guide for heavy ordnance and projectiles, warships and torpedo development. This group explored foreign as well as domestic information sources "to inquire as to the capacity of steel-producing works in the United States to make steel of suitable quality and sufficient in quantity to furnish metal for guns of high power, and metal plates and other material for the construction of vessels of war, and for the armor or sheathing for such vessels." It examined "the character and sufficiency of machinery and machine tools in the navy-yards, and also in private foundries and machine shops in the United States," for constructing engines, steel hulls and armaments of such vessels, and for the seacoast defenses of the country. The group wanted "the best locations in the United States for manufacturing guns, engines, and armor," iron and steel warships, and the best method of manufacturing and building them, whether by "the Government or by contract with private persons."[19]

By the time the Hawley Committee finished its business, the navy's own first and second policy boards had established direction, the first new-navy experimental ships (the so-called "ABCD" vessels) had been authorized, money appropriated to build them and construction contracts let, with the controversial but well-known shipbuilder John Roach of New York and Chester, Pennsylvania. Yet, if the die had been cast via this "Squadron of Evolution" (again, suggestive of experimentation), Hawley's group rendered more than just another "convenient sign post." Deliberations took two years. They set the country on a march to navalism. Moreover, the committee's findings sealed a pact between navalists on Capitol Hill and the bureaucracy. And, overall, Hawley's investigations tell us much. With Hawley (R-Connecticut) as chair, members Nelson Wilmarth Aldrich (R-Rhode Island), William Joyce Sewell (R-New Jersey), John Tyler Morgan (D-Alabama) and Matthew Calbraith Butler (D-South Carolina), assisted by two competent army and navy ordnance professionals, explored companies, works, and yards on the Atlantic and Pacific coasts as well as in England. Their comprehensive report included "the testimony or statements, of eminent manufacturers, scientists, and others as well as extracts from official American and English reports," along with summaries prepared by naval lieutenant W H. Jacques, and an attached catalogue or bibliography of recent official and unofficial publications supplying the latest information and opinions. From this data, the committee solemnly declared that the United States was "metallurgically independent for all purposes of warfare." Here was classic autarky of the industrial age! Hawley and colleagues further contended that "the manufacture of iron and steel for peaceful purposes has kept pace with the foremost science and skill of the world." Here too was classic American hubris.

Reality returned with the group's next sentence that for steel-making, the casting capacity was ample, "but the heavy forging and finishing of guns and armor will require new and costly plants." As to shipbuilding, the machinery and machine-tools of the navy yards were sufficient for building engines, although much of it was obsolete and uneconomical. But, the means for constructing iron or steel ships was lacking, and only one yard had a good plant of limited capacity for finishing steel guns, based on some experience. Hawley and company concluded that "ships in general should be built by private contract, and private yards are capable of doing the work." Some ships might be built in navy yards but only "as a resource in case of necessity. Nonetheless, some government facilities should be kept ready for repair work on these new vessels. "Armor plate and engines should be obtained wholly from private manufacturers." The politicians wavered on ship composition, recommending steel but with certain types a "composite of steel and wood." Either they were more conservative, or unsure of the country's ability to fabricate the latest in marine architecture.[20]

More specific in their observations on gun manufacture after "the costly experiments of twenty-five years," Hawley's committee felt such ordnance "should be made of open hearth steel, forged, breech-loading, chambered, of calibers ranging from 5 to 16 inches while armor and projectiles should also be made of forged steel, hydraulically forged not steam hammered." Gun manufacture suitable for ships and coast defense should be divided between private foundries and government shops; the former providing the forged and tempered parts, and the latter finishing those parts and assembling them. Two government processing plants for machine-finishing and assembling this new ordnance should be established at the Washington Navy Yard and Watervliet Arsenal "as the best sites for such factories." The senators finished their statements with two interesting conclusions. Their words, "All the needed private capital is ready for cheerful cooperation with the Government in whatever it may require," strongly suggested financial bonding between Wall Street and Washington. Moreover, armor and gun proposals "should require such quantities and extend over such a series of years as to justify private persons in securing the best plant." Government payments should demand completed work, said Hawley's committee, and contract with providers "having capital and experience." Such stipulations would produce numerous storms for the new military-industrial-congressional relationship which today we would call "the iron triangle."[21]

THE NAVY'S IMPERIAL BLUEPRINT AND AN "IRON TRIANGLE"?

With "initial industrialization of war" from 1840–1884 completed, technology historian William H. McNeill decided, "intensified military-industrial interaction would take over for the next twenty years down to 1914." Civil War and World War II business historian Mark R. Wilson declares the two decades before the first World War particularly as "the unacknowledged militarization of America." Others, like Koistinen and me, place the new American steel and steam navy and industrialization of the country as the birthplace of America's MIC. At this same time, a "pen-and-ink sailor," constantly at-odds with hide-bound naval superiors, gave it a strategic dimension. Instrumental in helping establish America's first war college, Captain Alfred Thayer Mahan wrote *The Influence of Sea Power upon History, 1660–1783*, which became the bible for a navalist/imperialist generation across the globe, but especially in America. A thinker rather than a doer, Mahan provided still another blueprint for his generation. Preaching commercial and military command of the sea, Mahan's work gelled the expansionism, imperialism, and social darwinism that swayed men's hearts and minds toward the end of the nineteenth century. Mahan's words especially stoked the already-glowing embers of navalism, the true consort to colonialism and imperialism. Yet, while Mahan spoke to geographical, economic and social factors of grand strategy, his was the rationale, not the plan, for converting elements to instruments of power in the ways-means-ends paradigm preached by generations of military planners and advocates. Officials needed something "actionable" for putting Mahan's theories into practice. Appointed civilian leaders gave it to them.[22]

Historians cite successive naval secretaries across the 1880s and 1890s and into the next century as naval rebuilders and acolytes of navalism and imperialism. Republicans William H. Hunt, William E. Chandler, Benjamin F. Tracy and John Davis Long were joined by Democrats William C. Whitney and Hilary A. Herbert. By stages they shepherded a new steel navy into being, working closely with like-minded legislators, and private sector steel producers and shipbuilders to overcome challenges of politics and policy, programs and budget, and technology and cost. They curried coastal-state favor and blunted hinterland opposition, courting allies on Capitol Hill which had naval partisans as well as anti-military advocates. They plied the preeminent lobbying group of the time, Civil War veterans, with calls to patriotism and memories of their sacrifice, while increasingly brandishing the flag in the remote realms abroad. As public servants they adhered to strict codes of quality, ethics and procedure. Tracy in particular, a decorated Civil War veteran, loyal New York Republican lawyer and true Mahanite became a symbolic father of the modern "American fighting navy."[23]

Tracy's tenure especially catalyzed grand strategy and policy with a Mahanist-tone annual report (if not actually ghostwritten by Mahan, suggests Walter Millis), official sponsorship in publication of Mahan's book itself, and singular negotiation with robber-baron steel magnate Andrew Carnegie to create a public-private partnership venture in naval armor fabrication. His expansionist naval policy board's report fused with final congressional approval to build "battle-ships." True, Tracy only got three when he and navalists wanted eight! Still, in Millis's words, "the vote was a turning point in military policy." It set the nation, eight years before the Spanish-American War, on the course toward global sea power and world politics. Millis might have added, a national security state too. Historian Paul E. Pedisch emphasizes neither would have been accomplished without a sympathetic Congress and its buying power. In 1898, Mahan and his disciples like Tracy finally got the "splendid little war" they had coveted, for testing theory, programs, and the new toys they helped create for America.[24]

After "years of bellicose posturing," Mahan and his disciples like Tracy finally got the "splendid little war" they coveted, in 1898. Largely fought by "General Tracy's Fighting Navy" with its armored steel hulls and modern heavier armament that wrested an empire from the Caribbean to the Philippines, the Spanish-American War destroyed two Spanish fleets and served notice to other European powers of America's appearance on the world scene. Ironically, its most enduring icon was not the battleship USS *Maine*, whose destruction is cited as the war's proximate cause, but rather the sleek, swift, protected cruiser USS *Olympia*: constructed on the west coast in a private San Francisco yard, equipped at the nearby Mare Island Navy Yard, fabricated from regional as well as continental materials, and manned by an array of native-born and immigrant young Americans led by Annapolis-trained Commodore George Dewey. *Olympia* provides a tangible link today to that era through preservation on the Philadelphia waterfront. Dewey is entombed in Washington's National Cathedral. The *Maine*'s mast towers above Arlington National Cemetery with a small inconspicuous urn-like memorial placed in the city's West Potomac Park. A more elegant statue of a period soldier, "the Hiker," graces the avenue from Memorial Bridge toward Arlington cemetery.[25]

Dewey's victory at Manila Bay and President William McKinley's prayerful decision to annex the Philippines for naval bases, useful to trade exploitation in China and the Far East, paralleled Rear Admiral William Sampson's similar success over a Spanish squadron at Santiago Bay, Cuba. American music halls reverberated to a lively ditty "There'll be a Hot Time in the Old Town Tonight." Actual "humanitarian" insertion of American soldiers proved less inspiring in both Cuba and the Philippines when American imperialism showed disturbing weaknesses, not just with mobilization and force projection, but more so in occupation and colonial suppression. From logistical foul-ups at Tampa, Florida—marked by "bully beef" spoiled rations, transportation logjams, and volunteers sent off to fight with old, converted trap-door 45/70 black-powder rifles instead of the better Krag-Jorgensen weapons, against Spanish first-class Mauser rifles—to a nagging, atrocity-strewn, prolonged Philippine native insurrection, perhaps the new MIPC showed some chinks. Still, strutting victoriously, America had her glamorous buff and white, steel and steam ships.[26]

American public and officials (including British, French, German, Belgian and other colonial masters), sobered, as naval renaissance merged with Rudyard Kipling's "white man's burden," bringing the dawn of "America's Century." Humorist-t Peter Dunne's caricature "Mr. Dooley" was told by his friend, Mr. Hennessey, "We are-re a gr-reat people" to which Dooley answered, "We ar-re that, We ar-re that. An th' best iv it is, we know we ar-re." Here was the crucial hubris churning modern America, in diplomatic historian Walter LaFeber's phrase, "laying the foundations of 'Superpowerdom' by searching for opportunities via militarism and dollar diplomacy, economic determinism and jingoistic public appeal." Diplomat/author Warren Zimmerman names five key public figures as heroic godfathers, epitomizing the audacity, arrogance, generosity, paternalism and vision fusing the process. President Theodore Roosevelt, Senator Henry Cabot Lodge, Secretary of State John Hay, corporate lawyer, sometimes colonial administrator and Secretary of War Elihu Root, and, of course, Mahan. The climate for American imperialism, spawned from earlier continental expansionism dating back to eighteenth-century colonial aspirations, depended upon military power. Everyone in Europe was doing it, Japan was doing it, and so, America's duty and place in the sun was to do it also. On the other hand, figures like Mark Twain, Booker T. Washington and Andrew Carnegie counseled restraint. Anti-imperialism also accompanied the journey.[27]

Trade and flag issues in the Americas, where fruit companies and mineral extractors drove the Stars and Stripes southward in the 1880s and 1890s, the fixation on Chinese markets (and human souls convertible to missionary Christianity), and then the Spanish-American War provided pathways to overseas possessions. As the United States government, in collaboration with business/industrial interests, moved outward from behind Atlantic and Pacific moats, its new influence, markets and possessions demanded stronger defense forces. If Dewey's *Olympia* heralded empire, so her newer sister battle wagons had overwhelmed decrepit Spanish warships at Santiago although the new naval-industrial complex's American steel navy was hardly tested by serious combat. Still, the Spanish-American war was the first stage in the fleet's coming of age.

The second stage came within the next decade when President Theodore Roosevelt sent the Atlantic battleship fleet around the world from 1907 to 1909. Grandstanding it was, mainly for the purpose of cowing a rival Japan in the Pacific. Nonetheless, the cruise signaled naval and strategic power projection of the United States. Again, no battle test of armor and armament, the cruise yielded invaluable lessons for fleet organization and training, mechanical reliability and fuel consumption, communication and logistics. Even then, TR's "Great White Fleet," not unlike Dewey's squadron, had to hire a fleet train of supply vessels, so unbalanced was America's naval construction program. Battleships not colliers made for more glamorous symbols to overawe natives and foreign ministries while titillating red-blooded Americans and congressional bill-payers. Once back home, the whole American navy was re-painted battle gray superseding the glitter and glamor of buff and white peace symbols. But, America's tandem rise to greatness from the 1898 war with Spain, reluctant acquisition of empire from 1899 on, a Roosevelt-brokered peace between a decadent Russia and emergent Japan in 1905 and the fleet's mission two years later signified a special providence that America could now evoke in international affairs.[28]

Not everyone felt that empire or even navalism was a good thing. Agrarian politicians like Georgian Tom Watson, Stanford University president David Starr Jordan, and Progressive journalist Oswald Garrison Villard, chorused against Roosevelt's chauvinism and war-profiteering by Wall Street's business elite. Special-interest moguls, from DuPont gunpowder scions, to Henry Frick, Joseph Wharton, Charles Schwab, and the steelmen and shipbuilders John Roach, William Cramp, all had their own perspectives. Obviously, Emilio Aguinaldo's independence-minded Filipinos provided another view of the invading but purportedly civilizing and benevolent Americans. The U.S. government eventually negotiated its empire in part by paying cash to the Spaniards after obliterating their fleets. Occupied peoples (Filipinos, Cubans, Puerto Ricans, et al.) became "protected" charges of the U.S. Army and Navy until such time as Washington deigned to grant them self-governance. Despite all the "huzzahs" when "hiker" American soldiers, sailors and marines returned from subduing Spaniards and insurgents, many Americans including farmers, non-plutocratic clergy, educators, and even some businessmen, protested the high costs of empire. Ultimately, in popular minds, the psychic thrill offset the odorous profit reaped by malefactors of great wealth. New York City victory parades, and the gilded-bow, stern-ornamented ships of the U. S. Navy overwhelmed the naysayers. Patriotism-guided navalists founded their own advocacy group in 1903, the Navy League of the United States, much as European counterparts similarly maneuvered to impact politics, programs and public opinion. Interestingly, the American lobby became more diverse, now not only retired naval officers, but also prominent financiers, corporate lawyers and captains of industry, "at least some of whom had a direct pecuniary interest in progressive naval expansion," said historians Harold and Margaret Sprout.[29]

A new elite controlled America's destiny. Budget battles for an ever more expensive navy, to counter perceived European and Asian threats to America's national interests, rippled a strident refrain. Securing best price underscored getting the best cost for a "golden mean" naval policy. Naval expansion itself was never in doubt—just how much, how fast and how costly. Construction and maintenance required larger shore establishments than before. Navy yards like Philadelphia were overwhelmed and needed more space. Old methods of raising public revenue struggled to keep pace with defense demand. Could traditional protective-tariff walls and treasury surpluses fund peacetime navalism forever? Imperial occupations, foreign interventions, gunboat diplomacy enforcing the Roosevelt Corollary to the Monroe Doctrine in the Caribbean, or defense of Asian-Pacific naval bases required more comprehensive planning, programming and budgeting. Whether American labor was "sacrificed on a cross of gold" standard through bank busts and economic downturns of the 1890s, or farmers paid the price of expanding plutocratic agendas of the nation and its government, surpluses still bulged the Treasury in 1901. Tariffs and excise taxes bankrolled navalism and imperialism until a progressive income tax became necessary through a constitutional amendment in 1913, largely because of naval costs.[30]

COLLABORATION IN SWADDLING CLOTHES

The early road to a Progressive Era MIPC birth was rocky. Contracting chronicler James Nagle likens it to a "shotgun marriage." Even Internal naval reformers such as gunnery innovator Rear Admiral William Simms in collaboration with artist/write and American editor of the British journal *Jane's Fighting Ships* (and who sailed with the Great White Fleet to observe) tried to pillory the navy's bureau establishment for faulty battleship design and other misdeeds only too have the traditionalists and their allies on Capitol Hill blow past that brouhaha in due course. Technology was the basic problem. "The first modern weapons system" was the "gigantic, expensive, steel-plated, steam-propelled, heavily armed warship." These ships, notes Nagle, required "large sums of money, specialized facilities, materials, and manpower as well as detailed and lengthy planning to synchronize their manufacture." In short, they "required a mobilization base." Yale research associate George T. Davis saw it another way opining that the navy was now "a vast organization and the need for modern industrial methods and for efficiency in assembling and equipping the fleet and planning for war strategy seemed imperative." But while the government expanded its own defense industrial base to ten arsenals and from five navy yards to seven, private shipyards constructing naval ships had shrunk from sixty-one to seven by the turn of the century. Foreign demand for American-built shipping continued to climb, although foreign trade carried by American-registered vessels went the other way. Congress might mandate all naval material be manufactured in America, but could industry respond easily? Where would high-grade, heavier steel for armor plate come from? Technology and innovation coupled with cost for autarky or self-sufficiency would not come cheap. Government needed to underwrite endeavor. While government subsidizing or ownership of process was possible, the private sector remained a reluctant partner. The Washington naval chiefs stayed immune to reform.[31]

Indeed, industry's initial disinterest in armor and ordnance, even to some extent steel warships in the first place, was a roadblock. Shipbuilder

John Roach of Chester, Pennsylvania had pioneered in less-than-perfect public-private collaboration with his ABCD ships. They were educational experiments, productive of "all the curses of modern procurement": cost overruns, design changes, breakdowns during sea trials, the navy's carping dissatisfaction with the results, as well as a chorus of discontent from politicians, competitors and newspapers. Naval secretaries like Whitney, Tracy, Herbert, Long, and their successors, battled steel moguls like Wharton, Carnegie (an enigmatic patriot always mindful of profit), Frick, and Schwab, over such issues as delivery deadlines, fair price, whistleblower accusations of fraud, waste and abuse, and competition. Production difficulties accompanied an evolving metallurgical gamble regarding the best steel plate (Harveyized, nickel, Krupp), naval-inspector adherence to "strict specification," and hyperbolic promises. Carnegie once told Secretary Whitney that there was no need to go abroad as his new steel mill "will roll the heaviest sizes you will require, with the greatest care," then backed out of contract bidding, leaving the navy scrambling to find a substitute.

Carnegie's transformation from an earlier business pacifism, mistrust of working with the government, plus a conviction that naval peacetime purchases of steel armor would never justify his startup costs, also occasioned his pause. Civilian markets for his steel suited him just fine, then a sudden revelation brought patriotism—and profit. Promising government subsidization of plant and process for making naval steel armor, as well as Secretary Tracy's reminders about Republican political loyalties and patriotism, occasioned a change of mind. Carnegie agreeably cooed to a subordinate "there may be millions for us in armor." Bethlehem's inability to deliver on its winning bid had forced Tracy to find a supplemental source, and both Carnegie and the navy became edgy about complaints of fraud by 1892–1893. Then, when President Grover Cleveland's second naval secretary Hilary Herbert explored collusion between Bethlehem and Carnegie over prices, the air of cooperation chilled noticeably by mid-decade. The question of fair price, underselling armor to Russia, government threats to construct its own armor plant and the escalating price of battleship production riled Capitol Hill. Congress wondered if the navy had expedited patent applications for armor production processes, and whether active-duty naval officers were illegally involved in contract or patent negotiations benefitting industry. Legislators reiterated the need for competitive bidding.[32]

Critics, anti-navalists, anti-imperialists and reformers of all stripes joined pockets of concerned congressmen in seeking "fraud, waste and abuse" in New Navy programs. If steel men would have willingly unloaded armor plants to government ownership, they also suddenly realized that government contracts provided convenient hedges against market recession and depression. The navy, always unhappy with private sector independence and attitudes, nevertheless needed its products when it dispersed shipbuilding contracts around the country. Creation of such economic dependency was good budgetary politics on the Hill. Whether constructing smaller warships (cruisers, torpedo boats, destroyers, even a submarine) through Bath Iron Works in Maine, or *Maine*-class battleships with Moran Brothers at Seattle in Washington state, developed a constituency. Newport News Shipbuilding and Dry Dock Company in Virginia as well as Fore River Shipbuilding at Quincy, Massachusetts also shared contracting largesse and the navy's growing economic stretch at congressional behest. Newport News particularly wanted to muscle on to the construction ledger in 1892, pointing out to the navy that distributing the work gave "encouragement to a new shipbuilding enterprise at the South." Management claimed to have "the largest and best equipped plant in America," adding that their company's exemplary commercial-ship construction and presence among competitors for government warship contracts would lower bidding in-general, thus saving upwards of a half-million on the latest projects. That would enable "the Navy Department to fully complete said vessels within the appropriations of Congress and at the same time do full justice to the work." A navy bureaucrat noted on Newport News's memorandum that government work, then at Cramp's yard in Philadelphia, was worth $14 million and at Union Iron Works on the west coast some $7,421,000. So, defense profits joined the agenda of Progressive reform after the turn of the century, drawing lines between excess and sufficiency, with lawyers and public servants duty-bound to find for the government, while maintaining public-private partnerships in securing steel, steam and ship. In 1902, Congress authorized government production of battleships in a public yard. Lower costs and speedier production through competition was the intent. The navy also employed its age-old method of "lead and follow." A lead yard would design and build the first ship, providing the model for follow-on vessels, ostensibly offsetting the fact that no two yards had precisely the same production layout or equipment for the common job.[33]

The main scuffle between the navy and steel industry centered on armor prices for the battleship *Arizona* in 1913. Midvale, Carnegie and Bethlehem companies submitted identical bids at $454 per ton while the government wanted $250 as the price. President Woodrow Wilson's new secretary of the navy, North Carolina newsman Josephus Daniels accused them of collusion, and Congress continued to vet the idea of a government armor plant. Senator "Pitchfork" Ben Tillman of Alabama, an agrarian opponent of Robber

Barons, threatened legislation to seize munitions plants in the event of war, or at-minimum threaten to do so. Steel spokesmen, in turn, promised to raise the price of armor with editors of the *Manufacturers Record*, labelling this move "one of the most unfortunate statements ever issued in this country by any great business organization dealing with the Government." Industrialist Schwab complained that if the government "had asked you to invest your money in a plant to supply government needs; and after the plant was built, and had become useful for no other purpose, the government built a plant of its own, making your plant useless and your investment valueless— would that seem fair?"[34]

Daniels and Tillman were far apart at this point. The secretary finally secured Midvale Steel as low bidder with a "winner take all" approach. He and Tillman engineered passage of a government armor plant bill in 1916, largely based on estimates that a ton of armor could be produced by the public facility at $314 per ton not the $454 demanded by the steel industry. Despite Schwab's massive public opposition campaign and Bethlehem's promise to manufacture armor plate at cost of operation plus any additional charges set by the Federal Trade Commission, public support rallied behind standing up to Big Business extortion. Gigantic-ism had met its match. A government armor plant at South Charleston, West Virginia proved short-lived, however. Costs for construction, machinery and raw materials brought on by World War I nearly doubled production expense per ton. The plant yielded only five over-priced armor plates and "closed quietly but ignominiously" in 1921, observes James Nagel.[35]

SYMBOLS OF THE AGE

Size denoted America by this stage, not by geography but by organization, production and progress. Business America embraced not only corporations but conglomerates called "trusts." The navy talked size too. Since 1903, its spokesmen touted a fleet of forty-eight battleships which its 1913 *Annual Report* proclaimed was, "to insure a fleet of measurable equality with the fleets of the principal foreign powers" (Germany and Great Britain). True, government budgets grew little after that "splendid little war" against Spain in 1898. Nonetheless, Congress authorized an increase in army size to 100,000 men (actually, it never got much above 75,000 for the first ten years of empire), and the navy did move closer to its goal, thanks to conglomerates like United States Steel keeping shipyards humming. Naval bureaucrats as well as agrarian congressmen from the heartland worried about production costs, contract procedures, fleet-maintenance costs, and excess profits, albeit from opposite ends of the political spectrum. Private foreign sales of the latest naval steel technology to Russia or Japan continued to fester. Yet, a true military-industrial-political complex or iron triangle was still on its maiden shakedown cruise.[36]

America's naval-industrial complex was in place by the outbreak of the European war in 1914. At this time, the army still experimented with the Wright brothers' aircraft, and the navy with machines from Glenn Curtiss. The nation's commitment to the new isthmian canal in Panama, its roles as "uncontested arbiter," even "semi-colonial master" in Latin America, as well as commercial "Open Door" interference in China, dictated naval power projection. Naval flexing in the Orient involved practical considerations of resourcing coaling stations. Technical opportunities beckoned with Italian Guglielmo Marconi's wireless-communication invention, intriguing the navy for shore-to-ship and inter-ship messaging. Yet, trepidation about paying royalties, outright technology ownership, and risk-aversion hindered progress. Officer-corps conservatism surfaced when the Great White Fleet's commander at first refused to deploy twenty-six De Forest radiotelephones aboard his ships on world passage. In the end, notes naval historian John R. Alden, wireless telegraphy performed successfully for the Fleet with messages sent between ship and shore over a thousand miles in favorable circumstances—radio had become "an integral part of naval operations."[37]

Industrialists, politicians and the military championed America's new internationalism and navalism. Industrialists facilitated the kluge. Fleet strength, counting vessels built, building and authorized, increased from 141 vessels in 1897 to 371 in 1910. but mere numbers were always deceptive. Navy department figures in 1897 still mentioned fourteen wooden and steam vessels, even if actually unfit for sea. A year later Secretary of the Navy John Long proclaimed 312 vessels of all kinds, of which 189 were "regular navy" and 123 "auxiliary navy" for the Spanish war. The latter were typically war-converted merchant vessels, yachts, tugs, colliers, revenue cutters, lighthouse tenders and fishing-commission vessels—shades of Civil War-style mobilization. While inventory numbers slipped lower by the end of 1908 (but climbing thereafter), within a half-decade, the United States Navy challenged the numbers game with European powers and Japan. The nation's "real dependence in time of war," the armored fleet advanced from twenty warships on the eve of the Spanish war—nine first-class battleships, two second-class battleships, two armored cruisers, one armored ram and six harbor-defense monitors in 1897—to fifty-eight warships eleven years later. Secretary Tracy's "fighting navy" now numbered thirty-five first-class battleships, one second-class battleship, twelve armored cruisers and ten harbor-defense monitors plus smaller vessels. Everything about the numbers reflected enthrallment with increases in tonnage, speed, armament, and production capacity of American domestic industry. The navy also entered the era of the colossus, with Dreadnought-class battleships.[38]

The navy's defense-industrial base now had Bethlehem, Carnegie, Midvale and Carbon Steel, and United States Steel supplying the material for armor and ordnance (finished heavy gun tubes from Washington Naval Gun Factory and Watervliet Arsenal) in addition to twenty-two navy yards and bases from the Atlantic to the Philippines. A subset of the ordnance complex included torpedo makers E. W. Bliss and Electric Boat for Howell and Whitehead torpedoes. By 1905 thirty-one ships were under construction by twelve shipbuilding companies: Neafie and Levy, and William Cramp and Sons of Philadelphia, Union Iron Works of San Francisco, Bath Iron Works in Maine, Newport News Shipbuilding and Drydock in Virginia, and Fore River Shipbuilding in Quincy, Massachusetts; in New Jersey were New York Shipbuilding and J. H. Dialogue and Son, both of Camden, plus Lewis Nixon, Crescent Shipyard, and Moore and Sons in Elizabethport, Columbia Ironworks of Baltimore, William Trigg of Richmond, Virginia, and in Morris Heights, New York were Gas Engine and Power Company, and Charles L. Seabury and Company Consolidated, all of them shouldering aside earlier ventures like Harland and Hollingsworth of Wilmington, DE and John Roach, which had served their purpose in initiating the more experimental phase of the naval buildup. With the government, the country now had a modern, industrialized public-private partnership.

Six different companies held contracts for battleships. On the one hand, proclaimed historian Charles Paullin, Cramp and Union Iron Works "have had the largest part in building the new fleet," and that "in 1903 it was said that one-half the larger ships of the navy had been constructed by the Cramps." Still, as time passed, Fore River and Newport News raced with Cramp for the honors. Torpedo boat, and torpedo-boat destroyer construction held more diversity, with nineteen separate contractors at one point that included one German contractor and one British for the former craft, and seven for the latter. As submarines now entered the fleet picture, Electric Boat Company and J. B. Holland Torpedo Boat Company joined the ranks, although the craft were actually fabricated at Crescent Shipyard, Fore River Shipbuilding, and the Union Iron Works. A permanent naval industrial-base had begun to proliferate, contributing to maritime state economies and political establishments. And this contributed its share to the Progressive era of contest and reform.[39]

HARNESSING MEGA-VENTURE

After the Civil War and Reconstruction, the age of excess that prevailed had run its course by the end of the century. Americans now expected government at all levels to restrain and regulate "malefactors of great wealth." From "populists" to "progressives," expectations hinged on social amelioration by government action. From civil service reform (Pendleton Act of 1883) to taming railroads (Interstate Commerce Act of 1887) to a corporate-focused Sherman Antitrust act of 1890, the procurement studies of the 1893 Dockery Commission, incorporated into the Dockery Act of 1894, pointed toward regulation by an administrative state. The Food and Drug Act of 1906, and the Clayton Anti-Trust Act and Federal Trade Commission Act, both of 1914, were part of a "design" to establish national "rules of the game" for competition, profit and power. A naval-industrial complex also faced scrutiny to some degree.[40]

America has always been about size and splendor, grandeur and greatness, whether in scenery, waves of grain, or enterprise. Business evolution to "corporation" and "trust" suggest why historians Bryant and Dethloff titled a chapter "Giant Enterprise," or why the government's attempt to build a massive fleet flowed toward gigantism, even in that domain. They suggest that between 1895 and 1907, "a major organizational upheaval took place in the national economy" as "huge, professional, bureaucratic managements perpetuated themselves in impregnable positions in the marketplace." Monopoly and then oligopoly "challenged economic democracy, 'free enterprise,' and *laissez faire* as philosophical staples of a growth-oriented society." When the total economic power fell into the hands of a dozen powerful bankers like J. P. Morgan, Frank Vanderclip and Paul Warburg, fire-alarm bells awakened national pushback. What resulted was Jackson Lear's "embryonic regulatory state," or as Richard H. Holton observes, "it was becoming increasingly apparent that competitive behavior had to be policed in some degree." True, a particular breed of Progressive like Woodrow Wilson "would further empower the very banking class he disparaged," cites Nomi Prins. This was largely an effect from an international situation by 1914.[41]

The American navy's industrial expansion also became a natural target for anti-imperialist opposition, and various public-accountability demands of legislative and administrative remedies for social and economic problems stemming from industrialization. Concern for cost, collusion and irregularity have always attended government endeavor, public-private sector relations, and military-naval contracting. Add in the appearance of "giganticism" (even the term "dreadnought" connoted immensity), that only the "Big

Steel/Big Ship" American private-sector might produce for the spectacle of international Big Power competition. Consider the operative words of the era—competition, combination, enhanced by trusts and mergers to ensure profit and power—and the U.S. navy also was soon ensnared. There was little choice if imperialists, navalists, and other brokers of the epoch were to be accommodated. Military demand, industrial supply, political enablement, or executive/legislative branches of government, coupled to financial incentives for a growth industry in peacetime. Later on, it would seem like an interlocking complex. We may yet wonder just who truly threatened the nation's survival? Who would invade us? Or was it merely the cloak of national interests that led the way?[42]

Cost and size were handmaidens of that time. Steel ships to defend the realm were undoubtedly sinkholes from start to finish; from authorization to retirement. The price for procuring 233,400 tons of armored steel alone for the new navy consumed $102,531,620 from 1887 to 1910. The earlier part of the period may have been "blessed with huge federal budget surpluses," to underwrite such largesse say Bryan and Dethloff. But Edward Silsby, who compiled *The Navy Yearbook, 1920–1921*, calculated total appropriations to re-create or modernize the fleet from 1884 to 1921 at nearly $7.5 billion, with other tabulations drifting over the $8 billion mark. Once the United States entered the international naval arms race and helped flower anew public-private interdependency for armaments, the government became captive to business and industry control of prices, process and product. The navy wiggled manfully, but the fish had been hooked. A succession of naval secretaries under Roosevelt and Taft, such as William H. Moody, Paul Morton, Charles J. Bonaparte, Victor H. Metcalf, Truman H. Newberry, and George von Legerke Meyer merely tried to manage cost in the interest of continued naval buildup.[43]

Robert Hormats's catchy title, *The Price of Liberty* reconciles what was a peacetime "search for colonial acquisitions, the efforts to dominate trade routes, and the need for protected coaling stations," not war-preparation spending that enticed the public and wealth-acquisition magnet J.P. Morgan. To the public, it was the glitter and glamor of Marine bandmaster John Philip Sousa's marching medleys, the lure of "join the navy and see the world" while tempered by a healthy counterpoise anti-imperialism moderating the stridency. To Morgan, liberty meant freedom to amass a gigantic supercorporation comprising eight of the largest competitors controlling two-thirds of the nation's steel casings and ingots, integrating ore beds to finishing plants, all of which spun back to embrace perceived demands of national security and defense—his flirtation with America's imperialism. It was the largest and wealthiest industrial enterprise the world had ever seen, the first billion-dollar company in the country, and a powerful stock-merger deal worth more than the combined values of the individual corporations tucked into the endeavor. United States Steel brandished such power with one of its major customers, the U. S. Navy and its need for armor.[44]

Trust but verification stood close to the heart of the Big Navy–Big Steel relationship. Cooperation was essential. In fiscal year 1905 alone, the navy's Bureau of Construction and Repair handled 154 million pounds of steel supplied by sixty-five companies. The Bureau of Steam Engineering similarly worked 50 million pounds of engineering materials, provided by no less than 318 concerns. And, at the same time, private establishments manufactured large quantities of materials for the Bureaus of Ordnance and Equipment. Friction persisted between 1893 and 1913 over the one high-tech item most necessary to naval expansion: quality and price of armor plate. Starting with Carnegie, Bethlehem and other steel giants long before formation of Morgan's mega-venture, both sides continued to profess what was best price and best quality for product while decrying interference, private and public. Spain's defeat and acquisition of overseas possessions upset a balanced marriage between supplier and customer in favor of the steel men, as the navy needed more steel warships to police the waves. However, imposition of government regulations, inspections and quality standards affected cost. Government rules may well have "primed the industry to produce the high level of quality and quantity demanded for skyscrapers, automobiles, trucks and tanks that would be coming within a generation," according to acquisition historian Nagle. Yet, as industry bridled against the idea that it needed government contracts which came with oversight—rules and regulations, inspections, interference and stipulations, all constraints on independent action government, by contrast, sought competitive "best price and value" and smooth, expeditious procurement. Progressive Era concern for Gilded Age raids on the U.S. Treasury reflected distinct growing pains in public/private partnering. Then war and preparation for war changed the landscape.[45]

PROGRESSIVISM AND PREPAREDNESS

By Wilson's election in 1912, misgivings about imperial pretensions refocused public attention. Financial and government reform swept past issues of common defense. Professionalization crept through War and Navy department management, military staff, and war colleges. General staffs and strategic planning looked at potential threats more seriously and the means to counter them. The navy sought more ships while the army re-engaged its unrequited quest for turning a small expansible regular force into something mobilizable for wartime. It had finally found its distinctly American service rifle, the Springfield Armory-produced model 1903, as well as a basic field cannon that same year, and moved toward a machine gun but in inadequate numbers. A plant for producing smokeless powder opened at the Picatinny Arsenal in New Jersey in 1905. The navy's Washington, D.C., heavy-gun factory and the corresponding army plant at Troy, New York were joined by an artillery-carriage works at Watertown Arsenal near Boston. Frederick Taylor's famous scientific management experiments fueled consternation among workers and Congress. Naval torpedoes became commodities in contract competition between Bliss and Electric Boat companies, but by 1912 production was transferred to the naval gun factory in Washington. Army departmental reforms came from Secretary of War Elihu Root for war-policy planning and operational training, a general staff and a war college in D.C., and larger joint maneuvers. The navy finally overcame internal dissent among the admirals and established its own general board. Added-in were striking scientific and technological innovations in tropical medicine, mechanization, and aviation that, with time, would change overall philosophy, patterns and budgeting for national security.[46]

These innovations included not merely bigger, better weapons platforms but reflected developments in mechanization and industrialization of war. The military-technological revolution injected electrical communications, ballistic improvement in rate of fire, and applications of motorization to land, sea and air operations. Empire added tropical medicine as a scientific byproduct of health and human services. The army's Signal Corps signing of a $25,000 "flying machine" contract with inventors Orville and Wilbur Wright in 1908 introduced "incentive contracts"—demanding specifications coupled with time requirements that were attached to incentive/penalty provisions, the first "fly before you buy" conditional contract. In time, manned flight would add another legislative patronage, in addition to service infighting over budgets, costs, doctrine, organization, and control.[47]

Americans themselves essentially remained insular. Mobilization of treasury and the economy stood apart from American defense planning, although the income tax amendment of 1913, establishment of the Federal Reserve bank that same year, and the Emergency Revenue Act the next (that revived some of the excise taxes that paid for the Spanish war), spoke to a concern for making the national financial system part of peacetime national security. Then, the onset of "The Great War" in Europe proved indispensable for changing context by late 1914. Historians Harold and Margaret

Sprout perceived America's vow to remain neutral as "the indifference, if not actual hostility" of both the executive and legislative branches, "to all projects for military and naval preparedness" during that first winter of the conflict. America remained detached although avid readers about the war. Public opinion kept officials with a noninvolvement attitude in office. Polls continued to show Big Navy advocacy was strongest in seaboard cities, not small-town interior America. Accounts of European battles eventually gained space with something called the "Preparedness" movement to strengthen American defense. Nonetheless, preparedness defied prevailing public indifference.[48]

The national imagination, ignited by headlines screaming implications for American safety, eventually spawned public associations like the Navy League and newly formed National Security League (with notable members from political, industrial, financial and professional sectors). They began beating the drums of military preparation for any contingency. Within two years the navy's General Board moved from calling for a navy to "answer any challenge" to a fleet "equal to the most powerful maintained by any other nation of the world." The Wilson administration moved ahead with a measured armaments program in the face of strident preparedness advocacy from former president Theodore Roosevelt, army chief of staff Leonard Wood and Admiral of the Navy George Dewey. As the Sprouts concluded, not only was the preparedness movement having an effect, but also "the inexorable logic of Wilson's diplomacy" driving him toward military and naval expansion. Undoubtedly British and German intransigence, through blockade and submarine attacks, manipulated America's proclaimed neutrality. Wall Street's J. P. Morgan and other banking houses discovered how to underwrite the Anglo-French war effort, and American industry helped its profit-line with Allied war orders and raw materials. A popular storm of hyper-patriotism, citizens' training camps to prepare young men for service as well as military competence, and a tsunami of public speeches, press releases, books, pamphlets, cinema showings, and other publicity tools roiled the scene, tapping fears that sooner or later, America "would have to face a merciless foreign enemy at their very threshold," i.e., Germany.[49]

Europe's preoccupation with its own shooting war by 1914 had offset any direct threat to the American homeland. By the following year, Anglo-German naval attrition at Jutland, and huge expenditures of men and matériel in the trenches effectively neutralized any Central Powers ability to extend the conflict to the New World. Still, even rational congressional testimony by army and navy leaders failed to ease public fears. After all, Spanish warships allegedly had threatened the whole east coast only a decade before. So why not German invasion now? The preparedness movement alerted Americans to new-found vulnerability. Former officials Roosevelt, Root, Wood and Henry L. Stimson, together with eastern business and industrial elite, provided formidable spokesmen for preparedness activism. Few voices of support came from the rural south, the West, and strongly isolationist Midwest. Big Business, Big Banks, and costly militarism bothered them more. The German-American population particularly deplored Allied favoritism, while Secretary of State William Jennings Bryan's strong policy-advocacy of detachment (providing loans but not direct munitions supply to combatants), led to his principled resignation after the 1915 *Lusitania* crisis. Wilson's supporters wavered between noninvolvement and defensive preparedness. Secretary of War Lindley Garrison successfully moved the president into the preparedness camp, although he too eventually departed the cabinet over what kind of army reforms would best meet defense needs. Military planners plied Congress with requests for more men, equipment and training, and for reorganization. They parried any legislator qualms that such moves might prove detrimental in 1916 elections. In fact, Wilson would successfully campaign for reelection that year on the slogan, he kept us out of war.[50]

To the Sprouts, Wilson's conversion to the preparedness thunder "opened the way for an armaments program without precedent in American history." By mid-1916, convergence of preparedness and external pressures translated into two dynamic pieces of legislation signifying the new direction. Traditional patterns in American thinking about war and peace, as well as perceived threat, translated into "securitization" of America. The first bill, on naval legislation, marked Wilsonian conversion to preeminence not parity, capturing the General Board's long-held goal for "incomparably the greatest navy in the world." As the president informed his close confidante Colonel Edward House, let us build a navy larger than Great Britain's and do what we want to do in the world. Big-Navy advocates rolled over congressional "little navy" Democrats in Congress, with little concern for how the war was rapidly changing naval equations away from large battle fleets toward smaller, faster craft, even adding fleet auxiliaries into the calculus. Washington envisioned adding ten battleships, six battle cruisers, ten scout cruisers, fifty destroyers, nine fleet and fifty-eight coast submarines, and thirteen miscellaneous ships, even something for naval aviation, with a $300-million price tag. Here was six times the amount allocated to the navy in 1898. "Hysteria whipped into fury" was what drove bipartisanship "in the mad race for shelter in the biggest naval program ever adopted by any nation on earth," wailed Texas Democrat Rufus Hardy.[51]

Hardy was a small-navy bitter-ender, aghast at his president and his party's acquiescence to "the militarists, the jingoes, and the self-interested munitions makers of this country." Colleague Claude Kitchin from North Carolina, and others, deplored spending seven times more than Great Britain in the decade before the war, and sixty times more than Germany in the five years before 1914, and really, over 100 times more than during the three years immediately before the outbreak of the conflict. Registered "in dollars and sense," the United States would become "the greatest military-naval nation the world has ever seen" and naval appropriations would "never be reduced," only increased, from year to year. The administration soon went further, creating the U.S. Shipping Board to regulate sea transport, develop an auxiliary fleet, and stimulate the merchant marine. Was this not merely building a battle fleet but also a capacity for expeditionary intervention anywhere in this hemisphere and beyond? Few citizens saw any ominous connection at this point. Anti-expansion/anti-preparedness progressives, small-navy, and minimalist foreign policy persuasions worried more about defense profits and fledgling militarism.[52]

The second pivotal legislation of 1916 had to do with the land service. Mexican bandit Pancho Villa's intrusion into homeland space at Columbus, New Mexico on March 9, 1916 tipped preparedness scales: here was threat to the homeland. Mobilizing a punitive expedition again proved the army's unreadiness for modern field operations. Legislators' hesitancy about long-overdue army organizational reform, and controversial proposals concerning an expansible regular force versus a genuine citizen army vanished with the crisis. A new Secretary of War, Cleveland mayor and lawyer Newton D. Baker, applied his administrative talent to both industrial and manpower preparedness. He consulted with Daniels at the Navy Department, embraced internal War Department studies by Colonel Francis J. Kernan and Judge Advocate General Enoch Crowder as notions circulated of a permanent "council of national strength" embracing cabinet officials and "captains of industry and commerce" to catalogue industrial resources of the nation, issue peacetime "educational" contracts to develop a production base for national emergency, as well as emergency federalization of civilian plants "to take the profits out of war." Such militarization of American industry in wartime seemed congruent with Baker's advocacy of government arsenals as research and development facilities, and his objective of trained officers supporting civilian managers in an emergency, with arsenals serving as assembly plants for components supplied by a civilian industrial manufacturing base. Historian Daniel Beaver insists voluntary cooperation, not executive fiat, was Baker's intent as "militarizing industrial product was never a realistic proposal," given opposition from southern Democrats who controlled congressional committees, and midwestern colleagues "opposed to any redistribution or expansion of federal authority." Ironically, former Secretary of State Bryan now championed public-run munitions production.[53]

A compromise position emerged as part of the National Defense Act of 1916. Although historians have focused elsewhere in this landmark legislation, a portion of the act recommended large-scale procurement, but not through War Department control of industry. The secretary of war could conduct an industrialized inventory, procure gauges, jigs and dies for arms production, and make small educational contracts with industry. Frankly, posterity has identified the 1916 act more significantly with organizing human resources. The 1916 act updated the Militia (Dick) Act of 1903 concerning the states' National Guard, the president receiving authority to federalize that body in time of emergency, and also created federal officer and enlisted reserve corps, university and college-based Reserve Officers' Training Corps, and a volunteer army recruitable only in wartime. The act further created an Army Aviation Service, and distinct Chemical and Finance branches. It limited the number of staff officers assigned to Washington (apparently Wilson thought too much war planning was unhealthy), yet authorized raising peacetime strength of the regular army, over five years, from 125,00 to 175,000, and wartime strength close to 300,000. Still wedded to the "citizen" soldier idea, the National Guard was enlarged to 430,000, annually required to do forty-eight armory drills as well as fifteen days of training; in some ways an extension of Leonard Wood's Citizen Training Corps (Plattsburgh Camp) idea. The army chief-of-staff's 1916 fall review concluded that only compulsory service or conscription would answer the nation's future emergency needs. Of course, that would also engender the resourcing support of a larger industrial base.[54]

Bowing to European experience with industrial war, the 1916 act enabled the president to place "educational orders" for defense materials and ensure industrial compliance. The army remained hamstrung by Congress so that only government should manufacture weapons and munitions, "unless the private concerns could compete on price." In the words of logistics historian James Huston, "the whole approach generally was one of testing and screening ideas" rather than pushing them. The critical question, Huston continued, "was not the development of new ideas, but getting the new weapons in sufficient quantity to be effective." Of course, this was still peacetime. By August 1916, Wilson had used $200,000 and a rider to the army appropriation act of that year, to create a Council of National Defense. He reasoned that "the country is best prepared for war when thoroughly prepared for peace"—a strange twist of phrasing for a neutral head of state. The preparedness debate also prompted Congress to authorize two nitrate-manufacturing plants, an industrial village, and a dam to provide hydropower: Muscle Shoals in Alabama became that site. The 1916 legislation that directed the secretary of war to survey all private arms and munitions industries could be seen as the first government mandate for studying economic mobilization. Comprised of the secretaries of appropriate government departments, a dedicated-support staff, and a civilian advisory commission of prominent private-sector specialists, the Council "carried forward the Progressive themes of voluntary national cooperation and organizational efficiency in the public interest," said Beaver, "while it avoided the corporatist extremes of monopoly capitalism or state socialism."[55]

MAKING PROFIT FROM OTHER PEOPLE'S WAR

An additional component of the Progressive-Preparedness picture complicated matters. Earning profit by brokering other peoples' wars appeared in private-sector financing and materials production for the European combatants. As reflected by phrases like Nomi Prins' "bankers go to war," Paul Koistinen's citing J. P. Morgan and Company as "allied purchasing agent and financier" or even Stuart Brandes' characterization of "warhogs and warsows," suggests ethical dilemmas for the World War I generation. Quoting Senator George Norris's 1917 observation that "war brings prosperity to the stock gamblers on Wall Street," British officials claimed the Allies' armies owed their survival in 1915 to Bethlehem Steel, E. I. du Pont Nemours and J. P. Morgan companies. Loans brokered by the Morgan financial house ran up $48 billion in indebtedness that insured links at the hip between London, Paris and other European governments and American capital. Only later would the neutrality period 1914–1917 show huge profits by what post-World War I commentators called the "merchants of death." When J. P. Morgan's company could arrange survival financing for the Allies, then become the buying and paying agent in the United States for matériel to secure that survival, a Senate investigating committee would declare in the mid-1930s that the British government had "de facto ownership of American munitions plants," all with tacit U.S. government approval." Wilsonian neutrality was crassly hypocritical.[56]

Indeed, Wall Street, with Morgan in the cockpit and helped by a complicit Washington crew of Congress, comptroller of the currency, treasury secretary, and presidential advisers fostered a sympathetic relationship with the needs of Great Britain, France, and other members of the Grand Alliance.

It was all quite legal. Loans tied Europe to America. In turn, until America declared war in April of 1917, Wall Street simply could not afford to permit war debt default through any success by the Central Powers. Wall Street and Washington both understood this basic political and economic fact: Morgan and the private sector bankrolled, while manipulating Washington and Wilson's government. Yet it was in American interests, especially if one viewed the war as the enabler of the United States to replace Great Britain as the world's dominant economic powerhouse. Moreover, Morgan's private contract management of Anglo-French procurement actually may have had a salutary effect on American development of its own defense production base. Expanded facilities like Du Pont's Hopewell, Virginia plant drew upon European war contracts.

Carefully negotiated by Morgan's people and British equivalents, with Great Britain also as lead for other European powers, a so-called Commercial Agency Agreement was a natural result of years of trans-atlantic relations in the international financial sector. As fund manager of disbursement, the Morgan firm built upon its experience in both direct and indirect investment in American munitions companies like Remington Arms or Union Metallic Cartridge. Cautiously avoiding buyouts and anything else smacking of war profiteering, Morgan claimed perhaps only fifteen direct-investment companies in its portfolio (but including American giants United States Steel, International Harvester, Midvale Steel and Ordnance, Baldwin Locomotive Works, and General Electric, for instance). Yet, the array of trusts, interlocking directorships, cliques, networks and syndicates existed for peddling securities as other aspects of his enterprise. If Paul Koistinen is correct, Morgan "was interested in rationalizing the American economy." The Commercial Agency Agreement presented "the company with an unprecedented opportunity to work closely with leading manufacturers in almost every major category," through increased "influence over the economic system in general." American business and industry "like the state itself," was moved by power, prestige and profits suggests Koistinen.[57]

Almost overnight, Morgan and Company became the largest purchaser of goods in the world. As agent for the Allies, with Great Britain also a pass-through for funding from Russia, Italy, et al., nearly $3.16 billion flowed into corporate coffers, mostly between the first part of 1915 to the first quarter of 1917. Great Britain garnered sixty-six percent and France the rest, as some 4,000 prime contracts went to 948 firms, virtually all in the United States with perhaps 20,000 subcontractors involved. Ten contractors cornered about one-third of the dollar amount and, not surprisingly, the largest gainer was powder mogul E. I. DuPont de Nemours, reflecting that the bulk of sales were made in the American industrial northeast. Fifty-eight percent of all Morgan contracts involved munitions and other "essential war materials," while the remainder included hardware, machine tools, acids, food, draft animals and other goods which in the parlance of industrial war should have been termed "essential." To historians like Koistinen, Matthew Coulter and John Wiltz, at least, this enterprise gave Morgan and Company vast power with implications for the American economy and a mobilizable industrial base. Their point, guardedly based on the famous postwar investigative committee led by Senator Gerald Nye of North Dakota, remains arresting.[58]

One man and his 175-member subdivision of Morgan's empire seemingly held the key to the Allies' procurement program. This was Edward R. Stettinius, meticulous head of the Export Department. Formerly president of Diamond Match Company, he organized his new enterprise by function and drew upon techno-specialists such as engineers, and manufacturers well-versed in production and labor management, to tap American production of heavy ammunition, chemicals and equipment, propellants, explosives, and hardware as well as food and animals, among other items. The Morgan establishment worked closely with defense ministries in Great Britain and France, through its affiliates in those countries, to weave a web outside the normal government-to-government relationships blocked by official neutrality. In the process, procurement tended to go to few contractors in the elite of America's economy, well-known to Morgan circles. Names like Remington Arms (part of Midvale Steel), Winchester Repeating Arms and Remington Arms-Union Metallic Cartridge would seem familiar but generally speaking the Allied trade wanted artillery shell manufacture, which was marginal in the United States as of 1915. Opportunities beckoned; Baldwin Locomotive Company of southeastern Pennsylvania created Eddystone Ammunition Corporation in 1915 for production of munitions destined for Imperial Russia, underwritten not just by Morgan but also Chase, and Mechanics and Metals banks.[59]

In effecting contracts between American business and the Allies, Stettinius's Export Department apparently played a critical role in screening and selecting potential contractors, sometimes persuading companies to undertake new production lines, starting manufacturing, helping to establish prices, and other contract terms. The Stettinius team located qualified, reliable subcontractors, offered general advice and coordination to the Allies as well as Morgan insiders and helped secure financial assistance. Aside from materials inspection which was always done by government authorities, the Export Office fully engaged in all aspects of the vast Allied purchasing program in the United States. Most of the powder, high explosives, and a huge number of artillery shells sent to the British came through such channels while the French tended to negotiate more for raw materials and semi-finished products. Koistinen concludes, "the [overall] purchasing effort extended far beyond [high explosives and weaponry] touching nearly every industry in the United States."[60]

The Allies did not attempt to transport machinery back to their own domestic war production in any quantity. Still, here was a privately orchestrated military-industrial endeavor outside normal boundaries of state sovereignty. It was not material resource procurement that unsettled neutral Washington. Officials realized that what was good for Europe was good for American business. Rather, private financing by Wall Street touched sensitive chords when by April 1917, Allied indebtedness to America's private investors totaled approximately $432.7 billion in addition to the $800 million in outstanding contracts with business firms. Assistant Secretary of State, Counsellor Robert Lansing, Treasury secretary William G. McAdoo, Federal Reserve governor Benjamin Strong and even the ubiquitous Colonel House squirmed as to how to adjust official neutrality rules to suit fluctuating needs of the United States and Entente Allies. A clue lay with McAdoo's advice "to maintain our prosperity, we must finance [the war trade]. Otherwise, it may stop and that would be disastrous."[61]

Washington was about politics, Wall Street about profits. Both worried about how America's economics might benefit from war but remain disentangled from the actual fighting. Morgan and Company was part of the mix as the complexities of neutrality, international relations and economic mobilization increasingly took center stage after the 1916 election. At issue too, notes Koistinen, "the type of economic leadership required of corporate America in using hostilities to benefit itself and the nation" might be another way of seeing it. Of course, providing the Allied powers with munitions also created, "well before United States became a belligerent—the nation's first armaments industry," claims another historian, James L. Abramson. Before 1914, that sector had consisted only of "a few shipyards, some small-arms manufacturers, and several government arsenals." He moves toward Brandes' reference to "warhogs and warsows" in explaining America's ramp-up to war, Koistinen, Coulter even Wiltz looking less at U.S. Steel and more to Wall Street and especially to the role of the U.S. Chamber of Commerce, along with "initiatives of business associations, the navy and army, management specialists and other professionals," as well as individuals "seeking to advance their political ambitions"—an opaque national security state in the making.[62]

A foreigners' war catered to America's need. The U.S. economy had suffered through nearly two years of slump commencing in 1913, remaining unimproved by the outbreak of the European war in the following year. A twenty-three percent decline in stock prices, six-month closure of the stock exchange, a modest bank crisis, forty-one per cent decline in exports, some industrial stagnation, and unemployment reaching eleven percent all signified the need for action. Given philosophies of the time, it would require private not public sector action. Then the war kicked into its attritional phase as foreign actions provided the fillip necessary for recovery. Transfer of $41 billion in gold, loan requests and war purchases provided welcome returns in exports, industry and employment. American agriculture boomed again for 60 million European males under arms, when home-front deficiencies meant hungry mouths that only distant suppliers of wheat, corn and other goods could offset. American trade also flowed to Latin American markets left wanting by departure of European competitors. Full economic recovery in America rode on the back of European carnage. Neutrality and economic recovery coexisted by late 1916.[63]

Virtually all idle American resources had been put into production by the spring of 1917. The rate of expansion generated by European orders then slowed, even declined, as American military and naval preparedness competed with Allied need. The European conflict, developments during American neutrality, and the eventual imperative to actively intervene itself, put the United States in a unique position. In April 1917, preparedness gave way to mobilization when the United States formally declared war. Perhaps it had only been a matter of time, given the attritional stalemate of Europe's industrial war and the fortuitous appearance of that conflict as a stimulus for American economic recovery. Wilson's August 20, 1914 plea for Americans to be "impartial in thought as well as action" could never be sustained once profit appeared to capitalists capable of circumventing neutrality laws to ensure Allied survival to the benefit of their own firms and nation. As John Petrie implies, "August 1914 probably marks the zenith of impartiality in U.S. foreign relations in the twentieth-century." But, was impartiality ever part of America's actual equation?[64]

On the other hand, the U.S. declaration of war in April 1917 merely changed the dynamics. Mobilization—that inherently governmental act—traditionally constituted a declaration of war. So, the Wilson government previously had to tread cautiously with any government efforts or programs in that vein during Preparedness/Neutrality. Economic mobilization may well have grown out of the Progressive political economy, as Frank A. Vanderclip, president of the City Bank of New York, discovered what it meant for a nation to prepare for and then go to war. This was certainly much different than merely supplying funds and facilitating somebody else (European powers) doing so or merely enabling resourcing of raw materials from a ready market. Or was it? Morgan's enterprise "mobilized" a military resourcing base of vastly greater dimension than had heretofore existed in peacetime America. Whether or not the U.S. Chamber of Commerce, the navy's Consulting Board, the army's General Staff, or even the Council of National Defense, constituted prime enablers, may best be viewed in retrospect, when the country actually went to war in 1917. Whether or not large-scale organizational response—which would become as typical a twentieth-century American way of war as mass production and total victory—would serve the country any better than the state-national coalition approach of the Civil War, remained to be seen. What was apparent at the time was Washington's discreet approach which incorporated Progressive concern that the government's role might exceed statutory planning and procurement, with a measurable assessment of peacetime industrial strengths capable of ratcheting up to support military effort in a national emergency. American leaders faced a decision for intervention that required "wise central direction to mobilization." Yet, says James Abrahamson, "no federal agency had a comprehensive understanding of the needs of the armed services, of the productive capacity available to meet those needs, of the best methods to expand output and to reconcile civil, military, and Allied demands or of the appropriate agencies to determine policy and supervise its implementation." America "sailed into a sea of troubles with little knowledge of the best course to its destination."[65]

* * *

Unrestricted German submarine warfare sent America to war. On April 2, 1917, Wilson asked Congress for a declaration of war. Four days later, he had it. A "responsibility to protect" national interests, in this case loans and investments, drove participation despite official neutrality. Senator Gerald Nye, investigating the war's culpability, would pronounce blandly in 1939: "no member of the Munitions Committee to my knowledge has ever contended that it was munitions makers who took us to war." Nevertheless, he clarified that he and his Capitol Hill colleagues repeatedly suggested "that it was war trade and war boom, shared in by many more than munitions makers, which played the primary part in moving the United States into a war." Because they stood "to make money out of war," thought Nye, "any portion of the banking industry which is engaged in financing the armament industry is just about as dangerous to peace as the armament industry itself."[66]

Ironically, modern industrial war technology would change perception of state-organized violence. Years of exorbitant capital-ship arms race cloaked more cost-effective U-boats, torpedoes, and mines. Since the impact of canvas-and-paste airplanes to capital-ship obsolescence remained untested and unappreciated, American politicians continued to fund expensive naval and coastal-defense armaments to protect national sanctuary. Preparedness worries excited the populace and perceived battle-fleet peers kept domestic steel furnaces stoked with claims that defense industrial base sufficiency could help diplomacy in a dangerous world. Progressive America concerned itself with managing gigantic corporations and untrammeled wealth. In Washington, public officials civilian and military became handmaidens with Wall Street and corporate board rooms in modernizing policy and organization reform toward a subtle militarization. Sensed best when reading what Walter Millis discerned as American military thought for the period, public pronouncements caused him to portray "the transformation of the Army from a more or less ritualistic military order into an instrument for waging war in the new world emerging after 1900." Innovation spawned a war college for studying the higher art of conflict, a general staff for shaping bureaucratic response, rationalization of militia and national guard reserves, better promotion and training policies and a joint army and navy board for cooperative coordination. Building on such improvements, the army moved inexorably toward advocating continental militarization patterns such as preparedness, resourcing devices like citizen training camps and manpower conscription. The navy went on planning and lobbying for its battle fleet to "answer any challenge," and subsequently "a navy second to none" even well past lessons of Jutland and budgetary sanity. Defense of homeland and empire hardly dictated extravagance. Yet, security rested on such.[67]

The federal government did its bit to balance public-private equity. One *American Machinist* writer told his readers in 1906, "the liberality of the government" had advanced steel-trade interests far beyond any point they could have attained by reason "of purely commercial influence." Government funding, intended to ensure domestication of heavy forging for armor and guns, as well as large-scale steel-warship engineering, experimentation with "exotic" nickel and chromium alloys, and expansion of open-hearth furnace production, came from government subsidies. Public subsidization helped wean industry off rails, thus diversifying commercial products for structural steel. Strict government inspection techniques, however onerous to steelmakers, "were the real means of producing the quality of material now so universally used in the industry," thought Charles Schwab following his stint as a Carnegie armor-plant superintendent when he had fought the issue. To the *American Machinist* commentator, however, government specifications for armor and projectile products had caused "a demand with incomparably more value than just the making of guns and the forging of armor." Public-private partnering had spun off civilian benefits on a broader scale during "neutrality" and by 1917 seemed ready to win a war it had helped make necessary.[68]

Chapter 5

ARSENAL OF DEMOCRACY IN TWO WORLD WARS, 1917-1945

The twentieth century was the Age of Industrialization. It was also the Age of Mechanization and Mobilization. Mechanization became the military's handmaiden. Mobilization was tantamount to war, war tantamount to mobilization–of people and things, organization and process. The epoch additionally identified with the Age of the Administrative State. Writing after the First World War, the director of America's Council of National Defense, Grosvenor B. Clarkson, observed: "war is no longer a phenomenon in which the military alone are called," no longer "chiefly a pageant of marching troops and tragic fields." War had become "a contest of all the powers of the antagonists–intellectual, moral, and industrial." Befitting a civilian who had suddenly discovered eternal truth, Clarkson intoned: "to the romance of armed men moving upon the stage of history has been joined the drama of industry militant, of titanic economic forces loosed and then governed to the need of the nation in arms." Size was the key. The government and the people embraced industrialization and mechanization but were unready for the enormity of mobilization and a security state. Two world wars made them ready.[1]

TOWARD A NEW STRATEGIC SYNTHESIS

The United States was still trying to finalize itself in 1917. Progressive era reform from previous Gilded Age excess and "ambivalent colonialism" claimed headlines and agendas. The Age of Big Business—the "Age of the Octopus," say some business historians, others suggest "Giant Enterprise" as a more palatable label—wrestled with the Age of Regulation by an administrative state. Also present were labor's protest of unbalanced capitalism, and paranoid murmurs about dissenters, socialists and International Workers of the World, known as "Wobblies." Political historians tout reform of big business as the prevalent guiding theme. Diplomatic historians deny isolationism, preferring to call it limited involvement with regional concerns in Latin America or the distant Pacific and China, with some setting that context as a search for world order through mission diplomacy. The problems of Old Europe tested America's power pretensions and disengagement as goals of foreign policy and economy joined in a sort of "geo-economics" of principle and pragmatism. Grand strategy became mottled, through use of diplomatic tools, private-sector interests, and the state's naval and military arms. Ira Katnelson and Martin Shefter framed the essence of America as "shaped by war and trade." It became an "arsenal of democracy" in defense of "the four freedoms," in route to the Power, Principle and Global Activism of today: an epic story that seems to stretch on from World War I.[2]

Two world wars irrevocably changed America. The first conflict saw America's involvement principally in a single theater of operations, with two subsidiary interventions. The second war assumed what today would be styled requirements for "globally integrated operations." By choice, deemed necessity, the nation embraced crusades against what a later president, Ronald Reagan, would term "evil empire." Not the reference he would make to the Soviet Union, mind you, but rather to German and Japanese aggression, plus a perceived politico-economic-ideological threat to liberal values and capitalism. Communist Russia, an ally of convenience at one point, subsequently joined the list. In the process, sanctuary evaporated as America, embracing technological solutions, had to confront its own vulnerability. United States grand strategy joined with that of other powers, to dominate coalition contests. Preventing the victory of militarism joined redemption of Anglo-French loans from the first war. An interwar interlude projecting customary military austerity, arms limitations, and economic depression, obtained until even more existential threats of Nazism, fascism and communism confronted world order. America relied on mobilization of mass production for intervention in Europe and then the Asia-Pacific. Industrialized war melded grand strategy, market capitalism and technology, with surge of effort. Demand plus organization empowered Enterprise.[3]

War's immensity above all required popular acceptance and public funding on an unsurpassed scale. Whether Americans responded to actor Douglas Fairbanks and songwriter George M. Cohan patriotism against the "Wicked Hun" in 1917 or a jitterbugging Gasoline Alley generation's pragmatism vanquishing Hitler's Germany, Mussolini's Italy and Hirohito's Japan a quarter-century later, nostalgic legend rests on "Doughboys" and "GI Joes" in uniform. Yet, Rosie the Riveter's factory contributions coalesced fighting and home fronts even more. To Rebecca U. Thorpe and Mark R. Wilson, World War II, in particular, produced a "permanent military industry" that "created new opportunities for presidents to expand their power." It was a matter of public-private cooperation in muting dispute that led to wartime "military-industrial complex," and eventual acquiescence to some national security state, which might have been foretold even before the onset of hostilities. One could be "mobilized" if necessary; a command economy of the time yielded answers. Ramp-up and participation in world wars and confronting an economic depression in-between gelled experience and organizational response and channeled new direction once momentum led from progressivism to preparedness as economic mobilization showed the way. Radical intellectual Randolph Bourne predicted as much during President Woodrow Wilson's time. In the end, perhaps, Americans were overwhelmed by what they had wrought. Or, maybe they simply misunderstood the trajectory.[4]

FOLLOWING AN INEVITABLE TRAJECTORY

Americans either did not know or did not care that their country followed an inevitable path from 1914 to 1917, for instance. That path involved money and resources: ours put to use by others. The government avowed neutrality and avoidance of the Europeans' war, and the nation elected Wilson to a second presidential term in 1916 on the slogan that he kept us out of war. But then, America went forward on a slippery slope from peacetime to preparedness, from material and financial interventionism to military mobilization, and ultimately to war in April 1917. In many ways, the Central Powers dictated direction as much as partners Great Britain and France. In some ways it was guided by Wall Street, especially financial titan J.P. Morgan's banking empire loans to the Allies, and personal brokerage as their purchasing agent of raw materials. Those Allies were in debt to America and conversely America was in thrall to their victory for repayment. Billions were at stake as circumstances ripened for profiting from others' war. Preparedness fanciers and fanatics were in place, anti-military factions fractured and fractious, the determined eastern "elite" in charge, with politicians and the military moving relentlessly toward mutual esteem and commitment. Morgan's millions and America's raw resources, like Canada's, linked-up for capitalism and democracy as much as Wilsonian moralism and America's professed humanitarian interests. Americans eventually jumped aboard Wilson's war bandwagon because now, every sector of America had a stake in that winning. They repeated the feat two decades later when Wilson's war became Franklin Roosevelt's crusade. Statistics illustrated tangible American contributions to both conflicts.[5]

Statistics are America's modern manna, the measurement criteria for industrial triumphalism. Yet, society's story is remarkable when measurement of losses in material and human resources is manipulated for some purpose. It sounded deceptively simple when World War I army chief of staff Peyton C. March declared that the country had spent approximately $24 billion and the War Department about $14 billion of that figure, for America's nineteen-month participation. One Marine Corps quartermaster, Brigadier General Seth Williams, told a 1938 audience at the Army Industrial College that "a need became apparent from the first that became more vital every day and that was the cause of great delay and confusion [as] embodied in the word STATISTICS [his emphasis]," A hundred times a day information was necessary that no one could produce quickly, he submitted. Perhaps the trade association could provide the answer, or– perhaps there was no trade association! In retrospect, the census bureau should have had raw data but only bureaucracy could translate that data to relevant meaning. World War II army mobilization historian R. Elberton Smith observed later that, "prior to World War I relatively little systematic effort had been made by the government to accumulate detailed information on the existence, location, and capacity of the nation's industrial establishments" for war. Unpreparedness was the result.[6]

Official non-involvement and geographical isolation providing sanctuary preceded how America gathered and employed military power from 1917 to 1945. Mobilization was rocky in creating, arranging and managing statistics that reflected that power. Sanctuary bought time for government and private sectors together to extract manpower and matériel, and moreover, to forge a national identity of shared experience and responsibility. Sanctuary enabled World War I Assistant Secretary of War and Director of Munitions Benedict Crowell to tell his boss, Secretary of War Newton D. Baker about "the whole teeming effort in its main outlines, its myriad ramifications, its boundless activity, its ten thousand enterprises, its infinite toil, its hosts of workers, its wonders of scientific achievement, its attainments, even its failure—in short that humming complex of work, planning, ambition, disappointment, triumph, shortcomings, ability, and driving force" reflecting "a mighty people concentrated with all of its powers upon a single objective." Or, as soldier Peyton March explained, "the idea that a force of one and one-half million men could be transported within six months 3,000 miles across a submarine-infested ocean and then maintained was one unconceived of not only in our own war plans but in those of any other country." That achievement came with shifting priorities from a capital-ship arms race to convoying expeditionary forces overseas in unanticipated effort. What it meant in statistics was striking.[7]

Logistics and supply won World War I," claims contract history expert

C. M. Culver. As financial and raw material provider, munitions and weapons manufacturer or extractor of human capital, the principal problem confronting the United States in the first conflict *was* truly logistics and supply. Thus, tangible statistics for World War I emerge; 4.8 million serving men and women, forty-two divisions of 28,000 officers and men each, delivered in-theater, 47,018 trucks, 68,694 horses and mules, 26,994 standard-gauge freight cars shipped to France, 227,000 Browning automatic rifles and machine guns, 10 million rounds of artillery ammunition and 1.8 billion rounds of small arms ammunition, 10,000 tons of poison gas, 13,574 Liberty engines, 3,227 aircraft, and 2.5 million rifles as well as 743,663 pistols. Government clerks passed those numbers to Baker and the public.[8]

The First World War took 16 percent of gross domestic product and 116,516 American lives in 503 days of combat to produce an armistice. Yet, most frustrating of all to that generation and posterity, America could not equip her own military contribution from domestic stocks. The rifles were re-chambered British Lee-Enfields, automatic weapons were mostly French (except American-made Browning and Vickers machine guns), as well as over 4,000 pieces of field artillery and howitzers, plus railroad artillery mostly procured from the Allies as were millions of artillery shells, mortar rounds and hand grenades. Aviation was dependent upon foreign frames and ordnance, six Allied to one domestic, a significant exception being the famous "Liberty" engine. Tanks were French and British, although thirty-six were manufactured by the U.S. By and large, America (like British and French colonies), supplied human resources for the slaughter. Of 3,685,458 mobilized American volunteers and conscripts, 2,000,000 had been shipped to France by the Armistice in 1918. Sixty-two divisions total were organized with forty-two going to the front.[9]

The American Expeditionary Force (AEF) was equipped and fought largely through Anglo-French acquisition systems, with Doughboys dying for common cause alongside the British and French. Allied combatants were fed from fruits of American and Canadian prairies, while fuel derived from the New World mines and oil derricks, as Maritime America made possible placing men in the trenches of France. They were the resource multiplier; the diplomatic clout to help dictate a peace. The navy also added its weight. It's original battle fleet projection for ten battleships, six battle cruisers, ten scout cruisers, fifty destroyers, and seventy-seven submarines, tankers and repair ships gave way to protecting the army's logistics chain with over two hundred destroyers. This was truly "command of the sea" from what maritime historian Thomas Heinrich styles "the largest warship construction in history," underscoring security implications at war's end. In sum, America's contribution to World War I really lay with statistics of power from raw materials, organized humanity and maritime capacity for an Allied victory.[10]

Statistics from a second World War added to what was begun in the first war, and then some. Advances in technology, nature of warfare and geopolitics notwithstanding, they reflected mobilization lessons studied and learned from the first experience. A different domestic context plus greater lead time in developing the capacity of government, military, industry and the public for eventual hostilities held the key. By mid-1945 (roughly between Victory in Europe and Victory in the Pacific), production statistics underscored Soviet premier Josef Stalin's toast at the 1943 Teheran conference in November 1943: "To American production, without which this war would have been lost." From July 1940 to August 1945, American industry contributed an estimated 88,000 tanks and self-propelled guns, 257,000 artillery pieces, 126,939 gun carriages and armored cars, 2,400,000 military trucks, 2,680,000 machine guns, 12,500,000 rifles and carbines, over 41,000,000,000 rounds of small arms ammunition, 29,000,000 heavy artillery shells, and in stark contrast to World War I, 310,000 aircraft of various types, sizes and purposes. Naval expansion included 141 aircraft carriers, 6 battleships, 45 cruisers, 358 destroyers, 504 destroyer escorts, 211 submarines, 5,600 (or fifty-two tons of) merchant vessels, and 82,000 landing craft. Nearly 300,000 aircraft, over 12,000,000 men and women under arms, nearly 41,600,000 rounds of small-arms ammunition, 434,000,000 tons of steel—and two atomic bombs—showed immense additional capacity.[11]

For World War II, the Treasury department computed $336.7 billion was spent by all government agencies from July 1, 1940 to August 31, 1945; $315.8 billion of that for the war program with $184.5 billion on munitions alone. Elberton Smith's detailed tables indicate that $44.8 billion flowed to aircraft production, $41.2 billion to shipbuilding, $9.9 billion to guns and fire control equipment, $18.1 billion to ammunition, $20.3 billion to combat and motor vehicles, $10.7 billion to communication and electronic equipment, and $39.5 billion to other equipment and supplies. Government-financed war construction totaled $1.4 billion, industrial buildings $8.2 billion, industrial machinery and equipment $7.9 billion, non-industrial military construction, housing, community facilities, and other construction $15.3 billion, with $60.5 billion in military pay and $10.6 billion to civilians in Federal war agencies, and such things as $5.8 billion in purchases of agricultural products for export , $3.3 billion for overseas purchases and construction, and $12.1 billion in transportation and other contractual services. Other figures put the cost of World War II in the $288–296 billion range, in 1940 dollar-values.[12]

Most of all, statistics from America's two industrial wars suggest an arsenal for forging partnering. In the first World War, loans, raw materials plus a 2 million-man expeditionary force styled the AEF provided contribution. Then, arms worth at least $50 billion plus more matériel through Lend Lease and even more prodigious outpouring of uniformed military, the second time around in the 1940s. The United States thus refuted British Prime minister David Lloyd George's caustic comment that the first conflict had been "one of the inexplicable paradoxes of history, that the greatest machine-producing nation on earth failed to turn out the mechanism of war after 18 months of sweating, toiling and hustling." There were no braver or more gallant men in any army than the Americans, he had groused, "but the organization at home and behind the lines was not worthy of the promptitude and efficiency." Not so from 1941 to 1945 as key concepts like "18 months for ramp-up," "organization," and "efficiency" commanded attention. America converted only forty-seven percent of its 1944 economic output to the war effort, claims Arthur Herman. Yet, it literally took from 1917 to 1945 to turn the lessons and the experience into what scholar Ronald Schafer terms "the warfare, welfare state." This was the public-private partnering success story in war and economic recovery from depression. Statistics show Americans bought military achievement as their standard. They forget the rest of the Free World, strong central government and incentivized business/industry were also part of the equation.[13]

PATRIOTISM ISN'T FUNGIBLE

Presidents Woodrow Wilson and Franklin D. Roosevelt faced a strategic dilemma. Public support of extracting resources for large industrial wars demands what historian Aaron Friedberg calls some "strategic synthesis," or memorandum of understanding between government and its people: "a set of inward-directed power-creating mechanisms" to generate military capabilities in support of U.S. strategy but "without doing grievous harm to American institutions or values." Although Friedberg referred to the Cold War, the synthesis began years before when the *casus belli* tripwire set it in motion, and in order to "to acquire the capacity to pull this off, the United States had to transform itself into a military-industrial state," thinks political scientist Aristide Zolberg. If the Yankee Doodle spirit came as a prerequisite, so too did the matter of how to pay for the experience. Making war became part of so-called shared responsibility. Scholar Sarah Kreps fetchingly calls it "the 'Liberty Bond' approach."[14]

Historians have taken great pains to explain how both Wilson and

Roosevelt shaped public opinion to accept the herculean effort when it took unprecedented imposition of taxes to pay for their wars. Perhaps the one made it easier for the other, to woo citizens to sacrifice in the name of security, although "never again" ideology complicated policy after the first war. Isolationism, non-involvement, and the "Merchants of Death" war-profits scandal, accompanied by twenty percent unemployment in the Depression, soured Americans on sacrificing much of anything until Pearl Harbor. The public was no more amenable to intervention before December 7, 1941 than before April 1917, although preparedness and mobilization were terms used by government in both situations to stir acceptance if not zeal. Complicating matters were the prohibitions of five neutrality acts passed by Congress from 1935 to 1939, until production for foreign military sales again became a fashionable policy tool by 1940. The Munich "appeasement" agreement between Germany, Great Britain, France and Italy in 1938 may have convinced Roosevelt of a need for "protective rearmament," but he had to sell that to a non-committed public. By the end of the 1930s, Americans had mostly embraced more activist government response to economic down turn like just before the first war. Yet, to fully participate in any new war was an anathema. Neither Wilson in 1916 nor FDR in 1940 could overtly ask for war preparation in an election year. Then the nation's enemies handed options to the two presidents. While prosperity through rearmament short of war suggested an acceptable alternative in both 1916 and 1940, within the year, submarines in 1917 and an enemy first-strike by air in 1941 changed all that.[15]

The World War I response seems sufficiently patriotic in retrospect. "Behind every American soldier," proclaimed one contemporary commentator Thomas H. Russell, "about fifty men and women were needed in order that he be supplied with everything his physical, moral and military well-being might require." "They were put there," as military draft took care of the army and "the enormous sums of money necessary to finance our allies as well as ourselves were promptly oversubscribed in a series of loans, the first and least of which ran to three billion dollars, the fourth into six billions." Such sums were larger than "any single loan ever floated by any other nation." Idleness was abolished; the order "work or fight" was strictly imposed upon rich and poor alike. Any attempt "to except any one or any class would have been blown away in a gale of laughter." In "an incredibly brief period of time," the country became a nation of workers, everyone doing his or her share "with good grace and no murmuring to be rationed." "Interstate utilities were taken over and operated by the government," including the railway, telegraph and telephone lines while the government "fixed prices on the necessities of life." It sounded so simple, so rational—even if autocratic.[16]

Soon after the first war's military and naval preparations had been set in motion, the United States Government, taking no chance, "began to regulate the lives and living of Americans at home," observed Russell. "A policy of conservation, so well-devised that it went into effect without the slightest disturbance of daily living and daily routine," took immediate effect. "Everything was subordinated to the one and only purpose of winning the war," passed for explanation at the time. "All that we were and all that we had was thoroughly mobilized behind the fighting arms, the army and the navy." From all parts of the country came assurances that the action of the government was approved. Organizations of every conceivable kind passed resolutions pledging support to all war measures. "One hundred million free-born people were at length aroused to action," commented Russell. American women "responded to the President's call for universal service, flocking to the Red Cross headquarters in every city and setting to work immediately in the preparation of comforts for the great army gathering on the horizon." Complaining about paying war taxes seemed knavish.

Music-maker George M. Cohan songs, and Hollywood personae Douglas Fairbanks, Jr. and Mary Pickford selling war bonds, set the tone. Yet, everything was about patriotism in 1917, about "what the Yankee Dude'll Do," announced in a popular ditty by T. H. Devereaux the next year. Further phrases spoke of girding on rifle and knapsack to beat back the Hun "to defend our nation's honor," and "for Liberty for all," rallying for the Red, White and Blue "as your fathers did for you," and following "the stars and stripes" of Old Glory. Frankly, it was also about domestic reconciliation (America had just marked the fiftieth anniversary of the Civil War, so Devereaux evoked the spirit, from the Golden Gate to the old Palmetto State and "way down in Dixie," to bind up festering wounds dating back a half-century. And the people responded, opening their purses in response to an April 14, 1917 congressional war appropriation totaling $7billion, by bond and certificate issue, floated among the populace. An initial $3 billion was intended to prop up the allies through loans (with the remaining $4b for the American military). By May and June popular enthusiasm had oversubscribed that first $3 billion of a so-called "Liberty Loan" idea by $1.6 billion. A second "Liberty Loan" eventually prompted nine million more Americans to contribute $5 billion in-total in response to a bond issue anticipating only $3 billion![17]

If patriotism could not be taken to the bank, profit would! Part of Wilson's job was to restore a flagging prewar American economy through new endeavor. His call to arms needed revenues to win the war yet prevent profiteering. American exports rose in value from $2.3 million in 1914 to $6.2 million in 1917 and the excess of exports over imports increased from

$435.8 million to $3.5 billion in the same period. The United States suddenly became a creditor nation for the first time. While a dip would occur during the first year of American participation, the upward pattern would return for 1919 and 1920. War could be good for all but the dead and maimed. Nevertheless, the conflict would ultimately cost the nation $35 billion including some $9.4 billion loaned to the Allied after April 1917. The national debt similarly rose from perhaps $1 billion to $26.5 billion by 1919. Within reason, most Americans accorded Wilsonian idealism and high-minded rhetoric much slack. Economists and Treasury department officials, if not Wall Street, were more concerned with how to meet these war-related financial obligations. The New York *Times* warned that paying for war would bring home to voters that "defense of this nation is going to cost them something." Here was "shared responsibility" cloaked in red, white and blue.[18]

One-third of the financial obligation was met immediately by taxation, and the rest by war-bond loans designed to induce wage earners to the support endeavor. An income tax, already increased in 1916 but yet again the next year, yielded perhaps two-thirds of the necessary revenue along with an excess-profits tax, increased or new excise taxes on such things as liquors, tobacco, and amusements, while five separate bond-issues, the famous "Liberty" and "Victory Liberty" loans alone extracted perhaps $433.5 million from 66 million patriotic Americans willing to do their bit. The devil lay in the details. As financial historians have discovered, the government's efforts to raise revenue showed poor anticipation of the war's duration and requirements, in addition to the abiding problem of the Progressive era: whether to soak the rich or spread the burden across the classes. In war, Capitol Hill and the White House struggled with common-cause flag waving and profit.[19]

Secretary of the Treasury William McAdoo later boasted that "we went direct to the people . . . we capitalized on the profound impulse called patriotism. It is the quality of coherence that holds a nation together. It is one of the deepest and most powerful of human motives." Still, hard-sell government enjoined that every American should buy bonds as an "expression of a fundamental patriotism" and pounded the public with the directive to "fight or buy bonds." Hyper-patriotism eventually went too far when coupled with George Creel's Committee on Public Information and enforcement of "sweeping coercive powers" stemming from executive orders, or legislated by Congress in the Espionage Act of June 1917, the Trading with the Enemy Act of October 1917 and the Sedition Act of May 1918." Directed at enemies of the state, this super-patriotism went beyond anti-German hysteria, attacking and discrediting radical and even Progressive organizations like the Midwestern farmers' movement, The Nonpartisan League. A paranoid government produced the witch hunts of Attorney General A. Mitchell Palmer and Postmaster General Albert S. Burleson, attacked Socialist leaders and the radical Industrial Workers of the World, on grounds of their overt opposition to the war (although their hidden motive was undoubtedly their anti-capitalist stance). Wilson was complicit in the name of security. On the other hand, observes Ronald Schaffer, as enthusiasm for this intolerance spread and intensified among a patriotic populace, "most dissidents learned to keep silent, and the American people became mentally prepared, not only to serve on the battlefronts but also to join the massive economic mobilization that the Great War demanded of belligerent nations." Revolutionary War pamphleteer Thomas Paine's maxim that "patriotism is the last refuge of scoundrels," or the state's use of such a cloak to hide America's weak sense of community and national solidarity seemed palpable.[20]

The road to how the United States financed and mobilized the militarized security state of World War II led directly through New Deal Keynesianism of the 1930s. The government financed the second war through heavy taxation that touched millions via payroll levies as never before. Extensive borrowing through more bond drives, points to budgets from 1941 to 1945 totaling $317 billion, with the national debt rising from nearly $49 billion to approximately $259 billion in that period. Taxes yielded perhaps $138.5 billion, with another $185.7 billion from purchases, either by individuals or banks and corporations, of redeemable government securities as loans. An immense amount of political wrangling between both ends of Pennsylvania Avenue enabled common cause. Nomi Prins also suggests that Washington and Wall Street "collaborated closely" thanks to patriotism and importance of public service, as "bankers facilitated the sale of war bonds," and "financed war production alongside the government," while reconnoitering in the rest of the world "to ascertain borrowing needs," before the U.S. even formally joined the fight. Administration sub-officials helped maneuver Japan into an untenable financial position that contributed directly to Pearl Harbor. Roosevelt's Secretary of the Treasury Henry Morgenthau and the president fought a cadre of ardent New Dealers, conservative Midwestern Republicans, and Southern "boll-weevil" Democrats (New Deal supporters, but racial desegregation opponents) over issues of tax sharing, sales revenues versus income and excise levies, deficit spending versus pay-as-you-go, and excess profits derived from lucrative wartime contracts. A new round of wartime bankers from Warren Randolph Burgess, Russell Leffingwell, Thomas Lamont to Winthrop Aldrich, helped Washington with taxation, inflation, recovery, and postwar finance. Once again, Eastern elites joined the national security apparatus for war.[21]

Beyond wage and price controls to combat inflation, "lending" the government citizen-dollars through bond drives once again proved efficacious for financiers. The patriotic "spirit of sacrifice" and right-thing-to-do mentality found media joining Wall Street with such Hollywood stars as Donald Duck and Betty Grable, singer Kate Smith, and composer Irving Berlin, to stir the hearts and minds in ways reminiscent of 1917. Smith's "God Bless America" sent shivers down patriotic American spines, although jitterbug tunes probably stimulated more involvement among the young. On the other hand, the heinous nature of the enemy, just as graphically portrayed as George Creel had done two decades earlier, gained equal heft from the infamy of Pearl Harbor and the Bataan death march in the Philippines. More practically, economic stimulus that began with prewar mobilization now surged. Patriotism mixed with recovery after years of Depression, this time with a Hollywood rather than Broadway cachet.

Taxation historian W. Eliot Brownlee advances that "their nation's security was at stake" and victory demanded "personal sacrifice through taxation and indulgence of the corporate profits that helped fuel the war machine." Novel approaches included payroll withholding and the concept of a mass rather than class tax, bolstering the moral argument for sacrifice from workers on the production line, equal to that of men drafted to the fighting forces. True, relocation centers for Japanese Americans, race riots in Detroit, and labor unrest similar to the post-World War I Red Scare, tainted the atmosphere. This second war reinforced McAdoo's earlier comment on how patriotism generates economic sacrifices during wartime and that such sacrifices contribute to the cohesion of society. Perhaps a new strategic synthesis had synchronized American values with a security state. An American general called it "Crusade in Europe." Historian Sarah Kreps paints varied, often controversial ways "in which attitudes about fiscal sacrifice shaped how leaders passed along the fiscal burdens to the public" for a war "of epic proportions."[22]

MANAGING A GOLIATH IN THE FIRST WAR

America always undertakes great enterprise with a will. It embraces growth with vigor, and likes to create, manage and control both. For the most part, America learned how to do so in twentieth century war. Government harnessed the administrative state through people-power, whether from notes in a little memo-book of Army chief of staff George C. Marshall, bureaucrat Ferdinand Eberstadt's "Good Man List," or contacts made by financier and adviser Bernard Baruch. These reference points pinpointed names of leaders, managers and organizers—an "old boy network"—which could be mustered on a scale far surpassing anything earlier. An even larger vehicle emerged from "mobilization" or "the act of assembling and organizing national resources to support national objectives in time of war or other emergencies." The World War I version opened the age of mobilization for total war. Combatants, including the United States, confounded themselves with the size and grandeur of the endeavor for death and destruction. Moreover, it seems likely that the mobilization experience of both world wars subliminally conditioned everyone to actual benefits of conflict, a testament to journalist Randolph Bourne's 1918 observation about war being the "health of the State," for only when the state is at war, "does the modern society function with that unity of sentiment, simple uncritical patriotic devotion, and cooperation of services, which have always been the ideal of the State lover."[23]

Questions of Statism or Anti-Statism in America's DNA aside, stronger central government reacting to existential crisis changed the political economy of the nation forever. Even robust response to economic depression between the two wars suggests linkage and continuity to both when viewed from a distance in time. In a sense, the period from 1917 to 1945 was a grand artistic expression of systemization, planning and organization or what Andrew Latham defines as "military Fordism." It was forged and fused through forces that patrician commentator Henry Adams considered "capitalistic, centralizing, and mechanical." Perhaps it was part of another great awakening of secular religiosity, a bow wave styled "corporatism" with mobilization merely the catalyst. More aptly, it was national mobilization in support of grand strategy.[24]

Where Latham sees America's military resourcing as a rite of passage from armory system to industrial manufacturing and production, others portray the change manifested, in form and structure, the power struggle between public and private sectors for control and direction as well as experimentation with theories and agendas in state-building. The story lay predominantly with economic mobilization of the nation through a dual, accommodating "partnership" posits historian Paul A. C. Koistinen or "industrial self-government." Beyond the ballyhoo of a triumph of production, statistics, and how private sector America won a war, the fact was one of war management as some 2,400 "permanent and emergency agencies" (branch, section, division, board, or the like), were created during the First World War, in the Federal government, and other inter-allied bodies in which the United States had representation and record-keeping authority. Today, what we call "whole of government" or "inter-agency," saw the Second World War produce two 1,000-page volumes just to guide users through the labyrinthine records from military and civilian agencies for one of the greatest enterprises in history.[25]

To logistics historian James A. Huston, World War II leaders and planners "took small advantage of the example and experience of the country's mobilization for World War I." Others like defense historian Thomas Hone, argue they learned only too well but that much from the first war would prove irrelevant or impractical in preparing for the second. Yet, make no mistake, prepare they did! Apparently, not sufficiently, as they also committed many of the same mistakes, and suffered the same frustrations as their predecessors. "This war is different" lies imbedded in human conscience. It excuses inefficiency and waste with the explanation that "no one could foretell what form the war would take," suggests Huston. Still, if no one could foresee the future in any detail, then, "neither could the future be left to chance and the enemy." Thus, the pattern of two industrial wars flows from Huston's thought that, with size and organization guiding the American experience, a way of war depended on decisions made for attaining strategic goals with technology, estimates of relative capabilities, learning experience, "and above all imagination." Organization, planning and response—for annihilation of the enemy–defined an American way of war.[26]

In fact, from 1914 on, Europe and America confronted maturation of the revolution in military affairs posed by industrialization. Mechanization and attrition of resources defied earlier concepts of quick, decisive battlefield success built purely upon mobilization of military manpower. Limited in scale and low-level in intensity, any familiar, traditional "way of war" gave way by 1915 to volume and immensity as expanded increased firepower, carnage and stalemate, providing a new self-perpetuating cycle. This revolution placed a tremendous and unanticipated burden on governments and their "home fronts." Firepower stopped maneuver warfare cold in Flanders. Rapid-firing field artillery, machine guns and barbed wire produced "a huge slugging match" in the trenches consuming unprecedented munitions and men, with battlefronts extending over hundreds of miles. Mechanization technology (motor car and truck, airplane and tank) promised magical breakthroughs to overcome this quagmire. However, mechanization required quantity manufacture, supply and maintenance, with additionally large amounts of petroleum products supplementing if not supplanting animal fodder and human food, to confound procurement and logistical systems. The effect was staggering, from "the Front" to "Blighty" back home.[27]

As economist Louis Hunter reminded a military audience studying economic mobilization in 1954, those weapons of 1914 not only presented complex production problems of great difficulty because of exacting specifications under which they were built but under the conditions of trench warfare between opposing armies of great size, "they consumed ammunition in incredibly large quantities." The intricacies of fabricating munitions in quantity and quality, especially high explosives, led historian William H. McNeill to refer to a "managerial metamorphosis" demanded by the first war, and "managed economies" in the second. He cited "far reaching changes in older patterns of management" acting rather independently "in the context of market relationships," that coalesced "into what amounted to a single national firm for managing war." He included not just corporations but labor unions, government ministries and military administrators "in defining new ways of managing national affairs."[28]

McNeill further explained that time-tested customs and institutions became "soft and malleable" to "rival technocratic elites," who made millions into soldiers and other millions into war workers. Family life, property rights, access to consumables, and relationships of locality and class changed drastically. Taken together, alterations in daily routines and encounters "added up to a social metamorphosis as remarkable as the metamorphosis of insects," and perhaps also as natural. The catalysts were national mobilization and shared sacrifice, as well as the conviction that normality would return at war's end. War had to be fought to the finish no matter the cost, while enlargement of public power so reduced individual and corporate freedoms to reach "the dawn of a new and juster [sic] society," as "a matter of faith and fear rather than of foresight."[29]

European belligerents found themselves "with supply crises of the first magnitude." Originally lacking plans or preparations for prolonged conflict, they suddenly realized they could as much win or lose "in the factories at the rear as in the battle lines at the front." Ordinary procurement methods through contract orders and funding proved inadequate for expeditiously obtaining critical supplies in needed amounts and at critical junctures. Shortages ranged from raw materials and finished goods to facilities and equipment, while speculation in scarce commodities, skyrocketing prices, improper scheduling, and competition between military and civilian demands produced confusion and slowed production, threatening to reduce "already limited supplies of key munitions." Financing also defied accepted norms. Consequently, everyone learned how an industrial system, like any complex and intricate machine, "might break down under heavy overload unless measures were taken to reduce the strain." Out of this 1915 crisis, Hunter observed, "a new concept in warfare and a new practice in production were born." He termed it "industrial mobilization."[30]

The European antagonists discovered that mobilization involved harnessing national resources through "assumption of extraordinary controls by the Central Government." They imparted this wisdom via liaison consultations to an America arriving late to the classroom. U.S. army ordnance colonel Frank Scott told an audience ten years after the Great War that while "we were not prepared to take the field," the U.S. had been "prepared in certain fundamentals, certain indispensable fundamentals," that made "the difference between success and failure." He cited the Federal Reserve System "without which we could not have financed the war," adding to this the National Defense Act 1916 legislation of June 3 and August 29, for "creating the Council of National Defense and the Advisory Commission of the Council," and following declaration of war, by May of 1917 "we had the Selective Service Act." Presidential war powers (added to those legislative pieces), had conferred "powers more extensive than are possessed by any other executive in the world." Here was a platform for building a war machine "that leaves little to be desired," although Scott admitted that "these acts and powers were not established with relation to each other." There was much that was not clearly defined. But, that "very indefiniteness" gave opportunity, since "it is certainly a defensible position that wherever Congress did not specify or specifically limit, it must have been the intention to allow freedom of action in the national interest in a time of great national emergency."[31]

America's greatest difficulty, claimed Scott, "rested not so much in lack of authority as in lack of general appreciation of the great power inferentially conferred by these enactments; lack of expansive power in the structure of our departments within the Army; lack of co-ordination of these departments with each other and with the Bureaus of the Navy, together with the presence on our statute books of numberless laws governing peacetime procedure that were not automatically repealed by a declaration of war." The army had its general staff and the navy its general board. From the two National Defense Act provisions derived the authority to create a General Munitions Board, which then became the War Industries Board (WIB), to establish the divisions of industry, headed by private sector luminaries like Daniel Willard, Bernard Baruch, Howard E. Coffin, Julius Rosenwald and Hollis Godfrey, and departments headed by Dr. Franklin H. Martin and Samuel Gompers. Further, through this legislation the U.S. government derived the power to fix prices, locate new facilities, establish priorities, and to appoint and utilize the vast lists of committees of industry which later also developed into subdivisions of the WIB. The power exercised by Secretary of War Newton D. Baker on April 9, 1917, declaring an emergency and ordering the army's supply branches to disregard the competitive system in instances when the national welfare demanded other methods (to save time or protect people), "made possible the war activities in the industrial, financial, and commercial fields" that preceded the heftier controls of the Lever Act of 1917 and Overman Act of 1918, said Scott.[32]

So, Americans discovered that prewar Progressive-era government tools applied to regulate prewar big industry and banks could thus expand to include wartime allocation of scarce raw materials, rationing certain consumer goods, plus price and export controls. The nation learned how the private enterprise system "had been substantially modified" to favor a controlled economy with respect to critical functions, as directed by central government. Nobody planned for this aspect of the national effort; improvisation of mobilization methods stemmed from the urgency of supply crises. European experience was not lost on American leaders, yet prewar non-belligerency had predisposed wartime action to be disconnected, sporadic and somewhat ineffective, as study boards and commissions produced useful surveys and reports with recommendations for action that saw little-follow-through, thought teacher Louis Hunter. When the United States entered the war, "it can be said with little exaggeration that there was almost a complete want of plans for mobilizing our industrial strength," he concluded. Results proved haphazard and makeshift, replicating the confusion of previous conflicts, thanks to disorganized procurement, chronic shortages and bottlenecks. Only by 1918 "did the full weight of our industrial might begin to be felt upon the battlefronts of Europe."[33]

In truth, the chaos of military procurement, explicable amateurish civilian-led mobilization, and Progressive political over-organization along with failures of logistical distribution systems from shipping to railroads to communication—much less the faux pas of production with its great promise, but limited conversion capability from consumer to military goods—all shaped a kind of World War I military-industrial complex. Stephen Skowronek asserts that such a "complex" (if it even existed) by the fall of 1918 "rested on the most precarious political and institutional foundations" with each part—political-bureaucratic, business and military—"scrambling for positions of advantage." He points to some kind of postwar consolidation as the target. By the time of World War II, analysts like Brian Waddell, Gregory Hooks and Mark Wilson paint an evolved tableau of Washington in-fighting and maneuvering by more veteran servants of the state against the peppery distrustful, yet indispensable, private-provider sector appointees. The prominence of business leaders incorporated into wartime governance alongside politicians and military bureaucrats, excessive profits, and tenuous productivity, plus an underlying philosophical dispute between public and private theorists for resourcing war through economic mobilization managed by the administrative state yielded a still volatile if haltingly effective mix. [34]

The World War I security state came to include prominent Americans from the public sector: Wilson's secretaries of War and Navy, Newton D. Baker and Josephus Daniels, also Treasury secretary William McAdoo, joined by captains of business and industry Eugene Grace, Charles Schwab, a new generation of Du Ponts and Bernard Baruch. Also present were financial titans J. P. Morgan, Daniel Lamont, James Stillman, Frank Vanderclip, and Charles Mitchell, as well such pillars of military supply and procurement as George W. Goethels and William Crozier; all effecting temporary accommodation in the interest of expediency. Patriotism and honor (as well as revenue incentives) enticed corporate leaders like Henry Ford to "do their bit" fabricating army aircraft. Public production advocates got their Emergency Fleet Corporation (for transport craft), a second torpedo factory, naval research laboratory, and naval aircraft factory, to go with as yet un-fulfilled pledges for steel armor and powder plants, all in a GOGO portfolio. But, government arsenals like Springfield, Frankfort, Watervliet, Watertown and Rock Island, and the eight construction and repair navy yards joined with expanding sectors for powder (DuPont, Hercules, Atlas), warships (Bethlehem Steel, New York Shipbuilding, Newport News, Bath Iron Works, Electric Boat, and Fore River Shipbuilding Corporation, a division of Bethlehem Steel. The pattern of contracting to prime corporations via "cost-plus-a-percentage-of-cost" arrangements led to vast new enterprises like Du Pont's Old Hickory plant and company town near Nashville, Tennessee (largest smokeless powder plant in the world and inducements of top private executives like Charles Schwab from Bethlehem Steel to head the Emergency Fleet Corporation, or Walter D. Hines from the Santa Fe Railroad to assist in managing a nationalized Railroad Administration. Financier Bernard Baruch headed the War Industries Board. Occupying flimsily built temporary government buildings on the National Mall, an influx of men from business and industry controlled the work of Washington's bureaucracy.

In retrospect, a historian like Hunter, at least, looked past America's detailed performance woes as stemming solely from absence of advance planning. He discerned deeper flaws, since neither European nor American leaders had anticipated the demands of large-scale industrialized war on the civilian economy. "Out of the crisis of 1915 [in Europe]," he intoned, "a new concept in warfare and a new practice in production were born—industrial mobilization." The very nature of American national development and experience, especially the tradition of assertive individualism, and the general hostility toward government interference with business then combined with ignorance of economic and administrative problems involved, limited resources of the national government, and lack of public understanding of the necessity for central controls, thus handicapping Wilsonian industrial mobilization. Business historian Thomas McCraw adds, "in the effort to mobilize the economy for all-out war," the challenge for finding the proper balance between centralized control and decentralized decision-making "became the biggest challenge" for public and private sector management. How could a "democratic capitalist country mobilize for war without having the central government dictate all business decisions," and wreck "the decentralized market mechanism on which the economy was based," McCraw asked. Conversely, how could laissez-faire government completely lacking economic powers "coordinate the independent industries to fight a massive war?"[35]

The Armistice intervened before anyone had answers. The year 1919 had become the target for maximum effort and success anyway. Spokesmen like wartime Army chief-of-staff Peyton March or War Industries Board administrator Bernard Baruch eventually suggested the country's real strength and contribution was "the complete and successful diversion to essential war work of practically every industry and activity of the country." Overstated, perhaps, as "a decisive factor in winning the war for civilization" and constituting "a national achievement of which we may well be proud," the effort proved that the country "can, in an emergency, be self-sustaining in all respects for an indefinite period." This was probably not true of any other great power, and certainly no other insular power, said March. Nonetheless, he felt such sentiments were only for public consumption anyway. More realistically, industry and government together proved incapable of putting distinctly American arms and equipment on the battlefield quickly and efficiently—an affront to America's prowess. British premier Lloyd George was right.[36]

DIVINING LESSONS FROM THE GREAT WAR

Largely left to postwar War and Navy establishments for correction through 1920 National Defense Act reform, and modified during what became an interlude of peace, there would be no perceptible postwar peacetime military-industrial complex per se. Strictly speaking, how could there have been? Demobilization, isolationism, disarmament and budgetary austerity dogged national security for nearly two decades thereafter. Yet, the return of peace hardly eclipsed a powerful administrative state, far more organized and centralized than before. Memories and agendas of participants like Baruch, Stettinius, Benedict Crowell, Herbert Hoover and FDR as well as the military leaders could not be simply erased. Business, industry and the state reverted to peacetime, the military stockpiled quantities of surplus matériel and returned to customary schooling or testing new theories—for aviation, armor (tanks) and submarine warfare. In traditional fashion, emergency wartime administration stood down, its experience archived. Only a small military-civilian alumni group were determined not to forget lessons learned. They provided institutional memory.[37]

For instance, Peyton March thought that "probably no great industry or activity exists in the country which has not gained, during the mobilization of the resources of the Nation . . . experience which, when analyzed and studied, will be of great and lasting benefit to it and to the Nation." Bernard Baruch (now back in private life while still an adviser to be heeded), urged establishment of "a little school house" to study mobilization and relations between military, government and industry. He got one—the Army Industrial College, set up in 1924. Elsewhere the army's ordnance establishment returned to "design, testing, experimentation and development conducted wholly in the arsenals and on the proving grounds," claims a Rand study. Maritime matériel was mothballed or dry-docked pending other demand, while the so-called "Treaty navy" scrapped tonnage, as navy yard work and budgets shrank accordingly. The army's proselytizing air service/air corps together with Congress and industry prevailed on "assembling America's private arsenal system," suggests expert Allen Kaufman. Paul Koistinen insists that "elaborate ties were growing between the armed services and the industrial community" as reflected in statute, planning, and military-business relationships stemming from that planning. A new informational forum for the exchange of ideas—the Army Ordnance Association—worked along with the Navy League to foster public-private contacts. Missing were large peacetime military budgets as a jaded public together with congressional opposition, exerted a powerful counterweight to any semblance of permanent war readiness. Yet, America had flourished on doubling gross national product in the war. Postwar consumerism looked to mass production of automobiles and other consumables that, ironically, retained large-scale industrialized war conversion potential. America's mantra of speed and decentralized production became baked into such mobilization potential.[38]

The Great War changed attitudes and process. A pool of veterans with their lobbying organizations, American Legion and Veterans of Foreign Wars, continued the drumbeat sounded earlier by Civil War survivors: patriotism and survivor benefits. The navy returned to its big battleship and battle-cruiser program authorized in 1916 but waylaid by the war. Still, the naval act of 1916 had called for a postwar international disarmament conference. The Conference on the Limitation of Armament and resulting naval limitation treaty of 1921–1922 represented as close as the United States got to disarmament and collective security. Secretary of State Charles Evans Hughes' opening address to the conference emphasized that economic crises due to an international system of armaments and "continual danger" which lay in the massing of war materials, "are transforming the armed peace of our days into a crushing burden, which the peoples have more and more difficulty in bearing." So, the world watched Senate rejection of the Versailles Treaty and a League of Nations and, eventually, some scrapping of major warships to avoid a new arms race. In 1925, President Calvin Coolidge appointed a board under banker-diplomat Dwight Morrow to report on "the best means of developing and applying aircraft in national defense." The next year, Congress responded with an Air Corps Act that, claims Alan Kaufman, "came close to designating the aircraft industry a private arsenal." Morrow's group of military and civilians was impressed by technological advances stemming from the World War just not necessarily that air power promised some breakthrough decisive weapon. The board rejected any autonomous air service or defense reform via an overarching defense department and super general staff. It advocated developing an aviation industry for dual civilian and military uses, capable of producing 15,000 aircraft after the first year of some "major emergency. It put off for ten years or more the amount and type of equipment to be purchased annually because "conditions change too rapidly." It opposed rationalizing and standardizing "a given type of machine to assure industry a continuous series of orders for a standard design, thus avoiding an excessive multiplication of types of equipment in service." Certainly, Congressional largesse to satisfy military needs and provide a "faltering industry" with steady demand, had been present for shipbuilders and steelmakers before anyone learned to call them "a national security asset." Nevertheless, the allure of an Air Age was palpable.[39]

The interwar period had its colorful moments. Insubordinate army brigadier Brigadier General William "Billy" Mitchell flouted "air power" in defiance of traditional army and navy high command, got courts martialed, while exciting barnstorming biplane flyers helped his cause. Yet, the Morrow Board was right, it took ten years to move technology as well as world events toward embrace of aviation as any breakthrough instrument. Unwanted intervention of the economic Great Depression by the 1930s as well as a controversial Army Air Corps conduct of the mail service put a dent in military aviation. Still, another civil-military board chaired by wartime secretary of war Newton D. Baker in 1934 cleared up the policies and organization of military aviation while speaking to establishing a "close liaison" between military and commercial aviation and, where possible, using converted commercial air transports for cargo and transport airplanes. Baker's group emphasized that "encouragement should be given to the further development of airways, air-navigation facilities, and ground facilities." Such increased airway facilities all over the entire United States "will be of value to the Air Corps from the standpoint of national defense," members argued, while "with increased operation a larger reserve will be developed" from which could be drawn trained personnel and flight equipment. Army aviators subsequently flying airmail delivery while the ground army gained organization and leadership experience managing Civilian Conservation Corps camps helping preserve environment and provide jobs training, discipline and civilian cohesion in New Deal response to out-of-work Great Depression labor needs. Roosevelt similarly used naval shipbuilding to provide succor in that sector of the economy. Talk in Washington may have been about investigations of Senator Gerald Nye and his Special Committee on the Munitions Industry and everywhere headlines screamed about so-called "Merchants of Death" as causing the world war. However, the Depression and New Deal remedies kept the public attention focused on practical day-to-day solutions as the world turned uglier by the mid-1930s.[40]

One of the major lessons coming from the Great War that resonated well in vicissitudes of the interwar period had to do with rebuilding civilian connections, contacts and readiness for demanding new emergencies. What was to come in a second World War resulted from army and navy procurement and economic mobilization planning between the conflicts. Such planning resulted from continuing moderate contact between military and industrial functionaries. Koistinen especially posits that the interwar years witnessed the most significant changes in civil-military relations relating to procurement, planning and administrative arrangements, which stemmed from the First World War experience. He views creation of Baruch's War Industries Board as the model of a "gigantic planning partnership of government and business that inextricably combined public and private interests." Total war and mass production, fused according to a system as "animating vision," now dictated an effort that was as much about standardized designs, special-purpose machinery, and moving assembly lines, as were its products of helmets, bayonets, tanks, aircraft, and shipping: in short, a medium for creating military-industrial works of art. Moreover, enlarged public administration had come via the WIB's incorporation of "dollar-a-year" businessmen and professionals, whose commodity-section and war-service-committee system eventually proved to be more efficient and effective than existing military supply channels. This experience provided models developed not only by Baruch, who would reappear as Roosevelt's shadow advisor, but also new, private sector transplants like Ferdinand Eberstadt, Robert Patterson, James Forrestal, William Knudsen and Donald J. Nelson, vital for any new conflict.[41]

Indeed, however weak the 1917–1918 performance had been, it provided a legacy. Wartime associates in business, industrial and financial areas of civilian life had shaped the system at all levels and across government. Republican administrations in the 1920s "attempted to achieve the benefits of wartime planning informally through the encouragement and guidance of concentrated economic power and trade association activity," Koistinen suggests. Roosevelt's subsequent New Deal Democrats "opted for direct economic planning" under the National Recovery Administration, patterned after the WIB and intended to help during the Great Depression, and which "validated War Department planning" and made it relevant to civilian life. Here also was a link, Koistinen offers, with a governmental, regulatory alliance that had begun in earlier Progressive years "as the principal, elitist mode of twentieth century American political economy." Political historians drew similar conclusions.[42]

William E. Leuchtenburg for instance, recognized how the first war "brought a dramatically new elaboration of governmental controls, which guided New Dealers in battling a domestic enemy, fifteen year later." Colleague Arthur Link also thought this New Deal generation realized that, despite pre-World War I Progressive efforts, "there had been remarkably little governmental intervention in the national economy before 1917." The war changed this, claimed Leuchtenburg, keynoting how that centralized power as facilitator marked the new era but still reflected Progressive politics and philosophy. To these scholars, while the "genealogy" of the later New Deal had distinct links to populist and progressive threads, it was the 1917–18 national mobilization for war that held the greatest significance. Recent scholars have substantiated Leuchtenburg's assertion that it was the war that "marked a bold new departure," and "occasioned the abandonment of laissez-faire precepts," raising the national government levels of "director, even dictator, of the economy." President Wilson had convened a special "War Cabinet" every Wednesday, the War Industries Board had molded production, the War Trade Board had licensed imports and exports, the Capital Issues Committee had regulated investment, the War Finance Corporation had lent funds to munitions producers, the Railroad Administration had rationalized the railways, the Fuel Administration had fixed prices and imposed "coal holidays," and the Food Administration had controlled production and consumption of food. Even the Emergency Fleet Corporation and the United States Housing Corporation that provided shelter for war workers served as precedents for the next crisis.[43]

Army colonel Frank Scott cynically thought sometime later that the first wartime experience "may well be treated as history for by this time they should have passed out of the domain of reminiscence and not yet have entered that of fable." And, if Leuchtenburg is correct, the end of the conflict left wartime administrators "with a sense of incompletion." The stock market crash of 1929 leading to the Great Depression caused Progressives to turn "instinctively to the war mobilization as a design for recovery." Businessmen and politicians called for a response based on procedures of the War Industries Board. President Herbert Hoover, himself a civilian administrator under Wilson, asked Congress to create a Reconstruction Finance Corporation patterned on the War Finance Corporation. Roosevelt turned even more to veterans of the war mobilization, notes Leuchtenburg, adding that "the summer of 1933 seemed like old times" to National Recovery Authority officials. Yet, why wouldn't their generation naturally have reached back to proven experience and methods for coping with crisis? A wartime practice reemerged for "shunting aside the regular line agencies and creating new organizations [emergency agencies] with dramatic alphabetical titles." Such work-arounds, which tapped precedent for establishing coordinating bodies like the National Emergency Council, proved useful in justifying the New Deal's emergency legislation in the courts. By decade's end when Roosevelt began rearmament and then "protective" or re-mobilization, all this transferred under the guise of preparedness for another war. Antiwar isolationism, meanwhile, also had been fed by concerns over corruption and collusion.[44]

INTERWAR ACCOUNTABILITY AND PROFITEERING CONCERN

Accusations of fraud, waste and abuse shone brightly on the Du Pont company at the end of World War I. Proving innocent of a barrage of charges in connection with the Old Hickory enterprise, accountability and profiteering never quite departed even as the company broadened its chemical portfolio beyond powder-making. Historian Stuart Brandes quotes President Warren G. Harding from his 1921 inaugural address, asking for an "ideal republic" where universal citizen service would involve sublime sacrifice for country, and not one penny of war profit "accruing to private individual, corporation or combination." Brandes suggests how "the wartime profits dispute," intruded upon "Republican politics of the New Era, the decade long quest for an effective arms control policy, and even into the literary imagination of Jazz Age culture." He thinks that the generation imbued with Progressive-era morality and reform purpose, had hoped "to obliterate the scourge of war" by legal action such as the Kellogg-Briand Pact for example, by parliamentary debate through the League of Nations, by arms reduction exemplified in the Washington Naval Treaty, and "by eliminating war profit." War-surplus and production overcapacity again accompanied demobilization.[45]

Issues of equitable settlements for wartime contracts certainly plagued the armed services. Cases with familiar names like Packard, Curtiss Airplane and Motor, and Du Pont, filled the private side of the ledger while Hollywood, pacifist intellectuals, and even new special-interest veterans' groups publicly banged the drums of reform. Absent visible collusion of any military-industrial complex, Brandes still senses a "growing cooperation between government and private industry," consisting of army concern for the health of a defense industry base, government promotion of foreign military sales by contractor companies as a means to maintain a "warm" mobilizable industry especially in the aviation sector, and widespread exploratory techniques of mobilization including official tours of ordinate facilities, promotion of "educational orders," and incorporation of businessmen into a newly organized "reserve corps". Collusion by the three largest warship-building companies—Bethlehem Shipbuilding, Newport News Shipbuilding and Dry Dock, and New York Shipbuilding—for "oligopolistic, semi-competitive control of production of capital ships," in Brandes' words, through a jointly owned, non-profit subsidiary, Marine Engineering Corporation, and also ardent navalist-lobbyist William Shearer's sabotage of the Geneva Naval Conference in 1927, played to navy interests. Passage of the Vinson-Trammel Act of 1934 attempted to restrict profits on government shipbuilding to 10 percent of cost, thereby reining-in navy and shipbuilder excess.[46]

Actually, "probe of war profits," became the most publicized matter during the troubled 1930s. Two new focal points investigating the issue surfaced, the Hoover administration's War Policies Commission of 1930, and congressional hearings of the Nye-Vandenberg Senate Munitions Investigation of 1934–1935. Brandes notes how the munitions question coalesced the Progressive "struggle against the evils of monopolistic capitalism." Hoover's exploration of public-private accommodation maneuvers "spotlighted war profits while defense profits became wrapped up with New Deal economic policies, interfered with public works' spending on accelerated naval construction and eventually the push for aviation surge and rearmament" in a new round of preparedness. Scorn heaped upon private business as a result of the 1929 Crash and resultant Depression, background noise from peace advocates and disgruntled veterans, geographical isolationism, and a hangover concern from the 1915–1917 neutrality period that munitions makers might help start some new war in order to maximize profits all provided atmosphere. The navy, at sixty-five percent of pre-treaty strength, seemed adequate for defense of palm and pine. Few Americans were enthusiastic about war planning, or were flatly "dead set against doing so," observes Brandes. But, they "gloried in scandal and sensationalism," ideal for pursuing profiteering.[47]

Revisiting the famous Nye committee investigations in the overheated climate of the mid-1930s shows how the hunt for any "merchants of death" conspiracy was clouded by agenda-driven, diversionary issues and some demagoguery typical of Capitol Hill. The hearings fed into the claim that munitions makers and bankers were hardly innocent witnesses to the calamity called war. Commercial bribery as a way of doing business (for example with Latin American countries seeking arms for their own wars, like between Bolivia and Paraguay over control of the Chaco Boreal), active partnering between American military officials and the Curtiss-Wright Export Corporation for arms sales abroad, controversial comparative costs between public and private yards for warship construction, exposure of World War I senior-leader manipulation, secrecy and maneuvering that made intervention inevitable if not premeditated, all stand out as prominent features from the period. More importantly, perceived-scandal, which grabbed headlines and made possible independent developments, like ratification of the Geneva Arms Traffic Convention of 1925, and the Neutrality Act of 1935 which established a National Munitions Control Board, also stimulated similar foreign investigations.[48]

Nye's investigation of munitions makers featured particular focus on Du Pont gunpowder, Bethlehem, Midvale and Carnegie steel companies, shipbuilders such as New York Shipbuilding Corporation, the Newport News Shipbuilding and Dry Dock Company and Bethlehem Shipbuilding Company—styled the "Big Three" as well as Curtiss-Wright Export Corporation and war financing more generally. The committee uncovered over 100 companies producing munitions for export and domestic use. Additional hundreds contracted with the army and navy for various goods and services. Here was a large and growing troubling, if not sinister, military-private establishment. Just what could be done when the march of hostile dictators and ideology soon provided more ominous background? The Nye committee uncovered nothing untoward. Lingering concern for war profiteering would accompany new preparedness planning and organizing for the next contingency. The mid-thirties still reflected peacetime—Sunday in America—and Nye's deliberations stretching over a three-year period eventually exhausted public attention. The witch hunt did reveal powder-mogul Pierre DuPont's "business pacifism" claim that wars were fundamentally bad for business since they were comparatively short, thus hampering bigger profits for company survival.

Wartime demanded hasty expansion which, in turn, drove up expenses for credit and labor during tight market conditions. Civilian product-line manufacture could not produce military goods with normal equipment, skills, or product line. Heavy taxes absorbed profit-margins, unskilled workers added to training costs, while safety concerns increased risk, and potential sabotage required extra security, hence effects on bottom-line, production time and so on. At war's end, demobilization and reconversion issues adversely impacted private suppliers. DuPont emphasized how profits mostly accrued for extractors, not producers, in time of conflict.[49]

The Nye investigations continued America's traditional anti-statist aversion to uncontrollable militarism. In Paul Koistinen's analysis, it "explicated most fully and convincingly, the dynamics of an emerging warfare complex." Yet, anti-war, anti-militarist individuals "were isolated from centers of power." Excluded from "the elite circles of the federal executive," and restricted mainly to the legislative branch, they might "make their voices heard, but their effect on policy was minimalized," because of the pluralized and dispersed nature of power on Capitol Hill. Despite Roosevelt's subtle money-shifting to improve and update government facilities like the Philadelphia Navy Yard (with predictable political overtones for the southeastern Pennsylvania economy), and provide a modicum of fleet modernization through limited Treaty-Navy shipbuilding, Congress did not fully embrace armaments production as an economic palliative for industry and labor in distress.[50]

That awaited a future emergency, when patriotic necessity and political accommodation combined to bring closure on the Great Depression. If Roosevelt announced in 1940 that he did not wish to see a single millionaire created as a result of world disaster but thought everybody was entitled to a reasonable profit, his administration together with Congress would still ride herd on the corporate elite, with the excess-profits taxes of 1940 and 1941. Missouri senator Harry S. Truman's Special Committee Investigating the National Defense Program would serve as guardian of the public trust. Catching a windfall-profit odor from wartime-tax amortization of facilities and machinery "necessary for national defense," here was one politician averse to this "legal profiteering." Nye committee, neutrality laws and economic depression dictating pecuniary notwithstanding, the "warhog" survived but there would be watchdogs, alert and willing to pounce, even in an emergency.[51]

PLANNING WAS THE KEY

America's military war planning after World War I was always "threat based" and "resource constrained." The army and navy earlier had developed so-called "color plans," color-coded to any possible enemy. War Plan Orange, against Japan, was the navy's fundamental national security document. The plans always underscored continental defense, or "homeland" protection of the resourcing base. Response to World War I was an expeditionary aberration, somewhat. Thanks to the National Defense Act of 1920, establishing an assistant secretary of war responsible for economic mobilization as well as army procurement, then, in 1922 creation of an Army-Navy Munitions Board to coordinate mobilization and logistics planning, and two years later establishment of an Army Industrial College to train officers in those arts, the way was paved for more sophisticated planning. By 1940–41, recognition of increasingly likely coalition partnering and multiple enemy threats eventually led to the so-called "Rainbow" schemes. The die was cast for an ever-expanding commitment, from continental, to hemispheric, to global allied involvements potentially meaning more expeditionary warfare. A series of military mobilization plans in the 1930s, provided resourcing elements to this planning system, resting on mobilization, cooperation and coordination with civilian agencies, and to some extent foreign partners. Finally, something styled a Protective Mobilization Plan emerged in 1937. While parsimonious in response to fiscal pecuniary, it relied on a War Reserve of munitions "before industry can obtain a rate of production adequate to meet then current military needs" of the plan. All the army plans ran afoul of Roosevelt politics. New Deal Democrats would not sanction a military planned mobilization with Republican businessmen and industrialists coming to Washington to run the show.[52]

While the goals were clear, the path remained crooked. Dismantling uncompleted ships of the so-called Treaty Navy, maintaining a tepid industrial base mainly for the navy, and waiving the fiscal cudgel of base reductions for naval shipyards and bases accommodated needs of the times. Fraught with political implications of business takeover on the one hand, or military control on the other, period mobilization documents became planning and training tools, not policy. The services remained tied to their own parochial supply chains and procurement practices. The interwar period provided a heyday for theorizing about armored and amphibious warfare, bombardment versus ground-support aviation, tanks versus horse cavalry and scientific contribution from chemistry to electronics that might revolutionize the next struggle. Before 1938, according to one historian, "the political isolationism that produced a posture of grand strategic indifference" engendered vague answers to uncertain threats. Mechanization and main battle fleets continued to populate meager Depression budgets while New Deal public-works programs like the Emergency Relief Act, National Industrial Recovery Act, and Public Works Administration, enabled maintenance of defense facilities and some ship construction but little more.[53]

Outside government, business and industry concentrated on wealth accrual via transportation, communication, and consumer consumption. The rise of advertising and public relations tied into the media radio, and automobiles, which fascinated Americans more than war plans. Perhaps, Baruch's advice to government officials investigating industrial mobilization, elimination of profiteering and distributing war burden drew more attention in Washington than out on the prairies. Occasionally issues touched upon responsible and accountable disposal of war surplus, as in 1924, or whether a constitutional amendment was necessary to authorize Congress to seize private property for public use during war, to remove the profits from war, and to equalize the burdens of war. But only scowling lawmakers replied to Baruch's lecture decrying confiscation as a useful compliance tool.[54]

No doubt Baruch remained one of the influential figures of the interwar. As an outsider and insider from Wall Street finance, he garnered attention in Washington for what he said and what he did, particularly by having been WIB chair, and part of Wilson's inner circle at the postwar settlement in Paris. He advised the worthies of the era, even if his later memoirs at times seem more a litany of name-dropping than policy illumination. Roosevelt held him at a political distance. Yet, he was part of the milieu that advocated preparedness, mobilization and close cooperation, between private and public sectors. His words carried weight, as to the industrial strength of the United States, saying it "is a delicate mesh of inter-related strands," that had evolved in response to the needs of the nation under natural economic law, but was dimly understood. "It is a sensitive living organism and the injection of arbitrary and artificial interference could be attempted only at the risk of starting a sequence of upheavals, the ends of which no man can foresee," he intoned. To approach it at the onset of conflict, "bearing in one hand demands for a vast stepping-up of output and a heavy draft on its manpower, and in the other, a broadax of governmental confiscation with which to wreck its vitals," said Baruch, "is no way to win a war."[55]

Preparedness and mobilization remained planning works-in-progress on paper, requiring modification according to unfolding events. From 1938 to 1940, American rearmament ratcheted upward in increments like a rheostat, as Eastern and Western Europe collapsed to German, Italian and Russian aggression, while the British Empire and Nationalist China held back Japanese expansion for the time being. Then in 1941, the Nazi juggernaut turned on its erstwhile partner the Soviet Union while Japan surged forth on its Greater Asia Co-Prosperity hegemony in the region. Behind a rather thin curtain of phony neutrality, economic mobilization supplanted the New Deal in America. Lend-Lease after March 1941 expanded to provide material aid to friendly foreign partners, as industrial mobilization for production of military matériel wrapped into concepts of "preparatory mobilization." The story of forging Anglo-American alliance despite neutrality and long before any declaration of war has been ably recounted by Gavin J. Bailey in his examination of aircraft supply and the American-British alliance from 1938 to 1942. FDR's "Doctor New Deal" gave way to building an "Arsenal of Democracy," perhaps inevitably lurching toward "Doctor Win-the-War" at some point. Questions reappeared—who might control administrative state mobilization, whether business and industry, bureaucrats and politicians or the military? How to get the private sector even to convert to armaments-production absent declaration of war, became Roosevelt's obsession. If participants later claimed that the 1939 Industrial Mobilization Plan was never put into effect, military officers, at least, "indoctrinated with its principles were later to exercise a very substantial influence on the actual course of industrial mobilization," in Louis Hunter's words. A Victory Program took shape but only Japanese aggression at Pearl Harbor truly answered many questions and tilted reluctant America to significant action.[56]

THE WAR LORDS OF WORLD WAR II

World War II Washington provided a theatrical stage for plutocrats, bureaucrats, and Colonel Blimps, thriving on production quotas, bureaucratic fiefdoms, carbon-paper and egos or "arsenic and red tape" to one commentator. Here would be a different kind of drama for what Michigan newsman and later Pulitzer prize-winning author Bruce Catton called "the warlords of Washington." Historian John Morton Blum termed them wartime vassals of the state. They fought bitterly over contract-award equity, whether only large or both large and small businesses should be part of the wartime team, government largesse, and especially whether the military, corporate elites, New Deal politicos or combinations of each should dictate mobilization and enterprise. Twenty-first century America has forgotten the power of Organized Labor in its heyday and how work stoppage (strikes) could hobble the best efforts at mobilization productivity. The picture from the 1940s was not pretty and political scientist Samuel Huntington and sociologist Gregory Hooks alluded to a "Battle of the Potomac." Before Pearl Harbor, plans alone proved insufficient for shifting prewar non-involvement—whether termed preparedness, protective or defense mobilization—into wartime production.[57]

After Pearl Harbor, the frame of reference became total involvement. Washington bureaucrats (civilian and military) and their field offices presided over a labyrinth (MIC) of government, contractor and subcontractor providers which delivered the goods. Aviation, for instance, would count not just Douglas, North American, Grumman, Glenn L. Martin, Consolidated-Vultee, Bell Aircraft and Boeing but also Ford Motor, Goodyear, Chrysler, Nash-Kelvinator while Hudson Motor subcontracted to supply pistons ad rocker arms to Wright Aeronautical and Briggs Manufacturing (another Detroit auto body-maker) supplied dorsal fins and stabilizers to B-29 assembly lines. Henry J. Kaiser might become famous for a fleet of "Liberty" cargo ships but the Detroit (Chrysler) Tank Arsenal, Fisher Body Division of General Motors, Cadillac and Ford produced tanks while amphibious vehicles (not landing craft) came from General Motors, Studebaker, White Motor, Autocar and Diamond T Motor, the famous general purpose "Jeep" from Willys-Overland and Ford, Willys, Ford, Dodge, Studebaker, REO, Chevrolet, White, Diamond T., Federal Truck, International Harvester and Mack Truck made cargo truck contributions to the effort. Similar enterprise worked for guns, shells bullets and other war goods while engines and propellers surfaced familiar company names from Wright Aeronautical to Pratt & Whitney and Allison Division of General Motors—even Rolls Royce/Packard with contracts and licensees ensuring further twists to wartime resourcing. Government controls and regulators guaranteed no civilian goods production for the duration. It became a gargantuan effort, notes Barton Hacker, "the climax of another long cycle in military history," of mechanization with friction temporarily resolved between labor and capital, enforcement of anti-trust laws, and size and scope of government. Fear of returning to economic depression lurked in the shadows with wartime government providing largesse against recession.[58]

Deferment of labor to production lines appeared alongside military conscription. Front-line service was more demanding, home-front was prosaic. Yet, fighting a multi-front war and providing an aid-cornucopia to the Free World, even to Communist partners, required far more organization and determination of needs, control, and direction than anyone imagined, and also generated stress between fundamental principles and practice of America's free-market capitalism greater than anyone recognized at the time or has, since. This was the cost of democratic capitalism fighting industrialized wars. The experience overwhelmed the Progressive generation that had confronted unexpected entry into the First War and botched mobilization. Taken in stride twenty years later, it would be overwhelming again. The Depression/New Deal, plus preparatory rearmament and mobilization effected test-bed and start-up, but "Rosie the Riveter" and "GI Joe" still needed eighteen months to get into gear. Neither cemeteries in foreign lands nor names on humble Arlington headstones, public monuments, fast-receding memories or memorabilia from attics not even insipid media testimonials, do justice to the robust public and private effort eventually mounted by the American republic from 1941 to 1945.[59]

But first, once again it was a struggle to actually manage enormity. As business historian Thomas McCraw observed about the many months stretching from 1939 to 1942, planners "set up one special body after another, but only a few of these agencies worked well." Should that have surprised anyone? The trial-and-error approach that had begun with the 1916 National Defense Act, years later seemed doomed to renewed trial and error, political control, and personal egos and agendas hiding behind military necessity. Resulting establishment of a Council of National Defense (still on the books a generation later), was designed "for the coordination of industries and resources of the national security and welfare." Roosevelt's resort to something similar—a National Defense Advisory Commission before settling on an Office of Production Management and followed by a parallel Office of Price Administration and Civilian Supply when the Warlords failed to play nicely in the sandbox showed that neither apparatus of the administrative state could only go so far absent official declaration of war. Nonetheless, under NDAC leadership, notes Charles Hyde, the rearmament effort of 1940/41 placed 920 defense contracts with 531 producers for a value of $2.85 billion by October 1940. Eight months later even the automobile industry alone counted $2 billion in defense work for 54 per cent of the dollar value for aircraft and parts and another 25 percent for trucks and tanks."[60]

American democracy would never be ready to go to war promptly or efficiently. Hard bargaining between government, business and industry, trial and error, political control, and egos overshadowed everything. Congress might originally have intended the Council of National Defense as a useful peacetime resource-planning tool and first-step coordination for actual mobilization, and so too, the 1920 Defense act and a storm of legislation in response to Roosevelt's Arsenal of Democracy much less preparedness demands. Both would prove inadequate for fighting wars beyond existing frameworks. Functional committees such as the General Munitions Board and the Committee on Supplies, like Wilson's War Industries Board under Baruch, might suffice as models for Roosevelt's later administrative and planning bodies. The "yellow brick road" led quite naturally through the New Deal response from leaders who had cut their teeth on World War I and nudged the administrative state toward a national security state. Roosevelt had learned well from Wilson, having been his Assistant Secretary of the Navy. Still, this approach literally needed to explode to meet the needs of a much larger second war.[61]

Then, too, there had been the military's own planning desire to be free of civilian interference and stormy petrel bureaucracies. By the late thirties, the War Department's "Protective Mobilization Plan" (PMP) (which envisioned an 80,000 regular force plus 180,000 National Guard adding 300–400,000 volunteers within a month, then going to 1.15 million at "M," or mobilization day, plus 20 months with an accompanying "Industrial Mobilization Plan," or IMP), could not provide equipment and support adequate for the immense task determined by actual events. Years of mobilization planning had identified thousands of plants and businesses that might support defense of the homeland plus outlying possessions but not some enlarged multi-theater expeditionary force plus defending friends and partners. Affixed to the political system, the plan was all about "national security" within boundaries of non-involvement. Nevertheless, on August 9, 1939, FDR had directed the assistant secretaries of war and navy to establish a War Resources Board advising the Joint Army and Navy Munitions Board, analyzing individual and committee reports on various aspects of industrial mobilization, and advising top Government officials. The IMP envisioned federal agencies regulating industrial facilities, essential commodities, manpower, overseas trade, wholesale and retail prices, domestic and oceanic transportation, energy sources, war finance, public relations, and selective service. The WRB recommended the blueprint subsequently followed, for several emergency agencies, established by and responsible to the president in the event of a war emergency, but not any superagency as proposed in the military's IMP. Politics and public attitudes were unready at that time to move to global power responsibilities.[62]

Circumstances changed the direction. As in 1916–17, with America remaining neutral, Roosevelt concentrated on organization. He instituted the Interdepartmental Committee for Coordination of Foreign and Domestic Military Purchases, otherwise known as the President's Liaison Committee, on December 5, 1939. Army, Navy and Treasury officials were involved as this body subsequently morphed into administrating the Lend-Lease Act by the spring of 1941. When Germany overran France and the Low Countries the year before, FDR had reactivated the National Defense Advisory Commission but it retained a first World War weakness as mainly an advisory body fraught with competing members, influences and directions. Donald Nelson eventually surfaced as yet, another government mobilization czar to stiffen mobilization backbone. Roosevelt probably wanted to maintain the same direct presidential control he had in the New Deal, so no competing authority would control mobilization (military or civilian) while he delicately maneuvered the country through neutrality, readiness for protective defense and measures short of actual participation in the war.[63]

By January 1941, FDR had moved to create the Office of Production Management (OPM) within an Office of Emergency Management, and a coterie of able liaison administrators like William H. McReynolds, Wayne Coy, and eventually Judge James F. Byrnes, battling service chiefs, their service secretaries, and other officials in a free-for-all style, bureaucratic all-out-war effort. Ultimately, decisions rested with the president. Skeptical if not downright anti-New Deal private-sector leadership eventually contributed redoubtable figures like William Knudsen of General Motors and head of the Amalgamated Clothing Workers of America Sidney Hillman, to represent management and labor, yet without direct authority over civilian goods production or any other coercive power sufficient to accomplish that demanding set of requirements. Even using innumerable persuasive tools to jog military production, or preference orders and priority ratings on raw material, OPM in peacetime still could not overcome the business preference for production of civilian over military goods for a country slowly reemerging from Depression and hungry for commodity goods. After all, when Americans went to the 1939 World's Fair in New York they flocked to pavilions promising peace and progress, not death and war. Pearl Harbor ended that illusion.[64]

No doubt, the framework was there for something bigger. Substituting military production and technology for manpower appealed to Roosevelt and American citizens, touching historians like David Kennedy as the "essence" of what was styled a neutral "arsenal of democracy." Roosevelt bought the concept of supplying the British and Russian fight for survival, but relying on a massive buildup of airpower was for America's own safety. Such "short-of-war" strategy might avert U.S. intervention, with attendant casualties, surely would strengthen partners' ability to survive, and also stimulate domestic recovery. Naturally, Lend-Lease coming on the heels of "cash-and-carry" demand for upfront payment for aid, a reversion to pre-World War I models for helping friends but avoiding active participation, triggered a bitter congressional battle. By the spring of 1941, Roosevelt was ready. He had won reelection the previous November, and his party held enormous majorities in Congress. Isolationist Republicans fought hard, but Lend-Lease passed that March. By December 1941, recounts money historian Robert D. Hormats, "$750 million in goods had been exported under the program," and eventually $51 billion in aid passed to America's friends and comrades in arms ($22 billion to Great Britain, $12 billion to Soviet Russia, for example). As in 1917, America had already economically entered the second war. Ideologically it had, too.[65]

"BIG M" PLUS "BIG L" EQUAL "BIG V"

Pearl Harbor abruptly jarred the country from complacency. From "lessons learned" planning to preparatory readiness, to the political realities within and beyond Washington, the nation passed from peace to war. Business historian McCraw bluntly observes that "many agencies created during the early years of the war had overlapping jurisdictions," and points to constriction of pre-war neutrality both in 1916 and after 1939 as well, as an inability to define "the precise relationship of public to private institutions during mobilization." Civilian and military Washington as well as the country learned the magnitude of overseas expeditionary warfare in 1917 and again in 1941. The lesson translated into Big Mobilization, Big Logistics and Big Victory in both instances.[66]

The difficulty of managing size of effort constituted to large measure the problem in a wartime command economy. FDR thought he could handle a plutocratic concentration of military-industrial power, for he believed his political nature could control both sectors—and probably so, in normal peacetime. Fortunately, centralized management deferred to decentralized execution. Resuscitating the original Council of National Defense and its successor NDAC had offered a necessary structural step but nothing more, and neither did a sense of urgency. Both army and navy had more power in 1941 than in 1917. Initiating the Selective Service System in September 1940 reintroduced yet another extractive emergency program with massive military impact and intrusion into American homes and factories. By mid-January of 1942 the pressure to increase defense production led to enforcing a priority system and substituting a War Production Board for the Office of Production Management, to manage industrial mobilization and authority shared with other agencies. Harnessing size unleashed forces that the jaunty smile and cigarette holder of the president, even in good health, might not resolve.[67]

Newly granted presidential war powers in early 1942 enhanced executive branch ability to curtail production of nonessential civilian goods, and strengthen a system of preference orders and priority ratings. To confront lagging acquisition of raw materials and production facilities, business incentives from new tax laws authorized depreciation over five years of costs to convert to war production, and ability to recover wartime excess profits, if a business incurred postwar losses. Other inducements included suspending military procurement competitive-bidding requirements, cost-plus-fixed-fee contracts to guarantee a profit (i.e. contracts structured to guarantee a profit, a system for financing conversion costs, and measures to guarantee retooling costs while contracts were still in negotiation), a thirty percent advance on contract value to finance conversion costs, letters of intent guaranteeing the cost of retooling for government work even while contracts remained under negotiations. Innovative approaches appeared, such as implementing a Production Requirements Plan. Eventually, Ferdinand Eberstadt's more sensible Controlled Materials Plan addressed bureaucratic log-jams over priorities not seen since 1918. Scholar James Abrahamson concludes that "after almost four years of mobilization and over eighteen months of war, the United States had a fairly satisfactory system for controlling industrial production."[68]

Abrahamson saw the emphasis on defense production as a detriment to the whole economy while leaving most procurement to the military. But this was wartime. The Great Depression had conditioned the country to austerity and people adapted accordingly. Americans took the military draft, civilian rationing and quotas in stride. The annoyances of war taxes, paperwork and red tape joined patriotism and shared sacrifice. Arguably poor coordination of civilian with Allied needs, little advanced planning, and a voluntarist approach to business, "emphasizing profit incentives rather than coerced central direction struck Abrahamson later. At the time, Washington bureaucrats fretted crucial parts of industrial mobilization like petroleum, rubber, prices and manpower, which fell under direction of agencies independent of War and Navy departments. Synthetic rubber and margarine made their debut as substitutes to consumer dismay. Production Requirements and Controlled Materials plans involved only a few scarce materials while imposing "an overwhelming paperwork burden on smaller manufacturers." The Controlled Materials Plan would transfer to a post-conflict "Cold War" as a Defense Materials System, its importance was so great. But, in the turbulent infighting between functionaries and their programs diverted effective prosecution of war matériel.[69]

Eventually, the 1943 appearance of Judge Jimmy Byrnes as head of the Office of War Mobilization (OWM), guaranteed "more effective coordination of the mobilization of the Nation for war." OWM supposedly assured the effective use of civilian manpower, the maintenance of a stable civilian economy, and the adjustment of that economy to war needs and conditions. OWM was to coordinate the activities of all federal agencies concerned with production, procurement and the distribution or transport of supplies, materials, and products. Additionally, OWM served to resolve controversies between such agencies, except those under the jurisdiction of the Director of Economic Stabilization, and to issue directives on approved policy, programs or operations to other agencies as necessary, to carry them out. On July 15, 1943, Byrnes' authority expanded to unify and coordinate Federal activities relating to foreign supply, procurement and other economic affairs, in conformity with foreign policy as defined by the Secretary of State. With Allied victory in sight, his agency morphed into a new Office of War Mobilization and Reconversion (OWMR) on October 3, 1944. As a wartime expedient for ultimate administrative-state management, here was what was styled later as a "whole of government" approach, absolutely indispensable to Big Enterprise achievement in the modern era.[70]

Whether the mechanics of government mobilization proved a help or a hindrance, seems academic now. By 1940, like in 1916, the requirements were set to rearm America and reinforce allies with resources. By 1941, as in 1917, declarations of war changed priorities to actively fight with U.S. assets. Still, if government plans and organization proved wanting, government nonetheless held the key to persuading the public, business and industry to join the Enterprise. True, it remained Sunday in America until presidents Wilson and Roosevelt asked Congress for war declarations. The requirement "to bring into the defense effort, as active co-operators" all of America, recalled Bruce Catton, was the gargantuan task. If the job could not be done without "the proprietors of the nation's chief physical assets," then "their fears and suspicions had to be allayed." Prior to what FDR called a "day that would live in infamy," thought Catton, "the game had to be played their way; whatever preparations the nation made had to be within the bounds of territory that was familiar to these men" which meant "the rules were not to be changed." As Secretary of War Henry M. Stimson wisely informed Roosevelt, if one were going to war or preparing for one "in a capitalist country, you have to let business make money out of the process or business won't work." America's regulatory/administrative state had to adjust to that notion. Even after 1941, one financial editor declared it difficult for some citizens to understand how the extra effort required by war could be made without "some stimulus other than the vague one that it is necessary to save the country."[71]

Patriotism could not be guaranteed; it could not be taken to the bank. Publicizing threat shaped citizen acceptance. So, the path to war inexorably climbed steadily to 1941. Flurries of War Department press bulletins, seemingly dictated by changing conditions abroad, signaled conversion of National Guard units from one combat branch to another. Transferring or repositioning air corps units around the country, calling up reserve officers for training and education, constructing new facilities at both municipal and military installations, and awarding contracts in staccato succession to large and small businesses in all forty-eight states signified something was afoot. And so it was: America was creating a new defense industrial base for itself. The range of products for the second war was more diversified and technologically advanced than in World War I. From Weyerhauser came lumber, and fuel from Tidewater Oil, while Cheney Brothers, American Silk Mills and Duplan Silk Company produced parachute material, and Myrtle Knitting Mills, sweaters. Bendix Aviation made maintenance parts, Goodyear Tire and Rubber provided hoses, trucks and fuel pumps were made by Yale and Towne, and E.I DuPont de Nemours even supplied 300,000 toothbrushes. Buick Motor Division of General Motors won a contract worth nearly $37 million to produce Pratt & Whitney aeronautical engines and spare parts. It cannot be understated, automakers General Motors, Ford, Chrysler, Studebaker, Hudson, Packard, Nash, Kaiser-Fraser, and Crossley all joined war work because of peacetime skills and products.[72]

Names like Caterpillar Tractor and Allis-Chalmers converted to ordnance and equipment, while quartermaster awards for infrastructure expansion on naval and army air corps bases went to such partnerships as McClosky and Company of Philadelphia, teaming with architectural engineers Graham, Anderson, Probst & White from Chicago, securing a new Cost-Plus-Fixed-Fee contract for nearly $5 million just to build an installation in Puerto Rico. Haggar Company was tapped for 100,000 khaki cotton trousers for a rapidly expanding force, which followed the call-up of reserves, National Guard, as well as new draftees. Companies listed for procurement also included Eastman Kodak for Air Corps filter units, General Electric for generator assemblies, Bell & Howell for aircraft cameras, DeVry for motion picture projectors, RCA for radio tubes, Stromberg-Carlson Telephone Manufacturing Company for telephone parts, Phelps Dodge Copper Products for wire, Dictaphone Corporation for code transmitters and recorders, Otis Elevator for steel castings, National Cash Register and Elgin National Watch Company for artillery ammunition components. Contracts awarded dotted a seemingly endless list. And, this was just the army story. The navy's differed somewhat.[73]

Government always retained the directing hand, ensuring that both navy facilities and private yards had production as well as other logistical responsibilities. Modeled on World War I experience at places like Philadelphia's navy yard, Cramp shipbuilding, and civilian-administered Hog Island, the design had been a diversified and responsive industrial base. So, in the second war, batching of orders, allocation of various classes of matériel, for aircraft and shipping for instance, went to specific producers, not just government-financed emergency plants. Further expansions of navy yards and other government-industry bases provide a fascinating portrait of enlarging the securitization of America. The navy's experience especially in World War II enables historian Thomas Heinrich to point out that "the navy yards launched fourteen percent of total combatant tonnage, including half of all battleship tonnage and a sizable number of aircraft carriers, cruisers, destroyers and submarines." Put another way, he cites "one-fifth of all destroyers . . . one-quarter of heavy fleet carriers, forty-five percent of submarines and half of all battleships" that fought in World War II were produced by U.S. navy yards. This maintained a million skilled workers in government shipyards. The arsenal of democracy required all hands on deck.[74]

Heinrich also referenced "the shipbuilding heyday of World War I" on the Delaware River, asserting how American entry had carried those shipyards out of a prewar slump. This ensured survival of shipbuilders like Cramp and New York Ship as well as other yards from Fore River of Massachusetts to Newport News in Virginia. Wartime surge contributions from the navy yards ranged from battleships to submarine chasers. Moreover, the first war witnessed urgent projects run not only by private providers like New York Ship's parent-company, American International Corporation, but also the government's Emergency Fleet Corporation which financed Hog Island shipyard downriver from Philadelphia. The second conflict enabled construction-magnate Henry J. Kaiser's national consortium of seven shipyards, which together comprised a total of fifty-eight shipways, to mass produce "Liberty" cargo ships on assembly-line regularity with prefabricated parts. The vessels became the unsung workhorses of the second war effort.[75]

Due to wartime demand and size of effort, over time Hog Island and Kaiser's ersatz shipyards linked up in business-government partnering, for speed in fabrication via standardization. Yet, wartime economic flush could not necessarily transfer to peacetime stability with postwar reconversion. Such was the case with the Philadelphia region until the onset of the New Deal when the Public Works Administration had pumped $238 million into naval shipbuilding in 1933 alone. The navy itself reopened Cramp to build heavy cruisers, which continued into the second war along with submarines. New York Ship made carriers and battleships. New assembly facilities on both coasts mass produced "Liberty," "C-Class," and "Victory" cargo ships, learning from the Hog Island experience with vessel-design changes, product obsolescence and subcontractors for hulls. Heinrich notes, however, how the Maritime Commission "rightly worried about the effects of excess tonnage on the postwar maritime economy." Still, in *Ships for Victory*, Frederick C. Lane underscores this singular, most-significant accomplishment of mass production as leading to victory. Despite passage of the Merchant Marine (Jones) Act of 1920, designed to bolster the country's maritime sector through conversion and regulation, the shipbuilding industry had slumped after World War I. Firms like Cramp, and Pusey and Jones foundered, while New York Ship survived only due to arms reductions and fascination with aviation potential, which enabled navy contracts for converting battle-cruisers *Lexington* and *Saratoga* to carriers.[76]

Indeed, it was the young aviation sector that became the darling of World War II. Roosevelt's May 16, 1940 call for production of 50,000 planes a year was met, to industry's disbelief. Prototypes were included in this output, along with production aircraft, although new plant and training facility construction advanced slowly until German blitzkrieg caused American generals to reevaluate speed and mobility and through active maneuvers re-fashion their own field doctrine and organization around machination technology on the ground and in the air. Automobile assembly-line aircraft production had achieved little success in the first war but it would in the second, with automotive production emphasizing massive aerial bombardment. The Army's Air Service-Air Corps and post-1941 Army Air Force's private-arsenal model epitomized what could be achieved in prolonged wartime. Private manufacturing for the second war, under government regulation and specification, supplied a diverse product-line from tanks to trucks and jeeps, but above all, aircraft manufactured by a GOGO/GOCO/COCO matrix. After Pearl Harbor, Bruce Catton's "active co-operators" would no longer hang back. Still, turning appropriations and contracts into viable aircraft always dogged bureaucrats like army under-secretary Robert Patterson, in charge of air procurement.[77]

Public and private partners shared rules, regulations, specifications, and guides, while advice to business also came from private advisory groups like The Research Institute of America. The group's executive secretary Leo M. Cherne provided "manuals" with titles like *Adjusting Your Business to War* (1939/1940) and *Your Business Goes to War* (1942), offering a roadmap for the private sector to ease the painful passage to war production. Enticing was a new tax-amortization law allowing annual depreciation of twenty percent of original cost on a defense plant, reducing the timeline from twenty to five years. Thus, observed Patterson, "the specter of an amortized plant or plant amortized only by the use of profits from which the government had already taken a large fraction for taxes—was removed." A major part of the munitions sector "built at private expense would be accorded this special permission." At least to the assistant secretary, while it was impossible to gauge with any precision how much influence this law actually had in expediting contract letting, "it seems a reasonable and intelligent judgment" that the law, "assisted by vigorous and intelligent administration," played a significant part in overcoming business/industry reluctance to shift from civilian to military programs.[78]

Sluggish bank-loan procedures also daunted contractors until a presidential order allowed the War Department to advance between $400 million to $1 billion in so-called V-loans. Utilization of the New Deal Reconstruction Finance Corporation credit idea was extended, through its Defense Plant Corporation, to enable loans and authorization for building factories of all kinds with public-funding assistance. Aluminum and magnesium plants, synthetic rubber works, chemical factories and a large Utah steel plant were the result, some operating on a fixed-fee arrangement directly for the government, noted Patterson. In one instance, Studebaker automobile company of South Bend, Indiana received nearly $40 million for new machinery, equipment and plant construction at its Fort Wayne and Chicago plants "under the terms of Defense Plant Corporation Agreements of Lease developed jointly by the Reconstruction Finance Corporation and the War and Navy Departments." Any sum above and beyond that portion of the cost for which DPC was not reimbursed through rental from Studebaker would come from the War Department. Plant title and equipment would remain with DPC until the end of five years when "the manufacturer will have the option to purchase the property at cost less some prearranged rate or depreciation or alternatives at some negotiated sum."[79]

Thus, Patterson observed, the government stepped in to help finance expansion of munitions plants in situations where private finance was risk-averse or too slow in procedure. Two-thirds of facilities built to fill War Department orders would be with government assistance. True, government contracts disproportionately went to large firms throughout the war. The government and financial institutions favored awards to those that offered financial stability and technical expertise as the "best guarantee to achieve both quality and speed of production." Shrinkage of critical materials, restrictive controls, labor demands, and questions of prime contractors versus demands of subcontractors, all added to difficulties in developing a defense industrial base. The rich American civilian market, said Patterson, as he underscored automobiles in particular, meant that even big companies from that sector remained reluctant to switch to munitions-making—until Pearl Harbor. They had been using materials and labor, and engineering tooling-up for the 1942 civilian sales year. After that, Patterson thought, "Detroit needed no further urging, automobile men converted far more rapidly "than we had dared hope."[80]

A UNIFYING AMERICAN EXPERIENCE?

Author Thomas Bruscino thinks that World War II "taught Americans to get along," through common cause, conscription, and what was once styled "war work." For many Americans, exposure to and participation in the exhilaration of belonging to a greater cause actually had begun earlier, during the World War I experience. Take for instance, farm girl Lou Cretia Owen from Henry County, Tennessee. Lured from a dead-end home experience, Owen joined and even helped manage 10,000 women of the 35–50,000 DuPont smokeless powder workforce at Old Hickory outside Nashville. Although her experience was short-lived, Owen and thousands like her manned other production plants, railroad yards as well as farms and businesses thanks to the exigencies of war. The twenty-two-year-old Owen found the experience liberating. Female cartridge makers as well as Treasury girls had served in Civil War Washington and both world wars mobilized female clerks who, like Owen at Old Hickory, discovered adventurous confidence-building, and a heady sense of distaff contribution and gender equality. Momentum built to women's suffrage in 1920 and conditioned civilians to defense work in national security.[81]

Yet, conversion of Americans to common cause called war work in either world war was never easy. Take for instance the army's 1940s Detroit tank plant or arsenal: Started from scratch in beet fields in Warren, Michigan, the plant was miles from downtown Detroit and bereft of worker housing, schools, and other amenities that meant commuting problems, housing shortages strained community race relations and distinctly unhappy government clerks when the central managing office moved from Washington to the Union-Guardian building in Detroit disrupting leave records while delaying paychecks and lowering morale. Thus, disruptions and dislocations in lives, routines, and life styles beyond rationing of food and gasoline and other commodities meant there were two sides of the story in 1917–1918 as well as 1940–1945. Washington cranked up its domestic inspirational programs while corporate America cultivated a participatory identity through all manner of activities including "production drive" issues of company magazines and newsletters like Douglas Aircraft's *Airview*. This approach supplemented government propaganda, war bond drives, scrap metal collection, remembrance banners in home windows and the ubiquitous ration booklets reminders to sacrifice. Together they contributed to the sense of belonging to one great effort. Shared sacrifice became a mantra worn with pride by what came to be called "the greatest generation" by later journalist Tom Brokaw. Aviation pioneer and corporate leader Donald Douglas energetically supported the war against the Axis powers. Why would he not? Douglas and his company held a $3 billion backlog in orders at some point.[82]

Douglas told his employees in February 1944 that the backlog "is our yardstick," for speedy victory, and asked: "will each and every one of you join me in a pledge to continue doing his job faithfully and on time?" Just two years before, he had told his employees that "we are not producing as many airplanes today as we are geared to produce because of shortages of parts and materials." Those shortages would not last, and he assured that "production will hum." "Let's pool our ideas and do it," he implored, "we want ideas and enthusiasm more than ever" and "we want to give full credit where credit is due," urging an inclusive, collaborative—hence American—Douglas team. This was the "great drama of the rivet gun and the slide rule," asking everyone to adhere to War Production chief Donald Nelson's requirements personally and responsibly as "the battles of tomorrow must be won in our shops today." Corporate pep talks like FDR's fireside chats bound Americans to a common weal.[83]

Douglas Aviation husband-and-wife workers Terry and Joe Hill graced the Kodachrome-color cover of one 1942 installment of the company magazine *Airview*, riding off to work on a bicycle built for two. The accompanying editorial comment from the corporate public relations department conveyed the message: "tires being what they are, such scenes will soon become common." Graphic artist Jack Campbell provided a grotesque caricature-character for the back cover named "Tokio Kid," maliciously fanged, and firing off reverse enjoinders like "much waste of material make so-o-o-o happy, Thank you" from a knife-like pen, dripping blood. The magazine had a fascinating array of feature stories connecting employees with the world beyond the headlines domestic and foreign, yet completely linked to what Douglas departments were doing at El Segundo, Santa Monica, and Long Beach, California and Tulsa, Oklahoma. There was sports coverage when world-champion swimmer from the 1932 and 1936 Olympics Ralph Flanagan joined the El Segundo family. A.M. Rochlen's public relations team combined photographs of pet cats, a monthly $1,500 prize contest for employee ideas to tap Americans' knack for ingenuity, tied to "whip out an idea to whip the Japs," details (unclassified) of how "trains without tracks" delivered parts and goods to production lines throughout a particular plant, with plenty of photographs of Douglas executives, managers and workers, providing all with name recognition reward for team play vital to production.[84]

Two years later, the Douglas workforce, as part of the wartime military-industrial effort, methodically produced the A-20/DB-7 "Havoc/Boston" light bomber from the Santa Monica plant, the B-17F "Flying Fortress" from Long Beach and its counterpart heavy bomber B-24 "Liberator" from the Tulsa facility, as well as the A-24/SDB "Dauntless" dive-bomber from El Segundo, and also the cargo-planes C-47 "Skytrain", C-53 "Skytrooper" and C-54 "Skymaster" from the facilities at Oklahoma City, Long Beach, Santa Monica and Chicago. Of course, the aircraft, like ships, tanks and other tools of war all had to carry monikers, part of the inspiring plan of attaching identities to what Americans were spending long work-shifts and sacrifices as part of the United Nations' Great Enterprise. "There must be no lag in production," declared Douglas in February 1944, with 145,000 aircraft scheduled for completion in the coming fifteen months.

Food recipes, pinup glamor of Douglas girls, selective combat-shots from the Pacific, articles on war correspondents, as well as "bobby-pins and girdles enlist" genuflection to distaff contribution, detailed cross-section illustrations of aerial bombs beside feature articles on performance of the C-47, indispensability of the A-30, and "Rube Goldberg" research-and-development gadgets from Douglas's own Research Hollow at the Santa Monica plant, although Lockheed's "Skunk Works" became even more famous. It was all self-serving of course, and a far cry from the civil-military feuding on the Potomac. At least in *Airview*, a reader might take heart that the Cause was justified, efficient and effective. Americans could read in "Wings for the Wounded" how the Douglas C-47 was the workhorse for Army Air Forces' evacuation of wounded, as other products of Douglas industry were sowing the havoc of death and destruction, in a multi-theater global war. Of course, the "Tokio Kid" still imparted corny and ethnically insensitive propaganda, like: "careful please of saving scrap it are creasing pants for Jap" as a bullet sped through his buttocks. The cartoon, like other similarly directed songs, ditties, poems and attitudes, must have caused Douglas team members to smile appreciatively in the 1940s![85]

Regional historian Gerald D. Nash has shown how World War II dramatically reshaped America's western states, especially economically. But, all across the nation from 1940 to 1945, just as in 1917–1918, citizens were enlisted for production line and conscripted for fighting front. Creating a mindset of contributing to something important as part of Team America changed the nation. Western states before 1940 were virtually "colonies" mostly supplying the maw of eastern and mid-western productivity. The war replaced Depression apprehension and hesitancy with economic growth and visions of a bright future. Western mining, shipbuilding, aluminum, magnesium, steel, oil, uranium, along with urban and scientific centers, shifted economic growth and westward migratory patterns, even altering cultural life built around Hollywood popularization. Could not similar transformational patterns be sensed for other regions, perhaps? The fact is, once U.S. leaders had committed to intervention in two foreign conflicts, there could be no turning back. Woodrow Wilson and his coterie, followed in time by Franklin Roosevelt and his New Dealers, supplemented by additional political stripes, were swept into the excitement of total commitment to total war. Huge human and resource extraction mobilized into armaments production and combat service also translated to full dinner-pails and employment in war industries after years of austerity. To a large extent the world wars were about jobs, promising plenty amid sacrifice. Yet, they were also inspirational, incentivizing and part of an uplift after the Great Depression and Pearl Harbor. They transformed despair to hope by means of nationalization. Of course, after victory, what then?[86]

How to get the genie back in the bottle? Demobilization and Reconversion entered government planning as early as 1943. A popular ditty at the end of World War I had queried "how are you going to keep [the Doughboys] down on the farm once they've seen Paree?" Making war was heady stuff. Americans of all ages, ethnicity and both sexes had experienced something truly different, had enjoyed belonging and contributing and succeeding in a Great Endeavor. From Hog Island and nearby Philadelphia Navy Yard, from arsenals and airfields spread out inland, prosperity accompanied war-making. Ending wars, making the world safer and better, and providing a brighter future were all worthy goals, but more basic was peacetime demand for "normalcy," like refrigerators, washing machines and automobiles—in short, a consumer economy that more than anything motivated the later GI Joes. That was what American business wanted too. Sufficient weapons stockpiles, a large labor pool of conscripted veterans, and reduced budgets and priorities after two world wars meant that the years 1917–1945 might join the Civil War on the shelf of celebration, memory and peace. The Army cancelled Chrysler's tank contract by October 1945, shut down the arsenal except for a maintenance contingent moved the last command personnel from downtown Detroit out to the empty Warren arsenal by the end of the year. Government leaders during World War II forged new international institutions to offset the interwar failure of the League of Nations.[87]

PASSING THE BATON TO SCIENCE

By mid-1945, wartime scientific and technological fusion came together in blinding light over two Japanese cities to end World War II. Less understood than other wartime achievements like radar, sulfa and penicillin drugs, much less firepower and airpower, the atomic bombs dropped on Hiroshima and Nagasaki represented victory of a new sort. America entered a new age. It had done so before, course, but this time it seemed beyond our ken. The industrial age had been about coal, steel, and oil. Now, science had changed everything more completely and frighteningly than ever before. Atomic physics via the government's "directed innovation," suggest technology historians Barton Hacker and Margaret Vining, reached fulfillment at the conclusion of two industrialized wars of mechanization in the first half of the twentieth century. Was this a waystation to a more orderly process of conscious decision, development, testing, and evaluation, asks historian I. B. Holley, but doomed to lag behind "the creative forces of science" ultimately gifted from the private sector? "Directed innovation", suggest Hacker and Vining, promised that not only could weapons and weapons systems be designed and built to meet military needs, but also to realize military desires. These weapons might even dictate peace.[88]

A flourishing National Advisory Committee for Aeronautics and an expanding Naval Research Laboratory pointed the direction. There were other innovation vehicles at arsenals and navy yards, as well as university and company labs. Army historian R. Elberton Smith posits in his economic mobilization history, the welding of manifold technologies from ballistics to "high-performance specifications required of military items," as suggestive of the complexity of the task and achievement that became the norm. The prosaic and the exotic came together in a fashion little-appreciated by the welter of statistics symbolizing victory. Yet, if the relationship of supplier to customer remained traditionally with a government arsenal and depot system complemented by private providers, where did wartime science fit on the mobilization rheostat-dial for war and peace? Were wonder-weapons just that—just another kinetic tool of destruction?[89]

Perhaps as historian Joel Davidson suggests, the Second World War "was the first war for which basic scientific research was harnessed to produce war-winning weapons." Yet, chemical weapons such as toxic gas, artificial nitrates, high explosives, even aviation facilitators such as oxygen equipment, and the mechanics accompanying mine and undersea warfare, had contributed in the 1918 war. Beyond military purposes, communications, medicine, engineering, and human psychology all took science to war. Hacker and Vining argue persuasively that in mobilizing American science, World War I "marked the beginning of a new relationship between scientists, who had their first taste of relevance in the corridors of power," and military officers, some of whom recognized the promise offered by science to revolutionize warfare. And, they specifically cited that it was the organizational approach of Progressive-era thinking that produced the Alva Edison-led Naval Consulting Board, National Advisory Committee on Aeronautics, and the National Defense Council's National Research Council, under the guidance of another scientist, Robert A. Millikan. All were instituted during the Preparedness phase before America formally entered the first war, but continued to function during the conflict. Millikan and colleagues effectively contributed to resolving the submarine-detection problem. Weaknesses at the time, Hacker and Vining admit, included lack of mechanisms for transferring military funds to civilian research, junior scientists were conscripted to work on specific projects, and "haste seemed to preclude delay," leaving little room for balanced programs or detached judgement.[90]

Science, too, had to demobilize from what Hacker and Vining call the "catastrophe of industrial war." But, taking their places beside the Army Industrial College, a flourishing National Advisory Committee for Aeronautics and an expanding Naval Research Laboratory, even the National Research Council, survived as government hothouses in the event of renewed conflict. Nonetheless, Hacker and Vining suggest that only NACA really flourished after World War I, moving the United States "to the forefront of aeronautical design and development," even becoming "a model for organizing American scientific research" by the end of the interwar period. Most of what might be termed mobilizable science, the discipline, facilities, and the players, like the business and industrial sector, remained in private hands. The groundwork was laid decades before and might survive past the latest struggle.[91]

Just as financier Bernard Baruch was to mobilization, Dr. Vannevar Bush of the Massachusetts Institute of Technology was to garnering attention and results from scientific mobilization by World War II. As president of the Carnegie Institute of Washington and chair of NACA, he subsequently headed a reactivated National Defense Research Committee which expanded to become the influential and productive Office of Scientific Research and Development during World War II, spurring such contributions as radar, the proximity fuse, blood plasma, and what came to be known as the atomic bomb. Most certainly, it was the army-managed "Manhattan Project" to produce the atomic bomb in the 1940s, which "helped turn scientific investigation into a national security endeavor that blurred the lines between industry, universities, and the armed force." From 1942 to 1946, the super-secret activity made its own contribution to the army and navy's labyrinthine conventional complex of yards, supply depots, airfields, and training camps across the nation. With thirty-seven facilities in at least fifteen states and two Canadian provinces, the Manhattan endeavor provided over 200,000 jobs. The J. A. Jones Company of Charlotte, North Carolina, which had constructed various army camps, built the main diffusion-plant for the project at Oak Ridge, Tennessee. Chemical giant E. I. DuPont de Nemours and Company of Wilmington, Delaware was part of a collaboration with the army for the Hanford Engineer Works at Richland, Washington. TVA projects of the New Deal provided conventional power sources the project's endeavor. Thus, chemistry in the first war, then physics in the second, culminated in a wedding of government, academic and military scientific application heretofore unanticipated and beyond previous, traditional government-owned-and-government-operated facilities, whether Springfield Armory or the David Taylor Model Basin near Washington, D.C.[92]

America's military-industrial complex had taken yet another step. How Hacker and Vining see it, arrangements made to exploit research in World War II permanently transformed relations among America's military, technological, and scientific institutions. Private sector academic and industrial laboratories became more dependent on government funding or even more formal contractual arrangements for services. A subset of the product providers, together they would become major sources of military-technological innovation, joined at the hip in the name of national defense. The Radio Research Laboratory at Harvard and nearby Radiation Laboratory at M.I.T., through wartime work on military radar and guidance systems, entered a new matrix; a natural progression from industrial war mechanization, but with new frontiers in the Atomic Age of automation and computerization. Merle Tuve's Applied Physics Laboratory at Johns Hopkins University became as indispensable to government work as the University of California's Berkeley radiation laboratory, which morphed into the more famous Los Alamos facility of the Manhattan Project. Science as much as production now undergird everything, if albeit on a different scale.

* * *

Two overseas ventures with an interlude between tested America's mettle but accustomed Americans to public-private partnering forged by a centralized administrative state. Did that mean Americans accepted an arsenal or security state as some new normal? Historian Koistinen finds politicians like Roosevelt unfazed about growth of industrial-military power during the second war. True, War Department seizure of over 600 plants, and hundreds of strikes costing millions in man-hour productivity may have soured the country on any permanent national security state. From North American Aviation and U.S. Rubber, to 565 railroads, textile mills, tool and traction companies, and even merchandise giant Montgomery Ward witnessed government interventions and the power of Big Labor even in wartime. But, proliferation of alphabet agencies, armed service layers and Treasury department reach for taxpayer purses introduced a dedicated and permanent defense production establishment in historian Joel Davidson's view. Large-scale organization and management technology, infrastructure, and an accommodating society slowly joined physical sanctuary between 1916 and 1945 so that a victorious American military giant could now stride the earth. The atomic bomb provided a capstone to a wartime military-industrial-political-scientific complex.[93]

After World War I, Du Pont's advertising director George F. Lord explained the impact of that experience on his own profession where "the war has surely taught the necessity and value of preparedness for any great undertaking." America "had within itself all the spiritual, physical and financial powers to protect itself and to help other nations needing protection, he concluded. Still, "we were like the manufacturer who has all the materials, machinery, money and workers to produce an important necessity, but no organization to market it." Lack of preparedness or national organization "cost us and our allies a lot of trouble, losses and expense." By 1940–1945, Du Pont had diversified and explosives no longer occupied much of the company's over-all production. But, nylon, cellophane, neoprene, dye-stuffs, plastics, paints and "the literally several thousand products of the other nine [company] departments dwarfed the explosives department." A second world war's "production miracle eventually "changed nearly every part of the economy in some way," adds business historian Thomas McGraw. He might have included American attitudes as well.[94]

Chapter 6

THE COLD WAR MIC AND EISENHOWER'S WARNING, 1945-1991

The day after Pearl Harbor, newspaper editor Charles A. Mosher of Oberlin, Ohio, told his readers it was something of a "be of good cheer" editorial: "our morale is high today. We are completely determined to win," and "completely confident of winning." At one point, he advanced that since the first surprise was over and "before becoming completely rapt in the war's execution," by which he meant the "battle of production here at home," he also warned his audience to think about the future. "It is inevitable," suggested this future Ohio congressman, that "when the shooting is over the United States will emerge as the most powerful nation in the world." It was not a question of our seeking this "dominant position," he claimed, but "a sort of irresistible centripetal force in the world affairs is whirling us inevitably to it." While America does not ask for it, said Mosher, "it is to be our destiny that in the post war settlement we probably shall be in a position to more powerfully influence the future of humanity than has any other nation in history." So, "let us not forget that such power, even though unsought, will burden us with moral and practical responsibilities beyond those ever borne by any other nations." Mosher concluded that if Americans "accept our responsibilities and act upon them wisely, there is great hope for the world." The United States had become the indispensable nation.[1]

STANDING DOWN FROM VICTORY

Allied industrial and human muscle eventually brought victory in World War II. The United States had the atomic bomb, a vast resource base, and a pool of war veterans, with no devastation to the homeland. It also had little inclination to maintain what was called a "garrison state." Most of the war surplus involved over millions of rifles, pistols and machine weapons, 2.5 million trucks and tracked vehicles, over 13,000 tanks, 61,000 pieces of artillery, 1,201 major naval vessels, 5,600 merchant ships and 64,546 landing craft, not to mention also 296,000 aircraft (34,400 heavy and 55,500 medium bombers plus 98,700 fighters), millions of tons of bombs (plus two unused atomic versions), shells and explosives, as well as some 41.6 million rounds of small-arms ammunition. Once again, statistics reflected production capacity, even as armament became surplus. So, too, did the 1,600 new government plants built to forge this armada, at public expense of $12.7 billion, with an $6 additional billion spent to finance private plants. An infrastructure of facilities, production lines, and machine tools, had consumed 434,000 tons of steel. Moreover, the government needed to prune over 150 war agencies acquired by the executive branch of the Federal government, and now a particular target of the postwar business community. Styled "demobilization" or "reconversion," the legendary "Arsenal of Democracy" faced dismantling. There appeared to be no need for it anymore.[2]

Like mobilization, previous demobilization experience had been chaotic and unplanned. Military production stopped and veterans went home, though destined to be a potent force in postwar politics. But, if Congress had been obligingly generous with service benefits after the Civil War, and most niggardly towards its saviors after the initial world crusade, now it proved more obliging with the Servicemen's Readjustment Act or "GI Bill" of 1944, providing a variety of incentives and assistance to help transition human resources from war to peace. While the bill added to the public debt, it reflected New Deal Keynesian economics and was widely viewed as a firewall against the nation slipping back into economic Depression. With Washington desperately seeking stabilizers, the push to full employment found government war spending trailing off anyway. Abrupt contract terminations were planned as early as 1943, but a Contract Settlements Act the next July pointed to a negotiated, orderly, rapid, and financed downsizing to assure prime and subcontractors "speedy and equitable settlement," with adequate transition monies until final settlement. A wartime military-industrial "complex" needed to stand down. Parts of the arrangement like aviation remained particularly worrisome.[3]

Major dislocation occurred in sectors like aviation, ordnance, and military research. Only a small cadre shifted to manage surplus inventories at the government's Detroit tank plant. Army-Navy joint regulations ensured that within two days of V-J Day 60,000 contracts worth $7.3 billion had been terminated. Business and industry eventually lost a total of $20,000,000 in revenue. Nonetheless, a year later, favorable government prices enabled 250 of the largest firms to buy 70.1 percent of surplus plants, and their contents. Reliance on a diminished military and mothballed weaponry still supported by continuing research and development for public-private partnered scientific labs, even retention of over 200 defense plants deemed vital to national security (with perhaps an additional 100 unsaleable plants as an industrial reserve), seemed sufficient to military needs. Industrial age mobilization theoretically had not ended with the atomic bomb. But the nuclear stockpile was nil and postwar policy placed confidence in the Bretton Woods economic institutions for international recovery and redevelopment, the United Nations for collective security, and a residue of conventional war supplies readily available in need. Historian James F. Nagle posits, even "a degree of government intervention and control," that business resented even before the war, had proven acceptable.[4]

In the immediate postwar period when the Soviet Union was just beginning to pose a threat, adjustments were made. A "fire sale" on machine tools at 15 cents on the dollar seems ridiculous when by 1951 U.S. machine-tool production capacity had fallen to only one-third of 1941 levels and thirty-four companies simply had closed their doors. Still, Congress passed a Strategic and Critical Materials Stockpiling Act in 1946 to ensure a future reserve of such materials likely to be in short supply. An executive order within a week of victory over Japan that year also reconstituted the Munitions Board (Army and Navy Munitions Board), charged with planning for military-industrial emergency and coordination of such plans between the armed services. The board laid foundations for postwar economic mobilization planning for the next two years. A reconstituted Army Industrial College beginning in 1944 had already begun studying the wartime experience with military mobilization and thus began an almost parallel study and planning effort as the ANMB. Frankly, national security officers across Washington debated the success or failure of pre-World War II industrial mobilization plans and policy and determined that reform was in order. But, new policies, organization and procedures were soon swept up in the overall question of the day, called "unification."[5]

Recognizing the pitfalls of permitting industrial-age institutions, functions and public-private partnering to atrophy, an Armed Forces Procurement Act of 1947, National Industrial Reserve Act of 1948, together with 1948 renewal of military selective service conscription, held promise. So too did reorganization of government support of science with the political savvy of Dr. Vannevar Bush trying to coax his wartime Office of Scientific Research and Development toward new frontiers with a National Institutes of Health complex and a National Science Foundation shepherding basic versus applied research in competition with scientific and technological programs in a new Atomic Energy Agency (succeeding the old Manhattan project). Above all, official Washington focused mostly on defense reorganization through the more famous National Security Act of 1947. Under so-called "unification," the army favored continuation of industrial mobilization as a military responsibility as it had been since the National Defense Act of 1920. Yet, veteran bureaucrats Ferdinand Eberstadt and James Forrestal, for instance, argued the navy's case for a separate civilian agency. Lost in the ultimate struggle for control and power, unification rested on the need for unified organizational response, adequate government-industry planning prior to any declaration of war, and advisability of phased approach rather than a 1930s-style "M-day" coincidental with a declaration of war. It reflected America's continued struggle over civil-military control of national security and pointed to the need for public appreciation of peacetime preparedness and mobilization planning for both military and industry. Not that the public particularly cared at this point. The army and navy did and if American industry recognized and accepted lessons of coordination and cooperation with government in peacetime, then as industrial-preparedness advocate Roderick Vawter later implied, previous experience created a management receptivity vital to what Secretary of Defense Forrestal clearly saw as requirements of modern total war. War had evolved into integrated approach of economic, industrial and financial strengths with the term "national security" applied more universally.[6]

The National Security Act of July 1947 which still stands more than seventy-five years later as the national blueprint for defense in an American Sparta, provided an elaborate organizational structure outside the military establishment. Americans, to this day, recognize a Joint Chiefs of Staff and separate army, navy and air force services managed by a civilian Secretary of Defense as key features. The act also held for outside tools—a Central Intelligence Agency (CIA), a strategic advisory National Security Council (NSC), a National Security Resources Board (NSRB), a Munitions Board (MB) and a Research and Development Board (RDB)—all tacitly embracing a wider interpretation of national security and war-making. Of course, by 1947, the Soviet Union and ideological Communism had emerged as the new common enemy. But, as Louis Hunter concludes, the wording of the act settled little on the resourcing dimension of the unified arrangement. It simply provided yet another general framework "within which planning, both within and outside the military establishment would be conducted." The same could be advanced overall as a National Military Establishment subsequently restyled as a Department of Defense moved forward. Frankly, the difficulties of rationalizing peacetime resource planning meant the NSRB and MB became dysfunctional and marginalized. On the other hand, government and industry continued inseparable.[7]

Airpower seemingly held the operational key. It was now in vogue, and a cheaper road to military success in the minds of fiscally conservative politicians. A new and separate Air Force emerged from NSA-1947 with its own facilities and industrial base constituency to add, to army and navy lobbies. The government generally wanted to stimulate postwar commercial aviation anyway, as the sector faced decline due to diminished market, advent of new jet-propulsion technology, and surplus military aircraft not necessarily convertible to civilian use. Aircraft plants declined from sixty-six during the war to sixteen, most going back to producing automobiles and other consumer items, while $21 billion in government wartime contracts shrank to a mere $1.2 billion in commercial sales. Fifteen of the largest manufacturers had $620 billion working-capital in 1945 with only $13 billion in bank debts, but by 1947 firms like Lockheed, Republic, Convair (a merger in 1943 of Consolidated and Vultee firms), Northrup, and others, claimed millions a year in lost revenue. While industry leaders had welcomed federal subsidies before the war, they were unsure of such entanglements afterward. However, Washington realized that a new strategy based on the war-winning combination of aircraft and atomic bomb would require public-private partnership. Air Force research and development and sponsorship of an acclaimed think-tank RAND corporation, the Atomic Energy Commission, the civilian aviation industry, as well as a public which equated aviation with progress equal to that of Ford and Chevrolet automobiles all pointed the way. Business historian Thomas K. McCraw terms American aircraft production, "as probably the most significant industrial feat of World War II," surpassing the Manhattan Project. The Truman administration "actively sought to integrate aviation into the national defense program."[8]

Thus, military and industry leaders forged "an alliance eagerly supported by small businessmen and local politicians," claim business historians Keith L. Bryant and Henry C. Dethloff. Capitol Hill legislators certainly sensed how shaping aviation and new technologies might translate to jobs and facilities in their home districts. The military may have once more bridled at civilian control over policy and procurement, and some industrialists once again pushed back at sacrificing civilian to military products in peacetime, but economic largesse, tied to strategic choice, eventually outweighed any qualms. Strategic direction and consumerism were themes of the postwar period. Yet, as economic historians Robert L. Heilbroner and Aaron Singer have pointed out, a third stage in the changing role of U.S. government beckoned. Measures like Truman's 1946 Employment Act which committed to "promotion of 'maximum' employment through fiscal and monetary means," suggested a role for government as *guarantor* not regulator. Would this objective of maintaining socially acceptable rates of growth and levels of employment through a domestic "Fair Deal" transfer to postwar provision for the common defense? At this point international upheaval again intervened to prompt answers.[9]

TOWARD NEW STRATEGIC CALCULATIONS

International stability proved elusive after World War II. Apparently, Soviet Premier Josef Stalin was no longer spellbound by his own wartime toast, "to American production, without which this war would have been lost." Slowly, perceptibly, and perhaps inevitably, the world slipped back into Great Power competition and potential for renewed conflict. Bilateral polarity came from a capitalist free world in contrast and conflict with a communist autarchic world. Eventually a "third world" appeared, emerging from colonialism, vying for attention, and permanently fragile. The United States and Russia offered lodestars of threats and promises based on the power of military victory and self-righteous confidence. Both sides would jockey for nearly five decades in acquisition of clients and satellites, utilization of the instruments of DIME power (diplomatic, informational, military and economic), carrot-and-stick in play at different times and places. Neither side dominated the other. Miraculously, the world escaped a third world war when Russia acquired the atomic bomb and provocatively tweaked the west over places like Berlin, Eastern Europe and the Middle East. China slipped into the communist orbit while American interventionism, through the Marshall Plan for nation rebuilding and the Bretton Woods economics arrangement, dampened but never completely ameliorated Third World chaos. Possibly, Franklin Roosevelt's grand design for a postwar-world global peace based on the United Nations regime, could not have survived his death. Over time, the UN proved utopian at best. What economic historian Hugh Rockoff calls "the War against Communism," including interventions like Korea and Vietnam, "was by far the longest, and in terms of financial resources the costliest, war in American history."[10]

Roosevelt's successor Harry Truman if nothing else was a pragmatist. In the wartime U.S. Senate, he had chaired the select committee exploring fraud, waste, and contracts and procurement abuses. Upon Roosevelt's death, he assumed the presidency to preside over what professor William C. Martel calls the "transformation" of the United States to the most powerful Western country in the postwar era, "the central accomplishment of Truman's grand strategy." His domestic Fair Deal aimed at initiatives for health care, government spending, and civil rights, no less related to national security as a broadened definition of "common defense" now obtained. He advocated "pay-as-you-go" taxation with possible deficit spending as-necessary in an emergency, but a sound economy was uppermost. He consistently vetoed Pentagon requests for lifting the $15 billion cap on the 1950 defense budget. However, emergence of the Soviet Union as the preeminent political, military and ideological threat to American global power eventually caused his administration to reorient America's grand strategy toward rearmament and a permanent national security state including a "military-industrial-political complex." The story, from a patience prescription of State department Sovietologist George Kennan and his Policy Planning Staff to successor Paul Nitze's hardline NSC-68 policy paper is well known. Truman's surprise victory in the 1948 election and the march of communism led to what Cold War historian John Gaddis and others term "militarization of containment." The formative period overlapped into the Eisenhower administration.[11]

In succession came collapse of democracy in much of Europe, the Berlin crisis, China passing into the communist orbit, the explosion of a Soviet atomic test-bomb, and eventually the Korean War in June 1950. Deterring Soviet aggression rested upon a rearming North Atlantic Treaty Organization coalition and American atomic-airpower. By early 1950, as Truman readied a decision on development of thermonuclear weapons to stay ahead of the Soviet atomic program, a response to warning signs appeared necessary. The resourcing panoply now extended from Marshall Plan aid and military assistance programs to enhance stabilization and formation of the North Atlantic Treaty Organization and on through conventional rearmament to sharply escalated nuclear weapons programs. American troops returned to European assignments as NATO was "collective security" at its most promising, restoring America's commitment to the defense of partnering. Collective military action by the United Nations remained to be proven, so this alternate pattern seemed obvious: $13 billion in economic recovery comported with strategic partnering, especially in Greece and Turkey, shielding NATO member states rearming for self-defense and trans-Atlantic collaboration. True, such direction conflicted with the administration's fiscal probity, and also with America's time-honored avoidance of entangling alliances. When war surpluses ran out, it proved a path to securitization of the American state and reinstituting "the arsenal of democracy" with new power and purpose.[12]

In a way, Korea provided the catalyst for America's new security state eventually based on a military-industrial-political complex. It started with a small group of State department planning experts and moved through months of deliberation to spell out a strategy for an unfolding "Cold War" between East and West. Eventually identified with staff director Paul H. Nitze, the famous National Security Council document 68 (NSC-68), first rejected by Truman as too costly until the North Korean invasion of its southern neighbor introduced panicky acceptance of militarized containment, rearmament, deterrence, and the guide by national government for implementation over the next four decades. The public knew nothing of NSC-68 but fell in line with the administration when Truman declared a national emergency upon Red China's joining the war in December 1950. Public paranoia suddenly jelled even though that conflict eventually stalemated in an inconclusive armistice. Visions of Russia's Soviet army knifing its way to the English Channel, Red Chinese hordes pouring across Asia and communist infiltration of U.S. government agencies like State and AEC gripped Capitol Hill and the media. Realization that the Free World had a daunting peer froze people with fear. Assuming the maintenance of present policies, a large U.S. advantage might remain, said Nitze's group, but "the Soviet Union will be steadily reducing the discrepancy between its overall economic strength and that of the U.S. by continuing to devote proportionately more to capital investment than the United States." While a full-scale American effort would "precipitately alter this trend, the USSR today was on a "near maximum production basis." As seen in a Soviet atomic capability, "the totalitarian state, at least in time of peace can focus its efforts on any given project far more readily than the democratic state." As long as the Soviet Union was virtually mobilized and the United States had scarcely begun to do so, U.S. capabilities "are to that extent inoperative in the struggle for power."[13]

Soviet conventional military power was one thing, but Soviet atomic potential scared U.S. planners the most. Admitting a high level of uncertainty, Central Intelligence, military, and Atomic Energy Commission analysts computed a Soviet production capability for a fission bomb stockpile at a five-year moment of maximum danger. Production of ten to twenty bombs by mid-1950, twenty-five to forty-five by the next year, forty-five to ninety by mid-1952 and seventy to one hundred and thirty-five by mid-1953 with two hundred by mid-1954 would yield a capability for delivering one-hundred atomic bombs on U.S. targets that "would seriously damage this country." Anticipating surprise attack, with no better defenses than the U.S. and its allies had programmed to date, Soviet development of thermonuclear capability would be even more serious. The U.S. military budget represented six to seven percent of its gross national product (GNP) while the Soviet Union was allocating forty percent of its gross available resources to military purposes and investment, much of it in war-support industries. The

United States was devoting only twenty percent to defense. Still, "if a dynamic expansion of the economy could be achieved," the necessary defense build-up could be accomplished without a decrease in the national standard of living, since required resources could be obtained "by siphoning off a part of the annual increment in the gross national product." Truman initially had wanted more cost estimates of anticipated programs, the president's reluctance evaporated with Chinese communist intervention. Korea seemed a prelude to world conquest.[14]

Korean intervention even under UN coalition banners eventually cost the United States nearly 140,000 casualties and upwards of $1.8 billion (in 2008 dollars computes economist Rockoff). Higher taxes paid for it, stringent price controls were again imposed, and public support sagged about the necessity of intervention with the rising tallies of costs in lives and outcome short of accustomed victory. The Russians never moved; communist China had intervened and the United Nations eventually brokered a stalemate. Korea rallied strategic consensus within the American government. So, communist and democratic orbits, Russia and the U.S. would warily joust with one another for the next half-century and beyond. From such came a cascade of strategic plans and iterations, provocations and responses with NSC-68 giving way to NSC 162/2 under the Eisenhower administration's "Project Solarium" by 1953 and endless other programs and implementation tools like economic assistance (aid-grants and loans), CSA sponsored clandestine operations, civilian defense, material stockpiling, propaganda, intelligence, and internal security—even relentless production of atomic weapons and Air Force delivery systems, as well as steady conventional military buildup. Price tags of $35.8 billion in fiscal year 1951 for the resultant security state with its defense industrial base and administrative apparatus escalated to $63.4 billion by 1953, with overtones for 1954 as the year of maximum danger. "No nation has ever had a greater responsibility than ours at this moment," Truman intoned, "we must remember that we are the leaders of the free world." Americans would never be allowed to forget it.[15]

America rallied around a strategy of containment of communism, deterrence of Soviet and other aggression, maintenance of alliances, avoidance of nuclear and thermonuclear war as well as excessive military preparations or complacency—a middle ground of military readiness both conventional and nuclear. Mobilization planning passed to an Office of Defense Mobilization in December 1950 via eclipse of both national security resource and munitions boards. The armed services and DoD willingly grabbed resourcing for what the Eisenhower administration's Project Solarium national-level exercise in strategy and foreign policy in 1953 subsequently envisioned as a "New Look" long haul. If the new approach rejected pro-active "roll-back strategy" for the Soviet adversary, it rested securely upon national security with military-industrial-political complex (MIPC) rearmament at its core and implicit buy-in from all sectors and strata of American society (perhaps carefully orchestrated by Establishment elites). Truman had never asked for a declaration of war, nor did his successors. Eisenhower rejected any more land wars like Korea but thought fiscal probity could ride on clandestine programs and threat of "Massive Retaliation." Henceforward, a "guns and butter" philosophy governed resourcing national security. Leon Keyersling, chairman of Truman's Council of Economic Advisers, laid it out in a December 8, 1950 memorandum to the president. The programs enumerated in NSC-68/3 "represent a relatively brief maximum effort toward a limited objective." A target-strength of 3.2 million men for June 1952 would be but 4.5 percent of the total labor force, compared with over seventeen percent, or 12.3 million men at the peak of World War II. Military production at its highest would absorb no more than fifteen to twenty percent of total steel supply, compared to well over fifty percent late in the Second World War. Absorption of copper would be less than one-third of supply compared to two-thirds in that conflict with aluminum less than one-third, compared with over eighty percent in World War II. Keyserling confidently asserted that NSC-68 "programs in terms of their economic implications fall about half way between 'business as usual' and a really large-scale dedication of our enormous economic resources to the defense of our freedoms," even when defining this large-scale dedication as "far short of an all-out war or all out economic mobilization for war purposes." With limited-wartime controls, military targets could be maintained indefinitely, civilian consumption levels restored relatively quickly, balances between programs maintained, and critical material stockpiles accumulated. Defense, civilian, and international needs "are of such a size that none can be given an absolute priority."[16]

Keyserling's confidence would undergird strategic guidance and planning for decades. Korea rendered atomic warfare practically unthinkable but no official dared admit it. The Soviets had "the bomb," as did Great Britain, France and Communist China for what was later dubbed "mutually assured destruction" (MAD). The Korean stalemate guaranteed MIPC's survivability and Solarium its expansion - profitability, if systematized and institutionalized "for the duration," in some larger Cold War contest. Would the blueprint have looked any different? Would some other crisis or series of crises have spawned or perpetuated a military-industrial complex? Ike's complex was inevitable, given the domestic stakes of power, Soviet intransigence, containment/deterrence strategy and Free versus Communist world ideological, political, economic and socio-cultural competition. Korea simply moved up the timetable and size. The detailed comparisons, statistics and conclusions always would have eluded average American taxpayers who had accustomed themselves to countering threats to America's way of life, economy and happiness, starting in 1917, even more so in 1941 and certainly by the 1950s. Korea and other domino threats to the Free World, portrayal of Communist expansionism undergird by Soviet military power and agenda, especially a strategic nuclear sneak-attack, sent chills down the spine of red-blooded, patriotic, hegemonic and democratic-capitalist Americans accustomed to anti-Red tirades from Right-Wing politicians like Joseph McCarthy stoking that fear. Any concern for limits on taxes, budgets, and World War II-like constraints, fell before the new mindset. Security concerns depicted mushroom clouds and "duck and cover" air raid drills for an impending apocalypse, and a nation "sadly wanting in real military might." Kennan's containment was bluff without rearmament. Nitze's containment promised survival. Ike's riposte represented perpetuity.[17]

Memories of the Red Scare after World War I, the Munich appeasement in 1938 or even Russian comrades as part of the World War II coalition lurked in the shadows. Of course, domestic bankruptcy through militarization of the state and even nuclear war always loomed. Historian William C. Martel points out that under NSC-68 guidance, annual U.S. defense spending would grow "from $14.3 billion [that Truman managed to restrain] to $50 billion," or a fourfold increase from 5 percent to 20 percent of GNP over the decade after Korea. Expenditure on nuclear deterrence alone would prove staggering; but, after all, NSC-68 was designed to shock top government into rearmament. Strong isolationist sentiment among Republican senators Robert Taft, Arthur Vandenberg or William Knowland, aversion to profligate New Deal/Fair Deal domestic spending, the basic American negativity toward "statism," and extending American engagement abroad, together provided backdrop. Historian Hal Brands notes up to 1950 almost nobody in Washington had thought South Korea "constituted a core U.S. security interest," but by this point they did and still would, seven decades later! "Containment" was here to stay. Whether other post-World War II options realistically included disengagement, rollback, spheres of influence as viable alternatives remained uncertain. In the words of yet another NSC policy paper, to withdraw and let Korea disintegrate would "be interpreted as a betrayal by the U.S. of its friends and allies in the Far East and might well lead to a fundamental realignment of forces in favor of the Soviet Union throughout that part of the world." Here was America's mantra heard 'round the globe. In time Korea became "the forgotten war," except for an eerily haunting monument image just off the national mall in Washington. There would always be tugs "between the stimulus of international pressures, a preference for limited liability, and the desire to remake the international order in America's own image," claims historian Colin Dueck. But, the Truman administration "finally closed the gap between capabilities and commitments by increasing defense spending after 1950." A military-industrial-political complex inevitably lay ahead.[18]

MOVING TOWARD IKE'S MILITARY INDUSTRIAL COMPLEX

Between 1945 and 1950, America spent over $115 billion on new plants and equipment to increase production capabilities. This investment raised overall output capacity by 40 percent although most of the money went to making consumer goods. Then, Korea had forced reallocation of industrial resources. Congress responded in September with the Defense Production Act of 1950. This act gave the president unprecedented authority to mobilize the economy through priorities and allocations, requisitioning and condemnation, expansion of production capacity and supply, price and wage stabilization, labor dispute settlement, control of consumer and real estate credit, and other general provisions for small business encouragement, authority to create new agencies, issue regulations, gather information, and administrate small defense plants and voluntary agreements. Chinese intervention in Korea waylaid Truman's original intent of using the National Security Resources Board and Munitions Board for conducting mobilization, instead instituting a new temporary agency, the Office of Defense Mobilization (ODM), to do so. The agency director became a member of the cabinet and National Security Council. Established customarily within existing departments, other temporary agencies followed, including the National Production Authority, Defense Production Authority, and Defense Manpower Administration. An exception was the Economic Stabilization Authority. It sounded like the world wars all over again.[19]

Indeed, naturally replicating the approach taken in World War II, with which that generation of government officials would have been the most familiar, NSC-68 called for a one-year war reserve with key provisions of the Defense Production System allowing for rapid amortization over 5 years of mobilization-related facilities. Congress and the administration provided additional incentives and support, through guaranteed markets and prices for machine tools and raw materials, encouraged expansion via government-directed and guaranteed commercial-loan programs, covered the cost of new facilities and special tooling, provided government-owned facilities and equipment, generally through leasing, for use by manufacturers (GOCO), and offered government grants for research and development. In short, claimed one study, under the DPA, the Revenue Act of 1950, and other enabling legislation flowing from NSC-68, the United States as a result of Korea "reconstituted the defense industrial base that had been allowed to deteriorate so quickly after World War II." It also had the recipe for a warfare state to enable endless wars.[20]

Expansion of military production claimed priority because of Korea. Still, the real challenge lay with building adequate war reserves and a production base to sustain prolonged confrontation and possibly fight a survivable full-scale conflict with the Soviet Union. Goals resembled those of World War II—expand production capacity to fabricate 50,000 airplanes and 35,000 tanks a year, as well as 18,000 jet engines a month. Issues soon surfaced: a scarcity of engineers, designers and draftsmen, limited output of machine tools and other production equipment, diversion of productive capacity to old or new models, and lead-time delays for electronic equipment rather than airframe. Nonetheless, the army activated a new Detroit Ordnance Tank-Automotive Center with auxiliary government ownership/contractor operation of the Lima, Ohio ordnance depot, and its own laboratories. Production of all types of military aircraft reached almost 1,000 per month by January 1953, and more than 100 shipyards worked on a naval rearmament program, with nineteen combat ships launched in late 1951 and 1952. The keel for the first atomic-powered submarine was laid, and artillery pieces appeared at increasing rates giving army divisions a seventy-five percent increase in firepower over World War II counterparts. Technological advances in weaponry complicated but did not confound America's industrial capacity. Making nuclear weapons integrated smoothly into this new buildup through the Atomic Energy Commission. Moreover, the superiority of American weapons supposedly offset the Soviet advantage in numbers. A new emphasis placed the need for constant and intensive research "along the frontiers of the physical sciences and for translation of that research into practical, producible weapons." As new weapons developed, "a balance had to be maintained between sustained qualitative superiority and volume production." Falling behind in either "could spell destruction." A shift also emerged for developing a common global mobilization base or capacity involving not only NATO, but also supplying aid money and sending arms and advisers wherever needed. Aiding NATO, integrating a Western European defense industrial base and strengthening European economic recovery were mutually shared goals.[21]

Under the "guns and butter" scheme, Korean War era mobilization had another purpose: to expand basic U.S. economy and industrial capacity, permitting simultaneous growth in both defense expenditures and gross national production. Improvement in the country's standard of living would reinforce public acceptance of higher defense expenditures and create a powerful industrial base capable of supporting an all-out war of indeterminate scope and duration. Focus went to steel, aluminum, petroleum and other vital nonferrous minerals, chemicals, and electric power. World War II had shown that expansion of basic capacity added flexibility to the economy and allowed later expansion of specialized capacity. In the end, the overall government program proved extremely broad, extending to infrastructure projects like transcontinental petroleum pipelines, heavy forging and extrusion presses principally useful to airframe construction, other machine tools, and transport capacity of railroad equipment, oceangoing tankers, and inland waterway containers. An interstate highway system would bond Americans as well as contribute to a permanent mobilization base, "the approach by which the United States addressed a new situation in the world, a national security need for military readiness to the constant threat from the USSR." As the director of Defense Mobilization outlined in November 1952, it was "that capacity available to permit expansion of production, sufficient to meet military, war-supporting, essential civilian, and export requirements in event of a full-scale war," including "elements of essential services, food, raw materials, facilities, production equipment, organization and manpower." It depended upon strength, character and flexibility, laid against relentless deadlines. Here were the world wars once more–only in peacetime.[22]

Deviations appeared as Korea stalemated. Certain DPA provisions were repealed, including agricultural-product restrictions and requisitioning, as well as condemnation. Moreover, Korean mobilization experience led certain officials to advocate production-capacity expansion, over stockpiling military end items. The idea became one of "a larger productive capacity to produce military end items [which] must be created and thereafter must be maintained in such a condition that can be quickly expanded in the event of an emergency by merely adding manpower and hours of operation." Timing was everything in mobilization, obsolescence of military equipment was a fact of late industrial-age warfare, while "the creation and maintenance of ample production capacity is not only less costly and more practical than depending chiefly on reserves of military material, it also represents a greater contribution to national security." Proponents argued for realistic mobilization requirements, expenditure on new production capacity and keeping such capacity modernized. They advocated new budgeting procedures bridging the gap between service funding of initial consumptive war reserves and mobilization production levels. They wanted healthy support of a production equipment industry, retention of capacity in certain types of large, heavy forging and casting beyond private commercial needs (as in heavy Army tank armor), and, in fact, modernization of all domestic industrial production facilities, whether specific to military need or not. ODM's advocacy actually led to a purely military mobilization base. Perhaps, suggests mobilization analyst Roderick Vawter, "the seeds of the ultimate deterioration of mobilization planning and capability were planted by the concept of a dedicated military mobilization base," or simply "by a natural outgrowth of policy recommendations." Here was another building block for a large, stabilized defense industry base as one pillar of a national security state.[23]

Americans, unhappy about Korea, gladly consigned the Truman administration to history in the 1952 election. Truman's successor, former General Dwight D. Eisenhower, brokered a Korean truce the next year. Yet, even then there could be no demobilization in the traditional sense. A subsequent generation of historians would credit Truman with redirecting American grand strategy to indicate "political will and economic and military capacity to lead the rest of the world in a struggle against communism and totalitarianism." William Martel views Truman's legacy as an ability to balance the political values of freedom and economic might along with U.S. military and technological power that eventually would transfer to a post-Cold War era. Thus, Truman, he claims, "is among the most significant and enduring of modern American presidents." Possibly so, although subsequent administrations had little choice given the momentum if not insidious influence of what Eisenhower would term an elite "military-industrial complex." Fellow scholar Colin Dueck thinks that from where Truman left off, the gradual escalation in costs and commitments of containment and deterrence over time "allowed both Congress and the American public to digest the awesome implications of this ambitious new strategy piece by piece." Premier authority on the political economy of American warfare, Paul A. C. Koistinen decreed that the MIC developed from "the militarized Cold War," and "eventually began to grow beyond the control of responsible authorities."[24]

Any Truman-era fiscal conservatism evaporated with fiscal year 1952 Defense authorization hitting $56.9 billion, another $5 billion for security-related projects, and $6 billion more for military assistance. Few in government, much less the general public, knew what was then being spent on the nation's super-secret nuclear warfare programs for R&D, fabrication of devices, maintenance of facilities, or testing and deployment. Even here the programs entailed a rush to production in quantity, with attendant dismissal or benign ignorance of health implications, and environmental damage at production plants, storage sites and test locations. The atomic/nuclear weapons program was the worst of all. Given the noxious air of McCarthyism, with its relentless pressure of perceived threat and labeling non-commitment as treason, few people dared question cost figures or need for an ongoing, consistent audit. Connecticut Democratic senator Brien McMahon claimed in 1951 that too little, not too much, went for nuclear programs. This was the era of "duck and cover" in school classrooms, public and private fallout shelters, and marriage of devices with weapons carriers (bombs, later, missile warheads). Up to 1953, the AEC spent roughly $1.7 billion, and the Air Force in the range of $352 to $363 billion, on their shares of nuclear-related programs. Development and deployment of nuclear munitions can be calculated as part of the Cold War defense industrial base. However, the most transparent part of the story remained the traditional armed forces, expanding around the world with human and material resources, as well as organization and missions. America's defense perimeter, blurred as "everywhere," had to be defended.[25]

Eisenhower embraced containment policy but bridled at its escalating costs. Fiscal probity, smaller government and bureaucracy, curtailment of domestic programs, and the growing nuclear capability as primary deterrent offered "more bang for the buck." This was Ike's "New Look" policy with "massive retaliation" via nuclear airpower as strategy and Secretary of State John Foster Dulles as its chosen apostle. After Soviet premier Josef Stalin's death in March 1953, though a temporary pause settled over Soviet-American relations, the Kremlin soon returned to testing western resolve with an ever-spiraling nuclear arms race, "Bison" intercontinental bombers and intercontinental ballistic missiles. Brutal repression of the Hungarian revolution in 1956 tested the viability of both "Massive Retaliation" and "rollback" interventionism. Senior American military leaders, aside from the Air Force, fought nuclear reliance tooth-and-nail and argued convincingly by the late 1950s for something styled the "New New Look," calling for greater expenditure on conventional arms. Russian launch of the Sputnik satellite in October 1957 and its implied technology gap between the USSR and US sent new shivers through Washington and the general public. A restive Congress soon embarked upon closing "a spending gap" with the USSR over what was called "the bomber gap," followed later by "the missile gap." Close lobbying by the service chiefs (often challenging their commander-in-chief and his strategic and fiscal wishes), plus the growing ties "between public and private bureaucratic organizations working together to further their own interests at the expense of the public good," deeply disturbed Eisenhower, claim business historians William M. McClenahan and William H. Becker. Maybe a pliant Congress adding $900 million to the Air Force budget during the FY 1957 budget process despite Ike's desire for fiscal restraint, caused so much White House consternation. What alarmed the president, they contend, was the size of military spending that would bring on the garrison state. Moreover, "the specter of military and industrial organizations forming an alliance with each other" together with powerful political leaders on both sides of the aisle in Congress, threatened the very political and economic freedom of the republic in the name of national defense. This came to public attention via Eisenhower's televised farewell advice about a "military-industrial complex." But as a distinct warning shot, his words failed to alter much of anything.[26]

Eisenhower's legacy, suggests Martel, lay with the word "balance." Cost-effective strategies for balancing the ends and means, meant "helping the United States mobilize just enough of its economy and society to deter war with Moscow without weakening the American economy with more defense spending than it could reasonably or prudently bear." Such might be said in hindsight. But, Russian plus Chinese intransigence, destabilization in a neutral "Third World" following decolonization (or dis-imperialism), provided opportunities for American and Russian adventurism, military equipment markets, and use of covert Central Intelligence Agency programs in places from Latin America to Iran and Africa. No American politician could stand to be accused of weakness on national defense. The Soviets only respected force and would talk and negotiate only when confronted with such force, Truman had stressed. No wonder historian Hal Brands attributes America's quadrupling of its atomic arsenal and saber-rattling via global American military presence, bases and cooperative partnering as "bound to be threatening to Moscow." That was built into deterrence policy as risk-taking and confidence-building even while American politics heralded cutting government programs, and maintaining economic probity. If the Truman-era grand strategy was often "a messy affair, and in some ways a deeply problematic one," Brands ventures, it was also a prophetic one. Truman, the "hard-money man" from Missouri, worried in private that "our resources are not inexhaustible," and wartime higher taxes and growing budget deficits were perennially an anathema to both he and Eisenhower. Brands labels the Truman years as a time of grand strategic "determination and accomplishment" as well as "one of frustration, errors, and trade-offs as well." The same might be said of his successors' terms in office also.[27]

Eisenhower's coining of the term "military-industrial- complex" has echoed sporadically ever since his farewell speech to the American people in 1961. Possibly, his interstate highway system was more enduring to the nation, in the long-term. But those travel arteries too had national security and military intent. Though much was made of his warning about the MIC on its fiftieth anniversary in 2011, all too few people thoroughly parsed his words either in 1961 or thereafter. Ike's successor, the more glamorous John F. Kennedy, promised new frontiers for facing "a hostile ideology, global in scope, atheistic in character, ruthless in purpose, and insidious in method." Kennedy and others embraced and used the power of what was handed to them in theory and form. Yes, Eisenhower particularly thought "we have been compelled to create a permanent armaments industry of vast proportions," devote 3.5 million men and women to the defense establishment, fund a permanently large security budget and a powerful elite of military and bureaucratic officials, legislators and defense contractors who would devote careers to growing missions and programs. "The total influence—economic, political, even spiritual—is felt in every city, every statehouse, every office of the federal government," he observed, adding "we recognize the imperative for this development," but "must not fail to comprehend its implications." The Silent Generation of the Fifties paid little heed. Perhaps Ike's solemn tone and style put off the general populace. Or perhaps defense economics via rearmament and defense industry had become too alluring to the American psyche. Perhaps everyone in America lusted for power, destiny and boundless endeavor. Time would tell.[28]

"Our toil, resources and livelihood are all involved," as was the very structure of society, promised the fatherly Eisenhower. The weight of this combination should not be allowed to "endanger our liberties or democratic processes." Nothing could be taken for granted as "only an alert and knowledgeable citizenry" could compel "the proper meshing of the huge industrial and military machinery of defense with our peaceful method and goals so that security and liberty may prosper together." The tasks of statesmanship, Eisenhower declared, was "to mold, to balance, and to integrate" forces new and old within the principles of America's democratic system—ever aiming toward the "supreme goals of our free society." The impulse to plunder "for our own ease and convenience the precious treasures of tomorrow" had to be shunned, lest the mortgaging of the material assets "of our grandchildren" also would risk loss of their political and spiritual heritage. Ike also spoke of the imperative of disarmament "with mutual honor and confidence" and how mankind needed to overcome differences, not with arms, "but with intellect and decent purpose." His final words to the American people suggested, "during the long lane of the history yet to be written, America knows that this world of ours, ever growing smaller must avoid becoming a community of dreadful fear and hate, and be, instead, a proud confederation of mutual trust and respect." In the end, Dwight David Eisenhower also fretted science and scientists (public and private) becoming too integrated with defense research and policymakers too addicted to a sponsored scientific-technological elite. But, for political reasons, he held back from adding Congress or politicians to any Complex. He should have done so, as it turned out.

Eventually scholars like Duke University historian Alex Roland gave Eisenhower's words a greater context. When the president referred to a military-industrial complex and a scientific-technological elite, what he really meant was what other commentators styled a "permanent war economy," "the garrison state," the influence of a power elite or, quite frankly, "militarism." In Roland's interpretation, Eisenhower was convinced that "the real contest" [between Soviet Union and the United States] was not between arsenals but between economic and political systems. America could only win against a garrison state if it did not become one itself. Yet, the next three decades witnessed the flowering of Ike's warning, dictated by events, resting on fear, domestic acquiescence, and a permanent war economy. "MIPC" stabilized the international system as well as a domestic prosperity. America's public and private elites promoted national security by relying on a strategy of global containment and deterrence, punctuated by occasional (and not always successful) intervention to counter communist expansion. Eisenhower's hawkish Keynesian successor John F. Kennedy, attached a full-growth economy and deficit-spending approach to a new strategy styled "flexible response." America welcomed relief from Ike's austerity and promise of all-or-nothing nuclear "massive retaliation" although the Cuban missile crisis was a close escape. The growing "MIPC" provided ever more tools for the new strategy and its contribution of conventional weaponry for full-spectrum contingencies coupled with misguided approaches of Presidents Lyndon B. Johnson and Richard M. Nixon eventually led directly into a Southeast Asian quagmire. Eisenhower's America had promised no more land wars like Korea. Kennedy's, Johnson's and Nixon's strategic version promised to go anywhere and pay any price to preserve friends and democracy. A glamorous "Camelot" rode on programs like the Peace Corps and Alliance for Progress, while consortia such as NATO, SEATO, and CENTO with the CIA and military held the ramparts of security, largely with armaments traceable to the American MIPC and the European Economic Community as well as military and economic aid all over the Free World including apartheid South Africa. Vietnam further proved the nation was capable of guns and butter, just not victory.[29]

Were there truly any options after Kennedy's assassination in 1963? Was the costly failure to prevent Vietnam from sliding into the communist orbit, "the mobilization that never was," or just another watershed that domestically soured Americans due to over 50,000 dead? Nixon and his shrewd Secretary of State Henry Kissinger achieved détente with Communist China, their actions suggesting a recognition that America's resources were no longer infinite. The Vietnam decade displayed its own political and economic determinism thanks to investment of perhaps $30 billion per year and half a million troops at a ten per cent casualty rate, with North Vietnam forcibly unifying that country's halves by 1975. Arkansas senator J. William Fulbright's warning about an "arrogance of power" resonated with an antiwar movement, a war-weary populace and a beleaguered leadership stretching beyond Johnson and Nixon. Vietnam, at least, ended America's experience with peacetime conscription. Although it hollowed out the military for over a decade and provided much angst in Washington about the defense of the nation, it hardly applied brakes to the MIPC. Any customary post-conflict dip in defense expenditures notwithstanding. MIPC controlled its own destiny from there on out.[30]

Historians Jerel A. Rosati and James M. Scott may be correct. The Cold War era contained two subsets. First, a fixed and firmly militarized period after World War II for containing and deterring the Soviet threat worldwide was based on American leadership of the international political economy, supported by a foreign economic policy solidly formed on the Bretton Woods system. Yet, this period also produced a modern "military-industrial complex" to underscore containment/détente resolve. Vietnam and a deterioration of the Bretton Woods system under Nixon (thanks to the relative decline in the U.S. economy, economic recovery of Europe and rise of Japan, as well as emergence of the powerful Organization of Petroleum Exporting Countries (OPEC) in the Middle East), occurred while the U.S. was preoccupied with Southeast Asia. American preeminence then gave way to a second Cold War subset when not only foreign economic policy regained importance, but traditional foreign policy appeared incoherent and inconsistent. The ever-present influence of MIPC adjusted smoothly in both cases. Call it the late Cold War whereby a certain accommodation with both the Soviet Union and Communist China offered a maturing east-west balance of power. Sobering experience and sanity now dictated that both sides could live with one another without resorting to major war. Détente, or mutually assured destruction (MAD), held sway, traceable to the contributions of the MIPC. Presidents came and went with Nixon, Gerald Ford, Jimmy Carter and Ronald Reagan, their grand strategies and ideals tested by unfolding events short of East-West confrontation. Disintegrating Iranian-American relations due to hostage-taking, an oil embargo challenging domestic drift at home, Camp David Accords temporarily reducing Arab-Israeli discord in the Middle East with Soviet adventurism in Afghanistan tempering both détente and strategic arms control. The cycle proved a resiliency to Eisenhower's adjustable, responsive strategy and "military-industrial complex," politicians fascinated by military strength, new and better weapons technology, professionalization of the "all-volunteer military," and constituencies sharing in security state beneficence.[31]

TECHNOLOGY AND A PERMANENT DEFENSE INDUSTRY

Research Development Test and Evaluation (RDT&E) was now the key for both the United States and the Soviet Union. Both sides relentlessly plied military, not commercial application. By the 1960-s and 1970s, the United States had mobilized for the Cold War's duration, with a peacetime defense industrial base in place. So had Russia. America's unique arrangement kicked in as it had in World War II. Its organic components joined by private contractors when, for example the army's original Springfield arsenal stopped producing firearms in 1968. The private roster still included names like General Motors, Ford, Consolidated Vultee, Douglas, United Aircraft, Bethlehem Steel, General Electric, Chrysler, Lockheed, North America, Boeing, AT&T, Martin, DuPont, Westinghouse, and Grumman, although mergers and changes were in the wind. By 1960, new names like Raytheon, Sperry-Rand and IBM appeared among the top players. Mobilization planning waned in the government bureaucracy as slowly the National Priorities and Defense Materials System faded, along with long-dormant mobilization plans. Even the lessons of World War II and Korea withered with predictable result. Traditional peacetime issues resurfaced, such as long lead times, civilian orders given priority by producers, military-service competition for contracts with the same producer, and "as might be expected, the low-profile buildup did nothing to encourage historically hesitant private industry to expand its defense-related facilities." Government resorted to incentives and reactivating its own reserve plants, for example twenty-two of twenty-four ammunition producers. However, increased orders to private industry firms absorbed scarce surplus capacity, thwarting long-term modernization at plant facilities. Did any of this make a significant difference? Strategic outcomes rested with a nuclear armaments race leaving heavily armed but fiscally overextended superpowers to manage proxy wars. A cowed public practiced "duck and cover" civil defense drills.[32]

The United States particularly began a sharply escalated, almost vertical production direction for nuclear devices by 1955, peaking at many thousands stockpiled by the time of Vietnam with peak deployment, however, coming much later. That said, concern for the big "M" (military) of "DIME" drove American national security policy. Yet, by the 1970s, budgets were slimmed, a so-called "hollow" military appeared, and public interest and willpower slumped. The MIPC elite weathered traditional highs and lows, and survived a chorus of complaints about its sinister role in promoting overseas expeditions while yielding only economic burden. This MIPC elite appeared protected, funded and stoked by Washington. Détente-like containment enabled sufficient defense budgets despite partisan complaint and some public dissent but a defense revival started late in the Carter presidency, before his winsome successor Ronald Reagan garnered most of the credit for rebuilding assertive, global military power. It was always a waiting game of relative feast and famine for weapons merchants anyway. Then, suddenly reintroduction of "mobilization" capability as a strategic ploy offsetting perceived Soviet numbers. for global containment translated to the threat and use of force reminiscent of the early Cold War. In succession, a resurgence of multilateralism with the advent of Soviet president Mikhail Gorbachev, the influences of Margaret Thatcher (Great Britain) and Helmut Kohl (West Germany), combined with Reagan's leadership to help fracture the Eastern Bloc. Economic pressures of a renewed Soviet–U.S. arms race over a "Star Wars" missile defense system were also at play. Even so, fascination with the macho Reaganesque style, and a conviction that unilateral American technological power and resolve ended the Cold War, became gospel. Was the real ending more Kennanesque than Nitzian, both represented in Solarium solutions? Or had Ike's military-industrial complex and resiliency of capitalism really tipped the scales? Answers to both questions were "yes."[33]

Scholars more recently have traced the ending to the beginning, in Truman's redirection of American grand strategy "to indicate political will and economic and military capacity to lead the world in a struggle against communism and totalitarianism." In effect, the Truman administration had set in motion a remobilized military-industrial complex from the world wars but now across a strategic spectrum. Revisionist scholars like Martell observe Truman's "legacy" that Truman's fundamental architecture continued, in "the next series of presidential administrations along these conceptual and institutional lines." Exuberance of enterprise and undertaking was offset by "cost effectiveness" and balance from Eisenhower to Reagan. Fellow scholar Colin Dueck thinks that escalation, stretched-out over time in terms of costs and commitments of containment and deterrence, permitted elites and public to resist its identification with any "garrison," "warfare," or "national security" state. Policy, in response and effect, ends, ways and means, ranges and varieties, sometimes assertive (Kennedy, Johnson, Reagan), sometimes passive or disorderly (Eisenhower, Ford, Carter), and occasionally brilliant (Nixon), all flexibly used the instruments MIPC provided. Aaron Friedberg explains this as a stable strategic synthesis based on "an outward-directed force posture and military strategy, and a supporting set of inward-directed power-creating mechanisms." It reached what Martel portrays as full circle by the Reagan presidency, in line with the Truman idea of "the primacy of local partners deriving always as support from nationalist movements against communist regimes" or the Truman Doctrine "on the offensive."[34]

But, at what price technology? Expensive technology not production as a permanent mobilization/war economy took over. Defense spending for Korea nearly tripled, as expressed in percentage of the Gross Domestic Product (GDP), while defense outlays never returned to anything approaching peacetime before World War II. Both Truman and Eisenhower, especially the latter, "insisted on budget discipline," to quote money historian Robert Hormats. Yet, it was a technology race with the Soviet Union that drove costs of common defense and national security. Ideologues, gallery-playing politicians of both parties and on both ends of Pennsylvania Avenue, together with engineers, scientists, and the voracious appetite of the military, set precedent on defense and national security. Who could rationally question the Truman-Eisenhower dictum that "a strong economy and sound national finances are vital to the country's security"? Deficits spinning out of control and spiraling inflation "would damage the productive sectors of the nation's economy," as well as weaken public will for staying the course over the long haul. Making guns could be added to making automobiles for economic benefit and domestic stability although as government social scientist Richard H. Stevens points out, only in 1980, for the first time since World War II did commercial aircraft production exceed that for military services.[35]

Conventional wisdom has long-identified defense spending as the determinant in militarization of America during the Cold War. As Rebecca U. Thorpe shows, defense outlays never fell below a $300 billion baseline after Korea "despite extended periods without major shooting wars." She views this as part of the accretion of executive branch power and the question of political manipulation of crises, patriotism, and freedom of action via financial and economic allocation, assuming strength and momentum, i.e., permanence, from 1945–1991. To her, due to World War II, America embraced a state of mind which became what Eisenhower saw as a sinister power manipulator. Thorpe suggests that, not only reaction to enemy threat but also the largesse from defense spending, weakened checks and balances between branches of government. She concludes that what started with World War II would continue past the Cold War, playing upon external pressures and internal exploitation of peoples' fears plus reliance on defense jobs as an economic stimulant and stabilizer. Although, "no one deliberately set out to create long-term structural reliance on a war economy," she contends, such was "an uncoordinated result of a national military mobilization strategy where multiple actors pursued their own immediate goals." Technology, cost and superpower competition became a ceaseless, upward spiral.[36]

In many ways the work of economist Hugh Rockoff best calculates the metrics of the Cold War. "I added international spending to what is normally counted as defense spending–the cost of munitions and the wages of military personnel," he comments, "because the greater part of foreign aid was motivated by the goal of containing Communism." Even then such funding was only about ten percent of defense spending, and seven percent "if we exclude immediate post-World War II years to aid reconstruction in America's allies in Western Europe." The hidden spending on nuclear weapons research, as well as expenditures of the Central Intelligence Agency remained elusive in Rockoff's calculations. Economic costs of veterans affairs and draftee taxation, much less the niches and nuances of Korea and Vietnam, forced some degree of underestimation. In fact, he separately tabulated those conflicts, yet in the end, his numbers showed that together, the Cold War ($5.193 billion), Korea ($1.186 billion) and Vietnam ($1.697 billion) totaled $8.076 billion, or nearly three times that of World War II. Rockoff quietly cautions readers to realize that the tremendous drain of the Cold War "was also felt in the Soviet Union–which attempted to match the United States–and in some of the allies of each of these two opposing powers." Of course, dollar figures alone cannot compute the lost economic benefits from approximately 95,395 dead and 256,587 non-mortally wounded, wrenched from the resources of the nation, despite rehabilitating some portion of the wounded to productive capacity. As Rockoff observes, the long war against communism "in terms of resources [was] the most expensive in American history." His post-Vietnam treatment of tertiary, unsung yet strategically pivotal problems of balance of payments, end of the Bretton Woods solution, and diversion of domestic resource extraction absent customary demobilization, remain an under-appreciated effect of costs associated with the period. Technology lay at the base.[37]

One of the most incredible costs held clues as to why "thinking about the unthinkable" was never audited. This was the technology-infused, massive nuclear weapons program from 1940 to 1996 that cost the United States government nearly $5.5 trillion. Perhaps the ultimate deterrence of the Soviet Union, and one supposes by association the People's Republic of China, was so striking that few people have expressed interest in either the cumulative or the annual costs, observes atomic auditor Stephen I. Schwartz. Given the program's highly secretive nature, explicable, complacent acceptance by elected officials in both executive and legislative branches, a careerist-mentality of program bureaucrats including scientists, bomb-makers, health officials, and administrators—of the Atomic Energy Agency, later named Department of Energy—addicted to programmatic efficiency and effectiveness (numbers, tests, expansion of facility infrastructure and delivery of various stockpiled products to armed-service customers), and most precisely with such acceptance from an uninformed public, this lack of accountability was deemed simply part of doing business against a ruthless, determined enemy. The Cold War was full of ironies.[38]

The assumption that monetary costs of some (nuclear) would be offset by or substitute for other (conventional) systems, (for instance Eisenhower's "bigger bang for the buck" massive retaliation strategy could offset number of ground divisions), eventually reached the insanity of mutually assured destruction (MAD) for both contestants by the later Cold War period. Even the ex-general as president, while worried about arms buildup, arms race, and threat of a "garrison state" enveloping America perhaps comprehended little of the illogic of runaway nuclear arms with production at Hanford, Oak Ridge, Los Alamos, and other nuclear sites, producing deadly contamination with ensuing impacts on health and environment. No presidents, from Truman to Reagan, contested the standoff game as long as it kept the enemy equally engaged. Schwartz discloses that the United States "spent its first $1 trillion on nuclear weapons within fifteen years of the end of World War II." In the end, with nuclear programs coming in at possibly half the cost of conventional arms in the period, America ran two parallel sets of books for its military-industrial complex: nuclear and conventional. Schwartz concludes that domestic and international pressures of the Cold War "made the financial aspects of the arms race of secondary importance to ensuring U.S. security." Extended across an evolving and expanding national security definition, President John F. Kennedy's enjoinder that no price was too high, burden too onerous, or hardship too tough to preserve liberty, made perfect sense.[39]

Science and technology drove ever-escalating costs of the military-industrial-political complex. Historians Barton Hacker and Margaret Vining suggest that World War II had "reversed" military ludditism toward research. Basic research and applied research had vied with one another as Americans mainly saw science as a vehicle to gain useful technology.

Military, political and business professionals in the elite core supporting containment were disdainful of theoretical scientists and academics. Possibly, they did not subscribe to enjoinders from founding director of Princeton's Institute for Advanced Study Abraham Flexner, about the "usefulness of useless knowledge," or the fact that scientific elites might well find sympathetic companions among the laity for, as Hacker and Vining suggest, the "influence flowed both ways." World War II and the permanent war economy thereafter "touched" technologists and scientists with jobs and status. Like the general public attracted to employment in defense production and service, scientists and engineers also found attractive "virtually unlimited resources" of military-funded research. Gone would be "the transient the past," or the hot-and-cold spigots from earlier periods dependent on a clear break between peace and war. Institutions emerged from the previous period "to convert wartime arrangements into permanent features of American government and society." Allen Kaufman, speaking to the Air Force postwar experience, posits that creating a "voluntary network of research centers and corporations mobilized research scientists to preserve peace by perfecting destruction."[40]

The super-secret Manhattan Project and then the Atomic Energy Commission programs set the pattern, although the armed services and even other government agencies recognized how technology in their spheres prompted new opportunities. The young Air Force founded a government-funded nonprofit research center (MITRE), tapping Douglas Aircraft Company's nonprofit spinoff (RAND Corporation), and quickly learned that specially designed, interdependent parts for the B-47 jet bomber required seamlessly planning and overseeing a weapon system from design through manufacturing and operation, which in turn led to internal organizational rearrangements for "systems integration" that went beyond the capabilities of any single "prime" production contractor. So, comments Kaufman, the service "reworked its relations with science and industry" over time." Hacker and Vining add that "preoccupation with technological sophistication led to weapons of enormous capabilities and equally enormous costs" thereafter. "Avionics" or the combination of electronic gear, detectors and computers would dwarf the mere mechanical hardware of warfare in all three traditional dimensions of land, sea and air, eventually taking on a life of its own. Claim Hacker and Vining, "the widespread assumption that better technology meant victory had made military-technological innovation, to a significant degree, an end in itself." Thus, from the Cold War, "unrestrained pursuit of technological perfection has produced a baroque arsenal, possessed of extraordinary capabilities at astronomical expense."[41]

Science and technology failed to "win" in a war like Vietnam. As part of a unified containment-deterrence effort, they could help bankrupt the other side. America's love affair with gadgetry and technology as the solution to efficiency and effectiveness resonates from this period. Technological resources were long viewed as substitutes for human slaughter, although, ironically helped produce that carnage. As the U.S. military emerged from a second world war "with an array of research and development skills and organizations, all trending to applied science development engineering and hardware" that reflected need not altruism, prominent government-military association with university-managed laboratories, from the Manhattan Project group to Johns Hopkins Applied Physics Laboratory and California Institute of Technology's Jet Propulsion Laboratory, pointed the way. Postwar science policy stood little chance against technology policy with strategic implications for national defense. The congressionally-mandated Office of Naval Research institutionalized control over the in-house, wartime Naval Research Laboratory, and counterparts in the other services blurred basic and applied research and accumulated a $10 billion military research bill between 1950 and 1965. This was "mission-oriented research," honed to a fine art during the Cold War.[42]

Dual application in military and civilian arenas could be found in crossovers with military and civilian applications of "the strategic atom," jet propulsion, and rotary-wing aircraft programs. The Soviet Union's lead in space technology via Sputnik in 1957 spawned yet another scientific agency in the American government, the National Aeronautics and Space Administration. Sputnik's attendant military-threat consequences fused with Pentagon panic to exert "increasingly strong effects on the direction of research and even the structure of universities." Sputnik also spawned passage of the National Defense Education Act of 1958. So, Eisenhower left the White House warning not only against military-industrial influence but also the "twin dangers of science too closely entwined with government," academic research coopted by excessive dependence on federal support, and government policy-making "surrendered to a scientific-technological elite." Costly technology also led to Secretary of Defense Robert McNamara's infusion of defense intellectuals into the Pentagon during the Kennedy-Johnson years. Rationalizing introduction of systems approaches and cost accounting applied to defense planning, for handling escalating costs of high-end technology weapons programs, shifting emphasis for military careerists from command leadership to business management yielded a controversial reform plan styled Planning, Programming and Budgeting System or PPBS. McNamara's Department of Defense increasingly exerted influence via contracts for research, development and engineering that "altered higher education and channeled key areas of technological development along lines of military interest." Hacker and Vining cite the new DoD ethos as impacting substitution of machine and quantification for humans in such critical production sectors as the machine-tool industry.[43]

Indeed, this application of what physicist Seymour Melman styled "Pentagon capitalism" turned the defense budget into "a device for central economic planning and profound consequence" for the conduct and content of both physical and social sciences, as well as engineering in the 1960s, claim Hacker and Vining. If correct, when asserting how "the Pentagon exerted ever greater control over the direction of American economic development," the march toward automated war seemed unstoppable. Military enchantment with microelectronics and computers, the irrepressible appetite for latest technology applied to what now were styled "weapons systems," and "systems of systems," in missiles, munitions, ordnance, equipment and latest iterations of platforms (aircraft, armored vehicles, ships), spiraled onward in type, function and cost. Hacker and Vining style it "technological enthusiasm" that may have reached a pinnacle in one particular militarized science initiative of the 1980s, the famous Reagan-era Strategic Defense Initiative (SDI) or "Star Wars" gambit to outspend and out-science the Soviets. Indeed, it became the apogee of the decades-old constant upgrading of deterrent-related technological weapons systems, set against periodic arms-control efforts and treaties designed to stymie the enemy. The MX land-based missiles in the 1970s, Trident sea-based ballistic missile system in the 1980s, and the B-2 manned bomber replete with stealth-based technology, constantly demanded huge new budget outlays. At the center of the SDI scheme stood the Department of Energy's Livermore National Laboratory, run by nuclear physicist Dr. Edward Teller and his circle of enthusiasts, for developing an "x-Ray laser" generated in a nuclear explosion, by a space-based weapon, which could take out an enemy missile at launch. SDI served its purpose, perhaps, soaking up a decade of science and billions in funding that amounted to little more than "a shield of faith." This shooting star may have been the last glimmer of Cold War scientific insanity, questionably workable, and other such wonders as orbiting satellites designed to provide early warning, reconnaissance, communications, navigation, and weather, some of which yielded more transferable "dual use" offshoots for civilian use. Nonetheless, precision-guided munitions (PGMs) and the whole "stealth" detection technology offered practical application of science public-private partnering just like Lockheed's Advanced Development Program, descendant of renowned "Skunk Works" created by Clarence "Kelly" Johnson years before.[44]

Permanent technological revolution underpinned the major part of a permanent war economy, as the Cold War streaked along its foreordained trajectory. For a time, Admiral Hyman Rickover's nuclear navy held the limelight. Then, it became missiles, satellites and electronic gadgetry, while quietly standing behind it all stood the sinister genie of the atom: a production line of 70,299 nuclear and thermonuclear warheads with accompanying munitions packages, delivery systems, extraction and production facilities (mines, plants, research laboratories, test sites, as GOCOs), disciples of bomb makers and physicists, health scientists and caretakers, strategists and deployment experts, in and out of uniform. Then there was the spider web of armed-forces bases, conventional production and storage facilities, logistics networks, training and stationing posts, within a framework of GOGO, GOCO and COCO management arrangements. Cost and workability were always twin benchmarks in the latest attempt to find a talisman, magic wand, war-winning weapon, a silver bullet. Perhaps technology enabled the one event that counted. The ending of the Cold War was understood as a combination of spending, economic overstretch and technological bluff. Technology capped mankind's march toward thermonuclear war. Perhaps technological innovation became "an end in itself." America always put its faith and money in its technological superiority, no matter the cost.[45]

For business historian Thomas K. McCraw, the three post-World War II decades found the federal government funding "about 70 per cent of all R&D [Research and Development] done in electronics," while eighty percent of federally sponsored industrial research as a whole, concerned military applications. The number of military-related research projects rose from 15,000 in 1950 to over 80,000 within a decade. Two other historians Mansel Blackford and K. Austin Kerr note that, between 1955 and 1965, federal spending for science rose from $3.3 billion to $14.8 billion, "most of which was defense related." In 1962, Minnesota senator Hubert H. Humphrey voiced concern that too much research talent was going toward military, space, and atomic energy, rather than commercial work, citing European competitors in the Dutch, Belgian, and even British economies forging ahead in trade. McCraw later downplayed the impact, observing that "for better or worse, in the minds of many scientists and engineers, it was more exciting to try to develop a hydrogen bomb or land a person on the moon than to invent or improve some everyday consumer product." As political scientist Charles A. Stevenson put it, "lawmakers tend to embrace promising technologies, especially when they offer dramatic improvements in military capability or local economic benefits."[46]

A PERMANENT DEFENSE INDUSTRY

In 1968, physicist Ralph E. Lapp ventured where Eisenhower did not go seven years before. He called it what it was, "the military-industrial-political complex" (MIPC), a not-so-hidden hand of Washington at play. Business and industry remained screened from public awareness until passage of years and multiple events raised questions. Would America have reacted against what was fast-becoming a way of life at some point if Vietnam had not built upon Korea and other overseas interventions? Yet, even radical "New Left" ranting eventually faded from view. Corporate, government, military, and civilian elites weathered the storms of the seventies and eighties despite a dearth of national mobilization planning (FEMA the responsible agency, conflicted by mission priorities), concern for an industrial base increasingly going offshore for production (Japan being the bogeyman de jour) and increased interpretation of a North American rather than purely U.S. defense industrial base arrangement. The inevitable cycles of surge and recession accompanying policy actions in response to crisis, real and contrived, unceasingly shaped an American way of security. By this point, MIPC was entrenched, fed by paranoia about the Soviet communism, and by profit and loss too ingrained in the American psyche to be overtly reined in, scaled back, or downsized by normal peacetime "demobilization," or even Eisenhower's warning. "Military-Fordist" production of arms morphed into ever more expensive "knowledge-intensive" weaponry-making (like precision guided munitions) as well as another military-industrial divide with the enemy constantly ahead of the U.S. in theory. When threat of a new arms race (Star Wars) combined with capitalism's "guns and butter," Soviet-American confrontation suddenly collapsed, with a whimper. How best to explain it?[47]

Of course, the benefit of hindsight always brings better focus. Historian Mark Wilson may be correct in asserting that business historians have been particularly slow to study the details of this all-important segment of Cold War entrepreneurial endeavor. Political economists and others filled the gap. Such works by Lapp, Thorpe and Jacques Gansler, to cite a few, clearly expose the extent of MIPC: prime military contracts awarded to U.S. companies from 1960 to 1967, defense contract awards and state-by-state payrolls in 1966, the top 124 U.S. defense contracts for fiscal year 1967, as well as the top 100 space contractors for NASA that year, total federal obligations to federal-contract research centers administered by colleges and universities in 1966, and DoD obligations for research and development at 100 colleges and universities in 1964. Thorpe further adds to Lapp's regional-local delineation of total federal obligations, by various MIPC agencies

(AEC, DoD, DHW and NASA), expressing the total intrusion and dependency of America on security dollars. The Under Secretary of Defense for Acquisition in 1988 pointed to a collection of 215 industries accounting for 95 percent of DoD peacetime procurement relying on international industrial competitiveness for survival. No wonder, Gansler, an electrical engineer by early training and later a defense official himself, portrayed Cold War vicissitudes of a sometimes Potemkin-like defense industrial base. [48]

Ironically, while government officials and Washington think-tank savants bemoaned the plight of the resourcing sector of national defense and dearth of study for mobilization, corporate America blithely went on simply making money on defense contacts. The standbys of aerospace (McDonnell Douglas, General Dynamics, Lockheed, General Electric, United Aircraft, Boeing, North American, Grumman, Hughes, Northrop, even a residual Curtiss-Wright), had joined traditional firms such as General Electric, General Motors, American Telephone and Telegraph, Newport News, Bethlehem Steel, Westinghouse, Chrysler, Goodyear, DuPont, and Hercules. New names joined the list: Textron, Sperry Rand, AVCO, Litton Industries, Thiokol Chemical, Dow Chemical, General Precision Equipment, Martin Marietta, TRW, and Texas Instruments. In each sector of MIPC could be found hopes and fears, wrapped in patriotism, scandal, and profit-and-loss that often drove many away from any business-pacifism tradition, and to a federally funded peacetime defense and aerospace welfare-system, ensuring stability, contracts, jobs, and influence. For business historian McCraw, "in the broader sense, the interpenetration of all the major players in national defense procurement—the 'revolving door' of retired military officers, civilian officials, defense contractors, lobbyists, and political candidates—had become a commonplace of public life in the United States." But Gansler excoriated both government and industry for failing to understand and correct problems at sub-prime levels where, in every funding down-cycle, numerous suppliers departed for more dependable civilian markets. To him, "for 200 years, the United States has not treated its defense industrial base as the vital national resource it is."[49]

Professor Aaron Friedberg's study of statism/anti-statism in the Cold War era, displays sub-themes such as the evaporation of planning and execution of mobilization, defense industrial policy, dispersal of plants, facilities and people, substitution of procurement preferences for defense protectionism, even institutional devolution. All might have been predictable thanks to rapidly changing technology. Woven into interminable operational details of government and the defense business are a variety of interpretations. What Robert Heilbroner suggested in 1977 as "a whole new philosophy of a 'mixed' economy . . . slowly replacing that of laissez faire," Friedberg interprets as "a prolonged struggle of privatization" of the means of arms production. Heilbroner sensed that government committed to the maintenance of economic growth and stability as a "major aim of its overall policy." "Guarantor" had replaced "regulator" for Federal governance during the Cold War, with national security at its core. Friedberg asserts that a $600 billion weapons tab from 1965–1975, resulting from public-private partnering, was every bit as essential to the American way of life as a $6 billion allocation for housing. To Heilbroner, there was "a new economic structure in the United States," contrasted with 1929, a structure that committed "to a much greater degree of publicly guaranteed economic guidance and welfare." Still, some opponents termed it corporate welfare for MIPC. Whether autarky, laissez faire or mixed enterprise, defense production was a key element.[50]

Few people sensed any danger from "Pentagon Capitalism" dependence. Friedberg's fulsome expostulation of privatization-cum-triumphalism legitimized the fact that public-private partnership in the mixed-economy contributed to public welfare, national survival under foreign threat if at the expense of the militarization of that American economy and polis via a defense industrial base, however it evolved and for how long it took to do so. It evolved as a subset of what Australian professor Linda Weiss sees as the transformation of America into a national security state during the Cold War era. Technological enterprise and "permanent preparedness in pursuit of perpetual innovation" advanced its purposes. Dwight R. Lee suggests that so-called "public choice" benefitting defense and MIPC may well merit two (of three) cheers foe public good as opposed to reallocation of national funding elsewhere.[51]

Those procedural changes that had begun on the eve of the second World War, i.e., the growth of large institutions involving public and private collaboration (if not outright accommodation) which were devoted to supervisory regulation (government procurement process, oversight bureaucracy), and government laboratories and programs, contracted to business and industry, plus research at universities), and which guaranteed R&D and production entitlements (cost-plus profit contracts, tax breaks, advance and progress payments, and negotiated contracts, as-contrasted with full and open competition), reached maturity by the Reagan era. Government "incentivization" financing of programs, plants and equipment led some interpreters to coin the term "private arsenal." Recognizing that government-owned, government-operated public arsenals and shipyards still survived in parallel with a more overpowering private sector (also originated decades earlier as a test-bed for quality and competitive pricing), this duality continued to characterize the Cold War MIPC. Whether termed a garrison state, warfare state, permanent war economy, or weapons culture, its costs could be borne, as long as threat existed to national survival. Government beneficence flowed to management, worker, stakeholder and community, through manageable taxes and sustainable economy. The executive and legislative branches handled the vagaries of international and domestic politics. The military-service procurement systems managed by the DoD bureaucracy fretted with cost, efficiency, weapons-effectiveness and human wealth (within an understood and practiced umbrella of ethics and laws). Other stove-piped agencies participated, from intelligence to atomic energy even the National Institutes of Health, Weiss suggests. She might have included all of government, imprecisely "mobilized" through sporadic coordination and cooperation of the national security planning process for the state's latest Great Endeavor.

A consistently adaptive MIPC moved through periodic whims of acquisition reforms and contracting revolutions, to sophisticated efficiency-seeking public-private partnering. Ronald Reagan's populist-appealing "evil empire" appellation thrilled a weary populace while a virtually privately-run, technology-industrial arm of the government responded as the private arsenal system. This was implicitly "industrial policy" for national security, although few in or out of the security community dared declare such politically unacceptable thoughts at the time. Maintaining the competitive edge economically, militarily, and technologically remained the goal while privatization increasingly defined residual redundancy for "mobilization," and relegated the government's role to maintenance, logistical support, and contract management. Technology as well as pressure for post-Vietnam change shunted aside the qualitative, comparative measurement tools of state managed capitalism that had been designed to insure competitive procurement. Reams of paper and gallons of ink were expended on public investigations, commissioned studies and analyses. But, obsolescing government facilities like the Philadelphia Navy Yard continued to pull their political weight alongside corporate giants.[52]

To emphasize a point, historian David Reynolds asserts that by the time of Pearl Harbor, many of the features that would later be associated with "the 'national security state' were already apparent in embryo." Thorpe claims that nearly all the leading military corporations in the mobilization-era of World War II and the early Cold War periods ranked among those also in the preparedness and sustainment era at the end of the Cold War period, unless principally civilian in function, such as automobiles or energy. Even then, Weiss's more comprehensive interpretation suggests virtually every extractive and productive sector of the American state and economy could be linked to national security. If Curtiss-Wright dropped off the charts, companies Boeing, Lockheed, General Electric, etc continued throughout the period, with such mergers as produced a General Dynamics absorbing Chrysler and General Motors defense divisions, McDonnell-Douglas, Northrop Grumman, Martin Marietta, and United Technologies retaining Sikorsky Aircraft, Hamilton Propellers, and Pratt & Whitney. They maintained market share while newcomers like missile producers Raytheon, Honeywell, and TRW, or even Unisys for information technology joined a dynamic defense industrial base by the epoch's end.[53]

Defense resourcing assumed a prosaic inward-looking quality with the Cold War's passage. A corps of defense analysts like James Fallows, James Golden, Lawrence Korb, Henry Leonard, Michael Gordon hammered home pet theories, with Gansler best capturing key aspects like strategic responsiveness, significance to the economy, and economic efficiency. The cyclical nature of defense procurement over time defied expectations thanks to the lack of structured institutional planning, inadequacy of industrial-planning, and actual industrial readiness. Importance of technology and research stood out, but so, too, did differences among industries which made up the base, a high concentration of business shares in only a few large firms, and heavy dependence on military assistance abroad. The rubric highlighted questions about production base versus war-reserve stockpiling, or the slow erosion of traditional self-sufficiency, the litmus-test of this key component in national sovereignty. "Hot base," "Cold Base," "Warm Base," and either government or corporate ownership, and operation—GOGO, GOCO, COCO—filled the jargon of the trade. Political and economic pillars blended seamlessly for the United States and its partners over such matters as NATO resourcing capabilities, budgets, and planning, while the competitor, the Warsaw Pact, seemingly enjoyed more standardization from Soviet-industry supplied matériel, than multi-provider defense industrial bases still nationally identifiable among western partners. By means of a mystifying, extensive listing of events, organizations and individuals in fifty-six separate entries, Sterling Michael Pavelec's encyclopedic work, *The Military-Industrial Complex and American Society*, testifies to the difficulty of codifying the MIPC. Scholar Paul Koistinen tried for more systematic identification in his fifth and final volume on the political economy of American warfare.[54]

Updated backdrop provided the eternal short war or long war quandary, continuous press to create new weapons, witch-hunts associated with fraud, waste and abuse such as Senator William Promise's vigilance on Capitol Hill in the tradition of predecessor Gerald Nye's "merchants of death" hearings in the Depression Era. Intensive mobilization preparedness versus "come as you are" realism accompanied purely military planning. "Erosion" of quantity and source competition, like cost, threatened acquisition goals. Perhaps the Army was most vexed about "industrial preparedness," but the Navy also worried about the largely adversarial process between its providers and itself, as customer. The Air Force, as a contributor to high technology, high costs, and high-profile scandals evidenced by infamous $400 toilet seats, also sought atonement. Confusion intermixed when Senator Proxmire introduced his "compendium of words"—"military-industrial-bureaucratic-trade association-labor union-intellectual-technical-academic-service club-political complex." In 1971, Soviet affairs analyst John Erickson wanted "a catalogue which leaves little untouched about the process and pressure groups of the modern state." It might be said that every partner in the Endeavor had the best interests of the country—as well as self—at heart.[55]

We continued to reside in a world beset with wars, rebellions, political and ideological differences, and economic inflation, intoned procurement historian C.M. Culver. Arms Control and Test Ban Treaties, the technological explosion highlighting sensational explorations of the solar system, subsidence of internal unrest over Vietnam, as well as lifting domestic wage and price controls that had not contained inflation anyway, a fast-breaking energy shortage, the Iranian hostage situation which inflamed Americans, as well as endless, recurring attempts at government-wide procurement innovations, reorganizations, and procurement initiatives, all underscored Erickson's words. Defense spending after Vietnam dropped and the fifty-two percent figure of 1960 bottomed out at twenty to twenty-five percent by the time Reagan assumed the presidency in 1981. One doctoral student in 1971 thought the military-industrial complex had proven "a remarkably persistent set of institutions with a powerful ideological foundation" since Korea. National security "continues to control a large share of the nation's resources and to exercise political power over questions essential to its survival." Bernard Brodie, a respected theorist with the Rand Corporation, saw nothing insidious or nefarious in that. His disingenuous response was disarming.[56]

Aside from a sound reputation for strategic thinking, Brodie was, after all, a Rand Corporation scholar in the influential Air Force club, and despite disclaimers to the contrary, a "kept" MIPC intellectual. Thus, he argued "the influence on national decisions of the *industrial* side of the well-known complex has been far less than legend seems bent on attributing to it." Computing that influence at "very close to zero," he simply dismissed any hand of American industry in foreign trade, hence influence on foreign policy. In a cavalier tone, Brodie asserted that economic causes of war were no more magical than other causes, and need not be "subsumed where the evidence tenaciously refused to expose them," nor are they "a *more profound* cause of war than the issues or factors," like patriotism, "or more pervasively present than other factors, or more ingeniously and deeply hidden, or that one is necessarily gullible or a 'tool of the interests.'" In the post-Vietnam atmosphere of denial, recriminations over President Carter's reversal of Candidate Carter's inclination to reduce defense budgets, actually raising them from $96 to $126 billion by Fiscal Year 1980, consistent bleating about warplanes the Pentagon did not ask for but which Congress legislated (the A-7D and F-111), or fierce lobbying for aircraft engine programs by General Electric and Pratt & Whitney, headlines proclaimed "business booms for weapons makers" thanks to new programs, foreign sales and commercial aircraft. Infrequently would firms like Bath Iron Works deliver a destroyer like *Oliver Hazard Perry* on time and under cost![57]

Brodie acolytes Jerome Slater and Terry Narden thought literature on the Complex of this period seemed to contain variants of main assumptions like (a) the complex as a ruling class, (b) as a power elite, (c) as a governing bureaucracy, and (d) as a loose coalition of powerful groups. Similar to Koistinen's five volumes he carried back to the country's origins, this pair found anti-MIPC literature castigated "groups with economic and institutional interests in cold-war policies and high military expenditures and linked by shared values and beliefs as well as overlapping or symbiotic positions in the economic, social, and political structure of American society." So, they rejected the idea that the Complex was "America's dominant institution" with influence over a broad range of military, foreign, and domestic policies "which have consequences for even seemingly remote aspects of American life." Rather, the inconsistencies of American foreign and military policies, insisted Slater and Narden, came from "a pattern of fears, misconceptions, myths, and desires, shared by elites and masses alike, and historically rooted in the structure of American norms, practices, and institutions." In a rush to lessen the impact of the Complex, the pair advanced the notion of an American national security state. But, they cautioned, "the inflation of observations about American politics into an overblown theory" exaggerated "the unity and coherence that exists among groups," and policy scope "affected by their actions." That, in turn, neglected other crucially important factors that limited understanding the military and American society. By tying "to a restrictive and misleading model," via "deliberate actions and powers of agents," the tendency was to oversimplify and misdirect analysis of "power and militarism in American politics." MIT physicist Kosta Tsipis joined the Brodie following, writing in 1972, "what one finds is not a conspiratorial complex but a number of synergistic factors, largely unrelated to the security of the country, but extending much beyond the military officer and industrial manager."[58]

To Tsipis, military contracts eliminated "uncertainty inherent in a product whose profitability depends on public acceptance." The Pentagon provided money and often production machinery and manufacturing as well as special contract clauses ensuring a firm could not actually lose money on a military order. "The notorious cost-overruns" were frequent outcomes of such arrangements, Tsipis admitted. But, these "most extraordinarily favorable conditions," he continued, induced a number of industrial concerns to switch from nonmilitary business and "concentrate on strategic weapons production." If short-sighted on the part of business directors, "since their companies lose their entrepreneurial independence to the military," one could hardly demand that they "transcend the profit motive which has been ingrained by education and social acceptance and see the wider implications of their practices." Shades of centuries-long argument about fair return on public monies, excess profits and patriotism for profit, Tsipis posited, that even the Soviet 'apparatchik' in the Russian techno-bureaucracy who is in charge of a weapons system was most probably motivated not by any ideological fervor but "the understandable desire to rise in the hierarchy of the Party's bureaucracy."[59]

Whatever the motivations, money could be made in the defense business despite market fluctuations and risk. Not without reason would General Dynamics executive vice-president James W. Beggs coo that "business hasn't been as good as this since the late 1950s and early 1960s," when ICBMs and civilian airline purchases stoked 1970s boom times. But to *Los Angeles Times* writer Clayton Fritchey, the Pentagon was "literally eating America out of house and home." An ever-larger sum going for ships, tanks and planes meant less for pressing domestic needs, such as housing. Quoting Founding Father Benjamin Franklin's 1784 warning that "an army is a devouring monster," Fritchey perceived civilians in danger of losing control of the Pentagon, and worse, saw defense-business moguls about to manage Republican Gerald Ford's 1976 presidential bid. Writing at mid-decade before Carter's response to Iranian events, Fritchey claimed the defense package exceeded "the biggest budgets of the Vietnamese and Koreans wars," and even those "at the height of World War II." Indeed, at $104.7 billion, military obligations for the next fiscal year "are greater than the cost of the entire government" during any of the years of World War II. By decade's end, Carter's requested $126 billion was nearly double the early 1950s $66.1

billion outlay for Korea. Since about 1960, that figure had never dipped below $150 billion.[60]

MANAGING A MATURE MIPC

One outstanding problem with MIPC was its self-perpetuation. The Third World and foreign markets always offered defense business. While preaching human rights and moving haltingly on arms control, the Carter administration also tried to curb the developed world's escalating trade in conventional arms. The president declared that the United States could not be "both the world's leading champion of peace and the world's leading supplier of weapons of war." Still, in 1975 alone, the United States supplied $4.85 billion or over double the amount of armament exports by other countries, with not even the Soviet Union close to that figure. NATO, Australia and New Zealand were the largest recipients, but many allies were now competitors, having continued to develop their own domestic arms production capacity, coupled to under-performing domestic budgeting for defense. By May 1977, Carter issued policies limiting American foreign arms sales but enforcement proved difficult. Some sixty to seventy percent of sales of the French-built *Mirage* looked to foreign markets, and British Aerospace also had a major stake in foreign sales. Over eighty per-cent of French arms exports went to non-NATO customers, while forty percent of U.S. exports went to NATO and Australia and New Zealand. In the early part of the 70s decade the arms trade was principally aircraft or related products. Soon, broader foreign sales provided a cushion through a cost-saving relationship between high technology systems unit-costs and stretching out order-series that could reduce such costs at least for the U.S. military customers. Traditional maintenance of a stable production base and "building relationships "also ensured against unfriendly embargoes on American defense products, price wars, and even terms-of-access to materials like crude oil. Thus, the arms trade had become a strategic tool for everyone.[61]

The old but still-existing Depression response Buy-American Act of 1933 protected domestic industry in one sense. When the American market was down, the defense industrial base (DIB) could look for customers, a perfect vehicle practiced implicitly by the MIPC since its beginnings. But, any such thinly disguised attempt to limit competitive sales to the Third World from European rivals carried inherent risks. Given the multi-billion-dollar trade, and its obvious benefits to military readiness, if the United States was serious about multilateral limits in arms exports, it would have to be prepared to "restrict her own production capacity" and "bargain with other suppliers about market share, and world market share at that." The practical problems of organizing world armaments markets "are and will remain legion," thought Lawrence G. Franko, but unless they were faced, "the notion of multilateral restraint in conventional arms exports will remain a mirage."[62]

The arms-trade conundrum reflected America's weakening power during the Carter presidency. Conservative columnist George F. Will quoted figures showing that the level of defense spending as a percentage of gross national product was about the same in 1979 as it had been in the disarmament rush of 1948 (4.6/4.5), although it had peaked at 13.2 % in 1952, hovering between 7.5 and 8.9 GNP percent from 1960 to 1975. Defense spending then started climbing late in Carter's term, and *Washington Post* columnist George C. Wilson had tagged him "the new Jimmy Carter" by his last year in office. But this rise in spending came even more so with Carter's successor Ronald Reagan. International instability in various forms such as human rights, Iranian hostages, SALT II arms limitation, Camp David Accords, Chinese communist leader Mao Zedong's death, superpower competition in Africa, and proxy wars like the Soviet invasion of Afghanistan populated the Carter years, set against the lingering ghosts of Vietnam. But, after 1981, those shadowy phantoms only dimly offset Reagan's proclaimed crusade against the Soviet "evil empire." MIPC and renewed interest in mobilization as a strategy became "a given" for "bankrupting Soviet communism" through dedicating unlimited resources "to restore military parity with the Soviet Union," as phrased by Casper W. Weinberger, Reagan's initial Secretary of Defense. By 1987, the Reagan years became "the greatest peacetime military buildup in American history," claims finance historian Robert Hormats, with budget historian Dennis Ippolito noting constant defense-dollar spending climbing to more than $370 billion by FY 1989. The Strategic Defense Initiative, known by SDI, or "Star Wars", reinstatement of the B-1 manned-bomber program killed by Carter, the expansive goal of a 600-ship navy and fifteen battle-carrier groups, joined with military adventurism in Nicaragua, El Salvador, and Grenada were among the moves under Reagan doctrine. True, the US was now a debtor-nation, thus the Reagan years were fraught with economic angst. Upward-bound military expenditures spoke to "revitalizing the arsenal of democracy," via a defense industrial strategy or policy.[63]

Not that the defense industrial base was all that healthy at the time. The House Armed Services Committee panel weighed-in at the end of 1980 with six ways MIPC was found to be unready for crisis response. The group, chaired by Congressman Richard H. Icord, saw the DIB as unbalanced, with excess production capacity at the prime level, but lacked a corresponding capacity at subcontractor levels. The industrial base was not capable of surging production in time to meet a national emergency. Lead-times for military equipment had increased over the previous three years. Skilled manpower shortages existed and were projected for the next decade. The United States was also becoming increasingly dependent on foreign sources for raw materials as well as some specialized components for military equipment. Capital investment in new technology, facilities, and machinery was constrained by inflation, unfavorable tax policies and management priorities. These same themes became an almost permanent mantra for the MIPC going forward, although mobilization expert Roderick Vawter suggested the Icord congressional panel simply applied a defense label "to many problems that are much broader in their implications." He considered "the defense industrial base will tend to mirror the economic health of the entire [economic] base" of the nation and, in the event of mobilization, would be handicapped by larger problems of that base. In an indirect way, said Vawter, Congress "recognized the truth of an up-front premise of the Korean War era mobilization— "the basic economy must expand to serve as a foundation for a healthy defense industrial capability." For this reason, Vawter (reflecting a then-current blending of industrial sector and national preparedness), echoed Harry J. Gray, chairman and chief executive of United Technologies Corporation, who had told the Icord group that it might be time to reestablish an office of mobilization planning, headed by a cabinet-level official, to work closely with DoD and industry. The 1978 government reorganization merging coordination of emergency preparedness and industrial mobilization in the Federal Emergency Management Agency (FEMA) as a residual coordinating authority for the Defense Production Act of 1950, lacked Icord panel-confidence that it was providing a robust leadership role. Gray and others had pressed the committee that FEMA's foundations should lie in "the commitment of the country to a certain level of preparedness for an emergency." *Government commitment was a continuous and unremitting problem.*[64]

Public furor about MIPC's existence and influence had largely dissipated by the 1980s. Occasionally, voices surfaced about how much security the defense budget was actually buying. "Contrary to the long-held and popular belief, military spending is not good for the economy," Marion Anderson, director of employment Research Associates in Lansing, Michigan held, as "it does not create employment–it generates unemployment." In her computation, every million-dollar increase in the military budget cost 10,000 jobs. Deep problems of the American economy could not be ameliorated until the military budget was cut, and money left in the hands of citizens through tax cuts, or spent on economically productive activities at all levels of government. Yet, when surveyed, Americans for years had displayed a degree of unpredictability about defense, the military, and how much spending should be for national security. The nadir of Vietnam had evolved into remorse and renewed respect for military institutions. A volunteer military had supplanted required-duty. Still, the percentage of Americans who said defense spending was too high, had decreased during the years 1969 to 1981. Then, according to Gallup Polls, public attitudes shifted once again from a January 1980 low of 14 percent who thought defense spending was too high to reach 47 percent five years later, before once more dropping below 40 percent by the end of Reagan's term. An independent Packard commission's viewpoint suggested what perhaps had always been an American attitude: positive about the military as an essential institution of the state, yet negative on the defense budget and the Pentagon's track record for getting its money's worth. Americans had made their peace with anti-statist tradition, begrudgingly accepted MIPC indispensability, and signed off on Reagan's strong defense prescription, as long as it did not bankrupt them.[65]

Washington Post columnist Nick Kotz told readers on June 28, 1988, that "special interests dominate and prevail because defense spending has become a staple in the American political economy that we believe we cannot do without." The cumulative effect was that many agendas were thus distorting the entire national defense effort. He reminded everyone that locally "no one wants any bases or programs to shut down," while the weapons manufacturing executives sought profits for shareholders. As to who gains the profits and who gets the dislocated economy, Kotz remarked that "often depends on who has the most clout rather than on which company has the best product and the lowest price" or for that matter, "even on whether the weapon is needed at all." Members of Congress too "must continually balance national defense needs against the interests of their constituents in sharing the pork barrel of job-producing defense bases and plants," along with influence peddling related to campaign funds, and lucrative speaking fees "lavished on them by defense contractors." Kotz cited the B-1 bomber case where contractors were known to spread parts of their projects around congressional districts, "whether or not this division of spoils led to the most efficient weapons production." Each service allowed parochial priorities "to exert raw political pressure," undermining DoD control of procurement decisions, Kotz decided.[66]

What would it take to untie this knot, wondered Kotz. Proper enforcement of ignored defense-reform laws, which could limit conflicts of interest, since public servants often passed through a revolving door into lucrative private industry? He also advocated protection for whistleblowers who pointed out problems, establishing a congressionally independent testing service to determine more objectively whether weapons actually performed to specifications, higher ethical standards that could build upon the 1986 Goldwater-Nichols defense-reorganization act representing "a thoughtful effort to limit service parochialism," or simply encourage a coherent national defense plan? He pilloried Congress for micromanaging hundreds of separate programs, rather than overall defense needs, and further cited advocacy for a bill that would insulate legislators from constituent pressures by creating a bipartisan commission on base closures, which could save $2 billion annually. Yet, most of all, Kotz offered, "it is unlikely that the country will really be able to rid itself of many wasteful and unneeded defense programs unless the government actively promotes development of meaningful economic alternatives to defense jobs." The nation should redirect its high-tech capabilities from defense "to compete in more peaceful and rewarding pursuits."

By the 1980s, defense had ensured its economic place beside domestic programs as a viable part of business, industry, labor, and its commitment to domestic tranquility, stability and prosperity as much as national protection. In short, most defense companies were publicly traded on Wall Street. A $689 million deal with General Motors to build thousands of utility cargo vehicles in mid-1982 promised to offset a three-year slump in automobile production and give jobs to 2,000 auto workers in the Flint, Michigan area. Company vice president Donald J. Atwood termed it their largest military contract since the end of World War II. So, Americans, especially those in the so-called defense sector rejoiced that the Defense department had come to a policy of placing maximum reliance on the private-sector industrial base, rather than its own "captive" public sector. Indeed, Washington neared the end of a massive disposal of facilities that over the previous twenty-one years had sold off 114 industrial plants for $388.8 million. Finding buyers was not always easy, given breakdowns of old equipment. Nevertheless, declared one involved General Services Administrator, "most of the huge heavy hammers and forges are still considered the 'state of the art' for the metal-shaping industry." Privatization of the arsenal had become a panacea by the Reagan years.[67]

The sum of $1.4 trillion was spent from 1981 to 1986 with aircraft, shipbuilding, tanks, electronics, and sub-primes all profiting from this largesse, styled rearmament by Reagan hawks. California, New York, Texas, Connecticut, Massachusetts, Virginia, Missouri, Pennsylvania, Washington and Florida were the top-ten states, and collectively already getting sixty-eight percent military spending in 1980. The new outlays supposedly would add a half-million new jobs, with the lion's share (445,000) going to private-sector defense workers. Judged in 1979, the top-ten biggest defense contractors already were: General Dynamics ($3.5 billion for jet fighters, submarines, and research), McDonnell Douglas ($3.2 billion for jet fighters, missiles, and space systems), United Technologies ($2.6 billion for helicopters and jet engines), General Electric ($2.0 billion for aircraft engines), Lockheed ($1.8 billion for missiles, aircraft, and research), Hughes Aircraft ($1.6 billion for research for missile and space systems, radar, and navigational aids), Boeing ($1.5 billion for research for missile, space, and radar systems), Grumman ($1.4 billion for jet aircraft and fighter gear), Raytheon ($1.2 billion for missiles and components), and Tenneco ($1 billion for warships). When Tenneco's Todd Shipyards reported that ships were essential for commerce, peace, defense, and the public good, furthermore, they had to be built domestically "at our own facilities, by our own people and under our control," *Washington Post* writer Thomas Lippmann observed that the message is the "gospel according to the shipbuilders, but the only true believer is the U.S. Navy."[68]

No wonder James W. Canaan, senior editor of *Air Force Magazine*, headlined a 1985 opinion-piece "The Profitability of Defense." The defense industry was riding high, netting award of "a whopping $84.6 billion in prime contracts, in just the first six months of Fiscal Year 1985." He cited the $146 billion in prime contracts racked up by industry in Fiscal Year 1984, as "almost exactly $100 billion more than the value of such contracts ten years ago in Fiscal Year 1976," $63 billion more than in Fiscal Year 1980 and $21.3 billion more than in Fiscal Year 1982. He foresaw dangers in allegations of fraud, waste, and abuse, as well as questions of excessive profits. Inside the MIPC bubble, both government and industry turned increasingly to the overall health of what they now styled the "defense industrial base." Could the base respond in crisis to something as fundamental as ammunition supply? Jacques Gansler questioned the lack of "dual-sourcing" to ensure competition in DoD procurement. Such questions always had surfaced in other peacetime eras, but new muckraking by this point underscored what military analyst Arthur T. Hadley called "America's Broken War Machine," and what Industrial College of the Armed Forces dean John E. Ellison termed "the Beleaguered Arsenal." In April 1983, Texas senator John Tower told an American Defense Preparedness Association audience how government spending from 1970 to 1982 had increased by ninety-seven percent for social programs while defense spending decreased by eight percent, while, at the same time, "the Soviet Union was arming at a rate unprecedented in peacetime." Strategic, regional and technological parity had been lost. The answer was Reagan's "steadfastness of his position on defense spending," not yielding to the pressures of popular whim."[69]

Despite the rush of contract money during the Reagan years, trade journals, news media and the occasional professional journal joined public organs like Icord's congressional panel in a chorus condemning lack of plans, procedures, organizations, and actions on the problem. House Armed Services Committee chairman Melvin Price bemoaned the fact that in the event of war, the DIB could not surge "suddenly or dramatically" in numbers necessary to sustain any prolonged war. To many like Gansler, given Soviet nuclear parity, something as basic as industrial preparedness "can and should play in all four prongs of America's national security posture." Mobilization even industrial preparedness re-surfaced in strategic deterrence equations. Moreover, analysts like James R. Kurth and Robert E. McGarrah joined Gansler preaching the new gospel of "multinational interdependence" for benefits to America's industrial sector.[70]

Frankly, U.S. officials, strategists, and policymakers desperately sought any attractive approach to offset seemingly never-ending Soviet power. Economic and defense resourcing attending alliances, coalitions, and cooperation, received new impetus via détente. Authors like McGarrah measured America's "arsenal of democracy" as a global arms-industry hegemony, and that, "compared to competitive, independent programs, each US-allied cooperative-arms program would create a larger common-defense market, with greater opportunities for sustained income and employment for all partner nations." American and allied contractors "would be free to compete, consort, or merge interests and improve productivity and industrial efficiency," thus enhancing overall military security. Surplus and redundant arms-production capabilities could be eliminated, along with associated costs. Arms-export competition also would be eliminated. Best of all, a substantial reduction could be made in America's burden of defending everyone else. Washington "could accrue significant savings that it could reinvest to reduce the federal deficit and to increase productivity, employment, and exports of consumer goods and industrial products." Results "would more than compensate for the decline in growth and employment in the US defense industry," thought McGarrah.[71]

James Kurth went even further, arguing for American industrial transformation—a model seen years earlier for the U.S. and German chemical, electrical, aviation, and automobile industries. The United States particularly "has had a long history of moving out of old industries and into new ones." New business could help revive the industrial base and renew competitive lead in the world marketplace, creating a strong tax base for military expenditures, with a regenerative American competitiveness in the world market serving to reduce pressures at home for protective tariffs, and on balance-of-payments from US military deployments abroad. He anticipated a new industrial sector to include semiconductors, computers, telecommunications and robotics in the 1980s, and biotechnology, lasers and "space industrialization" later on. High technology could even be integrated with older production technology, say, for instance, in the steel industry. Moreover, he predicted "an economic strategy based on industrial transformation" as likely "to generate pressures for a military strategy based upon precision guided munitions." A disciple of this new strategy weapon, Kurth claimed that "successive generations of PGMS might also provide technological spinoffs to civilian industry, such as helping to make the telecommunication of information rather than the transportation of persons as the central focus of the future economy." Here was potential for dual use new technologies from new industries to make simpler, more effective, more reliable weapon systems, providing "an opportunity to combine the best of the ideas of industrial transformation and procurement reform." The Reagan years resounded with such confidence.[72]

A cottage industry sprang up around prescriptions for MIPC's problems. They included addressing procurement scandal and reform, efficiency and effectiveness, and always cost, the shortage of critical parts suppliers in the subcontractor tier of the primes, with production in castings, forgings, electrical connectors, semiconductors and precision bearings dropping off. Thanks to the customary post-conflict (this time, Vietnam) slump cycle, that meant fewer suppliers, lower profits, smaller-volume and single-year orders, cyclical demand, special military requirements, market uncertainty, excessive regulation, and extensive government paperwork. At one point, Gansler raised DoD's idiosyncratic acquisition practices which discouraged prime contractors from developing multiple sources for lower-tier supplies. Saturation for the few specialized suppliers, and absence of expansion capacity whether at established firms or through new entries, caused bottlenecks that resulted in rising costs and increased lead times for the vast majority of completed weapons systems. Recourse to offshore procurement by defense primes, thus courting the eternal anathema of foreign dependency, had its own issues, leading to cozy "offset agreements" via foreign military sales. Oddly, the inverse problems of excess capacity and underutilized plants at the prime contractor level were traceable to lower-volume production lines, for example, fighter aircraft, because of complexity and cost, compared to simpler platforms in the 1950s and 1960s. Suddenly, now, surge-capacity could not be achieved in under three years, due to sub-prime bottlenecks.[73]

The plain truth, said Gansler, is that since the Department of Defense was "the sole buyer—as well as the banker (through progress payments), the regulator, the specifier, the sponsor of research and development, and even the court of claims (on protests)–the government has the *responsibility* [Gansler's emphasis] to concern itself with the structure, conduct, and performance of the industry that it creates." Government officials had been slow to realize this responsibility, having embraced the notion that free market forces would create economic efficiency and surge capability, but which became impossible when the market consisted of a single buyer, and generally a single or very few suppliers. Gansler's particular solutions included strengthening domestic industrial infrastructure, improving U.S. competitiveness worldwide, and reducing dependency, in turn achieving maximum U.S. economic gain from defense investments, encouraging major new technological advances, stimulating lower prices and improved quality through duplicate even multiple sources for many products, and implementing something styled "an industrial strategy." Such were the challenges with a now-mature military-industrial-political-complex.

Nonetheless, issues existed within the Complex. An always-articulate government insider-outsider, Gansler felt that the United States was the only nation "that does not explicitly treat its defense industry as a vital national resource." He cited a 1984 Aerospace Industries Association report that called for "a new commitment and a new philosophy–characterized by a more cooperative relationship between government and industry," based on clearly enunciated government policy with input from industry. Thus, DIB could take its place along with Joint Chiefs of Staff, budget, and procurement, for reform implementation. Everybody thought that the Reagan defense buildup demanded policy changes and DIB restructuring that could lead to both preparedness and efficient procurement of new weapons systems. Government studies like the David Packard Commission and congressional analysis, which produced the Goldwater-Nichols Defense Reorganization Bill in 1986, pointed toward to regulation and reorganization. But, reformers like Gansler wanted more done on the industrial side. Highest priority "must be given to defining and mapping courses of action required to enable U.S. industry to regain leadership" in the coming manufacturing revolution.[74]

Other commentators who took up the chant of "Lifeline in Danger," two years later would still admonish "the lifeline is still in danger." Halting steps were taken when Secretary of Defense Richard Cheney deprecated the adversarial atmosphere between Defense and industry as completely unnecessary and wasteful, and set up a new Defense Manufacturing Board (DMB) as a means of communication and cooperation. What it all amounted to was mostly cosmetic preaching about DoD as a "world class customer," acquisition streamlining, and a much-ballyhooed Total Quality Management program. The semantics from the chairman of the Quality Committee of the DMB, Christopher Galvin of Motorola, touted changing Congress's role from "constructive operations management" (micromanagement?), to a "kind of board of directors for the Department of Defense." Gansler's vision of a strengthened defense posture, while improving long-term economic competitiveness via "an integrated, national industrial strategy" spotlighting the nation's strengths of "a competitive economy and a free democracy," got lost in the shuffle. Decrying the "bits and pieces" approach of the Reagan administration—operating primarily through tax and trade policies, and agency stove-piping actions—Gansler still sought instead a coherent strategy for establishing a set of consistent implementation actions. That lay beyond political reality. Both Carter and Reagan administrations proved disjointed and hidden, or merely encouraged mergers and acquisitions.[75]

THE EXTRACTIVE RESULTS OF MIPC

Just what had MIPC accomplished by the time of the Reagan years? Did it effectively end the Cold War? Its armada of strategic systems, from B-36, B-47, B-52, and B-1 propeller and jet bombers to intermediate and long-range ballistic missiles for carrying nuclear weapons, had deterred the unthinkable. Whole naval battlegroups were formed from both conventional and nuclear-powered aircraft carriers, the *Midway, Oriskany, Forrestal, Enterprise*, and *Nimitz*, for example, accompanied by their supporting vessels. A nuclear submarine fleet, shepherded by Admiral Hyman Rickover and his successors, was an entirely different marriage of surface and subsurface systems and platforms. Armored land vehicles went from the World War II era M-26 to the M-1 "Abrams" main battle tanks, as well as a succession of armored personnel carriers from M-76 to M-2. The tactical fighter family of aircraft and their upgrades saw new platforms unveiled, from the venerable World War II prop-driven P-51 still useful in Korea and its F-80 jet comrades, down to the A-10, F-16, F-18, and AV-88 by the 1980s. Advancements in small arms and artillery (self-propelled and automotive-drawn), as well as supply vehicles and equipment were also legion. These fruits of the arms industry and arms trade could be seen across the globe in allied inventories. Out of public view, except during controversial testing in Nevada and the South Pacific, were the nuclear weapons programs of the Atomic Energy Commission and its successors Energy Research and Development Administration, and Department of Energy. Those civilian agencies managed eight primary nuclear-weapons processes at dozens of sites in uranium mining and refining, isotope separation, fuel and target fabrication, production reactor operations, research and development, and testing. Mining companies and facilities spread from Africa to across America, along with leftover plants and laboratories from the Manhattan Project era to newer installations, and health and environment activities not even on the nuclear weapons-complex charts. Finished devices totaled in the thousands, from tactical to strategic in nature.[76]

The Cold War MIPC additionally gave the nation a Continuity of Government system, infrastructure thanks to private-sector AT&T and public Federal Emergency Management Administration, as well as a civil-defense parallel (while slowly obsolescing to irrelevance), also with a corresponding infrastructure and mentality conditioning the American public toward a national security-state framework of fear. The physical interstate highways, as well as information-highway systems derived, too, from MIPC and NSS in these decades. The Reagan years were supposed to produce resource parity, nay even better, superiority, to the Soviet Union. Along the way, the defense industry expected not only ever more infusion of contracts and funding, but less government regulation, and less excessive auditing. What the private arsenal received was more money, but coming with intense contract scrutiny, Pentagon emphasis on cutting profit margins and forcing companies to assume more risk, including greater industry-share for research and development costs, up-front investments, and for costs not directly related to the contract. While a happier military went on thinking the defense budget would expand forever, the Soviet Union always provided a worst-case scenario requiring more money to buy technology to fight a war, at tops lasting only thirty days, and guarantee a bigger bureaucracy for administrating more headquarters to make "warfighters" more efficient. The country in turn received more controversy coming out of the Pentagon, the biggest peacetime defense budget in history at the time (promised to be about $318 billion for 1987), and national security *wunderkind*, the SDI program. This missile-defense program using high-technology weapons to shoot down potential Soviet missiles after they had been launched in a nuclear barrage, was to be the technology-showcase of the age. In concept it may well have been the final tipping-point that at least psychologically helped end of the Cold War. Soviet leaders perceived they could not outspend Washington on such costly military technology.[77]

The Strategic Defense Initiative reflected bureaucratic growth incarnate. From a few aides, to the Air Force three-star in charge when created in 1981, SDI bureaucracy grew to 200, and from 1983 to 1985 Congress approved $10.2 billion for the project, then engaged in cutting the figure, but eventually left the program with a hefty $3.1 billion for FY 1987. Even if the technology could be made to work, few anticipated actual deployment but even fewer also expected the program would ever be eliminated outright. Really a presidential whim, Reagan had spoken on television in March 1983 calling upon scientists to develop technology that would render nuclear weapons "impotent and obsolete," and the Complex responded dutifully. Within a couple of years Lieutenant General James A. Abrahamson's Strategic Defense Initiative (SDI) office had signed 3,300 contracts worth $10.9 billion, eight billion of that with corporations. Those corporations included some of the biggest defense contractors: Lockheed ($1 billion), General Motors ($734 million), TRW ($567 million), McDonnell Douglass ($485 million), and others like General Electric, Rockwell International, Raytheon, LTV, Grumman, Teledyne, Honeywell and Martin Marietta also at the trough. The appealing fact was that SDI was not a single weapons program, but hundreds of different projects spread across satellite systems, space-tracking sensors, command-and-control communications networks, and high-speed gun and laser weapons. Of course, SDI components might find other military or space-related uses. As one analyst underscored, profits would not roll in until production, but already more profits meant jobs and economic growth "which translates into political pressure to keep the program going." Perhaps that was MIPC's reason for being anyway.[78]

SDI was MIPC's poster child. It was, as Defense department historian Walter Poole has noted, truly "defining the limits of technology and what constituted the state of the art," the Pentagon drawing on its own arsenals and universities, "acting as federally funded research and development centers," but most of all, resources in the private sector. Moreover, "large, diversified corporations run by technically trained professionals dominated the U.S. economy" by the mid-twentieth century and beyond, administratively managed in diversified enterprise by "decentralized structures of autonomous divisions "that handled all the functions involved in creating a line of product and a general office that evaluated performance and allocated resources." This was what business historian Alfred D. Chandler saw as "by far the largest number of people" carrying out the technological innovation central to economic growth, while spending "the greatest part of the massive funds" that the U.S. government gave to R&D, absolutely indispensable to the defense industry and the military. One could appreciate this government-private compact that would yield America's ultimate strategic defense, even an "interim system" by the 1990s and possibly full-system by early in the twenty-first century. SDI promised: 3,000 rockets positioned on 300 to 500 satellites orbiting the Earth, another 1,000 to 2,000 in North Dakota, designed to shoot down missiles in their final minute or so of flight just before reentry into the atmosphere and explosion over US territory, and a dozen or so satellites plus ground sensors to guide these rockets to their targets. It was a project rivaling the Manhattan and H-bomb nuclear programs, or NASA's various space projects. Either a $76 to $100 billion interim or fully deployed shield at $500 billion to $3 trillion, set atop the normal defense expenditures, since no one was willing to forego normal war toys for some unproven SDI shield. Spin-off applications of potential SDI breakthroughs increased salivation in the scientific and technical community for areas like artificial intelligence and computing, lasers and directed-energy systems, and sensors. Such large-scale technology projects were always "in the same category as rivers and harbors, post offices, and other elements of the political pork barrel." The initial success of the SDI organization caused analyst Gerald M. Steinberg trepidation because of the bureaucratic competition with the rest of the military's R&D community. It could create the potential for both duplication and determining national priorities based on organizational interests and perspectives. Still that was always inherent in "providing for the common defense."[79]

Frank Spinney, a maverick Pentagon military analyst, entitled his 1988 exposé, "Look What $2 Trillion Didn't Buy for Defense." He thought that spending billions of taxpayer dollars was always a power struggle. But, spending against the perception that the Soviets outspent us on defense "puts political expediency before military needs and undermines our constitutional system of power." In his view, the Carter-Reagan bump in spending had "not produced an increase in military strength and preparedness proportional to the large claim made on public and private resources." Where had the $1.83 trillion spent since 1980 on military weapons, manpower, operations and maintenance gone, he asked. That money had not bought larger or newer forces for higher operating tempos. Furthermore, there was no proof "if the defense budget bought better, if fewer weapons," for in some cases they "were not subjected to rigorous and realistic tests of their ability to perform their wartime missions." What the defense budget did, said Spinney, was to buy "jobs, votes in elections and votes in Congress." Complicated weapons-systems designs and success-oriented weapons testing meshed with astute political engineering "to convert the defense budget into a giant, self-perpetuating public-works budget."[80]

Procurement spending between fiscal years 1980 and 1987 (the peak year), with inflation, increased by seventy-eight percent and the 1988 decline reduced this spending to a level still sixty-eight percent higher than the budget in 1980, Spinney claimed. Additional money did not build larger forces—aircraft and helicopter inventories remained constant and strategic nuclear forces declined slightly, but maneuver battalions remained about the same. While ship numbers increased by about fifteen percent, the navy had decided to prematurely retire sixteen frigates and forego the Secretary of the Navy's pie-in-the-sky "600-ship Navy." Equipment was generally older than in the 1980s, tanks being an exception, and the reason the seventy-eight percent increase in spending did not secure larger or newer forces, Spinney harped, "is that we used this money to buy smaller numbers of more expensive, more complex, less efficiently produced weapons, modernizing selectively and keeping older weapons to maintain inventories." Spinney aimed his ire at the "political engineering" of such Pentagon officials as Secretary of Defense Caspar Weinberger, who routinely countered budget-cut threats from Congress by citing out how they would cost defense industry jobs. But, between 1980 and 1988 a sixty percent increase in defense-related jobs, or about 3.25 million, cost the taxpayer on the average more than $50,000 each. The defense industry now employed more workers than at the peak of the Vietnam War, said Spinney. Weapons, more complex and expensive, even though fewer overall, equated to "more and more subcontracts flowing to more and more congressional districts." In the case of the B-1 bomber program, killed under Carter and restored under Reagan, "several thousand contractors, employing 40,000 workers, artfully dispersed among 48 states, produced 100 airplanes."

Spinney also raised concern about strategic missiles. Plans in 1980 to replace one-thousand strategically vulnerable, silo-based Minutemen ballistic missiles with two-hundred mobile MX missiles carrying slightly fewer warheads. Rising costs and a new twist,cenvironmental concerns, meant that only fifty of the new systems were procured and placed in silos. "So, in the end, after spending $9 billion, U.S. missiles are still in silos, we still have the problem of replacing a large number of aging Minutemen in the 1990s and now we have two new mobile missile programs, the Midgetman [somewhat laughable in title] and the MX Rail Garrison, as well as the requirement for large strategic budgets for the foreseeable future," he observed. Moreover, 19,000 separate parts comprising the MX's inertial measurement unit, the heart of its guidance system, were produced by 553 suppliers located in twenty-six states. Similarly, a glossy Air Force public-relations pamphlet boasted of benefits from the new cargo transport C-17 competition that "translated into a solid production base across the nation especially at the sub-vendor level where the industrial base needs rebuilding." Twenty-nine states were selected to receive production money, with twelve more "provocatively labeled as 'potential' recipients," noted Spinney. Thus, thanks to political engineering, the Pentagon perceived a compliant Congress "that tows the line, [and] one that is afraid to impose penalties on its constituents if they do not produce satisfactory products."

Spinney and others like him pressed the money-flow pattern. "In 1987, 75 percent of contract dollars flowed into 14 states having 50.2 percent of the electoral votes; 87 percent flowed into 21 states with two thirds of the electoral votes," he observed. Navy secretary John Lehman told a Brookings Institution audience in December 1982 how he had "front-loaded" his 600-ship navy scheme via "the time-proven techniques of spreading seed money around and downplaying the future obligations entailed by these commitments." Spinney suggested Lehman might thus extend "his brag to the entire defense budget" by proclaiming, "sorry, it's too late, we have 'front-loaded' the electoral college." To Spinney, political engineering corrupted the entire defense decision process, aiming to paralyze Congress by buying its constituents or public bit by bit. It subordinated military needs to political pork-barreling and "reinforces perverse behavior." It led to exaggerated threat perception like the "vulnerability" of Minuteman missile silos, which had set MX missile cash flow in motion, only ending with the MX in silos anyway, as "we underestimate costs to make it easier to get weapons into production" and also, softening test requirements, lest they would disrupt development and production. Most importantly, emphasized Spinney, by political engineering "we design overly complex weapons that maximize the number of sub-contracts and jobs." In such an environment, real defense issues like force structure, modernization, readiness and operational test fidelity fall by the wayside. Since it was an election year, Spinney speculated the time-bomb of the national debt might force the next administration's hand.

In October of 1988, Frank Spinney may not have been the direct object of Deputy Secretary of Defense William Taft's wrath over procurement "kibitzers" who had too much to say about weapon systems programs. But historian Stuart Brandes contends that while the Cold War devoured wealth "in previously unimaginable amounts, methods of control worked out over the centuries were at least able to keep profiteering in check." His assertion that military profits finally had become "reasonable" in the 1960s, since they were no more lavish than those of their civilian counterparts, might raise eyebrows. Yet, to Brandes, "profiteering had evolved into a matter of cultural interest rather than a leading political and economic problem," and was "a salutary and long overdue development." Still, *Washington Post* editors and others caught the scent of "information-buying" or "information peddling" by former high officials-turned-consultants, parlaying inside information to their contractor clients. Also, controversial and unresolved, was the question of whether an aerospace giant like Grumman, which acted like any other Fortune 500 corporation in the commercial world—aside from the fact that much of its plant and equipment was owned by DoD and of $7.9 billion revenue in 1987, $7 billion came from Pentagon funds— "should be regulated like a public utility or allowed the same freedom as a private company." Brandes' assertion that "after more than three centuries of effort, the American people had finally achieved an ability to manage economic sacrifice competently and evenhandedly," is debatable. But, MIPC has always raised the question.[81]

SETTLING INTO FAMILIAR PATTERNS

By the close of the Reagan years, the defense industrial base (DIB) portion of the military-industrial-political complex (MIPC) had become a fixture of American society. Was America concerned? Military rebuilding, a tax cut, and a slowdown in domestic spending, all provided diversion. In 1979, social entitlements, as direct benefits to individuals eventually would become styled, took thirty-seven cents of every dispersed dollar, to only twenty-four cents for national defense, and another fourteen cents for other Federal operations. A decade later, it was all about improving America's position in the world economy. Cognoscenti spoke of "mutual interdependence," and the elite's concern now, was how to maintain America's place in a rapidly changing global economy. The public translated this to jobs, standard of living, and education. "Competitiveness" permeated discussions of the defense-industrial base, along with talk of erosions, adversarial relationships, instability, productivity, cost, and need for a national attitude check. The MIPC no longer drew the fervent moral and ethical critiques that it had two decades before. The question of its overpowering influence slipped into history, replaced by internal worries about the diminishing U.S. defense arsenal, and how the procurement pendulum was swinging back to the "very hard times" of the year 1969 for the defense industry. Congress heard how a post-Vietnam "total force" volunteer military, active and reserves combined probably couldn't contain any Soviet breakthrough into Europe without going nuclear, due to lack of backup forces, ammunition and other war supplies. One set of analysts scoffed, "while Americans worried about a mythical 'military-industrial complex,' relations between government and the defense industry were deteriorating." MIPC's issues had acquired an insipid sameness.[82]

Survey, analysis and prescription became endemic. For instance, an Air Force Association and United States Naval Institute Military Database joint-study criticized the years up to 1987 as lacking in mobilization planning, with acceptance in the armed services of "come as you are" conflict and foreign competition seen as reducing critical industries to a fraction of their former size. Tank production-surge at the time of the 1973 Yom Kippur War had gone nowhere and weapons-aid, such as to Great Britain during the 1982 Falklands action, "would not be sustainable over extended periods of time without seriously damaging the viability of U.S. war reserves." Without the ability to support friends in time of need, "the credibility of American foreign policy, often tarnished in recent years, might suffer blows from which it could take years to recover." Elsewhere, war planners wanted lists of defense requirements to include the industrial base in their calculations, so the system "would be another way for the nation to show resolve during a crisis, thus reinforcing the probability that war will be deterred." Fundamental weaknesses had become endemic: dearth of raw materials, inability to sustain a surge production period, reliance on foreign sources of high-technology military components due to foreign penetration of U.S. markets, "offset agreements" with foreign allies, R&D shortfall, the clash of regulatory government and profit-possessed industry, as well as decline in technically qualified manpower. Dependency on foreign sources of minerals and fuels, declining viability of stockpiling, as well as questions of productivity and profitability in key segments of the base such as machine tools, aerospace, maritime industry, pharmaceuticals, semiconductors, and precision optics, also became repetitive issues. Since the flagship Defense Production Act of 1950, and subsequent ups and downs of implementation, the AFA/NI study felt government had remained flatly ignorant of the state of industry.[83]

The AFA/NI authors concluded that the nation needed to learn from foreign experience by not always assuming the best answers inevitably lay abroad. Still, American systems set the standard for the world. The nation must stop viewing the defense industry "with distaste and reexamine its fantasies about a 'military-industrial complex.'" American industry "deserves better support than it has been getting from American government." AFA-NI authors did not want a foreign trade ministry like those of Japan or Great Britain which would advocate on behalf of America's defense industry. But, "clearly, though, the U.S. government could do more than it does–and it should do more." Yet, AFA/NI recommendations were fairly basic. Topping the list was yet another presidential commission "to chart a course." This commission, the study's authors suggested, should reexamine the field of incentives and disincentives in defense production, and plan reform of "the tangled network of laws and regulations" that had led to the current conditions. Congress should not rush to legislate solutions since it had been hasty, ad hoc legislation that created "the tangle" in the first place. The Department of Defense should immediately identify "to the end of the supplier and subcontractor chain, the foreign dependencies involved for critical weapons and components" and then monitor and report such dependencies, discover foreign and domestic overlaps for sources, and surge production requirements for those critical weapons and components. Further, they said, DoD "should adopt a more objective stance in its dealings with the defense industry" by eliminating "the arrogance with which it has too often approached industry in the past few years." Prime contractors should themselves "nurture the supplier-contractor base," and should "shed the 'bunker mentality'" coming from the repeated assaults made on it in recent years. The Pentagon "has a strong case to make on its own behalf and an important perspective that the nation needs to hear." Finally, the AFA/NI study concluded that the government as a whole should do a major command-post exercise (or CPX) like "Nifty Nugget 1978" to diagnose and demonstrate the state of the defense industrial base. That CPX had revealed logistics problems "in convincing detail" which "finally gave the nation a basis on which to rebuild its military mobilization plans." A new defense industrial-based CPX could do the same for the larger acquisition problem, "a most useful step" on the road back to defense industrial preparedness.[84]

The AFA/NI list of reform recommendations, in particular, reflected internal government management concerns that supposedly could be addressed in classic fashion by a new array of boards, offices and bureaucratic efforts, less unique to any one period in the MIPC's long history. Only now, the number of outsider-advocates for solution nearly outnumbered government and industry implementers, proffering lists filled with many ideas about factory modernization investments, program stability through two-year budget cycles, multi-year contracts, a more realistically achievable five-year program, life-cycle costs as a basic evaluation technique, and quality control in furtherance of the Total Quality Management (TQM). And there were still others, like increasing use of commercial manufacturing process, product specifications in lieu of unique military specifications, greater emphasis on development and application of process technologies, to assure domestic supply of affordable electronic, computer, and software components, for rapid insertion into weapon systems, as well as proposals for addressing a major private-sector complaint about identifying and eliminating government barriers in motivating management to achieve manufacturing excellence and competitiveness. DoD already had a solution-response to this issue, by increasing progress payments, restricting use of fixed price R&D contracts, and more clearly defining the role of program managers vis-à-vis contracting officers and auditors. Less simple, if not downright impossible, reforms for DoD implementation to achieve were recommendations for a Production Base Impact Assessment. This would entail a substantial analytic capability within the Legislative Branch or Congress that would be dedicated to objective impact-evaluation of existing and proposed legislation on the domestic manufacturing base and its ability to compete internationally, and an examination of coherent tax, trade and domestic policies that would require whole-of-government, or interagency, coordination and cooperation.[85]

Looking back, many of these issues simply had matured, over the decades. Physicist Seymour Melman had concluded in 1971 that private corporations in the Complex had moved the concept of public-arsenal autarky to a private arsenal system for national defense. Citing a long-understood difference between ownership and control (stockholders own, managers control, although occasionally there was interchangeability), Melman had suggested that this separation between the two was also present in government management which oversaw $44 billion of industrial activity in 1968 and "is by far the largest industrial management in the land." The output of the DoD endeavor had exceeded the combined industrial activity of General Motors, General Electric, U.S. Steel and DuPont. Corporate America had been reduced to medium and small-sized firms. "The center of control over capital allocation" was no longer in the private board rooms of Wall Street banks and major industrial firms. Instead, he advanced, "the overwhelmingly largest single block of investment capital, hence of decision-power over production, is now vested in the new state management whose capital supply is drawn from the national income, allocated, year by year, by a willing Congress." Because the new industrial control-center, the Pentagon, was management, it had characteristics different from those of any military-industrial complex. It was even a post-MIPC.[86]

Melman had viewed MIPC as "a market network; while the new state management consolidated this network into a highly structured formal organization which it now operates." A market had no executive committee, made no production decisions, and executed no planning, while the state management operated no centralized network of controls over subsidiary enterprises. The Complex as a market "did not have a built-in mechanism for enlarging its own decision power." State management did all of these things. "Since enlarging decision power is the professional-occupational imperative of the industrial manager, there has been built into American society a new institution of decision power whose growth and health as a decision-making-entity rests upon the growth of military budgets, military organizations, military production and military operation," Melman declared, in a mouthful. If Vietnam "is by various criteria a tragedy and a many-sided disaster for American society as a whole," it was a success for state management for "it has made available to that entity "more capital funds, more people working under its direction, more capital under its control, more men in its armed forces and more territory and civilians within its sway." Since military spending proved good for the economy—growth from $45 billion in 1960 to over $80 billion by 1969—a doctrine of flexible response had emerged, with American arms seen as competent for varied political uses. One thing was clear to Melman. The word "defense "for shielding the United States, "is left only in the name of the Department of Defense." Twenty years later, Melman wanted a nonintervention policy not the burgeoning policy of wars of intervention "defined by past administrations." Depart the folly of planning and preparing to conduct three simultaneous wars, commit instead to strategic deterrence via existing weaponry, maintain a capability for guarding the homeland, competently adequate forces for international peacekeeping operations, and no more. $50 billion could be turned to other useful purposes.[87]

* * *

The defining characteristics of America's defense establishment over fifty years of Cold War peace were national security budgets of unprecedented size, a large standing military, and a "permanent" armaments industry. Millions for defense and not one cent for tribute literally translated into millions under arms, and a defense industrial base of absorbent proportions. In addition, the components of nuclear weapons, intelligence and foreign affairs contributed an array of "whole of government/inter-agency" mobilization for permanent war. The public-private partnership for creating instruments of power had distinct characteristics as well. Some of the defense industrial base constituted platform providers of aircraft, missiles, ships, land vehicles. Other portions concentrated on major systems like propulsion and electronics. Most of this decentralized at the sub-systems level into small to medium elements, and spread throughout the land. They formed part of a market system of distinct features: monosporic (one large buyer, the U.S. government) and oligopolic (relatively few suppliers able to develop and construct complex integrated systems, for example air-to-air missiles). Everything led from technology, research, and development, driven by military needs (jet propulsion, high-speed computing, nuclear fission, lasers, digital electronics, computer networking), but with dual-use spin-offs for civilian applications (from eye surgery to compact disks to the Internet). A traditional public sector remained via arsenals, depots, shipyards, laboratories with nuclear weapons production, processes, and with administration at the apex. Completing the Complex was the political dimension, forming an interlocking "Iron Triangle of Executive and Legislative Branches, the military and private industry with human communities, and the interests of all objectives (weapons, jobs, profits) subsumed in strategy, mission, and coincidence (rational, irrational or premeditated)."[88]

Thanks to MIPC, national survival was assured. Statistics proved that fact. Defense spending as a percentage of the gross national product from the outset of the Cold War, had shot up from 4.5 percent to 13.2 at the tail-end of Korea, then back down to 8.8 percent at the time of President John F. Kennedy's election in 1960, stood at 8.9 percent eight years later (Vietnam), 7.5 percent in the mid-1970s and settled at 4.6 percent at the end of that decade. In 1985 it stood close to that, at 4.1 percent, when Reagan military buildup and congressional pushback collided over "guns and butter." Total military procurement about doubled from $23.7 billion in 1960 to $45.8 billion when America detached from Vietnam in the mid-1970s. Under-Secretary of Defense Robert Costello proudly proclaimed later that almost $165 billion had been spent in 1985 across a broad spectrum of 215 industries, reflecting ninety-five percent of manufacturing goods purchased by the Pentagon. This may have been only 4.1 percent of GNP but was "21 per cent of the manufacturing gross national product." Official definition of "the national needs for defense" changed little from beginning to end of this epoch. To protect America's people, its institutions, and its riches was a fundamental precept that had not changed in 250 years, much less fifty. But, the tools of war were now economic tools for public good, private counting-house, and boardroom. What had transmogrified over a half-century was the American state, its people, society, and acceptance of the permutations and permeations of common defense and national security.[89]

Secretary of Defense Frank Carlucci and Under-Secretary Costello preached the gospel of "Safeguarding a Strategic Asset: The Defense-Industrial Base." Maintaining overall balance between the United States and its allies, and the Soviet Union and their allies, had not changed since mutually assured destruction entered the vernacular. Promoting peace and security through arms-limitations treaties had been added, as had budget realities, and a general search for "more stable relationships among countries, and negotiated settlements of disputers." Interagency was now a resource-multiplier, although under mobilization schemes it always had been. Gone were the days of self-sufficiency, of autarky, the goal of the Industrial Age. By the 1980s, the defense industrial base mixed many of the same manufacturers producing goods for the general public, as for the military. "Few of those industries relied primarily or completely on the Department of Defense as their principal market," intoned Costello in 1988. His domain depended on virtually every sector of the manufacturing base for matériel. Ironically, it always had to some degree. Moreover, he claimed "for those essential products the United States does not manufacture, we must rely on offshore sources or stockpiles." This wasn't new either, until stockpile maintenance costs defied Pentagon auditors. Dependence on foreign suppliers had always been an anathema, and the precept of "we can, however, offer incentives to establish domestic manufacturing industries for these products," Costello thought, would contravene the inexorable direction of growing "globalization."[90]

Between 1975 and 1990, "transformation" was always in the air for an American military. Emerging from its hollow-force, post-Vietnam status, planners embraced reliance on calling up Reserve components in the event of major need. The Department of Defense dutifully but unenthusiastically supplied requirements-data to FPA and FEMA for envisaged industrial war, and skipped into its own more-controllable world of production-surge planning and force-expansion analysis in a national mobilization-planning structure that looked good on a chart. When the Berlin Wall came down; the Soviet empire disintegrated. The question then became what to do with America's military power? Would there be traditional demobilization and conversion? Would the nation and its people see a peace dividend through budgetary, production, and institutional shrinkage, even eventual conversion to a civilian economy? Or would the American eagle continue to sally forth to slay new dragons with an MIPC untamed? Was a new "transformation" necessary for a still-grave new world?[91]

Chapter 7

COLD WAR LEGACY AND THE GRAVE NEW WORLD, 1991-2001

The Cold War ended with a whimper not a bang. The Iron Curtain disappeared, the Berlin Wall came down and Russian leader Mikhail Gorbachev played a prominent role in the result. So too did British prime minister Margaret Thatcher, West German chancellor Helmut Kohl and American president Ronald Reagan. The West watched and might have had choices—strategic disengagement, liberal humanitarian interventionism, aggressive response to aggression through multinational institutions, claims Colin Dueck. The Military-Industrial-Political Complex could have evaporated or, at least traditionally demobilized, at the end of the Cold War. That it did not was a tribute to its inherent strength and resilience. The Cold War had gone on too long. It had become a way of life. Scholars like Carl Boggs see this as permeation of the American psyche in a national security state. True, if the Cold War ended by 1991, Americans still lived in "a grave new world." Japan's meteoric rise to economic and technological competitiveness in the eighties, the quest for self-determination by newly free nations of the former communist orbit promised regional destabilization and ethnic confrontation. Nuclear arsenals downsized, yet four ex-Soviet republics retained about 30,000 nuclear devices. The American military went from "threat"-based to "capabilities"-based planning, and downsized but never demobilized. By one account, the United States still spent over $300 billion per year for military forces that included 530 ships, 16 active divisions, over 3,000 aircraft, and more than 25,000 nuclear warheads. Designed for two major, simultaneous regional conflicts without significant allied support, "that strategy seems more a justification for a large American military than a plausible scenario for future conflicts," claimed scientists Philip Morrison, Kosta Tsipis and Jerome Wiesner. Such massive forces placed an "unacceptable burden on the American economy," built around "an unrealistic scenario of vast global conflict," and required "prompt reduction and reform."[1]

With America's traditional affinity for limited liability, the previous half-century had spawned an expanded and entrenched military-industrial, political complex (MIPC) that Dwight D. Eisenhower had deplored. It had helped close out the Cold War and was now available to shape what President George H.W. Bush envisioned as a "New World Order." Cries of "we bankrupted them" reflected "triumphalism" that America's superior economic, social and political system had prevailed. A new Marshall Plan to help transition the former communist world, or any drastic draw-down of the MIPC and reallocation of funds, programs and process to domestic needs stood little chance. Hegemony and empire beckoned. Self-congratulatory victory laps took sway as America proceeded with its self-appointed mission of globally shaping democracy and free market capitalism. Political scientist/political economist Francis Fukuyama's "end of history" view went mostly unchallenged. Defense analyst Jacques Gansler reflected residual hawks thinking that the country had to be "prepared for and/or capable of deterring future conflicts—but with far fewer dollars." Historian Paul A. C. Koistinen simply observes that to meet Cold War and post-Cold War international challenges, the United States "for first time in its history, has maintained large military structures during years of relative peace." Eventually, national security outgrew the control of responsible authorities."[2]

THE PERSIAN GULF WAR: LAST OF THE OLD OR FIRST OF THE NEW?

Overlapping the end of the Cold War and the start of yet another "postwar" period, the Persian Gulf conflict of 1990–1991 tested the viability of an old defense resourcing base (MIPC), set against a so-called "revolution in military affairs" or RMA. On the one hand, it was a Fulda Gap focused NATO versus Warsaw Pact-model proxy confrontation, the last gasp of Soviet and American (plus coalition) conventional arms, absent resort to nuclear or even chemical and biological weapons. The navy, which had expended $1.5 billion to reactivate and upgrade four World War II battleships during the Reagan military resurgence, deployed the *USS Wisconsin* and *USS Missouri* off the Kuwaiti/Iraqi coast, capable of hurling 2,700-pound armor-piercing shells every second, as well as precision-guided munitions at targets twenty-three miles inland. The *Missouri* alone fired 800 rounds or 1 million pounds of ammunition as well as twenty-eight Tomahawk conventional land-attack cruise missiles. Yet, given six months of buildup, followed by a quick victory measured in hours or days, was the American public seduced into short-war expectations? High-tech gadgetry sloughed aside blemishes in battle management that entailed allied coordination of communication systems, niche-production shortages, and how this latest kind of interventionism was to be paid for.[3]

Providing government ammunition necessitated thirteen of fourteen plants accelerating production, hiring temporary workers in several, and working production shifts sixteen to eighteen hours long, and at times even 25 hours. Commercial defense firms helped meet munitions needs. Analyst Andrew Cordesman as well as *Air Force Magazine* editors John Correll and Colleen Nash claimed that though the conflict vindicated "the much-maligned U.S. defense industry," the base no longer existed. "Even as the nation watched the war on television," companies that produced the war-winning weapons, in many cases, "were releasing workers, closing plants and searching for nondefense business." While industry's support of the Persian Gulf conflict was excellent "and often spectacular," confusion existed as to whether any "surge" in military production under the guise of graduated mobilization response (GMR) could occur, short of a formally declared national emergency. The Pentagon had finally embraced GMR in the late 1980s as part of strategic government-wide preparedness planning and coordination effort, while speed-up of items already in the production pipeline sufficed for "maintenance and overhaul" purposes of the new short-war, said one Defense department study. But, production of major end items, excepting Patriot (PAC-2) and Army Tactical Missile System was not accelerated. "The 6-monh buildup provided time for limited industrial response," claimed one Army study. Even then, "production could not have met demand for items like batteries and other electronic items had it been a longer war."[4]

The industrial base response reinforced the need to refocus planning for short war but because of a declining industrial base and anticipated reduction in funding by Congress, the army needed to concentrate on "ensuring that a reconstitution capability remains," claimed Army analysts. Adequately funding war reserve stocks not supplied by the industrial base during emergency, reemphasizing General Mobilization Response (GMR) even explore more transfer of government-operated manufacturing and repair operations and transferring some depot repair operations to commercial industry—in short, accelerated privatization—also claimed attention. Nevertheless, some weapon systems simply had leapfrogged over development to operational status for the Persian Gulf war. The Joint Surveillance Target Radar System, for one, flew operational missions six years ahead of its official planned deployment date. One Pentagon principal for Production and Logistics declared that the war's requirements "did not really tax our industrial base." Existing inventories of weapon systems and munitions were adequate, proving "unnecessary to surge or mobilize production of the complex, long-lead items except on a very selective basis. "The Defense Production Act of 1950, which had been allowed to lapse, was quickly re-approved and selectively employed. Surge seemed confined to rations, desert boots and an antidote vaccine for nerve gas, all of which were also products of Cold War capacity. Sophisticated commercial products like Global Position System receivers served nicely when adapted to military use. Technology for new ways of war like precision-guided munitions, precision navigation, and stealth (platform signature reduction), simply achieved fantastic results.[5]

Strikingly, Desert Shield/Desert Storm was really an international strategic-resourcing effort. As Jacques Gansler later commented, spare parts became a problem, such that "DoD representatives were sent scurrying around the world begging for special arrangements to expedite the sale of these needed foreign parts." Other coalition nations defrayed the majority of U.S costs–Kuwait, $16 billion; Saudi Arabia, $16 billion; other Gulf states, $4 billion; even Germany at $6.6 billion and Japan, $10 billion, in lieu of military support. Internationally, the conflict was about energy anyway. Tin-cup or pass-the-hat funding by a total of twenty-seven nations allocated fifty percent to U.S. expenses, and fifty percent to ease the economic impact of embargo on the "front-line states" of Turkey, Jordan and Egypt (with the U.S. also forgiving $7 billion in the latter's debt). Arab countries contributed troops as well as money to a willing coalition-force total of 810,000 that included 50,000 British, 18,000 French and 540,000 Americans, arrayed beside 60,000 Saudis, 20,000 Egyptians, and 15,000 Syrians, with smaller contributions from Morocco, Kuwait, Oman, Pakistan, Canada, UAE, Qatar, Bangladesh, and others. Fifteen nations sent naval resources. Many of the partners drew upon American and European arms makers for weapons and equipment. For example, 444 coalition aircraft joined 1,376 American for control of the skies. American forces turned to foreign suppliers and access to foreign military facilities. Pentagon comptroller Sean O'Keefe hinted to the House Armed Service Committee that "product surge items might be needed for combat or replenishment afterwards," citing Patriot, Hellfire and TOW missiles, ATACMS missile system, MLRS rockets, HARM Maverick and Tomahawk missiles–the stuff of a high-tech, high-price revolution in military affairs, and not quickly replicable.[6]

Serious questions of expanded defense production and industrial mobilization never arose in the new vernacular of "come as you are war." Shock and Awe tactics and Raytheon's Patriot defense-missile system mesmerized Americans. The Cold War MIPC stepped up to the immediate challenge Still, no new evidence could be found to refute the previous wisdom that industry would need at least eighteen to twenty-four months to increase production for major military items in expanded conflict. Correll and Nash felt the Gulf War experience, when coupled to a new post-conflict defense strategy, might "stimulate a reconsideration of the need for expanded defense production and industrial mobilization in time of crisis." U.S. senators Jeff Bingaman and John McCain had declared in 1989 that they could find no industrial mobilization component in U.S. national security strategy. But after the Gulf War, Joint Chiefs chairman Colin Powell alluded to three elements in reconstitution—industrial capability, mobilization capability and force regeneration. Considerations, all industry-related, of short war versus long war, Vietnam versus Persian Gulf paradigms, war reserves, surge, and industrial base, all assumed renewed vigor. In October 1990, DoD authors of the required annual defense industry-base report to Congress admitted that "maintaining an ability to reconstitute production rates to support regional conflicts, including possible Foreign Military Sales, on short notice is a challenging new issue for DoD." Correll and Nash decided this was an open question, quoting Vice Chief of Staff Admiral David F. Jeremiah who asserted that reemergence of any new Russian threat would be preceded by a long mobilization and "therefore we will have time to reconstitute the necessary forces—provided we still have the infrastructure on which to build them." The United States seemed to being going forward "with a strategy that counts on the capability to reconstitute forces but with a defense industrial base that is declining on all fronts." Cold War technology from MIPC brought Gulf War victory. But, what then?[7]

FALSE GOD OF "PEACE DIVIDEND" AND THE TYRANNY OF EVENTS

Of course, the American taxpayer expected some reward for "winning the Cold War." After all, world leaders like George H.W. Bush and Margaret Thatcher employed "peace dividend" as a political slogan to tout economic benefits following the collapse of the Soviet Union. Calls for budgetary paring and reallocation of priorities came from all political sides both public and private. The post-Persian Gulf administration of President Bill Clinton reflected an opaque demobilization—a sharp reduction in military spending from six percent of gross national product in the mid-Reagan years to three percent ten years later. Anticipated reduction in active military forces of twenty-five per cent by 1995 had surfaced, from presidential verbiage three years before. Finance historian Robert D. Hormats thought it an "enormous peace dividend" that contributed to budget surpluses at the century's end, subsequently fueling adventurism in the first part of the next century. Aerospace analyst William Gregory compared it to a similar post-Vietnam downward adjustment. An Army War College writer adamantly held that nowhere was the word "demobilization" used in any official statement, or voluntarily offered unofficially. The decisions of the Bush administration took place under a "build-down," for "the mind-set was clearly not one of 'demobilizing' after the cold war." An unstable new environment seemed to demand strategy and forces suitable for the future. Still, Cold War military systems had pounded Saddam Hussein's Iraq into submission, and would keep it suppressed for another decade. MIPC would continue to shape policy.[8]

At the time, budget policy analyst Dennis Ippolito thought that any assessment of the Cold War peace dividend depended upon "plausible assumptions about what would have occurred to the defense budget if the Soviet threat had not disappeared." The reality of inflection-points in U.S. defense spending, from the onset of Korea (about $200 billion) to the height of that "police action" ($658 billion), the subsequent dip under $400 billion by 1958, then the rise at the peak of Vietnam ($562 billion), another retreat to about $400 billion by 1974–1976, followed by increase in the Reagan buildup ($582 billion), then down once more to an "historic defense bottom" of $380 billion in the late-nineties, suggested a customary war-peace cycle. Ippolito claimed that any peace dividend failed to account for actual defense and domestic military-oriented spending that occurred during conflict—ninety percent of the budget during World War II and seventy percent during Korea. Peace dividends, he argued, could not be measured by budgets or disbursements alone. Corporate boardrooms, shop floors, military bases, and their adjacent communities would not have welcomed a peace dividend anyway, in his view.[9]

Others, like economics Nobel laureate Joseph Steinmetz took a different approach, looking back on "the roaring nineties" in a fall 2002 *Atlantic Monthly* retrospective. Here was a *de-facto* peace dividend almost replicating the 1920s after World War I, with an economic boom hailed as "a period of unprecedented growth," for triumphant American capitalism. Globalization was in full swing and the nineties were good years, he announced, as "jobs were created, technology prospered, inflation fell, poverty was reduced." J. Bradford De Long had written five years before in "From Beast to Beauty," how domestic ripples stemming from the decline of government programs fostered a new public appreciation of the corporation as "less a beast and more a beauty than at any other time in recent history." De Long essentially focused on the nation's political economy and national political ecology, when he asked whatever happened to Progressive-era critique of the economic order, dredging the past like Steinmetz, to analyze the present. But, Steinmetz, a member of the Clinton administration from 1993 to 1997, observed, "we eagerly claimed what credit we could for the prosperity." The American people, "wanting to believe that the economic good times were a matter not just of luck but, rather, of good management," freely credited those responsible for shaping economic policy, in hopes "that under the continued stewardship of such policymakers this prosperity could be prolonged."[10]

As before in history, the tyranny of events quickly won out. The corpse of the Soviet Union was hardly cold when the nineties devolved into Persian Gulf war, Somalia intervention, and Balkan instability. NATO reinvented its *raison d'etre* by associating former Warsaw Pact countries a la "partnership for peace" programs to contain a new Russian Federation. Questions about NATO's survival became lost in the shuffle, as American presence in Europe was retained, and a military alliance paralleling the European Union economic arrangement transformed collective defense to collective security. NATO now became a tool for expanded interventionism, peacemaking and peacekeeping, as well as nation-building, outside Europe. Given the label "idealist internationalism", the approach by Clinton administration policymakers such as Madeleine Albright, Anthony Lake and Richard Holbrook, applied economic power, military strength and political influence to perceptible regional disputes, humanitarian needs, and the threat of environmental degradation. To others, the more apt terminology for America's post-Cold War role came in National Security Advisor Lake's words "engagement" and "enlargement." The first put to rest any notion of the remaining Superpower's withdrawal. The second, however, said British historian Richard Crockatt, "was the successor to containment-enlargement of the 'world's free community of market democracies.'" He asked whether this new doctrine might blur "any distinction between pragmatically conceived American interests and the others of other powers." MIPC would delineate that distinction.[11]

Primacy and liberal internationalism dominated post-Cold War U.S. foreign policy. Aside from defense, other international program spending hovered somewhere near $20 billion per year, far less in proportion to that spent by other industrialized democracies, claims Dueck. This included Department of State funding for maintenance of posts and embassies, U.S. contributions to the United Nations and its multiple operations, international developmental and humanitarian assistance programs, democracy promotion, economic and military aid to allies, and securing nuclear materials in the former Soviet Union. The term "national security" absorbed "common defense." The Pentagon's internal refashioning yielded the Base Force of the Bush years, and Clinton's Bottom Up Review (BUR). These moves trimmed spending cuts of ten percent, shrank active army divisions from twelve to ten, halved the number of reserve divisions from ten to five but retained the Marine Corps at the same 3 to 1 ratio. Navy battle forces lost 200 ships; aircraft carriers slipped from fifteen to eleven while Air Force active fighter wings slumped from twenty-four to thirteen and reserve equivalents lost five wings from twelve to seven. Civilian administrators let the military wrangle over the details for stationing 200,000 personnel as the forward presence in Europe and Northeast Asia to hedge against two major regional contingencies, plus smaller-scale operations, "due, in part, to the new predilection for humanitarian intervention." Department of Defense expenditures slipped from modernization, procurement, readiness and salary accounts. America's military stayed at about 1.4 million. Dueck called this "hegemony on the cheap." It certainly did not constitute traditional demobilization after a war.[12]

Some analysts like Sharon K. Weiner claimed defense spending declined "approximately 30 percent" by 1996 with possibilities for additional cuts of 10 to 20 percent. Energy scholar Michael Klare questioned the meaning of a new Pentagon strategy of preparing for mid-level conflict, the absence of a peace dividend, and the very premise of Gulf War success. Vietnam POW hero Senator John McCain proclaimed that American military power might "well remain the free world's insurance policy," but Klare refuted the notion of advancing America's geopolitical and economic interests, through a mammoth military and huge Pentagon budgets equal to those of the Cold War. None of this would likely result in a cooperative world order, thought Klare. Rather, like Imperial Rome and Great Britain, new Pax Americana legions might yield some benefits for regional stability, "but, we are also likely to pay a heavy price in blood, and in the continued decline of our cities, our non-military industries, and our natural environment." Defense analyst Andrew Cordesman countered that realistically America was the only nation capable of assembling and projecting enough power to meet any aggressor. Americans might not wish to be "the world's policeman," he suggested, but "they must consider what it could be like to live in a world without any policeman at all." In turn, said a California group of socialists, "the jump in Raytheon stock since the first Patriot missiles were launched" in the Gulf War suggested "quite neatly and dramatically the cozy, interdependent relationship between capitalism and war; the intermingling, in this case, of blood and oil." The "merchants of death" cry had not died out.[13]

Meanwhile, Pentagon cognoscenti bewailed a "raging peace and a merciless operations tempo." This denoted "global power projection," a buzzphrase resonating in the Nation's Capital. Washington University of St. Louis economist and defense hawk, Murray Weidenbaum, extolled American presence "in a dangerous world." Harvard's Kennedy School professor and future Secretary of Defense Ashton B. Carter referred obtusely to an "asymptotic state" world in the future (divergent, not convergent in nature) with "American strategy: the conceptual vacuum." The United States needed to admit the post-Cold War period "is over and [so] chart a course into the future." Lawrence Skibbie, editor of the National Defense Industry Association's *National Defense* journal, wanted debate on national security in the 2000 presidential election, while talk of revolutions in military and business affairs droned on incessantly. Demands of military operations other than war (MOOTW in Pentagon jargon) and frequent deployments for reservists alongside regulars for such expeditions beckoned, along with ever-present irritants North Korea, Iran, even Serbia as part of the disintegrating Balkans problem. Economist Weidenbaum and a colleague had wondered in 1966 what would have happened to the distribution of personal income among the various regions of the United States if defense contracts with private industry in 1963 had shifted to non-defense programs "in the proportions existing among these civilian programs prior to the shift." A generation later, hubris not dismantlement answered their question.[14]

"Demonstrating the capability to provide, if needed, a global warfighting" capacity, required the ability to form, train and field new fighting forces, initially from cadre-type units, as well as "activating the industrial base on a large scale," observed Army War College strategic analyst Don Snider. Alternatives against resurgence of Russian and former Soviet republics, it also articulated "a militarily valid, post-cold war mission for the very large and politically influential reserve forces of the United States." The updated approach accentuated technological lessons of the Gulf War. The Pentagon plumbed for this new "base force," falling back on military jargon, a "builddown" of the base force, like the twenty-five percent reduction structures between Fiscal Year 1990 and 1995. Chairman of the Joint Chiefs of Staff Colin Powell declared that while he "thought the greatest challenge facing us" was controlled slimming of U.S. capabilities, "the services offered plenty of evidence as to why they didn't need to do it."[15]

Chided by National Security Adviser Brent Scowcroft's frantic complaint, "this government is financially broke" and that "huge reductions" would be necessary in future defense plans and programs, everyone felt the need to assure allies about continuing U.S. leadership and steadiness. In the end, government gridlock over budget, the guns versus butter debate, produced funding that resulted in a 1990 Budget Enforcement Act compromise that also took the glare away from future defense funding. Cold War strategic synthesis showed signs of unraveling, when Republican administration key players Bush, Cheney, Wolfowitz and Powell aligned against a Democratic congress led by Senator Sam Nunn and Representative Les Aspin, on issues of who determined future defense policy. The question of how much to reduce the defense budget, twenty-five or forty percent, ultimately took second place in negotiations on lowering the budget deficit, when the timeline shifted, and the Gulf War temporarily settled the issue of paying for war. Reduction would not be held hostage to regular budget funding, yet, a dangerous precedent was set.[16]

Both Bush Sr. and his successor, Bill Clinton, could justify reduced military spending due to the absence of any major conflict. The military moved away from "high-intensity combat" (against the Warsaw Pact) and/or "low-intensity war" in Central America, to focus on "mid-intensity conflict" in regional clashes with rogue and renegade nations. Both presidents avowed economic and military power as, using Clinton's 1994 words, "indispensable to the forging of stable political relations and open trade." Yet, almost decreeing a self-fulfilling answer, the hawkish ambassador to the United Nations, Madeleine Albright, asked Colin Powell bluntly, "what's the point of having this superb military that you're always talking about if we can't use it?" Americans may have elected Clinton in 1992 largely because he promised to focus on domestic problems like the economy and disengagement may have appealed to Americans. Yet, Clinton's grand strategy of "Engagement and Enlargement" bolstered America's economic revitalization and promoted democracy abroad, as-formalized in his 1995 National Security Strategy. Exercising global leadership while not policing the world, greater reliance on multilateralism to counter threats before they reached America's shores also tied in to enlarging the community of democratic and free market nations, while supporting and even intervening to uphold human rights. Yet, Peter Trubowitz observes, the United States still gave more to its military "than the combined sum spent by all of its potential adversaries and more than all its main allies combined." The defense budget of about $380 billion, at its "historic defense bottom" in 1998, exceeded the total of Russia and China together. The rest of the world may have reaped some sort of peace dividend, just not the American people. Nevertheless, Daniel Ippilito posits that while the outlay for discretionary domestic programs and social welfare entitlements "changed very little during the 1990s," defense outlays actually dropped from 5.2 percent of GDP to 3.0 percent - "the lowest level since the late 1940s."[17]

SLIMMING THE DEFENSE INDUSTRY BASE

An essential question now was what to do with the defense industrial base? Quite frankly, how much was enough and to do what? Powerful government, corporations responsive to expanded profit lines, and a public accustomed to economic benefits deriving from national security - all grew complacent (or complicit?) with exactly what Eisenhower had warned about. Could it have been otherwise when, as Jacques Gansler suggested in 1995, the defense industry "is characterized by its enormous size and complexity" with DoD expending about $100 billion each year "in about 15 million separate contract actions" or "some two contract actions per second." From the state's side, how could DoD and the military continue with innovative designs and procure financially sound weapons with no peer competitor in sight? Could the Pentagon tap commercial technologies without risking both proliferation and loss of technological edge? Should the Defense department buy its weapons only from domestic sources or open global competition? Did foreign arms sales offer solution? The mantra for the Nineties at first, however, seemed to be conversion (or re-conversion, in the traditional war to peace cycle) of demobilization. It failed ultimately.[18]

Some large, specialized military contractors like McDonnell Douglas, Lockheed, Grumman, General Dynamics, Northrop, and Boeing, tried to diversify into the civilian market outside aviation and aerospace. They ultimately abandoned or sold off such ventures, since they operated at marginal levels, their products were over-engineered and costly, and their knowledge of civilian business was inadequate. Boeing tried converting its Vertol division from helicopter to subway cars, only to encounter "all sorts of grief in dealing with the Department of Transportation, several large cities and union restrictions." Grumman attempted to peddle a minivan years before Chrysler popularized that product, but failed at distribution. Curtiss-Wright had decided early on that diversification was the way to proceed, yet, it limped along in 1989 with only $212 million in sales, while rivals garnered billions from aircraft and missiles. General Dynamics stood as the model of staying totally within the defense business for its core competence and proficiency. Professor Weidenbaum told *New York Times* readers, that conversion failure lay with defense-company specialization. "They are very good at what they are set up to do: design and produce state-of-the-art weapons and related civilian aircraft," he felt but "woefully ignorant of the basics of commercial business" in such areas as products, production methods, advertising and distribution, financial arrangements, funding of research and development, and dealing with intractable customers. Experienced engineers and craftsmen went to maintaining military production potential.[19]

Broader issues confronted the defense industry as well as American industry overall. De-industrialization had struck the country generally toward the end of the Cold War, and continued from vulnerabilities to global supply chains, foreign ownership of domestic firms, and control of technological transfer. But, as long-time academic and public servant Jacques Gansler saw it, by the 1990s, "the nation had too many aircraft plants, shipyards, missile plants, etc. to support the greatly reduced demand." He viewed defense conversion as involving traditional issues that included community economic adjustment due to defense downsizing; defense plant conversion and retaining laid-off defense workers. Modern manufacturing-technology training for lower-tier suppliers and transferring defense technology to nondefense businesses added still others. Yet, several new twists intruded, like transformation of the unique defense industry into an integrated civil-military industrial base and shifting research and investments in defense into product and process technologies for dual-use. Gansler, for one, found little consensus on how any of this could be done, but right-sizing clearly bubbled to the surface. That meant restructuring, mergers, selling off assets, and simply closing excess-capacity shops and acquisitions. In 1993, major munitions firms like BAE Systems, General Dynamics, Alliant Techsystems, Chemring Group, Esterline, Day and Zimmermann all formed the Munitions Industrial Base Task Force, a nonprofit association with commercial goals of educating government and preserving key-sector capabilities. But otherwise, McDonnell acquired Douglas Aircraft, and Electric Boat merged with Consolidated Aviation to form the General Dynamics Corporation. North American Aviation and Rockwell Standard became Rockwell International, and United Technologies appeared from combining United Aircraft, Sikorsky Aviation, Hamilton-Standard, and other civilian-sector concerns like Carrier and Otis Elevator. The Persian Gulf War supposedly demonstrated that the United States still needed strong military and service contractors, just not at Cold War levels.[20]

The nation retained an organic and inorganic resourcing mixture of GOGOs, GOCOs and COCOs—what increasingly was styled the "defense industrial base." Discovering cost-benefits of more outsourcing of support functions, and even forward-deployed support infrastructure, had accrued slowly ever since "privatization" captured the government's imagination in the mid-1970s. The Defense department commissioned studies and corporate America, including firms Westinghouse, General Electric, Perot Systems, Bear Stearns and Military Personnel Resources Inc., responded with a stable of retired and active-duty military advisors plus think-tank experts as well corporate moguls. Furthermore, by the later nineties, outsourcing and privatization devotees pumped the idea that small-scale private-contractor deployments in locations like Haiti, Somalia and Rwanda, even expanded in the Balkans interventions saved money as well as uniformed military for more combat roles. Logistical chores like food service, garbage collection and water-suppliers could be added to others that included base construction and management in general. Even for purely fiscal reasons, contract personnel would soon be at or near the front lines as part of the "force multiplier," and "augmentation" equations, along with regulars, reserves, allies, and partners. The term "contractors on the battlefield" joined the MIPC lexicon for the service industry now assuming its place beside the equipment-creating legacy industry. For more traditional manufacturing, analysts spun civilian-industry benefits bleeding over into a defense counterpart, via lean and agile manufacturing, focused factories and mass customization. But, basically, Harvey Sapolsky and Eugene Gholz of MIT and Lawrence Korb of Brookings had little patience with the continuing bloat they still found in a new DIB. It was expanding if not deepening.[21]

A "rotating phalanx of corporate executives" plied the Pentagon, proclaiming how their companies from Boeing to Westinghouse, General Electric to Perot Systems, Bear-Stearns and Military Personnel Resource, Inc., could save budgetary bottom-lines and spare modern American legions the onus of prosaic, noncombat military functions. Eventually, outfits like DynCorp, and Brown and Root Services, garnered lucrative contracts performing such work in Bosnia and recruiting labor from former eastern-bloc countries. Eventually Halliburton, (Root Services parent company, with former defense secretary and future vice president Richard Cheney at its helm), secured a lucrative DoD program styled LOGCAP (Logistics Civil Augmentation Program), and thus an entire private military industry came of age in the Balkans, according to *Business Week* writers. Muckraker Rachel Maddox (later MSNBC newswoman), spins a splendid tale about how this tentacle of a new and improved, more-privatized post-Cold War MIPC had entrenched itself by 2000. Whether or not cost-savings ever offset questionable conduct in the field by DynCorp employees, or widely publicized cost overruns by others hung over the endeavor.[22]

The Bush administration determined that normal free-market forces were the way to stimulate the U.S. economy and right-size the post-Cold War defense industrial base. But sharp-eyed analysts still pointed out that defense industries did not operate in a free market. The government modestly reduced the defense budget, size of military forces and defense infrastructure. A Democratic Congress preferred stretching out existing defense production programs, while at the same time using provisions from the FY 91 Defense Authorization Act to implement defense economic adjustment, diversification, conversion, and stabilization. This legislation transferred $200 million out of DoD funds to the departments of Labor and Commerce for programs to assist downsized defense workers and communities. The legislative body initiated $1.7 billion in defense conversion programs that became a baseline for Clinton's more serious 1993 Defense Conversion program. In fact, he committed to a systematic expenditure of $20.3 billion as a "conversion program" for the 1994–1997 budgets focusing on defense-related worker assistance, community transition assistance, dual-use technology investment and non-defense technology investment. An interagency group, under co-chairs of Defense and the new National Economic Council, divvied up $4 billion for retraining displaced defense and civilian workers, $1 billion to aid communities hit by defense cutbacks, $5 billion to promote dual-use technology, and $10 billion to spur new civilian technology that would help wean companies from reliance on defense funding. As one 1998 government study observed, though initially slow to develop, whatever actual conversion was achieved plus the strength of the economy, may have been the major factor in successful post-Cold War industrial adjustment. Few people recognized this as any "peace dividend." Technology and economic development analyst Vernon W. Ruttan wondered, "is war necessary for economic growth?"[23]

From the government's standpoint, as Secretary of Defense William Perry had put it, "we will allow consolidations if it reduces costs to the DoD, and if adequate competition will still exist after the merger or acquisition." Competition between General Electric and Pratt and Whitney had always seemed evident in the aircraft engine business. Rolls Royce provided back-up. While the Department of Justice and the Federal Trade Commission fretted about declining numbers of available firms for competition, they allowed mergers and acquisitions to proceed, suggested Gansler, due to "the obvious shrinkage in the available business," and "'uniqueness' of defense market structure," exemplifying the monopoly buyer and the small number of oligopoly suppliers "fighting for the few, infrequent, major procurements." So, what had been 50 major defense suppliers (prime contractors and large subcontractors) eventually consolidated into only a half-dozen dominant firms. The aim had to be providing for "peacetime and crisis demands at a dramatically lower cost," he said. Otherwise, America would "end up with a small, highly subsidized, inefficient, ineffective, noncompetitive, and technologically obsolete defense industrial base" that would be lacking a surge capability in a crisis, or any civilian benefits from expenditures in defense research, development, and procurement. If the shrinkage of the DIB required that the Pentagon could no longer assume that it would always have an adequate number of competitive available suppliers, it also calmly accepted having only two or three suppliers in each critical sector of the

DIB as the new norm of the MIPC. Challenges to sustaining the DIB from technological superiority, the option of foreign suppliers, persisting redundancy of parallel public-sector facilities (arsenals, maintenance depots, navy yards and laboratories), and drift of private firms finding defense business no longer profitable enough in market and foreign military markets were all factors that would test a post-Cold War MIPC.[24]

At this same time, the military's global array of bases and facilities also experienced transition—closures to save money on unnecessary infrastructure or "BRAC-ing" (Base Realignment and Closures). Four separate rounds of BRACs in 1988, 1991, 1993 and 1995, via an independent commission, shut down almost one hundred major bases, and hundreds of smaller facilities, despite congressional opposition. Of course, as of 1996, the Defense department still owned and maintained sixty-one organic GOGO and GOCO industrial facilities. Decades of congressional resistance to closures of facilities in order to save billions of dollars, had largely succeeded, observed political scientist Kenneth P. Mayer. BRAC retained as many "not in my backyard" issues and as much congressional-presidential power-jockeying, as any other gridlocked budget process. Mayer claimed the use of an independent commission might mask, but would not eliminate, "the fundamental tension between the interests of local constituencies and the broader 'public benefit.'" It hardly made a ripple, when the military undertook its own internal acquisition reviews and reforms. But it did when the chopping-axe approached the sacred cows of DIB and MIPC through a BRAC.[25]

Budget battles over military spending fused with ever-accelerating costs of technology, downsizing unneeded forces and supporting infrastructure, and America's general disinterest in so-called industrial mobilization. The industrial age blended with the Information revolution and other ways of doing business. Precision-Guided munitions, precision navigation and stealth signified new ways of war. But, price tags were hefty. Organizational size and structure integrated with a production scheme for public/private partnering in aging facilities. Globalization pushed foreign producers toward competition rather than coordination or consolidation with American counterparts. Global supply chain integration further complicated U.S. industrial vulnerability. Constitutional precept "for the common defense" now signified "national security," as traditional peer-national threats gave way to the new peril of "clash of civilizations" and rogue state terrorism, however imperfectly perceived by policymakers. Obsession with technology was reflected by the remark from author-team Barton Hacker and Margaret Vining pointing out "the widespread assumption that better technology meant victory had made military-technological innovation, to a significant degree, an end in itself." A post-Viet Nam generation had begun "thinking anew about the tactical and organizational ideas that might guide technological innovation into more useful channels." Validated by its Persian Gulf experience, the Pentagon applied the term "Revolution in Military Affairs" to every aspect of military organization, training and logistics. To fast-paced advances in global communication networks and electronic data processing, DoD added precision-guided weapons and stealth technology. Discussion would shift "from revolution to transformation" or "the rise of stand-off warfare" by the end of the century.[26]

From the government's standpoint, acquisition reform almost always appeared on the agenda. Talk about more use of commercial products had been present ever since the second Hoover Commission of 1953, which preceded the Packard Commission in 1985, Defense Management Review of 1989, Section 800 Panel Report in 1993, and the National Performance Review that same year. And, so it went, unaltered. By 1995, the Pentagon touted the challenge of technological supremacy and affordable cost as achievable through five investment-strategy pillars: right-sizing infrastructure, reducing cost of weapon-system ownership, implementing acquisition reform, leveraging the national industrial base, and involving the industrial bases of international allies. This mantra sounded good; the jargon for seeking commercial processing and production efficiencies, through Non-Developmental Items (NDI), Commercial Off-the-Shelf (COTS) acquisitions, and use of common production facilities. Reduction of acquisition-cycle time-frames from fifteen to three or four years seemed sensible. International team competition with equal national work-shares could deliver the highest-value product at a price unattainable through any national "go it alone" approach. Reducing or eliminating the governmental arsenal system was another idea since high-technology could best be provided by a more sophisticated, well-funded private sector. Acquisition experts applauded; less-charitable denizens still decried systemic defense bloat.[27]

MERGER MANIA

Legend now took over the narrative. Martin Marietta chief executive Norman R. Augustine supposedly, and surreptitiously, gathered his management team every Friday in "his basement, only a short trip from the office, where they convened over sodas with a rotating cast of specialists in areas such as policy and Wall Street interests." They anticipated a drastically-altered landscape, following Reagan-era buildup in defense spending. More capital would be needed to outlast whatever change-of-course by government, and what actually turned out to be "the most significant contraction in the history of the defense industry." That event was precipitated by a publicized moment in 1993 when, over a Pentagon dinner, then-Deputy Secretary of Defense William J. Perry bluntly served notice that the five-year downward slide in defense spending was to fall farther and faster. The Pentagon wanted to see only half the number of companies and urged consolidation. DoD leadership proclaimed that "we expect defense companies to go out of business," proclaiming that "we will stand by and watch it happen." DoD would not pick winners and losers, nor would it obstruct defense firms from mergers and acquisitions. Industry officials felt betrayed. Norm Augustine dubbed it "the Last Supper," and soon sought to merge Georgia-based Martin-Marietta and California-based Lockheed "in a deal that not only reshaped the industry," but also shifted its center to the D.C. area. Before the end of the century, private arsenal system ripples were palpable.[28]

Nonetheless, the loss of an estimated $55 billion in government underwriting for the DIB from 1992 to 1997 hardly proved catastrophic. Industry captains like Augustine sensed opportunities. By 1995 Lockheed-Martin surged ahead of the flock, with $11.6 billion in military sales. McDonnell-Douglas, Northrop-Grumman, GM-Hughes Electronics, Raytheon, United Technologies, General Dynamics, Loral, Boeing, and General Electric rounded out the rest of the top ten. The shock-wave of "Primes" reduction to what was styled "The Big 5" continued until 1998 when, DoD suddenly became skittish of perceived monopoly as Northrop-Grumman tried to merge with Lockheed Martin. Augustine still wanted to acquire Northrup-Grumman (maker of the B-2 bomber) for $8.3 billion, to add to his $28 billion in sales accruing from acquisitions of Loral, Unisys Defense, and Ford Aerospace, in addition to Martin-Marietta. Along the way, he absorbed twenty-two weapons manufacturers, to become the second-largest mega-industry in the defense business. The dizzying process dropped civilian employment in the defense industry by over 2 million workers (1,000 per day at one point). Long-respected companies simply disappeared or became merely divisions, in what was billed as a "new and improved military-industrial complex." This was residual power. True, such power had been reduced in military sales statistics of the top ten between 1991 and 1994, from $617 billion to $414 billion. Yet, Boeing, Raytheon, Litton Industries, Lockheed-Martin, and Northrop-Grumman remained after three waves of consolidation. The story seemed to duplicate an earlier "Robber Baron" era in industrial America.[29]

Poets might have styled it "a merger of equals," or "a marriage made in heaven," for the story of Martin-Marietta's Norman Augustine and Lockheed's Dan Tellep formed the heart of the narrative. Both men had their respective company's best interests at heart. Tellep had fended off Texas businessman Harold Simmons' attempt to take over Lockheed, and picked up a downsizing Fort Worth division of General Dynamics, maker of the nimble F-16 jet-fighter plane. Augustine had married Martin-Marietta and General Electric's Aerospace division in the early stages of DIB devolution. Augustine, the outgoing big-picture type, and detail-oriented Tellep, were both engineers by profession. They came together with related spirit and ease of negotiation. Both men had the ultimate goal of making their two firms much stronger in the increasingly rigorous international competition for capturing the diminishing defense markets. Aviation historian Walter Boyne paints a picture of collaborative logos creating a new heritage-based corporate entity, with a genuflection to staff by both men for necessary legwork and soothing the transition hardships of individual employees. Augustine felt that, "on these uncharted waters, few institutions have found themselves in more bewildering circumstances," and the defense industrial base is "an institution with very special responsibilities to the nation, and, indeed the world, yet at the same time needing for its very viability to compete in the financial markets alongside Coca-Cola, Intel, Disney, and Microsoft." He announced "there are no asterisks on the New York Stock Exchange listing to indicate 'Granted Special Consideration—Member of the Defense Industrial Base.'"[30]

As Augustine told an Atlantic Council gathering in 1998, "we concluded that it was better to have two or three strong companies than five or six weak and inefficient companies. "It wasn't even evident that defense-procurement budgets could support that many in some areas. So, they had merged, "aiming at the kind of synergy and efficiency that would enable the newly created companies to prosper in the circumstances in which they found themselves." Even this was not easy, as Augustine confessed "that the leaders of the firms comprising America's defense industrial base were almost all engineers and as such were, putting it kindly, ill-equipped for the world of investment bankers, anti-trust reviewers, media reporters, and striped suit lawyers." He regaled his audience with little homilies about code-names among participants, and secret meetings on the 53d floor of the Rockefeller Center in New York that were well-known, even to passers-by on neighboring streets. Rejecting diversification into civilian markets "for canoes, buses, tractors, banjos, pagers and the like," Augustine and his team built a new empire from the ruins of America's Cold War DIB. Throughout this consolidation, Augustine claimed, "we had the support of an enlightened Department of Defense, which realized what had to be done and dealt with us forthrightly, always in the interest of the public, and tried to make the process as nondisruptive as practicable." Fortunately, those in government "recognized that our choice was not between a down-sized industry on the one hand and some hypothetical competitive Utopia on the other," but rather, "it was a choice between a downsized industry and diminishment to irrelevance."[31]

Was this a marriage of convenience or patriotic survival? Though Augustine was termed the most important figure in a public-private vision for the future, some commentators were not impressed by what was styled "Saint Augustine's Rules," describing them as "a government-subsidized consolidation that will leave the job of producing major weapons systems for the Pentagon in the hands of a few massive firms." The country may not have seen his like since the days of Andrew Carnegie, J.P. Morgan, Charles Schwab, and their trust-building a century earlier. Aerospace giant Augustine made no apologies about where he was going, either. William Hartung, a World Policy Institute senior fellow and student of the weapons game, declared that for most of Augustine's career, his hard-wiring into the Washington policy-making process made him "one of a handful of people drawing up the blueprints for American defense policies and deciding where the wiring should be placed." Few shifted as effortlessly as Augustine could, between chairs of the Defense Policy Advisory Committee on Trade and Defense Science Board, and president of the Association of the United States Army. At one time or another he was a business associate of Secretary of Defense William Perry and Central Intelligence Agency director John Deutch. Augustine epitomized the MIPC of the Reagan, first Bush and Clinton periods. Seemingly a Defense secretary surrogate at times, he lobbied Capitol Hill for his enterprise and was especially mindful of DoD sensitivities about manipulating laws, rulings, regulations, and money-pots, for the benefit of Lockheed-Martin Marietta.

In parallel, the Clinton administration used government bailout money as "relocation costs" to close plants, relocate equipment, pay severance to workers, and provide bonuses to executives and board members affected by the scope of the mega-merger game. Augustine, DoD secretaries Perry and Aspin, Deutch (when Undersecretary of Defense), and other industry heads like Tellup, C. Michael Armstrong of GM-Hughes, and Bernard Schwartz of Loral, tested government procedure but eluded anything illegal in the drive to assure a private arsenal system. Ethics and accountability scrutiny descended upon accelerated export subsidies, $1.1 million in political contributions, plus speaker and consultant fees, tax breaks through waiving fees to weapons clients to repay tax dollars, and a $15 billion government-guaranteed loan fund administered by the Pentagon. Lockheed-Marietta and its lobbyists argued that some 1,300 F-16s sold to twenty-four different countries now had to be superseded by more technologically advanced aircraft like the F-22 and successor F-35, to maintain America's own fighting edge and defense industrial base. Eventually the merger-mania evaporated when Augustine moved to capture Northrop-Grumman for $11.6 billion. The Pentagon suddenly decided that kluging first and third-largest suppliers would create "unprecedented anti-competitive concerns."[32]

Still, like Andrew Carnegie many years before him, Augustine also was adept at hiding behind the American flag in the interests of corporate profit. He received praise for the Lockheed-Martin merger as "truly trying to do the right thing for the country," according to National Air and Space Administration head Dan Goldin. If a non-defense business folds, some jobs might be lost and shareholders lose money, "but life goes on," yet, "If you are building Patriot missiles or night-vision goggles, the consequences are very different." Certainly, Augustine had little compunction about relocating a new, merged headquarters to Bethesda, Maryland outside Washington, D.C., seat of the new and improved MIPC. Displaced employees bridled at trading a legendary corporate headquarters in Southern California with its stunning views of the Santa Monica Mountains and canyon-paradise of flowers and hummingbirds, for Washington, D.C., a "dreary, work obsessed town that can't compare with L.A.," where, they pointed out, "you can wear flip-flops at Christmas." They deplored the delays in announcing transition and the $85 million payouts Lockheed would give Martin-Marietta officials under a decade-old procedure in the event of a merger. Predictable relocation angst (exacerbated by the previous year's earthquake damage affecting residential real estate sales markets in the Los Angeles area), mirrored similar instability across the land. Sub-primes, even more than primes, suffered this latest industrial devolution. Grumman engineers also echoed concern about cuts, mergers and location transfers from Bethpage, Long Island, just thirty miles from New York City. "We're into aircraft," said one, "We build aircraft—Top Gun—Tom Cruise running around in the sky, that's us. Is the country going to keep that, or is it a thing of the past?" Here was "the end of life as we know it," bewailed a Grumman engineer as Pentagon largesse replaced aerospace jobs with service-sector work in computers, medicine, and other fields.

AND WHAT ABOUT THE NUCLEAR WEAPONS COMPLEX?

One outlier was the nuclear weapons program and complex, managed in great secrecy through the Department of Energy. Facing nuclear arms-reduction agreements and parallel commitments since 1987 (START I and II), the department confronted monumental issues surrounding dismantling the nuclear weapons legacy of the Cold War. And, like the conventional industrial dimension of MIPC, nuclear dismantlement involved programs, facilities and personnel, plus remediation, health and cleanup requirements, being suddenly thrust into the public limelight. The United States additionally agreed to assist in closing down former-Soviet programs, mainly to prevent any residual materials from falling into the hands of rogue states and maverick bad-actors. A fairly comprehensive picture may be drawn from the work Stephen I. Schwartz and nine more colleagues wrote titled *Atomic Audit: The Costs and Consequences of U.S. Nuclear Weapons since 1940*. Weapons retirement had always been part of the program due to obsolescence, revised mission, targeting parameters, or safety concerns. Now it was more a concern for disposal and storage of tons of surplus fissile materials, principally plutonium 239 and enriched uranium. The costs of dismantling "the bomb" ran to a projected $31.1 billion. The DOE "began to pay serious attention to the back end of the arms race, the enormous quantities of long-lived, dangerous wastes generated as a result of large-scale nuclear weapons production activities."[33]

$365 billion price tag for nuclear waste cleanup far exceeded similar remediation requirements in normal BRAC facilities. An additional $2.05 billion projected to victims of the bomb—not just Hiroshima and Nagasaki, but also an estimated 500,000 to 600,000 people working in the nuclear weapons production complex over five decades, especially in the 1940s and 1950s, who might have been exposed to significant doses of radiation and toxic chemicals used in the manufacturing process. Overall, Schwartz and his colleagues determined seven categories of human exposure to environmental and health dangers, including workers in uranium mines and mills, in weapon design, production and testing facilities, people living near nuclear weapons sites, human-experiment subjects (deemed necessary to understand possible health effects of a Cold War nuclear exchange), armed forces personnel who participated in atmospheric weapons tests or were exposed, along with others, during deployment, transportation, and other weapons handling and maintenance within DoD, residents of Hiroshima and Nagasaki, in addition to what the authors termed "the world's inhabitants for centuries to come." Perhaps the $3.4 billion calculated to maintain nuclear secrecy would never be redeemed in post-Cold War downsizing, nor the projected $901 million costs for congressional oversight of the bomb program, either. Somehow, no one seriously suggested eliminating nuclear weapons altogether.

Especially troublesome was the possible conversion of nuclear production from defense to civilian products, or its translation to any real utility in a peace dividend. Conversion had never been contemplated when nuclear facilities were built, but security and physical isolation were. Technologies used in nuclear weapons manufacturing differed significantly from normal manufacturing. Many workers' skills were so unique that conversion was difficult in facilities constructed to build "esoteric weapons" and particularly when the government intended retaining nuclear weapons and the capability to remanufacture them indefinitely. This placed both technologies and facilities off-limits. Site contamination of buildings, other facilities, plus land and ground water (often defying estimated clean-up costs), as well as physical isolation, rendered little economic benefit to communities. Finally, for scientific and technical personnel, the vested interest in producing nuclear devices made them less inclined or even qualified to convert their highly specialized and classified skills to civilian work. All this promised high costs for cleanup and decommissioning that had to be passed to taxpayers, and a "future negative" value to a nation that had devoted so much time, money and resources to this type of deterrence.

The nuclear weapons effort always had been under tight security and administered from the beginning through a public/private government/contractor partnership. And since 1947, there had always been a matter of policy to avoid letting military production slip into military control. Examples included the Pennsylvania Apollo Plant, the Environmental Management Project in Fernald, Ohio, the Eniwetok Pacific Proving Ground, Paducah Gaseous Diffusion Plant in Kentucky, Ohio's Portsmouth Gaseous Diffusion Plant, the Pinellas Plant in Florida, and Weldon Spring Feed Materials Plant in Missouri, to name a few. Some were simply sunk-cost sites, of little to no conversion or dual-use capability. Still, any post-Cold War nuclear program would have to comprise residual facilities, along with their contractors: Ames Laboratory (Iowa State University), Argonne National Laboratory (University of Chicago and Argonne Universities Association), Bettis Atomic Power Laboratory (Westinghouse Bettis Company), Brookhaven National Laboratory (Brookhaven Science Associates and former Associated Universities Inc.), Holston Army Ammunition Plant (Holston Defense Corporation, subsidiary of Eastman Chemical, and managed for the U.S. Army), Idaho National Engineering and Environmental Laboratory (Lockheed Idaho Technologies Company, as the latest in a long line of contractors stretching back to 1950), Kansas City Plant (Bendix Kansas City Division of Allied Signal, formerly Bendix Aviation), Knolls Atomic Power Laboratory (General Electric), Lawrence Livermore National Laboratory and Los Alamos National Laboratory (both University of California Board of Regents), Nevada Test Site (Bechtel Nevada Corporation, latest in the long line starting in 1951), Nuclear Fuel Services, Inc., Oak Ridge Reservation (Lockheed-Martin Energy Research

Corporation as latest in the succession of contractors going back to 1942), Pantex Plant (Mason and Hanger-Silas Mason Company, Inc., formerly contracted by Proctor & Gamble Defense Corporation in the 1950s), Sandia National Laboratories (Sandia Corporation, a Lockheed Martin Corporation subsidiary), Savannah River site (Westinghouse Savannah River Company, Bechtel, Wackenhut Services, Inc., formerly contracted with E. I. Du Pont de Nemours and Company 1950–1989), Waste Isolation Pilot Plant (Westinghouse WIPP Company, subsidiary of Westinghouse Electric Corporation), and Yucca Mountain Project (TESS).[34]

Nuclear workers' feelings about downsizing and transition after the Cold War differed little from their conventional MIPC counterparts. There was psychological disillusionment for many, especially in the DOE labs, who had embraced the total Armageddon of nuclear war for its nuclear physics, engineering and scientific attractions. Now, challenges came in re-inventing themselves "to develop technology for the commercial sector to improve our economy and to raise our standard of living," as one group of Lawrence Livermore professionals informed management. Adjustment was difficult–writing manuals, collecting old shot-records, or writing books on past events and science was not exciting by comparison. However, in the absence of actual nuclear testing thanks to test ban treaties, another alternative loomed in the form of a proposed $700–800 million National Ignition Facility for using lasers to maintain physicists' skills and design abilities. But somehow, for every American respectful of the scientists' function as helpmates in winning the Cold War, there were others who now equated them with "oven builders of Auschwitz." Furthermore, one nuclear scientist working at Los Alamos who had mishandled classified documents, along with other allegations of lax DOE administration, prompted rearrangements in the nuclear complex by century's end.[35]

Congress proposed an independent agency, passing in 1999 legislation that created a National Nuclear Security Administration which was subsequently established as a subagency of the Department of Energy. In essence an expansion of the previous defense program organization of the Atomic Energy Commission and later Department of Energy) defense programs, nonproliferation, naval reactors, emergency response, defense nuclear security, and eventually counter-terrorism and counter-proliferation, would number among its responsibilities. Its major private-contractor partner would be controversial, profit-oriented Bechtel Corporation. No wonder so much unhappiness attended this direction leading away from scientific and educational management of the University of California system for Los Alamos, Livermore, and other activities in the field. Privatization had reached the MIPC pinnacle. Moreover, two decades later the Department of Energy would still be cleaning up sixteen highly-contaminated former nuclear-weapons sites, vestiges of the Cold War arms race, including Oak Ridge in Tennessee, Savannah River in South Carolina and Hanford, Washington, all requiring $6.1 billion in annual costs.

ASSESSING HOW MUCH IS ENOUGH?

People like Norm Augustine, the administration, the rump defense industry and the military, all got their way in the end. Perceived national need and mission joined with policies translating to local economic benefit prompted Georgia senator Sam Nunn's push for keeping the B-2 bomber production line warm when the Pentagon had capped it. Senator Joseph Lieberman of Connecticut persuaded President Clinton to promise purchase of two superfluous *Seawolf* submarines for $5 billion, just to preserve naval construction capacity. Other legislators voted for $200 million to buy more machine guns and carbines, under the argument of maintaining a healthy and resilient industrial base. They, too, could cite costs associated with the dispersal of trained technicians that attended closures, mergers and consolidations. Advocates of a defense industrial policy felt there was no market solution in defense. Professor Harvey M. Sapolsky of MIT bluntly declared that "the government cannot avoid having an industrial policy." For a good part of the aerospace industry, much of shipbuilding, and all of the tank market, the government was the only customer. "It has always picked winners and losers in defense," he argued, just "not necessarily very well." It was government's responsibility. Others saw a traditional argument for conscious transatlantic partnerships, even mergers, as economic insurance against universal downturns in defense budgets, sharing development costs and common production lines to provide economies of a scale that eventually would be found with international programs for radios, missile defense systems and the much-ballyhooed joint-strike fighter. Partnering required care, even in an insurance scheme through majority-investor control, of placing such a British aerospace giant as BAE Systems beside Boeing, Lockheed-Martin, Raytheon, General Dynamics, and Northrop-Grumman, as "Crown jewels" of the American DIB.[36]

Meanwhile, private contractors had found a profitable, continuing business with no public facilities created for technologies like satellites and jet aircraft. The private arsenal sector lobbied to keep production lines open even as the cost for excess capacity intruded on military readiness and new weapons development. Wishing the problem gone would not work. A conscious government industrial policy was the answer, believed Sapolsky and others, as the DoD should take steps to even buy out more of America's excess capacity in weapons production. Paying the costs of more than just merging lines when a contractor could demonstrate benefit to the government, paying companies in essence to go out of business through mergers, and authorizing DoD to buy any excess capacity seemed viable answers, although Lawrence Korb of Brookings questioned whether the Pentagon should actually pay for defense industry restructuring. Moreover, questions arose about the large cost of restructuring that was placed on workers and local communities. More than severance pay was needed to convince those affected that their sacrifices were for the good of the nation.

One could wonder if the U.S. did not have a de facto industrial policy regarding the DIB. Sapolsky at one point noted that the U.S. still consciously had eight lines producing military aircraft, six producing warships, five making helicopters and four manufacturing tactical missiles with a need for only half of those numbers. Administration claims notwithstanding, neither enactment of acquisition reform nor the development of lean production techniques offered much hope for dealing with the basic problem of overcapacity. Sapolsky, for one, felt an even smaller, more secure industrial base should be the goal, claiming the need to recreate the public arsenal system so recently dismantled. Naturally, the business community saw it differently. William Anders, chairman of General Dynamics, manufacturing giant of M1 tanks, jet fighters and nuclear submarines, had told an October 1991 audience that contractors should lobby for every military dollar they could squeeze from Congress, the administration, and from foreign sales, otherwise, weapons makers should shut down factories and send workers home, to eliminate over-capacity and improve efficiency. Other commentators stressed mobilization and industrial preparedness implications, privatization, and acquisition reform. The "military-industrial complex," thus became the Defense Technology and Industrial Base (DTIB). Augustine even exhorted in early 1998, "we will not have a national defense industry," adding "we'll have to draw on our [civilian] industrial base rather than having the defense capability of the past." Or as Gansler, having returned to public life as Under Secretary of Defense for Acquisition and Technology, saw the defense-industrial base as the U.S. industrial base.[37]

Whether styled "defense-industrial base," "defense technology industrial base," or more colloquially "the iron triangle," America still had its military-industrial-political-scientific complex at the close of the twentieth-century. True, defense spending and the size of the DIB had begun to change even prior to the end of the Cold War, and by now the budget in real terms supposedly was down by forty percent from its Cold War peak. Literally hundreds of defense firms had either departed defense work or had been consolidated through an avalanche of mergers and acquisitions that reduced to a mere handful the number of prime contractors in major sectors of defense production. More than 2,000,000 jobs were eliminated in the process. The government continuously sought internal acquisition reform and assessed the effects from strategizing to resourcing. The question remained, would the ongoing consolidation and reform attempts produce a stable, robust production base for future defense needs? Or as critics contended, would restructuring result in over-concentration of producers, monopolistic pricing, and a slowdown in innovation? There always seemed to be more questions than answers.[38]

In fact, devolution of the Defense Industrial Base may have run its course by the year 2000. There still was nothing approaching traditional demobilization and the "elite" exponents of preparedness could not clarify precisely what the threat was that necessitated a continuing behemoth. That behemoth itself—the MIPC—worked at internal adjustments for survival. Introduction of "competitive sourcing" for jobs that were not inherently government followed the lead of commercial and defense firms in a rash of cost-cutting methods. Meanwhile, an array of satellites—think tanks, trade associations, pundits and academics proclaimed solutions and prescriptions. The defense industries themselves seemingly had moved in one of three directions: exiting the military-industrial sector by selling off assets or abandoning certain defense business areas following Ford's lead; diversifying into non-military production or services, such as Rockwell International's purchase of the commercial electronics company, Reliant Electronics, or remaining in defense and even expanding military production, as did Lockheed Martin and Northrup Grumman through acquiring and expanding empires, and coopting DoD on anti-trust, so as to regulate less and buy into dual-use. The Clinton administration which loosened traditional antitrust policies to allow American defense giants to become more internationally competitive via cost reduction, also witnessed a bottoming-out of this procedure. One major commercial producer (Boeing) and three major weapons contractors out of twelve left at the beginning of the decade, with some major systems like tanks or submarines retaining only one production source, meant that DoD was no longer willing or able to integrate all the components and support-elements of major weapon systems. That function now resided with the so-called "primes."[39]

Vertical integration ended the mega-merger frenzy in 1998 when DoD (under Department of Justice guidance) decided to oppose the proposed

$12 billion Lockheed Martin-Northrop Grumman merger. The government wanted Augustine's outfit to shed $4 billion in assets; Lockheed offered only $1 billion. In essence, Secretary of Defense Warren Cohen and DoD now feared monopoly and adverse effects in defense electronics; Northrup Grumman's radar and electronics facility outside Baltimore, Maryland was a sticking point. But there were other issues of extensive horizontal and vertical integration, like Northrop Grumman's profitable aircraft business. DoD promised to continue supporting further consolidation, when transactions did not adversely affect competition. Defense Science Board reports warned about vertical corporate integration that could negatively affect defense-product cost, quality and performance. Some writers anticipated the next round of consolidation would clean out excess capacity still present in five shipbuilding firms, result in more layoffs, trigger possible consolidating among sub-contractors and third or fourth-tier suppliers and vendors, and perhaps increase entry of dual-use electronics and information technology firms at the subcontractor tier, not the primes.[40]

Meanwhile, from Pentagon perspectives, keeping domestic base production lines warm or hot looked increasingly to foreign military sales. By 1995 many systems like the F-16, F-15, M-1 tank and Patriot surface-to-air missile were dependent on such sales. The U.S. led the world in arms exports although they fell off by mid-decade and at that point "there is fierce competition for this global market from Europe." Implications included less competition, enormous leverage and lobbying power in the hands of a few companies, and fewer companies doing research and development. Three years later, the Senior Policy Panel of the Center for Strategic and International Studies predicted solemnly, "the 60 per cent reduction in defense procurement since 1985 guaranteed that there would not be sufficient funds to keep an industrial base sized and organized for the Cold War." Twenty-three weapons sectors would shrink appreciably. Manufacturers of fixed-wing aircraft for U.S. military consumption would go from nine in 1985 to five in 1995, then to four in 1997, and down to only three by 2010—a sixty-seven percent change. A similar downward shift for European companies went from seventeen in 1985 to thirteen in 1995, dropping to eight two years later with only five remaining by 2010, or a seventy-one percent change over the period. Supplying the rest of the world showed the twelve American makers of 1985 increasing to fifteen by 1995 and 1997, before again returning to twelve in 2010. Clearly aviation projections looked to selling and supplying rather than diversifying to dual-use or even civilian programs. Shrinkage in naval platform makers, and tracked and wheeled vehicles, seemed more alarming as shifts from four to sometimes two or one supplier were projected. Nobody but Newport News would be making nuclear aircraft carriers, and only one nuclear submarine manufacturer would be left by 2010. Reduction in tracked vehicle manufacturers took a similar turn. Ordnance and weapons both government owned/contractor-operated and company owned/company operated facilities would shift by as much as sixty-seven percent. Missiles, space-launch vehicles and satellite makers, even electronics and communication sector companies would also shrink, with a growth market only in aerial unmanned vehicles, as evidenced by no companies in that sector in 1985 up to three by 2010.[41]

Defense analysts bemoaned "no more recycling of petro-dollars, the use of sovereignty debt, or the desire and ability by Third World governments to convert revenue into the weapons purchases which had boosted the international arms trade in the past. Ann Markusen thought that the debt-financed buildup of the Reagan period had only increased industry dependence on the defense sector. She decried the more recent strategies of mergers and acquisitions inadequately and ineffectively funded or pushed by Washington, which increased a wall of separation between civilian and military markets rising higher and more difficult to overcome. She anticipated industry "dominated by a few very large firms with high defence-dependency rates and market power in major weapons systems final assembly, surrounded by a large pool of contractors who are relatively more diversified and 'dual use' in character." She saw the large contractors continuing to have disproportionate influence "helping to shape evaluations of future weapons needs and receiving favorable treatment on questions of arms-export policy, procurement policy and R&D spending commitments." Diversification of firms heavily dependent on defense into civilian markets could produce a more flexible base, less dependent on Pentagon cuts and less pressured by arms-export fluctuation. Military spending could decline more quickly, match new security realities, and slow conventional arms proliferation. Markusen and Harvey Sapolsky were two who stressed the benefits of rededicating skilled scientific, engineering and blue-collar manpower, toward opportunities in health, environmental and commercial arenas rather than defense.[42]

Writing in 1998, Norman Augustine estimated "that only about one-quarter of the 20,000 firms that once supplied the Department of Defense" still functioned in that capacity. To him, the U.S. defense industry had sustained "a far greater rate of market loss than any other industry in recent times, and a high conglomeration of human tragedy as well." He said, ironically, it was "all brought about by the welcome news of the end of the Cold War." Within the military world, weapons systems aged and their maintenance ultimately fell afoul of overseas expeditionary interventionism that ate dollars. By Clinton's second term, the acquisition reform community fancied attempts to squeeze more efficiency from major programs rather than eliminating them altogether as part of much vaunted Defense Reform Initiative measures. Still, a blizzard of questions continued about the future of American defense and its industry sector. Could defense industry consolidation have a downside in terms of war preparedness and rapid wartime mobilization? Would private companies dictate the next generation of weapons they (not the Pentagon), felt best suited the marketplace? Would industry consolidation lead to potential rise in the cost of defense systems, a potential loss of tech innovation or a dampening of international defense cooperation? Or was it more relevant to periodically publicize defense-spending largesse per state, per capita, touting the largest increases and decreases spent annually for defense contracts and work compensation which translated as "defense spending pumps large sums of money into state economies, making it a difficult item for Congress to cut in appropriations bills." After all, by the post-Cold War period, was not MIPC simply a gigantic jobs program? Analyst Jeffrey Record asked pointedly about a defense industry "ready for what and modernized against whom?" Answers may not have been readily apparent.[43]

A WAY FORWARD TO CENTURY'S END

Virtually everyone in the national security business had some prescription for a declining defense industry. After years of vertical integration and horizontal consolidation, the number of U.S. companies gleaning sixty percent of their sales from the Defense department shrank from twelve in 1992 to four at the turn of the century. They included Lockheed Martin, Boeing, Raytheon and Northrop Grumman. Add in General Dynamics for a first-tier of U.S. defense firms capable of providing main-system integration that numbered five: Lockheed Martin ($20 billion in annual military sales), Boeing ($20 billion), Raytheon NSD and Northrop Grumman (with $13 billion each), and General Dynamics (about $6 billion). A second-tier of subsystems suppliers with annual sales of $2—4 billion each included United Technologies, TRW, Honeywell, L-3 Communication, SAC, and others. Yet a third-tier accounted for annual sales below $2 billion that included Textron, ITTD, United Defense, GE for aircraft engines, Alliant, Harris, Rockwell Collins, and others. The merger-mania also spread to Europe, with serial consolidations within and across national boundaries, although in a somewhat different model from that of America. Various joint ventures produced three main groups acting as a European defense industry. BAe Systems became the world's biggest defense contractor after acquiring GEC Marconi. EADS regrouped into a joint venture with the French Aerospatiale-Matra, German Daimler-Benz, and Spanish Casa, to compare with Lockheed Martin (military and civilian), while a third group was Thales, essentially a French defense electronics company that acquired many companies in various European countries. Some joint ventures included BAE and EADS for commercial aircraft (Airbus), with MBD for missiles and Astium for space systems. British aerospace expert Keith Hayward suggested that while European defense industries had been carefully shielded as national assets by their governments since the end of the nineteenth century, this was now changing.[44]

Globalization, internationalization, trans-oceanic partnerships, shared ventures, access to foreign production markets, and the revolution in military affairs, together symbolized the new market. This, said Hayward, "was increasing the level, depth and complexity of global industrial integration," with governments attempting to maintain competition in national markets by soliciting bids for contracts from international suppliers. To him, governments "in the core states of the West would "have to adopt a new set of policies and attitudes that can reconcile national security with transnational industrial operations." Even the Pentagon in May 1995 admitted that it no longer subscribed to the mobilization-base concept that required a purely national emergency production capability. Rather, in an era of declining budgets and forces, Hayward prescribed "it can best meet the military need by assuming the role of world-class customer" interacting in a competitive and global market.

The Pentagon still thought it controlled direction. So, six years after Secretary Perry's domestic "Last Supper," a similar meeting took place in November 1999. This time hosted by Deputy Defense Secretary John Hamre, and including national armaments directors from France, Germany, Great Britain and the United States as well as heads of defense and aerospace industries in their respective countries. The Pentagon's intent was to assess and discuss the prospects going forward with an international base. Dubbed "the first dinner," the meeting's message was that, contrary to earlier appearances, the Pentagon now did not favor large-scale transatlantic mergers involving American and European companies. Joint ventures, cooperation agreements and other forms of limited *ad hoc* business alliances could continue and be encouraged. But, major mergers and straight acquisitions in both directions were not. Since the American defense and industrial sector remained the pacesetter because of high-technology, relatively more-unified structure, and sophisticated approaches to policy and process as well as market share, this gave the United States an advantage. The earlier Pentagon conviction that it was acceptable to have "US giants gobbling much smaller European national companies" now confronted emerging European mega-giants that might threaten reverse acquisition of American companies. Was the Pentagon rationalizing "the need to harmonize US/European regulatory issues," from facing prospects of "an alarmingly reduced competition basis," or ducking the "current delicate financial situation of the leading US defence and aerospace contractors," which might produce a domestic chorus of bailouts in the form of increased defense spending and contracts?

Any homogeneity to Eisenhower's military-industrial-political complex seemed wobbly at best. Defense companies were not making money for shareholders, and not even showing the management skills which would provide confidence that they could do so in the future, claimed critics. The Pentagon was to blame. It had ceased purchasing when the Cold War ended, and needed more leeway on antitrust policy and foreign mergers. Nobody could predict a market. The system lacked the flexibility of allowing industry to adapt to low demand levels. Aerospace and defense industries remained a more regulated and dependent sector of the economy at a time when barriers to global civil commerce were disappearing, putting companies at distinct disadvantage. DoD's solution of industrial downsizing had created illusory efficiencies, while the most visible result of the mergers seemed to be a decline in quality-control standards exemplified by Titan rocket explosions, Mars spacecraft malfunctions, C-130 transport aircraft cost overruns, and test failures of theater-missile defense systems plaguing Lockheed. Cutting-edge defense companies were vital more than ever but Congress needed to put money into multi-year contracts while continuation of an unpredictable system would cause investors and engineers alike to avoid the sector. Secretary of Defense William Cohen responded that struggling companies would rebound, as the FY 2001 budget promised an increase from $54.9 to $60.3 billion. He pointed to projects like Lockheed-Martin's C-130 build and other big-ticket items. Still, it was "a kind of caretaker's budget," declared a Business Executives for National Security observers, since "just spending more money on these companies is not going to make them viable."[45]

To an astute industry sector spokesmen like Philip Odeen, chairman of the Defense Science Board task force on the industrial base and executive vice president of TRW, Inc., the defense industrial base remained at risk very simply because of the paradigm shift out of Cold War demands where the Pentagon depended on "a captive defense industry," to set rules and conditions with companies developing the required technology and producing the weapons in quantity. Long production runs and a sort of defense entitlement program for industry had become a thing of the past. Now, he said, the Pentagon buys fewer new platforms, extends the life of older ones, and referencing top technological keys, "updates its 'black boxes.'" Much of the software, networking, biotechnology and communications "is developed and provided by the commercial sector." Whereas the U.S. government funded about a third of the nation's research in the 1960s, that figure would be less than five per cent by 2000. Defense contractors at this stage were more integrators, drawing upon technology and products from a variety of sources, many of them commercial. As Odeen emphasized, "a broad range of different suppliers who don't and won't do business on government terms." Moreover, as an increasing share of technology came from abroad, regulatory barriers made it difficult for the Pentagon to access those capabilities. Odeen also saw criminalization of regulatory areas via the Civil False Claims Act as hampering commercial firms from considering defense work. Yet, he found progress in reducing the use of military specifications, and expanding waivers and setting higher standards thresholds for cost-accounting.[46]

Odeen pointed to the obvious. Many American companies like Texas Instruments, General Electric, Chrysler, IBM, Hughes, and GTE simply had left the defense business because of limited growth potential, risk and low investment returns. Other firms would deal with the Pentagon only for commercial products. Everyone knew DoD business was cyclical: upturn in the 1960s and 1980s, reversal in the 1970s and 1990s. Defense traditionally had been a reasonable investment with modest profit margins, good cash flow, and returns on investment reflecting fair value and premium result, said Wall Street. But that had changed, with stock prices sharply down. The sector's profitability underwent pressure as acquisitions and mergers drove up interest payments and amortization costs. Major program problems hurt profit lines of the larger companies, with management blamed for lacking aggressiveness in rationalizing the consolidations of the 1990s. Odeen felt that cost savings attributable to consolidation of facilities and cuts in overhead, even introduction of new technology, mostly benefitted the government. Few new defense projects attracted interest for companies pressured to shave profit margins in hopes of being the low bidder in "must win" competitions. Cash flow had weakened at a time when interest rates were rising and many companies held heavy debts. Industry suffered too from changes in tax laws and progress payment levels. It had absorbed upfront costs of rationalizing programs that were then being reimbursed by the government over time-periods of three to five years. All of this led to investment returns below those of other sectors. Thus, "not surprisingly, defense stocks are depressed," although Odeen admitted it was not government's responsibility to shore up the market value of defense companies. But, the decline in financial performance made it more difficult and costly for those companies to raise capital. Exiting from defense, together with inability to recruit talent in a "new economy" threatened industry's ability to maintain its technological advantage.

Working with the private sector, the Pentagon viewed exports, international industry alliances, and regulatory and policy changes, as ensuring the financial health of its private arsenal system. DoD would not agree to raising progress payment rates from seventy-five to eighty-five percent, although the new acquisition czar, the ubiquitous Jacques Gansler, contended "if you pay it as a function of making progress, you are giving them a real incentive to make their progress on time or early because the main thing the defense industry is motivated by is cash flow." Clearly, he said, "If they have an incentive to do a better job earlier, to make schedule, or beat schedule, they'll get paid up front." Still, there was too much "them" and "us" on both sides of what had long been touted as seamless partnering. Industry could not see either presidential candidate in the 2000 election promising requisite relief. Lobbying was intense, as Tom Schivelbein of Newport News Shipbuilding declared "from our perspective Congress is more important" than the White House. Teal Group's military aircraft expert, Richard Aboulafia, observed "the issue that's shrouding over all this is that the political will for more defense spending just isn't there." Yet, was the situation really that dire?

The stock-value decline of 1999 evaporated by 2000. In 1999, the aerospace index had fallen eight percent while Standard and Poor rose twenty-one percent. The next year, the S&P Aerospace index rose by twenty-six percent, even though the S&P overall sagged by 2.2 percent. The defense industry itself undertook collaborative measures; a joint internet-commerce exchange for buying supplies and selling products. Lockheed Martin, Boeing, Raytheon and BAE Systems, PLC, partnered with e-commerce facilitator Commerce One, Inc., to pool huge purchasing power for extracting better prices from a large group of suppliers brought together in bidding over the internet. The companies also planned to sell goods like spare parts, equipment, and even weapons, although one source contended "U.S. government policy is going to play a big role in that regard." Perhaps a key lay not only with savings but also in the hope that "old economy" (legacy) defense companies could share the enormous stock valuations of internet companies. A shrinking arms market and slow payments from oil-rich countries like Saudi Arabia and the United Arab Emirates, plus a scarcity of funds in Latin America, weakened foreign sales plans of the Pentagon and DIB. But with the top-ten awardees of FY 2000 government contractors raking in $50.6 billion in new contract awards, up from $47.5 billion in 1999, and relatively little change in the top-ten, (styled "the contractor elite"), comprised of Lockheed Martin, Boeing, Raytheon, General Dynamics, Northrup Grumman, the University of California System, United Technologies, Westinghouse Electric, Litton Industries, and Science Applications International (SAIC), skeptic s might wonder at any ostensible plight of what was styled the nation's "contractor elite." MIPC. The *Government Executive* informed its readers about the top 100 defense contractors or separate listings for foreign contractors, foreign military sales and the breakdown via the various armed services or "other federal agencies" involved with national security. Still, the president of the Aerospace Industries Association believed problems to be so pervasive that nothing short of a presidential commission could assess the future of an industrial sector accountable for so much of the nation's recent prosperity.[47]

Election of President George W. Bush in November 2000 offered a roadmap for new strategies, policies and defense reform. Defense contractors rebounded, with Lockheed Martin winning a radar contract over competitor Raytheon, signing-on Denmark to the total number of countries engaged in Lockheed Martin's megabuck Joint Strike Fighter (JSF) project, in addition to acquisitions and mergers like Northup Grumman acquiring Litton Industries and General Dynamics securing Newport News Shipbuilding. New Secretary of Defense Donald Rumsfeld still trumpeted the decline of the defense industrial base as "a very serious problem." With the government buying rather than producing things, industry had to be there, and to be there, he said, "it has to be viable from an economic standpoint or people are not going to invest in it." Indeed, as Lockheed Martin worried about Pentagon cuts, the Marine Corps Osprey tilt-rotor transport illustrated much of what Eisenhower had feared about collusion of military and political interests, draining millions from the Treasury, and in dictating policy. Between the Corps, Osprey's contractors (Boeing, Bell Helicopter Textron), a nationwide collection of subcontractors, and an alliance of congressmen led by Pennsylvania Republican Curt Weldon (whose district included Boeing's helicopter division), the project had been kept alive for a decade or more, despite deadly accidents and complaints about an "entrenched politically motivated policy known as 'concurrent engineering and manufacturing development.'" Weldon explained that "we had a coalition that was broad and deep," coalescing as ex-Marines in Congress, the Retired Marine Reserve Officers' Association, the United Auto Workers Union, and "the civil aviation people." Who could fight city hall?[48]

Looking at the list of Top 100 Defense Contractors, collectively awarded over $132 billion in FY 2000 DoD contracts, MIT defense analysts Sapolsky and Gholz concluded that while "the Cold War is over, U.S. defense budgets are being absorbed in producing wasteful political benefits." Despite appearances of a post-Cold War drawdown, and even a procurement holiday, political pressures had kept government expenditures on the defense industry at Cold War levels. The two analysts cited the instance where two Pennsylvania senators had blocked a 1997 move by General Dynamics Land Systems to buy United Defense Limited so as to consolidate armored-vehicle production. Senators Rick Santorum and Arlen Spector had arranged UDL's sale to a Wall Street buyout firm, the Carlyle Group, which promised to leave all production in place, thereby perpetuating inefficient capacity, claimed Sapolsky and Gholz, also declaring that the armed services "have the responsibility, if not the clear authority, to shape a reasonable defense industrial policy." An "inclusive, pro-consolidation merger policy would enable political support for the elimination of defense industry overcapacity." Once that was wrung from the base, they said, "a new business-government relationship would be able to preserve needed research and design skills at lower cost." Meanwhile, the Carlyle Group joined the exclusive "Top 100" American corporations, the eclectic nature of which by 2001 still contained Federal Express, Motorola, MITRE, Massachusetts Institute of Technology, Johns Hopkins University, Exxon Mobil, AT&T, Proctor & Gamble, Rolls Royce, B.F. Goodrich, Philip Morris and, far down the ranking at eighty-seventh, E.I.F. DuPont de Nemours. More modern "merchants of death" like Lockheed-Martin, Boeing, Raytheon, Northrop Grumman, General Dynamics, United Technologies, TRW, General Electric, SAIC, and foreign contractor BAE were there too. As Brian Friel commented, the days when a government agency "simply paid a company to do a particular job are disappearing." Agencies now formed partnerships to seek contractor solutions and, in some cases, contractors even sought solutions from other agencies. He referred to civilian agencies, although the Bechtel group reflected a multi-agency, civilian-military mixture in the "Top 100."[49]

One of several defense-community panels recommended in 1997 that the defense industrial base should be transformed. So had academics Gholz, Sapolsky and others on various occasions. Achieving and maintaining technological superiority through time-based competition was the generally held view in the DIB, along with other practices: pursue commercial off-the-shelf opportunities, exploit dual-use technologies, encourage new enterprises, in order to set new rules and procedures that emphasize technology development and deemphasize large production quantities, as well as favoring established or legacy firms for developing innovative ideas, and penalizing pedestrian efforts. A Booz, Allen and Hamilton study "U.S. Defense

Industry Under Siege—An Agenda for Change" in the summer of 2000 again protested that while "the U.S. Defense industry remains the world leader and the American armed forces are indisputably the best equipped, the industrial base is deteriorating." Erosion of the financial health of the industry and increasing challenges to recruiting and retaining top science and engineering talent lay at the cause. If the trends remained unchecked, an eventual effect on national security would be felt. Here was an amalgam of old and new phrases and concepts of preparedness and national security— marginally dissimilar to arguments in 1800 and 1900. Some of the ideas seemed on track with the Pentagon, although industry appeared mired in its habitual "just send money" refrain. In 2000, President Eisenhower would have recognized a military-industrial-political complex solution to the nation's security ills.[50]

* * *

Perceptive British lecturer David Ryan felt that George W. Bush and Bill Clinton had searched for resource-hungry "monsters to destroy" following the Cold War. Then Francis Fukuyama's "end of history" had given way to Samuel Huntington's "clash of civilizations" while waiting off-stage lay "backlash states" challenging the western narrative of free trade, democracy and stabilization and non-state actors preaching nihilism to followers and non-followers alike. Globalism and world leadership (or Washington's preferred terminology of "engagement and enlargement"), tested American foreign policy at century's end. Meanwhile, having drunk the nectar of Mars, Americans found it impossible to relinquish the chalice. Forty years after Eisenhower's prophetic warning and a decade after the end of the Cold War period, aerospace analyst William Gregory wrote that, with its Cold War purpose gone, military alliances emptied of substance, its military research machine facing an uncertain future, the United States confronted "a test of national-industrial strategy." Historian John W. Dower commented later that the end of the twentieth century "closed with an explosive overlay of developments" including a fixation on Middle East oil and accompanying "apocalyptic visions of chaos" in that region, while "acceleration" of military interventionism, paired with wishful thinking that "monopolization of sophisticated military equipment" would assure "full-spectrum dominance" to some quick solution. U.S. policymakers proved inept at discerning undercurrents of tribal, ethnic and religious identities defying America's special providence visions of models and process leading to democracy, free enterprise and social comity. Scholar Elaine Tyler May recorded that there seemed little proof that Americans "are safer, or more empowered, as a result of their weapons, the number of their fellow citizens who are imprisoned, their gated communities, their protective gadgets, and their SUVs." Dower and May both penned their snapshots in 2017. What would happen in intervening years of the new millennium to create such unabashedly sanguine viewpoints and necessitate some new-blown military-industrial-political complex?[51]

Chapter 8

NATIONAL SECURITY SINCE 2001

The United States invaded Afghanistan on September 26, 2001, fifteen days after the "9/11" terrorist attacks in New York and Washington, D.C. On December 28, 2014, NATO forces, including American, collaboratively ended combat operations in that country and transferred security responsibility to a reconstituted Afghan government. American military remained as advisers and trainers. On March 20, 2003, an American-led coalition invaded Iraq, resulting in occupation of that country which supposedly ended on December 18, 2011. Involvement in a Syrian civil war became its corollary. In April, 2017, as another terrorist entity, the Islamic State or ISIL, supplanted al-Qaeda as the preeminent threat, 8,500 American and an additional 7,000 NATO troops were still in Afghanistan. In late 2020, an American president still spoke of bringing residual troops home by the end of the year. Together the two conflicts constituted "the longest war" in American history. Moreover, the nation maintains "a veritable empire" of military bases as "forward deployed military posture" throughout the world. Some 800 hundred installations in more than 70 countries suggested a "new" deterrence for threats subsequently labeled "4+1" (China, Russia, Iran, North Korea, plus terrorism), later altered to "2+3" by the Pentagon but retaining the same cast of characters if now led by China and Russia. A transitional, ever-transformational national security enterprise continued to sit atop an updated version of a military-industrial-political complex. Worst of all, as Mark Danner shows, the war on terrorism redefined America's values and not for the better.[1]

SEARCHING FOR PRUDENT BALANCE

New geopolitical realities intruded upon the millennial world. Terrorism, pandemics, rogue nuclear states, resource conflicts, insurgencies, mass migrations, economic collapse, climate change, and cyber-attacks all attracted policy wonks. This latest chapter in American national security reflected changes consistent with these new twists and challenges, alongside old "givens" of power, control, and "shaping" a now-aging "New World Order." That order lingered, perhaps past its due date, eventually buffeted by fierce counter-globalization, nationalism-populism, and a vaunted disengagement, while perpetuating critics' complaints about a lack of coherent American grand strategy, and directionless foreign policy. The influence of MIPC provided an *eminence grise*. If not a manifestation of America as Security State, it adjusted its identity to a global war on terror, countering threats from states regular and rogue, and pondering mystifying, evolving cyber.

How history judges the presidential administrations of George W. Bush (2001–2009), Barack Obama (2009–2017) and Donald Trump (2017—2021) remains to be seen. Inevitably they will be tied to "endless war," although realistically to merely expeditionary campaigns of hegemony or displays of power. Styled "contingency operations" by government, their counterparts could be seen in previous experiences of Roman, Persian and probably even Chinese empires, much less modern European equivalents. September 11, 2001 enabled a global war on terror with all of its instruments mustered from "elements of power" (animal, vegetable, mineral), and applied to secondary themes during the period from regime change, nation-building and democratization, eventually to an almost self-willed return of Great-Powers Competition. Kinetic and non-kinetic methods were used in new ways. Gone were the statistics of military Fordism in World Wars I, II and Cold War mobilizations. New methods of extraction, even definition of the resourcing base, came into play. "War" truly blended politics and conflict in symbiosis. "Security" short of war, however, became the mantra for power across the world.

The promise of freedom, democracy and economic opportunity, quickly springing from the ashes of overthrown autocratic regimes, emerged as one of the most tragic theories of the young millennium. Beneath the rhetorical panacea of state commitment to international code-based rights and responsibilities, the mutual interests of nations and people, self-determinism plus economic opportunity shifted like tectonic plates. The equality/equity battles of economists, the clashes of civilization—popularized by political scientist Samuel P. Huntington, though debunked, but never completely refuted—and the pure barbarities of a new wave of extremism, terrorism, and anarchy, all tested the state-sovereignty system. The nuclear genie still held court while international and domestic consumerization of weaponry threw fresh fuel upon smoldering fires of instability. Agendas of state and non-state actors both dominated the scene. Perhaps continuity not change was the *leitmotiv* of this era of perpetual violence, fear and war. Elites and special interests played a role.[2]

As the new century advanced, policymakers and scholars mixed phrases like "delicate balance," realism, liberalism, constructivism, state and non-state actors, containment, preemption, unilateralism, and humanitarian intervention, while pushing some agenda or explanation of "Bush doctrine," "Obama doctrine," or eventually, a Trump version. The Great Recession of 2007, or Michael Lind's substitution of "the American way of trade" for "the American way of war" always confronted geopolitical realities. Withdrawal of American troops from Iraq while forever "assisting" somewhere else (from Afghanistan to the Korean peninsula, and Yemen to Niger), wariness of Iranian nuclear proliferation, an uncomfortably resurgent Russia, or an irrepressible China provided official backdrop. Issues like transnational crime and drugs, global warming, with spinoff socio-cultural and economic ramifications built upon religious extremism, restless dispossessed youth and war zone refugee migration. It was even unclear that stable nations from Europe to America might face national *insecurity*, with heavy legacy fragrances of populism, nativism, and even authoritarianism. Whether because of terrorism, economic disparity, or the democratization and marketing of communication technologies via globalization, the world was a fractious place. Fear formed an underpinning for a new dinner conversation in every American home. Academician Elaine Tyler May explained "Fortress America" showed "how we embraced fear and abandoned democracy."[3]

In her examination of innovation and enterprise, Linda Weiss claims that the post-9/11 state, was "considerably larger than its early-Cold War version." Arguably, impacts to the resourcing supply base of the new bureaucratization of response, the changing role of financialism, as well as technological omnipresence, renders the new epoch exciting. But as Weiss explains, "Security" encompasses virtually everything. It even melds the surveillance state with the warfare state, in "a new form of authoritarianism that imposes its own brand of terror and whose real enemy is not terrorism at all but democracy itself." By 2016, 8,000 residents polled in China, Egypt, France, India, Indonesia, Turkey and the United States indicated that terrorism was the number one challenge facing their country, noted expert Geoffrey R. Skoll in *Globalization of American Fear Culture*. Another observer felt the use of the term "homeland" sent "shivers up my spine" due to past European associations with" hypernationalism and chauvinism."[4]

The United States government responded to 9/11 by what it does best—it opened the money spigots, then reorganized and applied two models for a new bureaucracy. Congress appropriated $40 billion as energy and patriotism were thrown at the problem. One model of consolidation came with the Homeland Security Act of 2002, launching the most extensive reorganization of the U.S. government since the National Security Act of 1947. Building upon an initial White House office of homeland security, in January of

2003 the Bush II administration drew together a number of disparate agencies and 170,000 employees, to achieve unity of effort under a cabinet-level secretary similar to the Department of Energy oil-crisis response in 1977. Budget control of operations in the Secret Service, Coast Guard, Federal Emergency Management Agency, Transportation Security Administration, Immigration and Customs Enforcement, Customs and Border Protection, and Citizenship and Immigration Services was consolidated to achieve domestic security followed by its own homeland-security technologies facility which copied the Defense Advanced Research Projects Agency. FEMA and its contractors had reconstituted a Continuity-of-Government regime.[5]

A second, and different model for intelligence operations followed in 2004 with creation of the Office of the Director of National Intelligence, designed to introduce coordination, collaboration and coherence into eight separate intelligence organizations under Defense: four in total for each separate military service, plus four others, respectively based in the Defense Intelligence Agency, National Security Agency, National Reconnaissance Office, and National Geospatial-Intelligence Agency, as well as another seven intelligence components in departments of State, Justice, Homeland Security, Energy, and Treasury. Other government agencies such as The National Air and Space Administration, Department of Health and Human Services with its subsidiaries National Institutes of Health and National Science Foundation, as well as others, soon found a way aboard the largesse bandwagon. A new faucet of funding via threat and "war" had been opened. While this was no Sputnik effect, claims Weiss, the national security state nonetheless acquired new components, strategic synthesis, and popular support to resurgent "anti-statism" at the previous century's end. The picture clouded, however, when military and security agencies were joined by those more traditionally associated with foreign affairs and economic assistance. Everyone sought a slice of the budget for the counterterrorism mission, both overseas and at home.[6]

America signed on to "overseas contingency operations," or OCOs, in Afghanistan, Iraq and elsewhere. Traditional combat joined with post-conflict state-building activities by departments of State and Treasury, Export-Import Bank, and the Agency for International Development, plus a multitude of other programs outside the purview of "providing for the common defense." Diplomacy aggregated foreign assistance, public persuasion (information), economic assistance, and humanitarian relief, as viable parts of the new security enterprise. Contractors joined public servants both military and civilian, international military and civilian joined occupied nationals in an integrated effort of rehabilitating the Iraqi state. As Gordon Adams and Cindy Williams perceptively write, "global engagement funded through the national defense and international affairs budgets serves multiple objectives." Some were traditional and self-evident, such as protecting national sovereignty and territorial integrity of other states, sustaining a suitable level of U.S. global influence, supporting alliances like NATO, and ensuring the safe conduct of international commerce. Some seemed more transformative, such as helping countries to become capable partners in the global economy. Homeland security measures also served many purposes like "improving resilience" in the face of natural disasters, outbreak of pandemic disease as well as keeping citizens and infrastructure safe from threat of direct attack. After 9/11, focus seemed entail everything, everywhere, at all times. "Preparedness" replaced mobilization for a nation engaged in permanent war, permanent technological revolution and seemingly permanent paranoia.[7]

When Adams and Williams entitled their book *Buying National Security*, they backed into what the new epoch was mostly about. President George W. Bush urged the populace to respond to 9/11 by going out shopping, while eclectic scholar-practitioner David Rothkopf provocatively entitled a 2003 *Foreign Policy* essay "Business Versus Terror." People might have wondered, where was the traditional shared-sacrifice of wartime? Bush worried about the state of the economy based on public panic over losing affluent freedom. Rothkopf suggested that America's best weapons would "not be found in some musty Pentagon basement or arms manufacturer's warehouse." He trumpeted the mantra of yielding a public solution of the new problem to the private sector. He spotlighted "the briefcases of corporate CEOs and venture capitalists and the cubicles of high-tech start-ups." Nimble private-sector players could deploy innovative technologies and unlimited financing to fortify U.S. cities, effectively battle cyber threats, track the movements of terrorists, and disarm biological weapons, "if only Washington has sense enough to let them." Rothkopf knew that too many fiefdoms, too many agendas, and too much was at stake, for the state to protect its people after 9/11, when it had failed them before.[8]

Perhaps an escalation of defense spending reached its zenith of $754 billion by 2008. Unceasing foreign adventures, assumption of extraordinary legal powers and political arrogance, displays of precipitous acts of incarceration and interrogation, and an upsurge in police power and "securitization" of society that began with passage of "the USA Patriot Act" on October 26, 2001 all disturbed American tranquility. Even the legislation's full title reflected excess: "Uniting and Strengthening America by Providing Appropriate Tools Required to Intercept and Obstruct Terrorism," while "sunset clauses" simply perpetuated expiration dates by shrewd lobbying of a compliant Congress and a media-stoked popular frenzy. Any nouveau antiwar movement stayed with shadowy blogs and websites, or otherwise out of sight. A self-indulgent populace appeared content to wave flags, and allow the professional volunteer military and its contracted messmates to bear the brunt of foreign regime change, protection of oil oligarchies, and changing the hearts and minds of indigenous peoples mired in tribal feuds and religious fanaticism while resistant to western crusaders. Conflict eventually labeled the "longest continuous war in U.S. history" would cost taxpayers an estimated $4 trillion by 2014, although cost figures varied upward. It would drift to an era of mass surveillance, unmanned drone strikes and cyber warfare, said writer-filmmaker Oliver Stone. The dearth of returning body bags smothered another anti-Vietnam outburst in Americans' conscience.[9]

FUNDING WARS AND THE NATIONAL SECURITY ENTERPRISE

A critical issue for both the Bush and Obama administrations was simultaneously paying for the Security Enterprise (especially Defense) and Overseas Contingency Operations termed OCOs. Both directly tied to the military's fascination with weapons of enormous capabilities and staggering costs. The war on terror extended technological possibilities but also limited traditional public contribution of shared sacrifice. Conscription and mobilization devices of the Selective Service and Defense Production Act remained on the books as law but no real requirement was implemented. There would be no military draft, and tax revenues had multiple destinations. Leading industry experts believed terror attacks would mean new orders for the arms and aviation industry. Whatever form the new conflict took, it would be driven by information technology. Some corporate heads predicted that a lot of money would flow into intelligence infrastructure, others thought electronics. Still others proclaimed, overall, "it is not being projected that there will be a great need for new military equipment." The tempo and persistence of Afghanistan and Iraq soon contradicted post-Cold War abandonment of wartime-surge production requirements. Defense reliance on commercial industry for such components as computer chips or mine-resistant vehicles affected crisis response. Moreover, when fears of bioterrorism grew daily, anthrax in particular, the pharmaceutical sector even tasted patriotism for profit. With precision-guided munitions and technology driven stealth as part of war's landscape, Linda Weiss declares, a "powerful American cocktail created an encompassing political-economic system in which the national security state became intricately bound to the development of the private sector and its capacity of innovation."[10]

Opportunities beckoned but were pricey. Earlier wars had been financed by taxes, public bond sales and creating new money, each category in rising percentiles from the Civil War to the World Wars. Astronomical military and federal spending kicked in when post-World War II demobilization bottomed at $100 billion annually then took off again with Korea and never settled below $300 billion as a baseline before the end of the twentieth century, observes Rebecca Thorpe. Officially, in what was technically peacetime (no declared war), only random expeditions and humanitarian interventions semantically clouded the landscape. Calculating the "dynamics of defense budget growth from 1998–2011," co-director of the Project on Defense Alternatives Carl Conetta told a Naval War College symposium in 2010 that cost-surge for Iraq and Afghanistan was nearly as great as both Korea and Vietnam combined. He discounted any impact of the actual campaigns, emphasizing rather their combination in service support of a volunteer force coincidental to military modernization and cost growth. Todd Harrison, senior fellow at the Center for Strategic and Budgetary Assessments added, a "new guns versus butter debate is also an intergenerational struggle—a question of providing benefits to those who served in the past or funding the equipment and training needed for those who will fight tomorrow's wars." When the 2008 Great Recession occurred, he says, "every dollar going to pay for health care, pensions, and other retiree benefits is a dollar not available to ensure tomorrow's troops are the best equipped and trained military force in the world."[11]

Parsing the nature of costs aside, paying for the war against terrorism prompted little resistance from the public or its elected officials: ninety-four percent of surveyed citizenry supported military action against those responsible for the 9/11 attacks, with eighty-four percent in favor of doing so against any state sponsoring such actions. Some respondents thought the new conflict would be long (ninety-two percent) and difficult (ninety-four percent). The president had said so. Yet, the public at times actually believed that wars now would be short and cheap, again thanks to technology. David Von Drehle's "rallying 'round the flag" piece in April 2006 suggested that since al-Qaeda declared war on the country, rather than meet any hardship, "we have loosed the fateful charge cards of America's fat wallet." A few economists began to question the "war's stunning price tag" since Afghanistan and Iraq were already "more costly than 'the war to end all wars,'" referring to World War I. *Financial Times* pundit Martin Wolfe declared that America had "failed to calculate the enormous costs of war" and, for about five years, security spending rose with little protest. Then pushback began, suggesting the days of open checkbooks were numbered for the Pentagon and other security agencies. Congress responded: it might provide everything for the wars but the basic defense budget faced significant reductions. Potential targets included missile defense, a new destroyer, the army's future-combat system and the Marines' V-22 tilt-rotor helicopter.[12]

Part of the problem was the Defense department's separate bookkeeping—one set for regular defense spending and another for war expenses. On Capitol Hill they were called "Shadow budgets," supplemental or emergency appropriations quickly passed with all due deference to the president's war effort. Still, escalating costs of endless conflict could not be conveniently bracketed while what the Pentagon would eventually invent as "hybrid war" synthesized with post-conflict stabilization, reconstruction and nation-building. Millions anticipated for short war turned into billions for long war, and eventually into trillions including country rebuilding. Conscious political decisions of the Bush administration for continuing pre-9/11 tax cuts by underwriting operations through supplemental appropriations postponed any reckoning concerning budget and debt problems. "Supplemental" circumvention of the regular budget process had been used before on an emergency basis, before in Korea, Vietnam and Bosnia, but not as a calculated method of securing "guns *and* butter *and* tax cuts." Bush tax cuts represented "an abrupt departure from the customary U.S. practice of increasing taxes during times of war," claim historians Steven A. Bank, Kirk J. Stark and Joseph J. Thorndike. But such borrowing against future generations seemed an amenable device.[13]

This really wasn't traditional "war" anyway. Politically marginalized fiscal discipline, or opposition to excessive reliance on deficit-financing, came into vogue. Mobilizing financial assets "to respond to the 9/11 attacks, topple the Taliban, and round up or kill Al Qaeda forces did not require the enormous tax increases, domestic spending cuts, or patriotic bond-drives seen during World Wars I and II," declares war financing expert Robert Hormats, also admitting that it should have occasioned "a reassessment and revision" of fiscal priorities to determine "what portion of the tax cuts and spending commitments that seemed affordable before 9/11 were no longer so." The administration (primarily worried about a flattened economy, hence necessary stimulus measures), might have rallied the people behind comprehensive energy-conservation efforts thus neutralizing Middle East oil considerations. Underestimates of costs, overestimates of Iraqi oil revenue for rebuilding that country, and the feebleness of international financial help, compared to the 1990 Gulf War, stood out.[14]

After 9/11, U.S. defense-spending resumed customary up and down cycles due to crises, emergencies and interventions. The budget low point of under $400 billion started upward in earnest after the terrorist attacks, settling in between $500 to $600 billion during the Obama years. Yet, as Hormats posits, if the war on terrorism was considered the nation's highest priority, it was not reflected in U.S. fiscal policies for freeing up resources to pay for it. The 9/11 attacks required heightened spending for national security and economic- measures, then came the Afghan and Iraqi contingencies, and by 2006 the two together hiked military and homeland security spending to nearly five percent of GDP. Would allocation of money to traditional weapons projects help offset risk, vulnerability, or any additional attacks on the homeland? When Treasury Secretary John Snow told Congress in March 2003 that war costs would be small, and a policy that "we can afford the war, and we'll put it behind us" merged with the feeling that much of the war would be fought out of sight by commandoes, diplomats and intelligence agents, would a self-indulgent nation stay focused? The answer, to acquisition-guru Jacques Gansler, suggested a peculiar response to the astronomical expansion of defense spending by the Bush administration, which defied control measures by his successor Barack Obama's directed tax cuts and "far less concern about economic considerations," whether on Capitol Hill, at the White House and Pentagon or out in the heartland. Economic security and national security hardly even connected with the Great Recession of 2008–2009.[15]

Washington politicians, policymakers and bureaucrats faced the complex fiscal challenge of prosecuting elective combat while still meeting regular costs of government and growing costs of retirement and healthcare benefits (termed "entitlements"), plus interest payments on rising government debt. National security now comprised more than outlays for defense or even war alone. Intelligence, diplomatic initiatives, efforts to interdict terrorist financing, foreign assistance even domestic state and local first responders, police departments, homeland protection vied for funding with nation-building and re-building, "public diplomacy" and veterans' costs. The three-tiered American system of governance cloaked securitization for all levels. Response even to domestic violence seemed to summon armored vehicles with assault-rifle bearing, camouflaged, jack-booted police deployed in streets and backyards. Author Radley Balko dared talk openly of a militarization of America's police forces and a possible militarized police-industrial complex. Thanks to Second Amendment gun-rights fervor stoked by the National Rifle Association and the iconic image of a right-wing cowboy nation perpetually at High Noon in Dodge City—who needed al-Qaeda or its franchises, when America seemed bent on drifting into anarchy, all on its own?[16]

OCOs, normal security-agency commitments and weapons procurement all stimulated portions of MIPC and might have set off alarm bells in Washington. Some commentators thought that the substantial budget surplus left over from the Clinton presidency gave the government great leeway for relief, reconstruction and economic stimulus, as well as subsequent overseas interventions and enhanced homeland defense after 9/11. Yet, Senators like John Kerry and George V. Voinovich chirped that curbing explosive social security and Medicare growth was indispensable to sound financial stewardship. The Government Accountability Office worried that an "unsustainable path will gradually erode, if not suddenly damage, our economy, our standard of living, and ultimately our national security." If military allocations accounted for a relatively small portion of GDP and the overall budget, it consumed a large share of discretionary spending. Yet, as the pat refrain of observers like Robert Hormats went, "while American servicemen and women are sacrificing their lives, the thought that companies are making untoward profits due to the mismanagement of contracting and procurement damages Pentagon credibility." Security expert Andrew Cordesman found little "to celebrate in a President and Congress that have done the worst job of fiscal management in our nation's post-World War II history, if not our nation's entire history," adding that excessive entitlements and health costs seemed "to be more of a threat to US security" than foreign enemies."[17]

Winslow Wheeler, defense-budget analyst at the Center for Defense Information, also suggested that "what constitutes defense spending depends on your point of view." The costs of maintaining the nuclear stockpile added $16.4 billion, for instance. When Congress passed the FY 2006 defense budget in December 2005, the "commonly advertised budget figure" had been $453 billion for FY 2006 ending September 30. But the United States would actually spend nearly $670 billion "defending and protecting American interests," a figure "about $220 billion more than the narrowly defined defense spending," Wheeler contended. Suddenly, by mid-decade, people awoke to "the crisis in defense spending." Deficit pressures, controversy involving defense contracts, congressional unease with Pentagon bookkeeping for war costs, along with the increased unpopularity of Bush and his antiterrorism policies, contributed "to end defense spending's status as the budget's sacred cow." Expenses for overseas contingencies would remain favored, but the rest of the defense budget could be squeezed. Treasury pursuit of terrorist money at the expense of law enforcement and intelligence functions suggested further targeted savings. Few talked about fiscal discipline or stress to the defense-industry base, only supporting military deployments.[18]

Conservative hawks remained dissatisfied. "Winning in Iraq and Afghanistan and the global War on Terror, having the arms and men to react to a new crisis—be it with Iran, North Korea, or an imploding Pakistan—and preparing the military to hedge against a rising China," became a steady drumbeat for those like American Enterprise Institute scholar Gary J. Schmitt. Dedicating five percent of the GDP—"a nickel on the dollar"—to defense was a wise investment. To Jeffrey Tebbs at rival Brookings Institution, "since September 2001, the Department of Defense (DoD) budget has increased $179 billion in FY 2006 dollars, or 56 percent," plus defense spending now exceeded "totals at the peak of the Korean War and approaches a real level of resource expenditure not witnessed since the Second World War." With Pentagon plans for another budget increase in 2009 (before tapering back to 2008 levels over four years), analysts fretted about long-term affordability and significant mismatch between plans and funding levels. They never lacked answers.[19]

One business-leader group, with cost-cutter Lawrence Korb writing its position, touted how $60 billion could be flushed by eliminating Cold War-era weapons systems designed to thwart the former Soviet Union but no longer useful in defending the country from extremists or other threats. Some $21 billion could be saved by paring the nuclear arsenal to no more than 1,000 warheads, $8 billion by cutting the National Missile Defense program to basic research, about $28 billion found in scaling back R&D and construction of weapon systems like the F/A-22 fighter plane, and the new *Virginia* class submarine, with another $5 billion chopped by eliminating two active Air Force wings and a carrier-group, plus about $5 billion more "would be saved if the giant Pentagon bureaucracy simply functioned in a more efficient manner and eliminated the earmarks in the defense budget." Other observers thought the FY 2008 proposed budget, at 4.4 percent of GDP, "should be adequate to meet America's immediate national security needs," although a question of sustainability would remain as ongoing terrorism costs would test Bush's plan for defense budgets to decline to 3.2 percent of GDP by FY 2012. Writing with Miriam Pemberton, Korb also advanced that while strategy documents were one way to comprehend a nation's security priorities, "budget allocations are another." They advocated a "united security budget," allowing better congressional recognition of three dimensions: offensive (military), defensive (homeland security) and preventive (nonmilitary international engagement). Predictably, Boeing's defense-business head Jim Albaugh still preached that any decline in strictly defense budgets would leave the country relying on old and worn-out weapons systems. Furthermore, what would happen when we left Iraq and Afghanistan and the supplementals dried up, he groused.[20]

Mid-decade found analyst Fred Reed wondering "why we fund unneeded weapons" and that we lived in an age of technological dinosaurs. These projects never could justify their costs in money or mental effort, had become embedded in our culture and would endure, just because "killing them off would have a drastic effect on the economy." Among those he cited the international space station, bombers and fighters for the Air Force, and the airborne laser as candidates, while dual-use technology particularly at the research stage might also no longer converge as before. He faulted advanced-weapons engineers, always ready to find another design challenge. The *New York Times* on February 4, 2008 revealed that not only was the $600 billion already approved in supplemental budgets to pay for Iraq, Afghanistan and other counterterrorism operations, but the Pentagon was about to unveil a proposed 2009 budget of $515.4 billion which omitted any new round of supplemental appropriations specifically for those efforts or for nuclear weapons. Military spending, when adjusted for inflation "will have reached its highest level since World War II," claimed Thom Shanker, stating this was a five percent increase over the 2008 budget, a thirty percent increase since 2000, and "a figure sure to be noted in coming budget battles as the American economy seems headed downward and government social spending is strained, especially by health-care costs." The 2009 request might be the peak for defense spending, thought Lexington Institute's Loren Thompson. The proposed amount of merely four percent of the 2008 economy (counting nuclear weapons and supplemental war costs, with base-line Pentagon spending of about 3.4 percent of GDP), was acceptable to new Secretary of Defense Robert M. Gates and Joint Chiefs chairman Admiral Mike Mullen. Analyst Steven Kosiak thought spending limits made it easier for the Pentagon to avoid trimming programs. The fate of the defense industry might depend on the 2008 ballot box, advanced Standard and Poor analyst Richard Tortoriello. So too might the fate of OCOs.[21]

RECESSION, AUSTERITY, AND STRATEGIC PIVOT

Clinton-era budgeteer Gordon Adams doubted much would change from electing either 2008 presidential candidate. Rather, he said, deep into that campaign and years into Afghanistan and Iraq, "the US national security debate is missing the point." Instead of focusing on a strategy that engaged the world differently after Iraq, politicians argued over the cost of that episode, who could be trusted to execute the next war, and who could expand the military and "raise the defense budget to handle it." Such instinctive yet mindless fixation might well "sink U.S. national security policy in the next administration," Adams insisted. Because the candidates offered few alternative strategies using all the tools of statecraft, America was "slouching" toward ever-higher military budgets, expanded forces, weakened diplomacy, and a declining international reputation. The political candidates "are tiptoeing around this debate for fear of being attacked as weak on defence," he decided. "Be strong on disciplining defence budgets and forcing a strategic rethink," Adams counseled, otherwise, once in office they would simply inherit a swelling budget that "lacks sufficient oversight and strategic foresight."[22]

Suggesting just that, Government Accounting Office analysts found multiple cost overruns. Ninety-five major systems had exceeded their original budgets by a total of $295 billion. Particular offenders included Boeing/SAIC's Future Combat systems, Lockheed Martin's Joint Strike Fighter, Virginia-class attack submarine, chemical demilitarization, and the Evolved Expendable Launch Vehicle, along with other programs including C-17 A, Expeditionary Fighting Vehicle, the *Arleigh Burke*-class destroyer, C-5 transport re-engineering, and BIRS satellites. These overruns resulted from inflation and changes in support, engineering, scheduling and estimates, but other analysis also suggested plain erosion of Pentagon buying power. The GAO found it was cheaper to cancel than continue a number of such huge weapons programs, since by 2012 the top-ten weapons programs were expected "to eat up 64 percent of the funds that currently pay for all 95." However, defense firms also chased a lucrative $1.3 trillion global market, undecided whether budgetary flush or hard times beckoned.[23]

Fall 2008 proved unsettling, with Barack Obama's election to the presidency and the continuing conflicts abroad. Then, a severe recession hit the economy. Predicted spending cuts even threatened the defense enterprise. Some savants hoped Democrat Obama would defang the MIPC but feared he would simply enhance ground forces, "which makes an increase in spending almost inevitable." Defense industries themselves were literally awash in $20 billion free-cash flow. Increasing defense capital spending and recruiting through science and technology initiatives like the Defense Education Act of 2006 led Air Force secretary Michael Wynne to anticipate "a call for investing in America's defense and research to create the opportunity for economic recovery, [to] reward those who have completed their studies and get something immediately for our investment." With Congress pumping $3.4 billion to Lockheed Martin for twenty F-22 Raptor aircraft and $6.32 billion for fourteen F-35 II Joint Strike fighters, to Boeing for the C-17 Globemaster III cargo plane ($318.8 million in multiyear procurement), $3.6 billion to Boeing/SAIC for the Future Combat Systems, $1.5 billion to Northrop/Grumman for Zumwalt class destroyer, and $41 billion to Lockheed Martin/General Dynamics for two Littoral Combat Ships, was the DIB recession-proof?[24]

DoD ultimately received considerably more than the combined total given other "security" agencies. In FY 2006, Project on National Security Reform writers singled out the Department of Defense ($419.3 billion), Department of State ($31.8 billion), the overall intelligence community an estimated $60 billion and the Office of the Director of National Intelligence $1 billion, Homeland Security ($29.3 billion), and Treasury, $11.6 billion. Indeed, a $553 billion "national security" budget may well have been a more insightful index for the confluence of 9/11 and growth of the national security state than any traditional defense budget tying into a military-industrial-political complex or even a "defense industry base." Proponents of identifying defense as a low proportion of GDP or of government expenditure would not concede that "national security" costs of defense and homeland security alone accounted for fifty-two percent of discretionary spending for FY 2007. Security reform proponents asserted that "the actors in U.S. national security policy today already include government departments that have not traditionally had front-row seats" like Treasury, Justice, Agriculture, Interior, and Health and Human Services or even elements of state and local governments and the private sector. Still, this twenty-first century "whole-of-government" or "interagency" approach hardly resembled journalist Bruce Catton's mobilized World War II "warlords of Washington."[25]

Obama did what Democrats had long advocated. He pared defense, vowed to withdraw U.S. forces from Iraq and close down the terrorist incarceration facility at Guantanamo Bay while touting the role of "soft power." His new defense secretary Robert Gates, a Bush holdover, told the Senate Armed Services Committee, "the spigot of defense spending that opened on 9/11 is closing." Nonetheless, like in the Clinton years, there would be no draconian drawdown of the MIPC. "There was a war on" so Gates and his acquisition czar Ash Carter aimed at accountability, re-negotiating more favorable contacts for programs like the JSF and air refueling tanker. However, their primary concern lay with "supporting the troops." Defense contractors immediately lobbied Congress and advised against cutbacks in a suffering economy. Observers expected some maneuver for a "stimulus" bill to help nondefense portions of businesses but not a dramatic decrease in total spending. Said Loren Thompson, "this White House does not believe in stimulating the economy by buying more weapons," although cutting weapons programs "could eliminate tens of thousands of jobs, causing further damage to the economy." Marion C. Blakey, president of the Aerospace Industries Association, claimed her sector was so "fundamental to national security," that undercutting it by shutting down production lines would cost "good, middle-class jobs." To Larry Korb: "When you've got a $1 trillion debt and you have an $840 billion stimulus package to pay for [it] and you're trying to boost your economy, people will say, 'do you really want to have this big fight to cut something like the F-22 now?'"[26]

In fact, big defense contractors reacted by strengthening their nondefense business areas, like healthcare servicing and retrofitting federal buildings for greater energy efficiency. Lockheed Martin prepared to expand its information technology division to help government computerize healthcare records, while also planning to bid on cybersecurity and renewable energy projects favored by the new administration. Northrop Grumman, anticipating federal support for nuclear-power construction, retooled its Newport News shipyard to manufacture heavy components for nuclear plants in a joint venture with a French company, Areva. MIPC proponents thought weapons production was a stimulus program in disguise anyway—timely, targeted, if temporary, while economically and strategically smart, occasioning bipartisanship, and "a part of a political solution that saves the Obama administration's first—and perhaps most important—initiative." Officials tried to eliminate war supplementals. Gates sought systems with maximum flexibility for the broadest possible range of conflict. It became "politically taboo to discuss reducing or rearranging Pentagon spending requests in the years after September 11," thought Travis Sharp of the Center for Arms Control and Nonproliferation.[27]

The Obama administration, with Gates as its herald, hoped that long-term deficits and economic stagnation would prompt "a renewed vigor for lawmakers and military officials alike" to endorse meaningful reform policies. A proposed $663.7 billion FY 2010 defense bill (including war costs and DOE nuclear-weapons programs) was about four percent more than the previous year. Analyst Frida Berrigan declared that, "despite the sort of economic maelstrom not seen in generations, the defense industry insulated by an enduring conviction that war spending stimulates the economy, remains almost impervious to budget cuts." To comprehend why military spending was no longer a stimulus driver meant "putting aside memories of Rosie the Riveter and the sepia-hued worker on the bomber assembly line and remembering instead that the Great Depression came *before* 'the Good War,'" and to recall in World War II that the massive military buildup was "labor intensive, employed millions, and was accompanied by rationing, austerity, and very high taxes." Oklahoma senator James Inhofe blasted, "never before has a president so ravaged the military at a time of war." Loren Thompson felt that Gates merely repeated predecessor Donald Rumsfeld's error by proposing changes "without a strategic framework or a political plan for getting them implemented." Gates did not have the interests of the defense industry "first and foremost in his mind," claimed critics.[28]

Pentagon spokesman Geoff Morrell felt that "the priorities in the Pentagon's 2010 budget request "aren't changes on the margins; it is a fundamental shift in direction." Reshaping the MIPC could be seen as a hidden benefit of cost control when congressional knives carved into Gates's budget. Defense experts like Michael O'Hanlon excoriated administration moves to use the budget not just to reform acquisition but also to shape strategic priorities. Gates countered, "every dollar spent to over ensure against a remote or diminishing risk—or, in effect, to run up the score in a capability where the United States is already dominant—is a dollar not available to take care of our people, reset the force, win the wars we are in and improve capabilities in areas where we are underinvested and potentially vulnerable." Hoping congressmen would rise above parochial interests and consider the best interests of the nation as a whole, Gates gained support from Democratic representative Ike Skelton and Republican senator John McCain for "a good faith effort" and "step in the right direction." Still, Skelton pointed out, "the buck stops with Congress" which would get to decide whether to support these proposals. That was evident on April 2, 2010 when Alabama Republican senators Richard Shelby and Jeff Sessions held up Ashton Carter's nomination as DoD's next acquisition chief after a spat with the Pentagon over an Air Force tanker contract imbroglio. By year's end, Washington had added $100 billion to the 2011–2012 base budget. Legislators on the Hill still drove the MIPC bus![29]

A pattern continued. The Center for Defense Studies released "A Nation at War, An Administration in Retreat," which touted how the congressionally-mandated 2010 Quadrennial Defense Review report failed to answer "how much was enough," substituted "risk management" for victory, reflected "unanticipated" war costs, froze forces and deferred modernization, and held defense at historic lows while the debt and deficit, or so-called fiscal cliff, reflected entitlements, not defense costs. To Tom Donnelly and Tim Sullivan, a "Four Ps" Pentagon philosophy—first, prevail in the wars, second, prevent or deter via alliances and partners, third, prepare in multi-theaters and multi-domains, and fourth, while also preserving or preparing to reduce dwell-time, sustainable rotations, and accept risk in preventive efforts—was out of step with budget plans. Then "Sequester" struck.[30]

Was this a new type of induced demobilization? Unable to fiscally discipline itself, the U.S. government entered an austerity period with the Budget Control Act of 2011. Reductions in spending authority ($85.4 billion or some $40 billion in actual cash outlays) were to be duplicated each successive year until 2021, and divided evenly between defense and non-defense categories. Subsequent manipulation of figures resolved little, for what originally had been designed as a compromise for tackling a debt-ceiling crisis. Instead, it became an argument over how the country had become addicted to entitlements (sixty-six percent of mandatory spending), compared with merely eighteen to twenty percent for discretionary spending on domestic and international programs. Economic problems as a national security issue continued with recession persisting amid a slow recovery, increasing national debt and debt-to-GDP ratio, and growing polarization between political parties. DoD officials like Gates, and his successors Charles Hagel and Leon Panetta, saw this as a chance to "fundamentally reshape the defense enterprise to better reflect 21st century realities." The public saw only government gridlock. A Republican election-year platform blasted a failed National Security Strategy, declining conventional forces, and "Nuclear Forces and Missile Defense imperiled." A new Obama doctrine promised an Asian pivot and "turning the page on a decade of war." Pentagon budget cuts would make a difference predicted pundit David Ignatius.[31]

The spring of 2013 found the Secretary of Defense warning of deeper cuts ahead. The search for waste joined defense reform as the Obama administration kept a $526.6 billion 2014 defense budget relatively steady, while calling for the Pentagon to find $150 billion in savings over the next decade. Costly ground wars supposedly would wind down and new priorities like cybersecurity take hold. Some citizens advocated shifting money from defense to public infrastructure projects and social programs. The Pentagon hoped automatic sequestration spending cuts would evaporate in congressional repeal by the end of the fiscal year. Politically, few wanted to touch "limiting combat power, reducing readiness and undermining the national security interests." A pro-defense congressional group led by Californian Buck McKeon, petitioned leadership for redress from defense cuts, claiming that defense represented only seventeen percent of the national budget, but absorbed fifty percent of the cuts to date. A Bipartisan Budget Act (BBA) of 2013 was hammered out eventually. Many termed this "fiscal cliff deal" a bad bargain, a rollback of sequestration only for the Pentagon, and praised solely by "the beltway elite." A reduction in the cuts scheduled under the Budget Control Act of 2011, the BBA specified $498 billion for defense, $469 billion for non-defense, and it reduced sequester penalties so that defense would come in at about $521 and non-defense at $491. BCA arrangement for FY 2015 held $512 billion for defense, $483 billion for non-defense when the compromise dust settled. Agreement reduced sequester by $9 billion each, raising defense to $521.4 billion and non-defense to $491.8 billion. With the same caps in place for 2016–2021, the budget was essentially flat but a return to regular budget order.[32]

Analysts labeled the 2014 budget period chaos and uncertainty. Yet, reports of devastating effects from sequestration on national security appeared exaggerated. If defense industry CEOs concluded anything from the budget game, except for an insulated joint strike-fighter project, most of the military's modernization plan was on shaky ground, observed Sandra I. Erwin, senior editor of *National Defense magazine*. Defense spending had become just another line item in the budget, increasingly disconnected from strategic interests and rational threats. It was a "money pit of possible reductions to pay for burgeoning retirement benefits, mainly Social Security and Medicare, which are largely immune to cuts." The BCA was taking "nearly $1 trillion out of then-projected military spending over a decade," thought economist Robert Samuelson, and that since 2010, inflation-adjusted defense spending "has declined 21 percent" if the Iraq and Afghanistan OCOs were included, or twelve percent without them. Defense spending in 2014 was but 3.4 percent of GDP, compared with a post-World War II average of 5.5 percent, and unless the caps were lifted by 2019 would fall below 2.5 percent of GDP, the lowest since 1940. Of course, it was a specious argument—Cold War containment versus twenty-first century interventionism. However, Russian aggression in Ukraine, the rise of the Islamic State and rogue regimes in North Korea, Syria plus autocratic China and Iran underscored the folly of BCA and the budget deal, claimed "deficit hawks."[33]

A chorus of derision took over Washington. The National Defense Panel (a bipartisan commission chartered by Congress), decided that BCA 2011 was a "serious strategic misstep," that "dangerously tied the hands of the Pentagon leadership," with universal cuts in defense spending "subjecting the nation to accumulating strategic risk." The threat of sequester was never meant to be carried out claimed NDP members Michele Flournoy and Eric Edelman. BCA "was supposed to be a 'sword of Damocles' ensuring that lawmakers would reach an agreement on ways to cut the federal deficit." Those efforts failed, holding national security hostage at a particularly dangerous moment in world affairs. It was a matter of DoD as an emasculated hollow force, or a trimmed but still-bloated cash cow. Senator John McCain called upon his own consultants from among former national security luminaries who solemnly declared that present threats were complex although far less dangerous than the Cold War's potential nuclear exchanges. The Obama administration countered that the DoD $585.3 billion FY 2016 budget request was strategy-driven. Deputy Secretary of Defense Robert O. Work suggested that multi-dimensional threats required more innovative and agile investments in nuclear weapons, space-control capabilities, sensors, communications, cybertechnology, munitions and missile defense, unmanned undersea vehicles, high-speed strike weapons, and aeronautics. Columnist Walter Pincus observed wryly, "this is why there is an increase in the defense budget, from high-tech to low-tech and everything in between." NDIA's Sandra Erwin felt, "the new foreign policy mantra in Washington is that the world is on fire," so "the nation's weapons procurement machine, meanwhile, keeps partying like its 1999."[34]

Despite dire predictions in February 2015 that the $585 billion FY 16 defense budget request would likely die a long and complicated death, it survived as part of another budget deal that eased the full impact of the BCA. Whether or not this spelled "the beginning of the end of [BCA] caps" remained questionable. A waning war on terror kept future costs of the "Longest War" chimerical. Everything was 'budget-driven" with no clear plan or program. Readiness remained a "trust me" Pentagon mystery, as did shaping the force to fit the mission. Modernization was not tied to any distinct future-year defense plan or Quarterly Defense Review. The FY 2016 DoD budget concentrated on securing sequestration funding, with similar efforts for Homeland Security, State/AID, and Intelligence agencies. And, the budget proposal from Obama's final defense secretary Ash Carter seemed driven principally by technology and resurgent threats from Russia and China.[35]

Scoring at $580 billion, it was "a better, not bigger" military budget, suggested *New York Times* editors. The Pentagon "got most of what it wanted in the decade after 9/11, yet America still struggles to keep Afghanistan and Iraq from falling to insurgents." DoD had wasted billions on misguided programs. Congress needed to reform the military healthcare program and a planned thirty-year modernization of a nuclear arsenal, contrasted with conventional weapons to fight the Islamic state and other threats. A budget crisis was coming since many new systems under development would reach peak funding years in the 2020s. One public survey found citizens favoring cuts of $121 billion by eliminating the F-35 and an aircraft carrier. Congressional analysts saw deferral and innovation as budgetary watchwords instead. Jittery contractors saw billions pared from previous procurement spending. Matthew Goldberg of the Congressional Budget Office posited that if weapon-systems costs continued to rise, "funding required to implement the Administration's plans would exceed the Budget Control Act caps by $262 billion (in 2016 dollars) over the 2017–2020 period." Controversy slogged on.[36]

TRANSITIONING THE SECURITY STATE ENTERPRISE

Editor of *the Independent Review*, Robert Higgs re-titled "MIPC" to "SICC" or Security-Industrial-Congressional Complex, for greater clarification of "the more menacing apparatus," sitting alongside the "entrenched predatory monstrosity" of MIPC. Indeed, MIPC was now a hydra-headed monster with sub-sector homeland security, intelligence in addition to the defense industrial bases, constituencies, congressional advocates and dependent general public. The increase in DoD funding between FY 2001 and 2006 by sixty-nine percent (forty-nine percent after allowance for inflation), from $217 to $366 billion, was a bonanza whereby "nearly all of this money finds its way into the pockets of owners, employees, and suppliers of military-contracting companies." More appalling to Higgs was the economic incentive passed in homeland security contracts. They numbered 3,512 in 2003, three years later 33,890, with a registered lobbyist corps growing from three in 2001 to 671 in 2004. "America is in the grip of a business based on fear," as Higgs observed the government was "sparing no expense ostensibly to protect all Americans from every known form of threat and from many threats yet undreamt of, too." Americans expected no less from "their savior of first resort." Nobody was upset "by the bogus quality of most of the goods and services procured under the rubric of 'homeland security"—"little more than a gigantic exchange of *pork* for items that merely purport to protect Volk and Vaterland."[37]

The new official phrase Overseas Contingency Operations, or OCO, replaced Global War on Terror in 2013. It still mirrored the fact that since President Franklin Roosevelt, the country had lived "in a permanent state of national insecurity, always at war with or against someone or something, because there is always someone or something to be afraid of." Even before Obama entered office, the DoD's Quadrennial Defense Review (QDR) spoke to how the nation was engaged in a multi-theater, long-term conflict against militant extremists, "seeking to erode the strength and will of the United States, our partners, and our allies through irregular and asymmetric means." Analysts with Washington's Center for Strategic and International Studies (CSIS) later admitted that the 2014 QDR "presaged very little of the major happenings of 2015," with the global environment that year "almost as confounding as the American political scene." Global trends and regional realities created "a kaleidoscope of pressing and slow-burning challenges" with Obama strategists shifting from "hard power" interventionism to "soft power" bolstering of fragile states. Conflict had been routinized, as MIPC and its defense industrial base (DIB) adjusted. The tenth anniversary of 9/11 found Americans accepting almost everything about a security-surveillance state.[38]

Tough questions went unasked about the nation's direction toward an Orwellian-like "1984," much less a unique American brand of empire. The terrorists lost, opined blogger Frank Rich, but then, who had won? Paranoia at home stoked propaganda about militant Islam and atrocity-prone terrorism. All this avoided an inconvenient truth that a home-grown corporate variety had savaged America's middle-class investment in 2008 while "24/7" news deluged viewers with domestic violence as well as ethnic and class conflict. Some future historian might think that like ancient Rome, observed legendary consumer advocate Ralph Nader, "the empire is eating itself." A Bipartisan Policy Center's National Security Preparedness Group (a follow-on to the original national 9/11 Commission), decided America was "undoubtedly safer." Yet, Nader urged Americans to "recognize–or unlearn," reactions and overreactions to 9/11. From exaggerating adversary strength to produce a climate of hysteria resulting in repression of civil liberties via the USA Patriot Act, to immense damages to the economy by "the massive diversion of trillions of dollars from domestic civilian needs because of the huge expansion and misspending in military and security budgets," he inveighed against leaders disobeying federal statutes and international treaties, pursuing unlawful, misdirected quicksand wars, and allowing Congress to "write a blank check outside the normal Appropriations Committee hearing process" for demands of Iraq, Afghanistan-Pakistan and "other undeclared wars."[39]

But, was Nader's diatribe lost on the indispensable nation? "Permanent war" had the United States "working feverishly" to make "terrorism-justified powers of detention, surveillance, killing and secrecy permanent." This war would continue indefinitely, as any notion of the US government "putting an end to any of this is a pipe dream, and the belief that they even want to is fantasy." Echoing Nader, activist Glenn Greenwald declared that "only outside compulsion, from citizens, can make an end to all of this possible." Almost reinforcing such criticism, Obama reintroduced and then expanded a military advisory presence in Iraq of 170 in June 2014 to 4,087 by June of 2016. One California congresswoman suggested that "Congress is missing in action." Neither America nor its representatives called the state's hand on "these endless wars unchecked." The Afghan-Iraq/Middle East continued to be America's tar-baby. Did they help underpin MIPC's purpose?[40]

Washington Post columnist Walter Pincus in late 2014 offered that Americans had to realize that U.S. military power "won't decide the issue." Officials only begrudgingly conceded that "this is a long-term effort," (Secretary of Defense Hagel) with Army chief-of-staff Ray Odierno suggesting that "the long-term war against [the Islamic State] needs to be fought by the indigenous capability there," referring to the nations of the Middle East. That Afghans, Iraqis, and others would not, could not, or did not do so became apparent, despite abundant American aid, military support, and equipment.

Vacillation between regime overthrow or support of Assad's dictatorship in Syria, unwillingness to accept Saudi intransigence, or "declare victory and end the 'global war on terror'" once 9/11 mastermind Osama bin Laden had been killed in 2011, left cost-analysis to only a few Americans. Six years later, what author Henry Giroux facetiously termed "the national insecurity state," refused to accept any rise of "blowback," or "price for the 'War on Terror." The national security state was too entrenched.[41]

As Obama prepared to leave office in 2017, the campaigns in Iraq and Afghanistan had not fully ended, and the Guantanamo prison had not been closed. Though Bin Laden was dead, the campaign to counter the Islamic State threat alone was topping $3 billion with no end in sight for, even if uncharitable, what was being termed "Washington's Twenty-First Century Opium Wars." Supposedly, American citizens wanted no more nation-building. A seemingly unresolvable Syrian civil war also remained on the table, with more Russian involvement possibly escalating to an impasse reminiscent of the Cold War. Nobody overtly calculated costs, although the *Financial Times* on May 5, 2011 noted a figure of $2 trillion as bin-Laden's direct cost to taxpayers, "and the indirect burden may be much higher." Iraq consumed $806 billion more, Afghanistan still $43 billion additionally, with extra homeland security costs at $690 billion, perhaps much of it expensive and excessive. Still, so-called soccer-moms at home could feel safer absent any new 9/11.[42]

So, perspectives shifted once again. Observations by economist Joseph Stiglitz and statistics from academic think-tanks like Brown University's Eisenhower Study Group (which tallied monetary costs at $3.2 to $4 trillion and 225,000 mostly indigenous lives lost by the OCO operations) added to 2012 election-year trepidations, causing Washington to weigh troop levels for continuing commitments. Certainly, Gideon Rachman of the *Financial Times* put a strategic floodlight on implications when he pointed out that, while America poured money and resources into the global search for terrorists, "the truly epoch-making changes of our time were taking place in east Asia." The economic rise of China and India, paralleling "the relative decline" of the US, would "ultimately shape the next century far more than the terrorist threat." Anxiously staring at job loss, companies, and influence to China, Americans wondered whether the nation that had outspent and outlasted the Soviet Evil Empire could do the same fighting Islamic militants, while neglecting other vital interests.[43]

The Pentagon eventually scrapped counterinsurgency and nation-building for hybrid warfare, with everything shaped by a "Third Offset" strategy, announced Secretary of Defense Hagel in November 2014. Offset meant asymmetric compensation for some perceived military disadvantage. In the Eisenhower era, "First Offset" had been nuclear weapons to counterbalance Soviet conventional forces. "Second Offset" followed with Jimmy Carter, when development of precision-guided munitions offset ostensible quantitative, conventional-force inferiority. Intelligence, surveillance and reconnaissance platforms, stealth technology, and space-based military communications and navigation complemented precision-guided munitions, as shown in the First Iraq war of 1990–1991, campaigns in the Balkans, Iraq II, Afghanistan, Syria, and Global War on Terror in general. Now, "Third Offset" arrived, with persistent hybrid conflict, robotics, system autonomy, miniaturization, big data, and advanced manufacturing, to shape improvements to the U.S. military's collaboration with innovative private-sector enterprises. Naysayers might call this "fairy dust" strategy. Technological innovation not actually in-hand was nothing more than wishful thinking. However, central to all the offsets was a strong, responsive defense industry resting upon that talisman.[44]

A MORPHING MIPC AND DIB

MIPC was now a way of life, planted and nurtured with the defense industrial base nested in a distinctively American security state. Henceforth, attention riveted on the details of the comprehensive power of that state. On May 3, 2011, the Senate Armed Services Committee's Subcommittee on Emerging Threats and Capabilities held a hearing on the "Health and Status of the Defense Industrial Base and its Science and Technology-Related Elements." Testimony from DoD officials for acquisition, technology, and logistics, to private-sector icons like Augustine and Gansler highlighted what government knew or did not know about its own private arsenal system. Designated an educational event by committee chair Senator Kay R. Hagan, the hearings showed DoD understood its prime defense contractors but not their supporting sub-primes. It acknowledged the fragility of globalized supply chains. The Pentagon worried about limited competition "within a heavily consolidated" defense industrial base faced with global competition," loss of skilled domestic expertise, and manufacturing capability offshore, as well as "the negative impacts of an outdated export control regime." Still, testimony claimed that there would be no "precipitous decline like the one DoD and industry experienced" at the end of the Cold War. Market forces as "the primary mechanism by which industry responds to this change" of stable but static budgets, while improved "mapping" of the complex horizontal and vertical nature of the DIB itself, seemed encouraging. Less so were comments on reversing scientific and engineering brain drain and loss of experienced government-acquisition professionals. Pentagon czar for acquisition, technology and logistics, Frank Kendall, for one, tried to reassure congressmen that the government intended a healthy DIB for the long haul, had no intention of replacing industry's profit motive, yet wanted to ensure MIPC's reinvigoration of research and development.[45]

Two decades had now passed since the "last supper" meeting between industry and senior DoD officials. This earlier "downsizing" had led to an estimated seventy percent of companies (or parts thereof), exiting the defense business entirely. DoD supposedly had gained billions in efficiencies from that exodus but at the expense of competition. The situation demanded a new approach testified Norman Augustine with five areas needing attention: financial, human and knowledge capital, manufacturing capability, and a DIB ecosystem with its turbulent changes in schedule, requirement and people that made it "almost impossible to manage the industrial base efficiently and effectively." He and others took MIPC's existence for granted. Yet, he was not sanguine when American firms spent twice as much on litigation as research, more on healthcare for employees and retirees than production materials, paid the second-highest corporate tax rate in the world, while also facing daunting patent laws, export regulations, and immigration restrictions on retaining qualified foreign expertise. Prevailing tax laws and market structure encouraged short-term outlook and dis-incentivized long-term research investment, he observed, singling out the demise of widely-acclaimed Bell Laboratories, home to inventions of laser and transistor, and numerous Nobel Laureates. Augustine ripped an inadequate U.S. educational system, while preaching for a return to 1960s- prototypical systems to keep technical skills active. He urged investing in manufacturing *process* technology, not manufacturing *product* technology.

Augustine was joined by the indefatigable Jacques Gansler, repeating the 2008 Defense Science Board Task Force conclusion that "the Nation currently has a consolidated 20th century industry, not the required and transformed 21st century national security industrial base needed for the future." He saw a new configuration "flexible, adaptable, agile, responsive, innovative while providing "high quality goods and services at affordable prices," and "most important, in the quantities required." Government had to reform its laws, regulations, policies, and acquisition procurement practices. Gansler prescribed that "DoD has to articulate a national security industrial vision and adopt policies that match this vision and secure incentives for industry to achieve that vision." Elsewhere, Gansler observed that with the National debt piling up, the public tiring of the Iraq war, growing moves toward protectionism and a potential return to excessive regulation, "the future trends for the U.S. defense industrial base are very much uncertain."[46]

Actually, a resilient and responsive Military-Industrial-Political Complex (MIPC) arose after 9/11 on the bedrock of overseas contingencies, homeland security and, eventually, economic recession. Perhaps it no longer bore Eisenhower's original triangular stigma. Congress was more participatory through its budget and spending oversight, incorrigible special interests and constituents, internal fiefdoms and staff expertise. The National Security Enterprise "whole of government" now included, if not all cabinet departments and sundry agencies reminiscent of industrial age mobilization, then at least those of defense, state, intelligence and homeland security. Its dimensions dipped through state homeland-defense regimes, to communities with military bases and private and public defense-related businesses, first responders and law enforcement at local and state levels, as well as hyper-patriotic citizenry. The commercial media pandered to a public that conveniently forgot "those brave soldiers sacrificing so much" overseas were actually professional volunteers supported by thousands of paid contractors, not friends and neighbors conscripted from hearth and home. A corps of defense intellectual cognoscenti joined civilian society giants. The numbers of public and private scientists and engineers supposedly shrank in comparison to the attractions of working at the national security cutting-edge during the Cold War. Yet, the defense industry base displayed two parallel public/private segments—service as well as manufacturing. Congressional Research Service authors observed, "since 2000, the term defense 'industrial base' has obscured the increasing role that service contracting plays in the defense world." Gansler's congressional testimony cited fifty-seven percent of acquisition costs in FY 2009 went to non-material services, yet regulations, policies and practices still rested on buying goods.[47]

Anticipated security-sector growth after 9/11 proved good news for defense companies. For six years after 2007, while fewer vendors entered federal contracting ranks, they had to adapt to "transformational technologies," and still provide legacy hardware. Four months after "September Eleventh," Defense Deputy Undersecretary for Industrial Policy Suzanne Patrick observed that "we are veritably at the watershed between the more known, conventional forms of warfare and new ways of pursuing warfare that will undoubtedly be less platform and more network centric." It should surprise no one, she ventured, that "we will have a dwindling supplier base of the old-style platforms and systems." However, while "prudent" to maintain the maximum level of competition" for building nuclear attack submarines, it was imperative "to adequately fund the futuristic systems that will take us to this new form of warfare" without imprudent risk to current requirements. Narrowing the fighter aircraft industrial base to but one team" did not appear to take disproportionate risk. Defense supplier flexibility was vital, she maintained, citing Boeing's choice to pursue contracts for unmanned aircraft after having lost out to Lockheed Martin for the Joint Strike Fighter project. Overseas contingencies and homeland security would infuse significant funding, while a new Priority Allocation of Industrial Resources Task Force would "ensure the smooth and equitable allocation of key warfare requirements among multiple programs." Like some mobilization-era throwback, this group would monitor industrial capabilities and assign "production priority to key systems and subsystems." This time, mobilization would be done inside the Pentagon.[48]

Patrick reflected conventional wisdom at the time—"winner take all" on Joint Strike Fighter, but disallowing merger of the country's only two nuclear shipyards. The government was strongly committed "to the principles of market economics and our confidence that these market forces and companies' responsibilities to shareholders will generally result in cost-effective, innovative behavior," she beamed, adding, and the ability "to look as far into the future as practical to assess our decisions." Winner-take-all to Lockheed-Martin was one way, despite Congressional pressure to award a residual share to Boeing as a redundancy for duopoly "warm" base competition. Defense department endorsement of the Department of Justice's fear that merging Newport News Shipbuilding with General Dynamics-Electric Boat would create a monopoly for shipbuilding seemingly clashed with Northrop Grumman's acquisition of Newport News, in terms of keeping "the maximum level of competition in this sector." Lessons of the Persian Gulf, Kosovo and Afghanistan proved "much less platform centric and more UAVs or unmanned aerial vehicles," hence limiting the aircraft industrial base to one company was acceptable. Maintaining two separate ship-providers, however, was necessary to secure "a competitive base both for the potential requirement of a next generation attack submarine as well as the Trident nuclear boat replacement.

The DoD's challenge lay with shaping an industrial base that had shrunk from roughly fifty major defense suppliers in the 1980s to five "highly-consolidated, cross-Service, cross-platform prime contractors," that could help achieve six operational goals for the 21st century. Those goals reflected grand strategy—protect homeland and bases, project power, deny sanctuary, protect information networks and achieve C4ISR interoperability, and gain unhindered access to space. Defining the defense industry's new architecture became a fundamental part of DoD thinking when "consolidation spanning less than ten years fused and fundamentally changed an industry nearly a century in the making." The ten largest companies in 1985 had garnered over thirty-four percent of all prime contract awards ($75 billion in FY 2002 dollars), but twenty-eight percent of direct DoD revenues in 2003 was spread across an additional forty firms. The Cold War "ten" (McDonnell Douglas, General Dynamics, Rockwell, General Electric, Boeing, Lockheed, United Technologies, Hughes, Raytheon and Grumman) became the War on Terror "five" (Lockheed Martin, Boeing, Raytheon, General Dynamics and Northrop Grumman). DIB consolidation, begun in the 1990s, also had "proceeded in lockstep" with the fifty-one percent decline in DoD funding for research and development, and procurement, from 1985 to 1998. Altered "nameplates" included Westinghouse and Texas Instruments, while General Electric divested defense-specific business since "the defense market environment of decreasing budgets and slim profit margins did not support growth-oriented market dominance objectives to be the number one or number two player in a given market."[49]

One problem was that revolutionary innovations in military technology traditionally came from second-tier or niche organizations that went on to dominate the market, while a previous era's largest firms themselves had made infrequent monumental leaps. In 2003, DoD expected transformation to produce "new entrants to the global defense industrial base," staking the future on evolving current primes, companies already twinned with those primes (like iRobot and Foam Matrix), companies forming around defense requirements, (for instance the pharmaceutical industry by effect of chemical biological warfare and associated vaccination programs), or security (SpaceX). Outliers like entertainment companies might replicate the 1930s promise in Westinghouse for a technological breakthrough like radar; by efforts to "apply their ability in visualization to the battlefield of tomorrow." Nothing was fixed, however as the Pentagon expected "all companies within the defense industrial base, regardless of size, type, location or socio-economic category" to be nimble enough to affect policy, program evaluation and merger-acquisitions.[50]

Shrinking budgets after the Great Recession of 2008–2009 and onset of Sequestration hardly helped untangle what perhaps even DoD failed to appreciate. Bloomberg government analysts suggested that all of the top five primes "have at least one relationship with one of their cohorts." Yet, it took elaborate color-coded charts to discern how Boeing, Lockheed Martin, Northrop Grumman, General Dynamics and Raytheon were inextricably imbedded with the same sub-prime suppliers, even many that were not exclusively U.S. companies. Mergers and acquisitions might continue, given budget flux, but on a case-by-case basis. Apparently, DoD had completed thirty-three significant transaction reviews, from almost 300 defense-related mergers and acquisitions deemed relevant the year before. The largest in the history of the defense and aerospace industries included United Technologies' divestiture of four business units, including Goodrich Electrical Power Systems and Goodrich Pump & Engine Control Systems. Carpenter Technology's acquisition of Latrobe Specialty Metals was also significant. DoD's main industrial-sector interests, and concern for the health of U.S. business and industry now cut across a spectrum of providers and products including aircraft, electronics, contract services, ground vehicles, materials, munitions and missiles, shipbuilding, and aerospace. Advanced manufacturing initiatives (i.e., technology), expanded efforts to incorporate industrial-base impacts in budget deliberations, continuation of acquisition reform, and increased cooperation on industrial-base materials assessments (the same critical-materials issue demanding attention since the 1920s)—all cut across sectors.[51]

Even DoD's industrial capability assessments of the Obama years projected blandness. The DIB base had seen "erosion in multiple sectors, including missiles, electronics, ground combat vehicles, and materials," with associated decreases in design engineering and manufacturing capability. The Department "relies on an industrial base that is now far more global, commercial, and financially complex than ever before," intoned Pentagon spokesmen. The defense industry overall was "viable and competitive," with primes "carefully managing shareholder value through equity buybacks, debt reduction, reduced capital expenditures, and reductions in the labor force." Concern continued that future budget levels could partially impact companies' investments in their defense portfolios and sometimes deter new firms from working with defense. Yet, additions to shipbuilding and space sectors offset Under Secretary Kendall's gloom that the dramatic reduction in the number of prime contractors since the 1980s could "reduce competition, weaken the pool of prospective suppliers and maximize prime contractor leverage over suppliers." DoD enthusiastically embraced its "private arsenal system," preached technological superiority, acquiesced to global supply chain reality, and genuflected towards more commercial products. Firms had to remain profitable and RD & T investments were as much private as public responsibility claimed government spokesmen.[52]

Indeed, the DIB or Private Arsenal System had become fairly static. Major aircraft acquisition programs firms included Boeing and Lockheed Martin (incorporating Sikorsky), Northrop Grumman, Bell Helicopter, Airbus Helicopter, General Atomics, Beechcraft, and Eurocopter. Prime contractors for major ground-vehicle programs numbered BAE, and General Dynamics Land Systems. Also included were British Aerospace Systems, Science Applications International Corporation, NAVISTAR, and Oshkosh Defense, with the first two dominating combat markets and Oshkosh the tactical market. The shipbuilding industrial base comprised seven shipyards owned by four companies and their suppliers, segmented by ship type and included Bath Iron Works, Electric Boat, NASSCO, Newport News Shipbuilding, Ingalls, Marinette Marine and Austal, with two additional companies, Dakota Creek Industries and VT Halter Marine, building an oceanographic research ship and an oceanographic surveying ship respectively. Simplicity ostensibly governed the munitions and missiles sector, with Raytheon Missile Systems and Lockheed Martin accounting for roughly ninety percent of the department's procurement funding, while the C4-sector included General Dynamics, Raytheon, Northrop-Grumman and collaborators Thales/General Dynamics, Rockwell Collins/BAE and Harris/Viasat. Far less clear were public-private providers for electronics, materials and space sectors. As for mergers and acquisitions, while the revenue of transactions had fallen since the 2012 high (influenced by an $18.4 billion acquisition of Goodrich by United Technologies), the number of transactions themselves had remained steady. Lockheed Martin's $7.1 billion acquisition of Sikorsky, Orbital's $5 billion merger with ATK and Harris's $4.75 billion acquisition of Excelis seemed noteworthy.[53]

Meanwhile, defense critics relentlessly pleaded their case. Danielle Brian of the watchdog group Project on Government Oversight nailed the F-22 Raptor fighter, B-1 bomber, V-22 tilt-rotor aircraft, Comanche helicopter, and Crusader self-propelled artillery (a 40-ton behemoth reminiscent of World War I railroad cannon), as" five of the most wasteful and ineffective weapons systems" that could be scrapped. Senate Armed Service Committee chair Carl Levin, a Michigan Democrat, commented that long-standing management problems in areas such as financial, acquisition, information technology, and personnel had not disappeared just because" we are now fighting a war." *Christian Science Monitor* reporter Brad Knickerbocker invoked Eisenhower's undue-influence warning, citing Republican-establishment ties to the defense industry. Military writer James Fallows felt the country was back where Ike had started, "with a renewed appreciation" of the problem posed by a military-industrial complex and that "'only an alert and knowledgeable citizenry' could bring it under control." *The Wall Street Journal* and *The Economist* both wondered where all the money would go as Iain Carson opined that "since September 11th, the world's interest in defense has revived for the first time since the end of the cold war." Anne

Marie Squeo noted that before 9/11 economists before had long debated whether military spending actually boosted the economy. "They're still debating it," she observed.⁵⁴

On the other hand, maintaining at least a warm, if not hot, production base seemed irrefutable. If having somebody else pay for overseas excursions was preferable, better still having them help produce the expensive weapons sustaining America's defense industrial base. Bringing NATO members into the Joint Strike Fighter endeavor, even if gaining influence in shaping the aircraft's final requirements and capabilities based on level of financial contribution made sense. Lockheed Martin ascended to the top of the "100 Companies receiving the Largest Dollar Volume of Prime Contract Awards" from DoD at $42.7 billion. Boeing was next with $26.6 billion in FY 2002 as all prime contract awards totaled $170.8 billion, $26 billion more than in the previous fiscal year. As *Business Week* correspondent Stan Crock advanced, what stood out was that previous massive industrial mobilization planning and practice was over. High performance had replaced high output. Commercial companies devoted to technology for the most part had supplanted the government's organic industrial base. This was now "public-private partnership." Writing also for the *Washington Post* at the end of August 2003, Crock claimed that "while hardly anyone was watching, the infamous American military-industrial complex died." True, Lockheed Martin and General Dynamics would not disappear, "but the notion of an all-powerful military-industrial complex is a vestige of the Cold War." He sought "a new paradigm" to organize the defense industrial base. Industry needed overhauling; it was in a death spiral simply because, without a large standing military, there was no need for a large, commensurate supporting industry, that had been Eisenhower's concern. "Without a seismic change, the industry is headed into a death spiral," he proclaimed.⁵⁵

Crock overestimated while less passionately, his fellow commentators Pierre Chao and Loren Thompson, added their take on DIB. Chao thought in March 2005 that "the defense industry is at the crossroads of international relations, business, and technology." Its stakeholders included employees, investors, and various customers, like taxpayers, the armed services, and Congress, and a unique external environment created by the defense budget, foreign competition, and technological change. He admitted fundamental disconnects in the industry, principally tension between public goods and private ends. Taxpayers wanted the high quality but cheapest possible defense goods, while corporations sought high returns and as much of a monopoly position as was possible. Shareholders generally rewarded efficiency, but the defense industry was inherently inefficient. Economies of scale might call for fewer shipyards, "but the navy likes shipyards and the political support of twelve senators they bring." A year later Thompson added that the "arsenal of democracy" that had "made America unstoppable in World War II" flatly appeared "to be going out of business." His conclusion that "as a result, industrial decline is becoming a political issue," paralleled that of Crock.[56]

Thompson, like Norman Augustine and others saw industrial troubles stemming from "homegrown reasons" like high healthcare costs, and burdensome environmental rules plaguing carmakers, shipbuilders, and equipment manufacturers. But he also cited "Pentagon incompetence" as handicapping "the largest purchaser of U.S. manufactured goods" in aircraft, space and ships. "Most countries with aerospace industries work hard to protect them," Thompson argued, "but in America, policymakers seem determined to destroy theirs." Aside from one or two programs, for example the Space Tracking and Surveillance System, "the Pentagon has managed to foul up all of its next generation satellite programs." As for maritime industries, "when the world's biggest trading nation doesn't produce any oceangoing commercial vessels, something is definitely wrong." And the array of networks or supply chain ("an opiate of the elites"), were so complex and costly that they lacked commercial relevance. With military transformation becoming "the biggest market distortion in the infotech sector," enticing competitive companies "into dead-end projects that they can't sell abroad," he wondered how the nation and its security establishment had gotten into such a fix. To columnist Sebastian Mallaby, with the shift from manufacturing to services, the gallop of globalization, and the rise of information technology that flattens corporate hierarchies—"these forces had come together to create an American moment." A gluttonous MIPC was part of that moment.[57]

The events of 9/11, Afghanistan and Iraq provided "a showcase" for defense firms in both domestic and export markets. The slack "procurement holiday" (and consequent equipment aging) of the 1990s had seen DoD increasingly moving to privatization. Traditional manufacturing turned to the high-technology sector of semiconductors and computers for communications systems, aircraft and space technology, and biotechnology. In September 2003, Pierre Chao estimated that growth opportunities lay with systems integration, defense information technology, knowledge management, C4ISR, training/simulation, UAV/CAV and missile defense. At the same time, terrorism stoked homeland defense, intelligence gathering and analysis, electronic surveillance, as well as the security apparatus of police and first responders. When carefully separated and delineated sectors of military defense, civil defense, disaster relief, law enforcement and public safety of the Cold War era coalesced to create a heady environment of government and corporate investment and profit after 9/11, money spigots of a "New Patriotism" opened to entice private-sector firms. Homeland defense was a lucrative market, with leading contractors taking advantage of a growth-industry. "Securitization" supplanted "defense" in everyone's lexicon.[58]

Defense Primes adjusted to the global war on terrorism by using existing technologies and systems, together with new ones, for applications to border and port security, combatting the threat of shoulder-fired missiles, emergency communications, and detecting chemical, biological and nuclear terrorism. This market tapped Raytheon Systems, Boeing, Lockheed Martin, and Northrup Grumman, among others. Yet, defense technology did not automatically translate to non-defense security needs. Of immediate concern were competitiveness, DoD demands from its primes for "system-of-system" development, and production of IT, semiconductors, and biotechnology innovation, that threatened national advantage in both military and economic arenas. The Pentagon's Office of Industrial Policy urged more attention to communications and other "network-centric" technologies, than traditional weapons and platforms. Lists of top earners from 2004 showed traditional defense firms like Bechtel, Lockheed Martin and Loral Satellite suddenly overshadowed by a security-service community handling protection, reconstruction, and development, as well as communications in the overseas contingencies. Aegis, Bering Point, BKSH & Associates, Caci & Titan, Custer Battles, Halliburton, and Qualcomm now counted among the American and British companies. The Pentagon also looked abroad, softening "buy American" practices thus throwing the market into some turmoil. British Rolls Royce sought to partner with American General Electric to compete with Pratt and Whitney for engines of the planned F-35 Joint Strike Fighter, and European-based EADS hustled the state of Alabama to build a plant near Mobile, in order to muscle into the American defense market. Lockheed redesigned the presidential helicopter amidst soaring costs and profits, while Northrop and Raytheon saw military research and development spending boosting their own profits for investors.[59]

The Top 100 Defense Contractors retained "Big Five" names like Lockheed Martin, Boeing, Raytheon, Northrop Grumman, and General Dynamics (which often avoided the competitive process because of uniqueness, sole-source status for product, or in DoD's "best interest.") Only one of the top ten, Science Applications International Corporation (SAIC), secured contracts through full and open competition. Halliburton in the top twenty had unique connections with the Bush II administration. The least competitive categories lay with ships, aircraft, communications and detection, as well as guided missiles and engines. Most competitive were construction, equipment maintenance and repair, fuels, oils and lubricants, as well as medical services. Cost-Plus contracts continued to pervade thirty-three percent of the market for 737 biggest Pentagon contractors, but only eleven percent for smaller contractors. Joint ventures of multiple partners to manage specific contracts provided another example of concentration of defense contractors. Competitors Lockheed Martin and Northrop Grumman teamed as Longbow LLC for the Longbow Hellfire missile system, for example. Forty-three joint ventures worth $100 million had four earning more than $1 billion apiece, and four such ventures reverberated top names like Lockheed Martin, Northrop Grumman, General Dynamics, General Motors, United Technologies and Raytheon. Ninety-five foreign companies or government agencies testified to defense-industry globalization, with top names like DaimlerChrysler, Royal Dutch Shell and Tyco International. Darker clouds appeared by 2005/06 when costs and a stubborn budget deficit, fueled by hurricane-relief bills and rising costs of post-9/11 defense spending, prompted anxiety that record-high values of defense stocks faced retrenchment. Expensive projects risked scrutiny, so stocks retreated. Acting DoD deputy secretary Gordon England bluntly told military leaders to find $32.1 billion in budget savings over the next five years.[60]

The plain fact was that post-9/11 was a "boom time" for defense contractors. Companies producing bullets and repair equipment enjoyed profits from service-support opportunities in Iraq and Afghanistan. At the same time, the Pentagon continued spending billions on new weapons development. Jacques Gansler cited profits of 9.6 percent for the top four defense companies, in contrast to comparably large commercial firms with profits of only 6.69 to 7.3 percent. The president of the National Defense Industries Association, Larry Farrell, asked quaintly, "When combat operations end and the supplemental dollars dry up, what will the financial 'big bang' look like?" With real pressures on the nation's resources, tough choices appeared inevitable, he thought. Industry, for its part, would continue toward greater consolidation and vertical integration. Mergers, acquisitions and partnerships would accommodate the Pentagon's anticipated pattern of acquiring fewer expensive items that were underwritten by complex engineering and integration efforts. Such a pace might result in fewer domestic suppliers. Overseas firms increasingly would seek out opportunities in a marketplace becoming ever more globalized.[61]

Periodic news stories spotlighted a litany of Pentagon/DIB faux pas like spending too much money on an "unproved jet fighter" (F-35 JSF), or reliance on single suppliers, which drove up costs. A $6 to 11 billion new presidential helicopter from Lockheed added to the din. Lockheed-Martin program managers and factory foremen rallied, touting production-projections of one JSF per day from Fort Worth manufacturing facilities by 2016. A questionable Air Force plan to lease refueling aircraft from Boeing provided a *cause celebre* for the moment. Executive management was pilloried, from top levels of DoD to that of Boeing. The years-long $30 billion imbroglio illustrated a classic power struggle, even within the "Iron Triangle" of DoD, Congress, and private provider. In the context of defense procurement, Senator John McCain's invoked memories of Eisenhower's warning about the military-industrial complex as well as earlier watchdog Senator William Proxmire's 1969 enjoinder of "a revolving door," describing "the easy movement of high-ranking military officers into jobs with major defense contractors and the reverse movement of top executives in major defense contractors into high Pentagon jobs as solid evidence of the military industrial complex in operation." Few people doubted the need to replace decades-old aircraft, but cozy deals with Boeing raised eyebrows over legal/ethical questions. Rebidding battles tested professed Pentagon seriousness about transatlantic market-sharing for Northrop Grumman and European partner EADS (which initially beat out Boeing over cost and delivery schedule), and the whole mess was deferred to a new administration with eventual Northrop withdrawal by March 2010. Boeing and "its loyal crew of Washington allies" had advertised 230 U.S. suppliers positioned in forty-nine states, while Northrup announced its successful bid would support 48,000 U.S. jobs (double its previous estimate). The tanker affair smacked of "jingoism, protectionism and outright hypocrisy," cried Steven Pearlstein. Gansler asked, "why compete" when splitting the tanker buy could still save money?[62]

Industry was reportedly "unscathed" when the Iraq drawdown appeared imminent by 2008. By 2009, observers wondered, could Obama take on the mega-budgeted and mega-powered Pentagon much less the DIB, Iron Triangle, MICPC or whatever else it was now called? Cutting budgets meant more than trimming useless, costly high-tech weapons systems, decided activist Frida Berrigan, offering that weapons come second to rebuilding the nation's place in the world through international cooperation. Yet, programs from F/A-22 Raptor fighter aircraft to SSN-774 Virginia Class Submarines, DD(X) Destroyers to the infamous V-22 Osprey and C-10J transport aircraft, the ever-controversial F-35 JSF as well as Space-Based Offensive Weaponry, and questionable Future Combat System (FCS), had all been termed "investment programs," by Larry Korb and a group of business leaders targeting military spending in February 2007. Industry fortune-tellers suddenly turned skittish at prospects of boom and bust dictated by contingency costs and the election cycle. Links in the Private Arsenal system (DIB) found suppliers like Intel and IBM even raising the U.S. military as an unreliable customer. Lockheed Martin began looking to state and local governments for non-military, information-based contracts. Returning veterans from the fighting-fronts expressed concern about a marginally responsive, non-mobilized home-front. Focus should be on "current and potential problems in ordnance maintenance, critical materials, research and development, procurement policy, and foreign competition," said one. Former Defense Science Board member and Motorola executive William Howard Taft told a Washington seminar in July 2006 that DoD officials expected that "contractors will fix the problem."[63]

The Defense Science Board suddenly wondered if the defense industry had over-consolidated in the 1990s, leaving an insufficient number of players to sustain the benefits of competition a decade later. It seemed unclear if it could sustain more than a half-dozen large players anyway. Nontraditional suppliers from abroad might weaken the only companies "truly committed to the military customer," thought Loren Thompson. Moreover, using taxpayer money to build up foreign suppliers at the expense of American workers was anathema. Trade associations urged Congress to reverse cuts to vital weapons programs, yet various voices observed that the recession-directed American Recovery and Reinvestment Act of 2009 still spoke to Buy-American protectionism dating back to 1933. This might actually hurt American strength in the global economy, and the Pentagon alone could not put America back to work with a stimulus package. Reformist defense secretary Robert Gates disputed figures that 100,000 jobs would be cut in weapons programs. Life might become more difficult for some defense contractors, but Pennsylvania representative Jim Murtha's House Appropriations subcommittee responded to the demands of constituents with earmarks benefitting the Five Primes plus homeland-security providers. If industry remained unconvinced, few disputed that the Primes were the great benefactors of "permanent war."[64]

The General Accounting Office warned that lack of strong leadership for planning and executing stable weapons programs had led to a cumulative cost jump of $296 billion in DoD's major programs portfolio. But shortly after Secretary Gates unveiled his plan to rein-in spending, defense executives decided that there would not be "enough work to keep every company in business, or to satisfy the demands of shareholders who have been spoiled by a decade of double-digit growth," claimed Sandra Erwin of the National Defense Industrial Association. Talk of mergers and acquisitions came back into fashion, the workforce (halved over the previous decade), looked to drop another ten percent. Key second and third-tier suppliers became critical bottlenecks "wielding significant power over much larger prime contractors." The U.S. defense budget was expected to level off and international demand for U.S. technology would expand. So, advice for industry professionals included acquisition of knowledge and expertise in "export laws, foreign markets' regimes and protocols, partnership building and understanding of cultures." As if to prove the point, the U.S. and Saudi Arabia cemented military ties with a massive arms-deal for high-end fighter jets, helicopters, radar and missiles. Politicians and business groups scrambled to benefit home states like Massachusetts or Washington. However, a workforce dependent on cyber and mobile communication-information technology worried defense officials.[65]

The Obama administration wanted a $400 billion reduction in national security spending spread over the next twelve years. Authoritative Price Waterhouse Cooper estimates were $500 billion or 10 percent. DoD acquisition leader Kendall, proclaimed "the sky will not fall." But, by mid-2011, Pentagon officials were taken aback that their recession-proof department was anything but that. Another new Secretary of Defense, Leon E. Panetta, found himself fighting the very reductions that he had once advocated as chairman of the House Budget Committee and later, as budget director in Clinton's administration. Deputy Defense Secretary William J. Lynn III told a Royal Bank of Canada Defence and Aerospace Conference that "the challenge for us is to manage this slowdown in defense spending without disrupting the capabilities of the world's most effective fighting force." The best outcome would be for contractors to continue "to earn fair profits for superior performance, the department to get quality products for an affordable price, and the taxpayer to be able to underwrite our security at an acceptable cost." Making tough choices early, prioritizing now, balancing reductions, and avoiding precipitous cuts was Lynn's answer. Still, Price Waterhouse Cooper thought "the mood in defense might be pensive due largely uncertainty over the prospect of sequestration." Defense companies faced more pressure than ever to improve productivity, increase transparency, respond to increasingly complex government regulations and oversight, tighter schedules and generally higher expectations. In the end, Lockheed Martin still garnered 2011 sales of $46.5 billion, up almost two percent from 2010 sales of $45.7 billion. Boeing registered a seven percent revenue increase to $68.7 billion, up from $64.3 billion the year before. General Dynamics too was up slightly from $32.5 to $33.7 billion, but Raytheon posted a loss of one percent. Lockheed's clout killed a resolution of Montgomery County, Maryland council (its headquarters location), which called for the Pentagon to drastically cut military spending and end wars abroad. All Lockheed had to do was make its displeasure known through possible headquarters relocation to Virginia.[66]

Similarly, when Boeing announced plans to close its Wichita, Kansas plant in January 2012 with a loss of 2,000 jobs, Jayhawk legislators cried foul. They accused Boeing of reneging on promises to boost its presence in the state in return for their help in winning the $335 billion contract for the Air Force refueling aircraft. The Pentagon vowed to ease contractor pain from cuts to cybersecurity, and it appeared that there would be an Air Force budget battle between F-35 supporters and drone interests. Continuing purchase of the army's Abrams tank garnered strong support on Capitol Hill, with 173 House members asking Defense secretary Panetta to sustain tank production in the 2013 budget, claiming cutbacks ignored the combat-vehicle industrial base which "is a unique asset that consists of hundreds of public and private facilities across the United States." The Lima, Ohio production line of General Dynamics Land Systems (GDLS) was the focus. Just because the army wanted to finish its Abrams tank buy in 2014, and defer fleet upgrade until 2017, did not impress lawmakers. It was all about jobs, they claimed, as they angled a $255 million purchase of forty-two more tanks in the 2012 appropriations bill, and an additional thirty-three M1As System Enhancement Package (SEP) tanks, enough to keep the Lima plant open. "To believe that you can shut it down for three years and turn it back on is not a realistic statement," contended Bruce Barron, president and CEO of a metal casting and machining company. The army sought foreign buyers and pleaded that doing best for the soldiers "each and every day" posed not only a fiscal challenge but also understanding "the right technologies." One general contended, you don't want to be in the 1939 position where you say, "we've got to go out and protect the saber and the saddle industries, because our cavalry is going to need them for the future."[67]

Shrewd company executives once again began spinning off less profitable units and otherwise preparing for a "fiscal cliff." General Dynamics third-quarter profits rose slightly but overall profits declined by eight percent toward the end of 2012. Another presidential election year found corporate cash-hoarding as a hedge against further cuts in federal spending. Still, the Aerospace Industry Association contended its sector had a productive year and one of the bright spots in the 2012 economy. Overall sales were projected up by 3.3 percent from $211 to $218 billion, and employment improved by nearly 5,000 jobs, rising to 629,000 "mainly well-paid, high-skilled workers and professionals with technical and scientific proficiency." Some analysts noted how automatic U.S. spending cuts and tax rises in 2013 would translate to a four percent dip in GDP with a ten percent cut to most defense programs, $130 million falling on Northrop Grumman and a $55 million cut to Lockheed Martin. Whether or not the defense industrial base was truly hurting depended upon who was asked. Defense giants complained even when in March 2013, DoD announced contracts valued at nearly $39.4 billion that were "71 percent more than the prior month, even as automatic federal budget cuts started taking effect." Upgrades were in vogue with the aircraft carrier *Abraham Lincoln* leading the way for Huntington Ingalls' Newport News, Virginia shipyard. Management decried "any further delay in receiving the contract would have negatively impacted our workforce" of 3,800 employed on the project. Even with sequestration budget cuts, the Pentagon could expect to spend at least $300 billion on contracts before the end of the fiscal year in September as Lockheed Martin profited by at least $1.8 billion and Austal got the nod for the Navy's next four Littoral Combat ships at $682 million. London-based BAE Systems secured a five-year $781 million contract for explosives manufactured by its GOCO Holston Army Ammunition Plant in Kingsport, Tennessee. Even the intelligence community depended upon fifty-eight publicly traded private companies (from weapons producers like Lockheed Martin, Raytheon and General Dynamics, to advanced technology providers such as supercomputer-maker Cray, unmanned aircraft makers Elbit Systems Ltd., and AeroVironment), so that seventy percent of its budgets went to private firms. Millions of uniformed military, civil servants and contractors performed classified work or operated 13,300 secure facilities and over 18,000 classified computer systems. Neither White House nor Congress had an appetite for reducing that part of the National Security State.[68]

Less money but still business-as-usual making, selling, scrapping, even trading surplus equipment in the war zones (a time-honored solution to shipping it home), accompanied DoD business affairs. America's "wars" were fought with aging but reliable systems like B-52 and B-1 bombers and tomahawk cruise missiles, with "boots on the ground" increasingly special operatives, with military aid, to include training. Trade-association articles featured "vertical lift" as a shot in the arm for the stagnant military helicopter market, and a new generation of manned bomber for the aerospace industry. Still, many corporate executives appeared unready to gamble on unmanned vehicles. Survival was tied to repurchasing their own stocks and paying out dividends to shareholders, rather than investing in the research and development desired by Pentagon. The Primes pictured only fewer programs for bidding, small production runs, and procurement officials squeezing contractors' profit margins.[69]

Lockheed Martin, Boeing, Raytheon, General Dynamics and Northrop

Grumman together distributed dividends and bought back stock valued at $18.6 billion, eighty-eight percent of their cash from operating activities in 2014. They plowed back only $5.2 billion in R&D that year, not unlike the top five companies in Standard & Poor's 500 Index. While commercial firms invested because of potential profit dividends where no clear future payoff existed, defense contractors were deterred from making further investments in R&D until that model changed, said Bloomberg analysts, as "government may need to pay for R&D above and beyond what the market will bear." Still, blogger-critic Glenn Greenwald quickly pointed out in mid-November 2015, after an ISIS attack in Paris, France, that stock prices of weapons manufacturers had soared. Citing a *Fox Business* note on the causal connection, Greenwald opined, "The private-sector industrial prong of the Military and Surveillance State always wins, but especially when the media's war juices start flowing." Top Pentagon contractors weathered Sequestration remarkably well; their financial performance exceeded expectations. Perhaps not so much small and mid-size companies selling equipment to the military.[70]

AND THE NEW PLAYERS

A newer service sub-sector of MIPC also demanded consideration. OCOs had dictated using what were variously termed private military contractors, or contractors on the battlefield, even "corporate warriors." Such entities had functioned with the American military since the Revolution, but never so much as after Vietnam. The advent of the warrior-class volunteer military for service in the Persian Gulf and the Balkans, and especially following 9/11, led Congressional Research Service authors Daniel H. Elsen and Sean I. Mills to tabulate that in 2014, the Defense department "spent 45% of its contracting dollars on services, 45% on manufactured goods, and 10% on RDT&E [Research, Development, Technology, Engineering]." Ninety-two percent of contract work was domestically performed, continuing historical trends. Overseas operations in Afghanistan and Iraq caught much of the public's attention because more defense contractors were in combatant commands than military personnel. Yet, shift in the federal arena towards service-sector contractors in A-76 programs was a broader phenomenon. Lieutenant General Joseph Heiser had cited Vietnam where contracted trucking, terminal and marine purposes "provided the extra punch needed" for success as "augmentees" to regular uniformed personnel.[71]

The philosophy of smaller government became synonymous with general outsourcing by the Reagan and first Bush administrations. The idea that market not government could provide goods and services more cheaply appealed to resource-constrained bureaucrats and their superiors, while blowing past the short first Gulf War (which saw a ratio of only about one to fifty-five in contractors to troops) and on into the downsizing nineties. Coalition forces were contracted strategically through "cup-in-hand" gyrations for Gulf War I, but further privatization, outsourcing and downsizing really came during the Clinton years. The army employed the firm Military Professional Resources, Inc. or MPRI, a subsidiary of L-3 Technologies, to support education and training, for example the Reserve Officer Training Corps program. That experiment proved controversial but Secretary of Defense William Cohen was a privatization exponent, and his Pentagon reduced not merely administrative bureaucracy but also applied "peace dividend" demobilization to cutting troops, military bases and substituting contractors for some support roles. Contracted labor increasingly undertook supply and maintenance chores in the field and also acquisition, unwittingly removing government management supervision. Officials had little recourse but to turn to such support in Bosnia and Kosovo. Firms flocked to contracts, with DynCorp training indigenous police forces and security forces, Kellogg, Brown and Root (KBR) doing military base and refugee-camp construction as well as logistical support, Vinnell Corporation and Bechtel concentrating on military infrastructure, and CACI International handling intelligence gathering. This experience led to claims that contractors could be deployed more quickly than the military, remain longer than rotational military assignees, bring greater expertise for servicing complex weapons systems, and arguably were more cost-effective.

Law Professor Laura Dickinson suggests that conditions were ripe for a radically different kind of war and postwar nation-building by the time of Afghanistan and Iraq. Now available for circumventing scrutiny and accountability under international law, plus supplying necessary augmentation to combat-focused regular military professionals, contractors conveniently filled a post-conflict void. The Department of State joined DoD use of contractors. Beyond customary aspects of military support in food-service and sanitation, to functions of managing "black sites" incarceration centers and prison interrogation operations - in short, a broader range of logistics or infrastructure responsibilities- foreign and domestic contractors absorbed $16 billion in 2007 Pentagone contracts alone, with an almost-equal ratio of private to uniformed personnel in Iraq, for instance. Adding in departments of Justice and State (including USAID), and the Central Intelligence Agency, the footprint was even larger. P.W. Singer's 2003 website-listing of corporate providers numbered seventy citations. Deborah Avant's 2005 listing of operational military and security companies between 1990 and 2004 cited more than thirty specifically American companies that were spread across activities in military advice and training, operational support, logistics support, site and personnel security, crime prevention, and intelligence. Names like Blackwater, Booz Allen, CACI, DynCorp, Parsons, SAIC and Wackenhut were joined by familiar firms like Bechtel and Raytheon. A more-international 2007 listing contained names of fifty American companies, represented among those by Vinnell, SAIC, Executive Outcomes (although soon to be defunct), Erinys, and the notorious Blackwater USA. Still another study the next year featured Kellogg, Brown and Root (later renamed KBR, subsidiary of oil-services giant Halliburton), EO, Blackwater Worldwide (ultimately also renamed due to unwanted controversy), and MPRI, a subsidiary of legacy firm, Lockheed Martin.[72]

Perhaps all too visible in Afghanistan and Iraq were Blackwater Services, DynCorp, and Triple Canopy. In 2004–2006, KBR culled $16 billion in contracts, along with State-department servicer DynCorp, a distant second at $1.8 billion in federal money. Subsequent extensive examination by congressional committees, as well as agencies themselves and some scholars, regarding their uncontrollability/unaccountability made such contractors ripe for a new phase of MIPC introspection. As did Senator John McCain on the weapons side, New York Congressman Henry Waxman kept alive Senator Harry Truman's World War II legislative-style oversight for the contingency-service aspect. Although indispensable partners in American expeditionary operations, and by February 2008 tucked into the DoD's Quadrennial Defense Review as part of the "Total Force," writer Jeremy Scahill scathingly suggests that the rise of Blackwater's private army "is nothing short of the embodiment of the ominous scenario" that Eisenhower warned about, with grave implications for "the rise of misplaced power" of a military-industrial complex. Blackwater, Halliburton and Bechtel provided costly examples of private security, military and contingency contractors working battlespace.[73]

Details on these privatized-services sector "primes" points to all the wily entrepreneurship, insider dealings, crass exploitation of situations, contract arrangements and, in some cases, questionable practices of their traditional manufacturing brothers. Their record also suggests that the customer, i.e., government, got what it wanted: freeing in-uniform resources for other missions, but at a cost. The Bechtel family and its collateral managers Erik Prince and Richard Cheney (former secretary of defense and Vice President of the United States and sometime Halliburton CEO) might be seen as robber barons in this sector. Once Afghan and Iraqi operations subsided, Blackwater rebranded itself Xe, trying to leave its sullied corporate image (if not its history) behind, and DynCorp secured $20 million LOGCAP IV task-orders from the army, despite protests from the General Accounting Office about its performance. Contracting numbers decreased after FY 2009 from 767,000, "the estimated number of full-time equivalent contractors performing services" for $255 billion to 655,000 for a price of $127 billion by the end of FY 2015. With the attraction of contractors as "force multipliers," reformed management and careful oversight seemed the preferred course of action. Some observers draw ominous lessons, however. Such signs of nation-state sovereignty decay "are symptoms of a large, dangerous challenge to the aspirations for order in the world," wrote Jackson Nyamuya Maogoto in 2006.[74]

* * *

National Defense senior editor Sandra Erwin told readers in 2010 that a stormy decade lay ahead for national security. America would still be involved in Afghanistan and Iraq, neither of which would culminate in victory parades. Budget pressures would be severe, with national debt continuing to rise. A Quadrennial Defense Review of that year would set the tone for renewed cuts, although "ultimately what will be real or perceived threats to U.S. security" might be Iran, North Korea, or somewhere else. Climate change might also emerge as a national security concern, or we might "witness another financial meltdown." The only certainty was "that nobody can predict the next crisis." The final decade of the nineties had seen "sweeping, profound and often excruciating change" for the American military and its supporting industrial base. But, September 11, 2001 "will always be remembered as the day that changed everything," followed thereafter by "a landmark period of commotion in the business of defense." Budget woes in particular had shaken MIPC complacency. Still, by the Stockholm International Peace Institute's 2016 computation of the top one-hundred largest defense contractors with $374.8 billion in wealth, thirteen of the top twenty were U.S. companies. Erwin might have recast President Calvin Coolidge's famous 1925 quip that "after all, the chief business of the American people is business," was now national security.[75]

Postscript

THE NATIONAL SECURITY STATE FOR POSTERITY

If September 11, 2001, defined a generation, the world has *not* been entirely freed from terrorism two decades later. In 2018 computed one writer, "seventy-six countries are now involved in Washington's War on Terror." Another commentator suggested the U.S. had troop presence in 177 countries. Estimates vary, but the Defense Department postulated that as of mid-year 2017, "American taxpayers have spent $1.46 trillion on wars abroad since 9/11." That amounted to $250 million per day for sixteen years. Two years later, an Army War College study group contended that only Iran emerged strategically victorious from the Iraq intervention that, alone, cost the US more than $2 trillion, along with 4,500 service members dead and an additional 32,000 wounded in action. Afghanistan seemed to be on perpetual life-support and a post-Saddam Iraqi military arguably capable of surmounting any Islamic State mutation of al-Qaeda without continued American assistance. Syria tottered on its own brink as a pawn between Russia and the United States, with American military presence there in hushed tones. Elsewhere, the United States chased "terrorists" across the globe while populism, authoritarianism and nationalism thwarted globalization. Washington bureaucrats broadcast a threat paradigm that featured China, Russia, North Korea, Iran, plus Terrorism—all helping funnel more dollars to the Pentagon. By the twentieth anniversary of 9/11, research for Brown University's Watson Institute Costs of War project calculated U.S. Post 9/11 War Spending (FY 2001–FY 2022) at $8 trillion! Human cost for Afghanistan and Pakistan, Iraq, Syria, Yemen and other war zones rounded to 897,000–929,000 deaths of which 8,189 could be termed U.S. military, civilians or contractors. Calls to end "the forever wars" and assume more assertive posture against peer threats China and Russia resulted in hasty and controversial American and allied military withdrawal from Afghanistan in August 2021. The Taliban quickly resumed control amidst world angst. What would this mean for the American Leviathan and its preeminence as Super Power?[1]

STATE OF THE UNION

Just under fifty percent of voters seemingly approved the advent of a New Age in the 2016 elections. The "military-industrial-political complex" (MIPC), or "security-industrial-congressional complex" (SICC), applauded "happy days are here again," anticipating a lifting of Budget Control Act sequestration, a renewal of Department of Defense largesse, and a friendlier business climate in general. The American public was strong on defense but not military interventionism in the tradition of no more Koreas, Vietnams, or anywhere else. *Washington Post* writers suggested that 2017 opened with a Donald Trump presidency marked by turmoil, extremism abroad and at home, and worldwide refugee crises. An Age of Fear found new vigor with hordes of Latin Americans shuffling north in some diaspora to reach haven across the southern border of the United States. The Pentagon decreed this would be the era of a Renewed Great Power Competition with China and Russia. Only then could a nation be rallied, more money flowing, and the MIPC satiated. Four years later and one of the most tempestuous and disputed presidential elections in the nation's history in 2020, it appeared that domestic and international comity might not return for the country, controversial national security policies reversed and defense contractors "comfortable" with a new president and administration. Prognosticators think defense budgets will be flat without significant decline, "changes around the edges" in nuclear modernization and possibly more attention paid to biodefense and climate change. A COVID pandemic fixates a deeply divided American people. Russia and China will remain indefinitely as existential power threats.[2]

One Department of Defense intern calculated a national security state in 2016–2017 at 2.89 million Defense department, military and civilian workers absorbing $580 billion in Federal monies. The Department of Justice added 63,000 employees expending $13 billion. He also included the Central Intelligence Agency ($215 billion, 21,575 employees), Homeland Security ($60 billion, 250,000 employees), State Department ($65.9 billion, 73,000 employees), and even the Veterans Administration ($218 billion, 354,000 employees), but did not include the nuclear-defense programs of Energy, or agencies with budgets less than $1 billion, such as National Security Council, Selective Service, or Federal contractors (39,000 as of September 2011). Foreign aid added another $34 billion to the Federal level (which also included reservists of the National Guard). He then calculated total law enforcement as of FY 2008, at $73 billion and 93,000 people at state-levels, with $11 billion and 1,300,000 more at local levels. Even more enlightening was inclusion of the top eleven defense corporations that constituted the "private arsenal system" of the U.S. national-security matrix. Here were arrayed America's security elite, such as Lockheed Martin, Boeing, Raytheon, General Dynamics, Northrop Grumman, Leidos, Huntington Ingalls, L-3 Communications, United Technologies, and BAE Systems, at $308 billion in revenue with 832,000 employees. With that, the intern concluded that "the United States expends roughly $1.35 trillion (8 percent of GDP) on national security and has 5.6 million people (4 percent of workforce) engaged in such enterprise." Three years later, a DoD budget at well over $700 billion reflected the military-industrial-political complex.[3]

Trump's election as forty-fifth president of the United States in 2016 seemed to be another defining moment. Just what this moment would hold for American security remained unclear, then or subsequently. "America First," new Gilded Age-like scandals, technology and innovation promise, investigative controversy, and contradictions all stand out. Yet, the state of the nation, its institutions, its citizenry, and its politics always adjusts to defining new epochs. Americans today accept a new normalcy, defined by an evolving security state, belligerence, and sensationalist exposé. Hardly a note of dissent has been raised, observes academic Andrew Bacevich, or as filmmaker and writer Oliver Stone thought, "wars around the world rage, both Republicans and Democrats speak of muscle, power, and violence." Violence seems to define American values, whether domestically as gun rights and surveillance state, or abroad as policeman, with "the Pentagon as a global NRA [National Rifle Association]." Characteristically rowdy and robust, American politics wallow in vulgar and profane discourse, public discord and discontent, governance deadlock, self-doubt about economic decline and continuing social inequality, with domestic ghosts of slavery and foreign enemies new and old defining every shadow. Big-media stokes frenzied accounts of gunshots on domestic streets and in school corridors, and a violence-prone opioid epidemic (although supplanted by Covid flu pandemic in fear-driven America). Car-bombing terrorism and Lone-Wolf extremism complimented by organized domestic terrorism at the Nation's Capitol building in Washington raised new international paranoia about racism, nationalism, and xenophobia. If a poll by Charles Koch Institute and Center for the National Interest of 1,000 Americans showed voters' faith in diplomacy and trade, Trump eschewed the former, and embraced the latter with inflammatory rhetoric, use of sanctions and a trade war with China.[4]

Some voters in 2016 also wanted Trump to audit the Pentagon, encourage NATO members to increase burden-share for their own defense, press North Korea and Iran on nuclear matters, as well as revisit and revise the North American Free Trade Agreement. "Collective Security" that had conditioned international affairs since the 1920s evaporated in the polemic of "America First or America alone?" Trump's talismans were arrogant blunt power and acumen for personal transaction. *Financial Times* writer Philip Stephens openly declared that today's global system, designed and guaranteed by the United States, was endangered by the president's intention to make his own rules. New Pied Pipers beckoned with autocratic nationalism/ populism and anti-establishmentarianism. Was this fact, fable or merely the foible of citizens desperately trying to understand themselves while staving off national and imperial decline? Anti-globalization translated to Great Britain exiting the European Union, neo-rightist amnesia in eastern Europe, and a Russian leader mesmerized by past glories of Czarist Empire. "The year of the demagogue" proclaimed *Financial Times* editor Lionel Barber, citing a "new brand of politics that is nativist, protectionist and bathed in cultural nostalgia." Colleague Martin Wolf sensed a tectonic shift where the era of globalization under an American-led order was drawing to a close, replaced by "the fading light of liberal democracy around the world." National Defense Industrial Association president Craig R. McKinley called it "a world of disorder." Richard Haas at the Council on Foreign Relations saw a world in disarray. By 2020, acceptance of "the breakdown of the neoliberal consensus" was perceived truth.[5]

Perhaps uncertainty was more apt. Guns not butter defined "carnage America." "America, land of the free and home of the gun," was the way *Washington Post* columnist Courtland Malloy characterized the situation in 2015. Two years later, James Ragland in the *Dallas Morning News* suggested: "We boast less than 5 percent of the world's population but more than 40 percent of all civilian-owned guns," citing among them 630,000 fully automatic weapons. Malloy facetiously had asked "need a gun? Artillery, too?" and then answering, "Uncle Sam has your back!" What an awesome country we are, he preached, birthed in a blaze of black-powder, forged in civil war, and tempered by use of atomic bombs. America stands as the world's undisputed superpower with "a bullet on pretty much every global weapons chart—and proud of it," he stampeded. We are exceptional, Malloy suggested, with more than 300 million privately owned firearms that are "but a tiny inward reflection of the massive publicly owned armament we use to protect our strength abroad." "Don't mind our half-hearted 'gun control,' advocates," he thundered, Americans "are also owners of a military whose $600 billion-plus budget is larger than the military budgets of China, Russia, Saudi Arabia, France and the United Kingdom and India combined." We underwrite NATO by an additional $582 billion, three times more than the rest of the twenty-seven member countries. "When they need a gun and someone who knows how to shoot it, we are on speed dial," he added. Omit thirty-five mass shootings in as many days, but let the world beware as "such a high tolerance for spilling our own blood shows only that there is no limit to the hemorrhaging we are willing to inflict on others." And "we mourn, if ever so briefly, for innocent victims of a mass shooting, but we will not flinch when a U.S. drone unleashes Hellfire missiles on, say, a wedding party in Yemen."[6]

Malloy touched upon the sensitive ethical dilemma of using unmanned aerial vehicles in a war zone. Bacevich still pounded on the drone issue late in 2017, exclaiming "if chickens start coming home to roost, so help us, Smith & Wesson," illustrating a blurring in American minds concerning the nature of conflict. Filmmaker Jeremy Cahill said it best about Americans' view of drone strikes, that "they're just zapping people, you know, in acts of pre-crime." The rounds of domestic shootings and terror acts that came home stood out, from June 2016 mass shootings at Orlando, Florida, at Las Vegas the next year, and periodically thereafter. Between the usual blame that was passed around, among overseas terrorist groups like ISIL, domestic finger-pointing between pro and anti-gun advocates, customary anguish, and political jabbing, America seemed to accept a new reality. State surveillance in the name of fighting terrorism found a high-profile tussle between Apple and the FBI over smartphone encryption, WikiLeaks vetting of Democratic Party e-mails and, from government hacking to predictive "big data," to "the internet of things," all suggested a gray-zone technological revolution affecting battlefront and homeland alike. How might Americans react to Russian cyberattack interference in the 2016 and 2018 elections? Special Justice Department investigation mostly achieved only public shrugs.[7]

Then, just when the country had all but forgotten nuclear deterrence as a relic of the Cold War, president-elect Trump called for its strengthening, not its retirement. The price tag for a nuclear renaissance reputedly would cost billions, maybe $1.2 trillion or more spread over three decades, compared to annual Medicare expenditures of about $650 billion and about $550 billion for Medicaid, claimed the Congressional Research Service. Steven Aftergood's posting of Department of Energy data showed as of September 30, 2015, the U.S. nuclear stockpile stood at 4,571 weapons, and that only 109 nuclear weapons had been dismantled in that fiscal year. These new figures "underscored the striking gap between Mr. Obama's soaring vision of a world without nuclear arms," which he had laid out during his first months in office, wrote William J. Broad in the *New York Times* on May 27, 2016, "and the tough geopolitical and bureaucratic realities of actually getting rid of those weapons." With North Korea possessing "The Bomb" and testing intercontinental missiles, no wonder journalist Garrett Graff published *Raven Rock:*

The Story of the U.S. Government's Secret Plan to Save Itself—While the Rest of Us Die. The dialogue returned to "thinking about the unthinkable." The pro-nuclear modernization band girded to struggle the anti-nukes principally concerning upgrading critical nuclear production and process facilities like the Y-12 National Security Complex, the Los Alamos National Laboratory and the Savannah River Site.[8]

Truthfully, nobody could be sure where the state of the nation or world was going. William D. Hartung, director of the Arms and Security Project at the Center for International Policy in New York, suggested that "the Age of Trump" was built on "a bundle of contradictions," with early signs indicating the usual suspects, "the arms industry and its various supporters and hangers-on in the government," as well as Washington's "labyrinth world of think-tank policymakers and lobbyists." In short, Hartung wrote of a refreshed MIPC. Trump's eagerness to "pump vast sums into a Pentagon already spending your tax dollars at a near-record pace," replacing Obama's funding uncertainties but competing with a Mexican border wall, increases for immigration enforcement, private migrant-incarceration centers, and a trillion-dollar infrastructure program. His proposals for steep military spending increases and deep tax cuts, said Hartung, look like "Reaganomics on steroids." A Democratic Congress and citizens' movements like the nuclear freeze campaign had blunted many of Reagan's proposals decades before. Could something similar stop Trump's "own exercise in fantasy budgeting?"[9]

GRAND STRATEGY, BUDGET-BUSTING, AND A CROSSROADS

Trump's "Grand Strategy" in late 2017 had America addressing Principled Realism, a return to nationalism (for others too, not just the U.S.), America First, populist pushback against globalization, homogeneity and enforced socio-economic leveling, and the thought that liberal internationalism had reached the point of diminishing return. Later, "authoritarian capitalism" joined the rubric of possible trends by the end of Trump's four-year presidency. Themes like Bringing Back Jobs and Growth, Making the Military Strong Again, Rebuilding America's Infrastructure, Repealing and Replacing Obamacare, Standing Up for the Law Enforcement Community, and Trade Deals That Work for All Americans—all resonated with certain elements of the populace. According to the 2019 Chicago Council on Global Affairs survey, significant numbers of Americans were not ready to abandon traditional allies or rule of law, were against corruption, would rally to safeguard cyberspace and elections, and put authoritarian world leaders on the defensive. The media only reflected citizens from all walks of life and all levels of society remaining deeply divided by Trump's rhetoric even as rollout of a formal National Security Strategy just before Christmas 2017 marked a document that was "hard-nosed" and "realistic," yet also less ambitious, idealistic and "soft," than Obama's counterparts.[10]

The new mantra captivating foreign policy Washington became "An Era of Renewed Great Power Competition." Underscoring China and Russia, in particular, National Security Advisor at the time, Lieutenant General H. R. McMaster couched it more benignly in terms of protecting the American homeland and people, advancing American prosperity through growth, trade, and expanding the American industrial base, plus "preserving peace through strength." Nothing particularly new here, reclaiming "our strategic confidence" (as commentators called it), as well as "echoes of Reagan" and "less a coherent policy framework than a strained justification of some of [Trump's] prejudices and an attempt to wish away others." Appearance of a complimentary National Defense Strategy in late January 2018 promised "sharpening the American Military's Competitive Edge" while other strategy pronouncements cascaded down for cyber, homeland defense, even economic security. Nonetheless, funding held the key; subject to raising caps of the Budget Control Act of 2011.[11]

Hardly a strategy at all, concluded Andrew Bacevich about the proclamations. Unimaginative and distinctly uncreative, "only weapons manufacturers, defense contractors, lobbyists, and other fat cat beneficiaries of the military-industrial complex" would celebrate its implementation. Responsive to industry, lobbyist and trade association lament ever since enactment of BCA, fiscal gridlock on Capitol Hill seemingly relaxed enough by 2017 to promise a 350–355-ship "Trump navy" (up from the 279-ship Sequestration fleet), addition of five Air Force fighter squadrons, and larger ground forces (increasing a 540,000-person army and Marine Corps by four battalions), at an additional cost of $683 billion spread over the next ten years. Pundit J. P. Sottile blasted the U.S. military as the "biggest 'Big Government' entitlement program on the planet." Tennessee congressman John Duncan proclaimed "there is nothing patriotic or conservative about our bloated defense budget." Yet, few people blanched when the Congressional Budget Office pronounced weapons costs "have been, on average, 20 percent to 30 percent higher than DoD's initial estimates." Reversing Obama-era stagnation equated with what was always the MIPC's true nature—profits for the Primes (plus a few other preferred suppliers) and jobs to placate labor(and politicians). Trump's proposed $1.15 trillion government discretionary budget found the military portion at fifty-four percent of the pie-chart, and "international affairs" at another four percent. Of proposed total spending, shifting $54 billion from domestic and international aid to the Pentagon (a ten percent increase), boosting Homeland Security by seven percent and nuclear weapons funding by eleven percent, reflected Trump-era thinking, even a compromise defense bill that was $80 billion over the budget caps, and billions more than Trump requested. Congressman Duncan wondered if "there are any fiscal conservatives at the Pentagon."[12]

Defense department insiders dismissed this "timeless problem" as "requirements always exceed budgets." There was much truth in National Defense editor Sandra I. Erwin's blunt observation, "that after 15 years of war and numerous studies on the subject, we still don't know how much national defense really costs." Indeed, something was askew in the way calculations were done, implied Defense Program Senior-Fellow analyst Steven M. Kosiak, of the Center for a New American Security, speaking to a House of Representatives budget committee hearing on February 7, 2019. A question of "defense" versus "security," eighty-four percent of total discretionary spending was going to everything from international affairs, veterans affairs, homeland security, justice, centers for disease control and prevention, food safety, even non-defense portions of energy, aeronautics and space, National Institutes of Health, transportation, corps of engineers, and education programs in government. He could even see expanding the list to Department of Labor training programs, Department of Treasury funding relating to tax collection within the Office of Terrorism and Financial Intelligence, and the Commerce Department's National Oceanic and Atmospheric Administration (providing critical climate-change data). Conversely, Kosiak observed, "generating a substantially smaller list, or a substantially smaller funding total, would require a different, and significantly narrower, set of assumptions concerning the kinds of investments that contribute to our country's physical and human capital, and economic strength," i.e., security.[13]

Funding manipulation had become a political art, with Capitol Hill and White House subversion of normal spending limits, and procedural differentiations between "emergency" and "base" line-budgeting evading citizens, blissfully unaware "that defense costs are far bigger than most people realize," thought analyst Todd Harrison. As finally passed, and signed by Trump, the budget-cap busting, $1.3 trillion omnibus bill promised to jump Pentagon spending to almost $700 billion. Euphoria erupted in the National Defense Industrial Association which sensed a bonanza for defense big business contractors. Other Security windfalls included $58.8 billion for contingency funding, $20.5 billion for nuclear weapons and naval reactors run by the Department of Energy, $8 billion for FBI forensics supplied to DoD, and homeland security adding another $52.25 billion. As conventional wisdom echoed Republican representative Kay Granger of Texas that "our military is trying to recover from sixteen years of war," a lion's share would go to Lockheed Martin which received $3 billion for more F-35s and $1 billion for missile defense systems, $740 million to Boeing for F-18 Super Hornets, $676 million for additional V-22 helicopters, and $510 million for three additional KC-46 tanker aircraft, plus another $3.4 billion to naval construction. Watchdog Steven Ellis of Common Sense scolded, "more is not a strategy," for there was no underlying theme or rationale except "they had money to spend." Defense giants like General Dynamics prepared to grow even larger, looking to acquire CSRA, a government information-technology services conglomerate.[14]

The fact was that FY 2017 Federal spending showered four times as much money on mandatory/entitlements as defense and international programs. No wonder one analyst opined that the best way to more effectively provide for the national defense might not be a new weapons system or military unit, "but rather support of comprehensive, long-term entitlement and budget reform." Nonetheless, a large defense budget needed critical restructuring "to provide clear direction and a path forward" for future national security. Yet, a proposed 2020 budget provided $738 billion that both overfunded the F-35 gambit and recapitalized the F-15 fleet, while also advancing procurement funds (against army wishes), for the newest variant of a cargo helicopter—thus asserting congressional power of the purse while undercutting Trump's desire for the homeland security southern border wall by $5 billion. Whimpers about hawkish hypocrisy on military deficit-spending, and the most progressive defense bill in history, gave way to excitement on Capitol Hill for separate enactment of a new Space armed service standing alongside army, navy, air force and Maine Corps. Absent new wars (despite periodic Trump posturing against Iran), America spent far more on defense than the next fifteen countries in the world, and more than double that of China and Russia. *Rolling Stone* oppositionist Matt Taibbi implied, MIPC was clearly back in the driver's seat.[15]

MIPC'S NEW NORMAL

Although statistics are constantly amassed, reinterpreted, manipulated, even abused, analysts Jomana Amara and Raymond Franck laid estimated global defense expenditures at $1.7 trillion in 2017 and US. Defense expenditures at around $610 billion, accounting for "approximately 36 percent of total global defense expenditures for that year. The Center for Strategic and International Studies computed that from 2013 to 2017, the Five Big Primes increased their share of defense-contract dollars from twenty-eight to thirty percent. The Pentagon's 2016 military sales to foreign partners of $33.6 billion, down from $47 billion the previous fiscal year, or the $58 billion the Pentagon had sunk into canceled major-weapons development projects for the past twenty years, raised few qualms. The highly respected Stockholm International Peace Research Institute calculated a forty-four percent increase in arms sales from 2002 to 2017, with the United States as the world's biggest arms exporter at thirty-four percent of market share, or a fifty-eight percent lead over competitors. During Trump's first year in office, U.S. arms sales as a conscious and conspicuous policy choice, increased by thirty-three percent, reflecting relaxed legal restraints. Candidate Trump had railed about the revolving door of military and civilian public servants engaged in such activities, and then promptly populated his cabinet with individuals straight from the MIPC. An updated Conventional Arms Transfer policy reflected arms-industry influence on government, and CATO Institute analysts A. Trevor Thrall and Caroline Dorminey underscored the risks of arms sales in U.S. foreign policy. Still, increasing the arms trade reenergized a traditional defense industrial base at home. Trump would not interfere as it ensured domestic jobs and industries plus votes.[16]

Hardliner John Bolton replaced McMaster as National Security advisor in April 2018, and people worried that this would unleash the dogs of war against North Korea, Iran, or whoever got caught in the administration's crosshairs. Trump stridency about higher tariffs for strategic materials like steel and aluminum against all but the obsequious few, while a 2017 DoD estimate that Congress had appropriated $1.6 trillion for "war-related operational costs of the DoD since the terror attacks of September 11, 2001," seemed to faze no one. Adding to that, State Department and U.S. Agency for International Development had garnered an additional $123.2 billion, bringing the grand total to an estimated $1.7 trillion "for activities and operations in support of U.S. response to the 9/11 attacks." Only World War II cost more. Ever contentious, the ten most-expensive weapons, amalgamated nearly $1 trillion, and in-part, unending in spiraling costs. Such cost controversy traditionally signified budget wrangling, as with the price tags of earlier era frigates and battleships, now completely dwarfed by the navy's Ford-class aircraft carriers coming in at $11 to $12 billion apiece. The War on Terror has cost $250 million per day for sixteen years admitted the Pentagon. But, by 2018, the administration looked to Great Power competition for a Reaganesque revitalization, not to post-9/11 sugarplums for anti-terrorism.[17]

Cost, controversy and contradiction accompanied the Trump administration. The price for the Air Force One replacement-aircraft program originally drew Trump's ire as "ridiculous." By spring of 2018 Lockheed's president claimed costs had come down 2.4 percent, or about $13 million, to $5.06 billion and appeared to be on-schedule. But the Government Accounting Office disputed the claim. Trump had promised close scrutiny of cost and waste across government and bluntly termed the F-35 project "out of control." Even before entering the oval office, "the tweeter president" would take on giants Lockheed and Boeing, with contradictory signals that he would be a firm supporter of larger defense. Within the first week of his inauguration, Trump boasted of forcing defense giant Lockheed to squeeze $600 million out of the next batch of ninety F-35's (a per-unit drop from $100 to $85 million each). Skeptics immediately claimed that it was difficult "to parse the president's influence with reductions already planned." Lexington Institute's Loren Thompson (Lexington had consulting arrangements with Lockheed Martin), thought Trump was merely "saying they better stay on that path if they want this program to be successful." The new president's proclamation, "if we don't get the prices down, we're not going to order them," sounded hollow, but resonated well with opponents of massive military spending. Still, astute researchers as far away as the Australian Strategic Policy Institute thought Trump was "taking retrospective credit for program improvements made over five years ago."[18]

On the other hand, disagreement between Trump and conservative Republican allies over budget-busting tax and spending plans were only part of his new approach. By February 2018, Trump talked of some massive and costly military parade to inspire national unity. But replicating France's Bastille Day and the old Soviet Union's May Day extravaganzas of brawn and hardware seemed problematic. America snickered. Later in the year and into the next, it was all about billions for an anti-immigrant southern border wall. Pentagon disclosure of $125 billion in administrative waste hidden from public view vied with pronouncements from congressional watchdog-monitor, Senate Armed Services Committee chair John McCain outlining $123 billion in wasted defense spending. The Navy's Littoral Combat Ship headed the list that also included inappropriate travel-expense reimbursements, unused and inoperable Missile Defense Agency targets, Navy experiments with alternative fuel sources for its "Great Green Fleet," expense claims for travel entertainment, and research on mating habits of African rats. At the same time, Democratic senators from Virginia Mark R. Warner and Tim Kane, urged Republican leaders to approve $500 million in new spending to keep parts-fabrication alive for the carrier *Enterprise* at their home state's

Newport News Shipbuilding. Kane thought Trump put "shipbuilders in limbo" by asking Congress to delay action until after he took office.[19]

Watching MIPC requires a sharp eye for breaking down big numbers, like the contracts for two aircraft carriers from Huntington Ingalls's Newport News division. Aside from the $15.2 billion contract, the navy claims taxpayers will save $4 billion on four such projected capital ships, the real importance lies with understanding the true meaning of today's MIPC. The certainty of a two-carrier purchase, observes local-area newsman Hugh Lessig, is that it will enable the shipyard "to avoid the temporary business downturns that have led to layoffs." It will help "the hundreds of small businesses that supply products and services" to the shipyard, for both carriers and submarines. Or, as a Congressional Research Service report noted in November 2018, the two-ship purchase "would provide economic stability to approximately 130,000 workers across 46 states within the industrial base." By 2019, the issue boiled down simply to domestic employment, local economy, and political influence, as it had for nearly two centuries. To MIT history professor emeritus John W. Dower, Americans accept "a rich and spectacularly weaponized nation of high-rhetoric, enormous might, overweening hubris, profound paranoia, and deep failings and pathologies." One such pathology, according to Michigan State University professor Mark Skidmore was the Pentagon's appalling accounting that allowed $21 trillion to disappear without a trace over a seventeen-year period. Or as sometime Defense "secretary at war" Robert Gates has held, DoD's history of acquisition and development of new programs was "rich in over-cost, overdue, and flawed programs.[20]

TECHNOLOGY, INNOVATION, AND THE DEFENSE INDUSTRIAL BASE

Analysts Amara and Franck charted the cycle of DoD procurement outlays—up with the Reagan buildup, down with a "procurement holiday" of the 1990s, up again with post 9/11 overseas contingency operations and then down again after the budget control act strictures. They suggested the great corporate mergers and acquisitions of defense giants did not diversify portfolios between military and civilian market products. With the U.S. government as "a sovereign monopsonist" passing risk to industry, "only large, diversified and solvent defense companies can afford to be primes for major acquisition programs," claim Amana and Franck. Notwithstanding the intriguing domestic and international operating environment, their 2019 analysis of the United States and its defense industries featured the delicacy of foreign arms trafficking in an environment of bureaucratic impediments or export control while the Pentagon toyed with a "Third Offset Strategy" emphasizing asymmetric advantages of disruptive technologies and operational innovations like hypersonic systems, quantum computing, human machine collaboration and combat teaming, network enabled cyber systems, big data, and biological sensors, growing custom organisms and bio-inspired engineering. These would require a different kind of "industrial" base, more toward Silicon Valley. For a time, denizens there vacillated over supporting the military establishment at all.[21]

Following presidential signing of a 2018 national security-laden budget, talk turned to even having the military build Trump's Mexican border wall since it now had so much money. The Pentagon's Inspector General's Office had other priorities, above all cyber management. Iranian-backed "sleeper cell" militants hibernating in the United States caused sleepless nights for the Pentagon. Protecting key defense infrastructure, developing full-spectrum, total-force capabilities, building and sustaining readiness, and meeting a liturgical "main global strategic challenges," drove the defense acquisition process. Robots would revolutionize military operations, said National Defense Industrial Association president McKinley observing that this migration toward greater automation "is inevitable and expansive." Officials talked about using the latest tools of artificial intelligence (AI) and machine learning to create robot weapons or "human-machine teams" and enhanced super-powered soldiery. "Our adversaries, quite frankly, are pursuing enhanced human operations," and "it scares the crap out of us, really," exclaimed Deputy Undersecretary of Defense Robert Work. Innovation became the new Pentagon watchword (frankly, it had never been absent over the decades). Still, missile defense-technology contracts with Boeing ($6.5 billion for "accelerated delivery of a new missile field with 20 additional silos" in Alaska), Raytheon-built Standard Missile-3 (an unproven "new capability" that had slipped a two-year delivery date), Lockheed Martin (for 200 additional missiles), and even a small cybersecurity contract with Decisive Analytics ($59 million), to ensure ballistic-missile defense systems information components including proper cybersecurity controls sounded good.[22]

Certainly not everything in Trump Security World exclusively involved high-tech military superiority. The companies finally selected to build the 2,000-mile Mexican border-wall prototypes were ordinary construction firms like Caddell of Montgomery, Alabama, Fisher Sand and Gravel/DBA Fisher Industries of Tempe, Arizona, Texas Sterling of Houston, and W. G. Yates and Sons from Philadelphia, Mississippi. Still, the Pentagon worried about its DIB, not helped by the National Defense Industrial Association starting an annual assessment of its own called "Vital Signs" and awarding the DIB a flat "C" rating mainly because of poor industrial security and production inputs to include skilled labor, intermediate goods and services and raw materials used to manufacture or develop end products and services for the Pentagon. Think-tanks and an interagency task force pushed forward ideas about updating legacy manufacturing. The Center for a New American Security's 2014 project called "Future Foundry: Forging New Industries for Defense" sounded old-fashioned—a combination of government-produced, government-contracted and commercially acquired products with the usual talk about constrained competition with organic government arsenals, shipyards and federally funded research and development centers, low production quantities, high barriers to market entry, significant capital intensity requirements, and adapting private technology to military use (offering). Analysts continued the complaint that DoD insufficiently uses "purely commercial capabilities." It was a start and fit with the relatively new concept of "the National Technology and Industrial Base" (NTIB)—a post-Cold War combination of people and organization engaged in security and dual-use R&D, production, maintenance etc. within the U.S., Canada, Britain and Australia, designed for sharing among allies while countering potential adversaries.[23]

Critics scoffed since over decades, technology had provided the glue for more than just the military dimension of national security. Architect of post-Cold War defense industry consolidation, former defense secretary William J. Perry, and subsequent undersecretary for acquisition, technology and Logistics (AT&L) Frank Kendall both fretted that the so-called "last supper" of the nineties had not produced "a leaner industry rather than one simply consolidated into a few large firms." Earlier, when United Technologies had wanted to sell its Sikorsky Helicopter unit to Lockheed Martin, Kendall had offered, "with size comes power and the department's experience with large defense contractors is that they are not hesitant to use this power for corporate advantage." Kendall had professed neutrality on that deal as long as it did not affect prices too much. But Big Enterprise projecting Big Power in corporate America threatened Pentagon control. Mergers—especially at tiers lower than the Primes—gathered momentum especially with budget caps abrogated and the Trumpian climate right for corporation money-making from defense.[24]

Of the "Top Twenty" (out of the top 100) defense contractors in the world as of 2016, thirteen were American. Familiar corporate-welfare names included Lockheed Martin, Boeing, Raytheon, Northrop Grumman, General Dynamics, L-3 Communications, United Technologies, Huntington Ingalls

Industries, Bechtel, Textron, Leidos, Harris, and Booz Allen Hamilton. Two years later Boeing's revenue as a company broke the $100 billion mark, although not because of defense work, but rather commercial sales. Nonetheless, defense reflected annual revenue increase by twelve percent, or about $23 billion, over 2017, that included a series of unexpected wins against Lockheed, offsetting among other things, the Air Force tanker controversy. The government's own "intrusive reporting and auditing requirements" posed the greatest barrier to new firms entering the U.S. defense market, claimed trade association spokesmen. Moreover, roughly 17,000 companies comprising twenty percent of first-tier prime vendors supplying the military ostensibly had left the defense market, noted another expert. To industry lobbyists like the NDIA, it was better to focus on attracting new firms to the defense market by aggressively eliminating barriers to entry, claiming that it is in the nation's best interest "to have a competitive and technologically vibrant defense industry that is geographically dispersed and diverse." That the U.S. defense industrial base is a "major strategic asset and key competitive advantage that extends U.S. influence and enhances the nation's capabilities" was familiar. "Industry, Government: Enduring Partners" *is* gospel, said NDIA president Hawk Carlisle, while corporate executives complained that stopgap funding only from Capitol Hill hurt the economy. The MIPC had reached a kind of stable maturity.[25]

The Enterprise could be confusing at times. For Raytheon's Patriot missile system or the F-35 Joint Strike Fighter, the path pointed to attracting new customers. In fact, U.S. defense companies eyed "partnerships" with India and revamping and streamlining International Traffic in Arms Regulations, along with the Export Administration Regulations from the Department of Commerce which control weapon sales and sharing of technical data overseas. Owen B. McCormack's characterization of Obama's "lesser-known legacy" as "arms dealer in chief" would attach to his successor. Yet, the defense industry remained jittery, and munitions-making capacity shaky thanks to surplus material in storage, obsolete and expensive manufacturing equipment, and aging workers. Private military service contractors remained players although strictly speaking, the road from 1976 privatization legislation and securing government contracts via influential middle-man companies like Deltek, reached a peak perhaps in Iraq. Over time, the Army declared that its heavy reliance on civilian contractors was "eroding the skills and cohesion of units deployed to the country." Some of the most egregious actions by firms like KBR, Halliburton, Blackwater (and its successor Xe), ARINC, Carlyle Group, URS, Electronic Data Systems, Harris, and others, surfaced under congressional and government accounting investigations. Yet, the damage had been done, helping suck money from the cumulative national security tab of $4.4 trillion since 2003. Ten years later Blackwater founder and symbol Erik Prince embarked on new international work, having been ostracized from U.S. government markets. By 2018, his latest venture Frontier Services Inc. made news with security-training arrangements for the Chinese government. Prince even approached Trump about hiring his personnel to replace America's regular military services. To Sean McFate, author of *The Modern Mercenary*, Prince "is the hood ornament of the new era of the military-industrial complex and a set of mercenaries who work for countries, oligarchs and random billionaires." Perhaps, Prince should have been hired to sort out the 2021 Afghanistan mess.[26]

Meanwhile, Trump's initial kerfuffle with Lockheed-Martin over F-35 costs as symptomatic of "war on the defense industry," settled into a more normal MIPC relationship. Concern for the DIB was simply a "message to the industry of potentially more risk-sharing on costs," a potentially new paradigm for the industry. So, when Boeing transferred its defense-division leaders to Washington headquarters in Arlington, Virginia, leaving 14,000 workers still in St. Louis, it was "all driven by being closer to the customer," declared company spokesman Todd Bleecher. Boeing joined Lockheed Martin, General Dynamics, and Northrop Grumman in nestling close to the Pentagon and NASA, and especially Capitol Hill. DoD awarded a tenth production-lot of ninety F-35 aircraft to Lockheed Martin, sans engines separately awarded earlier in the year, with possible lower costs between lots indicating a response even before Trump's initial concern. But, when Lockheed Martin and Boeing also moved to manufacture legacy fighter-jets in India, this scheme threatened to lose Texas jobs and Trump's focus on domestic employment preservation.[27]

One *Boston Globe* reporter proffered, President Dwight D. Eisenhower "might be stunned at how completely his prophetic [military-industrial complex] warning has been ignored." By 2016, analysts of the Congressional Research Service confirmed broad agreement on two points. First, the defense industrial base did not operate in a free market but rather the U.S. government is a monopsonist (sole buyer) in a defense market with an oligopoly (limited number) of key suppliers. Second, "it is not an autocratic 'military-industrial complex,' since the decision-making process for industrial procurement is decentralized between Congress, the Secretary of Defense and U.S. military departments." Thus, "a distinctive market structure and decision-making process impacts industry" more than combat operations formed a basic background for discussing the defense industrial base. Obama's last defense secretary Ashton Carter professed that the defense industrial base had to be treated as a key part of the force structure, along with the armed services themselves and the Pentagon. It had already become a normal part of Wall Street. Resourcing decisions affected dimensions of equal gravity in military policy, strategy development, budget formulation, and industrial readiness and capacity, thought NDIA president McKinley. Two years in, the Trump administration comfortably did MIPC bidding, surveying America's whole of industry under the guise of innovation, pushing strategic conventional-arms transfers (the arms trade), hawking a healthy collaborative Joint Strike Fighter Program across the globe, and ensuring "a dynamic defense industrial base" employed more than 1.7 million contented people.[28]

On July 12, 2017, Trump's Executive Order 13806 seeking clarity on America's manufacturing sector came like manna from heaven for industry and business. This order, titled *Assessing and Strengthening the Manufacturing and Defense Industrial Base and Supply Chain Resilience of the United States*, conformed to MIPC desires. Fifteen months later, the final interagency report captured all that defense industrial base analysts had been grousing about for at least a decade. It reflected the ever-present perplexing budget cycle of feast and famine, as well as the periodic post-conflict downsizing and pre-conflict upsizing. It provided a think-piece for the MIPC elite, mobilization sequence, defense acquisition and whole-of-government coordination and response. Perhaps, it captured the private-sector prism. Numbered among its concerns were visibility, a platform to counter the cyclical nature of defense spending, especially the impact of BCA 2011, as well as the decline of overall manufacturing capability, capacity and employment. Yet, the report also represented something else. Like similar studies through the years, it was a first-step return toward preparedness, rearmament, and rejuvenation of the all-important resourcing dimension of national security. It enabled DoD to confront DIB issues.[29]

Report authors identified impacts and risks primarily affecting sub-tier rather than prime contractors. They uncovered a "surprising level of foreign dependence on competitor nations," and underscored the domestic decline of STEM and manufacturing trade-skills. The authors cited key capabilities moving offshore to capture foreign-market share and advantages in cost-saving opportunities. All this derived from cases not merely in traditional defense sectors but also "cross-cutting" sectors like electronics and cybersecurity. The study decided that the Pentagon has enough tools to mitigate some of the identifiable risks, it could correct current business and procurement policies and practices straining the industrial base, and reduce incentives to meet national security demands. Contractors, not just government, needed to pay more attention to the cyber-threat, as well as Chinese products and components in the defense supply chain. The role of allies loomed in the final report, despite self-sufficiency prescriptions and overall nationalist primacy associated with the Trump administration. The study mostly enabled government to look at weaknesses in its private resourcing auxiliary although to any member of the general public, the effort must have seemed an affair best addressed within what was increasingly called the Iron Triangle (a euphemism for MIPC).[30]

Meanwhile, the very nature of the multi-national Joint Strike Fighter Program seemed to conflict with Trump's prescription for "America First" and protective favoritism for domestic industry. Yet, it was all quite clear. The program belongs to Lockheed Martin which builds the aircraft's forward-section in Fort Worth, Texas, Northrop Grumman constructs the midsection in Palmdale, California. and BAE Systems fabricates the tail in Great Britain. Final assembly of components takes place in Fort Worth, but final assembly and checkout facilities have also been set up in Cameri, Italy and Nagoya, Japan. The F-35 engine comes from Pratt & Whitney in East Hartford and Middletown, Connecticut, but British Rolls-Royce builds its F-35B lift-system in Indianapolis, Indiana. Here is the incarnate global supply chain interlock reflected in the Trump-commissioned industry study. The Pentagon seeks efficient adjustments to the defense industrial base (as part of MIPC), yet internationally mobilizes against peer competitors via centralization and attitude, planning, and process. Competition ostensibly would drive productivity and value. At least two firms must be retained in every critical sector continue as dogma, although not all need be domestically headquartered. Belated Pentagon interest below the primes to "lower tier" contractors should concern primes themselves. The Pentagon might devote more attention to the "services" sector, encourage new entrants to the DIB and an open market to all outsiders, while striking an appropriate balance with "America First," said government spokesmen. But, America First still represented America Supreme.[31]

Then, the National Defense Industrial Association working with "a decision science company" Govini, commissioned successive "Vital Signs" studies in 2020 and 2021 on the declining health and readiness of the Defense Industrial Base. It received only a "C" report card. In an effort to annually monitor (but mainly to bring the government's 13806 report findings to public attention, Vital Signs studies hammered key issues like inability to attract workers in key fields like science, technology, engineering and mathematics essential to meeting challenges of "a volatile and uncertain future" and impact of a raging health pandemic on the DIG. Industry generally wanted clear guiding government strategic policy and stable financing for sustaining the defense base (and had been saying so for years). It also desired continuous assessment of the industrial base from a more strategic perspective. It sought improvement in a cholesterol-plagued government acquisition and planning, programming, budgeting, and execution system, reinvigorated Congressional review of DIB issues, and ensuring that both public and private sectors focused research and development on competitive design and development, as well as efficient production. Some commentators (even before "Vital Signs"), like Erich Fischer, an aerospace and defense analyst at Deloitte Consulting, pictured the major defense companies as still risk-averse after a quarter-century of strategies and business models "that more or less 'stayed the course,'" despite significant changes in the environment and market needs. He cited democratization and globalization of technology, massive private investments spurring innovation, and companies introducing commercially derived platforms at lower cost, as factors opening doors for "more nimble competitors and new entrants" to defense markets. Meanwhile, the DIB locked on shareholder desires based on business models and methods wedded to long-term, expensive, largely outdated programs.[32]

In short, national preparedness, military readiness and sustainment have always demanded some type of defense industrial base, just not necessarily one of today's size, influence and cost. The history of MIPC and America's progression to a security state never has been a straight line. Rather it has been a series of rises and dips, even circles, conditioned by periodic mobilizations, wars and demobilizations, and vested interests. America has been permanently mobilized since the 1940s and in a state of perpetual conflict since 9/11, if not 1945. Then, suddenly in 2019 and 2020 it encountered an unexpected test not adequately met either by government, private industry or the general public. This, of course, was the Great Worldwide Pandemic of Covid-19 virus. Woefully managed at all levels of government, even an updated Defense Production Act of 1950 as emergency response to bolster supply and distribution of vaccines seemed inadequately invoked in timely or effective fashion. The MIPC or DIB like America generally suffered when health was neglected as a national security priority.[33]

Meanwhile, MIPC's organic arsenal and depot, naval shipyard and logistics base vied with the private arsenal system. Today, the state expects both its generic and its private components to function as a "modern, cost effective and highly responsive Enterprise that provides the resources, skills, and maintenance and manufacturing competencies necessary to sustain the lifecycle readiness of warfighting systems ... worldwide in a reliable and efficient manner while also maintaining the capability to surge as required to meet the demands of future contingency operations." DoD's private partners continue to focus more on bottom-line shareholder returns and reducing the number of competitors for the large Defense pie. Pentagon insiders will complain that congressional spending has become "so unpredictable" that the defense industrial base is shrinking and "the weapons systems of tomorrow are not being developed today." Research and development will fluctuate as national security is threatened, and politicians and analysts harp on costs. The same refrains have echoed down the ages. So too have strains of reevaluation and reform, or at least how the defense industry needs to do business or even if the Air Force, for instance, might need a new defense industry base model of its own.[34]

On April 13, 2017, U.S. forces dropped the largest, most lethal non-nuclear weapon in history when a modified C-130 Hercules cargo aircraft delivered a GBU-43/B "massive ordnance air blast" (MOAB) munition against ISIL warriors in Afghanistan. What irony; a propeller-driven aircraft and a conventional munition reflecting both the old and the new of warfare. Two years later a newer "new" came, with a U.S. cyberattack on ISIS heralded as the first large-scale effort that "is likely a template for similar efforts against Russia, China and others." In March 2019, the Pentagon's Office of Economic Adjustment released FY 2017 data breaking down the impacts of defense spending by state to the county level. The Pentagon spent $407 billion on contracts and payroll in all fifty states plus Washington, D.C., or $1,466 per U.S. resident. This accounted for 2.3 percent of the gross domestic product. Still, in three years, the Trump presidency had increased defense spending 19 percent from $619.5 billion to $740 billion and the Border Security industry could be worth that much by 2023 insisted *Congressional Quarterly* analyst Michelle Chen. The Trump administration pointed to $709 billion for defense alone in its final FY 2021 budget despite Progressive Democrats demanding a 20 per cent reduction in defense in the 2020 election year. The Congressional Budget Office decided that with the deficit remaining large over the next decade and growing substantially after that and the end of the BCA not necessarily reducing pressure on defense spending, defense budgets would remain constrained by rising costs for operation, maintenance, and military personnel. Actual buying power of defense dollars would diminish each year, with particular impact on research and development. Few experts anticipated a drop in any overseas contingency operations account below FY 2019 level of $69 billion especially when that money had become a customary "plus-up" for defense spending generally. Along with a $13 billion military-construction list, Brookings Institution analyst Molly Reynolds thought new data "provides a window into congressional districts that have the most skin in the defense spending game."[35]

The advent of nimble weapons, thanks to robotics, AI, cyber, and 5G, as brought forward by new-age tech firms like Space X, might increase costs. But, with the Covid-19 pandemic ravaging the country's economy as well as health, commentators screamed that the defense industry remained in dire straits and needed more relief from Congress. DoD cited "30–40 percent inefficiency" across the DIB due to worker COVID absences with sectors like shipbuilding "experiencing 50–60 percent inefficiency." Blue-collar shipbuilding worker attendance ranged from only 50 to 70 percent proclaimed Pentagon spokesmen. Reuter's Michael Stone thought in November that a new commander-in-chief would struggle to cut defense since such spending "supports countless U.S. jobs during the coronavirus recession."[36]

* * *

No doubt, nations will constantly go forth to slay dragons, real or perceived. America certainly reflects "armamentism" (defined as continuous pursuit of military superiority over perceived opponents whether such opponents are real or not). Noted particle physicist Neal A. Homer was convinced that "more than any other event in U.S. history," Sputnik focused America's attention in 1957–1958 on "creating government policies" in support of science and education, "with the aim of maintaining U.S. scientific, technological, and military superiority over the rest of the world." *Financial Times* columnist Simon Kuper assured readers just before President Joe Biden's inauguration over six decades later that the United States was no longer a superpower, overseas expeditions were politically impossible and pointless while no enemy would "ever attempt to invade America." The country's military now served three main purposes, he thought; "a rationale for the state-funded defense industry; a need-blind stimulus programme for places with military bases; and a jobs and welfare programme for military personnel." Amara and Franck inferred the defense industry "represents a unique case due to its sheer size; its largest customer, the U.S. Department of Defense and the non-defense industries engaged in defense related work." Prognosticators thought maybe the Biden administration might cut at least 10 percent of the defense budget. In the end, what would Eisenhower say? America *has* become the national security state as a way of life, a mindset, a complacency driven by chosen economic identity, defined by an elite and subject to the whims of international instability if not irrationality. With a $741 billion defense appropriation and $13 billion aircraft carriers as well as $175 billion in arms sales abroad in FY20, Military-Industrial-Political-Complex armamentism undergirds an American Sparta.[37]

The founder of the Business Executives for National Security, Stanley A.

Weiss, told the Dallas *Morning Herald* in 1989, that "all too often, the Congress and the Pentagon are not sufficiently focused on defense, but rather on pork, parochialism and promotions." He claimed that his BENS had "simply tried to bring business sense to the business of defense." In the year of his death, 2021, there seemed no let-up to either Weiss's earlier perception or resolution via his group's prescription. Perhaps an armed mob storming the U.S. Capitol building on January 6, 2021—more reminiscent of Third World antics—suggests the threat may lie here, not abroad.[38]

In any event, America ignominiously withdrew from Afghanistan in August 2021. COVID pandemic and supply-chain fiascoes of the year suggested shifting from just-in-time response back to mobilization/industrial age "just-in-case" stockpiling; and the evolving geography of the DIB promised "further isolation of the Defense establishment from American society." Then, the reality of Great Power competition turned dangerous in the winter of 2022 when Russia invaded neighbor Ukraine, disturbing equilibrium with NATO even as Biden's national security budget promised to increase significantly, not decrease. "Costco drones" (cheap, off-the-shelf weaponized commercial AVs) joined the migration of war into cyber, disinformation and organized crime, artificially intelligent conflict, and prospect of civil disorder in America's future. As the Russian-Ukraine conflict assumed an even uglier cast when Vladimir Putin hinted at a nuclear solution, the *Bulletin of the Atomic Scientists* was already moving the hands on its famous Doomsday Clock, although adding climate change and disruptive technologies to their calculus. The National Defense Industrial Association and collaborator Govini published their annual "Vital Signs" health and readiness report in February 2022 and excoriated the DIB for "less than Passing" grades, mainly due to COVID-19 impact. In fact, the industry base failed five of the eight criteria with "significantly improved" markers reflecting only recent growth in the defense budget. Still, the "Big Five" continued to dominate the top-contractor playing field. As author James Carroll once remonstrated in his *House of War*, the Cold War produced, then protected, tremendous levels of influence, wealth and prestige for whole segments of American and Russian society. He cited the military brass, national security bureaucrats, weapons manufacturers and their workers, as well as political leaders "whose scope of action was always wider when the governed were afraid." A generation later, America's governed are even more so.

As with everything else in a centuries-old, constantly evolving military-industrial complex and national security state—stay tuned![39]

Notes

PREFACE

1. Charles Debenedetti, "American Historians and Armaments: The View from Twentieth-Century Textbooks," *Diplomatic History* 6, no.4 (Fall 1982), 329–337 esp. 327–328, 331–334 and Charles Debenedetti with introduction and postscript by Charles F. Howlett, "Educators and Armaments in Cold War America," *Peace and Change*, 34, no. 4 October 2009), 425–441.

2. Robert D. Hormats, *The Price of Liberty Paying for America's Wars* (New York: Henry Holt, 2007), introduction; Steven A. Bank, Kirk J. Stark and Joseph J. Thorndike, *War and Taxes* (Washington: The Urban Institute Pres, 2008), introduction and conclusion; Sarah Kreps, *Taxing Wars: The American Way of War Finance and the Decline of Democracy* (New York/Oxford: Oxford University Press, 2018), chaps. 1 and 2.

3. Ethan B. Kapstein, *The Political Economy of National Security: A Global Perspective* (New York: McGraw Hill, 1992), 13–15 especially; James F. Nagle, *A History of Government Contracting* (Washington, DC: The George Washington University, 1994), 5–9; William S. Dutton, *Du Pont: One Hundred and Fort Years* (New York: Scribner, 1949), 100–103.

4. On Koistinen, see note viii; also Robert F. Smith, *Manufacturing Independence: Industrial Innovation in the American Revolution* (Yardley, PA: Westhome, 2016, especially chaps 2, 3, 8; John A. Alic, "The Origin and Nature or the US 'Military-Industrial Complex,'" *Vulcan* 2 (2014), 63–97; James Ledbetter, *Unwarranted Influence: Dwight D. Eisenhower and the Military-Industrial Complex* (New Haven: Yale University Press, 2011, 17–18; Kurt Hackemer, *The U.S. Navy and the Origins of the Military-Industrial Complex, 1847–1883* (Annapolis, MD: Naval Institute Press, 2001, introduction.

5. Memorandum, To CSIS Board of Trustees, Advisers and Friends, From John J. Hamre, "An Honest Look at the 'Military-Industrial' Complex," [Number 380], May 10, 2013, Washington, DC, Center for Strategic and International Studies, 2013).

6. Keith L. Nelson, "The 'Warfare State': History of a Concept," *Pacific Historical Review*, XL (May 1971), 127–143; see also Michael S. Sherry, *In the Shadow of War: The United States Since the 1930s* (New Haven, CT: Yale University Press,

1995) in toto; William T. R. Fox, "Representativeness and Efficiency Dual Problem of Civil-Military Relations," *Political Science Quarterly* 76 (September 1961), 354–366; Renaud Bellais, *Production d'armes et puissance de nations* (Paris/Montreal, Editions L'Harmattan, 1999); Aaron L. Friedberg, *In the Shadow of the Garrison States: America's Anti-Statism and Its Cold War Grand Strategy* (Princeton, NJ: Princeton University Press, 2013) passim; Brian Waddell, *Toward the National Security State: Civil Military Relations during World War II* (Westport, CT, Prager Security International, 2008), conclusion

7. For Paul A. C. Koistinen's repeated thesis, see introductions in *Beating Plowshares into Swords, 1606–1865* (Lawrence, KS: University Press of Kansas, 1996); *Mobilizing for Modern War, 1865–1919* (Lawrence, KS: University Press of Kansas, 1997); *Planning War, Pursuing Peace, 1920–1939* (Lawrence, KS, 1998); *Arsenal of World War II, 1940–1945* (Lawrence, KS: University Press of Kansas, 2004); and *State of War: The Political Economy of American Warfare, 1945–2011* (Lawrence, KS: University Press of Kansas, 2012); Keith L. Bryant, Jr. and Henry C. Dethloff, *A History of American Business* (Englewood Cliffs, NJ; Prentice Hall, 1983), 15; Graham K. Wilson, *Business and Politics: A Comparative Introduction* (New York/London, Chatham House Publishers, 2003 edition), introduction, especially 4, 6. Carlos Lozada, "9/11 was a test. We failed." September 5, 2021 accessed at Washingtonpost.com/Outlook, Section B; Thomas J. Brown *Civil War Monuments and the Militarization of America* (Chapel Hill: University of North Carolina Press, 2019, passim.

CHAPTER 1

1. Robert D. Hormats, introduction to *The Price of Liberty: Paying for America's Wars* (New York: Henry Holt, 2007); Steven A. Bank, Kirk J. Stark and Joseph J. Thorndike, introduction to *War and Taxes* (Washington: Urban Institute Press, 2008).

2. Ethan B. Kapstein, *The Political Economy of National Security: A Global Perspective* (New York: McGraw-Hill, 1992). Chapt. 1, especially pages 13–15, provides a solid place to begin exploration.

3. Fundamental to understanding the ageless themes are the following sources. Bank, Stark and Thorndike, *War and Taxes*; Stuart D. Brandes, *Warhogs: A History of War Profits in America* (Lexington: University Press of Kentucky, 1997); Hormats, *Price of Liberty*; Paul A. C. Koistinen, *Beating Plowshares into Swords: The Political Economy of American Warfare, 1606–1865* (Lawrence: University Press of Kansas, 1996). This work is the first in Koistinen's 5-volume set. See also: C. M. Culver, *Federal Government Procurement: An Uncharted Course Through Turbulent Waters* (McLean, VA: National Contract Management Association, 1985), 1; James F. Nagle, *A History of Government Contracting* (Washington: George Washington Uni-

versity Press, 1994), 5–8 and Joyce Lee Malcom, *To Keep and Bear Arms: The Origins of an Anglo-American Right* (Cambridge, Harvard University Press, 1994), 135–143.

4. Richard D. Brown, *Modernization: The Transformation of American Life, 1600–1865* (New York: Hill and Wang, 1976), 36, 38, 61–73. Chapt. 2, especially pages 36 and 38, and chapt. 3, especially pages 61–73.

5. Brown, *Modernization*, 67–73.

6. John Shy, *Toward Lexington: The Role of the British Army in the Coming of the Revolution* (Princeton: Princeton University Press, 21965), 338–339, 342–343; Julian Gwyn, "British Government Spending and the North American Colonies, 1740–1775," *Journal of Imperial and Commonwealth History* 8, no. 2 (January 1980), 74–84, especially 77; Barton C. Hacker and Margaret Vining, *American Military Technology: The Life Story of a Technology*, 2–5; Alan I. Marcus and Howard P. Segal, *Technology in America: A Brief History*, 6–9.

7. Aaron L. Friedberg, *In the Shadow of the Garrison State: America's Anti-Statism and Its Cold War Grand Strategy* (Princeton, NJ: Princeton University Press, 2000), chapt. 1; James F. Nagle, *A History of Government Contracting* (Washington, DC, The George Washington University, 1992), 10–12; Donald M. Snow and Dennis M. Drew, *From Lexington to Desert Storm: War and Politics in the American Experience* (Armonk, NY/London, UK, M.E. Sharpe, 1994), 33–35; James C. Bradford, "The Navies of the American Revolution," in Kenneth J. Hagan, editor, *In Peace and War: Interpretations of American Naval History, 1775–1978* (Westport, CT, Greenwood, 21978), 3–4.

8. Esmond Wright, "A Question of Duty," pp 33–34 and John Mollo, "A Shilling for a Redcoat," pp. 87–89 both in Kenneth Pearson and Patricia Connor, compilers, *1776: The British Story of the American Revolution* (London, Times Books, 1976); Fred Anderson, *Crucible of War: The Seven Years War and the Fate of Empire in British North America, 1754–1766* (New York, Alfred A. Knopf, 2000), especially 560–562; R. Arthur Fowler, *Logistics and the Failure of the British Army in North America, 1775–1763* (Princeton: Princeton University Press, 1975), 3–11.

9. Useful primers include Albert Manucy, *Artillery Through The Ages: A Short Illustrated History of Cannon, Emphasizing Types Used in America* (Washington; Government Printing Office 1949), 1–10; Harold L. Peterson, *Round Shot and Rammers* (New York, Crown, 1969), chapt. 2, especially 32–38; Jeffrey M. Dorwart with Jean K. Wolf, *The Philadelphia Navy Yard: From the Birth of the U.S. Navy to the Nuclear Age* (Philadelphia: University of Pennsylvania Press, 2001), 9–14.

10. James. A. Mulholland, *A History of Metals in Colonial America* (University, AL: University of Alabama Press, 1981, introduction, especially x; Charles Winthrop Sawyer, *Firearms in American History, 1600 to 1800* (Boston, By Author, 1919), chapt. "The Colonial Period (1660–1775), 1–3.

11. James A. Huston, *The Sinews of War: Army Logistics 1775–1953*

(Washington, Office of the Chief of Military History, United States Army, 1966), pp. 3–6; Joyce Lee Malcom, *To Keep and Bear Arms: The Origins of an Anglo-American Right* (Cambridge, MA, Harvard University Press, 1994), ix; Ian C. Hope, *A Scientific Way of War: Antebellum Military Science, West Point, and the Origins of American Military Thought* (Lincoln, NE: University of Nebraska Press, 2015), 17–26; Hacker and Vining, *American Military Technology*, 4.

12. Robert F. Smith, *Manufacturing Independence: Industrial Innovation in the American Revolution* (Yardley, PA, Westholme, 2016), xii–xiii and chapt. 1; M. L. Brown, *Firearms in Colonial America: The Impact on History and Technology 1492–1792* (Washington, DC, Smithsonian Institution Press, 1980), appendix 7, 399–403; Alan I. Marcus and Howard P. Segal, *Technology in America: A Brief History* (New York: Harcourt Brace Jovanovich, 1989), chapt. 1; Hacker and Vining, *American Military Technology*, 4.

13. Sawyer, *Firearms in American History*, 20–30, 32; Arcadi Gluckman, *United States Martial Pistols and Revolvers* (Buffalo, NY, Otto Ulbrich, 1948), 27–28 and *United States Military Muskets, Rifles and Carbines* (Buffalo, NY, Otto Ulbrich, 1948), 41–42; Larrie D. Ferreiro, *Brothers at Arms: American Independence and the Men of France & Spain who Saved It* (New York, Alfred A. Knopf, 2016), 57–58.

14. E. Wayne Carp, *To Starve the Army At Pleasure: Continental Army and Administration and American Political Culture 1775–1783* (Chapel Hill/London: University of North Carolina Press, 1984), prologue; Marcus and Segal, *Technology in America*, 22–28, 29–31, 34–36.

15. Jeffery M. Dorwart with Jean K. Wolf, *Philadelphia Navy Yard: From the Birth of the U.S. Navy to the Nuclear Age* (Philadelphia, PA: University of Pennsylvania Press, 2001), chapt. 1.

16. Malcom, *To Keep and Bear Arms*, 145–147

17. Smith, *Manufacturing Independence*, x.

18. Keith L. Bryant and Henry C. Dethloff, *A History of American Business* (Englewood Cliffs: Prentice Hall), 13; Christopher M. Dent, "Economic Security," in *Contemporary Security Studies*, 2nd ed., ed. Alan Collins (Oxford; New York: Oxford University Press, 2010), 241.

19. Letter, Benjamin Franklin to Peter Collinson, quoted in Esmond Wright, *Franklin of Philadelphia* (Cambridge, MA: The Belknap Press of Harvard University Press, 1986), 96, also 84–101 and H.W. Brands, *The First American: The Life and Times of Benjamin Franklin* (New York, Doubleday, 2000), 232–240, 247–251; Alan Calmes, "The Lyttleton Expedition of 1759: Military Failures and Financial Success," *The South Carolina Historical Magazine*, volume 77, number 1 (January 1976), 10–33; Harry D. Berge, "Economic Consequences of the French and Indian War for the Philadelphia Merchant," *Pennsylvania History*, volume 13, number 3 (July 1946), 185–193; Bradford, "Navies of the American Revolution," 4–7; Max M. Edling, *A Rev-*

olution in Favor of Government: Origins if the U.S. Constitution and the Making of the American State (Oxford/New York: Oxford University Press, 2003), 54–55.

20. Huston, *Sinews of War*, 18–19.

21. Staughton Lynd and David Waldstreicher, "Free Trade, Sovereignty, and Slavery: Toward an Economic Interpretation of American Independence," *William and Mary Quarterly*, Third Series, volume 68, number 4 (October 2011), 597–630; Robert F. Smith, *Manufacturing Independence: Industrial, Innovation in the American Colonies* (Yardley, PA, Westholme, 2016), chapt. 1; Nagle, *Government Contracting*, chapt. 1. "S.H.," "Rebirthing the Revolution," *The Pennsylvania Gazette* [University of Pennsylvania Alumni Magazine], volume 112, number 2, pages 21–23.

22. Bank, Stark and Thorndike, *War and Taxes*, 2–3 and Sarah E. Kreps, *Taxing Wars: The American Way of War Finance and the Decline of Democracy* (Oxford UK/New York: Oxford University Press, 2018), 8, 30, 37, 55–56, 58, 60, 151; Esmond Wright, "A Question of Duty," in Pearson and Connor, compilers, *1776: The British Story of the American Revolution* (London Times Books, 1976), 34; for the text of the Declaration, see Center for Civic Education, *American Legacy: The United States Constitution and Other Essential Documents of American Democracy* (Calabassas, CA, Center for Civic Education, 2005), 6–10.

23. For the text of the Declaration, see Center for Civic Education, *American Legacy: The United States Constitution and other Essential Documents of American Democracy* (Calabassas, CA, Center for Civic Education, 2005), 6–10.

24. Carp, *To Starve an Army at Leisure*, chaps. 1 and 2.

25. From Fred Anderson, *Crucible of War: The Seven Years' War and the Fate of Empire in British North America, 1754–1766* (New York, Alfred A. Knopf, 2001), especially 560–562, Smith, *Manufacturing Independence* inter alia, significantly updates and expands the work of James Huston and Edna Risch; Huston, *Sinews of War*, 6.

26. Smith, *Manufacturing Independence*, 34, 40, 47, 48.

27. See E. James Ferguson, *The Power of the Purse: A History of American Public Finance, 1776–1790* (Chapel Hill, NC: University of North Carolina Press, 1961), chapt. 5 and 142; William L. Downard, "The Web of Government and Business: Nathanael Greene and His Associates," *Indiana Military History Journal*, v. 6, number 2 (May 1981), 19–27.

28. Gluckman, *United States Muskets, Rifles and Carbines*, chapt. 2 and 56–64; Gluckman, *United States Martial Pistols and Revolvers*, 27–31.

29. Darwin H. Stapleton, "General Daniel Roberdeau and the Lead Mine Expedition, 778–1779,:" *Pennsylvania History*, v. 38, no. 4 (October 1971), pp. 361–371; David L. Salay, "The Production of Gunpowder in Pennsylvania During the American Revolution," *Pennsylvania Magazine of History and Biography*, vol. 99 (October 1975), number 4, pp. 422–442; Larry Bowman, "The Virginia County Committees of Safety, 1774–1776," *Virginia Magazine of History and Biography*, v. 79 (July

1971), number 3, especially 334–336; Larry G. Bowman, "The Scarcity of Salt in Virginia During the American Revolution," *Virginia Magazine of History and Biography*, volume 77 (October 1969), number 4, 464–472; G. Melvin Hendon, "A War-Inspired Industry: The Manufacture of Hemp in Virginia During the Revolution," *Virginia Magazine of History and Biography*, volume 74, number 3 (July 1966), pp. 300–311.

30. William Fowler, "The Business of War: Boston as a Navy Base, 1776–1783," *American Neptune*, v. 42, no. 1 (January 1982), 26–27; Manucy, *Artillery Through the Ages*, 10.

31. Huston, *Sinews of War*, 22–23; Peterson, *Round Shot and Rammers*, 57–60.

32. Paullin, *History of Naval Administration*, 8–10; Dorwart/Wolf, *Philadelphia Navy Yard*, chapt. 2.

33. Paullin, *History of Naval Administration*, 11.

34. Dorwarts/Wolf, *Philadelphia Navy Yard*, 25, 28, 29; Paullin, *History of Naval Administration*, 11–12, 18, 26, 28, 37, 47, 52–53; Fowler, "Boston as a Navy Base," 27.

35. Huston, *Sinews of War*, 85; Fowler, "Boston as a Navy Base," 27; Bellesiles, *Arming America*, 207.

36. Marvin A. Kreidberg and Merton G. Henry, *History of Military Mobilization in the United States Army, 1775–1945*, reprint of DA Pamphlet 20–212, Department of the Army, Washington, DC, 1955 (Washington: US Army Center of Military History, 1989), 22.

37. Bank/Stark/Thorndike, *War and Taxes*, 2–3; Daniel Marston, *The American Revolution 1774–1781* (Osprey Publishing, 2002), 372; Merrill Jensen, *The Founding of a Nation: A History of the American Revolution 1763–1776*. (New York/London: Oxford University Press, 1969), 82; John Shy, *A People Numerous and Armed: Reflections on the Military Struggle for American Independence* (New York: Oxford University Press, 1976), 249–20; John Whiteclay Chambers, II, editor in chief *The Oxford Companion to American Military History* (New York/Oxford: Oxford University Press, 1999), 849.

38. Compare Carp, *To Starve the Army at Pleasure*, chaps. 1–3 and conclusion especially with Smith, *Manufacturing Independence*, conclusion, 208, 213; Ferreiro, *Brothers at Arms*, 335–336; Brown, *Firearms in Colonial America*, appendix IX, 404–409.

39. Benjamin Lincoln memorandum regarding arsenals and academies, March 5, 1783 and Lincoln to President of Congress, June 14, 1783, quoted in Smith, *Manufacturing Independence*, 176–177; Carp, *To Starve the Army at Pleasure*, 222; Malcom, *To Keep and Bear Arms*, 147–153 passim.

CHAPTER 2

1. Charles R. Ritcheson, "The Earl of Shelbourne and Peace with America, 1782–1783, Vision and Reality," *International History Review* 5, no. 3 (1983): 322–345.

2. Max M. Erdling, *A Revolution in Favor of Government: Origins of the U.S. Constitution and the Making of the American State* (Oxford/New York: Oxford University Press, 2003), chapt. 3.

3. Alan R. Millet, "The Constitution and the Citizen-Soldier," especially 96–100 and Lawrence Delbert Gross, "A Question of Sovereignty: The Militia in Anglo-American Constitutional Debate, 1641–1827," especially 123–134 in John Elsberg, editor, *Papers on the Constitution* [The U.S. Army Bicentennial Series], Washington, D.C., U.S. Army Center of Military History, 1990); Ian C. Hope, *A Scientific Way of War: Antebellum Military Science, West Point, and the Origins of American Military Thought* (Lincoln, NE: University of Nebraska Press, 2015), 26–30; Letter, Secretary of War—President, April 3, 1797, Joseph McHenry papers, LC-III- A- 1 as reprinted in Benjamin Franklin Cooling, editor, *The New American State Papers: Military Affairs, Volume 1, Policy and Strategy of National Defense* (Wilmington, DE, Scholarly Resources Inc., 1979), 5–7, 8–12; M. L. Brown, *Firearms in Colonial America; The Impact on History and Technology 1492–1792* (Washington, DC, Smithsonian Institution Press, 1980), 366–371.

4. John Steele Gordon, *An Empire of Wealth; The Epic History of American Economic Power* (New York/London, Harper, 2004), Part 2; *American State Papers, Military Affairs*, Series Five, Volume 1, pages 7–8.

5. Robert F. Smith, *Manufacturing Independence: Industrial Innovation in the American Revolution* (Yardley, PA, Westholme, 2016), page 48 and chapt. 8; James Biser Whisker, *The United States Armory at Springfield, 1795 -1865* (Lewiston, NY, Edward Mellen Press, 1997, pages 12–16; Office of Archeology and Historic Preservation, National Park Service, *Springfield Armory: Evaluation Under Provision of Historic Preservation Act of 1966* (Washington, DC, U.S. Department of the Interior, August 1, 1967), 97.

6. Michael A. Bonura, "A French-Inspired Way of War: French Influence on the U.S. Army from 1812 to the Mexican War," *Army History* (Winter 2014), pages 7–23; Ian C. Hope, *A Scientific Way of War: Antebellum Military Science, West Point, and the Origins of American Military Thought* (Lincoln, NE: University of Nebraska Press, 2015), introduction, chapt. 1; Brown, *Firearms in Colonial America*, 360, 381.

7. Marvin A. Kreidberg and Merton G. Henry, *History of Military Mobilization in the United States Army, 1775–1945* (Washington, DC, US Army Center of Military History, 1989 edition), pages 23–25; James F. Nagle, *A History of Government Contracting* (Washington, DC, The George Washington University, 1992), pages

57–59; James A. Huston, *The Sinews of War: Army Logistics 1775–1953* (Washington, DC, US Army Center of Military History, 1966), chapt. 7; Erna Risch, *Quartermaster Support for the Army, 1775–1939* (Washington, DC, US Army Center of Military History, 1962), 78–81; Charles Oscar Paullin, *Paullin's History of Naval Administration, 1775–1911* (Annapolis, MD, US Naval Institute, 1968), 52–53; Terry Sharrer, "The Search for a Naval Policy, 1783–1812," in Kenneth J. Hagan, editor, *In Peace and War: Interpretations of American Naval History, 1775–1978* (Westport, FT, Greenwood, 1978), 27.

8. Walter Millis, editor, *American Military Thought* (Indianapolis, IN, Bobbs-Merrill, 1966), 16–28; Dave R. Palmer, *Provide for the Common Defense: America, Its Army and the Birth of a Nation* (Novato, CA, Presidio Press, 1994), 26–29; Hope, *Scientific Way of War*, 27–29.

9. Palmer, *Common Defense*, 29; also Richard H. Kohn, *Eagle and Sword: The Beginnings of the Military Establishment in America*. (New York, Free Press, 1975), 50–70.

10. Center for Civic Education, *American Legacy: The United States Constitution and other Essential Documents of American Democracy (Calabasas, CA, Center for Civic Education, 2005)*, 12–26; Millis, *American Military Thought*, 28–32; Joyce Lee Malcom, *To Keep and Bear Arms: The Origins of an Anglo-America Right* (Cambridge, Harvard University Press, 1994), 150–164 passim.

11. Millis, *American Military Thought*, 32–67; Center for Civic Education, *American Legacy*, 7–29.

12. Hope, *Scientific Way of War*, 30–35; Edling, *A Revolution in Favor of Government*, conclusion.

13. Particularly focused is Edward Mead Earle's classic if now neglected essay, "Adam Smith, Alexander Hamilton, Friedrich List," in Peter Paret, editor, with the collaboration of Gordon A. Craig and Felix Gilbert, *Makers of Modern Strategy from Machiavelli to the Nuclear Age* (Princeton, NJ: Princeton University Press, 1986 edition), especially 230–242; Hamilton's report can be found in Jacob E. Cooke, editor, *The Papers of Alexander Hamilton* (New York, Harper and Row, 1964), 116–158; also Keith L. Bryant, Jr. and Henry C. Dethloff, *A History of American Business* (Englewood Cliffs, NJ, Prentice Hall, 1983), 56–58; Alan I Marcus and Howard P. Segal, *Technology in American: A Brief History* (San Diego, CA: Harcourt Brace Jovanovich, 1989), 43–46; Lois M. Hacker, *The Triumph of American Capitalism: The Development of Forces in American History to the Beginning of the Twentieth Century* (New York, McGraw-Hill, 1965 edition), 188–195.

14. See John Avlon, *Washington's Farewell: The Founding Father's Warning to Future Generations* (New York: Simon & Schuster, 2017), section II and appendix.

15. John C. Fitzpatrick, editor. *The Writings of George Washington* (Washington, DC, Government Printing Office, 1932), volume 6, pages 234–236, 314–317.

16. Millis, *American Military Thought*, 70–74

17. Millis, *American Military Thought*, 74–78; John J. Carrigg, "Benjamin Stoddert, 8 June 1798–31 March 1801," in Paolo E. Coletta, editor, *American Secretaries of the Navy, Volume 1, 1775–1913* (Annapolis, MD: Naval Institute Press, 1980), 59–77, especially 64–65, 69.

18. United States Bureau of Statistics, *Historical Statistics of the United States* (Washington, Government Printing Office, 1951), Series Y, 718–720.

19. Brown, *Firearms in Colonial America*, 360–364.

20. Sharrer, "The Search for a Naval Policy," 28–32; Paullin, *Naval Administration*, 90–91; Percival Perry, "The Naval-Stores Industry in the Old South, 1790–1860," *The Journal of Southern History* 34, number 4 (November 1968), 510–512; also see Robert D. Hormats, *The Price of Liberty: Paying For America's Wars* (New York, Holt, 2007), chaps. 1, 2; Steven A. Bank, Kirk J. Stark, Joseph J. Thorndike, *War and Taxes* (Washington, The Urban Institute Press, 2008), chapt. 1, pages 7, 20.

21. Jeffrey Dorwart with Jean K. Wolf, *The Philadelphia Navy Yard: From the Birth of the U.S. Navy to the Nuclear Age* (Philadelphia: University of Pennsylvania Press, 2001), chapt. 3; Marshall Smelser, *The Congress Founds the Navy, 1787–1798* (South Bend, IN: University of Notre Dame Press, 1959), 12–13; Maury Baker, "Cost Overrun, An Early Naval Precedent: Building the First U.S. Warships, 1794–98," *Maryland Historical Magazine*, volume 72, number 3 (Fall 1977), 361–372; Bank, Stark, Thorndike, *War and* Taxes, 9–11; Paullin, *Naval Administration*, 93–95.

22. Baker, "Cost Overrun," 364–371; Paullin, *Naval Administration*, 96–97.

23. Baker, "Cost Overrun," 371–372; Paullin, *Naval Administration*, 97–98; Sharrer, "Search for a Naval Policy," 33–34; Dorwart and Wolf, *Philadelphia Navy Yard*, chapt. 2.

24. Walter Millis, "Benjamin Stoddert Calls for Massive Naval Expansion," in Millis, editor, *American Military Thought* (Indianapolis, IN, Bobbs-Merrill, 1966), 73–78 especially 73; John J. Carrigg, "Benjamin Stoddert, 8 June 1798–31 March 1801," in Paolo E. Coletta, editor, *American Secretaries of the Navy, Volume 1, 1775–1913* (Annapolis, MD: Naval Institute Press, 1980, 59–77, especially 64–65, 69.

25. Carrigg, "Stoddert," 69; Charles R. Fisher, "The Great Guns of the Navy, 1797–1843," *The American Neptune* 36 no. 4 (October 1976), XXXVI, # 4, 278–279.

26. Larry J. Sechrist, "Privately Funded and Built U.S. Warships in the Quasi-War of 1797–1801," *The Independent Review* 12, no. 1, Summer 2007, 101–113.

27. Dorwart and Wolf, *Philadelphia Navy Yard*, chapt. 4; Sharrer, "Search for a Naval Policy," 38; Paullin, *Naval Administration*, 98–118, 127; Fisher, "The Great Guns of the Navy,", 278–279; Louis F. Gorr, "The Foxall-Columbia Foundry: An Early Defense Contractor in Georgetown," in Francis Coleman Rosenberger, editor, *Records of the Columbia Historical Society of Washington, D.C, 1971–1972* (Char-

lottesville, VA: University of Virginia Press, 1973), 35; Sechrest, "Privately Funded and Built," 111–113; Charles R. Fischer, "The Great Guns of the Navy, 1797–1843," *The American Neptune,* 36 no. 4 (October 1976), 278–279.

28. Edling, *A Revolution in Favor,* 227–228; Joseph G. Henrich, "The Triumph of Ideology: The Jeffersonians and the Navy, 1779–1807," unpublished doctoral dissertation, Duke University, 1971.

29. Paullin, *Naval Administration,* 119, 132–135; Dean R. Mayhew, "Jeffersonian Gunboats in the War of 1812," *The American Neptune,* XLII, number 2 (April 1982), 101–117; Gorr, "The Foxall-Columbia Foundry," 40–48.

30. Linda Maloney, "The War of 1812" What Role for Sea Power?" in Hagan, *In Peace and* War, 46; Ronald Mosley, *Blood Relations: The Rise and Fall of the Du Ponts of Delaware* (New York, Atheneum, 1980), 26, 28; Mayhew, Jeffersonian Gunboats," 101–105; Paulin, *Naval Administration,* 144–148.

31. Paullin, *Naval Administration,* 144–148; Sharrar, "Search for a Naval Policy", 43–44; and Maloney, "The War of 1812: What Role for Sea Power?" both in Hagan, *In Peace and War),* 19, 46; Ronald Mosley, *Blood Relations: The Rise and Fall of the Du Ponts of Delaware.* (New York, Atheneum, 1980), 26–29; William S. Dutton, *Du Pont: One Hundred and Twenty Years* (New York, Charles Scribner's Sons, 1949), 48–50; Dorwart and Wolf, *Philadelphia Navy Yard,* 53–60.

32. Bank/Stark/Thorndike, *War and Taxes,* 9–21 especially 20–21 citing W. Elliott Brownlee, *Federal Taxation in America: A Short History* (New York/Cambridge: Cambridge University Press, 2004), 219; Donald R. Hickey, *The War of 18122: A Forgotten Conflict* (Urbana, IL: University of Illinois Press, 1990), 2; Hormats, *Price of Liberty,* chap. 2; Stuart D. Brandes, *Warhogs: A History of War Profits in* America (Lexington, KY: University Press of Kentucky, 1997), 53–62.

33. Paullin, *Naval Administration,* 148–158; Maloney, "The War of 1812," 54, 56.

34. Taylor Peck, *Round-Shot to Rockets: A History of the Washington Navy Yard and U.S. Naval Gun Factory* (Annapolis, MD, United States Naval Institute, 1949) 47–68; Gore, "Foxall-Columbiia Foundry," 40–48.

35. Maloney, "The War of 1812," 61; David F. Long, "The Navy under the Board of Navy Commissioners, 1815–1842," in Hagan, *In Peace and War,* 64.

36. Nagle, *A History of Government Contracting,* 89; Tennessee governor quoted in Ellis F. Lenz, *Muzzle Flashes* (Huntington, WVA, Standard Publications, Inc., 1944) 112; Kreidberg and Henry, *Military Mobilization,* chap. 2; J. Mackay Hitsman, "David Parish and the War of 1812," *Military Affairs* 26, no. 4 (Winter 1962–1963), pp. 171–177; Huston, *Sinews of War,* 102–112; Risch, *Quartermaster Support of the Army,* 117–133 and chap. 5.

37. Kreidberg and Henry, *Military Mobilization,* 59–60; Edling, *A Revolution in Favor,* conclusion.

38. Millis, *American Military* Thought, 121; Bryant and Dethloff, *American*

Business, 58–59; Brian Bralogh, *A Government Out of Sight: The Mystery of National Authority in Nineteenth Century America* (Cambridge/New York: Cambridge University Press, 2009), chaps. 1, 2, 3; Max M. Edling, *A Hercules in the Cradle: War, Money, and the American State, 1783–1867* (Chicago/London: University of Chicago Press, 2014), chaps. 4, 5.

39. Robert L. Heilbroner, *The Making of Economic Society* (Englewood Cliffs, NJ, Prentice-Hall, 1962), chapt. 4; Robert L. Heilbroner and Aaron Singer, *The Economic Transformation of America* (New York: Harcourt Brace Jovanovich, 1977), chapt. 2; Thomas C. Cochran, *Frontiers of Change: Early Industrialism in America* (New York: Oxford University Press, 1981), chaps. 5 and 6 and *Business in American Life: A History* (New York: McGraw-Hill, 1972, part 2; Alan Marcus and Howard P. Segal, *Technology in America: A Brief History* (San Diego, CA: Harcourt Brace Jovanovich, 1989), chaps. 2 and 3; Bryant, and Dethloff, *A History of American Business*, chaps. 4–6; Matthew Karp, *This Vast Southern Empire: Slaveholders at the Helm of American Foreign Policy* (Cambridge, MA, Harvard University Press, 2016); Frederick S. Weaver, *An Economic History of the United States* (Lanham, Md. Rowman and Lttlefield, 2016), part 2; John Steele Gordon, *An Empire of Wealth: The Epic History of American Power* (New York, Harper, 2004), chaps. 7–10.

40. Millis, *American Military Thought*, 90–102; original documents pertinent to strategy, military policy and contribution to nation building can be found in Benjamin Franklin Cooling, editor, *The New American State Papers—Military Affairs*, volumes 1 and 2, both Policy and Strategy of National Defense (Wilmington, DE, Scholarly Resources, Inc., 1979, henceforth (NASP-MA) with appropriate reference to volume.

41. Millis, *American Military Thought*, 79–117.

42. Millis, *American Military Thought*, 102–111; Hope, *A Scientific Way of War*, 54–59; original documents pertinent to fortification development may be found in Cooling, editor, *NASP-MA*, volume 3, Policy and Strategy of National Defense.

43. Dorwart and Wolf, *Philadelphia Navy Yard*, chapt. 5.

44. Marcus and Segal, *Technology in America*, chaps. 2 and 3; Walter Licht, *Industrializing America: The Nineteenth Century* (Baltimore, Md., The Johns Hopkins University Press, 1995), chaps. 1–3, especially 42–43.

45. Barton C. Hacker and Margaret Vining, *American Military Technology: The Life Story of a Technology* (Baltimore, MD, The Johns Hopkins University Press, 2006), 19–20; James C. Haslett, Edwin Olmstead and M. Hume Parks, *Field Artillery Weapons of the Civil War* (Urbana, IL: University of Illinois, 2004 edition), 23; Fisher, "The Great Guns of the Navy," 279–280.

46. M.L. Brown, "Early American Manufacture: American armories played

a prominent role in the early mechanization of industry," *National Defense*, LXVIII (July/August 1983), 59–62; Felicia Johnson Deyrup, *Arms Making in the Connecticut Valley: A Regional Study of the Economic Development of the Small Arms Industry 1798–1870* (York, PA; George Shumway, Publisher, 1970), 3; Hacker and Vining, *American Military Technology*, 20–25; Robert A. Howard, "Interchangeable Parts Reexamined: The Private Sector of the American Arms Industry on the Eve of the Civil War," *Technology and Culture* v. 19, number 4 (October 1978), 633–649 and "Communication: Interchangeable Parts revisited," *Technology and Culture*, v. 21, number 3 (July 1980), 549–550; Donald R. Hoke, *Ingenious Yankees; The Rise of the American System of Manufactures in the Private Sector.* (New York, Columbia University Press, 1990), chaps. 1, 6; Dutton, *Du Pont*, 81–83.

47. Bonura, "A French-Inspired Way of War," *Army History* (Winter 2014), 7–22; Hacker and Vining, *American Military Technology*, 10; Whisker, *Springfield Armory*, 2–63 inter alia; Clive Bush, *The Dream of Reason: American Consciousness and Cultural Achievement from Independence to the Civil War* (New York, St. Martins, 1979), 127–129; Hope, *A Scientific Way of War*, chaps. 1, 3, 5.

48. Gluckman, *Pistols*, 48–49 and *Muskets*, 82–94, 123–124; Whisker, Springfield *Armory*, 20–21.

49. Merritt Roe Smith, "The American System of (Interchangeable) Manufacturing. Ca. 1815–1854," mimeograph chart, no date, author's files; definitive studies of the firearms dimension of the early MIC remain Deyrup, *Arms Making in the Connecticut Valley*, Whisker, *Springfield Armory* (who delineates the GOGO as of the mid-1820s on page 80) and Merritt Roe Smith, *Harpers Ferry Armory and the New Technology: The Challenge of Change* (Ithaca, NY: Cornell University Press, 1977). On changing mission as illustrated by Frankford, see James J. Farley, *Making Arms in the Machine Age: Philadelphia's Frankford Arsenal, 1816–1870* (University Park, PA, Pennsylvania State University Press, 1994). Frederic D. Schwartz, "Arms and the Man; Notes from the Field," *Invention and Technology* 12, no. 3 (Winter 1997), 6–7 seems justified in his Silicon Valley—Connecticut Valley allusion.

50. Whisker, *Springfield Armory*, 15–16; Merritt Roe Smith, "George Washington and the Establishment of the Harpers Ferry Armory," *The Virginia Magazine of History and Biography*, v. 81, number 4 (October 1973), 415–436; Arthur P. Wade, "Mount Dearborn: The National Armory at Rocky Mount, South Carolina, 1802–1829," *South Carolina Historical Magazine*, v. 81, number 3 (July 1980), 207–231 and number 4 (October 1980) 316–341; Edward A. Battison, "Eli Whitney and the Milling Machine," *Smithsonian Journal of History* v. 1, number 2 (Summer 1966), 9–34; Merritt Roe Smith, "Eli Whitney and the American System of Manufacturing," in Carroll W. Pursell, Jr., *Technology in America: A History of Individuals and Ideas* (Cambridge, MA: MIT Press, 1981), 45–61; R. T. Huntington, *Hall's Breech-*

loaders (York, PA: George Shumway, publisher 1972); Peter A. Schmidt, *Hall's Military Breechloaders* (York, PA, George Shumway publisher, 1972); John E. Jessup, "Problems in Selecting a Standard Weapon for the Army: The Breech loading Issue," in International Commission of Military History, *Acta Number 5*, Volume 8, 1908 (Bucharest, Romania; Romanian Commission of Military History, 1981), 10–17; R. Gordon Wasson, *The Hall Carbine Affairs: A Study in Contemporary Folklore* (New York, Paddick Press, 1948), 55–65.

51. James F. Nagle, *A History of Government Contracting* (Washington, DC, The George Washington University, 1992), 78–79; Hazlett, Olmstead and Parks, *Civil War Artillery*, 24–25.

52. Joel W. Grossman, "High-Caliber Discovery," *Federal Archeology* 7, no. 2 (Summer 1994), 38–43; Hazlett, Olmstead and Parks, *Civil War Artillery*, 26–46.

53. Gluckman, *American Martial Pistols and Revolvers*, part 1, chaps. 1–4 and part 2, chapt. 1; Martin Rywell, *United States Military Muskets, Rifles, Carbines and their Current Prices* (Harriman, TN, Pioneer Press, 1956), 16–21, 30; Taylor Peck, *Round-Shot to Rockets: A History of the Washington Navy Yard and U.S. Naval Gun Factory* (Annapolis, MD, United States Naval Institute, 1949), 104–110.

54. Robert A. Howard, "Interchangeable Parts Reexamined: The Private Sector of the American Arms Industry on the Eve of the Civil War," *Technology and Culture*, v. 19, no. 4 (October 1978), 633, 649 and "Communication: Interchangeable Parts Revisited," *Technology and Culture* 21, no. 3 (July 19890), 549–550; for Dobbins' report, Millis, *American Military Thought*, 137–142.

55. Dorwarts and Wolf, *Philadelphia Navy Yard*, chapt. 5.

56. Geoffey S. Smith, "An Uncertain Passage: The Bureaus Run the Navy, 1842–1861," in Kenneth J. Hagan, editor, *In Peace and War: Interpretations of American Naval History, 1775–1978* (Westport, CT: Greenwood Press, 1978), 79–106; Kurt Hackemer, *The U.S. Navy and the Origins of the Military-Industrial Complex, 1847-1883* (Annapolis, MD: Naval Institute Press, 2001), introduction, chapt. 1; Frank M. Bennett, *The Steam Navy of the United States* (Westport, Ct: Greenwood Press, 1968 reprint of New York: W. T. Nicholson Press, 1896), iv; Oscar Paullin, *Paullin's History of Naval Administration, 1775–1911* (Annapolis, Md., United States Naval Institute, 1968), 209–211; Michael A. Bellesiles, *Arming America: The Origins of a National Gun Culture* (New York, Knopf, 2000), chaps. 7–9; Thomas R. Heinrich, *Ships for the Seven Seas: Philadelphia Shipbuilding in the Age of Industrial Capitalism.* (Baltimore/London, The Johns Hopkins University Press, 1997), 13–25.

57. Bennett, *Steam Navy*, chap. 9, quoting Dobbins 138–139; Paullin, *Naval Administration*, chaps. 5 and 6; Kurt Hackemer, *The U.S. Navy and the Origins of the Military-Industrial Complex*, 2001), chaps. 2 and 3; K. Jack Bauer, "Naval Shipbuilding Programs, 1794–1860," *Military Affairs* 29, no. 1 (spring, 1965), 29–40; Nagle, *Government Contracting*, 112–122.

58. Bennett, *Steam Navy*, 166–169 and appendix B; Kurt Hackemer, "Building the Military-Industrial Relationship; The U. S. Navy and American Business, 1854–1883," *Naval War College Review* 52, no. 2 (Spring 1999), 89–111.

59. Mark F. Cancian, "Cost Growth: Perception and Reality," (Fort Belvoir, VA, Defense Acquisition University, 2010), 391–392 extrapolating I. W. Toll, *Six Frigates: The Epic Story of the Founding of the United States Navy* (New York, W.W. Norton, 2006); Heinrich, *Ships for the Seven Seas*, 19, 23–24; Peck, *Round Shot to Rockets*, 105–112.

60. Nagle, *Government Contracting*, chaps. 5, 6, 7; Huston, *The Sinews of War*, chaps. 8–10; Risch, *Quartermaster Support*, chaps. 6–8; C. M. Culver, *Federal Government Procurement—An Uncharted Course Through Turbulent Waters* (McLean, VA, National Contract Management Association, 1984), 2; Huston, *Sinews of War*, chaps. 8–10.

61. Rebecca U. Thorpe, *The American Warfare State: The Domestic Politics of Military Spending* (Chicago/London, The University of Chicago Press, 2014), 8–10; Brandes, "*Warhogs*, 54–56

62. Raymond W. and Mary Lund Settle, *War Drums and Wagon Wheels: The Story of Russell, Majors and Waddell* (Lincoln, NE: University of Nebraska Press, 1966), chaps. 2–4, 7 especially; Thomas T. Smith, *The U.S. Army and the Texas Frontier Economy, 1845–1900* (College Station, Texas A&M University Press, 1999), chapt. 1, 2, and 10 especially.

63. U.S. Congress, 36th, 1st Session, House of Representatives, Report 650 to accompany Bill H.R. No. 844, "National Foundries in Pennsylvania and Alabama," June 18, 1860, in Cooling, ed., *ASP-MA*, 346–348.

64. Volume 18; Harold D. Langley, "James Cochrane Dobbin, 8 March 1853–6 March 1837," in Coletta, editor, *Secretaries of the Navy*, 285 citing Senate Executive Documents, 1st Session, Volume 3, *Annual Report of the Secretary of the Navy*, 1853, 307–311.

65. Edward D. Tippett, Letter to "Honored Sir," May 11, 1861, entry 994, file In-Misc.-177, Records of the Office of the Chief of Ordnance, Record Group 156, National Archives and Records Service (NARS), Washington, D.C., quoted in Michael P. Musick, "War in an Age of Wonders: Civil War Arms and Equipment," *Prologue*, v.27, # 1 (Winter 1995), 348.

CHAPTER 3

1. Walter Millis, editor. *American Military Thought* (Indianapolis, IN, Bobbs-Merrill, 1966), page 143; Russell F. Weigley, *The American Way of War: A History of United States Military Strategy and Policy* (New York, Macmillan, 1973), especially chapt. 7; see Brian M. Linn, "The American Way of War Revisited," *The Journal of Military History*, volume 66, Number 2, April 2002, pages 501–530

and Weigley's response, 331–333; Antulio J. Echevarria II, *Toward an American Way of War* (Carlisle, PA, US Army War College: Strategic Studies Institute, March 2004).

2. Thomas F. Army, Jr., *Engineering Victory: How Technology Won the Civil War* (Baltimore, MD, Johns Hopkins University Press, 2016), part 1; Barton C. Hacker and Margaret Vining, *American Military Technology: The Life Story of a Technology* (Baltimore, Md., The Johns Hopkins University Press, 2006), 30–31; Barton C. Hacker, editor. *Astride Two Worlds: Technology and the American Civil War* (Washington, DC, Smithsonian Institution Scholarly Press, 2016), chapt. 1; James A. Huston, *The Sinews of War: Army Logistics 1775–1953* (Washington, DC; Office of the Chief of Military History, 1966), 71, 76; Jeffrey D. Wert, *Civil War Barons: The Tycoons, Entrepreneurs, Inventors, and Visionaries Who Forged Victory and Saved a Nation* (New York, Da Capo, 2018), prologue, epilogue, postscript.

3. Richard Franklin Bensel, *Yankee Leviathan: The Origins of Central State Authority in America 1859–1877* (Cambridge/New York: Cambridge University Press, 1990), chaps. 1–3; Max M. Edling, *A Hercules in the Cradle: War, Money, and the American State, 1783–1867* (Chicago/London: University of Chicago Press, 2014), chapt. 6, conclusion; Brian Balogh, *A Government Out of Sight: The Mystery of National Authority in Nineteenth Century America* (Cambridge/New York: Cambridge University Press, 2009), chapt. 7; Alan I. Marcus and Howard P. Segal, *Technology in America: A Brief History* (San Diego, CA: Harcourt Brace, Jovanovich, 1989); Hacker and Vining, *American Military Technology*, 33, 34.

4. Allan R. Nevins, *Ordeal of the Union, Volume 2: House Dividing, 1852–1857* (New York, Charles Scribner's, 1947), 243–245 and *The War for The Union, Volume 1: The Improvised War, 1861–1862* (New York, Charles Scribners,1959), v, 342–343; Roy F. Nichols, *The Stakes of Power, 1845–1877* (New York, Hill and Wang, 1961) and *The Disruption of American Democracy* (New York, Macmillan, 1948) which secured the 1949 Pulitzer Prize in history.

5. Marvin A. Kreidberg and Merton G. Henry, *History of Military Mobilization in the United States, 1775–1945* (Washington, DC, US Army Center of Military History, 1986 edition, 6, 17, 138; Nicholas Onuf and Peter Onuf, *Nations, Markets and War: Modern History and the American Civil War* (Charlottesville, VA: University of Virginia Press, 2006), 345; Michael Brem Bonner, *Confederate Political Economy: Creating and Managing a Southern Corporatist Nation* (Baton Rouge, LA, Louisiana State University Press, 2016), introduction and Paul D. Escott, *Military Necessity: Civil-Military Relations in the Confederacy* (Westport, CT, Prager Security International, 2006), preface.

6. Joseph C. G. Kennedy, *Preliminary Report on the Eighth Census, 1860*, [US Cong., 57th, 2d Sess., Senate] (Washington, DC, Government Printing Office, 1862), 118–119, 137.

7. Kreidberg and Henry, *Military Mobilization*, 138; James M. McPherson, *Embattled Rebel: Jefferson Davis as Commander in Chief* (New York, Penguin, 2014), 18–21.

8. Kennedy, *Eighth Census*, 2–12; Army, *Engineering Victory*, conclusion.

9. Merritt Roe Smith, "Yankee Armorers and the Union War Machine," 25–30 in Hacker, editor, *Astride Two Worlds*.

10. Earl J. Hess, *Civil War Logistics: A Study of Military Transportation* (Baton Rouge, LA, Louisiana State University Press, 2017), chaps 3, 4, 5 passim; Seymour E. Goodman, "Information Flow and Field Armies," 87–114 in Hacker, editor, *Astride Two Worlds*.

11. Kennedy, *Eighth Census, 1860*, 103–106, Appendix Table 38, 214–237; George Rogers Taylor, *The Transportation Revolution, 1815–1860* [Volume 4, The Economic History of the United States] (New York, Rinehart and Company, 19561), chaps. 4 and 5; John E. Clark Jr., *Railroads in the Civil War: The Impact of Management on Victory and Defeat* (Baton Rouge, Louisiana State University Press, 2001), introduction; William G. F. Thomas, *The Iron Way: Railroads, the Civil War and the Making of Modern America* (New Haven, CT: Yale University Press, 2011), prologue, chaps. 1, 2; Louis G. Hunter, *Steamboats on Western Rivers: An Economic and Technological History* (Cambridge, MA: Harvard University Press, 1949), part 3 especially; Byrd Douglas, *Steamboatin' on the Cumberland* (Nashville, TN: Tennessee Book Company, 1961), chaps. 1–4, Robert Gudmestad, *Steamboats and the Rise of the Cotton Kingdom* (Baton Rouge, LA: Louisiana State University Press, 2011), 5.

12. Stuart D. Brandes, *Warhogs: A History of War Profits in America* (Lexington, KY, The University Press of Kentucky, 1997), chapt. 4; Marcus Cunliffe, *Soldiers and Civilians: The Martial Spirit in America, 1775–1865* (Boston, MA: Little, Brown, 1968), 413–423; Charles R. Shrader, editor. *United States Army Logistics, 1775–1992* (Washington DC, US Army Center of Military History), 193–194.

13. Lincoln's first inaugural address December 3, 1861 quoted as title for Aaron Sheehan-Dean, *Struggles for a Vast Future* (Botley, Oxfordshire, UK, Osprey, 2006); Donald Stoker, *The Grand Design: Strategy and the U.S. Civil War* (Oxford, UK: Oxford University Press, 2010), 16–17, 19; Kreidberg and Henry, *History of Military Mobilization*, chapt. 5.

14. See John H. Beeler's chapter in Leonard L. Lerwill, *The Personnel Replacement System in the United States Army* (Washington, DC, U. S. Army Center of Military History, 1954), 73.

15. William B. Edwards, *Civil War Guns; The Complete Story of Federal and Confederate Small Arms: Design, Manufacture, Identification, Procurement, Issue, Employment, Effectiveness, and Postwar Disposal* (Harrisburg, PA, Stackpole, 1962), chaps. 21 and 22; John D. Bennett, *The London Confederates: The Officials, Clergy,*

Businessmen and Journalists Who Backed The American South During the Civil War (Jefferson, NC, McFarland, 2008); and R. J. M. Blackett, *Divided Hearts; Britain and the American Civil War* (Baton Rouge, Louisiana State University Press, 2001), chaps. 1, 3; Howard J. Fuller, *Clad in Iron: The American Civil War and the Challenge of British Naval Power* (Annapolis, MD: Naval Institute Press, 2008), 42–43, 81–83, 126–127, 157–158, 174–175, 263–285.

16. Gary W. Gallagher and Joan Waugh, *The American War: A History of the Civil War Era* (State College, PA,FLIP Learning, 2015), 131–139; Richard Franklin Bensel, *Yankee Leviathan: The Origins of Central State Authority in America, 1859–1877* (New York/Cambridge University Press, 1990), 88–237; Brian Balogh, *A Government Out of Sight: The Mystery of National Authority in Nineteenth Century America* (Cambridge/New York: Cambridge University Press, 2009), 285–299; Max M. Edling, *A Hercules in the Cradle: War, Money, and the American State, 1783–1867* (Chicago/London: University of Chicago Press, 2014), chapt. 6; Mark R Wilson, *The Business of Civil War: Military Mobilization and the State, 1861–1865* (Baltimore, MD, Johns Hopkins University Press, 2006).

17. Robert D. Hormats, *The Price of Liberty: Paying for America's Wars* (New York: Henry Holt, 2007), 60–61; Huston, *Sinews of War*, 176.

18. Paul D. Escott, *Military Necessity: Civil-Military Relations in the Confederacy*, Westport, CT, Praeger Security International, 2006), preface, chapt. 2; Michael B. Bonner, "Expedient Corporatism and Confederate Political Economy," *Civil War History* 51, no. 1 (2010), 33–65 as expanded in *Confederate Political Economy: Creating and Managing a Southern Corporatist Nation* (Baton Rouge, Louisiana State University Press, 2016); David T. Gilchrist and W. David Lewis, *Economic Change in the Civil War Era*, Greenville, DE, Eleutherian Mills-Hagley Foundation, 1965), 166–194; J. Matthew Gellman, *The North Fights The Civil War: The Home Front* (Chicago, Ivan Dee, 1994), 93; Louise B. Hill, "State Socialism In The Confederate States of America," *Southern Sketches*, First Series, Number 9 (Charlottesville, Va., The Historical Publishing Co., 1936), 1; Kreidberg and Henry, *Mobilization*, 137; E. Merton Coulter, *The Confederate States of America, 1861–1865* (Baton Rouge, LA, Louisiana State University Press, 1950), chaps. 10–13; Paul A. C. Koistinen, *Beating Plowshares into Swords: the Political Economy, of American Warfare, 1606–1865* (Lawrence, KS: University Press of Kansas, 1996), preface, 102–103, 158; John Solomon Otto, *Southern Agriculture During the Civil War Era, 1860–1880* (Westport, CT, Greenwood Press, 1994), chap. 2; Richard D. Goff, *Confederate Supply* (Durham NC, Duke University Press, 1969), chap 9.

19. Charles R. Shrader, "Field Logistics in the Civil War," in Jay Luvaas and Harold W. Nelson, editors., *The U.S. Army War College Guide to the Battle of Antietam: The Maryland Campaign of 1862* (Carlisle, Pa., South Mountain Press, 1987), 258; Gallagher and Waugh, *American War*, 132

20. Koistinen, *Plowshares into Swords*, 195 as his thorough dissection of the Civil War experience may be followed in chaps. 5–9.

21. Koistinen, *Plowshares into Swords*, chapt. 9, especially pages 228–230.

22. Brandes, *Warhogs*, chapt. 4; "TP," "Champion of the Bureaucrats," *The Pennsylvania Gazette* (Jan/Feb 2015), 21–22; James F. Nagle, *A History of Government Contracting* (Washington, DC, The George Washington University, 1992), 181; Steven A. Bank, Kirk J. Stark and Joseph J. Thorndike, *War and Taxes* (Washington, DC, the Urban Institute Press, 2008), 24–26.

23. Koistinen's comprehensive coverage can be found in *Plowshares into Swords*, chs 5–9, passim; Nagle, *Government Contracting*, 182–198, especially 184–185 and C.M. Culver, *Federal Government Procurement—An Uncharted Course through Turbulent Waters* (McClean, VA, National Contract Management Association, 1984), 2.

24. Kreidberg and Henry, *Mobilization*, chap. 4; Paul A. C. Koistinen, *Beating Plowshares into Swords: The Political Economy of American Warfare, 1601–1865* (Lawrence, KS: University Press of Kansas, 1996), 104–106.

25. Hormats, *The Price of Liberty* chapt. 3 provides a convenient starting point on the issue; Ethan Barnaby Kapstein, *The Political Economy of National Security: A Global Perspective* (New York, NY: McGraw-Hill, 1992), 16.

26. Stephen Daggett, *Costs of Major US Wars* (Washington, Congressional Research Service, 2010), 1 cited by Sarah E. Kreps, *Taxing Wars: The American Way of War Finance and the Decline of Democracy* (Oxford/New York: Oxford University Press, 2018), 77; Huston, *Sinews of War*, 182–182 and James M. McPherson, *Battle Cry of Freedom: The Civil War Era* (New York: Oxford University Press, 1988), 442–447, especially 447–448; Edling, *A Hercules in the Cradle*, 181–221.

27. Keith L. Bryant, Jr. and Henry C. Dethloff, *A History of American Business* (Englewood Cliffs, NJ, Prentice-Hall, 1983), 223–224; Bank, Stark, Thorndike, *War and Taxes*, 26.

28. Hormats, *Price of Liberty*, 74, 78–79, 86–87; McPherson, *Battle Cry of Freedom*, 437–448, esp. 437–438; Bank, Stark, Thorndike, *War and Taxes*, 35–44.

29. Bank, Stark, Thorndike, *War and Taxes*, 26–35, 169, 181 n 15–16, 182 n 35, 183 n 32, 183 n 50; Hormats, *Price of Liberty*, 77–79.

30. Bank, Stark, and Thornton, *War and Taxes*, 183 n. 50; On the tax in kind problem, see Confederate States of America, Office of the President, "Message of the President to House of Representatives, November 11, 1864, 2–5, 18, copy, author's files.

31. Hormats, *Price of Liberty*, 78–79, 87; McPherson, *Battle Cry*, 437–442, especially 437–438; John Steel Gordon, Gordon, *An Empire of Wealth: The Epic History of American Economic Power* (New York, Harper Collins, 2005), 192–197, 199–200, 203; Maury Klein, "The Boys Who Stayed Behind: Northern Industrialists

and the Civil War," in James I. Robertson, Jr. and Richard M. McMurry, editors. *Rank and File: Civil War Essays in Honor of Bell Irvin Wiley* (San Rafael., CA, Presidio, 1976), 137–156; Philip Leigh, *Trading with the Enemy: the Covert Economy During the American Civil War* (Yardley, PA, Westholme, 2014), conclusion.

32. Stanley Lebergott, "Through the Blockade," *Journal of Economic History* 41, no. 4 (December 1981), 867–888, especially 872–873.

33. Edward S. Miller, *Bankrupting the Enemy; The U.S. Financial Siege of Japan Before Pearl Harbor* (Annapolis: Naval Institute Press, 2007), introduction, conclusion.

34. Typescript, 'Letter with Accompanying Currency, John Glenn Hart III—To Whom It May Concern, n.d., author's collection; Mary Elizabeth Massey, *Ersatz in the Confederacy: Shortages and Substitutes on the Southern Homefront* (Columbia, SC: University of South Carolina Press, 1952, 1993; especially chapt. 10; Bell I. Wiley, *The Plain People of the Confederacy* (Baton Rouge, Louisiana State University Press, 1943), chaps. 2 and 3; Charles W. Ramsdell [Wendell H. Stephenson, editor] *Behind the Lines in the Southern Confederacy* (Baton Rouge/London, Louisiana State University Press, 1944/1972), forward especially; William Blair, *Virginia's Private War: Feeding Body and Soul in the Confederacy, 1861–1865* (New York/Oxford: Oxford University Press, 1998) passim.

35. Gordon, *An Empire of Wealth*, 192, 199–200, 203; Leigh, *Trading with the Enemy*, chapt. 9.

36. Mark R. Wilson, *The Business of Civil War: Military Mobilization and the State, 1861–1865* (Baltimore, The Johns Hopkins University Press, 2006), Chapt. 6; for more details, see U.S. Congress, 40th, Second Session, House of Representatives Executive Document 99, *Message from the President of the United States in answer to a resolution of the House of 15th March last* [1867] *asking for information concerning the ordnance department and its transactions* (Washington, Government Printing Office, 1868) published as Stuart C. Mowbray, editor, *Civil War Arms Purchases & Deliveries; A facsimile reprint of the master list of Civil War weapons purchases and deliveries including small arms, cannon, ordnance and projectiles.* Lincoln, RI, Andrew Mowbray Publishers, 200; Stuart C. Mowbray and Jennifer Heroux, editors, *Civil War Arms Makers and their Contracts: A Facsimile Reprint of the Report by the Commission on Ordnance and Ordnance Stores, 1862.* (Lincoln, RI, Andrew Mowbray Publishing, 1998); John H. Tillman, *Civil War Cavalry & Artillery Sabers: A Study of United States Cavalry and Artillery Sabers, 1833–1865.* (Lincoln, RI, Andrew Mowbray Publishers, 2001), introduction; 358–361.Warren Ripley, *Artillery and Ammunition of The Civil War* (New York, Van Nostrand Reinhold Company, 1970) and Merritt Roe Smith, "Yankee Armorers and the Union War Machine," in Hacker, editor, *Astride Two Worlds*, 25–54.

37. Maurice Melton, *Major Military Industries of the Confederate Government*

(Ann Arbor, MI: University Microfilms, 1979), conclusion; Steven A. Walton, "Heavy Artillery Transformed," in Hacker, editor, *Astride Two Worlds*, 55–87.

38. U.S. War Department, *The War of the Rebellion: Official Records of the Union and Confederate Armies* (Washington, DC, Government Printing Office, 19801901), Series 3, Volume 5, page 145; William S. Dutton, *Du Pont: One Hundred and Forty Years* (New Yok, Charles Scribner's Sons, 1949), 90–100.

39. Mary A. DeCredico, *Patriotism for Profit: Georgia's Urban Entrepreneurs and the Confederate War Effort* (Chapel Hill/London: University of North Carolina Press, 1990), chaps. 2 and 3; Martin Rywell, *Confederate Guns and Their Current Prices* (Harriman, TN, Pioneer Press, 10–11; Ken R. Knopp, *Confederate Saddles and Horse Equipment* (Orange, VA, Publishers Press, 2001), 14–15 and *Made In The "C.S.A": Saddle Makers of the* Confederacy (Hattiesburg, MS, By Author, 2003), 9–10, appendices II, III, V; Matthew W. Norman, *Colonel Burton's Spiller and Burr Revolver: An Untimely Venture in Confederate Small-Arms Manufacturing* (Macon, GA, Mercer University Press, 1996) passim; William Harris Bragg, *Griswoldville* (Macon, GA, Mercer University Press, 2000), chaps. 1–3; Ralph W. Donnelly, "Local Defense In The Confederate Munitions Area," in Editors, *Military Affairs Analysis of the Civil War: An Anthology* (Millwood, NY, KTO Press, 1977), 239–251.

40. Melton, *Confederate Military Industries*, 499; Larry J. Daniel and Riley W. Gunter, *Confederate Cannon Foundries* (Union City, TN, Pioneer Press, 1977), iii, 85–90; Ripley, *Artillery and Ammunition* 361–365.

41. Charles Oscar Paullin, *Paullin's History of Naval Administration 1775–1911* (Annapolis, MD, U.S. Naval Institute, 1968), 250, 260, 279; Dana M. Wegner, "The Union Nay, 1861–1865," in Kenneth J. Hagan, editor, In *Peace and War: Interpretations of American Naval History, 1775–1978* (Westport, CT; Greenwood Press, 1978), 124.

42. Confederate Special Orders, Adjutant and Inspector General's Office, Richmond, August 22, 1862, Item 63 and Letter, Secretary of the Navy to ?, February 5, 1862, Item 206, both Catalog Raynor's Historical Collectible Auctions, Burlington, NC, June 2016, pages 16 and 50 respectively.

43. Paullin, *Naval Administration*, 284–285, 293–297, 302–304; Jeffrey M. Dorwart with Jean K. Wolf, *Philadelphia Navy Yard: From the Birth of the US. Navy to the Nuclear Age* (Philadelphia: University of Pennsylvania Press, 2001), 81–92.

44. Paullin, *Naval Administration*, 280, 305–307

45. Paullin, *Naval Administration*, 289–291; Kurt Hackemer, The *U.S. Navy and the Origins of the Military Industrial Complex, 1847–1883* (Annapolis, MD: Naval Institute Press, 2001) chaps. 3, 4, 5.

46. Paullin, *Naval Administration*, 284–288.

47. Hackemer, Origins of the Military-Industrial Complex, conclusion.

48. Thomas R. Heinrich, *Ships for the Seven Seas: Philadelphia Shipbuilding*

in the Age of Industrial Capitalism (Baltimore, Johns Hopkins University Press, 1997), chapt. 2. For the best overall study of Union naval industrialization see William H. Roberts, *Civil War Ironclads: The U.S Navy and Industrial Mobilization* (Baltimore/London, The Johns Hopkins University Press, 2002) and for encapsulated histories of the various types and categories of vessels procured by both sides, see Paul H. Silverstone, *Warships of the Civil War Navies* (Annapolis, Md. Naval Institute Press, 1989); Dorwarts/Wolf, *Philadelphia Navy Yard*, 91–92.).

49. Raimondo Luraghi, *A History of the Confederate Navy* (London, Chatham, 1996), especially chapt. 3; William N. Still, Jr., *Iron Afloat: The Story of the Confederate Armorclads* (Nashville, TN, Vanderbilt University Press, 1971), chaps. 1 and 2; Tom Henderson Wells, *The Confederate Navy: A Study in Organization* (University, AL: University of Alabama Press, 1971), chaps. 7–12; George M. Brooke, Jr., editor, *Ironclads and Big Guns of the Confederacy: The Journal and Letters of John M. Brooke* (Chapel Hill, NC: University of North Carolina Press, 2002), chaps. 5–7.

50. Gordon, *Empire of Wealth*, 201–202.

51. Luraghi, *Confederate Navy*, 35, 54.

52. Joseph W. McGuire, *Business and Society* (New York: McGraw-Hill, 1963), 37; DeCredico, *Patriotism for Profit*, chaps. 2, 3, 4 passim; Michael Thomas Smith, *The Enemy Within: Fears of Corruption in the Civil War North* (Charlottesville, VA: University of Virginia Press, 2011), chap. 1, 4–6. passim.

53. Wilson, *Business of Civil War*, introduction, especially 2; Keith L. Bryant, Jr. and Henry C. Dethloff, *A History of American Business* (Englewood Cliffs, NJ, Prentice Hall, 298), 216–117.

54. Louis M. Hacker, *The Triumph of American Capitalism: The Development of Forces in American History to the Beginning of the Twentieth Century* (New York, NY, Simon and Schuster, 1940), 373; Walter Licht, *Industrializing America: The Nineteenth Century* (Baltimore, MD, Johns Hopkins University Press, 1995), 96–101, esp. 97; George Rogers Taylor, "The National Economy Before and After the Civil War," in Gilchrist and Lewis, editors, *Economic Change in the Civil War Era*, 1–22; Koistinen, *Plowshares into Swords*, 195–196.

55. Robert L. Heilbroner, *The Economic Transformation of America* (New York, NY: Harcourt Brace Jovanovich, 1977), 57–58; Thomas C. Cochran, "Did the Civil War Retard Industrialization?" *Journal of American History* 2 (September 1961), 197–210; Richard D. Brown, *Modernization: the Transformation of American Life, 1600–1865* (New York, NY, Hill and Wang, 1976), especially 176.

56. Huston, *Sinews of War*, 186–187; Samuel Bernard Thompson, *Confederate Purchasing Operations Abroad* (Chapel Hill: University of North Carolina Press, 1935). chaps. 2 and 4 passim.

57. Daniel Faber, *Lincoln's Constitution* (University of Chicago Press, 2003), chaps. 5–8 passim; Daniel W. Hamilton, *The Limits of Sovereignty: Property*

Confiscation in the Union ad Confederacy during the Civil War (Chicago: University of Chicago Press, 2007), chaps. 2–7 passim; Harold Melvin Hyman, *Era of the Oath: Northern Loyalty Tests During the Civil War and Reconstruction* (Philadelphia: University of Pennsylvania Press, 1954), chaps. 1–12 passim; Aaron Sheehan-Dean, *The Calculus of Violence: How Americans Fought the Civil War* (Cambridge, Harvard University Press, 2018) chaps 2, 3, 5 passim; Jonathan M. Steplyk, *Fighting Means Killing: Civil War Soldiers and the Nature of Combat* (Lawrence: University Press of Kansas, 2018), intro, chap. 2, epilogue, passim; Joan E. Cashin, *War Stuff: The Struggle for Human and Environmental Resources in the American Civil War* (New York: Cambridge University Press, 2018), chaps. 3–7 passim; Mark E. Neely Jr., *Lincoln and the Triumph of the Nation: Constitutional Conflict in the American Civil War* (Chapel Hill: University of North Carolina Press, 2011); chaps 2, 3, 7, 8 passim; Mark E. Neely Jr., *The Fate of Liberty: Abraham Lincoln and Civil Liberties* (Oxford: Oxford University Press, 1991), chaps. 1, 3, 8 passim; Christian G. Smith, ed., *Changes in Law and Society during the Civil War and Reconstruction: A Legal History Documentary Reader* (Cambridge, Southern Illinois University Press, 2009), chaps. 2–5 passim.

58. Licht, *Industrializing America*, 97–98; Leigh, *Trading with the Enemy*, conclusion passim.

59. Goodlove Stein Orth quoted in Gordon, *An Empire of Wealth*, 204.

60. Smith, "Yankee Armorers," in *Astride Two Worlds*, ed. Hacker, 48; Kreidberg and Henry, *Military Mobilization*, 139–140; Unknown statistician, unpublished note, "Cost of the Rebellion," undated, author's collection.

61. Wert, *Civil War Barons*, Prologue, Epilogue and Postscript, passim; Koistinen, *Plowshares into* Swords, 278–284; Ian C. Hope, *A Scientific Way of War: Antebellum Military Science, West Point and the Origins of American Military Thought* (Lincoln, NE: University of Nebraska Press, 2015), chap 8, passim.

CHAPTER 4

1. Peter N. Stearns, *The Industrial Revolution in World History* (Boulder: Westview, 1993), 49; Marcus and Segal, *Technology in America*, 129–134; Hacker, ed., *Astride Two Worlds*, ch. 1 passim; Bensel, *Yankee Leviathan*, 418–419.

2. U.S. War Department, *The War of the Rebellion: Official Records of the Union and Confederate Armies*, Ser. 3:5, 145; Lance C. Buhl, "Maintaining 'An American Navy,'" in *In Peace and War: Interpretations of American Naval History, 1775–1978*, ed. Kenneth J. Hagan (Westport: Greenwood Press, 1978), 146.

3. James F. Doster, "The Chattanooga Rolling Mill: An Industrial By-Product of the Civil War," *East Tennessee Historical Society Publications*, no. 36 (1964): 45–55; Edwards, *Civil War Guns*, ch. 33 passim; Nagle, *Government Contracting*,

220–227; Kreidberg and Henry, *Military Mobilization*, 141; Risch, *Quartermaster Support*, 453–456; Robert. W. Coakley, *The Role of Federal Military Forces in Domestic Disorders, 1789–1878* (Washington, U.S. Army Center of Military History, 1988), chaps. 13, 14, 15 and epilogue, passim.

4. Nagle, *Government Contracting*, 221–227; Heather Cox Richardson, *West from Appomattox: The Reconstruction of America After the Civil War* (New Haven: Yale University Press, 2007), ch. 1.

5. Wert, *Civil War Barons*, Epilogue and Postscript.

6. Richardson, *West from Appomattox*, Introduction and Epilogue; Jackson Lears, Introduction, in *Rebirth of a Nation: The Making of Modern America, 1877–1920* (New York: Harper Collins, 2009), passim; Gordon, *Empire of Wealth*, ch. 11; Hormats, *Price of Liberty*, 99; Joseph W. McGuire, *Business and Society* (New York: McGraw Hill, 1963), 36–43.

7. Russell F. Weigley," American Strategy from Its Beginnings Through the First World War," in *Makers of Modern Strategy from Machiavelli to the Nuclear Age*, ed. Peter Paret (Princeton: Princeton University Press, 1986), 436–443 and Weigley, *Towards an American Army: Military Thought from Washington to Marshall*, 1st ed. (New York: Columbia University Press, 1962), 137–161; Buhl, "Maintaining 'An American Navy,'" 147.

8. Robert G. Angevine, *The Railroad and the State: War, Politics and Technology in Nineteenth Century America* (Stanford: Stanford University Press, 2004), chs. 8 and 9, passim, and Conclusion, esp. 192–193.

9. Hacker and Vining, *American Military Technology*, 35; Nagle, *Government Contracting*, 224–227.

10. Mansel G. Blackford and K. Austin Kerr, *Business Enterprise in American History* (Boston: Wadsworth Cengage Learning, 1994), chs. 5 and 6, passim; Paul A. C. Koistinen, *Mobilizing for Modern War: The Political Economy of American Warfare, 1865–1919* (Lawrence: University Press of Kansas, 1997), 9–18.

11. Licht, *Industrializing America: The Nineteenth Century*, chs. 5 and 6, passim; Heilbroner, *Economic Transformation of America*, chs. 4–6, passim; Hacker, *Triumph of American Capitalism*, chs. 25 and 26, passim; Gordon, *Empire of Wealth*, chs. 11–13, passim; Hormats, *Price of Liberty*, ch. 4 passim; Clayton D. Laurie and Ronald H. Cole, *The Role Federal Military Forces in Domestic Disorders, 1877–1945* (Washington, D.C. U.S. Amy Center of Military History, 1997), chaps 1–8 passim; Walter A. McDugall, *Throes of Democracy: The American Civil War Era, 1829–1877* (New York, Harper, 2008), 162–164.

12. Walter LaFeber, *The New Empire: An Interpretation of American Expansion, 1860–1898* (Ithaca, NY, Cornell University Press, 1963), passim; Walter Russell Mead, *Special Providence: American Foreign Policy and How It Changed the World* (New York, Routledge, 2002), 23, 47, 62, 122; Huston, *Sinews of War*, 252; Kreidberg

and Henry, *Mobilization*, 141–179; Marcus and Segal, *Technology in America*, 133. Nagle, *Government Contracting*, 225.

13. no author, *Du Pont: The Autobiography of an American* Company (Wilmington, DE, E. I. Du Pont de Nemours and Company, 1952), 44–45, 50–52; Brandes, *Warhogs*, 109–111; National Endowment for the Humanities, "In Search of New Wars, 'Winding Down'–After Appomattox," *Humanities* 3, no. 3 (June 1973): 1, 2, 5; Nagle, *Government Contracting*, 221–223; United States Congress, 42d, 2d sess., House of Representatives Executive Document 89, *Letter, from the Secretary of War relative to the sale of arms and ordnance stores*, January 24, 1872 (Washington: Government Printing Office, 1872), 1–23; Koistinen, *Mobilizing for Modern War*, chs. 3 and 4, passim; Dutton, *Du Pont*, ch. 5. Edwards, *Civil War Guns*, ch. 33 passim.

14. Joseph Bradley, *Guns for the Tsar: American Technology and the Small Arms Industry in Nineteenth Century Russia* (Dekalb: Northern Illinois University, 1990), chs. 4 and 5, passim.

15. Gluckman, *United States Muskets, Rifles and Carbines*, chs. 5, 6, and Appendix 8, passim (see note 13, ch. 1); also Gluckman, *United States Martial Pistols and Revolvers*, Part 2, ch. 2 passim (see note 13, ch.1); Hacker and Vining, *American Military Technology*, 38–41; Sidney B. Brinckerhoff and Pierce Chamberlin, "The Army's Search for a Repeating Rifle, 1873–1903," *Military Affairs* 32, no. 1 (Spring 1968): 20–30.

16. Nagle, *Government Contracting*, 225; Huston, *Sinews of War*, 255; Nagle, *Government Contracting*, 223–235; Gluckman, *Muskets, Rifles and Carbines*, 274–275; National Endowment for the Humanities, "Winding Down," in *Humanities*, 2, 5 (see note 13).

17. Hacker and Vining, *American Military Technology*, chaps. 2, 3, passim

18. Buhl, "Maintaining 'An American Navy,'" in *In Peace and War*, ed. Hagan, ch. 8 passim (see note 2), and Buhl, "Mariners and Machines: Resistance to Technological Change in the American Navy, 1865–1869," *Journal of American History* 61, no. 3 (December 1974): 703–727; Paullin, *Naval Administration*, ch. 9, esp. 340; Hackemer, *Origins of the Military-Industrial Complex*, ch. 7 passim; Frank M. Bennett, *Steam Navy*, chs. 31–48 passim (see note 58, ch. 2); Harold and Margaret Sprout, *The Rise of American Naval Power 1776–1918* (Princeton: Princeton University Press, 1939), ch. 11 passim; Walter R. Herrick, Jr., *The American Naval Revolution* (Baton Rouge: Louisiana State University Press, 1966), ch. 1 passim; Hacker and Vining, *American Military Technology*, ch. 3 passim; Gluckman, *Muskets, Rifles and Carbines*, 330; Katherine C. Epstein, *Torpedo: Inventing the Military-Industrial Complex in the United States and Great Britain* (Cambridge: Harvard University Press, 2014), ch. 1, esp. 18; Rogers Birnie, Jr., *Gun Making in the United States* (Washington: Government Printing Office, 1918), chaps. 2, 3, 4, 6, 7, appendices A, B, C passim; U.S. Congress, 40th, 3d sess., Rep. Com. No. 266,

Joint Committee on Ordnance, *Report*, February 15, 1869 (Washington, Government Printing Office, 1869); Robert F. Bradford, *Mode of Fabricating the XV-Inch guns Contracted for by the Chief of the Bureau of Ordnance, Navy Department with the "Knap Fort Pitt Foundry," Pittsburg, Pennsylvania, 1870 and 1871* [Naval Ordnance Papers No. 3] (Washington: Government Printing Office, 1872); U.S. Congress, 47th, 1st sess. Senate, Executive Document 178, *Report of the Board on Heavy Ordnance and Projectiles* (Washington; Government Printing Office, 1882); U.S. Congress., 47th, 2d sess. Senate, Report 969, Select Committee on Heavy Ordnance and Projectiles, *Report* February 9, 1883 (Washington: Government Printing Office, 1883); U.S. Congress, 48th, 1st sess. House of Representatives, Executive Document 97, *Report of the Gun Foundry Board*, February 20, 1884 (Washington: Government Printing Office, 1884); U.S. Congress, 49th, 1st sess., Senate, Select Committee on Ordnance and War Ships, *Report* (Washington: Government Printing Office, 1886); Dorwarts and Wolf, *Philadelphia Navy Yard*, 90–98.

19. U.S. Congress, 49th, 1st sess., Senate, Select Committee on Ordnance and War Ships, *Report* (Washington: Government Printing Office, 1886), xiii; Paul E. Pedisch, *Congress Buys a Navy: Politics, Economics, and the Rise of American Naval Power, 1881–1921* (Annapolis: Naval Institute Press, 2016) in toto.

20. Committee on Ordnance and War Ship, *Report*, xiii–xxx.

21. Ibid. xxx; Important works on the development of the steel industry include Duncan Burn, *The Economic History of Steelmaking, 1867–1939* (Cambridge: Cambridge University Press, 1961), books 1 and 2, Peter Temin, *Iron and Steel in Nineteenth Century America: An Economic Inquiry* (Cambridge: MIT Press, 1964), part II, and William T. Hogan, *Economic History of the Iron and Steel Industry in the United States* (Lexington: Lexington Books, 1971) vol. 1, part 2.

22. A. T. Mahan, *The Influence of Sea Power Upon History, 1660–1783* (Boston: Little, Brown, 1890), 25–89; Philip A. Crowl, "Alfred Thayer Mahan: The Naval Historian," in *Makers of Modern Strategy from Machiavelli to the Nuclear Age*, ed. Peter Paret (Princeton: Princeton University Press, 1986), 444–477; Mark Russell Shulman, *Navalism and the Emergence of American Sea Power, 1882–1893* (Annapolis: Naval Institute Press, 1995), 77–84; William H. McNeill, *The Pursuit of Power: Technology, Armed Force, and Society Since A. D. 1000* (Chicago: University of Chicago Press, 1982), chs. 7 and 8, passim; Koistinen, *Mobilizing for Modern War*, 55–58; B. Franklin Cooling, "The Formative Years of the Naval-Industrial Complex: Their Meaning for Studies of Institutions Today," *Naval War College Review* 26 no. 5 (March/April 1975): 53, as well as B. Franklin Cooling, *Gray Steel and Blue Water Navy: The Formative Years of America's Military-Industrial Complex, 1881–1917* (Hamden: Archon Books, 1979), in toto. Also useful are Herrick, *American Naval Revolution*, in toto and Paolo E. Coletta, ed. *American Secretaries of the Navy, Volume 1: 1775–1913* (Annapolis: Naval Institute Press, 1980), 389–522 passim.

23. Benjamin Franklin Cooling, *Benjamin Franklin Tracy: Father of the Modern American Fighting Navy* (Hamden: Archon Books, 1973), chaps. 4, 5 ; U.S. Congress, 51st, 1st sess., House of Representatives, House Executive Documents, *Annual Report of the Secretary of the Navy, 1889* (Washington: Government Printing Office, 1889), 3–6, 10–14 and U.S. Congress, 51st, 1st sess, Senate, Senate Executive Document, *Report of Policy Board*(Washington, Government Printing Office, 1890), 3–7; Walter R. Herrick, "Benjamin F. Tracy," in Coletta, ed., *American Secretaries of the Navy, Volume 1: 1775–1913*, 415–460; Koistinen, *Mobilizing for Modern War*, 26–38.

24. Paul E. Pedisich, *Congress Buys a Navy: Politics, Economics, and the Rise of American Naval Power, 1881–1921* (Annapolis: Naval Institute Press, 2016), 106; Millis, American Military Thought, 226–227.

25. Benjamin Franklin Cooling, *USS Olympia: Herald of Empire* (Annapolis: Naval Institute Press, 2000), chaps. 3, 4, 8 passim; John D. Alden, *American Steel Navy: A Photographic History of the U.S. Navy from the Introduction of the Steel Hull in 1883 to the Cruise of the Great White Fleet, 1907–1909* (Annapolis: Naval Institute Press and New York: American Heritage Press, 1972), 320–331.

26. Stephen Kinzer, *The True Flag: Theodore Roosevelt, Mark Twain, and the Birth of the American Empire* (New York: Henry Holt, 2017), joins others of note like Lears, *Rebirth of a Nation*, chs. 5, 6 and 7, passim; Robert L. Beisner, *From the Old Diplomacy to the New, 1865–1900* (Arlington Heights: Harlan Davidson, 1986), chs.3–6, passim; Howard Jones, *Crucible of Power: A History of American Foreign Relations to 1913* (Wilmington: SR Books, 2007), chs. 10–13, passim; Walter La Feber, *The American Age: U.S. Foreign Policy at Home and Abroad, 1750 to the Present* (New York: W.W. Norton, 1989), chs. 6–8, passim, and his earlier *The New Empire: An Interpretation of American Expansion, 1860–1898* (Ithaca: Cornell University Press, 1963), esp. chs. 3–6, passim; Walter Russell Meade, *Special Providence: American Foreign Policy and How It Changed the World* (New York: Routledge, 2002), chs. 1 and 2, passim; David F. Task, *The War with Spain in 1898* (Lincoln: University of Nebraska Press, 1981); and Richard E. Welch, Jr., *Response to Imperialism: The United States and the Philippine-American War, 1899–1902* (Chapel Hill: University of North Carolina Press, 2016) both in toto.

27. Warren Zimmerman, *First Great Triumph: How Five Americans Made Their Country at World Power* (New York: Farrar, Straus and Giroux, 2002), Introduction, passim; Finley Peter Dunne, *Mr. Dooley in Peace and in War* (Boston: Small, Maynard, 1898), 5, 6.

28. Robert A. Hart, *The Great White Fleet: Its Voyage Around the World 1907–1909* (Boston, Little, Brown,1965) passim; James R. Reckner, *Teddy Roosevelt's Great White Fleet* (Annapolis: Naval Institute Press, 1988), x, xi, ch. 15, passim; Kenneth Wimmel, *Theodore Roosevelt and the Great White Fleet* (Washington, D. C./Brassey's, 1988), in toto, passim

29. Sprout and Sprout, *Rise of American Naval Power*, 259–261, 267 n 58, 285–290, 302–311, 313–317 passim; Brandes, *Warhogs*, 111–120; and Gordon Carpenter O'Gara, *Theodore Roosevelt and the Rise of the Modern Navy* (Princeton: Princeton University Press, 1943) in toto.

30. Hormats, *Price of Liberty*, 94–105.

31. Nagle, *Government Contracting*, esp. 229–231; Reckner, *Great White Fleet*, 65–70; Wimmel, *Roosevelt and the Great White Fleet*, 231–236, 238; Davis, *Navy Second to None*, 183–188; Cooling, *Gray Steel and Blue Water Navy*, 90–97.

32. Nagle, *Government Contracting*, 255–257; Brandes, *Warhogs*, 116–120; Heinrich, *Ships for the Seven Seas*, ch. 5 passim; Newport News Memorandum, n.d. [in 1892], Subject File AC Const.–U.S. Ships 1871–1910 A 2, Folder, Misc. 1871–1910, Record Group 45, National Archives and Records Service, Washington, DC; for Carnegie, see various undated letters such as Andrew Carnegie to W. L. Abbott, October 1889–April 1890, Andrew Carnegie papers, vol. 240, Library of Congress, Washington, DC, cited in Cooling, *Gray Steel and Blue Water Navy*, 96, also see 90–97; Bank, Stark and Thorndike, *War and Taxes*, 50–52.

33. Robert Hessen, *Steel Titan: The Life of Charles M. Schwab* (New York: Oxford University Press, 1975), 217–224; Paolo Colletta, Ed., "Josephus Daniels, 5 March 1913–5 March 1921," in *American Secretaries of the Navy, Volume 2: 1913–1972*, 1st ed. (Annapolis: Naval Institute Press, 1980), 534–535.

34. Nagle, *Government Contracting*, 274–275; Cooling, *Gray Steel and Blue Water Navy*, 203; Hessen, *Steel Titan*, 226; Koistinen, *Mobilizing for Modern War*, 38–40, 48–57; U.S. Navy Department, *Annual Reports, 1913* (Washington: Government Printing Office, 1914), 30–33; Brandes, *Warhogs*, 11–125; Heinrich, *Ships for the Seven Seas*, ch. 5 passim.

35. Nagle, *Government Contracting*, ch. 13; Richard H. Holton, "Business and Government," *Daedalus*, 98, No. 1 (Winter, 21969), 42–43; C.M. Culver, *Federal Government Procurement—An Uncharted Course Through Turbulent Waters* (McLean, VA, National Contract Management Association, 1984), 3; John Micklethwait and Adrian Wooldridge, *The Company: Short History of a Revolutionary Idea* (New York, Random House, 2003), 65–73; Alden, *American Steel Navy*, appendices, 360–382; O'Gara, *Roosevelt and the Rise of the Modern Navy*, 115–126 using statistics in the Secretary of the Navy's *Annual Reports* for 1884–1899 and 1900–1915 and Edward A. Silsby, compiler, *Navy Yearbook, 1920–1921* (Washington, D.C., Government Printing Office, 1922), 805; Letter, D. W. Knox–E. S. Duffield, Navy Department, May 10, 1944, ZV files, Box 11, Shipbuilding, Naval–Submarines–Ind. Histories C2–552, Folder, Ship Force Levels, Center of Naval History, Washington Navy Yard, Washington, D.C.; Heinrich, *Ships for the Seven Seas*, chs. 5 and 6, passim; Brandes, *Warhogs*, ch. 5.

36. Alden, *American Steel Navy*, 234; Hacker and Vining, *American Military Technology*, chap 4, 5, passim; Thomas Schoonover, *Uncle Sam's War of 1898 and*

the Origins of Globalization (Lexington, KY: University Press of Kentucky, 2003), 120–121; Richard W. Turk, "Defending the New Empire, 1900–1914," in *Peace and War: Interpretations of American Naval History, 1775–1978*, ed. Kenneth J. Hagan (Westport, Greenwood Press, 1978), ch. 10.

37. Paullin, *Naval Administration*, 474–475; Cooling, *Gray Steel and Blue Water Navy*, Postscript and Appendix, passim; Alden, *American Steel Navy*, Appendices passim; Epstein, *Torpedo*, chs. 1, 3, 5, and Conclusion, passim.

38. Licht, *Industrializing America*, ch. 6; Heilbroner, *Economic Transformation of America*, chs. 5 and 6, passim; Koistinen, *Mobilizing for Modern War*, part II; Silsby, comp., *Navy Yearbook, 1920–1921*, 805; Cooling, *Gray Steel and Blue Water Navy*, 222–232; Nagle, *Government Contracting*, ch. 12; Coletta, *Secretaries of the Navy*, 431–495; Paullin, *Naval Administration*, chap. 12; Nagle, *Government Contracting*, ch. 10 passim; Cooling, *Gray Steel and Blue Water Navy*, chs. 6 and 7, passim.

39. Silsby, *Navy Yearbook*, 804–806.

40. Heilbroner, *Economic Transformation of America*, 110–112; Nagle, *Government Contracting*, 271–275; Bryant and Dethlof, *History of American Business*, 286, Hormats, *Price of Liberty*, 94–105; Stephen Skowronek, *Building a New American State: The Expansion of National Administrative Capacities, 1877–1920* (New York: Cambridge University Press, 1982), ch. 4; Hugh G.J. Aitken, *Scientific Management in Action: Taylorism at Watertown Arsenal, 1908–1915* (Cambridge, Harvard University Press, 1960), chaps. 3, 4; Epstein, *Torpedo*, chs. 1, 3, and 5, passim; Taylor Peck, *Round Shot to Rockets*, chs. 5 and 6, passim.

41. Nomi Prins, *All the President's Bankers: The Hidden Alliance that Drives American Power* (New York, Nation Books, 2014), 31; Richard H. Holton, "Business and Government," *Daedalus*, 98, no. 1 (winter 1969), 42–43; C.M. Culver, *Federal Government Procurement – An Uncharted Course Through Turbulent Waters* (McLean, Va., National Contract Management Association,1984), 3; John Micklethwait and Adrian Wooldridge, *The Company: A Short History of a Revolutionary Idea* (New York, Random House, 2003), 65–73.

42. Sprout, *American Naval Power*, ch. 16, 17, passim; Davis, *A Navy Second to None*, 183–215.

43. Silsby, *Navy Yearbook, 1920–1921*, 805; Cooling, *Gray Steel and Bluewater Navy*, 222; Bryant and Dehtloff, *History of American Business*, 286–287; Coletta, ed. *Secretaries off the Navy*, II, 431–495 passim.

44. Culver, *Federal Government Procurement*, 3; Taylor Peck, *Round Shot to Rockets*, chs. 5 and 6, passim (see note 36, ch. 2); Epstein, *Torpedo*, chs. 1, 3, and 5, passim; Stephen Skowronek, *Building a New American State*, ch. 4 passim (see note 45); Aitken, *Scientific Management in Action*, chap 3, 4 passim; Hormats, *Price of Liberty*, 94–105, passim.

45. Nagle, *Government Contracting*, ch. 10; Cooling, *Gray Steel and Bluewater Navy*, ch. 6, 7 passim,

46. Sprout and Sprout, *American Naval Power*, 317–329, esp. 326–327; U.S. Navy Department, *Annual Report, 1913*, 30–33, and *1915*, 73–76, and 79–81 (Washington: Government Printing Office, 1913, 1915); U.S. War Department, *Annual Report, 1912 (Washington, Government Printing Office, 1913)*, 71–83, 93–99, and 126–128, and *1916* (Washington, Government Printing Office, 1918), part 1, 155–162; also Leonard Wood, *Our Military History* (Chicago: Reilly & Britton, 1916), 193–213.

47. Nagle, *Government Contracting*, 266–269; Davis, *A Navy Second to None*, 218–232; Hacker and Vining, *American Military Technology*, 45–46, 67.

48. Sprout, *American Naval Power*, 317–324; Koistinen, *Mobilizing for Modern War*, ch. 6.

49. Prins *All the President's Bankers*, 38–47; Koistinen, *Mobilizing for War*, 124–138, passim; Brandes, *Warhogs*, ch. 6 passim.

50. Arthur S. Link, *Woodrow Wilson and the Progressive Era, 1910–1917* (New York, Harper and Row, 1954), ch. 3, 6, passim.

51. Sprout, *American Naval Power*, 332–349 passim; Davis, *Navy Second to None*, 200–232 passim.

52. Sprout, *American Naval Power*, 338–339; Nye committee *Report*. Sen. Rept. 944, part 6, 44. Brandes, *Warhogs*, 116–140; US Congress, 64th, 1st session, *Congressional Record* (Washington, DC, Government Printing Office, 1917), volume 53, 273 dd, 1215, 11312, 11330, 11341, 12669–72, 12672–4, 12679–80, 12683–6, 12697–98, 12698–700, Appendix, 113; *Navy Yearbook, 1916*, 480–481 and *Navy Yearbook, 1917*, 400, 401, 418ff, 426ff, 466, 673.

53. Daniel R. Beaver, *Modernizing the American War Department: Change and Continuity in a Turbulent Era, 1885–1920* (Kent, OH, Kent State University Press, 2006), 68–76 passim; Daniel R. Beaver, *Newton D. Baker and the American War Effort, 1917–1919* (Lincoln, NE: University of Nebraska Press, 1966), ch. 1, passim.

54. Millis, ed. *American Military Thought*, 240–50 passim.

55. Beaver, *Modernizing the American War Department*, 73–74; James A. Huston, *The Sinews of War: Army Logistics, 1775–1958* (Washington, D.C., Office of the Chief of Military History, 1966), 266, 268.

56. Matthew Ware Coulter, *The Senate Munitions Inquiry of the 1930s: Beyond the Merchants of Death* (Westport, CT, Greenwood, 1997), 131; Koistinen, *Mobilizing for War*, 114–138, passim; Prins, *All the President's Bankers*, ch. 2; Brandes, *Warhogs*, ch. 6; Dutton, *Du Pont*, chap. 5.

57. Koistinen, *Mobilizing for War*, 125, table 6.1; David Kennedy, *Over Here; The First World War and American Society* (New York: Oxford University Press, 1980), ch.5.

58. Coulter, *Senate Munitions Inquiry*, 108–124, 140; John E. Wiltz, *In Search*

of Peace: The Senate Munitions Inquiry, 1934–36 (Louisiana State University Press, 1963), 199–201; Koistinen, *Mobilizing for War*, 110, 114–118, 120–138, 178, 189.

59. Koistinen, *Mobilizing for War*, 121–138, passim.

60. *Ibid.*, 126.

61. Coulter, *The Senate Munitions Inquiry*, 109, 130; Koistinen, *Mobilizing for War*, 135–136.

62. Abrahamson, *American Home Front*, 87–90; Koistinen, *Mobilizing for Modern War*, 138–146.

63. Hugh Rockoff, *America's Economic Way of War: War and the US Economy from the Spanish-American War to the Persian Gulf War* (Cambridge: Cambridge University Press, 2012), 99–108.

64. John N. Petrie, *American Neutrality in the 20th Century: The Impossible Dream* (Washington, D.C., National Defense University, 1995), 50; Woodrow Wilson, "An Appeal by the President of the United States to the Citizens of the Republic Requesting Their Assistance in Maintaining a State of Neutrality During the European War," in James D. Richardson, ed. *A Compilation of the Messages and Papers of the Presidents, 1789–1917* (Washington, D.C., By Authority of Congress, 1909–), XII, 7978–7979.

65. Abrahamson, *American Home Front*, 101–102; Aaron L. Friedberg, *In the Shadow of the Garrison State: America's Anti-Statism and Its Cold War Grand Strategy* (Princeton, NJ: Princeton University Press, 2000), 62–66.

66. Nye quoted in Wayne S. Cole, *Senator Gerald P. Nye and American Foreign Relations* (Minneapolis: University of Minnesota Press, 1962), 96; U.S. Cong., 74th 2d sess., *Congressional Record* (1936), 2616–2619, and 10152 and 76th, 1st sess. (1939), 10405–10406 and 78th, 2d sess. (1944), 9686.

67. Millis, *American Military Thought*, 240–350, in toto.

68. Thomas J. Misa, *A Nation of Steel: The Making of Modern America, 1865–1925* (Baltimore, Johns Hopkins University Press, 1995),129–131 quoting "Pilgrim," "The Demands of War Influence the Requirement of Peace," *American Machinist*, 29 (July 19, 1906), 81–82.

CHAPTER 5

1. Grosvenor B. Clarkson, *Industrial America in the World War: The Strategy Behind the Line, 1917–1918* (Boston, Houghton Mifflin, 1923), 3.

2. See Ira Katznelson and Martin Shefter, editors, *Shaped By War And Trade: International Influences on American Political Developments* (Princeton/Oxford: Princeton University Press, 2002), part III; Hugh Rockoff, *America's Economic Way of War: War and the US Economy from the Spanish-American War to the Persian Gulf War* (Cambridge/New York: Cambridge University Press, 2012), chaps. 3–5;

Jerel A. Rosati and James M. Scott, *The Politics of United States Foreign Policy* (Boston, Wadsworth Cenage Learning, 2014 edition), 14–15, 22–24; Frederick S. Weaver, *An Economic History of the United States* (Lanham, MD, Rowman and Littlefield, 2016), chaps. 7 and 8; Mansel G. Blackford and K. Austin Kerr, *Business Enterprise in American History* (Boston, Wadsworth Cenage Learning, 1994), chaps. 7, 8; Keith L. Bryant, Jr. and Henry C. Dethloff, *A History of American Business* (Englewood Cliffs, NJ, Prentice-Hall, 1983), chaps. 10, 16 and 17; Regina Lee Blaszcsyk and Philip B. Scranton, editors. *Major Problems in American Business History* (Boston, Houghton Mifflin, 2006), chaps. 7–10; Howard Zinn and Anthony Arnove, *Voices of a People's History of the United States (New York, Seven Stories Press, 2004),* chaps. 11 and 12; Howard Jones, *Crucible of Power: A History of American Foreign Relations From 1897* (Wilmington, DE, SR Books, 2001) chaps. 1–3; William C. Martel, *Grand Strategy in Theory and Practice: The Need for an Effective American Foreign Policy* (Cambridge/ New York: Cambridge University Press, 2015), chapt. 8; Michael Lind, *The American Way of Strategy* (Oxford/New York: Oxford University Press, 2006), chapt. 11; Eugene R. Wittkopf, Charles W. Kegley, Jr. and James M. Scott, *American Foreign Policy* (Belmont, CA, Wadswoth/Thomson Leaning, 2003), chapt. 3.

    3. Joyce Appleby, *The Relentless Revolution: A History of Capitalism* (New York, W. W. Norton, 2010) 283–287, especially 284; Paul Kennedy, *The Rise and Fall of the Great Powers: Economic Change and Military Conflict from 1500 to 2000* (New York, Random House, 1987), chaps. 5, 6, 7; Philip Scranton and Patrick, Friedenson, *Reimagining Business History* (Baltimore, MD: Johnson Hopkins University Press, 2013), 22–26.

    4. Randolph S. Bourne, "The State," in Carl Resek, editor. *War and the Intellectuals: Essays by Randolph S. Bourne, 1915–1919* (New York, Harper and Row, 1964), 71; Rebecca U. Thorpe, *The American Warfare State: the Domestic Politics of Military Spending* (Chicago/London: University of Chicago Press, 2014), 11; William C. Martel, *Grand Strategy in Theory and Practice: The Need for an Effective American Foreign Policy* (Cambridge/New York: Cambridge University Press, 2015), 222–243; Michael Lind, *The American Way of Strategy* (Oxford/New York: Oxford University Press, 2006), 88–94; Robert J. Art, *A Grand Strategy for America* (Ithaca, NY, Cornell University Press, 2003), 181–191.

    5. Paul A. C. Koistinen, *Mobilizing for War: The Political Economy of American Warfare: 1865–1919* (Lawrence, KS: University Press of Kansas, 1997), 105–198; Nomi Prins, *All The President's Bankers: The Hidden Alliances That Drive American Power* (New York, Nation Books, 2014), chapt. 2.

    6. R. Elberton Smith, *The Army and Economic Mobilization [United States Army in World War II—The War Department]* (Washington, US Army Center of Military History, 1991), 9–27, 37–38; Brigadier General Seth Williams, USMC, "Thoughts on Industrial Mobilization Based on My Experience With the War Industries

Board During 1917–1918," March 25, 1938, Lectures, Army Industrial College, v. 14, 919l, Special Collections, National Defense University Library, Washington, DC; March's comment in U.S. War Department, *Annual Report, 1919* (Washington, DC, Government Printing Office, 1920), 471–478 as reprinted in Walter Millis, editor *American Military Thought* (Indianapolis, Bobbs-Merrill, 1966), 360–362, especially 361.

7. US War Department, *Annual Report, 1919*, in Millis, editor, *American Military Thought*, 356; Benedict Crowell, *America's Munitions 1917–1918* (Washington, Government Printing Office, 1919), 585.

8. Crowell, *America's Munitions*, 32, 33, 36, 54–55, 69, 71, 73, 75. 79, 81, 82, 86, 89, 90, 102, 129–134, 176, 190, 191, 199, 217, 220, 242, 253, 255, 264, 278, 293, 468, 492; see also C. M. Culver, *The Federal Government Procurement—An Uncharted Course Through Turbulent Waters* (McLean, Va., National Contract Management association , 1985), 6; Alan Gropman, editor, *The Big L: American Logistics in World War II* (Washington, National Defense University, 1997), introduction.

9. Marcel Vigneras, *Rearming the French* [United States Army in World War II—Special Studies]. Washington, Center of Military History, United States Army, 1989), 1–6 especially, Table 1; Alan W. Dowd, "Lessons & Leftover from the Great War," *Providence*, III (Fall 2018), 12, 20.

10. Thomas R. Heinrich, *Ships for the Seven Seas: Philadelphia Shipbuilding in the Age of Industrial Capitalism* (Baltimore/London, The Johns Hopkins University Press, chapt. seven, especially, 170; James A. Huston, *The Sinews of War: Army Logistics, 1775–1953* (Washington, DC, Office of the Chief of Military History, 1966), 374–375; Smith, *The Army and Economic Mobilization*, 37–38; Marvin A. Kreidberg and Merton G. Henry, *History of Military Mobilization in the United States Army 1775–1945*. (Washington, D.C., US Army Center of Military History, 1989 edition, Part II, pages 374–375 especially; Geoffrey Perret, *A Country Made by War: From the Revolution to Vietnam—The Story of America's Rise to Power* (New York, Random House, 1989), 322.

11. Alan Gropman, "Industrial Mobilization," in Gropman, editor, *Mobilizing U.S. Industry*, 96, 128–131, 131–145 citing Stephen Donadio, Joan Smith, Susan Mesner, Rebeca Davison, editors, *The New York Public Library Book of Twentieth Century Quotations* (New York, Warner Books, 1992), 184 and Gropman, editor, *The Big L: American Logistics in World War II* (Washington, National Defense University Press, 1997), 59, 89–93.

12. Smith, *Army and Economic Mobilization*, tables 1, 2, 3, pages 6–7.

13. Ronald Schaffer, *America in the Great War: The Rise of the War Welfare State* (New York: Oxford University Press, 1992), chaps. 1 and 2; James L. Abramson, *The American Home Front: Revolutionary War, Civil War, World War I, World War II* (Washington, National Defense University Press, 1983), 137; Francis Walton, *Mir-

acle of *World War II: How American Industry Made Victory Possible* (New York, Macmillan, 1956); 3, 5, 521; Smith, *The Army and Economic Mobilization,* chapt. 1; David Lloyd George, *War Memoirs* (London, Odhams Press, Ltd., 1942), Volume 2, pages 1831, 1833; Arthur Herman, *Freedom's Forge: How American Business Produced Victory in World War II* (New York, Random House, 2013), 335–336.

14. Sarah E. Kreps, *Taxing Wars: The American Way of War Finance and the Decline of Democracy* (Oxford/New York: Oxford University Press, 2018), chapt. 4; Aristide R. Zolberg, "International Engagement and American Democracy; A Comparative Perspective," in Katznelson and Shefter, *Shaped by War and Terade,* 42–43; Aaron L. Friedberg, *In the Shadow of the Garrison States: America's Anti-Statism and Its Cold War Grand Strategy* (Princeton: Princeton University Press, 2000), 62.

15. Kreps, *Taxing Wars,* 94–106; Michael G. Carew, *The Impact of the First World War on U. S. Policymakers: American Strategic and Foreign Policy Formulation, 1938–1942* (Lanham, Md., Lexington Books, 2014), 110–116, 124–128,

16. Thomas H. Russell, et al., *America's War for Humanity: Pictorial History of the World War for Liberty* (New York, L. H. Walter, 1919), 23–24, 29.

17. Russell, *America's War,* 26, 40, 52, 484–488; Schaffer, *American in the Great War,* 213, 14, 218–219,

18. *New York Times* quoted in Hormats, *The Price of Liberty,* 111. On the contest for American minds, see Schaffer, *America in the Great War,* chaps. 1 and 2; Melvin Small, "Woodrow Wilson and U.S. Intervention in World War I," in John M. Carroll and George C. Herring, editors, *Modern American Diplomacy* (Wilmington, DE, SR Books, 1996), 42–43; Kennedy, *Over Here,* chapt. 1; US *Statistical Abstract of the United States,* 1921, 840, 847, 849; Francis G. Walett, *Economic History of the United States* (New York, Barnes and Noble, 1954), 196–197.

19. Hormats, *The Price of Liberty,* 111–133; Steven A. Bank, J. Stark Kirk and Joseph T. Thorndike, *War and Taxes* (Washington, Urban Institute, 2012), chapt. 3; Kreps, *Taxing Wars,* 77–93.

20. Schaffer, *America in the Great War,* 30; Kennedy, *Over Here,* 87–88; Hormats, *Price of Liberty,* 126; Robert L. Morlan, "The Reign of Terror in the Middle West," in Arthur S. Link, editor, *The Impact of World War* I (New York, Harper and Row, 1969), 71–90 and Link's own preliminary comments 4–5.

21. On financing World War II, see Hormats, *Price of Liberty,* chapt. 5 and Stephen A. Bank, Kirk J. Stark and Joseph J. Thorndike, *War and Taxes* (Washington, DC, Urban Institute Press, 2008), chapt. 4; Nomi Prins, *All the President's Bankers: Hidden Alliances that Drive American Power* (New York, Nation Books, 2014), chapt. 2 and 8 especially; and Kreps, *Taxing Wars,* 93–106.

22. Kreps *Taxing Wars,* 105; Hormats, *Price of Liberty,* chapt. 5 and quoting Brownlee on 164; Bank, Kirk and Thorndike, *War and Taxes,* chapt. 4; Walett, *Economic History,* 232; Brandes, *Warhogs,* chaps. 10 and 11.

23. Randolph Bourne, *The State*. (Tucson, AS, Sharp Press, 1998 edition), 9, 21 https://mises.org/library/state; Bourne, [Olaf Hanson, editor] *Randolph Bourne: The Radical Will, Selected Writings, 1909–1918* (Berkeley, CA; University of California Press, 2992 edition), 307–318; Jeffrey M. Dorwart, *Eberstadt and Forrestal; A National Security Partnership, 1909–1949* (College Station, TX, Texas A&M University Press, 1991), 4–6.

24. Adams, Henry, *The Education of . . .* quoted in Glenn Porter, *The Rise of Big Business, 1860–1920* (Wheeling, Ill, Harlan Davidson, 2006 edition), 104; Andrew Latham, "From the 'Armoury System' to 'Agile Manufacturing': Industrial Divides in the History of American Arms," unpublished doctoral dissertation, York University (Canada), 1997), 139–240, chapt. 4.

25. See for instance Mark R. Wilson, *Destructive Creation: American Business and the Winning of World War II* (Philadelphia: University of Pennsylvania Press, 20q6), chaps. 1, 2, introduction, chaps. 1, 2.

26. Huston, *Sinews of War*, 455; U.S. National Archives, *Handbook of Federal World War Agencies and Their Records, 1917–1921* (Washington, Government Printing Office, 1943), vii, appendix; U.S. National Archives, *Federal Records of World War II* (2 volumes). (Washington, Government Printing Office, 1950), ix-xii.

27. The impact on just one English community, already part of the Crown's military-industrial complex can be sensed from David Pom, *A Desirable Neighborhood [History of Enfield, Volume Three—1914 to 1939]* (Enfield, UK, Enfield Preservation Society, 1994), chapt. 1.

28. William H. McNeill, *The Pursuit of Power: Technology, Power, Armed Force and Society since A. D. 1000* (Chicago, IL: University of Chicago Press, 1982 chapt. 9; L. C. Hunter, "Economic Mobilization Planning and National Security (1947–1953), "Publication No. R172, Industrial College of the Armed Forces, Education Division, Washington, D.C., February 1954, 1–4; Koistinen, *Mobilizing For Modern War*, 288 and 370 f. n. 1 citing Ellis W. Hawley, *The New Deal and the Problem of Monopoly: A Study in Economic Ambivalence* (Princeton, NJ: Princeton University Press, 1966), 3–16 and his own earlier viewpoint in "'The Industrial-Military Complex' in Historical Perspective," in *Business History Review,* 61 (Winter 1967), 379–380.

29. McNeill, *Pursuit of Power*, 317, 330, 337

30. Hunter, "Economic Mobilization," 3–4.

31. Colonel F. A. Scott, Lecture, "Industrial Mobilization for a Great War," [1928], Volume 0, Miscellaneous, Army Industrial College Curricular materials, National defense University Library, Washington, DC.

32. Ibid., pp. 2–3; for in-depth insights, see Koistinen, *Mobilizing for Modern War*, chaps. 7–11.

33. Hunter, "Economic Mobilization 4–5; Koistinen, *Mobilizing for Modern War*, chapt. 13.

34. In addition to Koistinen, *Mobilizing for War*, especially part 2; Robert D. Cuff, *The War Industries Board: Business-Government Relations During World War I* (Baltimore, Md., Johns Hopkins University Press), 1973; and Daniel Beaver, *Modernizing the American War Department: Change and Continuity in a Turbulent Era 1885–1920* (Kent, OH, Kent State University Press, 2006), chaps. 4–7, 9–11 and *Newton D. Baker and the American War Effort, 1917–1919* (Lincoln, NE: University of Nebraska Press, 1966), chaps. 3 and 4; Schaffer, *America in the Great War*, chaps. 3, 4; David M. Kennedy, *Over Here: The First World War and American Society* (New York/Oxford: Oxford University Press, 1980); chapt. 2; Brian Waddell, *The War against the New Deal; World War II and American Democracy* (DeKalb, IL Northern Illinois University Press, 2001), 19–25; Gregory Hooks, *Forging the Military-Industrial Complex: World War II's Battle of the Potomac* (Urbana/Chicago: University of Chicago Press, 1991), 75–77; Wilson, *Destructive Creation*, 7–21; Stephen Skowroneck, *Building A New American State: The Expansion of National Administrative Capacities, 1877–1920* (New York/Cambridge: Cambridge University Press, 1982), 241.

35. Thomas K. McCraw, *American Business Since 1920: How It Worked* (Wheeling, Il., Harlan Davidson, 2009 edition), 63; Paul A. C. Koistinen, *Planning War, Pursuing Peace: The Political Economy of American Warfare, 1920–1939* (Lawrence, KS, 1998), 3–4, 319–320; Hunter, "Economic Mobilization," 4–6.

36. U.S. War Department, *Annual Report, 1919*, in Millis. Editor, *American Military Thought*, 351, 358.

37. Benedict Crowell, *America's Munitions, 1917–1918: Report of Benedict Crowell, The Assistant Secretary of War, Director of Munitions* (Washington, Government Printing Office, 2019). Benedict Crowell and Robert Forrest Wilson, *The Giant Hand: Our Mobilization and Control of Industry and Natural Resources, 1917–1918* (New Haven: Yale University Press, 1921); also Crowell and Wilson, *The Armies of Industry: Our Nation's Manufacture of Munitions for a World in Arms, 1917–1918* (New Haven: Yale University Press, 1921), vol. 1.

38. U.S. War Department, Report of Chief of Staff Peyton C. March, 1919 in Walter Millis, ed. *American Military Thought (*Indianapolis, Bobbs-Merrill, 1966) 350–373; McNeill, *Pursuit of Power*, 345–346; W. Michael Hix, et al., *Rethinking Governance of the Army's Arsenals and Ammunition Plants* (Santa Monica, CA, Rand, 2003, 22–25; The History Factory, "NDIA History Snapshots," *National Defense*, volume 103, no. 782 (January 2019), 7; Jordan A. Schwarz, *The Speculator: Bernard M. Baruch in Washington 1917–1865* (Chapel Hill: University of North Carolina Press, 1981), 335.

39. Allen Kaufmann, "Assembling America's Private Arsenal for Democracy, 1920–1961," *Business and Economic History*, volume 236, number 1 (Fall 1997), 252–264; Charles Evans Hughes, Remarks to Conference on the Limitation of

Armament," 1921, U.S Cong., 67th, 2d sess, Senate Docs., 42–49 in Millis, *American Military Thought*, 363–373 as well as Morrow Board, "*Aircraft in National Defense, 1925,U.S. Cong., 69th, First sess.*, Senate Documents, also in Millis, *American Military Thought*, 374–398.

40. U.S. Cong., 74th, 2d session, Senate Report 944, *Report on Munitions Industry* (Washington, DC, Government Printing Office 1936, parts 1–5; Newton D. Baker, *Report of the War Department Special Committee on Army Air Corps* (Washington, D.C. Government Printing Office, 1934), 61–75 in Millis, *American Military Thought*, 398–417; George T. Davis, *A Navy Second To None: The Development of Modern American Naval Policy* (New York: Harcourt, Brace and Company, 1940), chaps XII–XIV passim; Matthew Ware Coulter *The Senate Munitions Inquiry of the 1930s: Beyond the Merchants of Death* (Westport, CT, Greenwood Press,1997), chap. 3- 5 passim.

41. Koistinen, *Planning War, Pursuing Peace*, ch. 1–4 passim; Dorwart, *Eberstadt and Forrestal*, chs 1–3 passim.

42. Koistinen, Ibid., xv, 45–47, chs. 1, 2, 3, 4 passim

43. Leuchtenburg, "Impact on Political Economy," 60–70, passim.

44. Leuchtenburg, "Impact on Political Economy," 60–70; F.A. Scott, "Industrial Mobilization for a Great War," lecture typescript (1928?), volume 0, Miscellaneous, Army Industrial College Archives, National Defense University Library, Fort McNair, Washington, DC; William Dutton, *Du Pont: One Hundred and Twenty Years* (New York, Charles Scribers, 1949), chs. 7, 7 passim.

45. Brandes, *Warhogs*, chapt. 8; Mathew Ware Coulter, *The Senate Munitions Inquiry of the 1930s: Beyond the Merchants of Death* (Westport, CT, Greenwood Press, 1997); Koistinen, *Planning War, Pursuing Peace*, 177–178, 209–210.

46. Hyde, Arsenal of Democracy, 4–5.

47. Brandes, *Warhogs*, 198, 199–205.

48. U.S. Cong., 74th, 2d sess. Sen. Rept. 944, Special Committee on Investigation of the Munitions Industry United States Senate, *Report* and *Hearings* 1934–1936. (Washington, Government Printing Office, 1936), in toto; John E. Wiltz, *In Search of Peace: The Senate Munitions Inquiry, 1934–36* (Baton Rouge, Louisiana State University Press, 1963), in toto; Wayne S. Cole, *Senator Gerald P/ Nye and American Foreign Relations* (Minneapolis: University of Minnesota Press, 1962), 91–92, 65–96 passim; Senate Munitions Inquiry, In toto.

49. Coulter, *Senate Munitions Inquiry*, ch.3 and 4 passim; Koistinen, *Palling War, Pursuing Peace*, ch. 14.

50. Dorwart and Wolf, *The Philadelphia Navy Yard*, chapt. 9.

51. Brandes, *Warhogs* chaps. 10, 11, especially 226 and 261–262; Koistinen, *Planning War, Pursuing Peace*, 253–256, 318.

52. William Woodring, *Annual Report of the Secretary of War, 1938*. (Wash-

ington, Government Printing Office, 1939), 1–6, 29- 35, in Walter Millis, *American Military Thought.* (Indianapolis, Bobbs-Merrill, 1966), 418–435 Henry G. Gole, *The Road to Rainbow: Army Planning for Global War, 1934–1940* (Annapolis, MD: Naval Institute Press, 2003), especially introduction and conclusion as well as Charles E. Kilpatrick, *An Unknown Future and A Doubtful Present: Writing the Victory Plan of 1941* (Washington DC, U.S. Army Center of Military History, 1992); Hunter, *Economic Mobilization Planning,* 7–18.

53. Dorwart and Wolf, *Philadelphia Navy Yard,* chapt. 9; Rodney K. Watterson, *32 in '44: Building the Portsmouth Submarine Fleet in World War II* (Annapolis, Md. Naval Institute Press, 2011), 7–14; Alan Beyerchen, "From Radio to Radar: Interwar Military Adaptation to Technological Change in Germany, the United Kingdom and the United States," in Williamson Murray and Alan R. Millett, editors, *Military Innovation in the Interwar Period* Cambridge, UK/New York: Cambridge University Press, 1996), 287; Thomas C. Hone, Norman Friedman and Mark D. Mandeles, *American and British Aircraft Carrier Development, 1919–1942* (Annapolis, Md. Naval Institute Press, 1999); Barton C. Hacker and Margaret Vining, *American Military Technology: The Life Story of Technology* (Baltimore, Md., Johns Hopkins University Press, 2006), chapt. 6; Theodore W. Bauer, *History of the Industrial College of the Armed Forces, 1924–1982* (Washington DC, Alumni Association of the Industrial College of the Armed Forces, 1983), chaps. 1, 2.

54. Kreidberg and Henry, *History of Military Mobilization,* part 3; Alan Gropman, *Mobilizing U.S. Industry in World War II: Myth and Reality* (Washington, Institute for National Security Studies, National Defense University, August 1996), chaps. 1–4; US Cong., 74th, 1st sess., Senate Committee Print Number 2, *Industrial Mobilization Plan Revised, 1933* (Washington, Government Printing Office, 1935); US War Department, Assistant Secretary of War, *Army Extension Course, Special Text No. 1229, Industrial Mobilization (Procurement of Munitions- Office of the Assistant Secretary of War* (Washington, Government Printing Office, 1934); Charles Lipsett, *U.S. War Surplus' Its Source and Distribution, 1917–1924* (New York, Atlas Publishing Company, 1924); US War Department, Ordnance Department, Requirements, Statistics and Progress Section, compiler, *Directory of Ordnance Establishments, November 1, 1920* and *March 15, 1924* mimeographs (Washington, War Department, 1920, 1924 respectively); Dorothy B. Howard, "Disposition of Artillery Plants: World War I," unpublished monograph # 76, "Disposition of Five Du Pont Munitions Plants, World War I, 1918–1926," unpublished monograph #77 and "History and Disposition of a Powder Plant Project, Nitro, West Virginia, 1917–1942," unpublished monograph # 78 (Washington, DC, U.S. Department of Labor, Bureau of Labor Statistics, Employment and Occupational Outlook Branch, 1944), 45.

55. Bernard M. Baruch, "Taking the Profit Out of War: Suggested Policies to provide, without change in our Constitution for Industrial Mobilization,

Elimination of Profiteering and Equalization of the Burdens of War," A Memorandum to Joint Congressional and Cabinet Commission Constituted pursuant to Public resolution No. 98, 71st Congress (Washington, Government Printing Office, 1960), 2; Bernard M. Baruch, *Baruch: The Public Years*, New York, Holt, Rinehart and Winston, 1960), chaps. 2-8, 15; Kreidberg and Henry, *History of Military Mobilization*, chaps. 12-16.

56. Edmund G. Love, *Arsenic and Red Tape*, New York: Harcourt, Brace, 1960); concerning arsenal of democracy, see Gavin J. Bailey, *The Arsenal of Democracy: Aircraft Supply and the Anglo-American Alliance, 1938–1942*. (Edinburgh, UK, Edinburgh University Press, 2013), chaps 2 -8 passim; Hunter, *Economic* Mobilization *Planning,* 16–18.

57. Bruce Catton, *The War Lords of Washington* (New York: Harcourt, Brace, 1948); John Morton Blum, *V Was For Victory, Politics and American Culture During World War II* (New York: Harcourt Brace Jovanovich, 1976), ch. 4; Wilson, *Creative Destruction*, ch. 2; Koistinen, *Planning War, Pursuing Peace*, ch. 2 and *Arsenal of World War II: The Political Economy of American Warfare, 1940–1945* (Lawrence, KS University Press of Kansas, 2004), in toto; Gregory Hooks, *Forging the Military-Industrial Complex: World War II's Battle of the Potomac* (Urbana/Chicago: University of Chicago Press, 1991), 338; Brian Waddell, *The War Against the New Deal*, chaps 1–4 and *Toward the National Security Security State: Civil-Military Relations* (Westport, CT, Prager Security International, 2008), chaps 1–4; Richard R. Lingerman, *Don't You Know There's a War On? The American Home Front, 1941–1945* (New York, Putman's 1976), chaps, 3, 4, 5; Latham, "Armoury System to Agile Manufacturing, 139–140, 175–178; Samuel P. Huntington, *The Soldier and the State: The Theory and Politics of Civil-Military Relations* (New York, Vantage Books, 1957), 338.

58. Barton C. Hacker and Margaret Vining, *American Military Technology: The Life Story of a Technology*, Baltimore, Johns Hopkins University Press, 2006), 53; Charles K. Hyde, *Arsenal of Democracy: The American Automobile Industry in World War II* (Detroit, Wayne State University Press, 2013), ch. 1–7 passim; Arthur Herman, *Freedoms Forge: How American Business Produced Victory in World War II* (New York, Random House, 2012), chaps 1–18; Michael W. R. Davis, *Detroit's Wartime Industry: Arsenal of Democracy* [Images of America] (Charleston, SC, Arcadia, 2007).

59. Koistinen, *Mobilizing For Modern War*, ch. 11; Maury Klein, *A Call To Arms: Mobilizing America For World War II* (New York, Bloomsbury, 2013), in toto; Blum, *V Was For Victory*, ch 4 and Mark R. Wilson, *Destructive Creation: American Business and the Winning of World War II* (Philadelphia: University of Pennsylvania, 2016. See also Donald L. Losman, Irene Kyriakopoulos and J. Dawson Ahalt, "The Economics of America's World War II Mobilization," in Gropman, *The Big "L,"* 145–192; Gropman, *Mobilizing U.S. Industry in World War II*, chapt.

10 especially; Huston, *Sinews of* War, chapt. XX and XXVIII; Smith, *the Army and Economic Mobilization*, chapt. XXX.; Kreidberg and Henry, *History of Military Mobilization*, par 4; Abrahamson, *American Home Front*, chapt. 4; Blum, *V Was for Victory*, chapt. 4.

60. Hyde, *Arsenal of Democracy*, 19.

61. James F. Nagle, *A History of Government Contracting* (Washington, DC, The George Washington University, 1992), 286–296; Thomas K. McCraw, *American Business Since 1920: How It Worked* (Wheeling, Il, Harlan Davidson, 2009 edition), 65–66.

62. Abrahamson, *The American Home Front*, 133; Albert A. Blum, "Roosevelt, the M-Day Plans, and the Military-Industrial Complex, *Military Affairs* 36 (April 1972), 44–46' Harry B. Yoshpe, "Economic Mobilization Planning between the Two World Wars," *Military Affairs*, 15 (Winter 1951), 201–204.

63. National Archives, *Federal Records of World War II*, 124–125.

64. Abrahamson, *the American Home Front*, 134–136; Richard Polenburg, *War and Society: The United States, 1941–1945* (Philadelphia, J. B. Lippincott, 1972), 9–13.

65. Koistinen, *Arsenal of World War II*, 67, 131, 266; Michael G. Carew, *Becoming the Arsenal: The American Industrial Mobilization for World War II, 1938–1942* (Lanham, MD: University Press of America, 2010), 206, 225–227; Hormats, *The Price of Liberty*, 145; Bank, Stark and Thorndike, *War and Taxes*, 85–90; Bailey, *Arsenal of Democracy*, ch. 4.

66. *McCraw, American Business Since 1920*, Alan Gropman, "Introduction and ch. 1, Industrial Mobilization," xiii–97 and Anthony W. Gray, Jr., "Joint Logistics in the Pacific Theater," ch. 6, 293–339 in Gropman, *The BIG L: American Logistics in World War II*.

67. Abrahamson, *American Home Front*, 136; Hyde, *Arsenal of Democracy*, ch 1.

68. Abrahamson, *American Home Front*, 136.

69. National Archives, *Federal Records of World War II*, 154, 165–168, 331–334, 630; R. Cuff, "From the Controlled Materials Plan to the Defense Materials System, 1942–1953," *Military Affairs*, volume 51, number 1 (January 1987), 1–6.

70. Hyde, *Arsenal of Democracy: The American Automobile Industry in World War* II, chaps. 1, 2 passim; Wayne D. Rasmussen, editor, *Agriculture in the United States: A Documentary* History. 4 volumes (New York: Random House, 1975), vol. 4, pp. 188–194; US Department of Agriculture. *Century of Service: The First 100 years of the United States Department of* Agriculture (Washington, Department of Agriculture, 1963), 273–323; National Archives, *Federal Records of World War II*, 574, 630

71. Stimson quoted in Kristine, *The Hammer and the Sword*, 580; Catton, *Warlords of Washington*, 29–30; financial editor of *New York* Sun quoted in Brian

Waddell, *The War Against the New Deal: World War II and American Democracy* (DeKalb, IL, Northern Illinois University Press, 2001), 54–55; Gregory Hooks, *Forging the Military-Industrial Complex: World War II's Battle of the Potomac* (Urbana/Chicago: University of Illinois Press, 11991), chs. 1–6 passim.

72. Keith L. Bryant Jr. and Henry C. Dethloff, *History of American Business* (Englewood Cliffs, NJ, Prentice Hall) 133–148, 289, 294–295; McCraw, *American Business Since 1920: How It Worked*, 13–15, 78–81.

73. Hyde, *Arsenal of Democracy: The American Automobile Industry*, chaps. 1–8 inter alia; Herman, *Freedom's Forge*; Michael W. R. Davis, *Detroit's Wartime Industry, Arsenal of Democracy* [Images of America] (Charleston, SC, Arcadia, 2007), chaps. 2, 3, 8.

74. See Thomas Heinrich, "'We Can Build Anything at Navy Yards:' Warship Construction in Government Yards and the Political Economy of American Naval Shipbuilding, 1928–1945," *International Journal of Maritime History*, XXIC, No. 2 (December 2012), especially 155, 178; Heinrich "Fighting Ships that Require Knowledge and Experience: Industrial Mobilization in American Naval Shipbuilding, 1940–1945," *Business History Review*, 88 (Summer 2014), 273–301 and Heinrich, "Jack of all Trades: Cramp Shipbuilding, Mixed Production, and the Limits of Flexible Specialization in American Warship Construction, 1940–1945," (New York: Oxford University Press/Business History Conference, 2010), 275–314, passim; Watterson, *32 in 44'*, foreword, conclusion; Hyde, *Arsenal of Democracy*, ch. 9; Dorwart and Wolf, *Philadelphia Navy Yard*, ch. 8.

75. Heinrich, *Ships for the Seven Seas*, ch. 7, and pages 164, 195; Bryant, Jr. and Dethloff, *History of American Business*, 291–293.

76. Heinrich, *Ships for the Seven Seas*, 223–224, ch. 8, and epilogue; Frederick C. Lane, *Ships for Victory: A History of Shipbuilding under the U.S. Maritime Commission in World War II* (Baltimore, MD, The Johns Hopkins University Press, 1951, passim.

77. Robert P. Patterson [Brian Waddell, editor] *Arming the Nation for War: Mobilization, Supply and the American War Effort in World War II* (Knoxville, TN University of Tennessee Press, 2014), chaps. 1 and 2; War Department Public Relations releases, January 18–24, 1941, mimeograph copies, author's personal files; Hyde, *Arsenal of Democracy*, chaps. 3 and 4.

78. Patterson, *Ibid*, 22–27; Leo M. Cherne, *Adjusting Your Business to War* (New York/Washington, The Research Institute of America, 1939, 1940) passim and *Your Business Goes to War* (Boston, Houghton Mifflin, 1942), passim

79. War Department Press Release, "Construction Under Defense Plant Corporation Agreements," Number 81, January 24, 1941, Mimeograph copy, Author's files; Patterson, *Arming the Nation for War*, 27–28.

80. Patterson, *Arming the Nation for War*, 33–35, 246–247 f.n. 35.

81. Deborah L. McConnel, "Lou Cretia Owen and the Old Hickory Munitions Plant During World War I," *Tennessee Historical Quarterly*, v. 58, no. 2 (Summer 1999), 228–239; Thomas Bruscino, *A Nation Forged in War: How World War II Taught Americans to Get Along* (Knoxville: University of Tennessee Press, 2010), especially chaps. 1, 7, conclusion; Kennedy, *Over Here*, passim.

82. Tom Brokaw, *The Greatest Generation* (New York, Random House, 1998), in toto; Bruscino, *A Nation Forged in War*, especially chaps. 1, 7 and conclusion; and sample issues of *Douglas Airview*, company organ of the Douglas Aircraft company, volume IX (1942) and XI (1944) for breadth and variety of topics directed at that firm's war workers; Kevin A. Thornton and Dale Prentiss, *Tanks and Industry: The Detroit Arsenal, 1940–1954* [A TASCOM History Office Publication] Waren, MI, U.S. Army Tank-automotive and Armaments Command, History Office, 1995), 32–33, 42–46.

83. See Douglas's editorials in *Douglas Airview*, IX, # 3, 1942, 3 and XI (February, 1944), # 2, and volumes IX (1942) and XI (1944).

84. *Douglas Airview*, IX, # 3, 1942, 1–6 inter alia as well as front and back covers.

85. *Douglas Airview*, XI (February, 1944), # 2, 1–42 inter alia as well as front and back covers.

86. Hyde, *Arsenal of Democracy: The American Automobile Industry*, chapt. eight; Gerald D. Nash, *The American West Transformed: The Impact of the Second World War* (Lincoln, NE: University of Nebraska Press, 1985), especially parts 1 and 3 and *World War II and the West: Reshaping the Economy*, Lincoln, NE: University of Nebraska Press, 1990), chaps. 1 and 11.

87. Nash, *The American West Transformed* and *World War II and the West* (Lincoln, NE: University of Nebraska Press, 1990; Thornton and Prentiss, *Tanks and Industry*, 55–56.

88. I. B. Holley, Jr., *Ideas and Weapons: Exploitation of the Aerial Weapon By the United States During World War I; A Study in the Relationships of Technological Advance, Military Doctrine, and the Development of Weapons*. (New Haven, CT: Yale University Press, 1953, reprint Washington DC, Office of Air Force History, 1983), v; Hacker and Vining, *American Military Technology*, 79.

89. Smith, *The Army and Economic Mobilization*, Introduction, especially 3–8, 28–31.

90. Barton C. Hacker and Margaret Vining, *American Military Technology: The Life Story of a Technology* (Baltimore, Johns Hopkins University Press, 2006), 65, 72–78; also Joel Davidson, "World War II and the Birth of the Military-Industrial Complex," in Regina Lee Blaszczyk and Philp B Scranton, editors, *Major Problems in American Business History* (Boston, Houghton Mifflin, 2006), 366–371.

91. Hacker and Vining, *American Military Technology*, chapt. 6; Davidson, "World War II," 370.

92. Davidson, "World War II," 370–371. On the Manhattan Project, see F. G.

Gosling, *The Manhattan Project: Science in the Second World War* (Washington, Department of Energy, August 1990); Vince C. Jones, *The Army and the Atomic Bomb [United States Army in World War II, Special Studies]* (Washington, United states Army Center of Military History, 1985); Richard G. Hewlett and Oscar Anderson, Jr., *The New World, 1939–1946 [A History of the Atomic Energy Commission*, Volume I] (University Park, Pennsylvania State University Press, 1962); Stephen I. Schwartz, editor, *Atomic Audit: The Costs and Consequences of U.S. Nuclear Weapons Since 1940* (Washington, Brookings Institution Press, 1998).

93. John H. Ohl [Clayton D. Laurie, editor], *Industrialists in Olive Drab: The Emergency Operation of Private Industries During World War II* (Washington, Center of Military History, United States Army, 1999), Conclusion, pp. 281–283 and Appendices A and B, pp. 315–320; Koistinen, *Arsenal of World War II*, chapt. 18; Davidson, "World War II," 367. 371.

94. McCraw, *American Business Since 1920*, 65; George Frank Lord, "War Will Make US Plan Advertising Further Ahead: The Advertiser Will Dig Deeper and Build Bigger," *Printer's Ink*, volume 102, number 10 (March 7, 1918, 25–26 in Blaszcsyk and Scranton, *Problems in American Business History*, 301–302; Dutton, *Du Pont*, 378.

CHAPTER 6

1. C. A. Mosher, "Lest We Forget," Oberlin (OH) *News Tribune*, Number 8, 1941.

2. Chairman, War Production Board, *Report: Wartime Production Achievements and Reconversion Outlook, October 9, 1945* (Washington, Government Printing Office, 1945), 7–9; Roderick L. Vawter, *Industrial Mobilization: The Relevant History* (Washington, National Defense University, 1983 edition, 7–8; Francis Walton, *Miracle of World War II: How American Industry Made Victory Possible* (New York, Macmillan, 1956), 5, 521; James L. Abrahamson, *The American Home Front: Revolutionary War, Civil War, World War I, World War II* (Washington, National Defense University Press, 1983) chapt. 4; Alan L. Gropman, *Mobilizing U.S. Industry in World War I* ([McNair Paper 50] (Washington, Institute for Strategic Studies, National Defense University, 1996), chaps. 8, 9 and pages 1241–165.

3. Hugh Rockoff, *America's Economic Way of War: War and the US Economy from the Spanish-American War to the Persian Gulf War* (Cambridge/New York: Cambridge University Press, 2012), 237–241; on reconversion see Mark R. Wilson, *Destructive Creation: American Business and the Winning of World War II* (Philadelphia: University of Pennsylvania Press, 2016), chap. 6; U.S. Department of the Treasury, Office of Contract Settlement, *A History of War Contract Terminations and Settlements* (Washington, July 1947), 1–66.

4. James M. Nagle, *A History of Government Contracting* (Washington,

George Washington University, 1992), 462–467; C. M. Culver, *Federal Government Procurement—An Uncharted Course Through Turbulent Waters* (McLean, Va., National Contract Management Association, 1984), 13; Vince C. Jones, *Manhattan: The Army and the Atomic Bomb [United States Army in World War II—Special Studies]* (Washington, US Army Center of Military History, 1988), chaps. 27 and 28; F. G. Gosling, *The Manhattan Project: Science in the Second World War* (Washington, Department of Energy, August 1990), part VI; Regina Lee Blaszcsyk and Philip B. Scranton, *Major Problems in American Business History* (Boston, Houghton Mifflin, 2006), 371; Michael W. Davis, *Detroit's Wartime Industry: Arsenal of Democracy [Images of America]* (Charleston, SC, Arcadia Publishing, 2007); 124–126; Kevin Thornton and Dale Prentiss, *Tanks and Industry: The Detroit Arsenal, 1940–1954* [A TACOM History Office Publication, 1995] (Warren, MI, U.S. Army Tank-automotive and Armaments Command, 1995), 53–57.

5. Louis C. Hunter, *Economic Mobilization Planning and National Security (1947–1953)* [Publication R172] (Washington, D.C, Industrial College of the Armed Forces, February 1954), 46–50.

6. Hunter, *Economic Mobilization* Planning, 22–38; Robert D. Hormats, *The Price of Liberty: Paying for America's Wars* (New York: Henry Holt, 2007), 178; Vawter, *Industrial Mobilization*, 8–12; The Munitions Board, National Military Establishment, *Report to the Congress on the National Industrial Reserve* (Washington, National Military Establishment, 17 March 1949), chaps. 1–3 passim.; Barton C. Hacker and Margaret Vining, *American Military Technology: The Life Story of a Technology* (Baltimore. Johns Hopkins University Press, 2006), chap 8 passim.

7. Hunter, *Economic Mobilization Planning*, chaps III, IV and V passim; US Congress, 80th, First session, *United Statutes at Large*, LXI, 496–507, in Walter R. Millis, "Congress Provides for the National Security," *American Military Thought* (Indianapolis, Bobbs-Merrill, 1966), 463–479; Herbert Hoover, *The Hoover Commission Report on Organization of the Executive Branch of the Government* (New York, McGraw-Hill, 1949) chap. 8, esp. pp.196–197.

8. Thomas K. McCraw, *American Business Since 1920: How It Worked* (Wheeling, IL, Harlan Davidson, 2009 edition), 79–83; Allen Kaufman, "Assembling America's Private Arsenal for Democracy, 1920–1961," *Business and Economic History*, Volume 26, number 1 (Fall 1997), 260–261.

9. Robert L. Heilbroner, *The Economic Transformation of America* (New York: Henry Holt, 2007), 178; Keith L. Bryant, Jr. and Henry C. Dethloff, *A History of American* Business (Englewood Cliffs, NJ, Prentice Hall, 1983), 294–296.Vawter, *Industrial Mobilization*, 8–12.

10. Rockoff, *America's Economic Way of War*, 265; Jerel A. Rosati and James M. Scott, *The Politics of United States Foreign Policy* (Boston, Wadsworth, 2014 edition), 26–27. See also Hal C. Brands, *What Good is Grand Strategy? Power and*

Purpose in American Statecraft From Harry S. Truman to George W. Bush (Ithaca, NY: Cornell University Press, 2014), chaps. 1–3; Colin Dueck, *Reluctant Crusaders' Power, Culture, and Change in American Grand Strategy* (Princeton: Princeton University Press,2006), chapt. four; Michael Lind, *The American Way of Strategy: U.S. Foreign Policy and the American Way of Life* (Oxford, UK: Oxford University Press, 2006), chapt. 6 and 7; William C. Martel, *Grand Strategy in Theory and Practice: The Need for an Effective American Foreign Policy* (Cambridge, UK and New York: Cambridge University Press, 2015), chapt. 9; Richard Crockatt, *The Fifty Years War: The United States and the Soviet Union in World Politics, 1941–1991* (London and New York, Routledge, 1995); Julian E. Zelizer, *Arsenal of Democracy: The Politics of National Security—From World War II To The War on Terrorism* (New York, Basic Books, 2010), chaps. 4, 5, 6.

11. John Lewis Gaddis, *Strategies of Containment: A Critical Appraisal of Postwar American National Security* Policy (Oxford/New York: Oxford University Press, 1982), chaps. 1–4; Steven A. Bank, Kirk J. Stark, Joseph J. Thorndike, *War and Taxes* (Washington, The Urban Institute Press, 2008), 110–111

12. Two studies are critical to this period, S. Nelson Drew, editor, *NSC-68: Forging the Strategy of Containment with Analyses by Paul H. Nitze* (Washington, National Defense University, 1994), 1–16, 33–99 for the basic study, 98–130 for the "family" labeled NSC 68–1 to NSC 68/4.

13. Drew, *NSC-68*, 49–50, 52.

14. Drew, *NSC-68*, 58–62.

15. Harry S. Truman, "Radio and Television Report to the American People on the National Emergency, December 25, 1950," *Public Papers of the Presidents: Harry S. Truman, 1950* (Washington, Government Printing Officer, 1965), 742–746; See Drew, *NSC-68*, 33–130, on war financing and costs, see Rockoff, *America's Economic Way of War*, 246–259, especially 254–256.

16. Drew, *NSC-68*, 115–120; Truman, "White House Statement Concerning a Meeting with Congressional Leaders to Discuss the National Emergency, December 13, 1950," *Public Papers: Truman*, 741.

17. Especially informative are Elaine Tyler May, *Fortress America: How We Embraced Fear and Abandoned Democracy* (New York, Basic Books, 2017), chapt. 1; Aaron L. Friedberg, *In the Shadow of the Garrison States: America's Anti-Statism and Its Cold War Grand Strategy* (Princeton, NJ: Princeton University Press, 2000), 58–61.

18. Dueck, *Reluctant Crusaders*, 112–113; Brands, *What Good is Grand Strategy*, 39–58; Martel, *Grand Strategy*, 247–254.

19. Aaron L. Friedberg, *In the Shadow of the Garrison State*, 217–218,

20. The Air Force Association and the USNI Military Database, *Lifeline in Danger: An Assessment of the United States Defense Industrial Base* (Arlington, Va., The Aerospace Education Foundation, September 1988), 9–10; Vawter, *Industrial*

Mobilization, 15–22; Federal Emergency Management Agency, *Resource Management: An Historical Perspective* (Washington, Government Printing Office, December 31, 1984), 6/13; Friedbeg, *Shadow of the Garrison State*, chapt. 6.

21. Vawter, *Industrial Mobilization*, 22–24; U.S. Office of Defense Mobilization, *Defense Mobilization—The Shield Against Aggression: Sixth Quarterly Report to the* President (Washington, Government Printing Office, July 1, 1952), 9–11; US. Office of Defense Mobilization, *The Job Ahead for Defense Mobilization: Eighth Quarterly Report to the President.* (Washington, Government Printing Office, January 1, 1953), 13–15; Hacker and Vining, *American Military Technology*, chaps., 8, 9 passim; Kevin Thornton and Dale Prentiss, *Tanks and Industry: The Detroit Arsenal, 1940–1954*, [A TACOM History Office Publication, 1995] (Warren, MI, History Office, U.S. Army Tank-automotive and Armaments Command, 1995), 64–67.

22. Vawter, *Industrial Mobilization*, 24–31.

23. Vawter, *Industrial Mobilization*, 31–36, especially 35–36. U.S. Office of Defense Mobilization, Advisory Committee on Production Equipment, *Production Capacity: A Military Reserve* (Washington, Government Printing Office, January 1853), 1, 5–17, 29.

24. Paul A.C. Koistinen, *State of War: The Political Economy of American Warfare, 1945–2011* (Lawrence, KS: University Press of Kansas, 2010), 8; Colin Dueck, *Reluctant Crusaders: Power, Culture, and Change in American Grand Strategy* (Princeton: Princeton University Press, 2006), 108–113; George C. Herring, *From Colony to Superpower: U.S. Foreign Relations From Colony to Superpower* (New York: Oxford University Press, 2008), 376–377; Martel, *Grand Strategy*, 254; Friedberg, *In the Shadow of the Garrison State*, chapts. 1 and 2 and 340–341 especially.

25. Stephen I. Schwartz, editor, *Atomic Audit: The Costs and Consequences of U.S. Nuclear Weapons Since 1940*. (Washington, DC, Brookings, Institution Press, 1998), 3–9, especially table 2, page 8 and Tables A-1 and A-2, pp. 560–565.

26. James Ledbetter, *Unwarranted Influence: Dwight D. Eisenhower and the Military-Indusial Complex* (New Haven: Yale University Press, 2011), chaps. 2, 3, 4; William M. McClenahan, Jr. and William H. Becker, *Eisenhower and the Cold War Economy* (Baltimore, The Johns Hopkins University Press, 2012), 37–42, 232; Martel, *Grand Strategy*, 254–264; Zelizer, *Arsenal of Democracy*, 121–144.

27. Brands, *What Good is Grand Strategy*, 46–58; Friedberg, *In the Shadow of the Garrison State*, chapts. 1 and 2; Dueck, *Reluctant Crusaders*, 110–112.

28. Eisenhower's farewell address is printed as an appendix in Ledbetter, *Unwarranted Influence*, 211–220; see also Evan Thomas, *Ike's Bluff: President Eisenhower's Secret Battle to Save the* World (New York, little, Brown, 2012), 3–4, 281, 308, 311–312, 399–400, 403; Brett Baier, *Three Days in January: Dwight Eisenhower's Final* Mission (New York, William Morrow, 2017), 125–126, 195–208, 233, 251, 283.

29. Martel, *Grand Strategy*, 264–269; Zelizer, *Arsenal of Democracy*, 143–177; Crockatt, *The Fifty Years War*, part III; Koistinen, *State of War*, in toto; Alex Roland, "The Grim Paraphernalia: Eisenhower and the Garrison State," in Dennis E. Showalter, editor, *Forging the Shield: Eisenhower and National Security for the Twenty-First Century* (Chicago, Imprint Publications, 2005), 13–21 and Alex Roland, *The Military-Industrial Complex* (Washington, Society for the History of Technology and the American Historical Association,2001), chap. 1.; Hacker and Vining, *American Military Technology*, 125.

30. See Martel, *Grand Strategy*, 273–288; Zeitzer, *Arsenal of Democracy*, chaps. 9–12; Crockett, *The Fifty Years War*, Part 4.

31. Rosati and Scott, *The Politics of United States Foreign Policy*, 30–31; Richard H. Stephens, *The Industrial Sector* [National Security Management] (Washington, DC, National Defense University, 1980).

32. Air Force Association/USNI Military Database, *Lifeline in Danger*, 11; Rebecca U. Thorpe, *The American Warfare State: The Domestic Politics of Military Spending* (Chicago, IL: University of Chicago Press, 2014), 61–62, Table 3.2

33. Rosati and Scott, *The Politics of United States Foreign Policy*, 31–32; Air Force Association and USNI Military Database, *Lifeline in Danger*, 11; Martel, *Grand Strategy*, 289–299; Zeitzer, *Arsenal of Democracy*, chaps. 13 and 14; Crockett, *The Fifty Years War*, Part V; James Carroll, *House of War: The Pentagon and the Disastrous Rise of American Power* (Boston, Houghton Mifflin, 2006), chaps. 1–8, provides a welcome non-academic perspective on the era.

34. Martel, *Grand Strategy*, 254–299 especially 254, 263–264, 268–269, 273, 281–282, 288–289, 296–29 and 297–299; Friedberg, *In the Shadow of the Garrison State*, 34–341; Lind, *The American Way of Strategy*, 115–124; Dueck, *Reluctant Crusaders*, 108–113, especially 110; George C. Herring, *From Colony to Superpower: U.S. Foreign Relations Since 1776* (New York: Oxford University Press, 2008), 376–377.

35. Stephens, *The Industrial Sector*, 32–34; also economic and financing aspects of the Cold War period are detailed in Robert D. Hormats, *The Price of Liberty: Paying for America's Wars* (New York: Henry Holt, 2007), chaps. 6, 7, 8 and see esp. 173–180 for stage setter as well as Steven A. Bank, Kirk J. Stark and Joseph J. Thorndike, *War and Taxes* (Washington, The Urban Institute, 2008), chapt. 5 that particularly centers on Korea and Vietnam.

36. Rebecca U. Thorpe, *The American Warfare State: The Domestic Politics of Military Spending* (Chicago/London: University of Chicago Press, 2014), 8–11, 181–182 and especially, figures 1.1, 1.2, 1.3 based on US Bureau of Census, *Historical Statistics of the United States 1789–1945*, "U.S. Treasury Expenditures, 1789–1945," (Washington, Government Printing Office, 1949); Office of Management and Budget, Historical Tables: Budget of the United States Government, "Composition of Outlays: 1940–2016" (Table 6.1) and "Outlays for Discretionary Programs: 1962–2016" (table

8.7) (Washington, Government Printing Office, 2014) (http://www.whitehouse.gov/omb/budget/Historical).

37. Hugh Rockoff, *America's Economic Way of War: War and the U.S. Economy from the Spanish-American War to the Persian Gulf War* (Cambridge/New York: Cambridge University Press, 2012, 272–275296–304, appendix 2.

38. See Stephen I. Schwartz, editor, *Atomic Audit: The Costs and Consequences of U.S. Nuclear Weapons since 1940* (Washington, Brookings Institution Press, 1998), Introduction and particularly the tables and figures; also Wikipedia, "Historical nuclear weapons stockpiles and nuclear tests by country," https://en.wikipedia.org/wiki/Historical_nuclear_weapons_stockpiles_and_nuclear_tests_by_country, accessed 11 August 2021.

39. Gregg Herken, "'Not Enough Bulldozers': Eisenhower and American Nuclear Weapons Policy, 1953–1961," and Alex Roland, "The Grim Paraphernalia: Eisenhower and the Garrison State," in Dennis E. Showalter, editor, *Forging the Shield: Eisenhower and National Security for the 21st Century* (Chicago, Il, Imprint Publications, 2005), 85–91 and 13–22 respectively.

40. Kaufman, "America's Private Arsenal For Democracy," 261–262; Abraham Flexner (and Robbert Dijkgraaf), *The Usefulness of Useless Knowledge* (Princeton/Oxford: Princeton University Press, 2017), 49–90; Barton C. Hacker and Margaret Vining, *American Military Technology: The Life Story of a Technology* (Baltimore, Md., Johns Hopkins University Press, 2006), chaps. 8–11, especially pages 164–165 and especially relevant, Thomas G. Mahnken, *Technology and the American Way of War* (New York, Columbia University Press,2008), chaps. 1–4.

41. Hacker and Vining, *American Military Technology*, chaps., 8–11; Kaufman, "America's Private Arsenal for Democracy," 262–263.

42. Hacker and Vining, *American Military Technology*, 112–122; Culver, *Federal Government Procurement*, 18–20, 22–26, 27–28, 30–31, 32.

43. Hacker and Vining, *American Military Technology*, chapt. 9 especially 124–125, 138–140.

44. Hacker and Vining, *American Military Technology*, 152–163; Culver, Federal Government Procurement, 35.

45. Hacker and Vining, *American Military Technology*, 164–165; Schwartz, editor, *Atomic Audit*, table 1–3, 86–91. See also Philip Shiman, *Forging the Sword: Defense Production During the Cold War* (Washington, DC, United States Air Force Air Combat Command and Department of Defense Legacy Program, Cold War Project, July 1997); Frederick J. Shaw, editor, *Locating Air Force Base Sites: History's Legacy* (Washington, DC, Air Force History and Museums Program, 2004); Neil deGrasse Tyson and Avis Lang, *Accessory to War: The Unspoken Alliance Between Astrophysics and the Military* (New York, W. W. Norton, 2019).

46. Charles A. Stevenson, "Congress and New Ways of War," in *Congress*

and Civil-Military Relations (Washington, DC, Georgetown University Press, 2015), 133; Thomas K. McCraw, *American Business Since 1920: How It Worked* (Wheeling, IL, Harlan Davidson, 2009 edition), 92–93; Mansel C. Blackford and K. Austin Kerr, *Business Enterprise in American History* (Boston, MA, Wadsworth, 1994), 322 and U.S. Congress, 87th, 2d session, Senate, Select Committee on Small Business, *Impact of Defense Spending on Labor Surplus Areas* (Washington, Government Printing Officer, 1962), 27–29 as abbreviated in Blaszczyk and Scranton, editors, *Major Problems in American Business History*, 388–389.

47. Ralph E. Lapp, *The Weapons Culture* (New York, W.W. Norton, 1968), chapt. 1, especially page 17; Andrew Latham, "From The 'Armoury System' To 'Agile Manufacturing': Industrial Divides in the History of American Arms Production," Ph.D. dissertation, York University, January 1997/Ann Arbor: University Microfilms, 1997, 208–214; Rockoff, *America's Economic Way of War*, 296–304.

48. See for instance, Jacques S. Gansler, *The Defense Industry* (Cambridge, MA, MIT Press, 1980) and *Affording Defense* (Cambridge, MIT Press, 1989); Thorpe, *The American Warfare State*, passim; Lapp, *The Weapons Culture*, appendices I–IX; U.S. Under Secretary of Defense for Acquisition, *Bolstering Defense Industrial Competitiveness* (Washington, Department of Defense, July 1988), passim.

49. Gansler, *Defense Industry*, 26–27; McCraw, *American Business Since 1920*, 86.

50. Robert L. Heilbroner, *The Economic Transformation of America*. (New York: Harcourt Brace Jovanovich, 1977), chapt. 11, especially 216, 218, 219, 220; Friedberg, *In the Shadow of the Garrison State*, chaps. 6–8.

51. Dwight R. Lee, "Public Goods, Politics, and Two Cheers for the Military-Industrial Complex," in R. Higgs, editor, *Arms, Politics and the Economy* (New York, Holmes and Meir, 1990), 22–36 passim; Linda Weiss, *America Inc? Innovation and Enterprise in the National Security State* (Ithaca, NY, Cornell University Press, 2014), 23–50; James Ledbetter, *Unwarranted Influence: Dwight D. Eisenhower and the Military-Industrial Complex* (New Haven, CT: Yale University Press, 2011), especially chaps. 1 and 8; Thorpe, *The American Warfare State*, 59–60; Heilbroner, *Economic Transformation of America*, 216; McCraw, *American Business Since 1920*, 86–87.

52. Jeffrey M. Dorwart with Jean K. Wolf, *The Philadelphia Navy Yard: From the Birth of the U.S. Navy to the Nuclear Age*, Philadelphia, PA: University of Pennsylvania Press, 2001), chapt. 11; Weiss, *America Inc?* 6, 3, 135, 162, 1569, 172, 174–175, 213–214 f. n. 7.

53. See David Reynolds, *From Munich to Pearl Harbor: Roosevelt's America and the Origins of the Second World War* (Chicago, Dee, 2001), 5; various essays in Lee D. Olvey, Henry A. Leonard and Bruce E. Arlinghaus, editors. *Industrial Capacity and Defense Planning: Sustained Conflict and Surge Capability in the 1980s* (Lexington, MA, Lexington Books, 1983), also Lapp, *The Weapons Culture*, appen-

dices V and V-A; Lisa Bromberg, *NASA and the Space Industry* (Baltimore/London, Johns Hopkins University Press, 1999), 9–13; Thorpe, *The American Warfare State*, table 3–2, pages 61–63; Weiss, *America Inc?*, table 2.3, p. 47 also 146–147 and Mary L. Dudziak, *War Time: An Idea, Its History, Its Consequences* (New York/Oxford: Oxford University Press, 2012), chapt. 3.

54. See Koistinen, *State of War*, especially chaps. 8, 9; Sterling Michael Pavelec, editor, *The Military-Industrial Complex and American Society* (Santa Barbara, CA, Denver, CO, Oxford, UK: ABC-CLIO, 2010), xv; Gansler, *Defense Industry*, 9–11.

55. J. Erickson, "The Military-Industrial Complex," *Science Studies*, v. I (1971), 225–233, esp. 226 reviewing William Proxmire, *Report from Wasteland: America's Military-Industrial Complex* (New York, Prager, 1970). For a sample of period commentary drawing upon prominent internal issues of the time, see Christopher S. Maggio, "Industrial Preparedness," [Student Essay], U.S. Army War College, 8 October 1971," Harold E. Bertrand, "The Defense Industrial Base: Executive Summary, Washington, Logistics Management Institute, August 1977; Association of the United States Army, "Army Industrial Preparedness: A Primer on What it takes to Stay Until the War is Over," Special Report, Washington, AUSA, 1979 and Brady M. Cole, *Procurement of Naval Ships: It Is Time For The US Navy To Acknowledge Its Shipbuilders May Be Holding A Winning Hand* (Washington, National Defense University, September 1979). On internal government attempts to manage requirements, process and production, see Federal Emergency Management Agency, *Resource Management: A Historical Perspective* (Washington, FEMA, May 1989).

56. Bernard Charles Alfred Cannon, "The Military-Industrial Complex in American Politics, 1953–1990," unpublished doctoral dissertation, Stanford University, 1975, University Microfilms, *Dissertation Abstracts* (Ann Arbor, MI: University Microfilms, June 1975), 7831-A; Michael J. Meese, "Strategy and Force Planning in a Time of Austerity," in Joseph Da Silva, Hugh Liebert, Isaiah Wilson III, editors, *American Grand Strategy and the Future of U.S. Landpower* (Carlisle Barracks, PA, Strategic Studies Institute and U.S. Army War College Press, December 2014), Figure 6–1 and 6–2, pp. 138, 140; Culver, *Federal Government Procurement*, 34.

57. Bernard Brodie, *War and Politics* (New York, Macmillan, 1973), 290–3023; Michael Getler, "The Great Warplane Charade," *The Washington Post*, September 20, 1974; George C. Wilson, "Destroyer Built on time, Under Cost," September 20, 1974, *The Washington Post*, December 5, 1978; George C. Wilson, "Business Booms for Weapons Makers," *The Washington Post*, January 21, 1979; George C. Wilson, "Aircraft Engine Program Sparks Fierce Lobbying," *The Washington* Post, March 12, 1979.

58. Kosta Tsipis, "Hiding Behind the Military-Industrial Complex, "*Bulletin of the Atomic Scientists*, v. XXVIII, Number 6 (June 1972), 20–23; Jerome Slater and

Terry Nardin, "The 'Military-Industrial Complex' Muddle," *The Yale Review*, v. LXV, No. 1 (October 1975), 1–23 esp. 1–6 and 22–23; Aaron L. Friedberg, *In the Shadow of the Garrison State: America's Anti-Statism and Its Cold War Grand Strategy* (Princeton: Princeton University Press, 2000), chaps. 3 and 6 passim; Robert D. Cuff, "An Organizational Perspective on the Military-Industrial Complex," *Business History Review*, v. 53, number 3 (Summer 1978), 250–252 passim.

59. Tsipis, "Hiding Behind the Military-Industrial Complex," 22–23.

60. Clayton Fritchey, "'The Devouring Monster,'" *The Washington Post*, July 15, 1975; Beggs quoted in George Wilson, "Business Booms for Weapons Makers," *The Washington Post*, January 21, 1979.

61. Gansler, *Defensed Industry*, 11, 212–218

62. Lawrence G. Franko, "Restraining Arms Exports to the Third World: Will Europe Agree?" *Survival*, v. XXI, No. 1 (January/February 1979), 14–25.

63. Robert D. Hormats, *The Price of Liberty: Paying for America's Wars* (New York: Henry Holt/Times Books, 2007), chapt. 8; Dennis S. Ippolito, *Why Budgets Matter: Budget Policy and American* Politics (University Park, PA, Pennsylvania State University Press, 2003), 223–225; George F. Will, ". . . Carter's Blessing," *The Washington Post*, January 31, 1980; see also; William P. Snyder and James Brown, editors, *Defense Policy in the Reagan Administration* (Washington, DC: National Defense University, 1988) and Daniel Wirls, *Buildup: The Politics of Defense in the Reagan Era* (Ithaca, NY, Cornell University Press, 1992).

64. Vawter, *Industrial Mobilization*, chapt. 6, especially 69–70.

65. Everett Carl Ladd and Karlyn H. Keene, "In Support of Defense," *Government Executive*, July 1989), 44–46.

66. Nick Kotz, "America's Defense Dependency," The *Washington Post*, June 28, 1988.

67. Myron Struck, "Pentagon Factory Disposal Running Down," *The Washington Post*, November 17, 1982; "GM gets largest military contact since World War II," Harrisburg, Pa., *The Evening News*, July 14, 1982; J. Frank Diggs and Carey W. English, *U.S. News & World Report*, September 27, 1982; Robert S. Dudney, "The Coming Battle Over Those Defense Dollars," *U.S. News & World Report*, February 15, 1982, 20, 21; William Raspberry, "Defense Costs Jobs," *The Washington Post*, January 13, 1982.

68. Thomas W. Lippman, "U.S. Navy: Shipbuilding Industry's Lifeline," *The Washington Post*, August 30, 1981; "Businesses That Gain Most in Defense Boom," *U.S. News & World Report*, March 23, 1981, 43, 46; Robert S. Dudney, "The Coming Battle Over Those Defense Dollars," *U.S. News & World Report*, February 15, 1982, 20, 21; William Raspberry, "Defense Costs Jobs," *The Washington Post*, January 13, 1982.

69. Michael Doan, "Defense Dollars Save Many a City," *U.S. News & World Report*, May 10, 1982; John G. Tower, "Address," April 14, 1983, in "Defense Communique," *National Defense* (May–June 1983), 222–224. For a sampling of commentaries

George C. Wilson, "Defense Contractors Zero In Sights on Profits," *The Washington Post*, January 17, 1980; T. R. Reid, "Tax Break Nears for Arms Contractors," *The Washington Post*, June 25, 1980; Jonathan Neumann and Ted Gup, "The Revolving Door"; George C. Wilson, "With Vietnam Defused, Weapon-Makers Ballyhoo Their Firepower," *The Washington Post*, November 25, 1980; John R. Ellison, "The Beleaguered Arsenal: The Need for a Revitalized National Indusial Policy," *Sea Power* (December 1980), 25–28, 32–37; Edgar Ulsamer, "The Alarming State of the US Defense Industrial Base," *Air Force* v. 644, No.1 (January 1981), 17–18, 21; Jack Anderson, "Fast Buck Operators Milk Sacred Cows," *The Washington Post*, March 4, 1981; Jay T. Edwards, "Time Ripe To Modernize Industry," *The Officer*, v. 57 (June 1981), 12–14; Tony Velocci, "Rearming: Can We Do It In Time? *Nation's Business* (July 1981), 25–32; George C. Wilson, "U.S. Plans to Beef Up Defense Industry," *The Washington Post* August 5, 1981; Maxwell D. Taylor, "How Much for Defense? Only What's Essential," *The Washington Post*, September 1, 1981; Michael Getler, "Navy, Submarine Builder End Dispute," *The Washington Post*, October 23, 1981; Michael Kovalsky, "Cities Under Siege," *Army Logistician*, v. 13 (November-December 1981), 6–11; Jacques S. Gansler, "Defense Spending: Some Competition Would Help," *The Washington Post*, April 4, 1982; Walter Pincus, "Helicopter Maintenance on the Hill," *The Washington Post*, March 14, 1982; Martha M. Hamilton and Mark Potts, "From Blue Notes to War Games, Area Defense Work Runs the Gamut," *The Washington Post* November 29, 1982 14, 1982; Werner Grosshans, "Ammunition—Can the Industrial Base Respond?" *Army Logistician* (September-October 1983), 14–18; James W. Canan, "The Profitability of Defense," *Air Force Magazine*, Vol.68, No. 11 (November 1985), 62–67 and John T. Correll, "Industry Under the Gun," *Air Force Magazine*, vo. 68, No. 11 (November 1985), 68–72.

70. Jacques S. Gansler, "Revitalizing the Arsenal of Democracy," *Air Force Magazine*, vol. 67, No. 4 (April 1984), 74–77; James R. Kurth, "Military Power and Industrial Competitiveness: The Industrial Dimension of Military Strategy," *Naval War College Review*, v. XXXV, No. 5 (September/October 1982), 33–47; Robert E. McGarrah, "US Strategies For Industrial Growth and Western Security," *Parameters, Journal of the US Army War College* v. XII, No. 4 (Fall 1982), 62–70; US Cong., 96th, 2d Session, HR Committee Print 29, *The Ailing Defense Indusial Base: Unready For Crisis: Report of the Defense Industrial Base Panel of the Committee on Armed Services, December 31, 1980* (Washington, GPO, 1980); Lawrence J. Korb, "A new look at United States defense industrial preparedness," *Defense Management* Journal, v. 18, 3d Quarter 1981, 2–7; Michael Kovalsky, "Cities Under Siege," *Army Logistician*, v. 13 (November-December 1981), 6–11; Ellison, "The Beleaguered Arsenal," *Sea Power* (December 21980), 25–28, 32–37.

71. Robert E. McGarrah, "US Strategies for Industrial Growth and Western Security, *Parameters, Journal of the U.S Army War College*, v. XII, No. 4 (Fall 1982),

62–70; James R. Kurth, "Military Power and Industrial Competiveness: The Industrial Dimension of Military strategy," *Naval War College Review*, vol. XXXV, No 5 (September/October 1982), 33- 47

72. Kurth, "Military Power and Industrial Competitiveness," 43–45; Jacques S. Gansler, "Needed: A U.S. Defense Industrial Strategy," *International Security*, volume 12, number 2 (Fall 1987), 45–49.

73. Jacques S. Gansler, "Needed: A U.S. Defense Industrial Strategy," *International Security*, volume 12, number 2 (Fall 1987), especially 45–49.

74. Ibid.

75. F. Clifton Berry, Jr., "The Lifeline Is Still in Danger," *Air Force Magazine* v. 72 A# 121 (November 1989), 108–111.

76. SYSCON GRAPHICS, *Correlation of East/West Leadership, Major Weapons Systems, and Conflict Since World War II* (Washington, DC, SYSCON Center for Modeling and Simulation Gaming, 1989), Chart; United States Department of Energy, *Linking Legacies: Connecting The Cold War Nuclear Weapons Production Processes to their Environmental Consequences* (Washington, Department of Energy, Center for Environmental Management Information, January 1997), Chart.

77. Fred Kaplan, "Second Look: 'Star Wars': The ultimate military-industrial compact," *Boston Globe*, September 14, 1987; Sandra Sugaware, "Defense: the Promise of 1980 remains Unfulfilled," *The Washington Post*, October 30, 1988; David Evans, "The Ten Commandments of Defense Spending," *Parameters, Journal of the US Army War College*, vol. XV, No. 4 (December 1985),76- 81; Garrett M. Graff, *Raven Rock: The Story of the U.S. Government's Secret Plan to Save Itself—While the Rest of Us Die* (New York, Simon and Schuster, 201), Introduction; Laura McEnaney, *Civil Defense Begins at Home: Militarization Meets Everyday Life in the Fifties* (Princeton, NJ: Princeton University Press, 2000), Conclusion; B. Franklin Cooling, *The Army Support of Civil Defense, 1945–1966: Plans and Policy* (Washington DC, U.S. Amy Office of the Chief of Military History, 1967), chaps. 2–6.

78. Gerald M. Steinberg, "SDI and Organizational Politics of Military R&D," *Armed Forces & Society*, vol. 13, No. 4 (Summer 1987), 579–598, 594–595 especially.

79. Steinberg, "SDI and Organizational Politics of Military R&D," 594–595; Walter S. Poole, *Adapting to Flexible Response, 1960–1968* (Washington, DC, Office of Secretary of Defense Historical Office, 2013), 14–15.

80. Franklin C. Spinney, "Look What $2 Trillion Didn't Buy For Defense," *The Washington Post*, October 30, 1988; "The Defense Budget: A Wasteful and Impregnable Bastion?" *Business Week*, October 10, 1988;Dina Rasor, "Sidetracking reform at the Pentagon," *The Washington Post*, July 1, 1988; Marcy Eckroth Mullins, "It's a 'back-scratching society,'" *USA Today*, June 24, 1988; Ken Adelman, "Cleaning Up The Mess," *Washington Times*, June 27, 1988; Malcom Gladwell, "Pentagon Paying High Price for Low Aircraft Production, *The Washington Post*, September 25, 1988;

A. Ernest Fitzgerald, *The Pentagonists: An Insider's View of Waste, Mismanagement, and Fraud in Defense Spending*. (Boston, Houghton Mifflin, 1988); Edward Luttwak, "Behind the Pentagon Scandal: The Real Problem Is a System That Treats Weapons Like Commodities," *The Washington Post*, June 26, 1988.

81. Brandes, *Warhogs*, 276; William H. Taft IV, "Serious About Cutting Costs," *The Washington Post*, October 13, 1987; "Taft Rails Over Procurement Kibitzers," *Defense Industry Report*, October 13, 1988, p. 5 and Editor, "The Pentagon Investigation," *The Washington Post* June 27, 1988; Malcom Gladwell, "The Procurement Pendulum Swings Back Again," *The Washington Post*, July 31, 1988.

82. The Air Force Association and the USNI Military database, *Lifeline in Danger: An assessment of the United States Defense Industrial Base* (Arlington, Va., The Aerospace Education Foundation, September 1988), David S. Broder, "The Issue for '88; America's competitiveness," *The Washington Post*, February 3, 1988; Richard Whittle, "U.S. defense arsenal eroding, study says," *Dallas Morning News* September 21, 1988; J. Ronald Fox, "Why the Military Can't Learn to Shop," *The New York Times*, September 4, 1988; US Department of Defense, Under Secretary of Defense, *Bolstering Defense Industrial Competitiveness: A Report to the Secretary of* Defense, July 1988, Summary, v-xiii; Industrial College of the Armed Forces, National Defense University, Mobilization Conference Committee, Class of 1988, coordinator, *Human and Materiel Resources Policies: A New Look at Enduring Issues: Proceedings Based on the Seventh Annual Mobilization Conference, April 14–15, 1988* (Washington; James M. Lindsay, "Congress and Defense Policy: 1961 to 1986," *Armed Forces & Society*, vol. 13, No. 3 (Spring 1987), 372–401; U. S. Officer of Management and Budget, *The United States Budget in Brief, Fiscal Year 1979* (Washington, Government Printing Office, 1978), 20–21.

83. AFA-USNI, *Lifeline in Danger*, 11–12, 62–63; Richard S. Whittle, "U.S. defense arsenal eroding, study says," Dallas *News*, September 21, 1988.

84. U.S. Under Secretary of Defense, *Bolstering Defense Indusial Competitiveness* (Washington, Department of Defense, July 1988), xi–xiii.

85. Office of Assistant Secretary of Defense (Public Affairs), News Release, Remarks Prepared for Delivery By The Honorable Frank C. Carlucci, Secretary of Defense To the National Security Industrial Association, Washington, D.C., Thursday, October 6, 1988, "Safeguarding A Strategic Asset: The Defense Industrial Base," copy, author's files; U.S. Under Secretary of Defense, *Bolstering Defense Industrial Competitiveness*, v-xiii; AFA-USNI, *Lifeline in Danger*, 61.

86. See Seymour Melman, "After the Military-Industrial Complex?" *Bulletin of the Atomic Scientists*, XXVII, No.3 (March 1971), 7–9.

87. Melman, "After the Military-Industrial Complex?" 8–9.

88. Linda S. Brandt and Francis W. A'Hearn, "The Proteus Syndrome: Transforming the Military-Industrial Complex in the Post-Cold War Era," in Deputy Under

Secretary of Defense For Acquisition Reform, *"Acquisition Reform—A Revolution in Business Affairs" (Special Focus on Civil/Military Interaction* [1999 Acquisition Research Symposium Proceedings (Washington, DC, Defense Systems Management College and the National Contract Management Association, 1999), 433; Gansler, *Defensed Industry*, figure 1, page 3.

89. United States Department of Defense, Under Secretary of Defense, *Bolstering Defense Industrial Competitiveness* (Washington, Department of Defense, July 1988), v-xiii, especially v; US Office of Management and Budget, *United States Budget in Brief, FY 1919*, 27–29; U, S, Department of Commerce, Bureau of the Census, *Statistical Abstract of the United States, 1977* (Washington, Government Printing Officer, 1977), 246, 356, 358–382 inter alia; George F. Will, "Carter's Blessing," *The Washington Post*, January 1, 1980; AFA-USNI Data Base, *Lifeline in Danger*, 61.

90. Office of Assistant Secretary of Defense (Public Affairs), News Release, Remarks Prepared for Delivery by the Honorable Frank C. Carlucci, Secretary of Defense To the National Security Industrial Association, Washington, D.C., Thursday, October 6, 1988, "Safeguarding A Strategic Asset: The Defense Industrial Base," copy, author's files; Under Secretary of Defense, *Bolstering Industrial Competitiveness*. v-xiii;

91. Timothy D. Gill, *Industrial Preparednes: Breaking with an Erratic Past* (Washington, National Defense University Press, 1984), 35–36, 44, 52–57

CHAPTER 7

1. See Carl Boggs, *Origins of the Warfare States: World War II and the Transformation of American Politics* (New York, Routledge, 2017), introduction; Philip Morrison, Kosta Tsipis and Jerome Wiesner, "The Culture of American Defense," *Scientific American*, vol. 270, no. 2 (February 1994), 38–45, esp. 38; Michael Brown, ed., *Grave New World: Security Challenges in the Twenty-First Century* (Washington, DC, Georgetown University Press, 2003), introduction; Colin Dueck, *Reluctant Crusader; Power, Culture and Change in American Grand Strategy* (Princeton/Oxford: Princeton University Press, 2006), chap. thirty-five, esp.125–127.

2. Paul A. C. Koistinen, *State of War: The Political Economy of American Warfare, 1945–2011* (Lawrence, KS: University Press of Kansas, 2012), 7, 8; Jacques S. Gansler, *Defense Conversion: Transforming the Arsenal of Democracy* (Cambridge, MA, MIT Press, 1995), 17; Francis Fukuyama, *The End of History and the Last Man* (New, Free Press, 1992), passim.

3. P.J. Simmons, "The Gulf War and the Revolution in Military Affairs," [Report No. 6] *The Woodrow Wilson Center*, vol. 6, no. 3 (November 1994), 1–2; John T. Correll, and Colleen A. Nash, "The Industrial Base at War," *Air Force Journal of the Air Force Association*, vol. 74, no. 12 (December 1991), https://www.airforcemag

.com/issue/1991-12/; John T. Correll and Colleen A. Nash, *Lifeline Adrift: The Defense Industrial Base in the 1990s: A Report to the Air Force Association* (Arlington, VA, The Aerospace Education Foundation, September 1991), 13–16; also "Navy Secretary Dalton's Pen Sinks Warships Kamikazes Just Scratched," *National Defense*, vol. LXXIX, No. 507 (April 1995), 8.

4. U.S. Army, Deputy Chief of Staff for Logistics, Logistics Management Institute (USADCL), et al., *Assessing The Adequacy of the Industrial Base* (Washington, DC, Office of the Assistant Secretary of Defense, May 1992), executive summary; Correll and Nash, *Lifeline Adrift*, 4–15.

5. DCSL, *Accessing the Adequacy of the Industrial Base*, executive summary, vii-xi, passim; John F. Starns and Paul W. Edwards, *A Logistics Management Plan for Mobilization Response* (Rosslyn, Va., The Analytical Sciences Corporation, 1992), chaps. 4, 5 passim; Scott S. Haraburda, *Conventional Munitions Industrial Base*, [Land Warfare Papers 113] (Arlington, Va, The Institute of Land Warfare, Association of the United States Army, August 2017), 6; Thomas G. Mahneken, *Technology and the American Way of War* (New York, Columbia University Press, 2008), 157–175.

6. Correll and Nash, *Lifeline Adrift*, 15–16, citing O'Keefe's statement to House Armed Services Committee, February 27, 1991; Bruce W. Watson, ed., *Military Lessons of the Gulf War* (London/New York, BC-A, 1991), appendices A, D, E, F; Gansler, *Defense Conversion*, chap. 3, esp. 44.

7. Correll and Nash, *Lifeline Adrift*, 16.

8. George H. W. Bush, former U.S. President, "Address to the Aspen Institute, Aspen, Colorado, August 2, 1992, quoted in Don M. Snider, *Strategy, Forces and Budgets: Dominant Influences in Executive Decision Making, Post–Cold War, 1989–1991* (Carlisle Barracks, PA, US Army War College, Strategic Studies Institute, February 1993), 1–3; Robert D. Hormats, *The Price of Liberty: Paying For America's Wars* (New York: Henry Holt/Times Books, 2007), 250, 262, 298; William H. Gregory, *The Price of Peace: The Future of Defense Industry and High Technology in a Post-Cold-War World* (New York, Lexington Books, 1993), preface, chap. 1; Koistinen, *State of War*, 1–34, 58–59, 87.

9. Dennis S. Ippolito, *Blunting the Sword: Budget Policy and the Future of Defense* (Washington, National Defense University Press, 1994), 150–157; Finmeccanica and Atlantic Council, Graph," Inflection Points in U.S. Defense Spending," http://www.bing.com/images/search?q=pentagon-++last+supper&view=detailv2&&id-33.

10. Joseph Stiglitz, "The Roaring Nineties," *The Atlantic Monthly* (October 2002), https://www.theatlantic.com/magazine/archive/2002/10/the-roaring-nineties/302604/; J. Bradford De Long, "From Beast To Beauty," *The Wilson Quarterly*, vol. 21, no. 4 (Autumn 1997), 70–81;

11. Richard Crockatt, *The Fifty Years War: The United States and the Soviet Union in World Politics, 1941–1991* (London, Routledge, 1995) 375–378 quoting

Anthony Lake, "Remarks to Johns Hopkins School of Advanced International Studies," (United States Information Service, US Embassy, London, September 22, 1993), 2–5; Brian Collins, *NATO: A Guide to the Issues* (Santa Barbara, CA, Prager, 2011), 86–90; "Tomgram": William Hartung, Trump for the Defense," *TomDispatch*, November 22, 2016, accessed at www.au.af.mil/au/awc/awcgater/nss/nss-9; Koistinen, *State of War*, chapt. 1.

12. Dueck, *Reluctant Crusader*, 144–145; William C. Martel, *Grand Strategy in Theory and Practice: The Need For An Effective American Foreign Policy* (Cambridge, UK: Cambridge University Press, 2015), 310–315; Daniel S. Ippolito, *Why Budgets Matter: Budget Policy and American Politics* (University Park, PA, Pennsylvania State University Press, 2003), 241–258.

13. Michael T. Klare, "The Pentagon's New Paradigm, 466–476, especially 469, 476; Andrew H. Cordesman, "Why We Need to Police the World," 477–479 and Marcy Darnovsky, L.A. Kaufman, Billy Robins, "What Will This War Mean" all in Micah L. Silfry and Christopher Cerf, ed., *The Gulf War Reader: History, Documents, Opinions* (New York, Random House/Times Books, 1991).

14. Murray L. Weidenbaum and Ben-Chieh Liu, "Effect of Disarmament on Regional Distribution," *Journal of Peace Research*, v. 3, no. 21 (March 1966), 93–94; also Weidenbaum, speech, "The Future of the U.S. Defense Industry: Two Different Approaches," to Western Economic Association, Seattle, WA, July 1, 1991 and Weidenbaum, "The U.S. Defense Industry After the Cold War," *Orbis*, v. 42, no. 24 (Fall, 1997), 591–601.

15. Colin Powell, *My American Journey* (New York, Random House, 1995), 578; Snider, *Strategy, Forces and Budgets*, 4–9, 57; Jeffrey P. Sahaida, "Reorganization after the Cold War, 1988–2003," in Frederick J. Shaw, ed. *Locating Air Force Base Sites: History's Legacy* (Washington, United States Air Force Air Force History and Museums Program, 2004), ch. 4, esp. 186–187; Lorna S. Jaffe, *The Development of the Base Force, 1989–1992* (Washington, DC, Office of the Chairman of the Joint Chief of Staff, Joint History Office, 1993) passim.

16. Snider, *Strategy, Forces and Budgets*, 10–39; Bruce W. Watson, Bruce George, Peter Tsouras and B. L. Cyr, *Military Lessons of the Gulf War* (London, BCA,1991), append. A passim; Ippolito, *Why Budgets Matter*, 241–258.

17. Julian Zelizer, *Arsenal of Democracy: The Politics of National Security—From World War II to the War on Terrorism* (New York, Basic Books, 2010), 382–487; William J. Clinton, *A National Security Strategy of Engagement and Enlargement* (Washington, The White House, February 1995), accessed at www.au.af.mil/au/awc/awegate/nss/nss-95.pdf), 2, 7, 22, 24; Powell, *American Journey*, 576.

18. Gansler, *Defense Conversion*, chaps. 2, 4, 5, 6 passim, esp.70–72; Weidenbaum, "Defense Conversion—An Empty Promise," *New York Times*, August 20, 1990; Ann R. Markusen and Sean S. Costigan, "The Military Industrial Challenge," chap. 1

in Markusen and Costigan, eds., *Arming the Future: A Defense Industry for the 21st Century* (New York, Council on Foreign Relations Press, 1999), 3–14.

19. Weidenbaum, "Defense Conversion—An Empty Promise," New York *Times* August 20, 1990; particularly useful is Gansler, *Defense Conversion*, chapt. 2, 4, 5, 6, especially pp. 70–72.

20. William H. Gregory, *The Price of Peace: The Future of the Defense Industry and High Technology in a Post-Cold War World* (New York, Lexington Books/Macmillan,, chaps., 3, 4, 5; Haraburda, *Conventional Munitions Industrial Base*, 7–8; Rebecca U. Thorpe, *The American Warfare State: The Domestic Politics of Military Spending* (Chicago: University of Chicago Press,2014), 65–66; Ann R. Markusen and Sean S. Costigan, eds. *Arming the Future*, passim; Gansler, *Defense Conversion*, 10, 40–41 and Gansler, *Democracy's Arsenal: Creating a Twenty-First Century Defense Industry* (Cambridge, MA, MIT Press, 2011), 33.

21. Harvey M. Sapolsky and Eugene Gholz, "Eliminating Excess Defense Production," *Issues in Science and Technology On Line A Publication of the National Academies, The University of Texas at Dallas*, Winter 1996, accessed at https://www.issues.org/13.2/sapols.htm; Harvey M. Sapolsky and Eugene Gholz, "The Defense Monopoly," Regulation; *The CATO Review of Business and Government*, v. 22, no. 3 (Fall 1999), 39–43; Harvey M. Sapolsky and Eugene Gholz, "Private Arsenals: America's Post-Cold War Burden," ch. 6, 191–206 in Markusen and Costigan, *Arming the Future*; Lawrence J. Korb, *"Merger Mania: Should the Pentagon Pay For Defense Industry Restructuring,"* Brookings "External Article," June 1, 1999, 1–7 accessed at https://www.brookings.edu/articles/merger-mania-should-the-pentagon-pay-for-defense-industry-restructuring; Cynthia R. Cook and John C. Graser, "Lean Manufacturing and the Defense Industry: Lessons for Cost Analysts," *Rand Research Brief* (Santa Monica, CA, Rand Corporation, 2001); Brown, *Grave New World*, introduction; and Ashton B. Carter, "Adapting US Defence to Future Needs," *Survival*, v. 412, no. 4 (Winter 1999–2000), 101–123; U.S. Department of Defense, Defense Science Board Task Force, *Report on Outsourcing and Privatization* (Washington, Office of the Under Secretary of Defense or Acquisition and Technology, August 1996), 2–13, 59–67.

22. Rachel Maddow, *Drift: The Unmooring of American Military Power* (New York, Crown, 2012), 160–184 passim; R. Philip Deavel, "The Political Economy of Privatization for the American Military," *Air Force Journal of Logistics*, v. 22, no. 2 (Summer 1998), 33–39; Allison Stanger, *One Nation Under Contract: The Outsourcing of American Power and the Future of Foreign Policy* (New Haven: Yale University Press, 2009), 84–98; Laura A. Dickinson, *Outsourcing War and Peace: Preserving Public Values in a World of Privatized Foreign Affairs* (New Haven: Yale University Press, 2011), 23–25.

23. Vernon W. Ruttan, *Is War Necessary for Economic Growth? Military

Procurement and Technology Development (New York/Oxford: Oxford University Press, 2006), esp. chaps., 1, 8; Gansler, *Defense Conversion,* chap. 4; Markusen and Yudken, *Dismantling The Cold War Economy,* chaps. 8 and 9; Ruth Stanley, "Employment effects of military restructuring," in Mary Kaldor, Ulrich Albrecht and Genevieve Schmeder, es. *Restructuring the Global Military Sector, Volume II: The End of Military Fordism* (London/Washington, Pinter, 1998), 55–59; Sanjeev Gupta, Benedict Clements, Rina Bhattaharya and Shamit Chakravanti, "The Elusive Peace Dividend," *Finance and Development: A Quarterly Magazine of the IMF,* v. 39, no. 4 (December 2001), 1–7; Lawrence R. Benson, *Acquisition Management in the United States Air Force and its Predecessors* (Washington, DC, Air Force History and Museum Program, 1997), 40–50.

24. Kenneth R. Mayer, "The Limits of Delegation: The Rise and Fall of BRAC," *Regulation: The CATO Review of Business and Government,* v. 22, no. 3 (Fall 1999), 32–38; Philip L. Shiman, "Defense Acquisition in an Uncertain World: The Post-Cold War Era, 1990–2000," in Shannon A. Brown, editor, *Providing the Means of War: Historical Perspectives on Defense Acquisition, 1945–2000* (Washington, DC, US Army Center of Military History and Industrial College of the Armed Forces, 2005), 283–315 esp. 283–290; Philip Shiman, *Forging the Sword: Defense Production During the Cold War* (Washington, DC, Department of Defense Legacy Program, Cold War Project and United States Air Force Air Combat Command, 1997), Appendix; Gansler, *Defense Conversion,* 238–239; Dorwart and Smith, *Philadelphia Navy Yard,* chap. 12.

25. Barton C. Hacker and Margaret Vining, *American Military Technology: The Life Story of a Technology* (Baltimore, The Johns Hopkins University Press, 2006) 165–166; also Mahnken, *Technology and the American Way of War,* 175–188.

26. Paul G. Kaminski, "The Defense Acquisition Challenge: Technological Supremacy at an Affordable Cost," speech before the Industrial College of the Armed Forces, January 27, 1995, Department of Defense News Release, January 27, 1995.

27. John A. Tirpak, "The Distillation of the Defense Industry," *Air Force Magazine,* v. 81, no. 7 (July 1998), 54–59 Jacques Gansler, "The U.S. Defense Industrial Base: From The End of the Cold War to the Present," in Lynne C. Thompson and Sheila R. Ronis, editors, *U.S. Defense Industrial Base: National Security Implications of a Globalized World* (Washington, DC, National Defense University, April 2006), 4–6, 12; Norman Augustine, *Augustine's Travels: A World-Class Leader Looks at Life, Business, and What It Takes to Succeed at Both* (New York, AMACOM, 1998), 145–146; and *Augustine's Laws* (New York, Viking/Penguin, 1986 edition), esp. 461–468; Marjorie Censer, "Defense companies brace for a different kind of consolidation this time around," *The Washington Post,* January 12, 2014.

28. John Mintz, "Defense Giants to Merge Today Amid Heartache," *The Washington Post,* March 15, 1995; Maryann Lawlor, "Defense Marketplace Changes

Cause Companies to Re-evaluate, Revamp," *Signal*, v. 52, No. 4 (December 1997), 59–62; Shiman, "Defense Acquisition," 300–301; Richard M. Weintraub and Sharon Walsh, "Toward a More Perfect Union," and Jay Mathews, "Defense Firms' Merger Plan Hailed," both in *The Washington Post*, August 31, 1994; Richard M. Weintraub, "Augustine's Imperative," *The Washington Post*, September 4, 1994

29. Norman R. Augustine, "Reengineering the Arsenal of Democracy," *The Atlantic Council of the United States Bulletin*, v. 9, No.6 (July 6, 1998), 1–6 especially 2; Walter Boyne, "Flying Out of the Cold War," *Cosmos: Journal of the Comsos Club of Washington, D.C.*, v. 9 (1999), 21–24, esp. 22–24; Chart, "Consolidation in the Defense Industry," Credit Suisse First Bank data as reported to the Defense Science Board, May 1997, author's files.

30. Augustine, "Reengineering the Arsenal of Democracy," 3–6.

31. William D. Hartung, "Saint Augustine's Rules: Norman Augustine and the Future of the American Defense Industry, *World Policy Journal*, v. 23, no. 2 (Summer 1996), 65–73.

32. Markusen and Yudken, *Dismantling the Cold War Economy*, chs., 6, 7, 8, 9, passim.

33. James E. Goodby, "Dismantling the Nuclear Weapons Legacy of the Cold War," *Strategic Forum*, [Institute for National Strategic Studies, National Defense University], No. 19 (February 1995), 1–4.

34. Stephen I. Schwartz, editor. *Atomic Audit: The Costs and Consequences of U.S. Nuclear Weapons Since 1940* (Washington, Brookings Institution, 1998), chaps. 8, 9, 10.

35. Leah Sottile, Lindsey Bever and Steven Mufson, "Near Hanford nuclear plant, residents smirk at scare," *The Washington Post*, May11, 2017, A 1, A 16; Sally Denton, *The Profiteers: Bechtel and the Men Who Built the World* (New York, Simon & Schuster, 2016), 156–159 and chap. 33; Jonathan Weisman, "Early Retirement for Weaponeers?" *The Bulletin of Atomic Scientists*, v. 50, no. 4 (August 1994) 16–22; Schwartz, *Atomic* Audit, appendix C.

36. Harvey M. Sapolsky, *Report of the Director, MIT Defense and Arms Control Studies Program* (Cambridge, MA, MIT, 1994–1995); Harvey M. Sapolsky and Eugene Gholz, "Eliminating Excess Defense Production," *Issues in Science and Technology*, (Winter 1996), http://wdww.issues.org/13.2/sapols.ht.gvc7vu; Sapolsky and Gholz, "The Defense Monopoly," *Regulation: The CATO Review of Business and Government*. 22, no1 (Fall 1999), 39–43; and Sapolsky and Gholz, "Private Arsenals: America's Post-Cold War Burden," chp. 6 in Markusen and Costigan, eds. *Arming the Future;* 191–206 passim; Korb, "Merger Mania," June 1, 1996, accessed at http://www.brookings.edu/articles/merger-mania-should-the-pentagon-pay-for-defense-inudstry-restructuring.

37. Weintraub, "Augustine's Imperative", *The Washington Post*, September 4, 1994; Mintz, "Defense Giants to Merge Today Amid Heartache," *The Washington*

Post, March 15, 1995; Weintraub and Walsh, "Toward a More Perfect Union, *The Washington Post,* August 31, 1994; "Indefensible Industrial Base," Editors, *The New York Times,* August 2, 1994; Gansler, "U.S. Defense Industrial Base," 4–5; Gansler, *Democracy's Arsenal,* 32–44, passim.

38. CSIS Senior Policy Panel on the U.S. Defense Industrial Base, *Defense Restructuring and the Future of the U.S. Defense Industrial Base* (Washington, Center for Strategic & International Studies, March 1998), 1–30 passim.

39. CSIS Senior Policy Panel, *Defense Restructuring,* 15; Industrial College of the Armed Forces, "Prime Contractors Forecast—January 1998," chart, Brandt and A'Hearn, "Proteus Syndrome," 435–440.

40. Ann Markusen, "The Post-Cold War American Defence Industry: Options, Policies and Probable Outcomes," 51–70, especially 51–70 and Ian Anthony, "Politics and Economics of Defence Industries in a Changing World," 1–27, especially 22–24, both in Efraim Inbar and Benzion Zilberfarb, eds., *The Politics and Economics of Defence Industries* (Portland: Frank Cass, 1998.); Sapolsky, *Director's Report, MIT Defense and Arms Control,* 6–7; U.K. Heo, *The Political Economy of Defense Spending Around the World* (Lewiston, NY, Edwin Mellen Press, 1999), 93–98, esp. 95–97.

41. Jeffrey Record, "Ready for What and Modernized Against Whom? A Strategic Perspective on Readiness and Modernization," *Parameters: The Journal of the Army War College,* v. 25, no. 3 (Autumn 1995), 20–30; Seth Hamblin and Robert Donnell, "Dividing Defense Dollars," *The Washington Post,* September 24, 1998, A-23; Leslie Wayne, "The Shrinking Military Complex," *New York Times,* February 27, 1998. Augustine, *Augustine's Travels,* 146; Erik Pages, "The New Defense Monopolies," *Armed Forces Journal International,* v. 136 (July 1998), 26–30; Shiman, "Defense Acquisition in an Uncertain World," in Brown ed., *Providing the Means of War,* 301–304; John R. Brinkerhoff, "The Late, Great Arsenal of Democracy," *Orbis,* v. 39, No. 2 (Spring 1995), 225–235; John H. Gibbons, *Building Future Security: Strategies for Restructuring the Defense Technology and Industrial Base* (Washington, US Congress, Office of Technology Assessment, 1992), iii; Michael e. Heberling, "Defense Industrial Base Policy: Revisited," *Acquisition Review Quarterly,* v. 1, no. 3 (Summer 1994), 238–249; Gordon Boezer, Ivars Gutmanis, and Joseph E. Muckerman II, "The Defense Technology and Industrial Base: Key Component of National Power," *Parameters: The Journal of the Army War College,* v. 27, No. 2 (Summer 1997), 26–51; Mike Austin, "Managing the US Defense Industrial Base: A Strategic Imperative," *Parameters: The Journal of the Army War College,* v. 24, No. 2 (Summer 1994), 27–37; 34–38.

42. Ian Anthony, "Review article; Arms procurement after the Cold War: how much is enough to do what (and how will we know)?" *International Affairs,* v. 74, no. 4 (1998), 871–882; John F. Shortal, "20th-Century Demobilization Lessons," *Military Review,* v. LXXVIII, No. 5 (September-November 1998), 66–73; Keith Hayward, "The Globalisation of Defence Industries," *Survival,* v. 42, no. 2 (Summer 2000), 115–132,

especially 115–116, 126–128; Keith Hayward, "The Defence Aerospace Industry in an Age of Globalization," *RUSI Journal* vol. 15, No. 3 (June 2000), 55–59; Gordon Adams, "The Transatlantic Defence Market and 'Fortress America': Obstacles and Opportunities," in Gordon Adams, Christopher Corns, Andrew James and Bernard Schmitt, editors, *Between Cooperation and Competition: The Transatlantic Defence Market* [Chaillot Paper 44] (Paris, Institut for Security Studies of the Western European Union, January 2001), passim; Terrence R. Guay, *At Arms Length: The European Union and Europe's Defence Industry* (New York, St. Martins, 1998/ Basingtoke, UK, MacMillan, 1998), 28–29; David M. D'Agostino, "Transatlantic Cooperative Weapons Development: How Can We Better Ensure Success?" *Acquisition Review Quarterly*, v. 3, no. 2 (Fall 2996), 131–146; Charles Gant, et al., "Global Defence Industry Survey," *The Economist*, June 2, 1997, 3–18; Ann Markusen, "Global Defense Mergers: Their Danger: Losing Control Of Leading-Edge Technology," *Christian Science Monitor*, August 5, 1998; David J. Louscher, Alethia H. Cook and Victoria D. Barto, "The Emerging Competitive Position of US Defense Firms in the International Market," *Defense Analysis*, v. 14, no. 2 (1998), 131–134; Anne Swardson, "French, German Defense Giants Plan Merge," *The Washington Post*, October 1, 1999, E1, E11; Michael Codner, "Just how far can we go?", Robin Laird, "A Giant Kick in the Pants on Both Sides of the Atlantic," 34–37, Sunjim Williams, "A Hopeful Voyage—or Rearranging The Deck Chairs?" 35–38 and Alison Wood, "BAe plans for success as a global player," all in *RUSI Journal*, v. 144, no. 2 (April/May 1999); Baroness Symons of Vernham Dean, "Creating a Competitive European Defence Industry—The UK Government View," *RUSI Journal*, v. 145, no. 3 (June 2000), 13–17; David G. Haglund, *Alliance Within the Alliance? Franco-German Military Cooperation and the European Pillar of Defense* (Boulder, CO, Westview, 1991), ch. 6; Markusen and Costigan, *Arming the Future*, 24–30.

43. Augustine, "Reengineering the Arsenal of Democracy, *The Atlantic Council of the United States Bulletin*, vol. IX, no. 6 (July 6, 1998), 1–6; Walter Boyne, "Flying Out of the Cold War," *Cosmos: Journal of the Cosmos Club of Washington D.C.*, vol. 9 (1999), 21–24; Chart, "Consolidation in the Defense Industry," Credit Suisse Bank data as reported to the Defense Science Board, May 1997.

44. Robert H. Williams, "Shrinking Arms Market Spurs Contest for Third World Sales," *National Defense* (December 1999), 34; Anne Marie Squeo and Thomas D. Ricks, "Pentagon Must Assist Suppliers Hit By Defense Consolidation," *Wall Street Journal*, November 20, 1999; John Donnelly, "Cohen: New Budget To Bolster Procurement," Defense Week, January 31, 2000, 3; Ezio Bonsignore, "From 'last supper' to 'first dinner,'" *Military Technology*, v. 23, no. 11 (November 1999), 3–4; John Lovering, "Loose Canons: Creating the Arms Industry of the Twenty-first Century," in Mary Kaldor, ed., *Global Insecurity: Restricting the Global Military Sector, Volume III* (London/New York, Pinter, 2000), ch. 6, especially 154–161.

45. Greg W. Schneider, "Pentagon Seeks to Aid Defense Contractors," *The Washington Post*, February 8, 2000, E1, E6 and "U.S. Urged for Defense Industry: Pentagon Panel Points to Profits, *The Washington Post*, May 18, 2000, E1, E7; John Donnelly, "Cohen: New Budget To Bolster Procurement," *Defense Week*, January 31, 2000, 3; Frank Wolfe, "Struggling Companies Will Rebound, Cohen Says," *Defense Daily*, January 31, 2000, 2; Kent Kresa, "Progress Through Process: The American Industrial Engine and the US Military," *Armed Forces Journal International* (December 1999), 124–127; Loren B. Thompson, "Plan for Defense Spending," *The Washington Post*, February 19, 2000; Thomas C. Donlan, "The Defense Industry needs less official help," *The Wall Street Journal*, March 13, 2000.

46. Philip A. Odeen, "Defense Industrial Base Remains at Risk," *National Defense* (June 2000) 4, https//www.nationaldefensemagazine.org/past-issues/2000 /June/2000; Greg Schneider, "Defense Industry Sees Gap in Both Candidates' Plans: Some Weapons Programs Threatened Under Bush or Gore, *The Washington Post*, October 19, 2000.

47. Tony Capaccio, "Pentagon Enacting Initiatives to Boost Defense Industry," *Defense Week*, October 20, 2000; Schneider, "Defense Industry Sees Gap in Both Candidates Plans," *The Washington Post*, October 29, 2000.

48. U.S. Department of Defense, Defense Science Board Task Force, "Preserving a Healthy and Competitive U.S. Defense Industry to Ensure our Future National Security," Final Briefing (Washington, Department of Defense) November 2000), 6 James Kitfield, "Military-Industrial Complexity," *Government Excecutive* (September 2000), 53–59; R. Pettibone, "Top 100 DOD Contractors," January 31, 2001, http://web1.whs.osd.mil/PEIDHOME/PROCSTAT/p01/fy2000/top100hm; Tony Cappacio, "Pentagon Enacting Initiatives to Boost Defense Industry," *Defense Week*, October 30, 2000 and "Pentagon To Implement Changes to Boost Industry," *Defense Week*, November 27, 2000, 5; Greg Schneider, "Four Defense Contractors to Join Forces; Joint Internet Exchange Planned for Buying, Selling," *The Washington Post*, March 23, 2000; Robert H. Williams, "Shrinking Arms Market Spurs Contest for Third World Sales," *National Defense* (December 1999), 35–35.

49. DSB Task Force, "Preserving a Healthy and Competitive Defense Industry, 28–48 passim, esp. 7, 22, 27; Under Secretary of Defense (Industrial Affairs), *Annual Industrial Capabilities Report to Congress*, January 2001, overview, 2–8; 51. Lawrence F. Skibbie, "Strategic Defense Review Should Address Industrial Base Concerns, *National Defense* (April 2001), 4; https//www.nationaldefensemagazine.org /articles/2001/4/1/2001april-strategic-review-should-address-industrial-base -concerns; Lawrence F. Skibbie, "Defense Secretary Says Industrial Base Decline is "A Serious Problem," *National Defense* (May 2001), 4, https://www.national defensemagazine.org/articles/2001/5/1/2001may-defense-secretary-says -industrial-base-decline-is-a-serious-problem; Katherine McIntire Peters, "Procure-

ment Outlook Still Cloudy," *Procurement Review* (2001), 48; Greg Schneider, "Northrop Buying Litton Industries: Big Defense Deal Has Local Tech Impact," *The Washington Post*, December 22, 2000 and "Shipbuilders to Merge; General Dynamics Buying Newport News," *The Washington Post*, April 26, 2001, E1, E17; Elizabeth G. Book, "Perceptions of Defense Sector Undermine Financial Health," *National Defense* (April 2001), 54–55, https://www.nationaldefensemagazine.org/articles/2001april-perceptions-of-defense-sector-undermine-financial-health; Franklin C. Spinney and John J. Shanahan, "Great Idea! Buy First, Then Find Out If It Flies," *The Washington Post*, February 11, 2001; Greg Schneider and Don Phillips, "Defense Contractors on Offensive; Lockheed Martin Hoping to Snatch Radar Contract from Raytheon," *The Washington Post*, March 13, 2001; Greg Schneider, "Allies Enlisted to Pay for Jet; Overseas Help May Make Warplanes Hard to Kill," *The Washington Post*, March 11, 2001; United States Commission on National Security/21st Century, "Road Map for National Security; Imperative for Change," draft report, January 31, 2001) (Washington, Commission on National Security/21st Century, 2001) passim; DFI International, *A Blueprint for Action Final Report* (Washington, DFI International, 2001), passim.

50. N.a., "Top 100 Defense Contractors" 50, 54–55; Also George Cahlink, "Replacing an Aging Fleet," 72–74 and "Equipping a Smaller, Lighter Forcer," 78, 80; Katherine McIntire Peters, "How Many Ships Are Enough?" 75, 76; Shane Harris, "Making Competition A Priority," 82, 83; Jason Peckenpaugh, "Doing Fewer Projects More Safely," 86–87; James Kitfield, "Uncertainty in the Skies," 90–91 and "Sowing the Seeds of a Revolution," 92–94 and "Leading the New Space Race," 96–97 as well as "Missile Defense Takes Center Stage," 98–99; all in *Procurement Review* (2001); Eugene Gholz and Harvey M. Sapolsky, "Restructuring the U.S. Defense Industry," *International Security*, 24, number 3 (Winter 1999/2000), 5–51, especially 45, 51; National Defense Panel, *Transforming Defense; National Security in the 21st Century* (Arlington, VA., National Defense Panel, December 1997), 78.

51. Elaine Tyler May, *Fortress America: How We Embraced Fear and Abandoned Democracy* (New York, Basic Books, 2017), 189; John W. Dower, *The Violent American Century: War and Terrors Since World War II* (Chicago, IL, Haymarket Books, 2017), 84; Gregory, *The Price of Peace*, 125; David Ryan, *US Foreign Policy in World History* (London/New York, Routledge, 2000), ch. 9, passim.

CHAPTER 8

1. Mark Danner, *Spiral: Trapped in the Forever War* (New York, Simon and Schuster, 2014), passim; John Glazer, "Withdrawing from Overseas Bases: Why a Forward-Deployed Military Posture Is Unnecessary, Outdated, and Dangerous," *Cato Policy Analysis No. 816*, July 18, 2017, 1.

2. This section draws upon Rosati and Scott, *Politics of United States Foreign Policy*, 33–38; Martel, *Grand Strategy in Theory and Practice*, 316–336; Brands, *What Good Is Grand Strategy?* ch. 4 passim; Colin Dueck, Conclusion in *The Obama Doctrine: American Grand Strategy Today* (New York: Oxford University Press, 2015), conclusion; Robert M. Gates, *Duty: Memoirs of a Secretary at War*. (New York, Alfred A. Knopf, 2014), passim; Ash Carter, *Inside The Five-Sided Box: Lessons Learned from a Lifetime of Leadership in the Pentagon* (New York, Dutton, 2020), ch. 1, 12, passim.

3. Elaine Tyler May, *Fortress America: How We Embraced Fear and Abandoned Democracy* (New York, Basic Books, 2017), 181–186, epilogue; Amanda Taub, "The Rise of American Authoritarianism," March 1, 2016, http://wwww.cvox .com/2016/3/1/1127424/trump-authoritarianism; Michael Lind, *The American Way of Strategy* (New York: Oxford University Press, 2006), ch. 13 passim.

4. Linda Weiss, *America Inc? Innovation and Enterprise in the National Security State* (Ithaca, Cornell University Press, 2014), 4; Robert D. Crook, "'Homeland' insecurity," *Washington Post*, April 21, 2017, A 20; Geoffrey R. Skoll, *Globalization of American Fear Culture: The Empire in the Twenty-First Century* (London, Palgrave Macmillan, 2016); Henry Giroux, "The National Insecurity State," excerpt from forward by Michel D. Yates in Giroux, *America's Addiction to Terrorism* (New York, Monthly Review Press, 2016), 32–45 and "Wanting it all: New Military Thinking Means More Cash or Fewer Options," *Financial Times*, December 12, 2003, 4.

5. Matthew J. Flynn, "The Department of Homeland Security," in Ty Seidules and Jacqueline E. Whitt, editors, *Stand Up and Fight: The Creation of U.S. Security Organizations, 1942–2005* (Carlisle Barracks, PA, United States Army War College Press, April 2015), 233–246; Garett M. Graff, *Raven Rock: The Story of the U.S. Government's Secret Plan to Save Itself While the Rest of the US Die* (New York, Simon and Schuster, 2017), chs 17–19 passim.

6. Weiss, *America Inc.?* 48–50; Gordon Adams and Cindy Williams, *Buying National Security: How America Plans and Pays for its Global Role and Safety at Home* (New York/London, Routledge, 2010), 120–121, 141–142, 145–148; Mark M. Lowenthal, *Intelligence: From Secrets to Policy* (Los Angeles, CQ Press, 2012 ed), ch.3, passim.

7. Adams and Williams, *Buying National Security*, ch. 1, especially 6, 7; Hacker and Vining, *American Military Technology*, 164–166.

8. David J. Rothkopf, "Business Versus Terror," *Foreign Policy*, 130 (May 1, 2002) 56–64 passim; Richard Falk, *The Great Terror War* (New York/Northampton, MA, Olive Branch Press, 2003), chs. 6, 7 passim; Charles Chatfield, "American Insecurity: Dissent from the 'Long War,'" in Andrew J. Bacevich, editor, *The Long War: A New History of U.S. National Security Policy Since World War II* (New York, Columbia University Press, 2007), 495–503, passim; Strobe Talbot and Nayan Chanda,

eds, *The Age of Terror: America and the World After September 11* (New York, Basic Books, 2001. 53–80. 143–170, passim.

9. Oliver Stone, "I believe Edward Snowden is Misunderstood by Americans," *Oliver Stone's Facebook*, October 27, 2016; Public Law, L. 107–56 (http://legtislikorg/us/pl-107–56).

10. Andrew Pollack, Reed Abelson, Milt Freudenheim, "A Delicate Balance: Patriotism vs. Business: Drug Makers Wrestle with World's New Rules," *New York Times*, October 21, 2001; "Industry Surge Hampered by Parts Suppliers, Air Force to Help Speed Ramp-up," *Defense Daily*, October 15, 2001, 6; Stark et al., Special Report From Forecast International," *Forecast International*, September 25, 3001, http://www.forecast1.com; Earle Eldridge, "Firms Prepare to equip Military," *USA Today*, September 19, 2001, 1B; Hamburg, Germany Financial Times, "Armament Industry Expects New Orders After Terrorist Attacks," *Hamburg Financial Times*, September 17, 2001, distributed by MiddleEastWire.com.; Julian E. Barnes, "War Profiteering," *U.S. News & World Report*, May 13, 2002, 20–23.

11. Carl Conetta, "The Dynamics of Defense Budget Growth, 1998–2011," and Todd Harrison, "The New Guns-versus-Butter Debate," both *Economics and Security: Resourcing National Priorities*, Ed. Richmond M. Lloyd, editor, [Ser. William B. Ruger Chair of National Security Economics Papers, no. 5] (Newport: Naval War College, 2010), 20–24; Thorpe, *American Warfare State*, 9–11; Frederick S. Weaver, *An Economic History of the United States*, 151, table 8.1.

12. Martin Wolf, "America Failed to Calculate the Enormous Costs of War," *Financial Times*, January 11, 2006; David R. Francis, "More Costly Than 'The War To End All Wars,'" *Christian Science Monitor,*, August 29, 2005; David Von Drehle, "Rallying 'Round The Flag," *Washington Post Magazine*, April 9, 2006, 10–16, 41–47; Art Pine, "Military Cutting Orders for Costly High-tech Weapons," Daily Briefing, *Government Executive*, February 5, 2007, accessed at http://govexec.com.

13. Bank, Stark and Thorndike, *War and Taxes*, ch. 6 and Conclusion, passim; Kreps, *Taxing Wars*, ch. 6 passim; Robert D. Hormats, *Price of Liberty*, ch. 9 passim *and*, esp. 275–279; Dennis S. Ippolito, *Why Budgets Matter*, 299–300; Jackie Calmes, "Pentagon's Blank Check May Be Withdrawn: Congressional Unease Mounts amid Off-Budget War Spending and Ballooning Deficits, *Wall Street Journal*, March 10, 2006.

14. Hormats, *Price of Liberty*, Conclusion passim; Bank, Stark, Thorndike, *War and Taxes*, Conclusion, passim; Ippolito, *Why Budgets Matter*, 241–258.

15. Hormats, *Price of Liberty*, ch. 9, passim and esp., 275–279; Jacques Gansler, "The U.S. Defense Industrial Base: From the End of the Cold War to the Present," in *The U.S. Defense Industrial Base: From the End of the Cold War to the Present; Symposium*, June 2, 2005 at Industrial College of the Armed Forces, Ft.

McNair, Washington, DC (Washington, National Defense University Press, 2006); Michael J. Meese, "The American Defense Budget 2017–2020," in R. D. Hooker, editor, *Charting A Course: Strategic Choices for a New Administration* (Washington, DC, National Defense University Press, 2016), ch. 4.

16. Radley Balko, Conclusion in *Rise of the Warrior Cop: The Militarization of America's America's Police Forces* (New York, Public Affairs, 2014), conclusion; May, *Fortress America*, chs. 3, 4, 5 passim; Steven M. Kosiak, Executive Summary in "Cost of the Wars in Iraq and Afghanistan and Other Military Operations Through 2008 And Beyond," (Washington, DC, Center for Strategic and Budgetary Assessments, 2008), passim.

17. Anthony H. Cordesman, "The Five Best 'Investments' Resource Decisions in National Security," (Washington, DC, Center for Strategic and International Studies, May 2, 2006 working draft revised), 2, 3 author's files; Hormats, *Price of Liberty*, 286–289.

18. Winslow Wheeler, "Ringing Up the Bill for America's Defense," *Star-Telegram*, Fort Worth (TX), March 4, 2007.

19. Greg Jaffe and Jonathan Karp, "Defense Spending Is Set For Sharp Rise," *Wall Street Journal*, February 6, 2007, 13; Jeffrey M. Tebbs, *Pruning the Defense* [2007 Budgeting Options Series] (Washington, DC, The Brookings Institution, January 2007), 3; Gary J. Schmitt, "Of Men and Materiel; The Crisis in Defense Spending," *National Security Outlook [AEI Online]*, November 1, 2006.

20. James Boxell, "Boeing Warns on Defence Budget," *Financial Times*, June 18, 2007; Lawrence J. Korb, "The Korb Report—A Defense for America," *Sensible Solutions pdf* (New York, Business Leaders for Sensible Solutions, 2006), 1, accessed at http://www.sensiblepriorities.org/pdf/korb_report_Finalb.pdf; Miriam Pemberton and Lawrence Korb, "Report of the Task Force on A Unified Security Budget for the United States, FY 2008," (Washington, DC, Foreign Policy in Focus Task Force of the Institute For Policy Studies, April 2007), 5–7, 55.

21. Fred Reed, "Why We Fund Unneeded Weapons, *Washington Times*, July 14, 2007, C9 and E.A. Merle, "Armaments and Investments," F 4; Thom Shanker, "Proposed Military Spending Is Highest since WWII," *New York Times*, February 4, 2008; Greg Grant, "Defense budget Reflects Cost of Maintaining Volunteer Force in Wartime," *Government Executive*, February 5, 2008 accessed at http://govexec.com.

22. Gordon Adams, "Greater Discipline Required on Defence Spending," *Financial Times*, March 19, 2008.

23. August Cole, "Defense Firms Chase Lucrative Missions in Global Market," *Wall Street Journal*, May 8, 2008; Sandra Erwin, "Preventive Care Prescribed for Pentagon Big Ticket Programs," *National Defense*, 92, no. 651 (February 2008), 8, accessed at https://nationaldefensemagazine.org/articles/2008/1/31/2008february

-preventive-care-prescribed-for-pentagon--bigticket-programs; Robert Brodsky, "GAO: Major Defense Contracts Cheaper to Cancel than Continue," *Government Executive*, March 19, 2008 accessed at. http://govexcec.comrbrodsky@govexec.com; Dana Hedgpeth, "GAO Blasts Weapons Budget: Cost Overruns Hit $295 Billion," *Washington Post*, April 1, 2008; A l, 4 and, "Balancing Defense and the Budget: After Eight Boom Years for Spending on Military Equipment, Contractors Expect a Slowdown," *Washington Post*, October 13, 2008, D 1; L. Dickerson, "Will Obama Cut Defense Spending?" *Forecast International*, November 7, 2008 and Shaun. McDougall, "Defense Spending strong Under Obama Administration," *Forecast International*, November 10, 2008, both http://www.forecastinternational.com.

24. Michael Wynne, "Investment Is Still Important: Increase Defense Capital Spending, *Defense News*, October 27, 2008 and Antoine Boessenkool, "In Down Economy, U.S. Defense Firms Face Unusual Problem, *Defense News*, November 17, 2008; Shaun McDougall, "Defense Spending Strong Under Obama Administration," *Forecast International*, November 10, 2008 accessed at http://www.forecast international.com.

25. N.a., "Limited Changes for Obama's First Defense Budget," *CQ Politics*, January 15, 2009 accessed at: http://www.cqpolitics.com; K. Chaisson, "Everyone Has Recommendations for Obama Administration," *Forecast International*, January 19, 2009, http://www.forecastinternational.com

26. Maya Schenwar, "The Push to Downsize Defense," *Truthout*, February 27, 2009; Tom Donnelly and Gary Schmitt, "Targeted Spending: Here's How to Make a Real Stimulus take Flight," *Washington Post*, February 8, 2009; Dana A. Hedgpeth and Steven Mufson, "A Retreat in Spending: As Obama's White House Shifts U.S. Priorities, The Defense Industry Prepares to Retrench," *Washington Post*, February 6, 2009, D 1, 2; Marion Blakey, Lawrence P. Farrell, Satan Soloway, "Defense Executives Assess Business Impact of Major Budget Cuts Conclude Further Reductions Will Deter Investment, Weaken Industrial Base," A Letter to Secretary of Defense Leon Panetta, November 13, 200, copy, author's collection; Gates, *Duty*, 460–465; Carter, *Inside the Five-Sided* Box, chap. 1.

27. Mary Louise Kelly, "Gates Calls for Shift in Defense Spending Priorities," *NPS News*, April 6, 2009; David W. Barno, Nora Bensahel and Travis Sharp, *Hard Choices: Responsible Defense in an Age of Austerity* (Washington, Center for a New American Security, 2011), passim.

28. Demeti Sevastopulo, "Gates Under Fire for Deep Defence Cuts," and Sylvia Pfeiffer and Sevastopulo, "Gates to slash military projects," both *Financial Times*, April 7, 32009, 1, 2; S; Frida Berrigan, "Is the Next Defense Budget a Stimulus Package?: Why the Pentagon Can't Put America Back to Work," *TomDispatch*, March 1, 209 accessed at http://TomDispatch.com; Tom Kauffman, "Stimulus Bill Gives DoD $7.4 BB." *Defense News*, 24, no. 1 March 30, 2009, 1, 8; Shaun McDougall, "Gates

Outlines Major FY10 Budget Decisions," *Forecast International*, April 6, 2009, accessed at: http://www.forecastinternational.com.; Daniel Dombey and Jeremy Lerner, "Obama's Defence Cuts Under Fire," *Financial Times*, May 12, 2011; Vago Muradian, "DoD Gains 100B in 2011–2015," *Defense News*, 2, no. 48 (December 1, 2009), 1, 6.

    29. Shaun McDougall, "U.S. Defense Budget Release," *Forecast International*, May 12, 2009; John T. Bennett, "'The Spigot Is starting To Close': DoD Hints at Spending Drop, but lacks 50-Year Details," *Defense News*, 24, no. 19 (May 11, 2009), 1, 8; Michael O'Hanlon, "Obama's Defense Budget Gap," *Washington Post*, June 10, 2009, A19; John T. Bennett and William Matthews, "Lawmakers Carve Marks on Gates' DoD Budget," *Defense News*, 24, no. 26 (June 29, 2009), 10.

    30. Tom Donnelly and Tim Sullivan, "A Nation at War, An Administration in Retreat: An Assessment of the 2010 Quadrennial Defense Review and the FY 2011 Defense Budget," Briefing. (Washington, Center for Defense Studies, 2011), passim; Vargo Muradian and John T. Bennett, "U.S. Budget Battle Begins; Hold on Carter Nomination Seen as First Punch," *Defense News*, 24, no. 14 (April 6, 2009), 1, 7.

    31. David Ignatius, "Obama's Pivot on Defense," *Washington Post*, January 8, 2012, AZ 17; Walter Pincus, "On Defense, GOP Platform Echoes Romney," *Washington Post*, August 23, 2012; Lawrence P. Farrell, Jr., "Administration's Defense Strategy Precedes Budget: A Good First Step," *National Defense* (February 2012), 3 accessed at https://www.nationaldefensemagazine.org/aicles/2012/2/1/2012february-administrations-defense-strategy-precedes-budget-a-good-first-step; Sandra I. Erwin, "It's Hobson's Choice: Dollars For Defense or for Education?" *National Defense* (February 2012), 8 accessed at https://www.nationaldefensemagazine.org/articles/2012/1/31/2012february-its-a-hobsons-choice-dollars-for-defense-or-for-education; Sandra L. Erwin, "Defense Drawdown: It's Been All Talk, Now It's Time to Walk," *Defense Week* (December 2012), 6; editor, "Shrinking Defense: Mr. Hagel's High-wire Act," *Washington Post*, April 8, 2013.

    32. Lawrence P. Farrell, Jr., "Budget Deal Gives Defense Breathing Room (UPDATED)" *National Defense*, January 2014, 7 accessed at https://www.nationaldefensemagazine.org/articles/2014/1/1/2014january-budget-deal-gives-defense-breathing-room-updated; Donna Cassata, "Budget Deal Stabilizes Pentagon Spending," *Washington Post*, December 12, 2013; Lawrence P. Farrell, "Sequester Impact More Than Meets the Eye," *National Defense* (September 2013), 6, accessed at https://www.nationaldefensemagazine.org/past-issues/2013/sep-2013; Sandra I. Erwin, "Sequester Sinks In, Extent of Fallout Unknown, *National Defense* (September 2013), 8, accessed at https://www.nationaldefensemagazine.org/past-issues/2013/sep-2013; Howard P. "Buck" McKeon, "Playing Chicken with Defense," *Washington Post*, July 12, 2013; Walter Pincus, "The Pentagon's Other Stash," *Washington Post*, April 22, 2013; Craig Whitlock, "More Cuts Ahead for Pentagon, Hagel Says: Defense Secretary Warns that

Military Must Rein in Soaring Costs," *Washington Post*, April 4, 2013; Ernesto Lonfono, "Proposed Defense Budget is About the Same as Last One; Plan Assumes Spending Cuts will be Averted," *Washington Post*, April 10, 2013.

33. Robert J. Samuelson, "Neglected Defense," *Washington Post*, September 8, 2014; 4; Lawrence P. Farrell, Jr., "Budget Sets Stage for Fight With Congress," *National Defense* (April 2014), accessed at ttps://www.nationaldefensemagazine .org/articles/204/4/1/April-budget-sets-stage-for-fight-with-congress; Center for Strategic & International Studies, "Discussion on the 2014 QDR and FY 15 Defense Budget," (Washington, CSIS, March 10, 2014/June 2014), passim; Brad Curran, et al., *US DoD 2015 Budget Assessment, Force Reduction and Limited Modernization* (Mountain View, CA, Frost and Sullivan, 2014), 5.

34. Sandra I. Erwin, "In '15 Budget, Red Flags for Contractors," *National Defense (April 2014)*, 6, accessed at https://www.nationaldefensemagazine.org /articles/2014/4/1/2014april-in-15-budget-red-flags-for-contractors; Walter Pincus, "Seeking a Strategy-driven Defense Budget," *Washington Post*, February 3, 2015; Office of The Under Secretary of Defense (Comptroller) Chief Financial Officer, "United States Department of Defense Fiscal Year 2026 Budget Request Overview," (Washington, Department of Defense, February 2015), 1–1 to 1–5; Robert Greenstein, "Commentary: What to Expect in the Coming Budgets—Regressive Policies, Gimmickry, and Budget Balance Only on Paper," (Washington, Center on Budget and Policy Priorities, March 15, 2015), passim; Walter Pincus, "Military's Duplicative Budgets Deserve Scrutiny," *Washington Post*, November 10, 2015; Michele Flournoy and Eric Edelman, "A Budget Deal that Hurt National Security," *Washington Post*, September 19, 2014; William J. Perry and John P. Abizad, co-chairs, "Ensuring a Strong U.S. Defense for the Future: The National Defense Panel Review of the 2014 Quadrennial Defense Review," (Washington, United States Institute of Peace, July 2014), ch. 5; Fred Hiatt, "A Military Budget for the Real World," *Washington Post*, May 18, 2015.

35. Craig R. McKinely, "The Year Ends on Some Positive Notes," *National Defense* (December 2015), 4 accessed at https//www.nationaldefensemagazine .org/articles; Sandra I. Erwin, "Should the Pentagon Rescue Ailing Suppliers?" *National Defense* (May 2014), accessed at https://www.nationaldefensemagazine.org /articles/2014/5/1/2014may-should-the-pentagon-rescue-ailing-suppliers; Paul McLeary, "US Defense Budget Request Will Change Drastically, Experts Say," *Defense News*, 30, no.4 (February 12, 2015), 1, 7; Anthony H. Cordesman, *The FY 2016 Defense Budget and US Strategy: Key Trends and Data Points.* (Washington, DC, Center for Strategic and International Studies, March 6, 2015), 3, 13, 20, 22, 28, 47, 55, 64, 72, 85, 91, 111, 119, 128.

36. Missy Ryan, "In Pentagon budget proposal, a new emphasis on countering Russia, China," *Washington Post*, February 2, 2016; Dan Lamothe, "Controversial Budgeting for the Military Persists: 'Supplemental' Funds Intended for Wars Pay for

Gear, Other Efforts," *Washington Post*, February 12, 2016, A5; Editorial Board, "A Better, Not Bigger, Military Budget," *New York Times*, February 29, 2016; Richard Lardner, "GOP Backers of Defense Budget Hike Got Millions in Donations," *Associated Press*, February 25, 2016, accessed at http://readersupportednews.org/news-section2/318-66/35394; Steven Kull, *Creating A Federal Budget For 2017: What the American People Would Do* (College Park, Program for Public Consultation, School of Public Policy: University of Maryland (February 2016), 16–19; Matthew Goldberg, *Prospects for DoD's Budget Over the Next Decade* (Washington, DC, Congressional Budget Office, May 3, 2016), passim; Katherine Blakeley, *Seven Areas to Watch in the FY17 Defense Budget* (Washington, DC, Center for Strategic and Budgetary Assessments, February 2016), passim; Sandra L. Erwin, "Jittery Times for Government Contractors," *National Defense* 100, no. 749 (April 2016), 6, accessed at https://www.nationaldefensemagazine.org/articles/2016/4/1/2016april-jittery-times-for-government-contractors; John Harper, "More Procurement Falloffs on the Horizon," *National Defense*, 100, no. 749 (April 2016), 9, accessed at https://www.nationaldefensemagazine.org/articles/2016/4/1/2016april-more-procurement-falloffs-on-the-horizon. Matteau Kramer, "Across-the-board budget cuts have had a much smaller impact on military spending than news reports suggest," *Facebook and Twitter* both on March 4, 2014, US Department of Defense, "Estimated Impacts of Sequestration-Level Funding," April 2014, 1–1; Todd Harrison, *Chaos and Uncertainty: The FY 2014 Defense Budget and Beyond* (Washington, Center for Strategic and Budgetary Assessment, October 2013), passim and *Analysis of the FY 2015 Defense Budget* (Washington, Center for Strategic and Budgetary Assessment, 2014), 1–4; Nick Turse, *The Complex: How the Military-Industrial Complex Invades Our Everyday Lives* (New York: Henry Holt/Metropolitan Books, 2008), in toto.

37. Robert Higgs, "The Security-Industrial-Congressional Complex (SICC)," *The Independent*, October 19, 2006, accessed at http://www.independent.review.org/newsroom/article.asp?id=1835.

38. U.S. Department of Defense, *Quadrennial Roles and Missions Review Report* (Washington, DoD, 2009, 2–4; Kathleen Hicks, Mark Cancian, Todd Harrison and Andrew Hunter, *Defense Outlook 2016: What to Know, What to Expect* (Washington, Center for Strategic & International Studies, January 2016), 2–7; Stephen J. Hadley and William J. Perry, "What needs to change to defend America," *Washington Post*, August 1, 2010, A19; Ira Chermus, "Requiem for the War on Terror," *TomDispatch*, April 9, 2009, accessed at TomDispatch.com; Trevor Timm, "If this is what an anti-war presidency looks like to you, you're detached from reality," *The Guardian*, March 30, 2009; Jeffrey Goldberg, "The Obama Doctrine: The U.S. president talks through his hardest decisions about America's role in the world," *The Atlantic*, 317, no. 3 (April 2016), 6; Colin Dueck, *The Obama Doctrine*, in toto.

39. Ralph Nader, "The Empire is Eating Itself," *CounterPunch*, September 2,

2011; Tom Sherwood, "Rethinking 'Securicat' America," *Northwest Current* [Washington, DC], April 4, 2012; Mark Karlin "Fear, Corporate Profiteering, and Government Expansion of the Security Surveillance State on the USA Borderland," *Truthout/News Analysis*, March 10, 2013; Falguni A. Sheth and Robert E. Prash, "Our Failed Security-State," *Reader Supported News*, April 27, 2013; Micah Zenko and Michael A. Cohen, "Clear and Present Safety; the United States Is More Secure Than Washington Thinks," *Foreign Affairs*, 91, no. 2 (March/April 2012), 79–93; Craig Hoogstra, "Taking Exception: When the Police and the Military Start to Blend Together," *Washington Post*, October 3, 2015; Frank Rich, "Day's End: The 9/11 Decade is Now Over. The Terrorists Lost. But Who Won?" *New York Magazine*, August 27, 2011; Ken Klippenstein, "Militarization of Police Is Not Just Dangerous—It's Wasteful Too, Study Finds," *Reader Supported News*, April 14, 2015; William Boardman, "Are Most Americans Still Afraid to Be Unafraid?" *Reader Supported News*, January 19, 2016; Leslie thatcher, "How the Powers That Be Maintain the 'Deep State': An Interview With Mike Lofgren," *Truthout*, February 21, 2016; Glenn Greenwald, "New Study Shows Mass Surveillance Breeds Meekness, Fear and Self-Censorship," *The Intercept/Reader Supported News*, May 1, 2016; National Security Preparedness Group, *Tenth Anniversary Report Card: The Status of the 9/11 Commission Recommendations* (Washington, Bipartisan Policy Center, September 2011), passim; Aaron B. O'Connell, "The Permanent Militarization of America," *New York Times*, November 5, 2012.

    40. Barbara Lee, "Congress is missing in action," *Washington Post*, May 4, 2016, A18; Anthony H. Cordesman, *Grand Strategy in the Afghan, Pakistan and Iraq Wars: The End State Fallacy*, October 14, 2010 (Washington, Center For Strategic & International Studies), October 14, 2010); Peter Rudolf, "War Weariness and Change in Strategy in US Policy on Afghanistan," [SWP Comments] *Stiftung Wissenschaft und Politik* (October 31,m 2011), 1–8; Walter Pincus, "Gauging the Price Tag for Afghanistan's Security," *Washington Post*, December 21, 2010 James K. Galbraith, Brenton Kenkel, "What Would a War with Iran help?, *Washington Post*, November 3, 2010; Rachel Maddow, "Reaching the limit in Afghanistan?" *Washington Post*, March 28, 2012; Walter Pincus, "Gauging the Military's Facts Behind a 'Daily Impact' Assessment," *Washington Post*, November 8, 20112; Nick Turse, "Wars of Attrition: Green Zones of the Mind, Guerrillas and a Technical Knockout in Afghanistan," *TomDispatch*, April 24, 2012; Glenn Greenwald, "The 'War on Terror' Designed to Never End," *The Guardian/Reader Supported News*, January 5, 2013.

    41. Mike Lofgren, "Blowback: Donald Trump Is the Price We Pay for the 'War on Terror,'" *Truthout*, March 1, 2016; Amanda Taub, "The Rise of American authoritarianism," *Vox*, March 1, 2016; Henry A. Giroux, "The National Insecurity State," *Truthout*, February 25, 2016 and *America's Addiction to Terrorism* (New York, Monthly Review Press, 2016); Alfred MCoy, "Washington's twenty-First-Century Opium Wars, *TomDispatch*, February 22, 2016; Walter Pincus, "Accepting limits on U.S. efforts in

Iraq, Syria," *Washington Post*, November 4, 2014; John Hanrahan, "A Cold Calculation": How Much is Too Much to Spend on Afghanistan?" *Nieman Watchdog*, June 125, 2011; Helene Cooper, "Cost of Wars a rising Issue as Obama Weighs Troop Levels," *New York Times News Service*, June 22, 2011; Walter Pincus, "Lessons from the Last 10 Years of Warfare," *Washington Post*, November 1, 2011; Alan Beattie, "Counting the Cost of al-Qaeda's Chief: Bin Laden's Death; the Aftermath; *Financial Times*, May 5, 2011; Bruce Berkowitz, "Strategy For A Long Struggle," *Hoover Institution Policy Review* (February & March 2007), passim; Charles Pena, *Winning the Un-War: A New Strategy For The War on Terrorism* (Washington, Potomac Books, 2006), passim.

42. Beattie, "Counting the Cost of al-Qaeda's Chief" and Rachman, "Declare Victory," both *Financial Times*, May 5, 2011.

43. Brown University, Eisenhower Study Group, Eisenhower Research Project, "Costs of War; The Costs of War Since 2001: Iraq, Afghanistan and Pakistan" (Providence, Watson Institute, June 2011), passim; Greg Jaffe and Missy Ryan, "'Exit strategy' for Afghanistan fades; U.S. Military Shifting Its Mind-Set, Officials see need for long-term troop commitments," *Washington Post*, January 27, 2016, A1, A 2; Jon Harper, "Counter-ISIL Campaign Tops $3 Billion," *National Defense* (September 2015), 10, https://www.nationaldefensemagazine.org/articles/2015/9/1/2015september-counterisil-campaign-tops-3-billion; Gideon Rachman, "Declare victory and end the 'global war on terror'?" *Financial Times*, May 3, 2011.

44. James Jay Carafano, "The Third Offset: The 'Fairy Dust' Strategy," *The National Interest*, November 2, 2014; Secretary of Defense Chuck Hagel, "Speech: Reagan National Defense Forum Keynote," November 15, 2014, accessed at http://www.defense.gov/Speeches/Speech.aspx?SpeechID=1903; Deputy Secretary Bob Work, "Speech to the 2014 CSIS Global Security Forum, November 12, 2014, accessed at http://www.defense.gov/Speeches/Speech.aspx?Speech ID=1899); Craig R. McKinley, "The Rocky Path to a Third Offset," National Defense, vol. C, No. 749 (April 2016), 4.

45. U.S. Congress, 112th, 1st sess., Senate Hearing 112–256, Committee on Armed Services, Subcommittee on Emerging Threats and Capabilities, "Health and Status of the Defense Industrial Base and Its Science and Technology Elements," May 3, 2011.

46. Gansler, "The U.S. Defense Industrial Base" ICAF Symposium, June 2, 2005), 12–19.

47. Daniel H. Elsen and Sean I. Mills, draft *U.S. Defense Industrial Base—Trends and Issus* (Washington, DC, Congressional research Service, 2016), 15; Margaret Sullivan, "Much of Media Marches to President's Military Tune," *Washington Post*, April 10, 2017, C 1, C3.

48. Elizabeth G. Book, 'War Will Change Industrial Priorities, Says Policy Chief," *National Defense* (January 2002), 14–15, accessed as nationaldefensemagazine.org/articles/2001/12/31/2002-january-war-will-change-industrial

-priorities-says-policy-chief; Elizabeth Book, "Pentagon Industrial Policy Rooted in 'Market Economics,'" *National Defense* (January 2001), 1–5, 6–8 accessed as https://www.nationaldefensemagazine.org/articles2001/12/31/2002january-pentagon-industrial-policy-rooted-in-market-economics.

49. Thorpe, *The American Warfare State*, 61–64.

50. U.S. Department of Defense, Under Secretary of Defense for Acquisition, Technology and Logistics, *Annual Industrial Capabilities Report to Congress, 2013*, Washington, DC, Department of Defense, October 2013), 1–12, and append. C and D; Philip Ewing, "DoD's 'industrial capabilities' dilemma," *DOD Buzz, Online Defense and Acquisition Journal*, October 4, 2011, accessed at https://www.dodbuzz.com/2011/10/04/dods-industrial--capabilities-dilemma.

51. Department of Defense, *Annual Industrial Capabilities Report, 2013*, 5–9, 13–43, 45–49; Robert Levinson, "Competition, Cooperation Among Defense Contractors: BGOV Insight," *Bloomberg Government*, January 23, 2014.

52. DOD *Capabilities Report, 2013*, 1–2.

53. DOD *Capabilities Report, 2013*, 14–67 inter alia.

54. James Fallows, "The Dustbin of History: Military-Industrial Complex," *Foreign Policy*, November 9, 2009, 46–48 accessed at htps://foreignpolicy.com/2009/11/09/the-dustbin-of-history-the-military-industrial-complex/; Brad Knickerbocker, "Return of the 'Military-Industrial Complex?" *The Christian Science Monitor*; Peter Cary, "The Pork Game," and Christopher H. Schmitt, "Wages of Sin," both in *U.S. News and World Report*, May 13, 2002, 25–26 and 28–34 respectively; Anne Marie Squeo, "Ready for Battle," R 4 and R 7 as well as "The Ripple Effect, R 5, *Wall Street Journal*, March 28, 2001; Ian Carson, et al., "A Survey of the Defence Industry," *The Economist*, July 20. 2002, 3–16.

55. Stan Crock, "An Arms Industry Too Big For The Task At Hand," *Washington Post*, August 31, 2003.

56. Pierre A. Chao, dialogue "The Structure and Dynamics of the Defense Industry," March 2, 2005, Washington, D.C. Security Studies Program Seminar, Center for Strategic and International Studies, 2005, v.

57. Loren B. Thompson, "Pentagon Incompetence Hastens U.S. Industrial Decline," Lexington Institute *Defense*, March 7, 2006; Sebastian Mallaby, "Why U.S. Business Is Winning," *Washington Post*, March 27, 2006, A15; also Editors, "The Business of Business: Expectations of the Company are Changing," *Washington Post*, June 26, 2006.

58. James Altucher, "Money in machines of war," *Financial Times*, February 15, 2005; Marianne Brun-Rovet, "A New and Lucrative Market Opens Up: Homeland Security," *Financial Times*, November 19, 2003, 5; Renae Merle, "Battlefield Is A Showcase for Defense Firms: Arms Exporters Could Thrive On Televised Success in Iraq," *Washington Post*, April 1, 2003, E 1, E 5; Talif Deen, "Arms Suppliers

Scramble into Iraq," *Truthout* via *Inter Press Servicer*, July 12, 2004' Kenneth Flamm, "Post-Cold War Policy and the U.S. Defense Industrial Base," *The Bridge Linking Engineering and Society.* 35, no. 1 (Spring 2005), 5–12; Pierre A. Chao, "The Structure ad Dynamics of the Defense Industry," unpublished paper (Washington, Center for Strategic and International Studies, 2005) and Loren B. Thompson, "The Future of the Defense industry," unpublished remarks to a Lockheed Martin Management Conference, October 5, 2005, both copies, author's files.

59. Renae Merle and Sara Kehaulani Good, "Aerospace Rivalry Expands: Airbus Parent to Build Alabama Plant In Bid to Wrest Defense Work from Boeing," *Financial Times*, June 25, 2005; Mark Jewell, "Northrop, Raytheon Beat Expectations: Military R&D Spending Boosts Profits," *Washington Examiner*, July 27, 2005; James Boxwell, "Rolls hopes for $8 bn from US contract," *Washington Examiner*, August 25, 2005; Christopher Bowsz, "Lockheed soars on Pentagon contracts," *Financial Times*, July 27, 2005; Renae Merle, "Pentagon's Global View: U.S. Increasingly Looks Abroad For Competitive Defense Contracts," *Washington Post*, March 8, 23005, E 1, E 5; Larry Makinson, "Outsourcing the Pentagon: Who benefits from the Politics and Economics of Security?" (Washington, Center for Public Integrity, September 2004); Dave Ahearn, "DOD Leader Backs Purchases of Systems from Abroad," *Defense Today*, February 24, 2005.

60. Renae Merle, "A Nervous Eye on Defense Firms," *Washington Post*, November 11, 2005, D 1, D5; Ago Muradian, "Pentagon Deputy Summons CEOs," *Defense News*, December 1, 2005 accessed at http://defensenews.com; Renae Merle, "Campaigning for the C-17; Long Beach Officials Look for Ways to Lower Boeing's Costs, Hang On to Jobs," *Washington Post*, December 28, 2004, D1, D2; Knut Royce, "Close ties at the Pentagon," *Newsday*, October 13, 2004; Makinson, "Outsourcing the Pentagon," charts "The 100 Biggest defense Contractors, FY 1998–2003," "Competition," "Least Competitive Categories," "Most competitive Categories," "Cost-Plus Contracts," "Joint Ventures," "Foreign Contractors."

61. Lawrence P. Farrell, Jr., "The Coming Challenge for Defense," *National Defense* (April 2006), 4 accessed aathttps://www.nationaldefensemagazine.org/articles/2006/4/1/2006april-the-coming-challenge-for-defense.; Gansler presentation, "The U.S. Defense Industrial Bas," ICAF symposium, 2005.

62. Shahnaz M. Punjani, *The Iron Triangle Manifested: U.S. Air Force Tanker Lease 2001–2005* [Industrial College of the Armed Forces Case Study] (Washington, D.C., National Defense University Press, January 2012), 1–34; Shane Harris, "Own the Sky," *Washingtonian*, November 1, 2010, 1–5; Eric A. Hollister, "Ike Warned Us About This: The MICC Stranglehold on Responsible Procurement," *Joint Forces Quarterly*, no. 59 (4th quarter 2010), 86–93; John McCain, Congressional Floor on the Military-Industrial Congressional Complex, December 15, 2011, accessed at: https://www.govinfo.go/content/pkg/CRECB-2011-pt15/pdf/CRECB-2011-pt15-Pgw02q87–2.

pdf; Steven Pearlstein, "Outrage is Wasted on Boeing's Snub by the Air Force," *Washington Post*, March 7, 2008; Jacques S. Gansler and William Lucyshyn, "Why Compete? Defense Department can split tanker buy and still save money," *National Defense* (June 2009), 16, accessed at: https://www.nationaldefensemagazine.org/articles/2009/6/6/2009june-defense-departmeny-can-split-tanker-buy-and-still-save-money; Dana Hedgpath, "A Mission To Rebuild Reputations: Upcoming Deals to Test Reforms at Air Force, Boeing," *Washington Post*, January 17, 2008, D-1, D-8 while on JSF criticism, see David Hammer, "Report: Pentagon Spending Too Much on Unproven Jet Fighter: Auditing Branch of Congress Criticizes Pentagon's Plan for F-35 Joint Strike Fighter," *Washington Post*, Mach 16, 2006; William Matthews, "Monopoly Money: Relying on Single Suppliers Could Cost in the Long Run," *Armed Forces International* (March 2006), 12; Robin Niblett and Pierre Chao, "The Strike Fighter Tests Transatlantic Ties," *Financial Times*, May 30, 2006; Guy Norris, "Power of Two: The Battle to Power the Joint Strike Fighter Harks Back to the "Great Engine War' Fought a Decade Ago Over the F-15 and F-16, but Will Competition Bring Benefits?" *Flight International*, no. 223 (29 May 2006), 34–35, 38–40; Bryan Bender, "Major Arms Soar To Twice Pre-9/11 Cost: Systems to Have Little Direct Role in Terror Fight," *Boston Globe*, August 19, 2006; Grace V. Jean, "F-35 Factory: One Aircraft Per Day by 2016," *National Defense*, 93 (July 2008) 41–44, accessed at: https://wwwnationaldefensemagazine.org/articles/2008/7/2008july-f35-factory-one-aircraft-per-day-by-2016.

  63. Frida Berrigan, "Weapons Come Second: Can Obama Take on the Pentagon?" *TomDispatch*, November 25, 2008, assessed at: http:// tomdispatch.com; Sandra I. Erwin, "Global Indusial Trends Spell Doom for Defense," *National Dispatch*, 90 (August 2006), 124, accessed at https://wwwnationaldefensemagazine.org/past-issues/2006/august-2006 and Sandra L. Erwin, "Industry Fortune Tellers See a Mix of Boom and Bust," *National Security*, 90 (November 2006), 12, accessed at https://www.nationaldefensemagazine.org/past-issues/2006/nov-2006; Renae Merle and Griff Witte, "Circling the Statehouse; Federal Spending Tightens, Contractors Scck Out New Clients: State, Local Governments Are in a Spending Mood," *Washington Post*, October 23, 2006, D1, D4; Glen W. Swanson, "Not Really Ready for War," (letter to Editor), *Washington Post*, December 16, 2006; Lawrence P. Farrell, Jr., "Manufacturing Edge Essential to Defense," *National Defense*, 91 (January 2007), 5 accessed at https: //www.natonaldefensemagazine.org/past-issues/2007/jan-2007; Renae Merle, "Weapons Maker Struggles To Survive: Money Trouble, SEC Inquiry Imperil Allied Defense Group," *Washington Post*, April 2, 2007; Lawrence P. Farrell, Jr., "Defense Industrial Base; Plans Needed to Ensure Soft Landing, *National Defense*, 92 (May 2008), 6, accessed at https://www.nationaldefensemagazine.org/past-issues/2008/may-2008; Sandra L. Erwin, "Industry Unscathed by Iraq Drawdown, Says Report," *National Defense*, 92 (June 2008) accessed at https://www.nationaldefensemagazine.org/articles/2008/6/1/2008june-industry-unscathed-by-iraq-drawdown-says-report.

64. Sandra I. Erwin, "Pentagon Must Avert 'Points of Failure' in Supplier Base, Says Industrial Policy Chief," *National Defense* (January 2010), accessed at https://www.nationaldefensemagazine.org/articles/2009/12/31/2010january-insourcing-efforts-require-careful-balanced-approach and Lawrence P. Ferrell, Jr., "In-Sourcing efforts Require Careful, Balanced Approach," *National Defense*, 5, accessed at https://www.nationaldefensemagazine.org/articles/2009/12/31/2010january-pentagon-must-avert-points-of-failure-in-supplier-base-says-industrial-policy-chief; U.S. Department of Defense, Office of Under Secretary of Defense for Acquisition, Technology and Logistics, Industrial Policy, "Annual Industrial Capabilities Report to Congress, May 2010," (Washington, DC, Department of Defense, 2010), 1–4. Yana Kunichoff, "Defense Spending the Top Priority, Critics Fear," *Truthout Report*, May 30, 2010; Bill Quigley, "Corporations Profit From Permanent War: Memorial Day 2010," and Camillo "Mac" Bica, "Corporatizing and Militarizing Memorial Day for 'Fun" and Profit," both *Truthout Op-Ed*, May 31, 2010; Kathleen Parker, "The Engine that Might," *Washington Post*, June 10, 2010; Government Printing Office, "Strong Leadership is Key to Planning and Executing Stable Weapon Programs," May 6, 2010, http:/www/gao.gov/new.items/d10522.pdf; Dana Hedpeth, "Defense Contractors Feel Pinch: Gates's Planned Cuts Spook Investors and Companies," *Washington Post*, August 11, 2010; Sandra I. Erwin, "Plans to 'In-Source' Contractor Jobs Collide With Fiscal Reality," *National Defense* (September 2010), 8, accessed at https://www.nationaldefensemagazine.org/articles/2010/9/1/2010september-plans-to-insource-contractor-job-collide-with-reality; Nick Mottern, "Calling Them Out: War Profiteer, Steven R. Loranger," *Truthout News Analysis*, August 27, 2010, accessed at http://truthout.com.

65. Lawrence P. Farrell, Jr., "For U.S. Defense Industry, Many Opportunities in the Middle East," *National Defense (November 2010)* 4, accessed at https://www.nationaldefensemagazine.org/articles/2010/11/1/2010november-for-us-defense-industry-many-opportunities-in-the-middle-east; Sandra I. Erwin, "Defense Downturn Sets Off Mergers and a Search for Non-U.S. Customers," *National Defense* (November 2010),6 accessed at https://wwwnationaldefensemagazine.org/articles/2010/11/1/2010november-defense-donturn-sets-off-merges-and-a-search-for-non-uscustomers; Carlyle Murphy, "US and Saudi Arabia Cement Military ties With Massive Arms Deal," *Global Post Report*, October 23, 2010; BERK and Associates, "Washington State's Defense Economy: Measuring and growing Its Impact" (Seattle, Economic Development Commission, September 2010, passim; University of Massachusetts Donahue Institute, Economic and Public Policy Research, "The Defense Industry in Massachusetts: Current Profile and Economic Significance" (Amherst, MA, UMASS Donahue Instituter, December 2010), passim.

66. Rachel Baye, "MontCo Lawmakers Kill Peace Bill," *Washington Examiner*, October 9, 2011; Marcus Weisgerber, "DoD Officials: Cutbacks Won't Hurt Indus-

trial Base," *Defense News* (May 3, 2011), Nathaniel H. Sledge Jr., "Viewpoint: Defense Acquisition in an Unaccountable World," *National Defense* (May 3, 2011), accessed at https://www.nationaldefensemagazine.org/articles/2011/5/1/2011may-viewpoint-defense-acquisition-in-an-naccountable-world; Lawrence P. Farrell, "What the Latest U.S. Budget Crisis Means for the Future of Defense," *National Defense* (May 3, 2011), accessed at https://www.nationaldefensemagaine.org/articles/2011/5/1/2011 what-the-latest-us-budget-crisis-means-for-the-future-of-defense; Sandra I. Erwin, "International Arms Sales, for Now, Remain Business-As-Usual," *National Defense* (April, 2011), accessed at https://www.nationaldefensemagazine.org/articles/2011/4/1/2011april-international-arms-sales-for-now-remain-business-as-usual; Aerospace Industries Association, "Defense Investment: Finding the Right Balance," (Washington, Aerospace Industries Association, May 2011), passim; David Berteau, et al., "DoD Workforce Cost Realism Assessment," (Washington, Center For Strategic & International Studies, May 2011), passim; Steve Mills, Scott Fouse, Allen Green, "Creating and Sustaining An effective Government—Defense Industry Partnership," *Defense Acquisition Research Journal*, 18, no. 3 (July 2011), 297–310; K. Chaisson, "Deputy Defense Secretary Gives Talk on How to Preserve the Defense Industrial Base," *Forecast International*, June 1, 2011; Marjorie Censer, "Amid Cuts, Options in Defense Industry Looking Uncertain," *Washington Post*, July 26, 2011, A18; n.a., "Defense Industry to See Decrease," *Frederick (Md.) News Post*, August 26, 2011; Craig Whitlock, "Ex-budget chief Panetta now on other side of Pentagon cuts," *Washington Post*, November 4, 2011; R. Pettibone, "Lockheed Martin Announces Fourth-Quarter and Full-Year 2012 Results," January 26, 2012, "General Dynamics Reports 2011 Fourth-Quarter, Full-Year results," January 25, 2012, "Raytheon Reports 2011 and 4th Quarter Results," January 26, 2012, and "Boeing Post Fourth-Quarter and 2011 results," February 25, 2012, all *Forecast International Government and Industry Group*; Barry D. Watts and Todd Harrison, "Sustaining Critical Sectors of the U.S. Defense Industrial Base," (Washington, Center for Strategic and Budgetary Assessments, 2011), in toto.

     67. Jeremy Learner, "Boeing To Shut Kansas Plant with Loss of Up to 2,000 jobs," *Financial Times*, January 5, 2012; Chris Strohm and David Lerman, "Defense Contractors Beef Up Cybersecurity, Space Programs," *Washington Post*, January 12, 2012; Nathaniel H. Sledge Jr., "Pentagon Resource Wars: Why They Can't Be Avoided," 18–20, Harvey M. Sapolsky, "Defense Industrial Policy Myths Debunked," 20–21, Dan Parsons, "Air Force F-35s, Drones May Square Off in Budget Battle," 28–29, Stew Magnuson, "Robot-Makers Ponder Next Moves as Wars Wind Down," 30–31 all *National Defense* (February 2012) accessed at https://www.nationaldefensemagazine.org/past-issues/2012/feb-2012.

     68. Sandra I. Erwin, "Pentagon, Contractors Clash Over Profits," *National Defense* (April 2013), accessed at https://www.nationaldefensemagazine.org/article

/2013/4/1/2013april-pentagon-contractors-clash-over-profits; Valerie Insinna, "Defense Industry to See Smaller Mergers," *National Defense* (April 2013), accessed at https://www.nationaldefensemagazine/articles/2013/4/1/2013april-defense-industry-to-see-smaller-mergers (Nick Taboree, "Defense Contracts Surge in March Despite Sequester," *Washington Post,* April 6, 2013, A13 and "Contractors Are Spinning Off Divisions as Pentagon Budget Cuts Take Hold," *Washington Post,* April 15, 2013, A12; "Pentagon Contracts Down 52 percent in April as Sequester's Cuts Take Hold," *Washington Post,* May 13, 2013, A 13; Sandra I. Erwin, "Firms Think Twice Before Investing in DoD," *National Defense* (May 2013), 6 accessed at httpls://www.nationaldefensemagazine.org/articles/2013/5/1/2023may-firms-thinkk-twice-before-investing-in-dod; Sandra I. Erwin, "Contractors Face Fight-or-Flight Decisions," *National Defense,* June 2013), 6 accessed at https//www.nationaldefensemagazine.org/aticles/2013/6/1/2013june-contactiors-face-fightorflight-decisionsm; Robert Levinson and Kevin Brancato, "US Intelligence Locked Into Federal Contractors: BGOV Insight," *Bloomberg Government,* June 12, 2013; Walter Pincus, "A New Vision of the Military's Role," *Washington Post,* June 13, 2013; Nick Taborek, "Defense Contractors Ditching Their Less-profitable Divisions," *Washington Post,* September 17, 2012 ; Robin Harding, "Investment hit as government contractors fear budget cuts," *Financial Times,* December 31, 2012.

69. Heidi Shyu, "Industrial Base: In Hard truth, New Opportunity," 5–7, Juan L. Millan, "Layers of Concern," 8–13, Kris Osborn, "Securing the Base," 14–19 and Christopher Calile, "Preparing for the Next Conflict," 20–24 all *Army AL&T* (January–March 2014); U.S. Department of Defense, Inspector General, "Northrop Grumman Improperly Charged Labor for the Counter Narco-terrorism Technology Program," May 13, 2014 (Washington, Department of Defense, 2014) passim; Ben Fitzgerald, Kelley Sayler, "Creative Disruption: Technology, Strategy, and the Future of the Global Defense industry," (Washington, Center for a New American Security, 2014) in toto; Sandra I. Erwin, "Hope and Despair in Government Procurement," *National Defense* (July 2014), 8, accessed at https://www.nationaldefensemagazine.org/articles/2014/7/1/2014july-hope-and-despair-in government-procurement; Ernesto Londono, "U.S. Selling and Scrapping Equipment in Afghanistan," *Washington Post,* August 5, 2014, A5; Joe Gould and Paul McLeary, "Shifting Gears; Companies Settle Into Sequestration Era by focusing on Upgrades," *Defense News,* October 20, 2014, 8, 11; John Harper, Battles Loom Over Nuclear Spending," *National Defense* (October 2015), 14, accessed at https://www.nationaldefensemagazine.org/articles/2015/7/1/2015julybattles-loom-over-nuclear-spending and John Harper, Analysts: Pentagon Overestimates Nuclear Costs," *National Defense* (October 2015) 14, accessed at https://www.nationaldefensemagazine.org/articles/2015/10/1/2015 october-analystspentagon-ovrestimates-nuclear-costs; Yasmin Tadjdeh, "Future Vertical Lift Could Be Shot in the Arm for Industry," *National Defense* (October 2015,

38, accessed at https://wwwnationaldefensemagazine.org/articles/2015/10/1/2015 october-future-vertical-lift-could-be-shot-in-the-arm-for-industry; Stew Magnuson, "New Bomber Will Be Boon For U.S. Aerospace Industry, *National Defense* (December 2015), 38, accessed at https://wwwnatinaldefensemagazine.org/articles/2015/11/30/2015december-new-bomber-will-be-boon-for-us-aerospace-industry; Mike Mccord, "Bipartisan Budget Act a Positive Step," *National Defense* (December 2015), accessed at https:/www.nationaldefensemagazine.org./articles/2015/11/30/2015-december-bipartisan-budget-act-a-positive-step; Stephen Snyder, "The US is Dropping Bombs Quicker Than It Can Make Them," *The World*, Public radio International, April 10, 2016.

70. Glenn Greenwald, "Stock Prices of Weapons Manufacturers Soaring Since Paris Attack," *Reader Supported News*, November 16, 2015; Sandra I. Erwin, "CEOs Not Yet Ready to Take a Gamble," *National Defense*, 100, no. 747 (February 2016), 6 accessed at https://www.nationaldefensemagazine.org/articles/2016/1/31/2016february-ceos-not-yet-ready-to-take-a-gamble; Sandra I Erwin, "Survival of the Fittest in the Industrial Base," *National Defense*, 100 (May 2016), no. 750, 6, accessed at https//www.nationaldefensemagazine.org/articles/5/1/2016may-survival-of-the-fittest.

71. Joseph M. Heiser, Jr., *Logistics Support in Vietnam [Vietnam Studies]* (Washington, Department of the Army, 1974), 45, 88–90, 139, 163, 192, 259; Elsen and Mills, *U.S. Defense Industrial Base—Trends and Issues*, 14–15; Laura A. Dickinson, *Outsourcing War and Peace: Preserving Public Values in a World of Privatized Foreign Affairs* (New Haven: Yale University Press, 2011), 24–35.

72. Kenneth Bredemeier "Thousands of Private Contractors Support U.S. Forces in Persian Gulf," *Washington Post* , March 3, 2003, E 1, E 10; Valerie Bailey Grasso, *Defense Contracting in Iraq: Issues and Options for Congress* [CARS Report for Congress, January 6, 2007] (Washington, Congressional Research Service, 2007), 7–8; Mary H. Cooper, "For Warring Nations, A Tradition of Armies Bought, Not Built," and "Private Affair; New Reliance on America's Other Army," both *Congressional Weekly*, September 18, 2004.

73. Nelson D. Schwarts, "The War Business," *Fortune*, March 3, 2003; Deborah Avant, "*Think Again: Mercenaries*," *Foreign Policy*, 143 (July-August 2004), 20–28; Jeremy Scahill, *Blackwater: The Rise of the World's Most Powerful Mercenary Army* (New York, Nation Books, 2007), 376–377; Suzanne Simons, *Master of War: Blackwater USA's Erik Prince and the Business of War* (New York, Harper, 2009), passim; John McCarthy, "Expanding Private Military Sector Faces Structural Change and Scrutiny," *Jane's Intelligence Review*, February 1, 2006; Roger D. Carstens, Michael A. Cohen, and Maria Figueroa Kupcu, *Changing The Culture of Pentagon Contracting* (Washington DC, 2008), passim; U.S. Department of State/Broadcasting Board of Governors, Office of Inspector General, Middle East Regional Office, *Status*

of the Secretary of State's Panel on Personal Protective Services in Iraq Report Recommendations, report, December, 2008, MEOO-IQO-09-01 (Washington, 2008), passim; James Cockayne and Emily Mears, *Private Military Security Companies: A Framework for Regulation* (New York, International Peace Institute, 2009), passim; Rolf Uesseler, *Servants of War: Private Military Corporations and the Profit of Conflict* (Brooklyn, NY, Soft Shell Press, 2008), ch. 4, passim; Scott Fitzsimmons, "The Market for Force in the United States," in Molly Dunigan and Ulrich Petersohn, *The Market for Force; Privatization of Security Across the World Regions* (Philadelphia: University of Pennsylvania Press, 2015) ch. 10, passim; Christopher Kinsey, *Corporate Soldiers and International Security: The Rise of Private Military Companies* (London/New York, Routledge, 2006), 5, 6; Dickinson, *Outsourcing War & Peace*, 36–9, 206–207; Peter W. Singer, *Corporate Warriors: The Rise of the Privatized Military Industry* (Ithaca, NY, Cornell University Press, 2003), appendix 1, 261–262; Peter W. Singer, *Can't Win With 'Em, Can't Go to War Without 'Em: Private Military Contractors and Counterinsurgency*. [Brookings Foreign Policy Paper 4] (Washington, Brookings Institution, 2007), Executive Summary, passim; Sandra Erwin, "For Contractors in War Zones, Business Will Keep Growing," *National Defense*, 92, no. 649 (December 2007), 8–9, accessed at https: //www.nationaldefensemagazine .org/articles/2007/11/30/2007december-for-contractors-in-war-zones-business -will-keep-growing.

74. Jackson Nyamuya Maogoto, "Subcontracting Sovereignty: Commodification of Military Force and Fragmentation of State Authority," *Brown Journal of World Affairs*, 13, no. 1 (Fall/Winter 2006), 157–158; Deborah D. Avant, *The Market for Force: The Consequences of Privatizing Security* (New York: Cambridge University Press, 2005), 30–37 and conclusion passim; Dickinson, *Outsourcing War & Peace*, 16–17 and conclusion; Marjorie Censer, "GAO: Number of DOD Contractors Falls to Lowest Level in Recent Years," *Inside the Pentagon*, November 3, 2016; U.S. Government Accounting Office, "DoD Inventory of Contracted Services: Timely Decisions and Further Actions Needed to Address Long-Standing Issues, [GAO-17–17], October 31, 2016,passim; John M. Bodner and James Risen, "Blackwater Mounts Defense With Top Talent," *New York Times*, November 1, 2007; Mike Baker, "Xe Tries to Leave History of Blackwater Behind," *Truthout*, March 2, 2009; ___,"Dyn-Corp International Wins $20 Million LOGCAP IV Task Order," February 24, 2009, Falls Church, VA, accessed at www.dyn-intl.com/media-center/predssd-releases/dyncorp -international-wins-30-million-logcap-iv-taskorder/; Sally Denton, *The Profiteers: Bechtel and the Men Who Built the World* (New York, Simon and Schuster, 2016), Parts 2, 3 and 4 passim; Pratap Chatterjee, *Halliburton's Army: How a Well-Connected Texas Oil Company Revolutionized the Way America Makes War* (New York, Nation Books, 2009), ch. 5 and Parts 2, 3 passim; Dan Briody, *The Halliburton Agenda: The Politics of Oil and Money* (New York, John Wiley and Sons, 2004), Parts II and III.

75. Sam Stebbins, "Twenty Companies Profiting the Most from War," Special Report, February 20, 2018, *24/7 Wall Street* accessed March 2, 2018 from MSN.com.24/7 Wall Street; Sandra I. Erwin, "Defense, Industry Upheaval Defined by 10 Key Moments, *National Defense, 674* (January 2010), 8–9 accessed at https//www.nationaldefensemagazine.org/articles/2009/12/31/2010january-defense-industry-upheavel-defined-by- 10-key-moments; Calvin Coolidge, "Address to the American Society of Newspaper Editors,, Washington, D.C., January 17, 1925 online by Gerhard Peters and John T. Wooley, *The American Presidency Project*, accessed at https://www.presidency.ucsb.edu/node/269410.

POSTSCRIPT

1. Neta C. Crawford, " plus chart "Estimate of U.S. Post-9/11 War Spending, in $Billions FY 2001-FY-2022 (Providence, RI, Brown University, Watson Institute for International and Public Affairs, September 2021), accessed at https://watson.brown.edu/costofwar/figures/2021/BudgetaryCosts and chart "Human Cost of Post-9/11 Wars," September 2021, accessed at https://watson.brown.edu/costofwar/figures/2021/WarDeathToll; Jeet Heer, "China Syndrome: Resisting the New Cold War in Asia," *The Nation,* 312, no. 2, January 25/February 1, 2021, 23–27; David Klion, "Foreign Policy: End the Forever Wars," *The Nation,* 312, no. 1, January 11–18, 2021, 27–28; Jon Harper, "Cost of Post-9/11 Wars Expected to Top $6 Trillion," *National Defense,* December 24, 2019, accessed at https://www.nationaldefensemagazine.org/articles/2019/12/24/cost-of-post-911/wars-expected-to-top-6-trillion. Andrew J. Bacevich, "The Real News We Ignore at Our Peril," http://www.theamericanconservative.com. January 11, 2018; Tom Engelbrecht, "Mapping a World From Hell, 76 Counties Are Now Involved in Washington's War on Terror," *TomDispatch,* January 8, 2018; Tim Fernholz, "The US Army says Iran is the only Victor of the Iraq War," https://qz.com/1530248/us-army-says-iran-winner-in-the-iraq-war/.

2. Jon Harper, "What a Biden Presidency Means for Defense," *National Defense* Magazine, December 14, 2020, accessed at https://www.nationaldefensemagazine.org/article/2020/1/14/what-a-biden-presidency-means-for-defense; Aaron Gregg, "Defense Contractors Appear Comfortable with Biden Win, *Washington* Post, November 9, 2020, A-18; Jay Cassano, International Business Times, November 1, 2017, http://readersupportecnews.org/news-section2/318–66/46618-defense-department-the-war. 11/2/17 citing Federation of American Scientists *Secrecy News blog*; Katrina Mason, "The Future of War," *Financial Times Weekend* 17/18 November 2018 (Life & Arts) 1, 21, 22); see also William W. Keller, *Democracy Betrayed: The Rise of the Surveillance Security State* (Berkeley, CA, Counterpoint.

3. Kevin Finn, compiler, "America as a Security State—Statistics," Unpublished study, circa 2016, author's files; Joe Brewer, "Shifting the Climate of Security,"

Truthout, May 15, 2007.Jomana Amana and Raymond Franck, "The United States and its Defense Industries," in Keith Hartley and Jean Belin, *The Economics of the Global Defence Industry* (London/New York, Routledge, 2019), 7–34 passim

4. Charles Koch Institute/Center for the National Interest, "POLL: This Holiday, Americans Wish for A More Peaceful Approach to Foreign Policy," (Arlington, VA, December 22, 2016); Oliver Stone, "As Wars Around the World Rate, Both Republicans and Democrats Speak of Muscle Power, and Violence," *Oliver Stone's Facebook*, January 6, 2016; Andrew Bacevich, "Still Waiting: A Harvey Weinstein Moment for America's Wars?" *TomDispatch*, December 10, 2017; Watson Institute, *Costs of War* (Providence, Brown University, November 2018; Philip Stephens, "Sanctions Are Trump's New Way of War," *Financial Times*, October 18, 2019.

5. Craig R. McKinley, "Contending With a World of Disorder," *National Defense* (May 2017), 4 accessed at http://www.nationaldefensemaazine.org/articles/2017/4/19/contending-with-a-world-of-disorder; Richard Haass, *A World in Disarray: American Foreign Policy and the Crisis of the Old Order* (New York, Penguin, 2017); Martin Wolf, "The March to World Disorder," *Financial Times*, January 6, 2017, 7 and Martin Wolf, "The fading light of liberal democracy," *Financial Times*, December 23, 2020, 17; Lionel Barber, "The Year of the Demagogue," *Financial Times Weekend* December 18, 2016, Life and Arts section, 1, 2; Philip Stephens, "America First or America Alone?" *Financial Times* January 10, 2017, 9; Andrew J. Bacevich, "The Age of Great Expectations and the Great Void: History After 'the End of History,'" *Reader Supported News*, January 9, 2017; Tom Hamburger, "How Military Rifles got to be a Civilian Commodity: NRA Lobbyist, Weapons Dealers Played Role in Legalizing Imports," *Washington Post*, May 4, 2013, A 1, A 6; Heer, "China Syndrome," *The Financial Times*, January 25 -February 1, 2021, 23–27.

6. Courtland Milloy, "America, land of the free and home of the gun," *Washington Post* December 9, 2015; Richard Eskow, "For Wall Street It's 'Peace on Earth, Goodwill toward Remington,'" *Campaign for America's Future* website, December 27, 2012; James Ragland, "We need to stop worshipping guns, *"News- Post* (Frederick, Maryland), October 7, 2017, A 5.

7. See Bill Gertz, *War and Peace in the Information Age* (New York, Threshold Editions/Simon & Schuster, 2017); The Cato Institute, "The 2016 Cato Surveillance Conference," Announcement on-line November 10, 2016; Greg Jaffe and Loveday Morris, "The High Toll of Obama's Low-cost Wars: As One Deadly Bombing in Iraq Shows, Even the Most Surgical of Strikes Can Result in Unintended Consequences," *Washington Post*, June 10, 2016, A1, A10, A11; Andrew Bacevich, "Still Waiting," *TomDispatch.com*, December 10, 2017; T. X. Hammes, "The Future of Warfare: Small, Many, Smart vs. Free & Exquisite?" *War on the Rocks.com* July 16, 2014.

8. Jon Harper, "Political Battle Brewing Over New Nuclear Program," *Na-

tional Defense, March 17, 2020, accessed at https://www.nationaldefensemagazine.org/articles/2020/3/17/political-battle-brewing-ovr-new-nuclear-program; William J. Broad and David E. Sanger, "Trump Plans for Nuclear Arsenal Require $1.2 Trillion, Congressional Review States," *New York Times,* October 31, 2017; Steven Aftergood, "Secrecy News: Updated Nuclear Stockpile figures Declassified," (Washington, Federation of American Scientists, June 2016), http://fas.org/blog/secrecy, posted on May 31, 2016 in Declassification (http://fas.org/category/declassification/), Department of Energy (http://fas.org/category/dept-of-energy/), Nuclear Weapons (http://fas.org/categoy/nuclear weapons/); http://www.//www.nytimes.com/2016/05/27/science/nuclear-weapons-obamma-united-states,html); Dallas Boyd, "Unconventional Thinking: Why Conventional Disarmament Must Precede Nuclear Abolition," *Bulletin of Atomic Scientists* (March/April 2016), 46–60; Garrett M. Graff, *Raven Rock: The Story of the U.S. Government's Secret Plan to Save Itself—While the Rest of Us Die* (New York, Simon & Schuster, 2017, in toto; Christopher Smith, "NDIA Policy Points: Reforms Needed to Aid US. Nuclear Enterprise," *National Defense,* May 8, 2019, accessed at https://www.nationaldefensemagazine.org/articles/2019/5/8/reforms-needed-to-aid-us-nuclear-enterprise.

9. William D. Hartung, "A Pentagon Rising; is a Trump Presidency Good News for the Military-Industrial Complex?" November 22, 2016, *TomDispatch.com*; Daniel Wasserby, "Trump's Defence Plans Thus Far Track Those of Republican Party," 5, Brooks Tigner, "Europe's Low Defence Spenders to Feel the Heat From a Trump White House," 6, Jon Grevatt, "Trump Victory Spells Uncertainty for Southeast Asia . . ." 7 and Gabriel Dominguez, ". . . As Well as for Key Allies Japan and South Korea," 7 all *Jane's Defence Weekly,* 53, no. 46, November 16, 2016, 5–7.

10. Robert B. Zoellick, "The Foreign Policy Americans Really Want," *Washington Post,* October 1, 2019, A 17; Michael Anton, "The Trump Doctrine *Foreign Policy,* April 20 2019. https://foreignpolicy.com/2019/04/20/the-trump-doctrine-big-think-america-first-nationalism.

11. National Security Issues, The White House, accessed on October 13, 2007, December 19, 2017, https://www.whitehouse.gov/; Jonathan Swan, "Trump Approves Core Elements of National Security Strategy," December 3, 2017, www.axios.com; Julian E. Barnes and Gordon Lubold," McMaster Gives Glimpse of New U.S. National Security Strategy," *Wall Street Journal* December 3, 2017; Rodger Baker, "The Echoes of Reagan in Trump's National Security Strategy," worldview.stratfor.com, December 19, 2017; Editors, Washington Post, December 20, 2017, A16.

12. David E. Mosher, "Prospects for DoD's Budget Over the Next Decade," [Presentation at the Professional Services Council's 2018 Federal Strategic Planning Forum] February 5, 2018 (Washington, DC, Congressional Budget Office, 2018); Office of Management and Budget, "President's Proposed $4.2 Trillion Total Spending (FY 2017) and "President's Proposed $1.15 trillion Discretionary Budget (FY 2017)

(Washington, DC, OMB National Priorities Project, 2017), Chart; John J. Duncan, Jr., "Rep. John Duncan: There Is Nothing Patriotic or Conservative About Our Bloated Defense Budget," *Antiwar. Blog*, November 16, 2017; Miriam Pemberton, "Huge Military Budget Makes Us Broke, Not Safe," *Other Words*, February 14, 2018; Jen DiMascio, "Trending Upward: US Defense Spending Grows to Meet North Korean Missile Threat," *Aviation Week & Space Technology* 179, no. 5, December 25, 2017–January 14, 2018, 42; JP Sottle, "The US Military Is the Biggest 'Big Government' Entitlement Program on the Planet," www.truthout.org, December 10, 2017; Maya Schenwar, "It's time to Dismantle Trump's Murder Budget and Defund Militarism," Michele Flournoy, "Here's the Right Way to Boost Defense Spending," *Washington Post*, March 20, 2017.

13. Steven M. Kosiak, Testimony before the U.S. House of Representatives Committee on the Budget, Hearing on ting in America's Economic and National Security," February 7, 2019, copy, author's files; Michael J. Meese, "The American Defense Budget 2017–2020," in R. D. Hooker, editor, *Charting A Course: Strategic Choices for a New Administration* (Washington, DC, National Defense University Press, December 2016), ch. 4.

14. Christian Davenport, "Budget Bill Includes Bonanza for Defense Contractors," *Washington Post*, March 24, 2018, A15 Kevin Brancato and Robert Levinson, " Charting Military Priorities: Winners and Losers from the Defense Drawdown and Strategy Shift," Bloomberg Government, *BGV Analysis*, May 24, 2013, 1–6; James C. Boozer, "Leverage Budget Agreement to Boost Defense," *National Defense*, 102I (April 2018), 6.; Aaron Gregg, "Big Defense Contractor Could Get Even Bigger," *Washington Post*, April 2, 1018, A 11; Joon Harper, "Defense Contracting Drawdown Now in Reverse," *National Defense*, April 25, 2017, accessed as; https://www.national defensemagazine.org/articles/2017/4/25/defense-contracting-drawdown-now in reverse; Annassa Brindley, Bob Wood and Tony Mullen, "Facing New Realities in the Defense Market," *National Defense*, April 21, 2017, accessed at https://www.national defensemagazine.org/articles/2017/4/21/facing-newrealities-in-the-defense.market.

15. Congressional Research Service, *FY 2020 National Defense Authorization Act: P.L. 16–92 (H.R. 500, S. 1790* (Washington, Congressional Research Service, January 2, 2020), https:// crsreports.congress.gov R46144; Bernie Sanders, "Deficit Hawks Once Again Show Their Hypocrisy on Military Spending," *Washington Post* December 17, 2019; Tony Bertuca, "Top Defense Dem Touts 'Most Progressive Defense Bill' in History," https://insidedefense-com.nduezproxy.idm.oclc.org/authors /ATony-Bertuca; Todd Harrison and Seamus Daniels, *Analysis of the FY 2019 Defense Budget*, [Center for Strategic and International Studies—Defense 360] (Lanham, Md., Rowman & Littlefield, 2018), 1–10; Matt Taibbi, "Trump Wants More Money Than Last Year and Democrats Don't Seem to Mind," *Rolling Stone*, March 21, 2019, Meese, "Charting a Course," 6, 73.

16. A. Trevor Thrall and Caroline Dorminey, "Risk Business: The Role of Arms Sales in U.S. Foreign Policy," CATO Institute, *Policy Analysis* no. 836, March 13, 2018; Peter Castagno, "The Arms Trade Is Intensifying Under Trump," *Truthout.com*, February 20, 2019; Sandra L. Ewin, "Industry Jittery About Defense Exports,: *National Defense*, March 21, 2017, accessed at https://www.nationaldefense magazine.org/articles/23017/3/8/industry-jittery-about-defense-exports; Yasmin Tadjdeh "Sales Taking Off: International Market for F-35 Heats Up (Updated)," *National Defense*, May 24, 2019, accessed at https://www.nationaldefense magazine.org/artifles/2019/5/24/international-market-or-f-35-heats-up; Jon Harper, "Bipartisan Support for Buying More Fighter Jets," *National Defense*, July 3, 2019, accessed at https://www.nationaldefensemagazine.org/articles/2019/7/3/bipartisan -support-for-buying-more-fighter-jets.

17. "The 10 Most Expensive Weapons in the Pentagon's Arsenal," *Wikipedia Commons*, November 7, 2016; Jason Sherman, "DoD Tallies $58B Sunk in Canceled Big-ticket Weapons Development Projects," *Inside The Pentagon*, October 27, 2016; Kristina Wong, "Pentagon: 2016 Military Sales to Foreign Partners Totals $33.6B," *The Hill*, November 7, 2016; Susan B. Epstein and Lynn M. Williams, *Overseas Contingency Operations Funding: Background and Status* (Washington, DC, Congressional Research Service, June 13, 2016), Summary; Barbara Salazar Torreon, *Instances of Use of United States Armed Forces Abroad, 1798–2015* (Washington, DC, Congressional Research Service, October 15, 2015), Summary, 16; Ashton Carter, Cabinet Exit Memo, January 5, 2017, copy author files; Jay Cassano, "Defense Department: The War on Terror Has Cost $250 Million a Day for 16 Years," readersupported news.org, November 1, 2017; Karen DeYoung, Greg Jaffe, John Hudson and Josh Dawsey, "Bolton, Arbiter of Policy, Puts his Stamp on NSC." *Washington Post*, March 5, 2019, A1; Jon Harper, "Trump's Defense Budget Ramp-Up in Doubt," *National Defense*, March 21, 2017, accessed at https.//www.nationaldefensemagazine .org/articles/2017/3/21/trumps-defense-budget-ramp-up-in-doubt; Majorie Censer, "CSIS: Fewer Vendors Entered Federal Contracting from 2007–20013," *Inside Defense*, February 6, 2019; Amara and Franck, "United States Defense Industries," 7.

18. Andrew Davies and James Mugg, "Trump and the F-35: the $600 Million Question," *The Strategist*, 1 Feb, 2017, accessed at https://www.aspistrategist.org .au/wp-content/uploads/2017/02/ADJM4.png. Christian Davenport, "Cost of Air Force One Program Chided, President-elect Trump Calls Amount 'Ridiculous,' but Canceling Boeing Contract Could Harm US Jobs, *Washington Post* December 7, 2016, A13; William D. Hartung, "Curb the Military Spending Binge," *Washington Post*. November 25, 2016; Christian Davenport, "A Year After Trump's Threat, Boeing Cements Air Force One Deal," *Washington Post*, February 24, 2018, A13; Colin Clark, "Lockheed's Prez Helo VH-92 Drops in Cost, but . . . ," *Breaking Defense*, April 30, 2018.

19. Craig R. McKinley, "Trump's Buildup: Easier Said Than Done," *National Defense*, 101, no. 61 (April 2017), 4; William D. Hartung, "The Pentagon's War on Accountability," *Reader Supported News*, May 24, 2016 6; Jenna Portnoy, "Senators: Budget Strife Puts Va. Shipyard Jobs in Danger," *Washington Post*, December 6, 2016, B1, B4;Craig Whitlock and Bob Woodward, "Pentagon Hid Study Revealing $125 Billion in Waste," *Washington Post*, December 6, 2016, A1, A 6; Robert J. Samuelson, "Just Cutting Waste at the Pentagon Won't Cut It," *Washington Post*, December 12, 2016, A 13; Editor, "Fighting Waste at the Pentagon: Efficiency Ideas Should be Aired, not Buried," *Washington Post*, December 8, 2016, A 18; Tony Bertuca, "Navy's LCS headlines McCain's 'Indefensible' Waste List," *Inside Defense*, December 19, 2016.

20. Robert M. Gates, *Duty: Memoirs of a Secretary at War* (New York, Vantage Books, 2014) 459; Matt Taibbi, "How to Blow $700 Billion: It's Easier Than You Think " *Rolling Stone*, March 20, 2019; John W. Dower, *The Violent American Century: War and Terror Since World War II* (Chicago, Il, Dispatch Books, 2017), x; Hugh Lessig, "Breaking Down the Big Numbers of Huntington Ingalls Two-Carrier Contract," *The Virginian Pilot* (Newport News), February 17, 2019; Robert Perry, "Democrats Are Now the Aggressive War Party," *Reader Sponsored News*, June 11, 2016.

21. Jomana and Franck, "The United Stares and its Defense Industries," 9–25; John Harper, "Silicon Valley Showing Support for Military," *National Defense*, January 28, 2019, accessed at://www.nationaldefensemagazine.org/articles/2019/1/28/silicon-valley-showing-support-for-military.

22. Aaron Gregg, "Air Force Cuts off Funds for Boeing's Missile Offering," *Washington Post*, October 28, 2019, A 12; Christian Davenport and Aaron Gregg, "U.S. Missile Contracts Balloon as North Korea Threat Grows," *Washington Post*, February 5, 2018, A12; Sandra I. Erwin, "Cold Dose of Reality on DoD Technology," *National Defense*, April 19, 2017 6;, accessed at https://www.nationaldefensemagazine.org/articles/2017/4/19/cold-dose-of-reality-on-dod-technology and Craig R. McKinley, "Robots to Revolutionize Military Operations," *National Defense*, March 21, 2017, 3, accessed at https://www.nationaldefensemagazine.org/articles/2017/3/21/robots-to-revolutionize-millitary-operations; Aaron Mehta, "Inside The 'Foundational' Future Technologies of the World's Largest Defense Company," *Defense News* 32, no. 21, November 6, 2017), 8; David Ignatius, "Arming Ourselves For The Next War," *Washington Post*, February 24, 2016; Morgan Chalfant, "Key Challenges Facing Trump's Pentagon Include Cyber, Acquisitions Management," *Washington Free Beacon (Washington D.C)*, December 23, 2016, citing DOD Inspector General FY 2017 oversight plan—http://www.dodig.mil/IGInformation/archives/2017 Oversight%20 Plan Final Signed 508.pdf; Adam Kredo, "Iranian-Backed 'Sleeper Cell' Militants Hibernating in U.S., Positioned for Attack," *Washington Free* Beacon (Washington, D.C. April 17, 2018, both accessed at https://twitter.com/freebeacon.

23. Congressional Research Service, *Defensed Primer: The National Technology and Industrial Base* (Washington, Congressional Research Service, September 17, 2019), 1–2; Adam Thomson, "Technology is Crucial in the Fight Against Terrorism," *Financial Times*, June 3, 2016, 4; Jill Aitoro, "DoD Could Bank On Virtues Of Commercial Manufacturing," *Defense News*, 32, no. 19 (October 9, 2017), 40; Tracy Jan, "Four Firms Picked to Build Border Wall Prototypes," *Washington Post* September 1, 2017, A 17; Ben Fitzgerald, Alexandra Sander and Jacqueline Parziale, *Future Foundry: A New Strategic Approach to Military Technical Advantage* (Washington, Center for a New American Security, December 2016), chart; Center for a New American Security, "CNAS Launches Project On 'Future Foundry: Forging New Industries For Defense," (Washington, CNAS, April 6, 2016, in toto; Ben Fitzgerald and Kelley Sayler,"Creative Disruption; Technology, Strategy and the Future of the Global Defense Industry," (Washington, Center for a New American Security, June 2014), in toto, all accessed at www.cnas.org.; Wesley Halllman and Christopher Smith, "Vital Signs 2020: Defense Industrial Base's Report Card Reveals 'C' Grade," *National Defense*, January 21, 2020, accessed at https://www.nationaldefen semagazine.org /articles/2020/1/21vital-signs-2020-defnse-industrial-bases-report-card-reveals-c -grade; Yasmin Tadjdeh, "Vital Signs 2020: Defense Sector Straining to Attract STEM Talent," *National Defense*, January 22, 2020, accessed at https://www.national defensemagazine.org/articles/2020/1/22/defense-sector-straining-to-attract-stem -talent; Jon Harper, "Vital Signs 2020: Industrial Base Could Struggle to Surge Production in Wartime," *National Defense*, January 24, 2020, accedssed at https://www .nationaldefensemagaziner.org/articles/2020/1/245/industrial-base-could-struggle -to surge-production-in-wartime

24. Craig R. McKinley, "New Blood May Stem Industry Consolidation," *National Defense*, February 1, 2016, 4 accessed at https://www.nationaldefense magazine.org/articles/2016/1/31/2016february-new-blood-may-stem-industry -consolidation; Linda Weiss, *America Inc.? Innovation and enterprise in the Nation al Security State* (Ithaca, Cornell University Press, 2014), 38, 60, 83, 88–89, 91, 175, 221 n 28; Daniel Goure, "Winning Future Wars: Modernization and a 21st Century Defense Industrial Base," in Dakota L. Wood, editor. *2019 Index of U.S. Military Strength*, Washington,, The Heritage Foundation, September 2018), 61–92, especially, 81–86; Juliet Eilperin, "Trump Signs Executive Order to Expand Critical Minerals Production in U.S.," *Washington Post*, December 21, 2017, A19; Office of the Press Secretary, the White House, "Presidential Memorandum for the Secretary of Commerce: Subject; Steel Imports and Threats to National Security," April, 20, 2017; Julian Sneider, "China: The Pentagon's Great Industrial Challenge," *The National Interest*, November 21, 2016; John C. Johnson, "Defense Community Must Help Lower-Tier Suppliers,' *National Defense*, July 10, 2019, accessed at https://www .nationaldefensemagazine.org/articles/2019/7/10/viewpoint-defense-community

-must-help-lower-tier-suppliers; Jon Harper, "The Budget Control Act is Dead. Now What?" *National Defense*, August 29, 2019, accessed at https://www.national defensemagazine.org/articles/2019/8/29/the-budget-control-act-is-dead-now-what; Mandy Mayfield, "Survey: More Mergers, Acquisitions to Come," *National Defense*, April 3, 2019. Accessed at https://www.nationaldefensemagazine.org/articles/209/4/3/survey-more-mergers-acquisitions-to-come.

25. Sam Stebbins, "Twenty Companies Profiting the most from war," *24/7 Wall Street*, 2 March 2018; Aaron Gregg, "For Contractors, No End in Sight to Funding Problems," *Washington Post* January 29, 2018, A 11; Hawk Carlisle, "Industry, Government: Enduring Partners," *National Defense*, June 16, 2017, 3 accessed at https://www.nationaldefensemagazine.org/articles/2017/6/16/industry-government-enduring-partners; Aaron Gregg, "Boeing Soars Past $100 Billion Mark Amid Banner Year," *Washington Post*, January 31, 2009, A 19.

26. Sean McFate quoted in Marc Fisher, Ian Shapira and Emily Rauhala, "Blackwater Founder's China Gambit," *Washington Post*, May 6, 2018, A 16; Scott S. Haraburda, *Conventional Munitions Industrial Base* (Arlington, VA, The Institute of Land Warfare, Association of the United States Army, 2017), preface; Owen B. McCormack, "President Obama's Lesser-Known Legacy: 'Arms Dealer in Chief,'" *Truthout*, March 23, 2016 accessed at truthout.com; Allyson Versprille, "Lockheed Seeking More International F-35 Sales To Reduce Cost of Fighter (UPDATED), *National Defense*, June 1, 2016, accessed at ttm://www.nationaldefense magazine.org/articles/2016/6/1/2016june-lockheed-seeking-more-international-F-35-sales-to-reduce-cost-of-fighter; John Harper, "Pentagon Budget Shortfall Is Greater Than Advertised," *National Defense*, June 1, 2016, accessed at httm://www.nationaldefensemagazine.org/articles/20016/6/1/2016june-pentagon-budget-shortfall-is-greater-than-advertised; Sid Ashworth, "National Security at an Inflection Point," *National Defense*, June 1, 2016, accessed at http://www.nationaldfense magazine.org/articles/3026/6/1/2016june-national-security-at-an-inflection-point; Sandra L. Erwin, "Facing Up to the True Cost of Defense," *National Defense*, June 1, 2016, accessed as httm://www.nationaldefensemagazine.org/articles/2016/6/1/2016june-facing-up-to-the-true-cost-of-defense; Scott Freling and Kathy Brown, "DoD's Antitrust Battle Ends Peacefully," *National Defense*, June 1, 20q6, accessed at httm://www.nationaldefensemagazine.org/articles/2016/6/1/2016june-dods-antitrust-battle-ends-peacefully; Kirk W. Smith, "The Enemy of Good Enough: A Different Way to Look at Emerging Technology," *National Defense*, May 1, 2016, 56 accessed at httls://www.nationationaldefensemagazine.org/articles/2016/5/1/2016may-the-enemy-of-good-enough-a different way-to-look-at-emerging-technology; Yasmin Tadjdeh, "U.S. Defense Companies Eye Partnerships in India," *National Defense*, June 1, 2016, accessed at httm://www.nationaldefensemagazine.org/articles/2016/6/1/2016june-us-defense-companies-eye-partnerships-in-india.

27. Annie Gowen, "U.S. Firms Maneuver to Build Fighter Jets in India," *Washington Post*, December 5, 2016, A 1, A 7; Gareth Jennings, "DoD Awards Lot 10 Production Contracts for F-35 Fighter," *HIS Jane's Defence Weekly,* November 3, 2016, 4; Christian Davenport, "Boeing to Shift Defense Division Headquarters to D.C. Area," *Washington Post*, December 14, 2016, A 14; Christian Davenport, "More Ups and Downs for F-35 Fighter," *Washington Post,* November 2016, A 14 and Christian Davenport. "Cost of Air Force One Program Chided," *Washington* Post, December 7, 2016, A16; Alwyn Scott, "Trump Attack on Lockheed Martin Foreshadows War on Defense Industry," *Reuters,* December 12, 2016.

28. Jeremiah Gertler, *F-35 Joint Strike fighter (JADF) Program* (Washington, DC, Congressional Research Service, April,13, 2018), 1, 25; Donald J. Trump Presidential Memoranda—National Security & Defense, "National Security Presidential Memorandum Regarding U.S. Conventional Arms Transfer Policy," April 19, 2018, https://www.whitehouse.gov/presidential-actions/. William D. Hartung, "Weapons for Anyone: Donald Trump and the Art of The Arms Deal," *Reader Supported News*, April 2, 2018; Erwin, "Red Flags Raised on Defense Industry Future," 6 and Artie Mabbett and John Kovach, "'Third Offset' Strategy Calls for Fresh Thinking," 17–18, both in *National Defense*, , CI, no. 758 (January 2017); Tony Bertuca, "White House Directs DOD to Run Government-wide Industrial Base Review," *Inside Defense* July 24, 2017.

29. Jennifer Santos, "Commentary: Defense Department Tackling Industrial Base Issues," *National Defense,* February 28, 2020, accessed at https://www.national defensemagazine.org/articles/2020/2/28/defense-department-tackling-industrial -base-issues; Richard L. Dunn, "Defense Industry Needs New Wy of Doing Business," *National Defense,* November 6, 2020, accessed at https://www.nationaldefense magazine.org/articles/2020/11/6/defense-industy-needs-new-way-of-doing-business.

30. Aerospace Industries Association, *Fostering the Manufacturing and Defense Industrial Base of the Future.* (Arlington, VA, Aerospace Industries Association, April 2018), n.p.; Jeff Bozman, Justin Ganderson and Zach Mears, "Key Takeaways from Industrial Base Report," *National Defense*, December 27, 2018, 41, accessed at https://www.nationaldefensemagazine.org/articles/2018/12/27key-take aways-from-industrial-base-report; Interagency task Force, *Assessing and Strengthening the Manufacturing and Defense Industrial Base and Supply Chain Resilience of the United States* (Washington, DC, Department of Defense, September 2018), esp. executive summary 1–6; Colin Clark, "It's Not Buy America: Admin Aide on Trump's Sweeping Industrial Base Study," accessed at https://breakingdefense.com/2017/07 /its-not-buy-america-admin-aide-on-trumps-sweeping-industrial-base-study/ (c. 2017).

31. Jacques S. Gansler, *Democracy's Arsenal: Creating A Twenty-First Century Defense Industry* (Cambridge, MA, MIT Press, 2011), chap 9; Gertler, *The F-35 Joint Strike Fighter Program,* 25.

32. National Defense Industrial Association/Giovini, *Vital Signs 2021: The*

Health and Readiness of the Defense Industrial Base, February 2021, accessed at https://www.ndia.org.policy vital signs; Yasmin Tadjdeh, "Vital Signs 2020: Defense Sector Straining to Attract STEM Talent," *National Defense*, January 22, 2020 accessed at https:www.nationaldefesemagazine.org/articles/2020/1/22/defense-sector-straining-to-attract-stem-talent.

33. Jon Harper, "Pandemic More Opportunities Exist to Leverage Defense Production Act (UPDATED), *National Defense*, April 20, 2020, accessed at https://www.nationaldefensemagazine.org/articles/2020/4/20more-opportunities-exist-to-leverge-defense-production-act; Jon Harper, "Defense Budgets Could Fall Victim to COVID-19," *National Defense*, May 19, 2020, accessed at https://www.nationaldefensemagazine.org/articles/2020/5/19/defense-budgets-could-fall-victim-to-covid-19; Connie Lee, "More Funding Sought to Offset COVID-19 Losses," *National Defense*, July 20, 2020, accessed at https://www.nationaldefensemagazine.org/articles/2020/7/20/more-funding-sought-to-offset-covid-19-losses; Yasmin Taddjeh, "Pentagon Examining Lessons Learned from Pandemic," *National Defense*, October 6, 2020, accessed at https://www.nationaldefensemagazine.org/articles/2020/10/6/pentagon-examining-lessons-learned-from-pandemic; Peter Emanuel, "Commentary: Pandemic Lays Bare Supply Chain Vulnerabilities," *National Defense*, June 23, 2020, accessed at https://www.nationaldefensemagazine.org/articles/2020/6/23/pandemic-lays-bare-supply-chain-vulnerabilities; Yasmin Tadjdeh, "Defense Industrial Base Rebounding From COVID-19," *National Defense*, June 16, 2020, accessed at: https://www.nationaldefensemagazine.org/articles/2020/6/16/defense-industrial-base-rebounding-from-covid-19.

34. Richard L. Dunn, "Defense Industry Needs New Way of Doing Business," *National Defense*, November 6, 2020, accessed at https://www.nationaldefensemagazine.org/articles/2020/11/6/defense-industry-needs-new-way-of-doing-business; Connie Lee, "Air Force Eyes New Industrial Base Model," *National Defense*, July 29, 2020, accessed at https://www.naionaldefensemagazine.org/articles/2020/7/29/air-force-eyes-new-industial-base-model; Rhys McCormick, Andrew P. Hunter and Gregory Sanders, *Measuring the Impact of Sequestration and the Drawdown on the Defense Industrial Base* (Lanham, MD, Rowman & Littlefield/Center for Strategic & International Studies, 2017), executive summary; Haraburda, *Conventional Munitions Base*, v and 18, quoting U.S. Department of the Army, *Army Organic Industrial Base Strategic Plan (AOIBSP) 2012–2022* (Washington, DC, Government Printing Officer, 2012), 3; John T. Bennett, "Trump Administration Ponders Demands of Wartime Footing," *Roll Call*, May 3, 2017 accessed at http://www.rollcall.com/news/politics/trump-administration-ponder; John Harper, "2020 Called Pivotal Year for Military Buildup," *National Defense*, January 31, 2018, accessed at https://www.nationaldefensemagazineorg/articles/2018/2/31/2020-called-pivotal-year-for-military-buildup; John Harper, "Trump Boosts Missile Defense Spend-

ing Plans," *National Defense,* February 22, 2018, accessed at https://www.national defensemagazine.org/articles/2018/2/22/trump-boosts-missile-defense-spending-plan; Vivienne Machi, "Strong Military Spending Propels Industry Mergers," *National Defense,* May 16, 2018, accessed at httm://www.nationaldefensemagazine.org/articles/2018/5/16/strong-military-spending-propels-industry-mergers

35. Jon Harper, "Supplementary War Funding Expected to Remain Robust," *National Defense,* February 1, 2019, accessed at https://www.nationaldefensemagazine.og/aticles/2019/2/10co-funding-expected-to-remainrobusy

36. Connie Lee, "Future Uncertain for Industrial Base as Pandemic Spreads," *National Defense* Magazine, February 3, 2021, accessed at https://www.nationaldefensemagaziner.org/articles/2021/2/3/future-uncertain-for-industrial-base-as-pandemic-spreads; Mike Stone, "Biden Will Struggle to Cut Defense Spending Despite Pressure," *Reuters,* November 25, 2020, accessed at https://www.reuters.com/articles/usa-biden-defense-spending/update-1-biden-will-struggle; Mackenzie Eaglen, "The Defense Industry Remains in Dire Straits, Congress Must Pass Another Relief Package," *Defense News,* August 18, 2020; Cmdr. Matthew Perry, "Cementing Silicon Valley Partnerships: A National Security Imperative," *National Defense,* June 18, 2018, accessed at httm://www.nationaldefensemagazine.com/articles/2018/6/18/viewpoint-cementing-silicon-valley-patnerships-a-national-security-imperative; John Harper, "U.S. Spending About $36 Billion on NATO," *National Defense,* September 11, 2018, accessed at httm://www.nationaldefensem-agazine.org/articles/2018/9/11/us-spending-about-36-billion-on-nato; Jon Harper, "Silicon Valley Showing Support for Military," *National Defense,* January 28, 2019, accessed at httm://www.nationaldefensemagazine.org/articles/2019/1/28/silicon-valley-showing-support-for-military; Jeffrey A. Green, "Industrial Base Gears Up for Great Power Conflict," *National Defense,* January 24, 2019, accessed at httm://www.nationaldefensedmagazine.org/articles/2019/1/24/viewpoint-industrial-base-gears-up-for-great-power-conflict; Aaron Mehta, "America sold $175 billion in weapons abroad in FY20," *Defense News,* December 4, 2020

37. Tony Bertuca, "Pentagon analyzes defense spending in all 50 states," *Defense News,* March 19, 2019; Department of Defense, Office of Economic Adjustment, *Defense Spending By State, Fiscal Year 2017, Revised Version, March 2019* (Washington, DC, Department of Defense, 2019), http://oea.gov/dsbs-fy2017; Thomas Gibbons Neff and Erin Cunningham, "U.S. Hits ISIS Target with Biggest Non-nuclear Weapon Ever Used in Combat," *Washington Post,* April 14, 2017; Congressional Budget Office, "Prospects for DoDs' Acquisition Budget Over the Next Decade," Professional Services Council, Vision Conference 2019, Panel on Platforms, PowerPoint; Michelle Chen, "The US Border Security Industry Could be Worth $740 Billion by 2023," *Truthout* October 6, 2019. Gopal Ratnam, "U.S. Cyberattack on ISIS was First Large-scale Effort Report," *CQ News,* January 21, 2020; Max Boot,

"Democrats Can't End 'Endless Wars,' Either," *Washington Post*, January 23, 2020, A 23; Amara and Franck, "United States and its Defense Industries," in Hartley and Belin, eds. *Global Defence*, 7; James Ledbetter, *Unwarranted Influence: Dwight D. Eisenhower and the Military-Industrial Complex* (New Haven: Yale University Press, 2011), chap.8, in toto; Eric Lipton and Kenneth P. Vogel, "Aides' Ties to Firms Present Biden With Early Ethics Test," *New York Times*, November 29, 2020, accessed at http://www.msn.com/en-us/news/politics/aides-ties-to-firms-present-biden-with-early-ethics-test; Homer A. Neal, et al., *Beyond Sputnik: U.S. Science Policy in the Twenty-first Century* (Ann Arbor: University of Michigan Press, 2008), 3; Terrell J. Staer, "Politics of the Defense Budget," *Outrider Organization* (February 11, 2021), accessed at https://outrider.org/nuclear-weapons/articles/politics-defense-budget.

38. Matt Schudel, "Prospector turned executive founded group to monitor defense spending," *The Washington Post*, September 2, 2021, B6.

39. Doug Berenson, "The Evolving Geography of the U.S. Defense Industrial Base," *War on the Rocks*, September 1, 2021. https//warontherocks.com/2021/09/the-evolving-geography-of-the-u.s.-defense-industrial-base; Brooke Masters and Andrew Edgecliffe-Johnson, "The Shift from 'Just In Time' to 'Just In Case,'" *Financial Times*, 21 December 2021, 15; Steve Coll and Adam Entous, "The Fall of the Islamic Republic," *The New Yorker*, December 20, 2021, 32–45; James Carroll, *House of War: The Pentagon and the Disastrous Rise of American Power* (Boston, Houghton Mifflin, 2006), 373–374.

Selected Bibliography

GOVERNMENT DOCUMENTS

Confederate States of America. Office of the President. "Communications from the Secretaries of the Treasury and of War . . . relative to the tax in kind and other taxes collected from the several States for the year 1863." Message of the President, November 11, 1864, Richmond, VA. Richmond: Confederate States of America, 1864.

Cooling, Benjamin Franklin. *The Army and Civil Defense 1945-1966: Plans and Policy*. Office of the Chief of Military History, Monograph 108. Washington: U.S. Department of the Army, 1967.

U.S. Bureau of the Census. Department of Commerce. *Historical Statistics of the United States*. Washington: Government Printing Office, 1951.

U.S. Congress. Congressional Budget Office. Report. *Contractors' Support of U.S. Operations in Iraq*, August 12, 2008. Washington: Congressional Budget Office, 2008.

———. House of Representatives. Committee on Oversight and Government Reform, Majority Staff. *More Dollars, Less Sense: Worsening Contracting Trends Under the Bush Administration*. Washington: U.S. House of Representatives, Committee on Oversight and Government Reform, June 2007.

———. House of Representatives. *Memorandum: Additional Information About Blackwater USA*, October 1, 2007. Washington: U.S. House of Representatives, 2007.

U.S. Congress 40th, 3d sess. Senate. Joint Committee on Ordnance. *Experiments on Heavy Ordnance*, February 15, 1869. Rep. Com. 266.

U.S. Congress 46th, 2d sess. Senate. *Memorial of the American Ordnance Company*, May 13, 1880. Misc. Doc. 89.

U.S. Congress 47th, 1st sess. Senate. *Report of the Board on Heavy Ordnance and Projectiles*. Ex. Doc. 178. Washington: Government Printing Office, 1882.

U.S. Congress 47th, 2d sess. Senate. *Report of the Select Committee on Heavy Ordnance and Projectiles*. Report 969. Washington: Government Printing Office, 1883.

U.S. Congress 48th, 1st sess. House of Representatives. *Report of the Gun Foundry Board*. Ex.Doc. 97. Washington: Government Printing Office, 1884.

U.S. Congress 49th, 1st sess. Senate. *Report of the Select Committee on Ordnance and War Ships*. Report 90. Washington: Government Printing Office, 1886.

U.S. Congress 64th, 1st sess. Senate. *Armor Plant for the United States: Hearings Before the Committee on Naval Affairs*. S-1417. Washington: Government Printing Office, 1916.

U.S. Congress, 74th, 2d sess. Senate. *Munitions Industry Multiple Parts*. Report 944. Washington: Government Printing Office, 1936.

U. S. Department of Defense. Deputy Assistant Secretary for Industrial Policy. *Annual Industrial Capabilities Report to Congress*. Washington, Department of Defense, 1994.

U. S. Department of Defense. Office of the Deputy Under Secretary of Defense, Industrial Policy. *Transforming the Defense Industrial Base: A Roadmap*. Washington: Department of Defense, February 2003.

U.S. Department of Defense. Office of Economic Adjustment. *Defense Spending by State: Fiscal Year 2017*, Revised Edition. Washington: Department of Defense, March 2019.

U.S. Department of the Navy. *Gearing Up for Victory: American Military and Industrial Mobilization in World War II*. Colloquium on Contemporary History, June 25, 1991, No. 5. Washington: Navy Historical Center, Department of the Navy, 1991.

U.S. Department of State. Broadcasting Board of Governors, Office of Inspector General, Middle East Regional Office. *Status of the Secretary of State's Panel on Personal Protective Services in Iraq: Report Recommendations*. Report Number MERO-IQ0-09-01, December 2008. Washington: Department of State, 2008.

U.S. Department of the Treasury. *Office of Contract Settlement. A History of War Contract Terminations and Settlements*. Washington: Department of the Treasury, Office of Contract Settlement, July 1947.

U.S. Federal Emergency Management Agency. *Resource Management: A Historical Perspective*. FEMA 167. Washington: Federal Emergency Management Agency, May 1989.

U.S. Government Accountability Office. Report to Congressional Committees. Rebuilding Iraq: Actions Needed to Improve Use of Private Security Providers. GAO-05-737. Washington: Government Accounting Office, July 2005.

U.S. National Archives. *Federal Records of World War II, Volume I: Civilian Agencies*. No. 51-7. Washington, National Archives and Records Service, 1950 and Westport: National Archives and Records Service, Greenwood Press, 1976.

U.S. National Archives. *Handbook of Federal World War Agencies and Their Records, 1917–1921*.Washington: Government Printing Office, 1943.

U.S. Small Business Administration. Office of Inspector General. *Review of Blackwater Worldwide Compliance with Small Business Laws as Requested by Congressman. Waxman.* Washington: U.S. Small Business Administration, July 25, 2008.

BOOKS AND PRINTED STUDIES

Abella, Alex. *Soldiers of Reason: The Rand Corporation and the Rise of the American Empire.* Orlando: Harcourt, Inc., 2008.

Abrahamson, James L. *The American Home Front: Revolutionary War, Civil War, World War I, World War II.* Washington: National Defense University 1983.

Adams, Doug. *The Confederate Le Mat Revolver.* Lincoln: Andrew Mowbray Publishers, 2005.

Adams, Gordon, Christopher Corns, Andrew James and Bernard Schmitt, editors. *Between Cooperation and Competition: The Transatlantic Defence Market.* Paris: Institute for Security Studies of the Western European Union, January 2001.

Adelman, Kenneth L. and Norman R. Augustine. *The Defense Revolution: Strategy for the Brave New World.* San Francisco: Institute for Contemporary Studies Press, 1990.

Agapos, A. M. *Government-Industry and Defense: Economics and Administration.* University: University of Alabama Press, 1975.

Air Force Association. *Lifeline Adrift: The Defense Industrial Base in the 1990s.* Arlington, VA, The Aerospace Education Foundation, September 1991.

Air Force Association and USNI Military Database. *Lifeline in Danger: An Assessment of the United States Defense Industrial Base.* Arlington, VA, The Aerospace Education Foundation, September 1988.

Aitken, Hugh G. J. *Scientific Management in Action: Taylorism at Watertown Arsenal, 1908–1915.* Princeton: Princeton University Press, 1960.

Anderson, Fred. *Crucible of War: The Seven Years' War and the Fate of Empire in British North America, 1754–1763.* New York: Alfred A. Knopf, 2000.

Angevine, Robert G. V. *The Railroad and the State: War, Politics, and Technology in Nineteenth-Century America.* Stanford: Stanford University Press, 2004.

Armstrong, Stephen. *War PLC: The Rise of the New Corporate Mercenary.* London: Faber and Faber, 2008.

Art, Robert J. *The TFX Decision, McNamara and the Military.* Boston: Little, Brown and Company, 1968.

Army, Thomas F. Jr. *Engineering Victory: How Technology Won the Civil War.* Baltimore: Johns Hopkins University Press, 2016

Association of the United States Army, *Army Industrial Preparednes: A Primer on*

What It Takes to Stay until the War is Over. Washington, Association of the United States Army, 1979.

Augustine, Norman R. *Augustine's Laws*. New York: Viking/Penguin, 1986.

Augustine, Norman R. *Augustine's Travels: A World-Class Leader Looks at Life, Business, and What It Takes to Succeed at Both.* New York: AMACOM, 1998.

Avlon, John. *Washington's Farewell: The Founding Father's Warning to Future Generations.* New York: Simon & Schuster, 2017.

Baier, Bret. *Three Days in January: Dwight Eisenhower's Final Mission.* New York: William Morrow, 2017.

Bailey, Gavin J. *The Arsenal of Democracy: Aircraft Supply and the Anglo-American Alliance, 1938–1942.* Edinburgh: Edinburgh University Press, 2012.

Balko, Radley. *Rise of the Warrior Cop: The Militarization of America's Police Forces.* New York: Public Affairs, 2014.

Baime, A. J. *The Arsenal of Democracy: FDR, Detroit, and an Epic Quest to Arm an America at War.* Boston, Houghton Mifflin, 2014.

Balogh, Brian. *A Government Out of Sight: The Mystery of National Authority in Nineteenth-Century America.* New York: Cambridge University Press, 2009.

Bank, Steven A., Kirk J. Stark, and Joseph J. Thorndike. *War and Taxes.* Washington: Urban Institute Press, 2008.

Barnet, Richard J. *The Economy of Death.* New York: Atheneum, 1970.

Baruch, Bernard. *American Industry in the War.* War Industries Board Report, March, 1921. New York: Prentice-Hall, 1941.

———. *Baruch: The Public Years.* New York: Holt, Rinehart and Winston, 1960.

Bauer, Theodore. *The History of the Industrial College of the Armed Forces 1924–1983.* Washington: Alumni Association of the Industrial College of the Armed Forces, 1983.

Beaver, Daniel R. *Modernizing the American War Department: Change and Continuity in a Turbulent Era, 1885–1920.* Kent: Kent State University Press, 2006.

———. *Newton D. Baker and the American War Effort 1917–1919.* Lincoln, NE, University of Nebraska Press, 1966

Bennett, John D. *The London Confederates: The Officials, Clergy, Businessmen and Journalists Who Backed the American South During the Civil War.* Jefferson: McFarland and Company, 2008.

Benson, Lawrence R. *Acquisition Management in the United States Air Force and Its Predecessors.* Washington: Air Force History and Museums Program, 1997.

Bertrand, Harold E. *The Defense Industrial Base: Executive Summary.* Washington, Logistics Management Institute, August 1977.

Biddle, Wayne. *Barons of the Sky: From Early Flight to Strategic Warfare, the Story of the American Aerospace Industry.* New York: Simon & Schuster, 1991.

Biody, Dan. *The Halliburton Agenda: The Politics of Old Oil Money*. New York: John Wiley & Sons, 2004.

Birnie, Rogers, Jr. *Gun Making in the United States*. Washington: Government Printing Office, 1918.

Bitzinger, Richard A., editor. *The Modern Defense Industry: Political, Economic, and Technological Issues*. Santa Barbara: Praeger Security International, 2009.

Blackett, R. J. M., *Divided Hearts: Britain and the American Civil War*. Baton Rouge: Louisiana State University Press, 2001.

Blackford, Mansel G. and K. Austin Kerr. *Business Enterprise in American History*. Boston: Wadsworth Cengage Learning, 1994.

Blair, William. *Virginia's Private War: Feeding Body and Soul in the Confederacy, 1861–1865*. New York: Oxford University Press, 1998.

Blaszczyk, Regina Lee and Philip B. Scranton, editors. *Major Problems in American Business History: Documents and Essays*. Boston: Houghton Mifflin, 2006.

Blum, John Morton. *V Was for Victory: Politics and American Culture During World War II*. New York: Harcourt, Brace, Jovanovich, 1976.

Boggs, Carl. *Origins of the Warfare State: World War II and the Transformation of American Politics*. New York: Routledge, 2017.

Bonner, Michael Bremm. *Confederate Political Economy: Creating and Managing a Southern Corporatist Nation*. Baton Rouge: Louisiana State University Press, 2016.

Bradley, Joseph. *Guns for the Tsar: American Technology and the Small Arms Industry in Nineteenth-Century Russia*. Dekalb: Northern Illinois University Press, 1990.

Bragg, William Harris. *Griswoldville*. Macon: Mercer University Press, 2000.

Brands, Hal. *What Good Is Grand Strategy? Power and Purpose in American Statecraft from Harry S. Truman to George W. Bush*. Ithaca: Cornell University Press, 2014.

Brandes, Stuart D. *Warhogs: A History of War Profits in America*. Lexington: University Press of Kentucky, 1997.

Brodie, Bernard. *War and Politics*. New York: Macmillan, 1973.

Brookmere Economic Service. *Economic Trends of War and Reconstruction, 1860–1870*. New York: Brookmere Economic Service, 1918.

Brooke, John M., Jr. *Ironclads and Big Guns of the Confederacy: The Journal and Letters of John M. Brooke*. Columbia: University of South Carolina Press, 2002.

Brown, Michael E., editor. *Grave New World: Security Challenges in the 21st Century*. Washington: Georgetown University Press, 2003.

Brown, M. L. *Firearms in Colonial America: The Impact on History and Technology 1492-1792*. Washington: Smithsonian Institution Press, 1980.

Brown, Richard D. *Modernization: The Transformation of American Life, 1600–1865*. New York: Hill and Wang, 1976.

Brown, Shannon A., editor. *Providing the Means of War: Historical Perspectives on Defense Acquisition, 1945–2000*. Washington: United States Army Center of Military History, Industrial College of the Armed Forces, 2005.

Brown, Thomas J. *Civil War Monuments and the Militarization of America*. Chapel Hill, University of North Carolina Press, 2019.

Bruscino, Thomas. *A Nation Forged in War: How World War II Taught Americans to Get Along*. Legacies of War Series. Knoxville: University of Tennessee Press, 2010.

Bryant, Keith L., Jr. and Henry C. Dethloff. *A History of American Business*. Englewood Cliffs: Prentice-Hall, 1983.

Bugos, Glenn E. *Engineering the F-4 Phantom II: Parts Into Systems*. Annapolis: Naval Institute Press, 1996.

Campbell, Colton C. and David P. Auerswald, editors. *Congress and Civil-Military Relations*. Washington: Georgetown University Press, 2015.

Campbell, Robert F. *The History of Basic Metals Price Control in World War II*. Ithaca: Cornell University Press, 1948.

Carew, Michael G. *The Impact of the First World War on U.S. Policymakers: American Strategic and Foreign Policy Formulation, 1938–1942*. Lanham: Lexington Books, 2014.

Carey, Omer L. editor. *The Military-Industrial Complex and U.S. Foreign Policy*. Pullman: Washington State University Press, 1969.

Carp, E. Wayne. *To Starve the Army at Pleasure: Continental Army Administration and American Political Culture, 1775–1783*. Chapel Hill: University of North Carolina Press, 1984.

Carroll, James. *House of War: The Pentagon and the Disastrous Rise of American Power*. Boston, Houghton Mifflin, 2006.

Catton, Bruce. *The War Lords of Washington*. New York: Harcourt Brace, 1948.

Chandler, Alfred D., Jr. *The Visible Hand: The Managerial Revolution in American Business*. Cambridge: Belknap Press imprint of Harvard University Press, 1977.

Chatterjee, Pratap. *Halliburton's Army: How a Well-Connected Texas Oil Company Revolutionized the Way America Makes War*. New York: Nation Books, 2009.

Clark, John E., Jr. *Railroads in the Civil War: The Impact of Management on Victory and Defeat*. Baton Rouge: Louisiana State University Press, 2001.

Clarkson, Grosvenor B. *Industrial America In the World War: The Strategy Behind the Line 1917–1918*. Boston: Houghton Mifflin Company, 1923.

Clayton, James L. *Does Defense Beggar Welfare? Myths Versus Realities*. New York: National Strategy Information Center, Inc., 1979.

———. *The Economic Impact of the Cold War: Sources and Readings*. New York: Harcourt, Brace & World, 1970.

Clem, Harold J. *Mobilization Preparedness*. Washington: National Defense University, 1983.

Coyne and Emily Spears Mears, *Private Military and Security Companies: A Framework for Regulation*. New York, International Peace Institute, March 2008.

Cochran, Thomas C. *Business in American Life: A History*. New York: McGraw-Hill, 1972.

Coit, Margaret L. *Mr. Baruch*. Boston: Houghton Mifflin, 1957.

Cole, Brady M. *Procurement of Naval Ships: It Is Time for The US Navy to Acknowledge Its Shipbuilders May Be Holding A Winning Hand*. National Security Affairs Monograph 79-5, September, 1979. Washington: Research Directorate of the National Defense University, National Defense University Press, 1979.

Cole, Wayne S. *Senator Gerald P. Nye and American Foreign Relations*. Minneapolis: University of Minnesota Press, 1962.

Collins, Brian. *NATO: A Guide to The Issues*. Santa Barbara: Praeger, 2011.

Converse, Elliott V. III. *Rearming for The Cold War, 1945–1960*. History of Acquisition in the Department of Defense. Washington: Historical Office, Office of the Secretary of Defense, 2012.

Cooling, Benjamin Franklin. *Benjamin Franklin Tracy, Father of the American Fighting Navy*. Hamden: Archon Books, 1973.

———. *Gray Steel and Bluewater Navy: The Formative Years of America's Military-Industrial Complex*. Hamden: Archon Books, 1979.

———. editor. *The New American State Papers–Military Affairs*. Wilmington: Scholarly Resources, Inc., 1979.

———. *USS Olympia: Herald of Empire*. Annapolis: Naval Institute Press, 2000.

———. editor. *War, Business and American Society: Historical Perspectives on the Military-Industrial Complex*. Port Washington: Kennikat Press, 1979.

———. *War, Business and World Military-Industrial Complexes*. Port Washington: Kennikat Press, 1981.

Coulam, Robert F. *Illusions of Choice: The F-111 and the Problem of Weapon Acquisition Reform*. Princeton: Princeton University Press, 1977.

Coulter, Mathew Ware. *The Senate Munitions Inquiry of the 1930s: Beyond the Merchants of Death*. Westport: Greenwood Press, 1997.

Crockatt, Richard. *The Fifty Years War: The United States and the Soviet Union in World Politics, 1941–1991*. New York: Routledge, 1995.

Crowell, Benedict. *America's Munitions 1917-1918*. Washington: Government Printing Office, 1919.

Crowell, Benedict and Robert Forrest Wilson. *The Armies of Industry: Our Nation's*

Manufacture of Munitions for A World in Arms, 1917–1918. 2 vols. New Haven: Yale University Press, 1921.

Crozier, William. *Ordnance and the World War: A Contribution to the History of American Preparedness*. New York: Charles Scribner's Sons, 1920.

Crum, William Leonard, John F. Fennelly and Lawrence Howard Seltzer. *Fiscal Planning for Total War*. New York: National Bureau of Economic Research, 1942.

Cuff, Robert D. *The War Industries Board: Business-Government Relations During World War I*. Baltimore: Johns Hopkins University Press, 1973.

Culver, C.M. *Federal Government Procurement–An Uncharted Course Through Turbulent Waters*. McLean: National Contract Management Association, 1985.

Daniel, Larry J. and Riley W. Gunter. *Confederate Cannon Foundries*. Union City: Pioneer Press, 1977.

Danner, Mark. *Spiral: Trapped in the Forever War*. New York, Simon and Schuster, 2014.

Davis, George T. *A Navy Second to None: The Development of Modern American Naval Policy*. New York: Harcourt, Brace and Company, 1940.

Davis, Michael W. R. *Detroit's Wartime Industry Arsenal of Democracy*. Images of America Series. Charleston: Arcadia, 2007.

De Mesquita, Bruce Bueno and Alastair Smith. *The Spoils of War: Greed, Power and the Conflicts that Made our Greatest Presidents*. New York: Public Affairs, 2017.

Denton, Sally. *The Profiteers: Bechtel and the Men Who Built the World*. New York: Simon & Schuster, 2016.

Dickinson, Laura A. *Outsourcing War & Peace: Preserving Public Values in a World of Privatized Foreign Affairs*. New Haven: Yale University Press, 2011.

Dickson, Keith D. *No Surrender: Asymmetric Warfare in the Reconstruction South, 1868–1877*. Santa Barbara, CA, Prager, 2017.

Dizard, Jan E., Robert Merrill Muth, and Stephen P. Andrews, Jr., editors. *Guns in America: A Reader*. New York: New York University Press, 1999.

Dorwart, Jeffrey M. *Eberstadt and Forrestal: A National Security Partnership, 1909–1949*. College Station: Texas A&M Press, 1991.

Douglas, Byrd. *Steamboatin' on the Cumberland*. Nashville: Tennessee Book Company, 1961.

Dower, John W. *The Violent American Century: War and Terror Since World War II*. Chicago: Haymarket/Dispatch Books, 2017.

Drew, S. Nelson, editor. *NSC-68: Forging the Strategy of Containment with Analyses by Paul H. Nitze*. Washington: National Defense University Press, 1994.

Du Pont: The Autobiography of an American Enterprise. Wilmington, DE: E. I Du Pont.

Dudziak, Mary L. *War-Time: An Idea, Its History, Its Consequences.* New York and Oxford, UK: Oxford University Press, 2012.

Dueck, Colin. *Reluctant Crusaders: Power, Culture, and Change in American Grand Strategy.* Princeton: Princeton University Press, 2006.

Duncan, Francis. *Rickover and the Nuclear Navy: The Discipline of Technology.* Annapolis: US Naval Institute Press, 1989.

———. *Rickover and the Struggle for Excellence.* Annapolis: Naval Institute Press, 2002.

Dunigan, Molly and Ulrich Petersohn, editors. *The Market for Force: Privatization of Security Across World Regions.* Philadelphia: University of Pennsylvania Press, 2013.

Dutton, William S. *Du Pont: One Hundred and Forty Years.* New York: Charles Scribner's Sons, 1949.

Edling, Max M. *A Hercules in the Cradle: War, Money, and the American State, 1783–1867.* Chicago: University of Chicago Press, 2014.

———. *A Revolution in Favor of Government: Origins of the U.S. Constitution and the Making of the American State.* New York: Oxford University Press, 2003.

Edwards, William B. *Civil War Guns: The Complete Story of Federal and Confederate Small Arms: Design, Manufacture, Identification, Procurement, Issue, Employment, Effectiveness, and Postwar Disposal.* Harrisburg: Stackpole, 1962.

Engelbrecht, Helmut C. and Frank C. Hanighen. *Merchants of Death: A Study of the International Armament Industry.* New York: Dodd, Mead & Co., 1934.

Epstein, Katherine C. *Torpedo: Inventing the Military-Industrial Complex in the United States and Great Britain.* Cambridge: Harvard University Press, 2014.

Escott, Paul D. *Military Necessity: Civil-Military Relations in the Confederacy.* Westport: Praeger Security International, 2006.

Fallows, James. *National Defense.* New York: Random House/Vintage, 1981.

Farley, Philip J., Stephen S. Kaplan and William H. Lewis. *Arms Across the Sea.* Washington: Brookings Institution Press, 1978.

Ferreiro, Larrie D. *Brothers at Arms: American Independence and the Men of France and Spain Who Saved It.* New York: Alfred A. Knopf, 2016.

Fitzgerald, Ben, Alexandra Sander and Jacqueline Parziale, *Future Foundry: A New Strategic Approach to Military-Technical Advantage.* Washington, Center for a New American Strategy, December 2014.

Fortune Magazine. *Arms and the Men.* Garden City: Doubleday, Doran and Company, 1934.

Fox, J. Ronald. *Arming America: How the U.S. Buys Weapons.* Boston: Harvard University Press, 1974.

Fox, J. Ronald and James L. Field. *The Defense Management Challenge: Weapons Acquisition.* Boston: Harvard Business School Press, 1988.

Friedberg, Aaron L. *In the Shadow of the Garrison State: America's Anti-Statism and Its Cold War Grand Strategy*. Princeton: Princeton University Press, 2000.

Fuller, Howard J. *Clad in Iron: The American Civil War and the Challenge of British Naval Power*. Annapolis: Naval Institute Press, 2008.

Gallagher, Gary W. and Joan Waugh. *The American War: A History of the Civil War Era*. State College: Flip Learning, 2016.

Gallman, J. Matthew, *The North Fights the Civil War: The Home Front*. Chicago: Ivan R. Dee, 1994.

Gansler, Jacques S. *Affording Defense*. Cambridge: MIT Press, 1989.

———. *Defense Conversion: Transforming the Arsenal of Democracy*. Cambridge: MIT Press, 1995.

———. *Democracy's Arsenal: Creating a Twenty-First Century Defense Industry*. Cambridge: MIT Press, 2011.

———. *The Defense Industry*. Cambridge: MIT Press, 1984.

Gates, Robert M. *Duty: Memoirs of a Secretary at War*. New York: Alfred A. Knopf, 2014.

Gertz, Bill. *War and Peace in the Information Age*. New York: Simon & Schuster, 2017.

Gilchrist, David T. and W. David Lewis, editors. *Economic Change in the Civil War Era*. Proceedings of a Conference on American Economic Institutional Change, 1850–1873, and the Impact of the Civil War, March 11–14, 1964. Greenville: Eleutherian Mills-Hagley Foundation, 1965.

Gill, Timothy. *Industrial Preparedness: Breaking with an Erratic Past*. Washington: National Defense University Press, 1984.

Goodwin, Jacob. *Brotherhood of Arms: General Dynamics and the Business of Defending America*. New York: Times Books, 1985.

Gosling, F.G. *The Manhattan Project: Science in the Second World War*, Energy History Series. Washington: United States Department of Energy, August 1990.

Graff, Garrett M. *Raven Rock: The Story of the U.S. Government's Secret Plan to Save Itself–While the Rest of Us Die*. New York: Simon & Schuster, 2017.

Graham, Otis L., Jr. *Losing Times: The Industrial Policy Debate*. Cambridge: Harvard University Press, 1992.

Grasso, Valerie Bailey. *Defense Contracting in Iraq: Issues and Options for Congress*. Washington, Congressional Research Service, January 2007.

Gropman, Alan L. *Mobilizing U.S. Industry in World War II: Myth and Reality*. McNair Paper 50, August, 1996. Washington: Institute for National Strategic Studies, National Defense University, 1996.

Gropman, Alan, editor. *The Big "L": American Logistics in World War II*. Washington: Industrial College of the Armed Forces, National Defense University Press, 1997.

Guay, Terrence R. *At Arm's Length: The European Union and Europe's Defence Industry*. New York: St. Martin's Press, 1998.

Gudmestad, Robert. *Steamboats and the Rise of the Cotton Kingdom*. Baton Rouge: Louisiana State University Press, 2011.

Haass, Richard N. *A World in Disarray: American Foreign Policy and the Crisis of the Old Order*. New York: Penguin, 2017.

Hackemer, Kurt. *The U.S. Navy and the Origins of the Military-Industrial Complex, 1847–1883*. Annapolis: Naval Institute Press, 2001.

Hacker, Barton C., editor. *Astride Two Worlds: Technology and the American Civil War*. Washington: Smithsonian Institution Scholarly Press, 2016.

Hacker, Barton C., with assistance of Margaret Vining. *American Military Technology: The Life Story of a Technology*. Baltimore: Johns Hopkins University Press, 2006.

Hacker, Louis M. *The Triumph of American Capitalism: The Development of Forces in American History to the Beginning of the Twentieth Century*. New York: McGraw-Hill, 1965.

Haglund, David G. *Alliance Within The Alliance? Franco-German Military Cooperation and the European Pillar of Defense*. Boulder: Westview, 1991.

Haraburda, Scott S. *Conventional Munitions Industrial Base*. Land Warfare Papers, No. 113, August 2017. Arlington: Association of the United States Army, The Institute of Land Warfare, 2017.

Harrison, Mark, editor. *The Economics of World War II: Six Great Powers in International Comparison*. New York: Cambridge University Press, 1998.

Heilbroner, Robert L. *The Economic Transformation of America*. New York: Harcourt Brace Jovanovich, 1977.

———. *The Making of Economic Society*. Englewood Cliffs: Prentice-Hall, 1962.

Heinrich, Thomas R. *Ships for The Seven Seas: Philadelphia Shipbuilding in the Age of Industrial Capitalism*. Baltimore: Johns Hopkins University Press, 1997.

Heo, U. K. *The Political Economy of Defense Spending Around the World*. Lewiston: Edwin Mellen Press, 1999.

Herman, Arthur. *Freedom's Forge: How American Business Produced Victory in World War II*. New York: Random House, 2012.

Hewlett, Richard G., Oscar E. Anderson, Francis Duncan, and Jack M. Holl. *A History of the Atomic Energy Commission*. 3 vols. University Park: Pennsylvania State University Press, 1962–1969. Berkeley: University of California Press, 1989.

Hicks, Charles J. and Roland N. McKean. *The Economics of Defense in the Nuclear Age*. New York: Atheneum, 1965.

Hill, Louise B. *State Socialism in the Confederate States of America*. Southern Sketches No. 9, First Series. Charlottesville: The Historical Publishing Co., 1936.

Holley, Alexander I. *A Treatise on Ordnance and Armor.* New York: D. Van Nostrand, 1865.

Holley, Irving B., Jr. *Ideas and Weapons: Exploitation of the Aerial Weapon by The United States During World War I: A Study in the Relationship of Technological Advance, Military Doctrine, and the Development of Weapons.* New Haven: Yale University Press, 1953. Washington: Office of Air Force History, 1983 reprint.

Hooks, Gregory. *Forging the Military-Industrial Complex: World War II's Battle of the Potomac.* Urbana, University of Illinois Press, 1991.

Hope, Ian C. *A Scientific Way of War: Antebellum Military Science, West Point, and the Origins of American Military Thought.* Lincoln: University of Nebraska Press, 2015.

Hormats, Robert D. *The Price of Liberty: Paying for America's Wars.* New York: Henry Holt, 2007.

Hunter, Louis C. *Steamboats on the Western Rivers: An Economic and Technological History.* Cambridge: Harvard University Press, 1949.

Hurly, Edward N. *The Bridge to France.* Philadelphia: J. B. Lippincott, 1927.

Huston, James A. *The Sinews of War: Amy Logistics 1775–1953*, Army Historical Series. Washington: Office of the Chief of Military History, United States Army, 1966.

Inbar, Efraim and Benzion Zilberfarb, editors. *The Politics and Economics of Defence Industries*, Portland: Frank Cass, 1998.

Ippolito, Dennis S. *Why Budgets Matter: Budget Policy and American* Politics. University Park: Pennsylvania State University Press, 2003.

Jacobstein, Meyer and Harold G. Moulton. *Effects of the Defense Program on Prices, Wages and Profits.* Washington: Brookings Institution Press, 1941.

Jaffe, Lorna S. *The Development of the Base Force, 1989–1992.* Washington: Office of the Chairman of the Joint Chiefs of Staff, Joint History Office, 1993.

James, Marquis. *Alfred I. DuPont: The Family Rebel.* Indianapolis: Bobbs-Merrill Company, 1941.

Jones, Vincent C. *Manhattan: The Army and the Atomic Bomb*, United States Army in World War II, Special Studies. Washington: United States Army Center of Military History, 1998.

Kaldor, Mary. *The Baroque Arsenal.* New York: Hill and Wang, 1981.

Kaplan, A. D. H. *The Liquidation of War Production: Cancellation of War Contracts and Disposal of Government-Owned Plants and Surpluses.* New York: McGraw-Hill, 1944.

Keller, William W. *Democracy Betrayed: The Rise of the Surveillance State.* Berkeley: Counterpoint Press, 2017.

Kennelson, Ira and Martin Shefter, editors. *Shaped by War and Trade: International Influences on American Political Development.* Princeton: Princeton University Press, 2002.

Kennedy, David M. *Over Here: The First World War and American Society*. New York: Oxford University Press, 1980.

King, Randolph, editor. *Naval Engineering and American Seapower*. Baltimore: The Nautical and Aviation Publishing Company of America, 1989.

Kinsey, Christopher. *Corporate Soldiers and International Security: The Rise of Private Military Companies*. New York: Routledge, 2006.

Kinsey, Christopher and Malcom Hugh Patterson, editors. *Contractors & War: The Transformation of US Expeditionary Operations*. Stanford: Stanford University Press, 2012.

Kinzer, Stephen. *The True Flag: Theodore Roosevelt, Mark Twain, and the Birth of American Empire*. New York: Henry Holt, 2017.

Kirkpatrick, Charles E. *An Unknown Future and A Doubtful Present: Writing the Victory Plan of 1941*. Washington: United States Army Center of Military History, 1992.

Klein, Maury. *A Call to Arms: Mobilizing America for World War II*. New York: Bloomsbury Press, 2013.

Knopp, Ken R. *Confederate Saddles & Horse Equipment*. Orange: Publisher's Press, Inc., 2001.

———. *Made In the "C.S.A.": Saddle Makers of the Confederacy*. Hattiesburg: By the Author, 2003.

Koistinen, Paul A. C. *Arsenal of World War II: The Political Economy of American Warfare, 1940–1945*. Lawrence: University Press of Kansas, 2004.

———. *Beating Plowshares into Swords: The Political Economy of American Warfare, 1606–1865*. Lawrence: University Press of Kansas, 1996.

———. *Mobilizing for Modern War: The Political Economy of American Warfare, 1865–1919*. Lawrence: University Press of Kansas, 1997.

———. *Planning War, Pursuing Peace: The Political Economy of Warfare, 1920–1939*. Lawrence: University Press of Kansas, 1998.

———. *State of War: The Political Economy of American Warfare, 1945–2011*. Lawrence: University Press of Kansas, 2012.

———. *The Military-Industrial Complex: A Historical Perspective*. New York: Praeger, 1980.

Kosiak, Steven M. *Cost of the Wars in Iraq and Afghanistan, and Other Military Operations Through 2008 and Beyond*. Washintgton, Center for Strategic and Budgetary Assessments, 2008.

Kreidberg, Marvin A. and Merton G. Henry, *History of Military Mobilization in the United States Army, 1775–1945*. Washington: United States Army Center of Military History, 1989.

Kunz, Diane B. *Butter and Guns: America's Cold War Economic Diplomacy*. New York: Free Press, 1997.

Lacey, Jim. *Keep from All Thoughtful Men: How U.S Economists Won World War II.* Annapolis: Naval Institute Press, 2011.

Lamb, Christopher J., Matthew J. Schmidt, and Berrit G. Fitzsimmons. *MRAPS, Irregular Warfare, and Pentagon Reform.* Occasional Papers 6. Washington: Institute for National Strategic Studies, National Defense University, June 2009.

Lane, Frederick C. *Ships for Victory: A History of Shipbuilding Under the U.S. Maritime Commission in World War II.* Baltimore: Johns Hopkins University Press, 1951.

Lapp, Ralph. *The Weapons Culture.* New York: W. W. Norton, 1968.

Ledbetter, James. *Unwarranted Influence: Dwight D. Eisenhower and the Military-Industrial Complex.* New Haven: Yale University Press, 2011.

Leigh, Philip. *Trading with the Enemy: The Covert Economy During the American Civil War.* Yardley: Westholme Publishing, 2014.

Lerwill, Leonard. *The Personnel Replacement System in the United States Army.* Washington: United States Army Center of Military History, 1954.

Lewinsohn, Richard. *The Profits of War Through the Ages.* New York: E. P. Dutton, 1937.

Lewis, George G. and John Mewha. *History of Prisoner of War Utilization by the United States Army 1776-1945.* Washington: United States Army Center of Military History, 1955.

Libicki, Martin C. *What Makes Industries Strategic.* McNair Paper No. 5. Washington: National Defense University Institute for National Strategic Studies, November 1989.

Licht, Walter. *Industrializing America: The Nineteenth Century.* Baltimore: Johns Hopkins University Press, 1995.

Lorell, Mark. *Troubled Partnership: A History of U.S.-Japan Collaboration on the FS-X Fighter.* New Brunswick: Transaction Publishers, 1996.

Lowenthal, Mark. *Intelligence: From Secrets to Policy.* Los Angeles: CQ Press, 2015.

Luraghi, Raimondo. *A History of the Confederate Navy.* London: Chatham Publishing, 1996.

Maddow, Rachel. *Drift: The Unmooring of American Military Power.* New York: Crown, 2012.

Mansfield, Harold *Vision: The Story of Boeing.* New York: Popular Library, 1966.

Markusen, Ann R. and Sean S. Costigan, editors. *Arming the Future: A Defense Industry for the 21st Century.* New York: Council on Foreign Relations Press, 1999.

Marolda, Edward J. *The Washington Navy Yard: An Illustrated History.* Washington: Naval Historical Center, 1999.

Marcus, Alan I. and Howard P. Segal. *Technology in America: A Brief History.* San Diego: Harcourt Brace Jovanovich, 1989.

Martel, William C. *Grand Strategy in Theory and Practice: The Need for an Effective American Foreign Policy*. New York: Cambridge University Press, 2015.

Massey, Mary Elizabeth. *Ersatz in the Confederacy: Shortages and Substitutes on the Southern Homefront*. Columbia: University of South Carolina Press, 1993 reprint of 1952 original edition.

May, Elaine Tyler. *Fortress America: How We Embraced Fear and Abandoned Democracy*. New York, Basic Books, 2017.

McClenahan, William M., Jr. and William H. Becker. *Eisenhower and the Cold War Economy*. Baltimore: Johns Hopkins University Press, 2011.

McCormack, Rhys, Andrew P. Hunter and Gregory Sanders. *Measuring the Impact of Sequestration and the Drawdown on the Defense Industrial Base*. Lanham, Md., Rowman and Littlefield for Center for Strategic and International Studies, 2017.

McCraw, Thomas K. *American Business Since 1920: How It Worked*. Wheeling: Harlan Davidson, 2009.

McDougall, Walter A. *Throes of Democracy: The American Civil War Era 1829–1877*. New York, Harper, 2008.

———. *The Tragedy of U.S. Foreign Policy: How America's Civil Religion Betrayed the National Interest*. New Haven: Yale University Press, 2016.

McEnaney, Laura. *Civil Defense Begins at Home: Militarization Meets Everyday Life in the Fifties*. Princeton: Princeton University Press, 2000.

McGuire, Joseph W. *Business and Society*. New York: McGraw-Hill, 1963.

McNaugher, Thomas L. *New Weapons Old Politics: America's Military Procurement Muddle*. Washington: Brookings Institution Press, 1989.

McNeill, William H. *The Pursuit of Power: Technology, Armed Force and Society since A.D. 1000*. Chicago: University of Chicago Press, 1982.

Mead, Walter Russell. *Special Providence: American Foreign Policy and How It Changed the World*. New York, Routledge, 2002.

Melman, Seymour. *Pentagon Capitalism: The Political Economy of War*. New York, McGraw-Hill, 1970.

Melman, Seymour. *The Permanent War Economy: American Capitalism in Decline*. New York: Simon & Schuster, 1985.

Micklethwaite, John and Adrian Wooldridge. *The Company: A Short History of a Revolutionary Idea*. New York: Random House, 2003.

Miller, John Perry. *Pricing of Military Procurement*. New Haven: Yale University Press, 1949.

Millis, Walter, editor. *American Military Thought*. Indianapolis: Bobbs-Merrill, 1966.

Misa, Thomas J. *A Nation of Steel: The Making of Modern America 1865–1925*. Baltimore: Johns Hopkins University Press, 1995.

Mosley, Leonard. *Blood Relations: The Rise and Fall of the du Ponts of Delaware.* New York: Atheneum, 1980.

Mowbray, Stuart C. and Jennifer Heroux, editors. *Civil War Arms Makers and Their Contracts: A Facsimile Reprint of the Report by the Commission on Ordnance and Ordnance Stores, 1862.* Lincoln: Andrew Mowbray Publishers, 1998.

Mowbray, Stuart C., editor, *Civil War Arms Purchases & Deliveries: A Facsimile Reprint of the Master List of Civil War Weapons Purchases and Deliveries Including Small Arms, Cannon, Ordnance and Projectiles.* Lincoln: Andrew Mowbray Publishers, 2000.

Mullins, James P. *The Defense Matrix: National Preparedness and the Military-Industrial Complex.* San Diego: Avant Books, 1986.

Murray, Williamson and Allan R. Millett, editors. *Military Innovation in the Interwar Period.* New York: Cambridge University Press, 1996.

Nagle, James F. *A History of Government Contracting.* Washington: The George Washington University, 1992.

Neal, Homer Alfred, Tobin Smith, and Jennifer B. McCormick, *Beyond Sputnik: U.S. Science Policy in the Twenty-First Century.* Ann Arbor: University of Michigan Press, 2008.

Nelson, Donald M. *Arsenal of Democracy: The Story of American War Production.* New York: Harcourt, Brace, 1946.

Norman, Matthew W. *Colonel Burton's Spiller & Burr Revolver: An Untimely Venture in Confederate Small Arms Manufacturing.* Macon: Mercer University Press, 1996.

O'Harrow Jr., Robert. *The Quartermaster: Montgomery C. Meigs, Lincoln's General, Master Builder of The Union Army.* New York: Simon and Shuster, 2016.

Palmer, Dave R. *Provide for the Common Defense: America, Its Army, and the Birth of a Nation.* Novato: Presidio Press, 1994.

Pam, David O. *A Desirable Neighborhood.* Vol. 3, *History of Enfield, 1914–1939.* Enfield: Enfield Preservation Society, 1994.

Patterson, Robert P., and Brian Waddell, editor. *Arming the Nation for War: Mobilization, Supply, and the American War Effort in World War II.* Knoxville: University of Tennessee Press, 2014.

Pavelec, Sterling Michael, editor. *The Military-Industrial Complex and American Society.* Santa Barbara: ABC-CLIO, 2010.

Peck, Taylor. *Round Shot to Rockets: A History of the Washington Navy Yard and U.S. Naval Gun Factory.* Annapolis: United States Naval Institute, 1949.

Pedisich, Paul E. *Congress Buys A Navy: Politics, Economics, and the Rise of American Naval Power, 1881–1921.* Annapolis: Naval Institute Press, 2016.

Penn, Mark J. *Views from Around the Globe: Countering Violent Extremism.* Washington, Center for Strategic and International Studies, 2016.

Perkins, Edwin J. *American Public Finance and Financial Servicers, 1700–1815*. Columbus: Ohio State University Press, 1994.

Poole, Walter S. *Adapting to Flexible Response, 1960–1968*. History of Acquisition in the Department of Defense. Washington: Historical Office, Office of the Secretary of Defense, 2013.

Porter, Glenn. *The Rise of Big Business, 1860–1920*. 3rd ed. Wheeling: Harlan Davidson Inc., 2006.

Powell, Colin. *My American Journey*. New York: Random House, 1995.

Prins, Nomi. *All the President's Bankers: The Hidden Alliances that Drive American Power*. New York: Nation Books, 2014.

Proxmire, William. *Report from Wasteland: America's Military-Industrial Complex*. New York: Praeger Publishers, 1970.

Ramsdell, Charles W., and Wendell H. Stephenson, editor. *Behind the Lines in the Southern Confederacy*. Baton Rouge: Louisiana State University Press, 1972 reprint of 1944 original edition.

Risch, Erna. *Quartermaster Support of the Amy: A History of the Corps, 1775–1939*. Washington: Quartermaster Historian's Office, Office of the Quartermaster General, 1962.

Ripley, Warren. *Artillery and Ammunition of The Civil War*. New York: Van Nostrand Reinhold, 1977.

Roberts, William H. *Civil War Ironclads: The U.S. Navy and Industrial Mobilization*. Baltimore: Johns Hopkins University Press, 2002.

Rockoff, Hugh. *America's Economic Way of War: War and the U.S. Economy from the Spanish-American War to the Persian Gulf War*. New York: Cambridge University Press, 2012.

Roland, Alex. *The Military-Industrial Complex*. Historical Perspectives on Technology, Society and Culture Series. Washington: American Historical Association, and Society for the History of Technology, 2001.

Rosen, Steven, editor. *Testing the Theory of the Military-Industrial Complex*. Lexington: D.C. Heath, 1973.

Rosenbloom, Morris V. *Peace through Strength: Bernard Baruch and a Blueprint for Security*. New York: American Surveys and Farrar, Straus and Young, 1953.

Russell, Thomas H. *America's War for Humanity: Pictorial History of the World War for Liberty*. New York: L. H. Walter, 1919.

Rywell, Martin. *Confederate Guns and Their Current Prices*. Harriman: Pioneer Press, 1952.

Sampson, Anthony. *The Arms Bazaar: From Lebanon to Lockheed*. New York: Viking Press, 1977.

Scahill, Jeremy. *Blackwater: The Rise of the World's Most Powerful Mercenary Army*. New York: Nation Books, 2007.

Schaffer, Ronald. *America in the Great War: The Rise of the War Welfare State*. New York: Oxford University Press, 1991.

Schulman, Bruce J. *From Cotton Belt to Sunbelt: Federal Policy, Economic Development and the Transformation of the South, 1938–1980*. Durham: Duke University Press, 1994.

Schrecker, Ellen, editor. *Cold War Triumphalism: The Misuse of History After the Fall of Communism*. New York: The New Press, 2004.

Scranton, Philip and Patrick Fridenson, *Reimagining Business History*. Baltimore: Johns Hopkins University Press, 2013.

Schwartz, Jordan A. *The Speculator: Bernard M. Baruch in Washington, 1917-1965*. Chapel Hill: University of North Carolina Press, 1981.

Schwartz, Stephen I., editor. *Atomic Audit: The Costs and Consequences of U.S. Nuclear Weapons Since 1940*. Washington: Brookings Institution Press, 1998.

Seidule, Ty and Jacqueline E. Whitt, editors. *Stand Up and Fight! The Creation of U.S. Security Organizations, 1942–2005*. Carlisle Barracks: U.S. Army War College Press, April 2015.

Settle, Raymond W. and Mary Lund Settle. *War Drums and Wagon Wheels: The Story of Russell, Majors and Waddell*. Lincoln: University of Nebraska Press, 1966.

Shaw, Frederick J., editor. *Locating Air Force Base Sites: History's Legacy*. Washington: Air Force History and Museums Program, United States Air Force, 2004.

Shiman, Philip. *Forging the Sword: Defense Production During the Cold War*. USACERL Special Report 97/77, July 1997. Washington: U.S. Air Force Air Combat Command and Department of Defense Legacy Program, Cold War Project, 1997.

Showalter, Dennis E., editor. *Forging the Shield: Eisenhower and National Security for the Twenty-First Century*. Chicago: Imprint Publications, 2005.

Silverstone, Paul H. *Warships of the Civil War Navies*. Annapolis: Naval Institute Press, 1989.

Simons, Suzanne. *Master of War: Blackwater USA's Erik Prince and the Business of War* (New York: Harper Collins, 2009.

Singer, P.W. *Can't Win With 'Em, Can't Go to War Without 'Em: Private Military Contractors and Counterinsurgency*. Washington, Brookings Institution, September 2007.

———. *Corporate Warriors: The Rise of the Privatized Military Industry*. Ithaca: Cornell University Press, 2003.

Skoll, Geoffrey R. *Globalization of American Fear Culture: The Empire in the Twenty-First Century*. London: Palgrave, an imprint of Macmillan, 2016.

Skowronek, Stephen. *Building a New American State: The Expansion of National Administrative Capacities, 1877–1920*. New York: Cambridge University Press, 1982.

Smith, Merritt Roe. *Harpers Ferry Armory and the New Technology: The Challenge of Change*. Ithaca: Cornell University Press, 1977.

Smith, R. Elberton. *The Army and Economic Mobilization*. United States Army in World War II Series, The War Department. Washington: United States Army Center of Military History, 1991.

Smith, Robert F. *Manufacturing Independence: Industrial Innovation in the American Revolution*. Yardley: Westholme Publishing, 2016.

Snow, Donald M. and Dennis M. Drew. *From Lexington to Desert Storm: War and Politics in the American Experience*. Armonk: M. E. Sharpe, 1994.

Spencer, Jack. *Focusing Defense Resources to Meet National Security Requirements*. Washington, The Heritage Foundation, March 2003.

Stearns, Peter N. *The Industrial Revolution in World History*. Boulder: Westview, 1993.

Sternberg, Fritz. *The Military and Industrial Revolution of Our Time*. London: Stevens & Sons, 1959.

Still, William N. Jr. *Iron Afloat: The Story of the Confederate Armorclads*. Nashville, Vanderbilt University Press, 1971.

Stockfisch, J. A. *Plowshares into Swords: Managing the American Defense Establishment*. New York: Mason & Lipscomb, 1973.

Stone, I. F. *Business as Usual: The First Year of Defense*. New York: Modern Age Books, 1941.

Stubbing, Richard A. with Richard A Mendel. *The Defense Game: An Insider Explores the Astonishing Realities of America's Defense Establishment*. New York: Harper & Row, 1986.

Swann, Leonard Alexander, Jr. *John Roach, Maritime Entrepreneur: The Years as Naval Constructor, 1862–1886*. Annapolis: United States Naval Institute, 1965.

Taylor, George Rogers. *The Transportation Revolution, 1815–1860*. Vol. 4, *The Economic History of the United States*. New York: Rinehart, 1957.

Tebbs, Jeffrey M. *Pruning the Defense Budget*. Washington, The Brookings Institution, January 2007.

Thayer, George. *The War Business: The International Trade in Armaments*. New York: Simon & Schuster, 1969.

Thomas, Evan. *Ike's Bluff: President Eisenhower's Secret Battle to Save the World*. New York: Little, Brown, 2012.

Thomas, William G. *The Iron Way: Railroads, the Civil War, and the Making of Modern America*. New Haven: Yale University Press, 2011.

Thompson, Lynne C. and Sheila R. Ronis, editors. *U.S. Defense Industrial Base: National Security Implications of a Globalized World*. Washington, National Defense University and Industrial College of the Armed Forces, April 2006.

Thorpe, Rebecca U. *The American Warfare State: The Domestic Politics of Military Spending*. Chicago: University of Chicago Press, 2014.

Tillman, John H. *Civil War Cavalry & Artillery Sabers: A Study of United States Cavalry and Artillery Sabers, 1833–1865*. Lincoln: Andrew Mowbray Publishers, 2001.

Toll, Ian W. *Six Frigates: The Epic History of the Founding of the United States Navy*. New York: W. W. Norton, 2006.

Turse, Nick. *The Complex: How the Military Invades Our Everyday Lives*. New York: Henry Holt Company, 2008.

Tyler, Patrick. *Running Critical: The Silent War, Rickover, and General Dynamics*. New York: Harper & Row, 1986.

Tyrell, C. Merton. *Pentagon Partners, the New Nobility*. New York: Grossman Publishers, 1970.

Uesseler, Rolf. *Servants of War: Private Military Corporations and the Profit of Conflict*. Brooklyn: Soft Shell Press, 2008.

United States Naval Historical Center, *Gearing Up for Victory: American Military and Industrial Mobilization in World War II*. Colloquium on Contemporary History, Number 5. Washington: Naval Historical Center, June 25, 1991.

Vawter, Roderick L. *Industrial Mobilization: The Relevant History*. Washington: National Defense University Press, 1983.

Verkuil, Paul R. *Outsourcing Sovereignty: Why Privatization of Government Functions Threatens Democracy and What We Can Do About It*. New York: Cambridge University Press, 2007.

Vigneras, Marcel. *Rearming the French*. United States Army in World War II, Special Studies. Washington: United States Army Center of Military History, 1989.

Vine, David, *The United States of War: A Global History of America's Endless Conflicts, From Columbus to the Islamic State*. Berkeley, University of California Press, 2020.

Waddell, Brian. *The War Against the New Deal: World War II and American Democracy*. Dekalb: Northern Illinois University Press, 2001.

———. *Toward the National Security State: Civil-Military Relations During World War II*. Westport: Praeger Security International, 2008.

Wall, John Frazier. *Andrew Carnegie*. New York: Oxford University Press, 1970.

Warren, Kenneth. *Triumphant Capitalism: Henry Clay Frick and the Industrial Transformation of America*. Pittsburgh: University of Pittsburgh Press, 1996.

Wasson, R. Gordon. *The Hall Carbine Affair: A Study in Contemporary Folklore*. New York: Paddick Press, 1948.

Weaver, Frederick S. *An Economic History of the United States: Conquest, Conflict, and Struggles for Equality*. Lanham: Rowman and Littlefield, 2016.

Weir, Gary E. *Building American Submarines, 1914–1940*. Washington: Naval Historical Center, 1991.

———. *Forged in War: The Naval-Industrial Complex and American Submarine Construction, 1940–1961*. Washington: Naval Historical Center, 1993.
Weiss, Linda. *America Inc.? Innovation and Enterprise in the National Security State*. Ithaca: Cornell University Press, 2014.
Wells, Thomas Henderson. *The Confederate Navy: A Study in Organization*. University: University of Alabama Press, 1971.
Wert, Jeffrey D. *Civil War Barons: The Tycoons, Entrepreneurs, Inventors, and Visionaries Who Forged Victory and Shaped a Nation*. New York: De Capo Press, 2018.
Wheeler, Winslow T. *The Wastrels of Defense: How Congress Sabotages U.S. Security*. Annapolis: Naval Institute Press, 2004.
Whynes, David V. *The Economics of Third World Military Expenditure*. Austin: University of Texas Press, 1979.
Wiley, Bell Irvin. *The Plain People of the Confederacy*. Baton Rouge: Louisiana State University Press, 1944.
Wilson, Graham K. *Business & Politics: A Comparative Introduction*. London: Chatham House Publishers, 2003.
Wilson, Harold S. *Confederate Industry: Manufacturers and Quartermasters in the Civil War*. Jackson: University Press of Mississippi, 2002.
Wilson, Mark R. *Destructive Creation: American Business and the Winning of World War II*. Philadelphia: University of Pennsylvania Press, 2016.
———. *The Business of Civil War: Military Mobilization and the State, 1861–1865*. Baltimore: Johns Hopkins University Press, 2006.
Wiltz, John E. *In Search of Peace: The Senate Munitions Inquiry, 1934–1936*. Baton Rouge: Louisiana State University Press, 1963.
Younger, Stephen M. *The Bomb: A New History*. New York: Harper Collins, 2009.
Zimmerman, Warren. *First Great Triumph: How Five Americans Made Their Country A World Power*. New York: Farrar, Straus and Giroux, 2002.

SELECTED ARTICLES AND ESSAYS

Specific journal, magazine, and newspaper articles cited in endnotes should be accessed online from publication archives.

Adams, Gordon. "Overview," in *Defense Industry Globalization: A Compendium of Papers Presented at a Conference on Defense Industry Globalization, 16 November, 2001*. Washington: The Atlantic Council of the United States, February 2002, vii–xxvi.
Anthony, Ian. "Arms Procurement After the Cold War: How Much is Enough

to Do What (and How Will We Know)?" *International Affairs*, 74, no. 4 (1998): 871–882.

———. "Politics and Economics of Defence Industries in a Changing World," in *The Politics and Economics of Defense Industries*. Efraim Imbar and Benzion Zilberfarb, editors. London: Frank Cass, 1998, 1–27.

Augustine, Norman R. "Reengineering the Arsenal of Democracy," *The Atlantic Council of the United States Bulletin* 9, no. 6 (July 6, 1998): 1–6.

Avant, Deborah. "Think Again: Mercenaries," *Foreign Policy* no. 143 (July/August 2004): 20–28.

Barber, Lionel. "The Year of the Demagogue," *Financial Times Weekend*, Life & Arts sec., December 18, 2016: 1, 2.

Barnes, Julian E. "War Profiteering," *U.S. News & World Report*, May 13, 2002: 20–24.

Bender, Brian. "Seminars Teach Senior Officers How to Land Industry Jobs," *Boston Globe*, December 26, 2010.

Berenson, Doug. "The Evolving Geography of the U.S. Defense Industrial Base." *War on the Rocks*, September 1, 2021.

Berry, F. Clifton, Jr. "The Lifeline Is Still in Danger," *Air Force Magazine* 72, no. 11 (November 1989): 108–110.

Bertuca, Tony. "Navy's LCS Headlines McCain's 'Indefensible' Waste List," *Inside Defense*, December 19, 2016.

Bonsignore, Ezio. "From 'Last Supper' to 'First Dinner,'" *Military Technology* [Bonn, Germany] 23, no. 11: 3–4.

Boyne, Walter. "Flying Out of The Cold War," *Cosmos, Journal of the Cosmos Club of Washington, D.C.* 9 (1999): 21–24.

Bredemeier, Kenneth. "Thousands of Private Contractors Support U.S. Forces in Persian Gulf," *Washington Post*, March 3, 2003: E1, E10.

Callum, Robert. "The Eurofighter Consortium: A Harbinger of Rationalization for the European Defense Industry?" *National Security Studies Quarterly* 4, no. 1 (Winter 1998): 21–40.

Cancian, Mark F. "Cost Growth: Perception and Reality." Fort Belvoir: Defense Acquisition University, July 2010.

Carmola, Kateri. "It's All Contracts Now: Private Military Firms and a Clash of Legal Culture," *Brown Journal of World Affairs* 3, no. 1 (Fall/Winter 2006): 161-173.

Carter, Ashton B. "Adapting US Defence to Future Needs," *Survival*, v. 41, no. 4 (Winter 1999-2000): 101–123.

Cary, Peter. "The Pork Game," *Christian Science Monitor*, May 13, 2002: 25-26.

Chandler, Alfred D., Jr. "The Role of Business in the United States: A Historical Survey," *Daedalus* 98, no. 1 (Winter 1969): 23–40.

Cochran, Thomas C., "Did the Civil War Retard Industrialization?" *Journal of American History*, 158, no. 2 (September 1961): 97–210.

Codner, Michael. "Just How Far Can We Go?" *RUSI Journal Journal* 144, no. 2 (April/May 1999): 31–33.

Coll, Steve, and Adam Entous. "The Fall of the Islamic Republic." *The New Yorker*, December 20, 2021, 33–45.

Connetta, Carl. "The Dynamics of Defense Budget Growth, 1998–2011," in *Economics and Security: Resourcing National Priorities*. Richmond M. Lloyd, editor. William B. Ruger Chair of National Security Economics Paper Number 5. Newport: Naval War College, 2010, 117–132.

Cooper, Mary H. "Private Affairs: New Reliance on America's Other Army," *Congressional Quarterly Weekly*, September 18, 2004: 2186.

Cuff, Robert D., "An Organizational Perspective on the Military-Industrial Complex," *Business History Review* 52, no. 2 (Summer 1978): 250–262.

D'Agostino, David M. "Transatlantic Cooperative Weapons Development: How Can We Better Ensure Success?" *Acquisition Review Quarterly* 3, no. 2 (Fall 1996): 131–146.

DeBenedetti, Charles. "American Historians and Armaments: The View from Twentieth-Century Textbooks," *Diplomatic History* 6, no. 4 (Fall 1982): 323–337.

———, with introduction and postscript by Charles F. Howlett, "Educators and Armaments in Cold War America," *Peace and Change*, 34, No. 4, October 2009), 425–440.

Dominguez, Gabriel. ". . . as well as for allies Japan and South Korea," *IHS Jane's Defence Weekly*, 53, no. 46 (November 16, 2016): 7.

Donnelly, John, "Cohen: New Budget to Bolster Procurement," *Defense Week*, January 3, 2000: 3.

Donnelly, Ralph W. "Local Defense in the Confederate Munitions Area," in *Military Analysis of the Civil War: An Anthology*. Editors of Military Affairs. Millwood: KTO Press, 1977, 239–251.

Edwards, Michael D. "Golden Threads to the Pentagon," *The Nation* 220, no. 10 (March 15, 1975): 306–308.

Evans, David. "The Ten Commandments of Defense Spending," *Parameters*, Journal of the US Army War College 15, no.4 (December 1985): 76–81.

Franko, Lawrence G. "Restraining Arms Exports to the Third World: Will Europe Agree? *Survival* 21, no. 1 (January/February 1979): 14–25.

Friedman, Milton. "The Role of War in American Economic Development: Price, Income, and Monetary Changes in Three Wartime Periods," *American Economic Review* 152, no. 2 (May 1952): 612–63.

Gansler, Jacques S., "Needed: A U.S. Defense Industrial Strategy," *International Security* 12, no. 2 (Fall 1987): 45–62.

———. "Revitalizing the Arsenal of Democracy," *Air Force Magazine* 67, no. 1 (April 1984): 74–77.

Garrah, Robert E. "U.S. Strategies for Individual Growth and Western Security," *Parameters, Journal of the U.S. Army War College* 12, no. 4 (December 1982): 62–70.

Gholz, Harvey M. and Eugene. "The Defense Monopoly," *Regulation: The CATO Review of Business and Government* 22, no. 3 (Fall, 1999): 39–43.

Gholz, Eugene and Harvey M. Sapolsky. "Restructuring the U.S. Defense Industry," *International Security* 24, no. 3 (Winter 1999/Spring 2000): 5-51.

Gibbs, David N. "The Military-Industrial Complex, Sectoral Conflict, and the Study of U.S. Foreign Policy," in *Business and the State in International Relations*. Ronald W. Cox, editor. Boulder: Westview Press, 1996.

Glaser, Elizabeth. "Better Late than Never: the American Economic War Effort, 1917–1918," in *Great War, Total War: Combat and Mobilization on the Western Front, 1917–1918*. Roger Chickering and Eric Forster, editors. Washington: German Historical Institute, Cambridge University Press, 2000, 389-408.

Golden, C. and F. Lewis. *"The Economic Cost of the American Civil War: Estimates and Implications,"* The Journal of Economic History, 35, no. 2 (June 1975): 279–326.

Gowen, Annie. "U.S. Firms Maneuver to Build Fighter Jets in India," *Washington Post*, December 5, 2016: A1, A9.

Grant, Charles, et al. "Global Defence Industry Survey," *The Economist*, June 2, 1997: 3–18.

Greenstock, Jeremy. "Private Security Companies in an Insecure World," *RUSI Journal* 151, no. 6 (December 2006): 42–44.

Grevatt, Jon. "Trump Victory Spells Uncertainty for Southeast Asia . . . ," *IHS Jane's Defence Weekly* 53, no. 46 (November 16, 2016): 7.

Gwyn, Julian. "British Government Spending and the North American Colonies, 1740–1775," *Journal of Imperial and Commonwealth History* 8, no. 2 (1980): 74–84.

Harrison, Todd. "The New Guns Versus Butter Debate," in *Economics and Security: Resourcing National Priorities*. Richmond B. M. Lloyd, editor. William B. Ruger Chair of National Security Economics Papers Number 5. Newport: Naval War College, 2010.

Hartung, William D. "Curb the Military Spending Binge," *Washington Post*, November 25, 2016: A22.

———. "Trump for the Defense," *TomDispatch.com*, November 22, 2016.

Hayward, Keith. "The Defence Aerospace Industry in an Age of Globalization," *RUSI Journal* 15, no. 3 (June 2000): 55–59.

———. "The Globalization of Defence Industries," *Survival* 423, no. 2 (Summer 2000): 115–132.

Holton, Richard H. "Business and Government," *Daedalus* 98 no. 1 (Winter 1969): 41–59.

Hooks, Gregory. "The United States of America: The Second World War and the Retreat from New Deal Era Corporatism," in *Organizing Business for War: Corporatist Economic Organization During the Second World War*. Wyn Grant, Jan Nerkkers and Frans van Waarden, editors. New York: Berg, 1991, 75–106.

Horwich, George and David J. Bjornstad. "Spending and Manpower in Four U.S. Mobilizations: A Macro/Policy Perspective," *Journal of Policy History* 1, no. 7 (1991): 173–202.

Husbands, Jo L. "The Arms Connection: Jimmy Carter and the Politics of Military Exports," in *The Gun Merchants: Politics and Policies of the Major Arms Suppliers*. Cindy Cannizzo, editor. New York: Pergamon, 1980, 18–48.

Jennings, Gareth. "DoD Awards Lot 20 Production Contract for F-35 Fighter," *IHS Jane's Defence Weekly* 53, no. 48 (November 30, 2016): 4.

Jones, Clive. "Private Military Companies as 'Epistemic Communities,'" *Civil Wars* 8, no. 304 (September-December 2006): 355–372.

Klein, Maury. "The Boys Who Stayed Behind: Northern Industrialists and the Civil War," in *Rank and File: Civil War Essays in Honor of Bell I. Wiley*. James I. Robertson and Richard M. McMurry, editors. Novato: Presidio Press, 1976, 137–156.

Knickerbocker, Brad K. "Return of the 'Military-Industrial Complex?'" *Christian Science Monitor*, February 13, 2002.

Kurth, James R. "Military Power and Industrial Competitiveness: The Industrial Dimension of Military Strategy," *Naval War College Review* 35, no. 5 (September/October 1982): 33–47.

Laird, Robin. "A Giant Kick in the Pants on Both Sides of the Atlantic," *RUSI Journal* 14, no. 2 (April/May 1999): 34–37.

Lawlor, Maryann. "Defense Marketplace Changes Cause Companies to Re-evaluate, Revamp," *Signal* 52, no.4 (December 1997): 59–62.

Lindemann, Marc. "Civilian Contractors Under Military Law," *Parameters* (Autumn 2007): 83–94.

Lindsay, James M. "Congress and Defense Policy—1961 to 1986," *Armed Forces & Society* 13, no. 3 (Spring 1987): 371–401.

Lord, George Frank. "War Will Make Us Plan Advertising Further Ahead: The Advertiser Will Dig Deeper and Build Bigger," *Printer's Ink* 102, no. 10 (March 7, 1918): 25–26.

Louscher, David J., Alethia H. Cook and Victoria D. Barto. "The Emerging Competitive Position of U.S. Defense Firms in the International Market," *Defense Analysis* 1, no. 2 (1998): 11–34.

Lovering, John. "Loose Cannons: Creating the Arms Industry of the Twenty-First Century," in *Global Insecurity: Restructuring the Global Military Sector, Volume III*. Mary Kaldor, editor. New York: Pinter, 2000.

Luck, Edward C. "The Arms Trade," *Academy of Political Science Proceedings* 32, no. 4 (1977): 172–183.

Lynd, Staughton and David Waldstreicher. "Free Trade, Sovereignty, and Slavery: Toward an Economic Interpretation of American Independence," *William and Mary Quarterly*, Third Series 68, no. 4 (October 2011): 597–630.

Maogoto, Jackson Nyamuya. "Subcontracting Sovereignty: Commodification of Military Force and Fragmentation of State Authority," *Brown Journal of World Affairs* 3, no. 1 (Fall/Winter 2006): 147–160.

Markusen, Ann. "Global Defense Mergers, Their Danger: Losing Control of Leading-Edge Technology," *Christian Science Monitor*, August 5, 1998.

———. "The Post-Cold War American Defence Industry: Options, Policies and Probable Outcomes," in *The Politics and Economics of Defence Industries*. Efraim Inbar and Benzion Zilberfarb, editors. London: Frank Cass, 1998, 51–70.

Masters, Brooke, and Andrew Edgecliffe-Johnson. "The Shift from 'Just In Time' to 'Just In Case.'" *Financial Times*, December, 21, 2021.

Mayer, Kenneth R. "The Limits of Delegation: The Rise and Fall of BRAC," *Regulation: The CATO Review of Business and Government* 22, no. 3 (Fall 1999): 32–38.

McCarthy, John. "Expanding Private Military Sector Faces Structural Change and Scrutiny," *Jane's Intelligence Review*, February 1, 2006.

McConnel, Deborah L. "Lou Cretia Owen and the Old Hickory Munitions Plant During World War I," *Tennessee Historical Quarterly* 58, no. 2 (Summer 1999): 128–129.

McNaugher, Thomas L. "Weapons Procurement: The Futility of Reform," *International Security* 12, no. 2 (Fall 1987): 63–104.

Meese, Michael J. "Strategy and Force Planning in a Time of Austerity," in *American Grand Strategy and the Future of U.S. Landpower*, December 2014. Joseph Da Silva, Hugh Liebert and Isaiah Wilson, editors. Carlisle Barracks: Strategic Studies Institute, Army War College Press, 2014, 135–150.

Melman, Seymour. "After the Military-Industrial Complex?" *Bulletin of the Atomic Scientists* 27, no. 3 (March 1972): 7–9.

Morrocco, John D. "Consolidation Poses Transatlantic Quandary," *Aviation Week & Space Technology* (July 24, 2000): 100–101.

National Defense Industrial Association/Govini. *Vital Signs 2022: The Health and Readiness of the Defense Industrial Base*. Arlington, VA, National Defense Industrial Association, February 2022.

Noone, Michael F., Jr. "The Military-Industrial Complex Revisited," *Air University Review*, 30, no. 2 (November-December 1978), 79–83.

Olson, William J. "The Slow-Motion Coup: Militarization and the Implications of Eisenhower's Presidency." *Small Wars Journal*, August 11, 2012.

Portnoy, Jenna. "Senators: Budget Strife Puts Va. Shipyard Jobs in Danger," *Washington Post*, December 6, 2016: B1, B4.

Rothkopf, David J. "Business Versus Terror," *Foreign Policy* no. 130 (May/June 2002): 56–64.

Samuelson, Robert J. "Just Cutting Waste at the Pentagon Won't Cut It," *Washington Post*, December 12, 2016: A13.

Sapolsky, Harvey M. and Eugene Gholz. "The Defense Monopoly," *Regulation: The CATO Review of Business and Government* 22, no. 3 (Fall 1999): 39–44.

Schmitt, Christopher H. "Wages of Sin," *Christian Science Monitor*, May 13, 2002: 28–34.

Shrader, Charles. "Field Logistics in the Civil War," in *The U.S. Army War College Guide to the Battle of Antietam: The Maryland Campaign of 1862*. Jay Luvaas and Harold W. Nelson, editors. Carlisle: South Mountain Press, 1987, 255–284.

Schwartz, Nelson D. "The War Business: The Pentagon's Private Army," *Fortune*, March 3, 2003.

Scott, Alwyn. "Trump Attack on Lockheed Martin Foreshadows War on Defense Industry," *Reuters*, December 12, 2016.

Singer, P.W. "Corporate Warriors: The Rise of the Privatized Military Industry and Its Ramifications for International Security," *International Security*, 26, no. 3 (Winter 2001-02): 186–220.

———. "Outsourcing War," *Foreign Affairs* 84, no. 2 (March-April 2005): 119-132.

Skibbie, Lawrence F. "Debate on National Security Should Play Role in 2000 Presidential Race," *National Defense* (December 1999): 2.

Slater, Jerome and Terry Nardin. "The 'Military-Industrial Complex' Muddle," *The Yale Review* 65, no. 1 (October 1975):1–23.

Squeo, Anne Marie and Thomas E. Ricks. "Pentagon Must Assist Suppliers Hit by Defense Consolidation," *Wall Street Journal*, November 30, 1999.

Sternberg, Gerald M. "SDI and Organizational Politics of Military R&D," *Armed Forces & Society* 13, no. 4 (Summer 1987): 579–598.

Swardson, Anne. "French, German Defense Giants Plan Merge," *Washington Post*, October 1, 1999.

Tigner, Brooks. "Europe's Low Defence Spenders to Feel the Heat from a Trump White House," *IHS Jane's Defence Weekly* 53, no. 46 (November 16, 2016): 6.

Tsipis, Kosta. "Hiding Behind the Military-Industrial Complex," *Bulletin of the Atomic Scientists* 28, no. 6 (June 1972).

Vernham Dean, Baroness Symons of. "Creating a Competitive European Defence Industry–The UK Government View," *RUSI Journal* 145, no. 3 (June 2000): 13–17.

Wasserbly, Daniel. "Trump's Defence Plans Thus Far Track Those of Republican Party," *IHS Jane's Defence Weekly* 53, no. 46 (November 16, 2016): 5.

Whitlock, Craig and Bob Woodward. "Pentagon Hid Study Revealing $125 Million in Waste," *Washington Post*, December 6, 2016: A1, A6.
Williams, Robert H. "Shrinking Arms Market Spurs Contest for Third World Sales," *National Defense*, December 1999: 34.
Williams, Sunjim. "A Hopeful Voyage–or Rearranging the Deck Chairs?" *RUSI Journal* 144, no. 2 (April-May 1999): 35–38.
Wilson George C. "A Larger Defense Budget for a Smaller Force," *National Journal*, February 9, 2002: 398–399.
Wood, Alison. "BAE Plans for Success as a Global Player," *RUSI Journal* 144, no. 2 (April-May 1999): 39–40.

UNPUBLISHED STUDIES

Baruch, Bernard. "Taking the Profit Out of War: Suggested Policies to Provide, Without Change in our Constitution, for Industrial Mobilization, Elimination of Profiteering and Equalization of the Burdens of War," A Memorandum submitted to the Joint Congressional and Cabinet Commission Constituted Pursuant to Public Resolution No. 98, 71st Congress. New York: private print, 1931.
Cannon, Charles Alfred. "The Military-Industrial Complex in American Politics, 1953–1970," unpublished doctoral dissertation, Stanford University, 1975. Ann Arbor: University Microfilms, 1975).
Clayton, James L. "A Comparison of Cold War Expenditures in the United States and the United Kingdom." Unpublished paper presented at the CPRH Southern Historical Convention The Costs of the Cold War, November 1970.
Donal, James Sexton. "Forging the Sword: Congress and the American Naval Renaissance, 1880–1890." Ann Arbor: University Microfilms, 1977.
Flamm, Kenneth. "Defence Industry and the Means of War." Unpublished paper presented at International Institute of Strategic Studies Fortieth Conference, September 3–6, 1998, Oxford, United Kingdom.
Latham, Andrew. "From the 'Armory System' To 'Agile Manufacturing': Industrial Divides in the History of American Arms Production," Unpublished PhD dissertation. Ann Arbor: Microfilm Dissertation Services, University of Michigan, 1997.
Maggio, Christopher S. "Industrial Preparedness," Unpublished Student Essay, October 8, 1971. Carlisle Barracks: United States Army War College, 1971.
Waddell, Brian Edward. "Economic Mobilization for World War II and the Transformation of the American State," doctoral dissertation, Ann Arbor: University Microfilms, University of Michigan, 1993.

Index

"ABCD" vessels, 98–99, 106
Aboulafia, Richard, 269
Abraham Lincoln, 312
Abrahamson, James, 124, 162, 225
Abramson, James L., 122
"Act to Aid in the Construction of Railroad and Telegraph Line . . . , 1862," 92
"Act to Provide Munitions of War and for Other Purposes, An," 65
Adams, 33, 34
Adams, Gordon, 278–79, 286
Adams, H. A., Sr., 79
Adams, Henry, 139
Adams, John, 20
Adams, Solomon, 74
Adjusting Your Business to War, 167
Administration of Justice Act, 7
Aegis, 306
Aerospace Industry Association, 222, 270, 288, 311
Aerospatiale-Matra, 266
Afghanistan, 197, 215, 275, 277, 280–81, 283–84, 286, 292–93, 295–97, 300, 305, 307, 313–17, 332, 336
Aftergood, Steven, 321
Age of Administrative State, 127
Age of Industrialization, 127
Age of Mechanization and Mobilization, 127
Age of Regulation, 127
Agency for International Development, 278
Aguinaldo, Emilio, 104
Air Corps Act, 147

Air Force, 202, 211; 1945–1991, 181, 185, 193; 2001-present, 285–87, 290, 327
Air Force Association, 229
Air Force Magazine, 219, 239
Air Service-Air Corps, 166
Airbus Helicopter, 266, 302
Airview, 169–70
al-Qaeda, 275, 281–83, 317
Alabama, 81
Albaugh, Jim, 285
Albright, Madeleine, 243, 246
Aldrich, Nelson Wilmarth, 99
Aldrich, Winthrop, 137
Alfred Jenks and Son, 72
Alger, Cyrus, 43, 73
Algiers, 29
Alliance, 16
Alliance for Progress, 195
Alliant Techsystems, 248, 265
Allies, 129, 162; favoritism, 116; procurement program, 121–22; survival financing for, 119
Allis-Chalmers, 164
Amalgamated Clothing Workers of America, 160
Amara, Jomana, 325, 328, 337
America, 16
American Defense Preparedness Association, 219
American Enterprise Institute, 285
American Expeditionary Force (AEF), 131
American International Corporation, 165
American Legion, 146
American Machine Works, 42

American Machinist, 125–26
American Recovery and Reinvestment Act, 309
American Silk Mills, 164
American System of Manufacturing, 40, 96
American Telephone and Telegraph (AT&T), 197, 224, 271
American Tobacco, 94
Ames, J. T., 72
Ames, Nathan Peabody, 43, 45
Ames, Nathaniel, 75
Ames foundry, 73
Ames Laboratory, 258
Ames Manufacturing Company, 42, 72, 91
Anders, William, 261
Anderson, Joseph Reid, 43, 44
Anderson, Marion, 216
Angevine, Robert, 92
Annapolis, 39
Annual Report, 108
anti-statism, 4, 19
Applied Physics Laboratory, 174
Appomattox, 71, 73–74, 81, 91
Appropriations Committee, 295
Areva, 289
Argonne Universities Association, 258
ARINC, 331
Arizona, 107
Arlington National Cemetery, 102
Armed Forces Procurement Act of 1947, 179
Armistice, 131, 145
Armour, 94
Arms Control Treaties, 211
arms manufacture: 1860–1866, 58, 71–72, 85; 1865–1917, 91, 96–97, 99–100, 110, 114, 121; 1917–1945, 131, 166; 1945–1991, 180–81, 183, 189, 197–98, 200–201, 204–5, 207, 212, 223, 225–27; Civil War, 72–73; Colonial America, 6, 8, 11–16, 18; France, 6, 12–13, 214; Great Britain, 6; interchangeable parts, 21, 37, 40–42, 44–45; standardization of, 13, 21, 37, 40–44
Arms Security Project, 322
Armstrong, C. Michael, 255
Army, 211, 258
Army Air Corps, 147–48, 166
Army Air Force, 166
Army Aviation Service, 118
Army Industrial College, 130, 146, 154, 173, 179
Army-Navy Munitions Board, 154
Army Ordnance Association, 146
Army Tactical Missile System, 239
Army War College, 241, 245, 317
Arsenal, the, 75
Arthur, Chester Allen, 98
Articles of Confederation, 10
Aspin, Les, 246, 255
Assad, Bashar Hafez al-, 296
Associated Universities Inc., 258
Association of the United States Army, 255
Astium, 266
Aston, H., 45
ATK, 303
Atlanta Arsenal, 75
Atlanta Naval Works August Arsenal, 75
Atlantic Council, 254
Atlantic Monthly, 242
Atomic Audit: The Costs and Consequences of U.S. Nuclear Weapons since 1940, 257
atomic bomb, 172, 174–75, 183, 186
Atomic Energy Agency, 179, 201
Atomic Energy Commission (AEC), 181, 184, 189, 192, 202, 223, 259
Atwood, Donald J., 218
Augusta Foundry and Machine Works, 75
Augustine, Norman R., 252–53, 254–56, 260, 263–64, 297–98, 305
Austal, 303
Australia, 214
Australian Strategic Policy Institute, 327

Austria, 4
Austro-Prussian War, 93
Autocar, 157
Avant, Deborah, 314
AVCO, 207

B. F. Goodrich, 271
Bacevich, Andrew, 319, 323
BAE Systems, 248, 260, 265–66, 269, 271, 303, 312, 319, 334
Bailey, Gavin J., 156
Baker, Newton D., 117, 130, 142–44, 147–48
Baldwin Locomotive Works, 120
Balkans, 243, 245, 248–49, 297, 313
Balko, Radley, 283
Balogh, Brian, 36, 55
Bangladesh, 240
Bank, Stephen A., 282
Barber, Lionel, 320
Barron, Bruce, 311
Baruch, Bernard, 138, 142, 144–46, 148–49, 155, 159, 173
Base Realignment and Closures (BRAC-ing), 251, 257
Bath Iron Works, 107, 110, 144, 212, 303
Bear Stearns, 248, 249
Beard, Charles, 83
Beaver, Daniel, 117–19
Bechtel Nevada Corporation, 258, 271, 306, 314–15, 331
Becker, William H., 193
Beechcraft, 302
Beeler, John, 61
Beggs, James W., 213
Bell & Howell, 164
Bell Aircraft, 157
Bell Helicopter Textron, 270, 302
Bell Laboratories, 298
Bellona Foundry, 43, 75
Bendix Aviation, 164, 258
Bendix Kansas City Division of Allied Signal, 258

Benet, Stephen Vincent, 96
Bennett, Frank M., 46
Bensel, Richard, 55, 89
Berdan, Hiram, 96
Bering Point, 306
Berlin, Irving, 138
Berlin Wall, 235, 237
Bernard, Simon, 38–39
Berrigan, Frida, 289
Bethlehem Shipbuilding Company, 151–52
Bethlehem Steel, 106, 108, 110, 113, 119, 144, 197, 207
Bettis Atomic Power Laboratory, 258
Biden, Joe, 337
bin Laden, Osama, 296
Bingaman, Jeff, 241
Bipartisan Budget Act (BBA) of 2013, 291
Bipartisan Policy Center, 295
BKSH & Associates, 306
"black sites," 314
Blackford, Mansel, 205
Blackwater Services, 315, 331–32
Blackwater USA, 315
Blackwater Worldwide, 315
Blakey, Marion C., 288
Bleecher, Todd, 332
Bliss, E. W., 110, 114
Bloomberg, 301, 313
Blum, John Morton, 156
Board of Navy Commissioners, 35
Board of Trade and Plantations, 4
Board of War, 8
Boeing, 157, 197, 207, 210, 219, 247, 249, 253, 260, 262, 265, 269–71, 285, 287, 300–302, 304, 306, 308, 310–11, 313, 319, 325, 327, 330–32
Boggs, Carl, 237
Boker, Herman, 72
Bolivia, 152
Bolton, John, 326
Bombard, James, 43
Bonaparte, Charles, 112
Bonaparte, Napoleon, 21, 38

Bonner, Michael, 62–63
Booz Allen, 315
Booz Allen Hamilton, 331
Border Security, 336
Bosnia, 282, 314
Boston, 15
Boston Globe, 332
Bottom Up Review (BUR), 243
Bourbon, 15, 16
Bourne, Randolph, 129, 139
Boyne, Walter, 254
Braddock, Edward, 6
Bradford, James, 4
Bradley and Company, 75
Brandes, Stuart, 49, 95, 119, 122, 150–51, 228–29
Brands, Hal, 187, 193
Bretton Woods system, 179, 182, 196, 200
Brian, Danielle, 303
Brierfield Arsenal, 75
Briggs Manufacturing, 157
British Aerospace, 214, 303
British Port Act, 7
Broad, William J., 321
Brodie, Bernard, 211, 213
Brokaw, Tom, 169
Brooke, John M., 81
Brookhaven National Laboratory, 258
Brookhaven Science Association, 258
Brookings Institute, 228, 249, 261, 285, 336
Brooklyn, 47
Brown, Adam, 35
Brown, M. L., 6, 18, 21, 27
Brown, Noah, 35
Brown, Richard, D., 3, 84
Brown and Root Services, 50, 249
Brown and Sharp, 42
Brown University, 296, 317
Brownlee, W. Eliot, 138
Bruscino, Thomas, 168
Bryan, William Jennings, 116, 118
Bryant, Keith, 36, 83, 111–12, 181

Budget Control Act (BCA) of 2011, 290–93, 318, 323–33
Budget Enforcement Act of 1990, 245
Buhl, Lance C., 92
Builders foundry, 73
Bulloch, James, 81, 85
Bureau of Construction and Repair, 113
Bureau of Equipment, 113
Bureau of Internal Revenue, 67
Bureau of Ordnance, 113
Bureau of Printing and Engraving, 84
Bureaus of Refugees, Freedmen, and Abandoned Lands, 64
Bureau of Steam Engineering, 113
Burgess, Warren Randolph, 137
Burleson, Albert S., 137
Burr, David, 75
Burton, James Henry, 43, 75
Bush, Clive, 40–41
Bush, George H. W., 238, 241–43, 245–46, 249, 255, 313
Bush, George W., 270, 272, 277–80, 282–85, 288, 306
Bush, Vannevar, 173, 179
Bushnell and Company, 79
Business Executives for National Security, 267, 338
"Business Versus Terror" (Rothkopf), 279
Business Week, 249, 304
Butler, Matthew Calbraith, 99
Buy American Act, 93, 214, 309
Buying National Security (Adams, Williams), 279
Byrnes, James E., 160
Byrnes, Jimmy, 163

Caci & Titan, 306
CACI International, 314–15
Caddell, 329
Cadillac, 157
Cahill, Jeremy, 321
Calhoun, John C., 20, 37–38

California Institute of Technology, 203
Camp David Accords, 196–97, 215
Campbell, Jack, 169
Canaan, James W., 219
Canada, 4, 240
Cancian, Mark, 48
Capital Issues Committee, 149
Capitol building, 34, 319, 337
Carbon Steel, 110
Carlisle, Hawk, 331
Carlucci, Frank, 234
Carlyle Group, 271, 331
Carnegie, Andrew, 91–92, 94, 101, 103, 106, 110, 113, 152, 255–56
Carnegie Institute of Washington, 173
Carp, E. Wayne, 7, 12, 17
Carpenter Technology, 302
Carrier, 248
Carroll, James, 338
Carson, Iain, 303
Carter, Ashton B., 245, 288, 290, 293, 332–33
Carter, Jimmy, 196, 198–99, 212–15, 223, 226–27, 297
Casa, 266
Caterpillar Tractor, 164
CATO Institute, 326
Catton, Bruce, 156, 163, 166, 288
Cecil Furnace, 43
Census Bureau, 94–95
Center for a New American Security, 324, 330
Center for Arms Control and Nonproliferation, 289
Center for Defense Information, 284
Center for Defense Studies, The, 290
Center for International Policy, 322
Center for Strategic and Budgetary Assessments, 281
Center for Strategic and International Studies (CSIS), 263, 294, 326
Center for the National Interest, 319
CENTO, 195

Central Intelligence Agency (CIA), 180, 184, 193, 195, 255, 314, 318
Central Ordnance Laboratory, 72, 87
Chaco Boreal, 152
Chaffee-Reese, 96
Chandler, Alfred D., 225
Chandler, William E., 101
Chao, Pierre, 304–5
Charles Koch Institute, 319
Charles L. Seabury and Company Consolidated, 110
Chase, 121
Chase, Samuel P., 67, 86
chemical weapons, 173, 240
Chemring Group, 248
Chen, Michelle, 336
Cheney, Richard, 222, 245, 315
Cheney Brothers, 164
Cherne, Leo M., 166
Chesapeake, 33, 34
Chevrolet, 157, 181
Chicago Council on Global Affairs, 322
China, 2, 103, 127, 156, 193, 201, 246, 275, 277, 285, 292–93, 296, 317–18, 320, 323, 332–34, 336; atomic bomb, 186; Communism, 182–86, 196; Korean War, 188; "Open Door" interference, 109
Christian Science Monitor, 303
Chrysler, 157, 171, 197, 207, 210, 268
Citizen Training Corps (Plattsburgh Camp), 118
Citizenship and Immigration Services, 278
City Bank of New York, 123–24
Civil War, 42, 46, 53–87, 89, 90, 92–93, 100–101, 111, 124, 135, 146, 168, 178, 281; African American recruits, 64, 65; Confederacy, 56–57, 60–65, 68; Confederacy, antebellum society, 62–63, 69–70; Confederacy, black market economy, 70; Confederacy, cannon manufacture, 72, 75; Confederacy, cotton reliance, 36–37, 39, 61–62, 68–70; Confederacy, currency, 68–69;

Civil War (*continued*)
  Confederacy, defense industry base, 71–75; Confederacy, national debt, 68–69; Confederacy, navy, 75–82; Confederacy, postwar economy, 83; Confederacy, slave labor force, 71; Confederacy, taxes, 68; Confederacy Treasury Department, 69; conscription, 63, 65; cost of, 86; expansion of military administration, 59–60; financing, 66–71; human capital loss, 54, 61; manufacturing and technology during, 54–55, 78–80; ordinance depots, 79; perceptions of, 53–54; postwar surplus, 89–90; taxes, 60, 63, 64, 66–71; "Treasury girls," 66, 168; Union, 62–65, 69, 71–82, 96; Union, black market, 78; Union, industrial superiority of, 54, 57, 59, 73–74; Union army's expansion, 71–72; Union navy, 75–82; Union postwar economy, 89; Union War Department, 72, 77; winter of 1864–1865, 69
Clarke, John, 43
Clarkson, Grosvenor, 127
Clayton Anti-Trust Act, 111
Cleveland, Grover, 106
Clinton, Bill, 241–43, 246, 250, 255, 260, 262, 265, 272, 284, 286, 288, 310, 314
Coast Guard, 278
Coca-Cola, 157, 254
Cochran, Thomas C., 83, 84
Cochran and Riggs, 49
Coercive Acts, 7
Coffin, Howard E., 142
Cohan, George M., 128, 135
Cohen, Warren, 263
Cohen, William, 267, 314
Cold War, 133, 162, 285, 292, 296, 299, 301, 321; end of, 205, 209, 223–24, 237, 247, 267; legacy, 237–73, 304–5; military industrial complex, 177–235;

military-industrial-political complex (MIPC), 186, 195, 209, 224, 240; peace dividends, 242
Collins, 265
Collinson, Peter, 9
colonial America: arms manufacture, 6, 8, 11–14, 18; arms possession, 6; artillery, 5, 14; colonial iron industry, 5; colonial military industrial complex, 7, 12; Connecticut, 14–15; conscription, 11; currency, 10; defense, 8–9, 14; demobilization, 16–17; Government Owned/Government Operated facilities, 8; heavy weapons manufacture, 14–16; Maryland, 8, 14; Massachusetts, 9, 12, 14; navy, 14; New York, 12, 14; Pennsylvania, 7–8, 12, 14, 16; Pennsylvania navy, 7; postwar slump, 16–17; Rhode Island, 14; security and weapons development, 4–11; shipyards/shipbuilding, 6, 7, 14–15, 16; state militias, 8; taxation, 8–9; Virginia, 12–14; war debt, 17, 19; war surplus, 17
Colorado, 47
Colt, 91, 96
Colt, Samuel, 43–44, 58, 72, 75, 96
Columbia, 34
Columbia Foundry, 44
Columbia Ironworks, 110
Columbia University, 55
Columbus Arsenal, 75
Columbus Naval Iron Works, 75
Commerce Department, 249, 324
Commerce One, Inc., 269
Commercial Agency Agreement, 120
Commercial Off-the-Shelf (COTS) acquisitions, 252
Commissary General of Military Stores (CGMS), 8, 12, 17
Committee of Observation, 15
Committee of Safety, 13
Committee on Public Information, 136
Committee on Supplies, 159

Common Sense, 325
company owned, company operated (COCO), 82; 1945–1991, 205, 210; 1991–2001, 248; World War II, 166
Compulsory Funding Measure of 1864, 68
Conetta, Carl, 281
Confederacy, 15
Confederacy, 56–57, 60–65, 68; antebellum society, 62–63, 69–70; black market economy, 70; cannon manufacture, 72, 75; cotton reliance, 36–37, 39, 61–62, 68–70; currency, 68–69; defense industry base, 71–75; national debt, 68–69; navy, 75–82; postwar economy, 83; slave labor force, 71; taxes, 68; Treasury Department, 69. *See also under* Civil War
Confederation Congress, 17, 20–23; 1787 meeting, 23
Conference on the Limitation of Armament, 147
Congress, 15
Congressional Budget Office, 293, 323, 336
Congressional Quarterly, 336
Congressional Research Service, 66, 313, 321, 328, 332
Connecticut Council of Safety, 15
conscription, 2; Civil War, 63, 65; Colonial America, 11
Consolidated Aviation, 248
Consolidated-Vultee, 157, 181, 197
Constellation, 29, 33
Constitution, 29
Constitution of the United States, The, 16, 23–24; 1st Amendment, 23; 2nd Amendment, 23, 283; 3rd Amendment, 23; 5th Amendment, 23; 14th Amendment, 67; Article I, 23; Article II, 23; Article III, 23; Article IV, 23–24; Article VI, 67; Bill of Rights, 24; military clauses, 23
Constitutional Convention, 24
Continental Army, 12, 14, 17

Continental Congress, 8–13
Contract Settlements Act, 178
Controlled Materials Plan, 162
Convair, 181
Conventional Arms Transfer policy, 326
Cooke, Jay, 67
Coolidge, Calvin, 147, 316
Cordesman, Andrew, 239, 244, 284
Correll, John, 239, 240
Cost-Plus-Fixed-Fee contracts, 164, 307
Costello, Robert, 234, 235
cotton production, 36–37, 39, 61–62, 68–70, 84; permits for trading, 70–71
Coulter, E. Merton, 62
Coulter, Matthew, 121, 122
Council of Economic Advisors, 186
Council on Foreign Relations, 320
Council of National Defense, 118, 124, 127, 142, 158–59, 161
COVID-19, 318, 334–35, 337
Cox, E. B., 49
Coxe, Tench, 28
Coy, Wayne, 160
Cramp, Charles, 48, 80, 104, 107, 110
Crash of 1929, 152
Cray, 312
Creel, George, 136, 138
Crescent Shipyard, 110
Crock, Stan, 304, 305
Crockatt, Richard, 243
Crossley, 164
Crowder, Enoch, 117
Crowell, Benedict, 130, 146
Crozier, William, 144
CSRA, 325
CSS *Hunley*, 82
Cuba, 102, 104
Culver, C. M., 131, 211
Cunliffe, Marcus, 59
Curtiss, Glenn, 109
Curtiss Airplane and Motor, 151
Curtiss-Wright aircraft, 207, 210, 247

Curtiss-Wright Export Corporation, 152
Custer, George, 91
Custer Battles, 306
Customs and Border Protection, 278

Dahlgren, John, 44, 47–48, 90
Daimler-Benz, 266
DaimlerChrysler, 307
Dakota Creek Industries, 303
Dallas Morning News, 320
Daniels, Josephus, 107–8, 117, 144
Danner, Mark, 275
David Packer Commission, 222
David Taylor Model Basin, 174
Davidson, Joel, 172, 175
Davis, George T., 105
Davis, Jefferson, 20, 37, 57, 59, 60, 62–63, 65, 69–70, 85, 87
Day, 248
de Lafayette (Marquise), 21
De Long, J. Bradford, 242
Declaration of Independence, 9
DeCredico, Mary A., 74
Defense Advanced Research Projects Agency, 278
Defense Authorization Act of 1991, 249
Defense Conversion program, 250
Defense Education Act, 287
Defense Intelligence Agency, 278
Defense Management Review, 252
Defense Manufacturing Board (DMB), 222–23
Defense Manpower Administration, 188
Defense Material System, 162
Defense Plant Corporation, 167
Defense Production Act of 1950, 188, 230, 239–40, 280, 335
Defense Production Authority, 188–89
Defense Reform Initiative, 265
Defense Science Board, 255, 263, 267, 298, 309
Defense Technology and Industrial Base (DTIB), 261

Delaware, 15
Deloitte Consulting, 335
Deltek, 331
Demologos, 47
Department of Agriculture, 84
Department of Commerce, 331
Department of Commissary General of Military Stores (DCGMS), 21
Department of Defense (DoD), 180, 203–4, 209, 217, 221–23, 229–33, 235, 241, 244, 247, 249, 254–55, 261–64, 267–69, 271, 287–88, 290–91, 293–94, 297, 300–302, 306, 310, 312, 314–15, 318, 325–26, 328, 337
Department of Energy (DOE), 201, 204, 223, 256–57, 259, 260, 277, 285, 289, 318, 321, 325
Department of Health and Human Services, 278
Department of Justice, 250, 314, 318
Department of State, 288, 293, 314, 318
Department of Transportation, 247
Deringer, Henry, 45
Desert Shield/Desert Storm, 240
Dethloff, Henry, 36, 83, 111–12, 181
Detroit (Chrysler) Tank Arsenal, 157
Detroit Ordnance Tank Automotive Center, 189
Deutch, John, 255
Devereaux, T. H., 135
DeVry, 164
Dewey, George, 102–3, 115
Deyrup, Felicia Johnson, 40
Diamond Match Company, 121
Diamond T Motor, 157
Dickinson, Laura, 314
Dictaphone Corporation, 164
DIME power (diplomatic, informational, military, and economic), 182, 198
Dimick, Horace E., 43
Disney, 254
Dobbins, James, 20, 37, 46–47, 51
Dockery Act of 1894, 111

Donnelly, Tom, 290
Dorminey, Caroline, 326
Dorwart, Jeffrey, 7
Doughty, William, 35
Douglas, Donald, 169
Douglas Aircraft Company, 157, 169, 170, 202, 248
Dow Chemical, 207
Dower, John W., 272, 273
du Pont, Eleuthere Irene, 28
Dueck, Colin, 188, 191, 198, 237, 243
Duke University, 195
Dulles, John Foster, 192
Duncan, John, 323, 324
Dunne, Peter, 102–3
Duplan Silk Company, 164
DuPont, Pierre, 153
DuPont, 74, 90, 94, 104, 120, 144, 168, 175, 197, 207, 232; war profit-making, 95, 150–52
Dyer, A. B., 74, 89
DynCorp, 249, 314, 315, 316

E. I. Du Pont de Nemours & Company, 33, 119, 120, 164, 174, 259; gunpowder, 46; "soda" blasting powder, 40
E. I. F. Du Pont de Nemours, 271
E. Remington and Sons, 72
EADS, 266, 306, 308
Eads, James B., 78
Earle, Edward Meade, 24
Early, Jubal, 73
Eastman Chemical, 258
Eastman Kodak, 164
Eberstadt, Ferdinand, 138, 149, 162, 180
Eckford, Henry, 35
Economic Stabilization Authority, 188
Economist, The, 303
Edelman, Eric, 292
Edison, Alva, 173
Edling, Max, 36, 55
Effingham, 15
Egypt, 240, 277

Eisenhower, Dwight D., 177, 183, 185–86, 191–95, 197–99, 201, 203, 206, 237, 247, 267, 270, 272, 299, 303–4, 308, 332, 337
Eisenhower Study Group, 296
El Salvador, 215
Elbit Systems Ltd., 312
Electric Boat Company, 110, 114, 144, 248, 303
Electronic Data Systems, 331
Elgin National Watch Company, 165
Elliott, J. D., 38
Ellis, Steven, 325
Ellison, John E., 219
Elsen, Daniel H., 313
Emancipation Proclamation, 63
Emergency Fleet Corporation, 144, 150, 165
Emergency Relief Act, 155
Emergency Revenue Act, 114
Employment Act of 1946, 181
Energy Research and Development Administration, 223
England, Gordon, 307
English Bill of Rights, 6
Eniwetok Pacific Proving Ground, 258
Enterprise, 223, 327
Environmental Management Project, 258
EO, 315
Epstein, Elizabeth, 97
"Era of Good Feeling, The," 36
Ericsson, John, 48, 79
Erikson, John, 211
Erinys, 315
Erlanger, Emile, 68
Erwin, Sandra I., 292–93, 309, 316, 324
Escott, Paul D., 63
Espionage Act of 1917, 136
Essex, 34
Esterline, 248
Etowah Works, 75
Eurocopter, 302
European Union, 320
Excelis, 303

Executive Mansion, 34
Executive Order 13806, 333
Executive Outcomes, 315
Export Administration Regulations, 331
Export Department/Office, 121–22
Export-Import Bank, 278
Exxon Mobil, 271

Fair Deal, 182, 187
Fairbanks, Douglas, Jr., 128, 135
Falkland Islands, 230
Fallows, James, 210, 303
Farragut, David, 92
Farrell, Larry, 307
Fayetteville Armory, 75
Federal Bureau of Investigation, 325
Federal Emergency Management Agency (FEMA), 206, 216, 224, 235, 278
Federal Express, 271
Federal Reserve Bank, 114
Federal Reserve System, 122, 142
Federal Trade Commission, 108, 250
Federal Trade Commission Act of 1914, 111
Federal Truck, 157
Federalists, 24, 28, 31, 32
Ferguson, E. James, 12
Ferreiro, Larrie, 18
Fessenden, William, 67
Financial Times, 281, 296, 320, 337
Finn, Kevin, 319
First Bull Run, 71
"First Offset" strategy, 297
Fischer, Erich, 335
Fisher Sand, 329
Flanagan, Ralph, 170
Flexner, Abraham, 202
Flournoy, Michele, 292
Flower, Benjamin, 12
Foam Matrix, 301
Fontaine, Mathew, 47
Food Administration, 149–50
Food and Drug Act of 1906, 111
Ford, Gerald, 196, 199, 213

Ford, Henry, 144
Ford Aerospace, 253, 262
Ford Motor, 157, 164, 181, 197, 262
Fore River Shipbuilding, 107, 110, 144
Foreign Policy, 279
Forrest, Nathan Bedford, 73
Forrestal, 223
Forrestal, James, 149, 180
Fort Donelson, 76
Fort Henry, 76
Fort Pitt, 21
Fort Pitt Foundry, 43, 44, 73
Fort Ticonderoga, 11
Fowler, William, 16
Fox Business, 313
Foxall, Henry, 44
Foxall Foundry, 34
France, 3, 4, 20, 266, 277, 320, 327; 1778 treaty, 13; 1783–1860, 24, 26, 29, 41, 44; American Revolution and, 18, 21; arms manufacture, 6, 12–13, 214; atomic bomb, 186; Civil War, U.S., 61; World War I, 119, 121–22, 129; World War II, 134, 160
Franck, Raymond, 325, 328, 337
Franco-Prussian War, 90, 93
Frankfort Arsenal, 35, 144
Franklin, Benjamin, 7–9, 23, 213
Franko, Lawrence G., 215
French and Indian War, 3, 4
Frick, Henry, 104, 106
Friedberg, Aaron, 133, 207–8
Friel, Brian, 271
Fritchey, Clayton, 213
"From Beast to Beauty" (De Long), 242
Frontier Services Inc., 332
Fuel Administration, 149
Fukuyama, Francis, 238, 272
Fulbright, J. William, 196
Fulda Gap, 238
Fulton I, 47
Fulton Iron Works, 47

Gaddis, John, 183
Galena, 79
Gallagher, Jerry, 63
Gallup, Poll, 217
Galvin, Christopher, 223
Gansler, Jacques, 206–7, 219–23, 238, 240, 247–48, 250, 261, 269, 283, 297–99, 307
Garfield, James A., 98
Garrison, Lindley, 116
Gas Engine and Power Company, 110
Gates, Robert M., 286, 288–91, 309, 328
GEC Marconi, 266
Gellman, Matthew, 62
General Accounting Office, 309, 316
General Atomics, 302
General Dynamics, 207, 210, 213, 219, 247–48, 253, 260–61, 265, 270–71, 287, 301, 303, 304, 307, 310–13, 319, 325, 330, 332
General Dynamics-Electric Boat, 300
General Dynamics Land Systems, 271, 303, 311
General Electric, 94, 120, 164, 197, 207, 210, 212, 219, 225, 248–50, 253–54, 258, 265, 268, 271, 301, 306
General Mobilization Response (GMR), 239
General Motors, 157, 160, 197, 207, 218, 225, 232, 307; Allison Division, 157; Buick Motor Division, 164; Fisher Body Division, 157
General Munitions Board, 142, 159
General Precision Equipment, 207
Geneva Arms Traffic Convention, 152
Geneva Naval Conference, 151
George, David Lloyd, 133
George, Lloyd, 145
George III, 11
Germany, 117, 128, 240, 266; Berlin crisis, 183; West, 198; World War II, 134, 160
Gholz. Eugene, 249, 271
GI Bill, 178

GI Joe, 158, 171
Gibbon, John, 91
Gilded Age, 86, 91–93, 97, 113, 127
Giroux, Henry, 296
Gladstone, William, 61–62
Glaze, William, 45
globalization, 242, 251, 266, 272; anti-, 275, 320
Globalization of American Fear Culture (Skoll), 277
Gluckman, Arcadi, 6, 42, 96
GM-Hughes Electronics, 253, 255
Godfrey, Hollis, 142
Goethels, George W., 144
Goldberg, Matthew, 293
Golden, James, 210
Goldin, Dan, 256
Goldwater-Nichols Defense Reorganization Bill, 218, 222
Gompers, Samuel, 142
Goodnow, 72
Goodrich Electrical Power Systems, 302, 303
Goodrich Pump & Engine Control Systems, 302
Goodyear Tire and Rubber, 157, 164, 207
Gorbachev, Mikhail, 198, 237
Gordan, Michael, 210
Gordon, John Steele, 71
Gorgas, Josiah, 74, 75, 81, 82
"Gospel of Wealth," 92
Government Accountability Office, 284
Government Accounting Office, 287, 327
Government Executive, 270
Government Owned/Company Operated (GOCO), 82; 1860–1866, 58, 82; 1945–1991, 189, 205, 210; 1991–2001, 248, 251
Government Owned/Government Operated (GOGO) facilities; Colonial America, 8; 1860–1866, 82; 1945–1991, 205, 210; 1991–2001, 248, 251
Govini, 334

Grable, Betty, 138
Grace, Eugene, 144
Graff, Garrett, 321–22
Graham, Anderson, Probst & White, 164
Granger, Kay, 325
Grant, Ulysses S., 92, 93
Gravel/DBA Fisher Industries, 329
Gray, Harry J., 216
Great Britain, 3, 4, 17, 20, 21, 156, 198, 230, 244, 266, 320; 18th century, 40; 1783–1860, 24, 32; arms manufacture, 6; atomic bomb, 186; Civil War, U.S., 61; Royal Navy, 5, 16; trade with, 19, 21; War of 1812, 32, 32–36; World War I, 119–21, 129; World War II, 134, 160–61
Great Crystal Palace Exhibition of 1851, 44
Great Depression, 129, 133–34, 138, 147–50, 152–55, 160, 162, 171, 211, 214, 289
Great Recession, 277, 281, 283, 286–93, 301
Great White Fleet, 103, 105, 109
Greece, 183
Green Green Fleet, 327
Greenwald, Glenn, 295, 313
Greenwood foundry, 73
Gregory, William, 241, 272
Grenada, 215
Griswold, Samuel, 75
Grumman, 157, 197, 207, 219, 225, 228–29, 247, 256, 301
GTE, 268
Guantanamo Bay, 288, 296
Gunpowder Trade Association, 96

H-bomb, 226
Haas, Richard, 320
Hackemer, Kurt, 46, 48, 80
Hacker, Barton, 3, 5, 54, 89, 93, 157, 172–74, 201–2, 204, 251–52
Hacker, Louis M., 83–84
Hackett, John, 28
Hadley, Arthur T., 219

Hagan, Kay R., 297
Hagel, Charles, 291, 295, 296
Haggar Company, 164
Haiti, 248
Hall, John H., 43
Halliburton, 50, 249, 306, 315, 331
Hamilton, Alexander, 20, 24–26, 28, 30, 36–37; "infant industry" argument," 27
Hamilton Propellers, 210
Hamilton-Standard, 248
Hamre, John, 266
Hancock, 15
Hanford Engineer Works, 174
Harding, Warren G., 150
Hardy, Rufus, 116–17
Harlan/Harland and Hollingsworth, 48, 80, 110
Harpers Ferry arsenal, 43, 47, 53
Harris, 265, 303, 331
Harrison, Todd, 281, 324
Hart, John D., 71
Hartford, 47
Hartung, William, 255, 322
Harvard University, 174, 244
Hawley, Joseph R., 98, 99
Hawley Committee, 98–99
Hay, John, 103
Hayward, Keith, 266
Heilbroner, Robert, 84, 181, 208
Heinrich, Thomas, 48, 80–81, 131, 165–66
Heiser, Hoseph, 313
Henry, Merton G., 11, 17, 57, 94
Henry N. Hooper foundry, 73
Herbert, Hilary A., 101, 106
Hercules, 144, 207
Herman, Oscar, 133
Hickey, Donald, 33
Higgs, Robert, 293–94
"Hiker, the,"102
Hill, Joe, 169
Hill, Terry, 169
Hillman, Sidney, 160
Hines, Walter D., 144

Hinkley, Williams foundry, 73
Hirohito, 128
Hitler, Adolf, 128
HMS *Warrior*, 79
Hodgdon, Samuel, 12, 21
Hoff, Charles, 14
Hoff, Joseph, 14
Hog Island, 165, 166, 171
Hogg and DeLamater, 48
Hoke, Donald, 40, 45
Holbrook, Richard, 243
Holley, I. B., 172
Holston Army Ammunition Plant, 258, 312
Holston Defense Corporation, 258
Holton, Richard H., 111
Homeland Security, 288, 293–94, 318, 324
Homeland Security Act of 2002, 277
Homer, Neal A., 337
Homestead Act, 63
Honeywell, 210, 225, 265
Hooks, Gregory, 143, 157
Hoover, Herbert, 146, 150–51
Hoover Commission of 1953, 252
Hope, Ian C., 5, 38, 40, 87
Hope Furnace, 43
Hopkins, Stephen, 15
Hormats, Robert, 1, 66, 68, 112, 161, 199, 215, 241, 282–84
Hotchkiss, 96
House, Edward, 116, 122
House Appropriations subcommittee, 309
House Armed Services Committee, 215–16, 240
House Budget Committee, 310
House Committee on Military Affairs, 50
House Committee on Naval Affairs, 30
Howard, Robert A., 45
Hudson Motor, 157, 164
Hughes, Charles Evans, 147
Hughes, Samuel, 43
Hughes Aircraft, 207, 219, 268, 301
Humphrey, Hubert, 205

Humphrey, Joshua, 7
Humphreys, Joshua, 28–29, 31
Hungarian revolution, 192
Hunt, William H., 101
Hunter, Louis, 140–41, 143–44, 156, 180
Huntington, Samuel, 157, 272, 276
Huntington Ingalls, 312, 319, 328, 330
Hussein, Saddam, 242, 317
Huston, James A., 10, 11, 49, 54, 67, 84–85, 94, 118, 140
Hutchinson, Thomas, 9
Hyde, Charles, 158

I. P. Morris, 483
IBM, 197, 268, 309
Icord, Richard H., 215–16, 220
Idaho National Engineering and Environmental Laboratory, 258
Ignatius, David, 291
Immigration and Customs Enforcement, 278
Independence, 34
Independent Review, 293
India, 4, 277, 296, 331
Indonesia, 277
Industrial College of the Armed Forces, 219
Industrial Mobilization Plan, 156, 159
Industrial Revolution, 1, 5, 19–51, 54; proto-, 16–17
Industrial Workers of the World, 137
Influence of Sea Power upon History, 1660–1783, The (Mahan), 100–101
Ingalls, 303
Inhofe, James, 289
Intel, 254, 309
Interdepartmental Committee for Coordination of Foreign and Domestic Military Purchases, 160
Internal Revenue Act of 1862, 67
International Harvester, 120, 157
International Traffic in Arms Regulations, 331

International Workers of the World, 127
Interstate Commerce Act of 1887, 111
interstate highway system, 190, 193–94
Ippolito, Dennis, 215, 242, 246
Iran, 213, 215, 245, 275, 285, 292, 316, 325–26, 329
Iraq, 242, 277, 280–84, 286, 288, 292–93, 295–98, 305, 307, 313–17, 331
iRobot, 301
Iron Act of 1750, 5
Iron Curtain, 237
Iron Triangle, 17, 100–101, 109, 234, 261, 308, 334
Isherwood, B. F., 47
Islamic State (ISIL/ISIS), 275, 292, 295, 313, 317, 336
Island No. 10, 76
Italy, 128, 134
ITTD, 265
Izhevsk armory, 96

J. A. Jones Company, 174
J. B. Holland Torpedo Boat Company, 110
J. H. Dialogue and Son, 110
J. P. Morgan and Company, 119, 121–22
Jackson, Andrew, 20, 36
Jacques, W. H., 99
Jane's Fighting Ships, 105
Japan, 104, 109, 128, 154, 156, 179, 196, 206, 240; Hiroshima, 172, 257; Nagasaki, 172, 257
Jefferson, Thomas, 20–21, 26, 31–34
Jenks, 72
Jeremiah, David F., 241
Jet Propulsion Laboratory (JPL), 203
Johns Hopkins Applied Physics Laboratory, 203
Johns Hopkins University, 174, 271
Johnson, Clarence "Kelly," 204
Johnson, I. N., 45
Johnson, Lyndon B., 195–96, 1998
Joint Army and Navy Munitions Board, 159

Joint Strike Fighter project, 260, 270, 287, 292, 300, 304, 306, 331, 333, 334
Jones, John Paul, 15
Jones, William, 34
Jordan, 240
Jordan, David Starr, 104

K-Mart, 94
Kaiser, Henry J., 157, 165
Kaiser-Fraser, 164
Kane, Tim, 327–28
Kansas City Plant, 258
Kapstein, Ethan B., 2, 66
Katnelson, Ira, 128
Kaufman, Alan, 147
Kaufman, Allen, 146, 202
Kellogg-Briand Pact, 151
Kellogg, Brown and Root (KBR), 314–15, 331
Kelvinator, 157
Kemble, Gouverneur, 43
Kendall, Frank, 298, 302, 310, 330
Kennedy, David, 160
Kennedy, John F., 194–95, 199, 201, 234
Kennedy, Joseph, 56–57, 59
Kennedy School, 244–45
Kennan, George, 183, 187
Kernan, Francis J., 117, 198
Kerr, K. Austin, 205
Kerry, John, 284
Keyserling, Leon, 186, 186
Kipling, Rudyard, 92, 102
Kissinger, Henry, 196
Kitchin, Claude, 117
Klein, Maury, 69
Knickerbocker, Bred, 303
Knolls Atomic Power Laboratory, 258
Knowland, William, 187
Knox, Henry, 12, 20–22, 28–29
Knudsen, William, 149, 160
Kohl, Helmut, 198, 237
Koistinen, Paul A. C., 12, 63, 87, 100, 119, 120–22, 139, 146, 148, 149, 153, 175, 191, 212, 238

Korb, Lawrence, 210, 249, 261, 285, 288–89, 308
Korea, 277; North, 184, 245, 275, 285, 292, 316, 317, 319, 321, 326; South, 184, 187
Korean War, 182–91, 206, 216, 223, 281–82; cost of, 185, 191, 199, 211, 213–14, 242, 281, 285
Kosiak, Steven, 286, 324
Kosovo, 300, 314
Kotz, Nick, 217–18
Kreps, Sarah E., 67, 133, 138
Kriedberg, Marvin A., 11, 17, 57, 94
Kuper, Simon, 337
Kurth, James R., 220
Kuwait, 240

L-3 Communication, 265, 319, 330
L-3 Technologies, 314
La Glorie, 79
Labor Department, 249
LaFeber, Walter, 103
Lake, Anthony, 243
Lamont, Daniel, 144
Lamont, Thomas, 137
Lamson, 72
Lancaster, 47
Lane, Frederick C., 166
Langdon, John, 15
Lansing, Robert, 122
Lapp, Ralph E., 206–7
Latham, Andrew, 139
Latin America, 127
Latrobe Specialty Metals, 302
Lawrence Livermore National Laboratory, 258
League Island, 77
League of Nations, 147, 151
Lebergott, Stanley, 70
Lee, Dwight R., 208
Lee, Richard Henry, 15
Lee, Robert E., 73–74
Lee, Roswell, 43, 47
Leffinwell, Russell, 137

Lehman, John, 228
Leidos, 319, 331
Leigh, Philip, 69, 70
LeMat, Jean Francois Alexander, 75
Lend-Lease Act, 133, 156, 160–61
Lenthal, John, 47
Leonard, Henry, 210
Leuchtenberg, William E., 149–50
Lever Act of 1917, 143
Levin, Carl, 303
Lexington, 166
Lexington Institute, 286, 327
Liberty Loans, 133, 135
Licht, Walter, 84, 85
Lieberman, Joseph, 260
Lincoln, Abraham, 51, 54, 60, 63, 69, 83, 85
Lincoln, Benjamin, 12, 18, 22, 59
Lind, Michael, 277
Link, Arthur, 149
Lippmann, Thomas, 219
List, Frederick, 25
Litton Industries, 207, 253, 270
Livermore National Laboratory, 204
Lockheed, 170, 181, 197, 207, 210, 219, 225, 247, 253–55, 267, 301, 330, 331; Advanced Development Program, 204
Lockheed Idaho Technologies Company, 258
Lockheed-Marietta, 255–56
Lockheed-Martin Corporation, 259–60, 262–63, 265–66, 269–71, 287, 289, 300–304, 306, 307–10, 312–13, 315, 319, 325, 327, 330, 332, 334
Lockheed-Martin Energy Research Corporation, 258–59
Lodge, Henry Cabot, 103
Logistics Civil Augmentation Program (LOGCAP), 249
Long, John Davis, 101, 106, 109
Longbow LLC, 307
Loral Satellite, 253, 255, 306
Lord, George E., 175
Los Alamos National Laboratory, 258, 322

Index 473

Los Angeles Times, 213
LTV, 225
Luraghi, Raimondi, 81, 82
Lusitania, 116
Lyman, Samuel, 31
Lynnn, William J. III, 310
Lyon, Hylan B., 73

M-Day, 180
Mack Truck, 157
Macon Armory, 75
Macon Foundry and Machine Works, 75
Macy's, 94
Madawaska, 78
Maddox, Rachel, 249
Madison, James, 20
Mahan, Alfred Thayer, 47, 100, 101, 103
Malcom, Joyce, 18
Mallaby, Sebastian, 305
Mallet, John W., 72, 87
Mallory, Stephen E., 76, 80–81
Malloy, Courtland, 320–21
Maloney, Linda, 34–35
Manhattan Project, 174, 179, 181, 202, 224, 226
Manifest Destiny, 20, 36, 92
Manufacturers Record, 108
Maogoto, Jackson Nyamuya, 316
March, Peyton C., 130, 145–46
Marconi, Guglielmo, 109
Marcus, Alan, 7, 55, 89
Mare Island Navy Yard, 47, 102
Marine Committee, 15–16
Marine Engineering Corporation, 151
Marines: 1991–2001, 244, 270; 2001–present, 182, 323
Marinette Marine, 303
Maritime Commission, 166
Markusen, Ann, 264
Marshall, George C., 138
Marshall, John, 20
Marshall Fields, 94
Marshall foundry, 73

Marshall Plan, 182, 183, 238
Marshall's, 94
Martel, William C., 182, 187, 191, 198–99
Martin, 197
Martin, Franklin H., 142
Martin, Glenn L., 157
Martin-Marietta, 207, 225, 252–56
Mason and Hanger-Silas Mason Company, Inc., 259
Massachusetts Government Act, 7
Massachusetts Institute of Technology (MIT), 173–74, 213, 244, 249, 260, 271, 328
May, Elaine Tyler, 272–73, 277
Mayer, Kenneth P., 251
Maynard, Henry, 43
MBC, 266
McAdoo, William G., 122, 136, 138, 144
McCain, John, 241, 244, 290, 292, 308, 315, 327
McCarthy, Joseph, 187, 192
McClenahan, William M., 193
McClosky and Company of Philadelphia, 164
McClung, Joseph, 43
McCormack, Owen B., 331
McCraw, Thomas, 145, 158, 161, 181, 205, 207
McDonnell-Douglas, 207, 210, 219, 225, 247–48, 253, 301
McDougall, Walter, 94
McFate, Sean, 332
McGarrah, Robert E., 220
McGraw, Thomas, 175
McGuire, Joseph M., 83
McHenry, James, 20
McKeon, Buck. 291
McKinley, Craig R., 320, 329, 333
McKinley, William, 102
McMahon, Brien, 192
McMaster, H. R., 323, 326
McNamara, Robert, 203
McNeill, William H., 100, 141

474 Index

McPherson, James, 57, 67–69
McRae, C. R., 85
McRae, John, 50
McReynolds, William H., 160
Mechanics and Metals banks, 121
Medicare, 284, 292
Meigs, Montgomery C., 78
Melman, Seymour, 204, 232–33
Melton, Maurice, 75
Memminger, Christopher G., 68
Memorial Bridge, 102
Mercantile Theory of Colonial regulation, 10
Merchant Marine (Jones) Act of 1920, 166
Merrick & Sons, 48, 79, 80
Merrick and Towne, 48
Merrimac, 47
Metcalf, Victor H., 112
Mexican border wall, 322, 325, 327, 329
Mexican War, 42, 44, 49
Meyer, George von Legerke, 112
Michigan State University, 328
Microsoft, 254
Midvale Steel, 107–8, 110, 121, 152
Midvale Steel and Ordnance, 120
Midway, 223
military industrial complex (MIC): Cold War, 177–235; congressional blueprint, 98–100; formation of, 89–126; Progressive Era, 105–8; 1991–2001, 261
Military-Industrial Complex and American Society, The (Pavelec), 210
military-industrial-political complex (MIPC), 98, 196, 199; codifying, 210; Cold War, 186, 195, 209, 223, 224, 240; extractive results of, 223–29; managing a mature, 214–23; new normal, 325–28; privatization of, 259–60; 1945–1991, 206–7, 211, 214–29, 234, 255; 1991–2001, 237–38, 242–43, 249, 251, 256–57, 259, 262, 265, 270; 2001–present, 276, 284, 287, 289–90, 293–95, 297–313, 322–23, 325

Military Personnel Resources Inc., 248, 249
Military Professional Services, Inc. (MPRI), 314, 315
Militia (Dick) Act of 1903, 118
Militia Act of 1757, 9
Militia Act of 1792, 24
Millikan, Robert A., 173
Millis, Walter, 23–24, 26, 37, 46, 101, 125
Mills, Sean I., 313
Minie, Claude-Etienne, 43, 58
Minnesota, 47
Minutement missiles, 227–28
Mirage, 214
Missile Defense Agency, 327
Mitchell, Charles, 144
Mitchell, William "Billy," 147
MITRE, 202, 271
Modern Mercenary, The (McFate), 332
Monitor, 79–80
"Monitor Row," 81
Monroe, James, 20, 37
Monroe Doctrine, 105
Montgomery, 15
Montgomery Ward, 94, 175
Moody, William H., 112
Moore and Sons, 110
Moran Brothers, 107
Morgan, George D., 78
Morgan, J. P., 94, 111–13, 115, 120–21, 124, 144, 255
Morgan, John Hunt, 73
Morgan, John Tyler, 99
Morgenthau, Henry, 137
Mormons, 54
Morning Herald, 338
Morocco, 240
Morrell, Geoff, 290
Morrill Land-Grant Act, 63
Morrison, Philip, 237
Morrow, Dwight, 147
Morton, Paul, 112
Mosher, Charles A., 177
Motorola, 223, 271, 309

MSNBC, 249
Mulholland, James A., 5
Mullen, Mike, 286
Munich Agreement, 134, 187
Munitions Board (MB), 179–80, 188
Munitions Industrial Base Task Force, 248
Murtha, Jim, 309
Mussolini, Benito, 128
mutually assured destruction (MAD), 186, 196, 201
MX missile, 227, 228
Myrtle Knitting Mills, 164

Nader, Ralph, 295
Nagle, James F., 2, 4, 49, 64, 72, 91, 105, 108, 113, 179
Napoleon, Louis, 44
Napoleon III, 44
Narden, Terry, 212
Nash, Colleen, 239–40
Nash, Gerald D., 170–71
Nash-Kelvinator, 157, 164
Nashville Plow Works Whitfield, 75
NASSCO, 303
"Nation at Wat, An Administration in Retreat," 290
National Academy of Sciences, 84
National Advisory Committee on Aeronautics (NACA), 172–73
National Air and Space Administration (NASA), 203, 206, 226, 256, 332
National Banking Act of 1863, 63, 67
national banking system, 67
National Cash Register, 164–65
National Cathedral, 102
National Defense, 245, 292, 316, 324
National Defense Act: of 1916, 118, 142, 158; of 1920, 145, 154, 159, 180; of 1958, 203
National Defense Advisory Commission, 124, 142, 158, 160–61
National Defense Council, 173
National Defense Industrial Association (NDIA), 245, 307, 309, 320, 324, 329, 330–31, 333–34

National Defense Panel, 292
National Defense Program, 153
National Defense Research Committee, 173–74
National Defense Strategy, 323
National Economic Council, 250
National Emergency Council, 150
National Foundry, 72
National Geospatial-Intelligence Agency, 278
National Guard, 118, 318
National Ignition Facility, 259
National Industrial Reserve Act of 1948, 179
National Industry Recovery Act, 155
National Institutes of Health, 179, 209, 278, 324
National Intelligence, 278, 288
National Missile Defense, 285
National Munitions Control Board, 152
National Nuclear Security Administration, 259
National Oceanic and Atmospheric Administration, 324
National Performance Review, 252
National Production Authority, 188
National Reconnaissance Office, 278
National Recovery Administration, 149, 150
National Research Council, 173
National Rifle Association, 96, 283, 319
National Science Foundation, 179, 278
National Security Act of 1947, 179, 181, 277
National Security Agency, 278
National Security Council (NSC), 180, 188, 318; NSC-68, 183–84, 186–89; NSC 162/2, 185
National Security League, 115
National Security Preparedness Group, 295
National Security Resources Board (NSRB), 180, 188
National Security Strategy, 246, 291, 323
Native Americans, 3, 5, 20, 22, 27, 91
Naval Act: of 1775, 16; of 1916, 147
Naval Committee, 15

Naval Consulting Board, 173
Naval Ordnance Works, 72, 75
Naval Research Laboratory, 172, 203
Naval War College, 281
NAVISTAR, 303
Navy, 211, 219; 1860–1866, 60–61, 71, 75–82, 108–10; 1865–1917, 90, 92–93, 95, 98–106, 107, 111–13, 115–17, 124; 1917–1945, 131–32, 142, 148, 152, 162, 165–66; 1991–2001, 260, 263; 2001–present, 285, 312, 323, 327; imperial blueprint, 100–101; nuclear, 205
Navy League of the United States, 104, 115, 146
Navy Yearbook, 1920–1921, The (Silsby), 112
Neafie & Levy, 110
Nelson, Donald J., 149, 169
Neutrality Act of 1935, 152
Nevada Test Site, 258
Nevins, Allan, 55, 57, 63
"New Americans," 37
New Deal, 137, 148–51, 154–56, 159–60, 165–67, 171, 174, 178, 187
New Haven Chemical Works, 79
New Ironsides, 79, 80, 81
"New New Look," 192
New World Order, 238, 275
New York Central, 94
New York Ship, 165, 166
New York Shipbuilding, 110, 144, 151–52, 157
New York Stock Exchange, 71, 254
New York Times, 247, 286, 293, 321
New Zealand, 214
Newberry, Truman H., 112
Newport News Shipbuilding, 269, 270, 289, 300, 328
Newport News Shipbuilding and Dry Dock Company, 107, 110, 144, 151–52, 207
Niagara, 47
Nicaragua, 215
Nichols, Roy Franklin, 55
Niger, 277
Nimitz, 223

9/11, 275, 277, 279, 281–84, 288–89, 293, 295–96, 299, 303, 305, 317, 326, 328
9/11 Commission, 295
Niter and Mining Bureau, 73
Nitze, Paul, 183–84, 187, 198
Nixon, Lewis, 110
Nixon, Richard, 195–96, 199
Noble Brothers and Company, 75
Non-Developmental Items (NDI), 252
Nonpartisan League, The, 136
Norris, George, 119
North, Simon, 28, 41, 43–44
North American Aviation, 157, 175, 197, 207, 248
North American Free Trade Agreement, 319
North Atlantic Treaty Organization (NATO), 183, 189, 195, 210, 214, 238, 243, 275, 279, 319, 320
Northrop, 181, 207, 247
Northrop-Grumman, 210, 253, 256, 260, 262–63, 265, 270–71, 287, 289, 300–303, 306–8, 312, 313, 319, 330, 332, 334
Northwest Ordinance of 1787, 22
Nuclear Fuel Services, Inc., 258
nuclear weapons, 183, 197–98, 200–201, 205, 223, 225–27, 318, 321–22; cleanup costs, 257, 258; reduction programs, 256–59; stockpile maintenance costs, 235, 260, 284
Nunn, Sam, 246, 260
Nye, Gerald, 121, 124, 148, 152, 153, 211
Nye-Vandenberg Senate Munitions Investigation of 1934–1935, 151–53, 211

Oak Ridge Reservation, 258, 260
Obama, Barack, 276–77, 280, 283, 287–89, 291, 293–96, 302, 308, 310, 321–23, 331–32
Odeen, Philip, 267–69
Odierno, Ray, 295
Office of Defense Mobilization (ODM), 185, 188, 190–91
Office of Economic Adjustment, 336

Office of Emergency Management, 160
Office of Immigration, 84
Office of Industrial Policy, 306
Office of Naval Research, 203
Office of Price Administration and Civilian Supply, 158
Office of Production Management, 158, 160–62
Office of Scientific Research and Development, 174, 179
Office of the Comptroller of the Currency, 84
Office of Terrorism and Financial Intelligence, 324
Office of War Mobilization (OWM), 163
Office of War Mobilization and Reconversion (OMWR), 163, 171
O'Hanlon, Michael, 290
O'Keefe, Sean, 240
Oliver Hazard Perry, 212
Olympics, 170
Oman, 240
Orbital, 303
Ordinance Boards, 44
Ordinance Department, 44
Organization of Petroleum Exporting Countries (OPEC), 196
Oriskany, 223
Orth, Goodlove S., 86
Oshkosh Defense, 303
Otis Elevator, 164, 248
Overman Act of 1918, 143
Overseas Contingency Operations (OCOs), 280, 286, 292, 294
Owen, Lou Cretia, 168

Pacific Railroad Act, 63
Packard, 151, 164, 217
Packard Commission, 252
Paducah Gaseous Diffusion Plant, 258
Paine, Thomas, 24, 137
Pakistan, 240, 285, 295
Palmer, A. Mitchell, 137

Palmer, Dave R., 22, 23
Palmetto Armory, 45
Panetta, Leon, 291, 310
Panic of 1857, 66
Pantex Plant, 259
Paraguay, 152
Parish, David, 35
Parker, Josiah, 30
Parker, Theodore, 49
Parrott, Robert P., 44, 47, 73
Parsons, 315
Patent Fire Arms Company, 72
Patrick, Suzanne, 299–300
Patterson, Robert, 149, 166, 167
Paullin, Charles, 97–98, 110
Paullin, Oscar, 16, 21–22, 32, 76, 78–80
Pavelec, Michael, 210
Peace Corps, 195
Pearlstein, Steven, 308
Pedisch, Paul E., 101
Pemmberton, Miriam, 285
Pendleton Act of 1883, 97, 111
Pennsylvania, 46
Pennsylvania Apollo Plant, 258
Pennsylvania Railroad, 94
Penrose, James, 7
Pensacola, 47
Perot Systems, 248–49
Perry, Oliver Hazard, 43
Perry, William, 250, 253, 255, 266, 330
Persian Gulf War, 238–41, 244–46, 248, 252, 282, 300, 313–14; cost of, 240; missiles, 239–40
Petersburg Iron Works, 75
Phelps Dodge Copper Products, 164
Philadelphia Navy Yard, 48, 81, 153, 165, 171, 209
Philip Morris, 271
Philippines, 102, 104; Bataan death march, 138
Phoenix Iron Works, 43, 73
Picatinny Arsenal, 114
Pickford, Mary, 135

Pillow, Gideon, 76
Pincus, Walter, 293, 295
Pinnelas Plant, 258
Pittsburgh, Pennsylvania Foundry, 43
Planning Programming and Budgeting System (PPBS), 203
Policy Planning Staff, 183
Poole, Water, 225
populism, 91, 94, 111, 149, 209, 276, 277, 317, 320, 322
Porter, Andrew, 92
Portland foundry, 73
Portsmouth Gaseous Diffusion Plant, 258
Powder Works, 72
Powell, Colin, 241, 245–46
Pratt & Whitney, 42, 157, 164, 210, 212, 250, 306, 334
precision-guided munitions (PGMs), 204, 221
"Preparedness" movement, 113–19
President, 34
President's Liaison Committee, 160
Price, Melvin, 220
Price of Liberty, The (Hormats), 112
Price Waterhouse Cooper, 310
Prince, Erik, 315, 332
Princeton, 48, 51
Princeton's Institute for Advanced Study, 202
Prins, Nomi, 111, 119, 137
Priority Allocation of Industrial Resources Task Force, 300
Private Arsenal System, 302, 309
Proctor & Gamble, 271
Proctor & Gamble Defense Corporation, 259
Production Base Impact Assessment, 232
Progressive Era, 91, 105–8, 127, 136, 149–50, 173, 242
Project on Defense Alternatives, 281
Project on Government Oversight, 303
Project on National Security Reform, 288
Project Solarium, 185–86

Promise, William, 211
Protective Mobilization Plan, 154, 159
Providence, 15
Providence Tool, 95
Proxmire, William, 211, 308
Prussia, 4, 61
Public Works Administration, 155, 166
Puerto Rico, 104
Pulitzer Prize, 55
Pusey and Jones, 166

Qatar, 240
Quadrennial Defense Review, 290, 294, 315–16
Qualcomm, 306
Quarterly Defense Review, 293
Quebec Act, 7
Quinby and Robinson, 75

Radiation Laboratory, 174
Radio Research Laboratory, 174
Ragland, James, 320
Railroad Bureau, 64
railroad(s), 144, 149; 1865–1917, 90, 92–93; Civil War, 58, 60, 83
Railroad Administration, 144, 149
Raleigh, 15
RAND Corporation, 181, 202, 211
Randolph, 15, 16
Raney & Archibold, 80
Ranger, 15
Raven Rock" (Graff), 321–22
Raytheon, 197, 210, 225, 253, 260, 265, 269, 270, 301, 306–7, 310, 312, 315, 319, 329–31
Raytheon Missile Systems, 303
RCA, 164
Reagan, Ronald, 128, 196, 198–99, 201, 208–9, 211, 215, 217, 218–20, 223–27, 229, 237, 242, 252, 255, 264, 313, 322–23, 326, 328
Reaney, Neafie & Levy, 48
Reconstruction, 71, 85, 86, 90–91, 97, 111

Index 479

Reconstruction Finance Corporation, 150, 167
Record, Jeffrey, 265
Red Cross, 135
Red Scare, 138, 187
Reed, Fred, 285–86
Reliant Electronics, 262
Remington, 72, 91, 96
Remington, Robbins, Kendall and Lawrence, 44
Remington Arms, 120, 121
Remington Arms-Union Metallic Cartridge, 121
"Report on Manufactures" (Hamilton), 24
Republic, 181
Research and Development Board (RDB), 180
Research Associates, 216
Research Institute of America, The, 166
Reserve Officers' Training Corps, 118, 314
Retired Marine Reserve Officers' Association, 270
Reuter's University, 337
Revenue Act of 1950, 189
Revere, Paul, 31
Revere Copper foundry, 73
Revolution in Military Affairs (RMA), 238, 252, 266
Revolutionary War, 7, 11–16, 28, 35, 66, 137; cost of, 17; public-private partnerships, 12; rationing during, 13
Reynolds, David, 209
Reynolds, Molly, 336
Rich, Frank, 5295
Richardson, Heather, 91
Richman, Gideon, 296
Richmond, 47
Richmond Armory, 75
Richmond Arsenal, 75
Rickover, Hyman, 205, 223
Rights of Man (Paine), 24
Ripley, Warren, 82
Roach, John, 98, 104, 106, 110

Roanoke, 47
Robbins and Lawrence, 42, 58
Roberdeau, Daniel, 13–14
Roberts, William H., 45
Rochlen, A. M., 170
Rock Island Arsenal, 144
Rockefeller, John D., 94
Rockefeller Center, 254
Rockoff, Hugh, 182, 185, 200
Rockwell Collins, 303
Rockwell International, 225, 248, 262, 265, 301
Rockwell Standard, 248
Rodman, Thomas J., 44, 74
Roland, Alex, 195
Rolling Stone, 325
Rolls Royce/Packard, 157, 250, 271, 306
Roosevelt, Franklin D., 70, 129, 133–34, 146, 148–50, 153–56, 158–61, 163–64, 166, 169, 171, 175, 182, 294
Roosevelt, Theodore, 103–4, 112, 115–16
Roosevelt Corollary, 105
Root, Elihu, 103, 114
Rosati, Jerel A., 196
Rosenwald, Julius, 142
Rosie the Riveter, 128, 158, 289
Rothkopf, David, 279
Royal Bank of Canada Defence and Aerospace Conference, 310
Royal Dutch Shell, 307
Rumsfeld, Donald, 270, 289
Russell, Major and Waddell, 50
Russell, Thomas H., 134–35
Russia, 104, 106, 109, 156, 245–46, 275, 292–93, 296, 317, 320, 323, 336; communism, 128; World War I, 120; World War II, 160–61, 187
Russia-Ukraine, 292, 338
Russian Federation, 243
Ruttan, Vernon W., 250
Rwanda, 248
Ryan, David, 272

S. Kresge, 94
SAC, 265
Saginaw, 47
"Saint Augustine's Rules," 255
Salay, David L., 13
Salisbury Arsenal, 75
SALT II, 215
Sampson, William, 102
Samuelson, Robert, 292
Sandia Corporation, 259
Santa Fe Railroad, 144
Santorum, Rick, 271
Sapolsky, Harvey, 249, 260–61, 264, 271
Saratoga, 166
Saudi Arabia, 240, 310, 320
Savannah River Site, 259, 322
Sawyer, Charles Winthrop, 5
Scahill, Jeremy, 315
Schafer, Ronald, 133
Schaffer, Ronald, 137
Schivelbein, Tom, 269
Schmitt, Gary J., 285
Schofield, John, 93
Schwab, Charles, 104, 106, 108, 125–26, 144, 255
Schwartz, Bernard, 255, 257
Schwartz, Stephen I., 201
Science Applications International Corporation (SAIC), 270, 271, 287, 303, 306, 315
Scott, Frank, 142–43, 150
Scott, James M., 196
Scowcroft, Brent, 245
SEATO, 195
Sechrest, Larry J., 31
"Second Offset" strategy, 297
Secret Service, 278
Section 800 Panel Report, 252
Security Enterprise, 280
Security-Industrial Congressional Complex (SICC), 293–94, 318
Sedition Act of 1918, 136
Segal, Howard, 7, 55, 89

Select Committee on Ordnance and War Ships, 98
Selective Service, 318
Selective Service Act, 142, 280
Selective Service System, 161
Selma Works, 75
Senate Armed Services Committee, 288, 297, 303, 327
Senate Finance Committee, 67
"Sentiments on a Peace Establishment" (Washington), 22–23
Serbia, 245
Servicemen's Readjustment Act, 178
Sessions, Jeff, 290
Settle, Mary Lund, 50
Settle, Raymond, 50
Seven Years War, 3, 4
Sewell, William Joyce, 99
Seyfort, McManus foundry, 73
"Shadow budgets," 282
Shanker, Thom, 286
Sharp, Christian, 43
Sharp, Travis, 289
Sharpe, 72
Sharps Rifle Manufacturing Company, 96
Shay, Daniel, 21
Shearer, William, 151
Shefter, Martin, 128
Shelby, Richard, 290
Shenandoah, 81
Sheridan, Philip, 92, 93
Sherman, William T., 73, 83, 90, 92–93
Sherman Antitrust Act of 1890, 111
Ships for Victory (Lane), 166
Shrader, Charles R., 59, 63
Shy, John, 3
Sikorsky Aircraft, 210, 248, 302–3, 330
Silsby, Edward, 112
Simmons, Harold, 254
Singer, Aaron, 181
Singer, Nimick foundry, 73
Singer, P. W., 314
Sixtieth Royal American Regiment, 4

Skelton, Ike, 290
Skibbie, Lawrence, 245
Skidmore, Mark, 328
Skoll, Geoffrey R., 277
Skowronek, Stephen, 143
"Skunk Works," 170, 204
Slater, Jerome, 212
slavery, 4, 20, 57–58, 60–61, 63, 69, 71
Smith, Adam, 25
Smith, John, 1
Smith, Kate, 138
Smith, Merritt Roe, 42, 58, 72
Smith, R. Elberton, 130, 132, 172
Smith, Robert F., 5–6, 12, 17–18
Smith, Timothy T., 50
Smith and Wesson, 96
Smithsonian Institution, 87
smokeless gunpowder, 97, 114, 168
Snider, Don, 245
Snow, John, 283
Social Security, 292
Somalia, 243, 248
Sottile, J. P., 323
Sousa, John Philip, 112
South Africa, 195
South Boston Iron Company Foundry, 43
Soviet Union, 128, 156, 183, 185–86, 189, 193, 196–98, 201, 213–15, 219, 224, 235, 242–43, 245, 285, 327; arms race, 183, 189, 192, 197, 199, 204, 206, 215, 260, 297; atomic program, 183–84, 186, 257; collapse, 220, 241; communism, 180, 187; post–World War II, 179, 182; WWII, 72
Space Tracking and Surveillance System, 305
SpaceX, 301
Spain, 3, 4, 10; 1783–1860, 32; 1865–1917, 101–5, 113; American Revolution and, 18
Spam, 157
Spanish-American War, 94, 101–5, 113
Special Committee Investigating the National Defense Program, 153
Spector, Arlen, 271
Spencer Repeating Rifle Company of Boston, 72, 91
Sperry-Rand, 197, 207
Spiller, Edward S., 75
Spinney, Frank, 226–28
Springfield Armory/Arsenal, 41, 43, 58, 86, 144, 174, 197
Sprout, Harold, 104, 114–16
Sprout, Margaret, 104, 114–16
Sputnik, 192, 203, 278, 337
Squeo, Anne Marie, 303–4
Stalin, Josef, 132, 182, 192
Standard and Poor, 269, 286, 313
Standard Oil, 94
Standish, Miles, 1
Stanford University, 104
STAR I and II, 256
Stark, Kirk J., 282
Starr, Nathan, 44
State Department, 278, 326
"stealth" detection technology, 204
steam engine, 46, 58, 80; coal-fired, 90–91; railroads, 58, 60, 83; steamboats, 78; "steam navy," 46–48, 100
Stearns, Peter, 89
Steinberg, Gerald M., 226
Steinmetz, Joseph, 242
Stephens, Philip, 320
Stettinius, Edward R., 121, 146
Stevens, Richard H., 199
Stevens, Thaddeus, 73
Stevenson, Charles A., 205
Stiglitz, Joseph, 296
Still, William N., 81
Stillman, James, 144
Stimson, Henry L., 116
Stimson, Henry M., 163
Stockholm International Peace Institute, 316, 326
Stoddert, Benjamin, 20, 26–27, 30, 35, 36
Strategic and Critical Materials Stockpiling Act, 179
Strategic Defense Initiative (SDI) "Star Wars", 198, 204, 215, 224; cost of, 225–26

Stromberg-Carlson Telephone Manufacturing Company, 164
Stone, Michael, 337
Stone, Oliver, 280, 319
Strong, Benjamin, 122
Stubblefield, James, 43, 47
Studebaker, 157, 164
Subcommittee on Emerging Threats and Capabilities, 297
Sullivan, Tim, 290
Sumter, 81
Syria, 275, 296–97, 317

T. M. Bannon, 75
Taft, Robert, 187
Taft, William Howard, 112, 228
Taft, William Howard (Motorola), 309
Taibbi, Matt, 325
Taliban, 282, 317
Tax in Kind laws, 69
Teal Group, 269
Tebbs, Jeffrey, 285
Teledyne, 225
Tellep, Dan, 253, 255
Teller, Edward, 204
Tenneco, 219
Tennessee, 78
terrorism, 275, 279–80, 282–86, 293, 313, 317; cyber, 275, 279, 333, 336; domestic, 319, 337; rogue state, 251
Test Ban Treaties, 211
Texas Instruments, 207, 268, 301
Texas Sterling, 329
Textron, 207, 265, 331
Thales, 266, 303
Thatcher, Margaret, 198, 237, 241
Thiokol Chemical, 207
"Third Offset" strategy, 296–97, 329
Third World, 182, 193, 214, 264
Thompson, Loren, 286, 288–89, 304–5, 309, 327
Thorndike, Joseph J., 282
Thorpe, Rebecca U., 128, 199–200, 206, 209, 281

Thrall, A. Trevor, 326
Tidewater Oil, 164
Tillman, "Pitchfork," 108
Tippett, Edward D., 51
Todd Shipyards, 219
Tokio Kid, 169–70
Toll, I. W., 48
Tortoriello, Richard, 286
Total Quality Management (TQM), 222–23, 231
Totten, Joseph G., 38
Tower, John, 219
Tracy, Benjamin F., 101, 106, 109–10
Trading with the Enemy Act, 136
Transportation Security Administration, 278
Treasury Department, 278, 288, 324
Treaty Navy, 153, 154
Treaty of Paris, 4, 19
Tredegar Foundry, 75
Tredegar Iron Works, 43, 72, 81
Trigg, William, 110
Triple Canopy, 315
Trubowitz, Peter, 246
Truman, Harry S., 153, 181–86, 188, 191, 193, 198–99, 201, 315
Truman Doctrine, 199
Trumbull, 15
Trumbull, Jonathan, 15
Trump, Donald, 276–77, 318, 320–329, 332–34, 336
TRW, Inc., 207, 210, 225, 265, 267, 271
Tryon, 44
Tsipis, Kosta, 213, 237
Tula armory, 96
Turkey, 183, 240, 277
Tuve, Merle, 174
Twain, Mark, 91, 103
Tyco International, 307

UDL, 271
Ukraine, 292, 338
Union Iron Works, 47, 110
Union Metallic Cartridge, 120

Union Pacific, 94
Unisys Defense, 210, 253
United Aircraft, 197, 207, 248
United Arab Emirates (UAE), 240, 269
United Auto Workers Union, 270
United Defense, 265, 271
United Kingdom, 320
United Nations, 170, 182, 185, 243
United States, 29
United States (1783–1860), 19–51; African Americans, 36; Alabama, 42, 50; armories, 28, 39; Army, 39, 49; arsenals, 39, 42–43; cannon manufacture, 39–40, 43–44, 48, 50; Capital security, 20; census, 1790, 27; Connecticut, 21, 40; currency, 25; defense spending, 25, 29–30, 33; exports, weapons, 43; firearms production, 21, 27, 35, 37, 40–41, 43–45; gunpowder mills, 28, 33; homeland defense, 39; identity, 20; industrialization, 36–40, 46–49; iron mines, 30; isolationism, 36–39; Louisiana, 42; Maryland, 42; Massachusetts, 21, 24, 42; Michigan, 42; military, peacetime, 20, 37–38; military budget, 49–50; military storage, 21; national debt, 1790, 27; national defense, 20, 27–32; national security, 22–27, 37; Navy, 26, 27, 29–33, 35, 39, 46–49, 51; navy yards, 39; New Hampshire, 30; New York, 21, 30, 42; North Carolina, 24; Pennsylvania, 21, 30, 42–43, 50; postal system, 24, 49; Rhode Island, 43; self-sufficiency, 25, 26, 30, 36, 51; service sector, 49–50; shipbuilding, 28–29; slavery, 49; South Carolina, 42; taxes, 32–34; Texas, 50; unification movement, 25–26; Vermont, 42; Virginia, 21, 28, 30, 42; War Department, 33, 35, 40; war surplus, 43
United States (1860–1866), 42, 46, 53–87; 1860 census data, 56–58, 65; aircraft, 109; banking, 67; cannon manufacture, 72; centralized state building, 61–66; Civil War, 42, 46, 53–87; conscription, 63; currency, 67, 68, 71; defense industrial base (DIB), 71–75; economy, 61–66; expansion of military administration, 59–60; firearms manufacture, 58, 71–72, 85; government Owned/Government Operated (GOCO) facilities, 58; human capital loss, 54; immigrant population, 58; manufacturing and technology during, 54–55; military budget and expenditures, 61–66, 71; national debt, 68; national security, 83; Navy, 60, 61, 71, 75–82, 108–10; people of color, 57–58; perceptions of, 53–54; slavery, 57–58, 60, 63, 71; taxes, 60, 63, 66–71, 68; war debt, 67–68; winter of 1864–1865, 69
United States (1865–1917), 89–126; aircraft manufacture, 114; Army, 92–93, 96–97, 104, 114, 124; Army Aviation Service, 118, 202; atomic bomb, 172, 174; cannon manufacture, 97, 114; economy, 123; firearms manufacture, 91, 96, 97, 99–100, 114, 121; imperialism, 100–101; industrialization, 89, 93–94; labor strikes, 90; military budget and expenditures, 112, 118–19, 199–200; military industrial complex, 89–126; National Guard, 118, 164; national security, 92–93, 116, 118–19; Navy, 90, 92–93, 95, 98–107, 111–13, 115–17, 124; postwar lethargy, 89–91; railroads, 92–93; steel production, 106–8; submarines manufacture, 110, 114; taxes, 94, 105, 114; torpedo manufacture, 110; War Department, 93–94, 117–18, 164; war surplus, 95; wealth inequality, 94; weapons sales to foreign countries, 109, 119–24; World War I, 115–24
United States (1917–1945), 127–75; automobile industry, 158, 166; aviation

484 Index

technology, 131, 147–48, 157, 160, 166, 170–71, 199, 223; defense production, 162–63; economy, 129, 133–38, 147–50, 152–55; exports, 135–36; firearms manufacture, 131; interwar accountability and profiteering concern, 150–54; isolationism, 127, 130, 150, 155; labor issues, 127, 157, 175; military budget and expenditures, 135; national debt, 136, 137; national defense, 148; National Guard, 164; Navy, 131–32, 142, 148, 152, 162, 165–66; patriotism, 133–38, 164; post-World War II peacetime, 172–74; scientific research, 172–74; shipbuilding, 165–66, 238; submarine manufacture, 166; tank manufacture, 131, 223; taxes, 137–38, 153, 167; War Department, 130, 159, 162, 167, 175; war planning after World War I, 154–56

United States (1945–1991), 177–235; Air Force, 181, 185, 193; arms exports, 214; arms race, 183, 189, 192, 197, 199, 204, 206, 215, 260; Army, 180; atomic bombs/power, 181, 183, 185, 191, 192, 195, 223; aviation technology, 180–81, 189, 204, 207, 212; defense industrial base (DIB), 214–16, 220, 222, 229, 234; economy, 178, 189–90; foreign aid, 230–31; FY 1957 budget, 193; FY 1980 budget, 212, 214; FY 1984 budget, 219; FY 1985 budget, 219; FY 1989, 215; "guns and butter" scheme, 189–90, 206; interstate highway system, 190, 193–94; military budget and expenditures, 184–85, 187–89, 191, 193, 197–205, 208, 211, 212–19, 224–27, 234, 252; national debt, 228; national security, 198; nuclear weapons, 183, 197–98, 200, 201, 205, 223, 225–27; permanent defense industry, 197–214; post-World War II, 177–82; procurement spending, 226–28; scientific research, 195, 197–205, 223–24; Star Wars missile defense system (SDI), 198, 215, 224–26; taxes, 183, 185; war surplus, 177–78; weapons systems, 204, 223

United States (1991–2001), 237–73; aviation technology, 239–40, 254, 256, 263–64, 267, 270; budget surplus, 241–42; defense industry base (DIB), 246–54, 260–62, 269; FY 2001 budget, 267, 294, 317; Marine Corps, 244, 270; military budget and expenditures, 240, 242, 244–46, 253, 261–62, 267, 271; missile program, 239–40, 260, 263; Navy, 260, 263; nuclear weapons, 237, 256–60; peace dividends, 241–46; space program, 267; weapons sales to foreign countries, 255–56, 263–64

United States (2001–present), 278–338; Air Force, 285–87, 290, 327; aviation technology, 282, 285, 293, 303, 307–9, 312, 327; defense industrial base (DIB), 294, 297–13, 328–37; entitlements, 283; FY 2002 budget, 301, 304; FY 2006 budget, 284, 288, 294; FY 2007 budget, 288; FY 2008 budget, 285, 286, 318; FY 2009 budget, 286, 299, 316; FY 2010 budget, 289; FY 2011 budget, 290; FY 2012 budget, 285, 290; FY 2014 budget, 291, 292; FY 2015 budget, 316; FY 2016 budget, 292–93; FY 2017 budget, 325, 336; FY 2018 budget, 329; FY 2019 budget, 336; FY 2020 budget, 325, 337; FY 2021 budget, 336; Marines, 182, 323; military budget and expenditures, 280–94, 296, 300–301, 303, 306–7, 313, 317, 320–21, 323–27, 329, 336; missile technology, 329; national security, 275–316, 332; Navy, 285, 312, 323, 327; nuclear weapons, 289, 321; security state, 293–97; shared sacrifice, 280, 282; taxes, 280, 282; weapons sales to foreign countries, 310, 326, 329, 331

United States Christian, 64
United States Colored Troops, 64, 65
United States Housing Corporation, 150
United States Military Academy, West Point, 21, 24, 39, 40–41, 43–44, 87
United States Military Railroads, 64, 83
United States Military Telegraph, 64
United States Sanitary Commission, 64, 65
United Technologies Corporation, 210, 216, 219, 248, 253, 265, 270–71, 301–3, 307, 319, 330
University of California Berkeley, 174
University of California Board of Regents, 258
University of California System, 270
University of Chicago, 258
University of Washington, 83
Upton, Emory, 91
URS, 331
U.S. Agency for International Development, 326
U.S. Chamber of Commerce, 122, 124
"U.S. Defense Industry Under Siege—An Agency for Change," 272
U.S. Rubber, 175
U.S. Shipping Board, 117
U. S. Steel, 94, 108, 110, 113, 120, 122, 157, 232
U.S. Treasury, 95, 113
USA Patriot Act, 279, 295
USAID, 314
USS *Maine*, 102, 107
USS *Missouri*, 238
USS *Olympia*, 102, 103
USS *Wisconsin*, 238

V-J Day, 178
V-Loans, 167
V Production Requirements, 162
Vandenberg, Arthur, 187
Vanderclip, Frank, 111, 123–24, 144
Vawter, Roderick, 180, 191, 216
Versailles Treaty, 147

Veterans Administration, 318
Veterans of Foreign Wars, 146
Viasat, 303
Victory Liberty loans, 136
Victory Program, 156
Vielle, Paul Marie Eugene, 97
Vietnam, 182, 195–96; North, 196
Vietnam War, 182, 195–96, 198, 203, 206, 211, 213, 215, 217, 221, 227, 232–34, 241–42, 281, 282, 313
Villa, Pancho, 117
Villard, Oswald Garrison, 104
Vining, Margaret, 54, 172–74, 201–2, 204, 251–52
Vinnell Corporation, 314–15
Vinson-Trammel Act of 1934, 151
Virginia, 15
Virginia/Merrimac, 79, 81
Vital Signs studies, 334, 335
Voinovich, George V., 284
von Clausewitz, Karl, 92
Von Drehle, David, 281
VT Halter Marine, 303

W. G. Yates and Sons, 329
Wabash, 47
Wackenhul, 315
Waddell, Brian, 143
Wadsworth, Decius, 44, 47
Wall Street: 1860–1866, 71, 104; 1917–1945, 136, 138; World War I, 119–24
Wall Street Journal, 303
War Finance Corporation, 149, 150
War Industries Board (WIB), 142, 144–45, 148–50, 159
War of 1812, 32, 32–36, 38, 44, 50, 51, 66
War on Terror, 284–85, 293–94, 296–97, 301, 306, 317, 326
War Plan Orange, 154
War Production Board, 161, 169
War Resources Board, 159
War Tax of 1861, 68
War Trade Board, 149
Warburg, Paul, 111

Warner, Mark R., 327
Warren, 15
Warsaw Pact, 210, 238, 243, 246
Washington, 15, 34
Washington, Booker T., 103
Washington, George, 11, 20–21, 29–30, 32, 36, 42; on coalitions, 25–26; farewell address, 25; "prescription for preparedness," 22–23
Washington Naval Gun Factory, 110
Washington Naval Treaty, 151
Washington Navy Yard, 34, 44, 47, 48, 76, 79, 97, 100
Washington Post, 215, 217, 219, 228, 295, 304, 318, 320
Washington University, 244
Waste Isolation Pilot Plant, 259
Waters, Asa, 43
Watertown Arsenal, 35–36, 114, 144
Watervliet Arsenal, 35, 97, 100, 110, 144
Watson, Tom, 104
Watson Institute Costs of War project, 317
Waugh, Joan, 63
Waxman, Henry, 315
Wealth of Nations (Smith), 25
Webster, Daniel, 20, 37
Wegner, Dana M., 75–76
Weidenbaum, Murray, 244, 247
Weinberger, Caspar, 215, 227
Weiner, Sharon K., 244
Weiss, Linda, 208–9, 278, 280
Weiss, Stanley, 338
Weldon, Curt, 270
Weldon Spring Feed Material Plant, 258
Welles, Gideon, 76
Wells, Thomas H., 81
Wert, Jeffrey, 63, 87, 91
West Point Foundry, 43–44, 47, 73
West Potomac Park, 102
Westevelt, Jacob, 47
Westinghouse, 94, 197, 207, 248–49, 301
Westinghouse Bettis Company, 258
Westinghouse Electric Corporation, 259, 270
Westinghouse WIPP Company, 259
Westinghouse Savannah River Company, 259
Weyerhauser, 164
Wharton, John, 7
Wharton, Joseph, 104, 106
Wheeler, Joseph, 73
Wheeler, Winslow, 284
Whiskey Rebellion, 24
whistleblowers, 217–18
"White Man's Burden," 92, 102
White Motor, 157
Whitman, Walt, 71
Whitney, 72, 96
Whitney, Eli, 28, 41, 43–44
Whitney, William C., 101, 106
Wickham, Marine T., 43
Wiesner, Jerome, 237
WikiLeaks, 321
Wilcox & Whitney, 80
Will, George F., 215
Willard, Daniel, 142
William Cramp & Sons, 110, 157, 165–66
Williams, Cindy, 278–79
Williams, Seth, 130
Willys-Overland, 157
Wilson, George C., 215
Wilson, Mark R., 63, 72, 100, 128, 143, 206
Wilson, Woodrow, 107, 111, 113, 115–16, 118–20, 124, 129, 133, 136, 144–45, 149–50, 155, 159, 163, 171
Wiltz, John, 121, 122
Winchester, 91, 96
Winchester Repeating Arms, 121
wireless communication, 109; De Forest radiotelephones, 109; wireless telegraphy, 109
Wobblies, 127
Wolf, Martin, 320
Wolfe, Martin, 281
Wolfowitz, Paul, 245
women's suffrage, 168
Wood, Leonard, 115, 116, 118
Work, Robert O., 292, 329

World Policy Institute, 255
World War I, 100, 108–9, 114–15, 127, 128–45, 159, 164–65, 168, 173, 186–87, 242, 276, 281, 286; cost in human lives, 131; cost of, 117, 130–32, 282; lessons from, 145–50; mechanization, 140–41; military industrial complex, 143; mobilization, 140–43; postwar investigative committee, 121; profits made during, 119–24; United States' formal entrance into, 123–24, 143; United States' neutrality in, 115–16, 119, 122, 126, 129, 152, 161; war bonds, 135; war planning after, 154–56; war surplus, 151; weapons technology, 140–41
World War II, 70, 72, 100, 128, 139–40, 143, 148, 156–61, 189, 196–97, 202, 209, 218, 223, 276, 281, 289, 292, 305, 315; cost of, 137, 213, 242, 282, 285, 326; Pearl Harbor, attack on, 134, 137–38, 156–57, 161, 166, 171, 177, 209; public support of, 128–29, 133–38, 158, 168–72

World's Fair, 1939, 160
Wright, Edmond, 4
Wright, Orville, 109, 114
Wright, Wilbur, 109, 114
Wright Aeronautical, 157
Wynne, Michael, 287

Xe, 315, 331

Y-12 National Security Complex, 322
Yale and Towne, 164
Yale of Windsor, 72
Yale University, 105
Yemen, 277, 317
Yom Kippur war, 230
Your Business Goes to War, 167
Yucca Mountain Project (TESS), 259

Zadong, Mao, 215
Zimmerman, Warren, 103
Zimmermann, 248
Zoldberg, Aristide, 133
Zuckerman, Michael, 10